A Practical Guide to Stage Lighting, 2nd Edition

A Practical Guide to Stage Lighting, 2nd Edition

Steven Louis Shelley

ELSEVIER

AMSTERDAM • BOSTON • HEIDELBERG • LONDON
NEW YORK • OXFORD • PARIS • SAN DIEGO
SAN FRANCISCO • SINGAPORE • SYDNEY • TOKYO

Focal press is an imprint of Elsevier

Focal Press is an imprint of Elsevier
30 Corporate Drive, Suite 400, Burlington, MA 01803, USA
Linacre House, Jordan Hill, Oxford OX2 8DP, UK

Notices

Knowledge and best practice in this field are constantly changing. As new research and experience broaden our understanding, changes in research methods, professional practices, or medical treatment may become necessary. Practitioners and researchers must always rely on their own experience and knowledge in evaluating and using any information, methods, compounds, or experiments described herein. In using such information or methods they should be mindful of their own safety and the safety of others, including parties for whom they have a professional responsibility.

To the fullest extent of the law, neither the Publisher nor the authors, contributors, or editors, assume any liability for any injury and/or damage to persons or property as a matter of products liability, negligence or otherwise, or from any use or operation of any methods, products, instructions, or ideas contained in the material herein.

Library of Congress Cataloging-in-Publication Data
Application submitted

British Library Cataloguing-in-Publication Data
A catalogue record for this book is available from the British Library.

ISBN: 978-0-240-81141-3

For information on all Focal Press publications
visit our website at www.elsevierdirect.com

09 10 11 5 4 3 2 1

Printed in the United States of America

Table of Contents

Foreword

At last. The second edition of the book that we in the theatrical lighting world have been waiting for has arrived. This new, greatly expanded edition includes a wealth of additional information, stepping through the design process from the beginning (contracts, budgets, bids, production schedules), through development of the plot and tech rehearsal, and on to the end (archiving). It includes helpful discussions of such disparate topics as what to do about transport, how to approach meetings, or how to cope with changes during load-in or tech. Whether you are a lighting designer on Broadway, off Broadway, in LORT theaters, for small or large dance companies who tour or give one time performances, or for any kind of theatrical venture, you will find a way to get a handle on your lighting process, both the craft and the design, in this book.

It is totally comprehensive and written in such a way that accomplished designers, as well as beginners, can find information, know-how, and stimulating ideas written in an organized and easily understandable manner. It is staggeringly complete and therefore hardly a volume for one's back pocket, but I am sure it will find its way into many a workbox, as well as the shelves of studios and classrooms alike. If you own the first edition there is more than enough additional material to warrant adding this second edition to your library.

In my experience as a teacher, I have learned that it is important for a student to learn one way well. Once that is done it becomes clear that any way—the student's way—is possible. Steve Shelley in *A Practical Guide for Stage Lighting, Second Edition*, has dissected his own carefully devised process and generously presented it to the reader. He shows us every aspect of lighting and how it becomes a part of a total production. The emphasis is on craft but his experience in design allows us to see how the two go hand in hand. The *how* may well determine a large part of the *what*.

It is through the light onstage that theater communicates with an audience. Only when one has a richly developed and organized language, a clear way of speaking, can one begin to express the light with a nuance and subtlety that will reveal the depth of fine performance. Once one has read and comprehended this second edition of *A Practical Guide for Stage Lighting*, one's ideas in light cannot help but become more organized and systematic, enabling one to communicate those ideas with greater depth and clarity. This organization, coupled with a developed eye for composition, is all that one needs to be a fine designer.

I have no doubt that this book will stimulate the designing of better light onstage, and make better lighting designers of us all. Bravo!

Jennifer Tipton
Lighting Designer

Preface

There are three defining moments in the course of any lighting design. The first is when the lighting designer is hired. The second is when the load-in starts and lighting instruments begin to get hung. The third and final moment is when the curtain opens to an audience.

In between, the realization of every lighting design requires a progressive sequence of tasks. In addition to completing the tasks, every design has to be adapted – no design is ever realized without some amount of change. Not only is every production different, the end result may even be completely different from the initial plan. In order for a design to be considered "complete," both the initial tasks and the adaptations must be executed.

The challenge is that both of these steps take place within a scheduled framework that's often referred to as "the production period," but is even more accurately named **stage time**. And this will come as no great surprise: There's never enough. Once the load-in starts and the show enters stage time, the countdown really begins. After that second moment, any time spent on stage trying to make a decision, rather than implementing a decision, is usually wasted time that can never be regained.

When I was a young student of lighting design, I wasted a lot of stage time. I had attended classes and read books, but no one said anything about time or any other constraints in a way that made me listen. From my perspective, no class stressed the need to streamline the process of lighting design. Without a system or enough experience, I started my career following production schedules that frequently resulted in unfinished products.

Eventually I analyzed these disappointments and came to realize that the unfulfilled designs were often my own fault. I ran out of time, typically because I couldn't quickly adapt to existing parameters or constraints. The constraints had always been there – I just didn't understand them, or I was locked in an ethereal mindset and chose not to understand them until they could no longer be avoided. And then, all too often, it would be too late.

Eventually I realized I had it backwards. I needed to first scrutinize the situation, acknowledge the constraints, and then construct a strategic design that not only addressed the ethereal needs of the show, but simultaneously addressed all of the parameters. Rather than walk in the door and slowly make decisions taking constraints into account, I began to construct tactical methods that pre-addressed the parameters before walking in the door.

Studying how constraints potentially impact the original design concept for a show allows many of the potential choices to be examined ahead of time. When adaptations are required, the choices are simplified, quickly made, and the design has a better chance to be completed on time.

After years of watching and analyzing missteps and mistakes (both my own and others'), I've developed these methods, tools, and techniques that I use to expedite the process. Doing the homework and producing lighting designs based on realistic parameters, the production process remains more focused on adapting a fully-conceived design into a realized product, instead of spending time on the distraction of knee-jerk reactions to information that should have been analyzed beforehand.

A Practical Guide for Stage Lighting illustrates these methods that I use to maximize the precious commodity of stage time and to create theatrical lighting designs. It presents nuts-and-bolts tools and techniques that address the realities of crafting or recreating a light plot with minimal space, tools, or time. Or, to put it another way, how to get the best lighting bang for your buck.

Steve Shelley
New York City
2009

Acknowledgments for the Second Edition

Like all books, this effort would not have been possible without the assistance and cooperation of a lot of folks. All of the organizations and individuals listed below had some hand in the realization of this book:

The manufacturers: Tony Sklarew and John Ryan at Altman Stage Lighting; Gary Fails at City Theatrical; Ken Romaine and Keith Gullum, lately of Color Kinetics; Sue Englund, Traci Kelliher, David North, Tony Romain, and at Electronic Theatre Controls; Joe Tawil at Great American Market; Debi Moen at High End Systems; Don Phillips at LeMaitre Special Effects, Inc.; Steve Lerman at Lycian Stage Lighting; Larry Beck at Martin; Beth Weinstein, Rob Morris, and Tom Morris at Ocean Optics; Josh Alemany, Joel Svendsen, and Chad Tiller at Rosco Labs; Jeremy Collins, Scott Church, and Marie (Deanna Troi) Southwood at Strand•Selecon Performance Lighting; Tom Folsom, Bobby Harrell, and Phil Foleen at Strand Lighting.

The lighting rental shops: Meghan Marrer at Scharff Weisberg Lighting; Al Ridella at 4 Wall Entertainment Lighting; Larry Schoeneman at Designlab Chicago and Interesting Products.

The organizations: United Scenic Artists 829 (Martha Mountain, Mitch Dana, Carl Baldasso, and David Goodman), ESTA (Karl Ruling and Lori Rubenstein), Noah Price and the rest of the Stagecraft List (WWFWD?), and the United States Institute for Theatre Technology.

The Usual Suspects: Kevin Linzey, Sam Jones, David KH Elliott, Cris Dopher, and Andrew Dunning, for their assistance with all questions regarding Vectorworks®. John McKernon for all matters Lightwright. Lorraine Hall, Suzie Elliott, and Mitch Tebo lent knowledge and support for matters regarding Word, Excel, or general grammaticism.

The Assisting Eyes: Aaron Copp, Judith Daitsman, David Fleming, Greg Goldsmith, Kevin Greene, Sabrina Hamilton, Ruth Hutson, Ellen Jones, Martha Mountain, Aaron Sporer, Nancy Schertler, and Jim Streeter.

The Assisting Ears: Julie Archer, Jimbo Griffith, Rhys Williams, and the staff and patrons of Acqua's. A special shout-out to Naz Aykent, Horace Beasley, and Bill Shapiro.

Filling in the blanks: Jim Bay, Sound Designer; Richard Cadena, editor of PLSN and author of "Automated Lighting; The Art and Science of Moving Light"; Mike Pitzer, Production Electrician; and Anne Valentino, Console Specialist.

Thanks to the ever-patient Ms. Cara Anderson and Ms. Danielle Monroe, both of whom garner the gratitude and bear the responsibility for making this second edition come to fruition. Thanks also to Ms. Maureen Moran, whose straightforward analysis and guidance kept this project on course. Finally, thanks to André A. Cuello, for his guidance and patience at the end of the publishing process.

Many thanks to the two people who helped inspire me into this strange business: Ms. Sara Boatman and Mr. Michael Orris Watson. Thanks also to Mr. Todd Randall, who provided a timely dose of confidence. As before, this book is dedicated to my family and my friends. Without their support, I might still be delivering laundry.

Finally, for her assistance, patience, and incredibly high tolerance level, big thanks to my Pookie,

Ms. Judith Schoenfeld. I could not have done this without you.

A Practical Guide for Stage Lighting, Second Edition, was written on Apple MacBook Pro, using an HP Officejet 5610 All-in-One, and an ancient HP Laserjet 6MP. The following applications were originally used to create the text and graphics used in this book: Adobe PhotoShop, Colorit!, Filemaker Pro, MacDraw, Microsoft Office 98, and ScanWizard. The second edition relied heavily on Microsoft Office 2004, Vectorworks®, Adobe Illustrator, Snapz Pro X, and Graphic Converter.

Some material in Chapter 1 initially relied on *Designing with Light*, by J. Michael Gillette; *Stage Lighting*, by Richard Pilbrow; and *Lighting Handbook*, by the Westinghouse Electric Corporation. Material in the shop order section made supplemental use of information from John McKernon's home page: www.mckernon.com. The production schedule format is based off templates created by Ms. Susie Prueter for Spoleto Festival USA.

The mannequin figure used in the wire frame focus diagrams courtesy of Mr. Andrew Dunning (www.landrudesign.com).

Images in Chapter 1 provided by a variety of very kind manufacturers: Images of Source Four instruments are courtesy of Electronic Theatre Controls; images of a gobo rotator and Rosco Designer Pattern #77733 are courtesy of Rosco Labs. Images of other instruments and devices mentioned in the text are included with the permission of Electronic Theatre Controls, High End Systems, Interesting Products, LeMaitre Special Effects, Lycian Stage Lighting, Ocean Optics, Strand Selecon Performance Lighting, and Strand Lighting. Remaining lighting instrument images courtesy of Altman Lighting. The digital photographs at the end of Chapter 8 were taken by Steven Louis Shelley of instruments focused for Steve Reich's *The Cave*, lighting designed by Matthew Frey. The original Front View High Side Beam Pool drafting provided by Martha Mountain.

All elements, concepts, and descriptions of *Hokey: A Musical Myth* by Steven Louis Shelley. All illustrations by Steven Louis Shelley.

All lighting symbols included in this text were created using either the Field Template™ or SoftSymbols™, both of which are designed exclusively by Steven Louis Shelley. Field Template is registered patent 5,033,333.

Visit the Field Template Home Page: www .fieldtemplate.com.

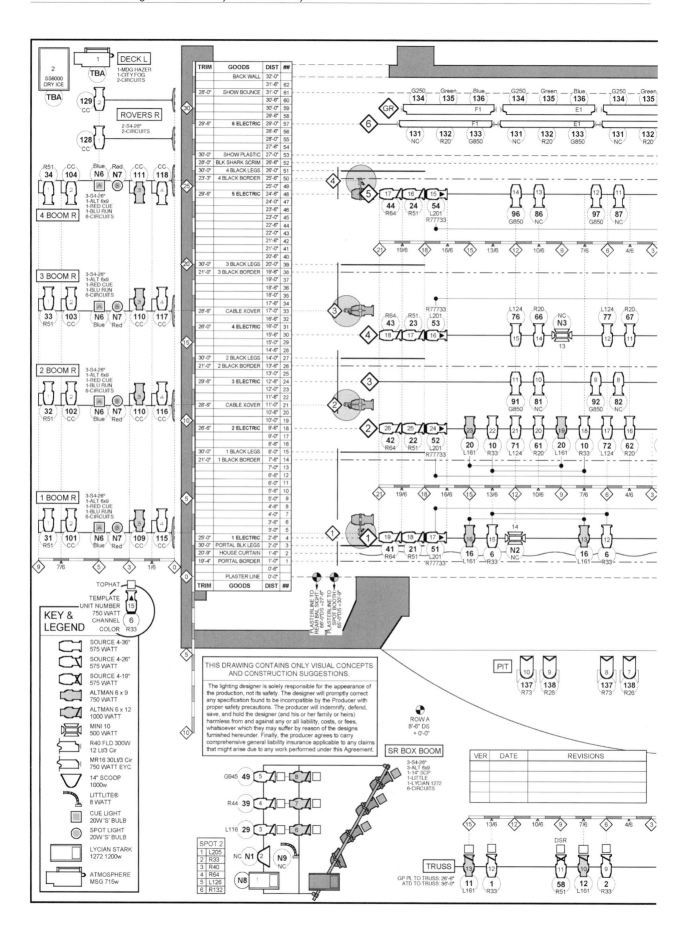

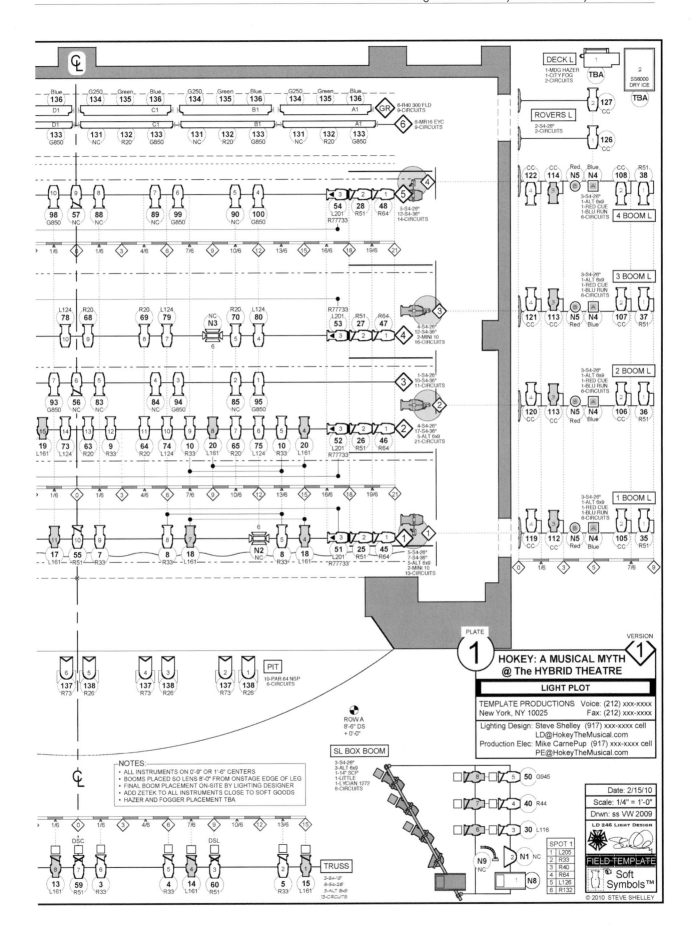

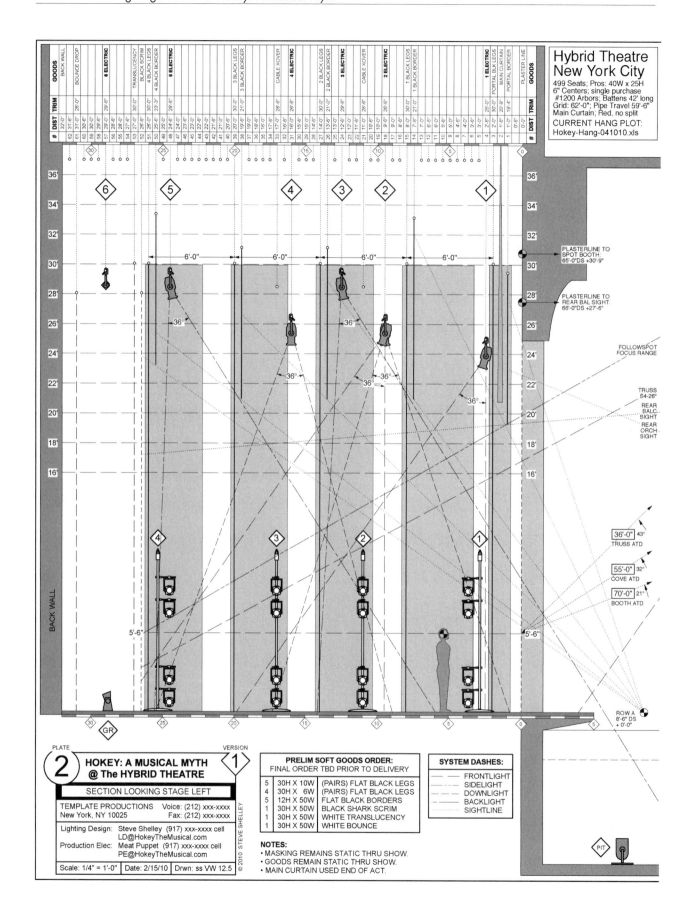

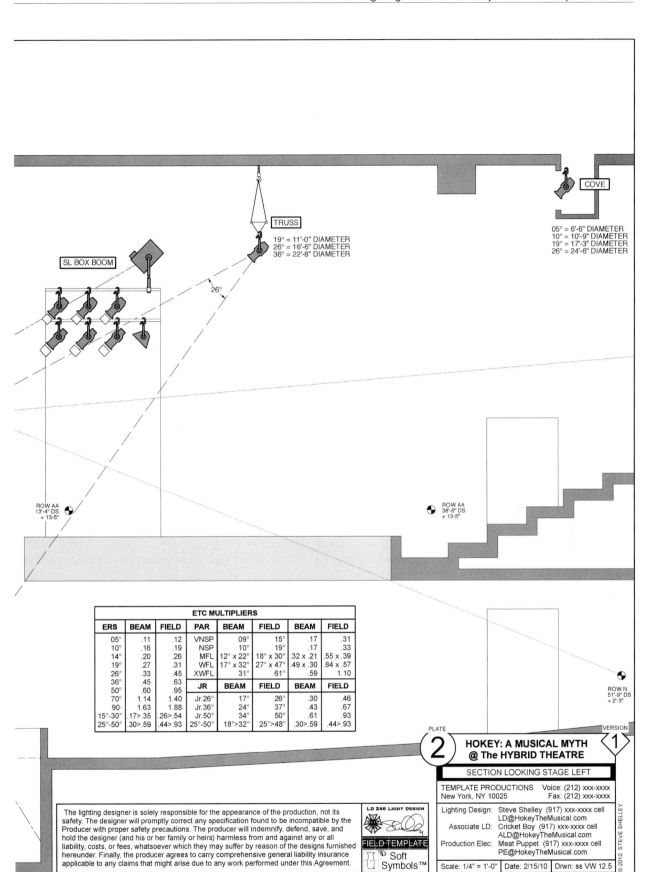

COVE

05° = 6'-6" DIAMETER
10° = 10'-9" DIAMETER
19° = 17'-3" DIAMETER
26° = 24'-6" DIAMETER

TRUSS

19° = 11'-0" DIAMETER
26° = 16'-6" DIAMETER
36° = 22'-8" DIAMETER

SL BOX BOOM

26°

ROW AA
13'-4" DS
+ 13-5"

ROW AA
38'-6" DS
+ 13-5"

ROW N
51'-9" DS
+ 2'-3"

ETC MULTIPLIERS

ERS	BEAM	FIELD	PAR	BEAM	FIELD	BEAM	FIELD
05°	.11	.12	VNSP	09°	15°	.17	.31
10°	.16	.19	NSP	10°	19°	.17	.33
14°	.20	.26	MFL	12° x 22°	18° x 30°	.32 x .21	.55 x .39
19°	.27	.31	WFL	17° x 32°	27° x 47°	.49 x .30	.84 x .57
26°	.33	.45	XWFL	31°	61°	.59	1.10
36°	.45	.63	**JR**	**BEAM**	**FIELD**	**BEAM**	**FIELD**
50°	.60	.95					
70°	1.14	1.40	Jr.26°	17°	26°	.30	.46
90·	1.63	1.88	Jr.36°	24°	37°	.43	.67
15°-30°	.17>.35	.26>.54	Jr.50°	34°	50°	.61	.93
25°-50°	.30>.59	.44>.93	25°-50°	18°>32°	25°>48°	.30>.59	.44>.93

LD 246 LIGHT DESIGN

FIELD TEMPLATE

Soft Symbols™

PLATE
2

VERSION
1

HOKEY: A MUSICAL MYTH
@ The HYBRID THEATRE

SECTION LOOKING STAGE LEFT

TEMPLATE PRODUCTIONS   Voice: (212) xxx-xxxx
New York, NY 10025   Fax: (212) xxx-xxxx

Lighting Design: Steve Shelley (917) xxx-xxxx cell
                    LD@HokeyTheMusical.com
Associate LD: Cricket Boy (917) xxx-xxxx cell
                    ALD@HokeyTheMusical.com
Production Elec: Meat Puppet (917) xxx-xxxx cell
                    PE@HokeyTheMusical.com

Scale: 1/4" = 1'-0" | Date: 2/15/10 | Drwn: ss VW 12.5

© 2010 STEVE SHELLEY

Introduction

A *Practical Guide for Stage Lighting* is intended for readers who want to understand the process and the tools used in theatrical lighting design.

This book is not written for the person only beginning to study theatrical lighting design. There's more introductory information that needs to be understood and practiced than can be presented in the Chapter 1 Review, and there are many other texts that provide that.

Likewise, this book is not written for those who want to learn about more specialized topics, like designing lights for television, film, or concerts. While a lot of information is included in this book, those topics aren't mentioned. There are also no examinations of touring, intimate discussions about moving lights, or inside dope on designing for Broadway. There are other books that cover those topics as well.

A *Practical Guide for Stage Lighting* is intended for the young designer who has some understanding of the lighting design process, the more experienced designer who's interested in viewing different techniques, or the mature designer who just keeps forgetting the list of things to remember. While I've been all of those designers, I now firmly place myself in the last category. This book got started long ago when it dawned on me how helpful lists could be. I'm not ashamed to admit that I've referred to this book numerous times before embarking on a process that I haven't encountered for a while.

While many of the methods and techniques I describe in this text are not the only way to achieve the desired end, they are the simplest ways I've found to successfully reach it. In some cases, those methods are presented merely as suggestions. Sometimes, they're *strongly* suggested. And in particular cases, they are ironclad – those are the Golden Rules.

To make it easy to distinguish one from the other, several icons are included to highlight portions of this book.

Checklist: This icon indicates a list of items. Though not every item is necessarily applicable to every situation, the list can be reviewed prior to addressing the task at hand.

Shelley's Notes: This icon points to notes based on my own experiences. They're included so others don't have to make the same mistakes I did.

Sneaky Tip: This icon indicates a piece of information that was a revelation when it was presented to me.

Shelley's Soapbox: This icon marks my own personal opinion regarding a particular topic that I feel strongly about.

Shelley's Golden Rule: This icon highlights a particular fact, situation, or method that I've found to be almost irrefutable.

Tales from the Road: This icon is used when a story is told. While the tire track implies the story is "from the road", it also indicates the pattern that's left after being run over. That's often how one feels after learning a painful lesson.

Chapter 1

A Review

INTRODUCTION

The general purpose of a theatrical presentation is to entertain, educate, and communicate ideas. That presentation is often comprised of a script, dance, or music, interpreted by performers, and design elements, all unified by the director's overall concept. Lighting is one of those design elements, and for a lighting design to successfully achieve its purpose, it can't conceptually, or physically, take place in a vacuum. Instead, it has to work in conjunction with the other design elements, the performers, and the directorial concept.

Similarly, the physical components of a lighting design must work in tandem with the other various elements of the physical and non-physical environment, including the theatrical space, the scenic components, various personnel, and the schedule. While the aesthetics of the design are the primary concern, the lighting designer must also possess a practical knowledge of the physical and conceptual framework of the theatrical lighting environment, in order to effectively communicate, coordinate, and execute those aesthetics.

The purpose of this book is to provide that non-aesthetic framework, by tracing the path of a single fictional lighting design from a practical point of view. Initially, the book will examine the preparation and adaptation process, viewing the graphic documents and written paperwork used to define, communicate, and facilitate the logistics of the lighting design. Then the book will follow the installation of the light plot and lighting design up through the hypothetical opening night.

Before tracing that path, however, this first chapter reviews basic theatrical lighting terminology, general theatrical staffing, and some of the parameters that potentially impact any production. The terminology includes basic nomenclature for the theatrical environment, basic electricity, and physical components of theatrical lighting, as it will be referred to in this text.

Experienced readers may find much of this redundant to their knowledge and skip ahead to Chapter 2, which talks about all of the paperwork potentially involved in designing and creating a lighting design. Chapter 3, on the other hand, jumps into a review of the basic information that needs to be acquired to form a basis of knowledge about a show, while Chapter 4 examines basic contractual components, budget estimates, and on-site surveys. While the inclusion of this chapter might seem redundant, including this review provides a basic framework for terms and explanations that are fundamental to lighting design using terms specific to this text. Terminology used later in this text may suddenly seem unfamiliar, but any misunderstandings or questions in later chapters can hopefully be referenced back and restored on track from information contained within this first chapter.

The first step of the review is to define the labels and terms for the various architectural elements of the theatrical space.

THE THEATRICAL SPACE

The theatrical space is described with a combination of architectural nomenclature and historical terminology. In general, theatrical presentations or performances can't exist without a public to observe the proceedings. To that end, most theatres have specific locations for the public called the **audience**, to watch the performance, and locations where the performers perform, called the **stage** or the **deck**.

Figure 1.1 shows simple overhead drawings looking down at the basic performance configurations. Figure 1.1A is the arrangement that allows an audience to view the stage from one side, as through a "picture frame," known as a **proscenium** configuration. Figure 1.1B shows the arrangement in which the audience views the stage from either side of the stage, generally known as an **alley** configuration, while Figure 1.1C illustrates the configuration where the audience views the stage from three sides, known as a **thrust** configuration. Figure 1.1D shows the audience viewing the stage from all four sides in an **arena** configuration, often referred to as "in the round." Arrangements that intertwine the stage and audience seating are often referred to as an **environmental**, or **organic** configuration. Since there are many possible combinations and variations of these configurations, one generic phrase used to describe a space used for theatrical presentations in any of these arrangements is a **performance facility**, or a **venue**. Although many of the discussions in this text have applications to other arrangements, the proscenium configuration is the principal environment used as a point of reference for this book.

Another term for the area containing audience seating is the **house**. The **main curtain**, which may be used to prevent the audience from viewing the entire stage until a designated moment, is often located immediately behind the proscenium, the architectural "picture frame" that separates the house from the stage area. In many cases, the proscenium isn't a rectangular shape; instead, the top horizontal frame edge curves into the two vertical sides, creating the **proscenium arch**.

Figure 1.2A is another drawing looking down onto the stage. The backside of the proscenium arch, concealed from the audience's view, is known as the **plaster line**. The plaster line is often used as a theatrical plane of reference. If the width of the proscenium opening is divided in half, that bisected distance produces a point on the stage. This point can be extended into a single line, perpendicular to the plaster line. This is the **centerline**, which is used as a second architectural plane of reference. The point where the centerline and the plaster line intersect on the stage is a point of reference called the **groundplan zero point**, or the **zero-zero point**. (In CAD drafting programs, this point is known as the **datum**.)

Two types of drawings are most commonly used to present the information about each space. One view looks down onto the performance space, compressing every object into a single plane. This drafting is called a **groundplan view**. The cross-section, commonly referred to as the **sectional view**, is the perspective produced after the entire space has been visually "cut in half" like a layer cake, often on centerline. After half of the "cake" has been removed, the inside of the remainder is viewed.

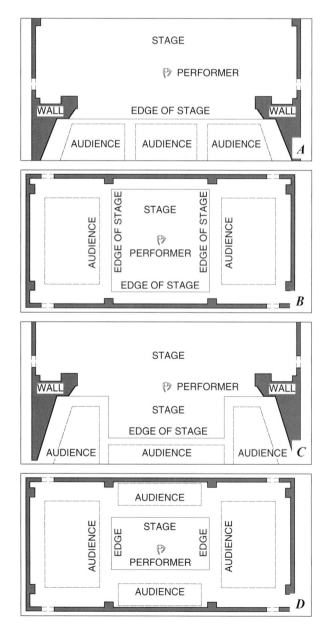

Figure 1.1 Basic Stage Configurations: A) Proscenium, B) Alley, C) Thrust, and D) Arena

THEATRICAL STAGE NOMENCLATURE

Figure 1.2A also shows the area between the plaster line and the edge of the stage, often referred to as the **apron**. In some theatres, a gap exists between the edge of the stage and the audience. This architectural "trench," acoustically designed to accommodate musicians and enhance sound, is often referred to as the **orchestra pit**. The area of the stage not concealed by masking, and available for performers, is known as the **playing area**, or the **performance area**. The rest of the stage, which is often concealed from the audience's view, is referred to as **backstage**.

Stage directions are a basic system of orientation. Their nomenclature stems from the time when stages were raked, or sloped, toward the audience. Modern stage directions can be illustrated from the perspective of a person standing at groundplan zero facing the audience.

Figure 1.2B illustrates this perspective; moving closer to the audience is movement **downstage**, while moving away from the audience is movement **upstage**.

Stage left and stage right are in this orientation as well. Moving toward centerline from either side is referred to as movement **onstage**, while moving away from centerline is movement **offstage**. Across the upstage and downstage edges of the performance space are the **light lines**, imaginary boundaries where light on performers is terminated. The upstage light line is usually established to prevent light from spilling onto backing scenery, while the downstage light line's placement may be established by a combination of factors. It often corresponds to the edge of the performance space, or it's established to prevent light from spilling onto architecture and creating distracting shadows. A point on centerline midway between the light lines is often referred to as **center-center**. While standing on this point, moving directly toward the audience is movement down center. Moving to either side is thought of as movement offstage left or right. Moving directly away from the audience is movement toward upstage center. Diagonal movement combines the terms, two examples being upstage left or downstage right.

Other terms are used to provide a relational placement system relative to centerline. Figure 1.2C is a groundplan showing a person standing on stage left, for example. All objects stage left of centerline can be referred to as **near** objects, or being on the **near side** of the stage. All objects on the opposite side of centerline, in this case stage right, are **far** objects, or exist on the **far side** of the stage. Objects on the far side can also be referred to as being on the **opposite side** of the stage. This orientation remains constant until the person moves to the stage right side of centerline, in which case all of the terms reverse. The same objects that were near are now far, and vice versa. Opposite is always on the opposite side of centerline.

Theatrical Rigging

Non-electrical objects hung in the air over the stage are typically referred to as **goods**, and are then divided into one of two categories. Backdrops, curtains, and velour masking all fall under the heading of **soft goods**, while built "flattage," walls, and other framed or solid objects fall under the heading of **hard goods**.

In most proscenium theatres, the area above the stage contains elements of the **fly system**, which allows goods and electrical equipment to be safely suspended in the air. Most modern fly systems are **counterweighted**; the weight of the load suspended in the air is balanced by equal weight in a remote location. Since many lighting instruments are often hung in the air over the stage, it's advisable to understand the basic components and mechanical relationships in a fly system.

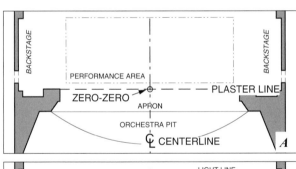

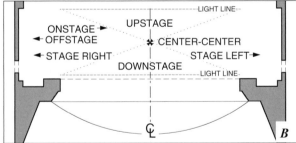

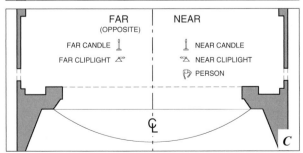

Figure 1.2 Stage Spatial & Relational Nomenclature: A) Basic Locations, B) Basic Directions, and C) Relational Placement

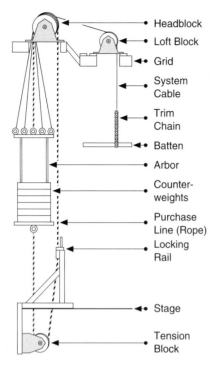

- Headblock
- Loft Block
- Grid
- System Cable
- Trim Chain
- Batten
- Arbor
- Counter-weights
- Purchase Line (Rope)
- Locking Rail
- Stage
- Tension Block

Figure 1.3 One Lineset in a Counterweight Fly System

Figure 1.3 illustrates a single lineset in a **counterweight fly system**. Goods are typically attached to **battens**, which often consist of lengths of steel pipe. The battens are held in the air by **system cables**. The system cables each trace a unique path up to the **grid**, which is typically a steel structure supporting the entire fly system and anything else that hangs in the air. Once in the grid, each system cable passes through a single unique pulley called a **loft block**, or a **sheave**. After passing through the sheaves, all of the system cables for one batten passes through a multi-sheaved pulley called a **head block**, and then terminate at the top of the **arbor**. The arbor, when loaded with sufficient **counterweight**, balances the weight of the goods attached to the batten. Rope tied to the arbor describes a loop, running from the bottom of the arbor down through a tension pulley near the stage, then up through the **locking rail** to the head block in the grid, and then back down again to the top of the arbor.

Pulling the rope, or **operating line**, adjusts the height of the arbor and, conversely, alters the height of the goods on the batten. Since the weight is counterbalanced between the batten and the arbor, the **rope lock** on the locking rail merely immobilizes the batten's location. Though not entirely accurate, this entire assembly, which controls a single batten, is often called a **lineset**.

This is the system that will be referred to through the course of this book, but it's only one kind of counterweight system. There are other counterweight

systems, and many other methods used to achieve safe theatrical rigging. They are discussed in much more detail in other books devoted to that topic, some of which can be found in the bibliography at the end of this book.

Now that counterweight fly systems have been examined, another term can be used which expands the playing area to include any portion of the stage underneath any lineset battens that may be lowered to the deck. This larger area is called the **hot zone**, and it becomes especially relevant when the show is initially being loaded into the performance space. Keeping the hot zone clear of equipment so that battens can be flown in and out as needed is no small task, making offstage space even more of a premium during that time.

Theatrical Backdrops

Large pieces of fabric that prevent the audience from viewing the back wall of the theatre are known as **backdrops**. Although they are usually located at the upstage edge of the playing area, any large piece of fabric "backing" a scene in the performance area is referred to as a backdrop or, simply, a drop. Several drops hung adjacent to each other, upstage of the performance area, are often referred to as the **scenic stack**.

Often the visual objective of a backdrop is to provide a surface that appears solid or unbroken by wrinkles. To achieve this, most drops constructed of fabric have a sleeve sewn across the bottom, known as **a pipe pocket**. The weight of pipe inserted in the pocket provides vertical tension to reduce the severity or number of wrinkles seen by the audience. Additional weights may be placed on top of the pipe pocket to increase this tension. Clamps, often dubbed "**stretchers**," may be attached to either of the side edges of the drop, in order to provide equal horizontal tension. The goal of these combined tensions is to achieve a smooth unbroken surface.

Backdrops can be constructed from a variety of materials, including canvas, muslin, plastic, bobbinet, or scrim. Backdrops that possess no visual design element are often lighted with washes of color. These drops are often referred to as **cycloramas**, or **cycs**. The techniques used in their construction often determine the method in which they are lit. Drops constructed of horizontal strips of fabric are often lit only from the downstage side (or the **front** of the drop), since the silhouettes of the horizontal seams will be seen if lit from the upstage side (or the **back**). Other drops are constructed from a single piece of material. This more expensive drop is known as a **seamless**, and, since there are no shadow lines created by horizontal seams, they may be lit from either the front or the back.

Viewing different types of backdrops is one way to compare the three different levels of theatrical visible transmission. When paint is so thick that it fills the tiny holes between the warp and woof of a fabric backdrop, light can no longer clearly pass through the fabric. Light projected onto the back of the drop is blocked, and will not be seen by the audience. In this first condition, the drop is considered **opaque**. An unpainted fabric backdrop, on the other hand, allows light to pass through the tiny holes. Light projected onto the back of the drop will be seen by the audience. In this second condition, the drop is considered **translucent**. (This term is often used as another name for a seamless drop. It can also be referred to as a **translucency**, or a **trans**.) An open-weave net drop called **scrim** can be used to illustrate the third level of transmission. If light falls solely on an object that is positioned upstage of a scrim, the audience can clearly see the object through the fabric. In this condition, the scrim is considered **transparent**. The method used to weave a scrim, however, allows light to change its visible transmission. If the upstage light is removed and replaced by a high angle wash of light projected onto the front of the scrim, the object disappears, and the scrim is now visually opaque.

Translucent drops are typically lit like shadowboxes, with rows of lights behind them. To make the drop as bright as possible, the rows of lights are sandwiched between the translucency and a second light-colored backdrop hung further upstage. In many cases the lights are pointed more at the second drop, which then reflects the scattered light back onto the trans. Usually the audience never sees this upstage drop, but it makes the trans visually "pop" to the audience's eye. Since its purpose is to contain and bounce all available light into the back of the translucency, its generic name is the **bounce drop**.

Theatrical Masking

The common convention in theatre is to hide the technical elements from the audience with large pieces of fabric or built flats generally called **masking**. Although many different types of fabrics are used for masking, it's generally accepted that black velour reflects the least amount of light. If the masking is unframed and can be folded for storage, it's generally categorized as "soft." If masking or scenery is framed or stiff, it's known as "hard." Figure 1.4 shows vertical masking placed on either side of the stage, which are called **legs** or **tormentors**, while units of horizontal masking hung above the stage are called **borders**, or **teasers**.

Legs and borders hung adjacent to each other create **masking portals** that mirror the proscenium arch. Typically, a series of masking portals prevent the

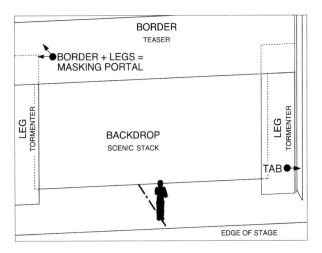

Figure 1.4 Masking Components

backstage area from being viewed by the audience. When fly systems are involved, a pair of masking legs of equal height is typically hung on a single batten. To hide the leg batten from the view of the audience, the accompanying masking border is typically hung on a separate batten downstage of the legs. Utilizing two independent battens allows the height of the border to be adjusted without altering the vertical placement of the masking legs. The two masking linesets are often hung adjacent to each other to allow room between masking portals for electrics or other flying pieces. If the masking legs aren't wide enough to conceal the backstage area, additional masking is often hung parallel to centerline, just offstage of the legs. These pieces are called **tabs**, and their name refers to their position and function; indeed, they're often a spare set of legs.

Additional scenery is often hung adjacent or in the middle of the masking portals. If scenic legs are a part of the design, they are often hung on a separate batten between the two masking linesets, so that the border hides the batten supporting the scenic legs. By hanging scenic legs adjacent to the masking legs, light can be cut off both sets of legs while providing optimum beam coverage. Midstage drops, or scrims, are often assigned to linesets immediately upstage of the masking leg battens. The masking border hides the batten, while the masking legs conceal the side edges of the drop.

The word "opening" can have two meanings when used in relation to masking. The distance from centerline to the onstage edge of two legs hung on the same batten is often referred to as the **width of the opening**, or the **leg opening**. The up- and downstage distance between two legs on the same side of the stage, on the other hand, is referred to either as the **depth of the opening**, or an "**in**." The "in" label is used to distinguish each opening that can be used as access between backstage and the performance space, each of which is assigned a sequential number starting at plaster line. "Stage Left In 1" is the first leg opening upstage of plaster line on stage left, and so on. If the entire performance space is masked in black velour legs, borders, and a black backdrop, the combined masking creates a **black surround**.

Theatrical Performance Surfaces

Performance surfaces are often used to cover the deck and create a surface that's easily installed, transportable, and often uniform in appearance. Large pieces of canvas, often painted, are called **ground cloths**. Rolls of flexible vinyl flooring, generically referred to as **dance floors**, may also be used to cover the stage. Platforms may be used instead to cover the entire playing area, and are collectively referred to as **show decks**. (Show decks often contain mechanical devices or tracks, which power turntables or transport other moving scenery.) On the other hand, rather than any of these, the stage may merely be painted.

HANGING POSITION AND FOCUS NOMENCLATURE

Contained in each theatrical venue are locations specifically designed to house the lighting instruments that illuminate the performers and other elements of the production, generically referred to as **hanging positions**. The lighting designer must understand the nomenclature and the order used to identify hanging positions, as well as the numbering systems employed to uniquely identify each lighting instrument. When lighting instruments are being targeted at specific points for use in a live presentation, the act of maneuvering and shaping each beam of light is referred to as **focusing** the instrument, which has its own vocabulary.

Hanging Position Nomenclature

To prevent confusion, each hanging position or location has a unique name. The nomenclature is defined by architectural location, the type of mounting position, and the location relative to groundplan zero.

The initial division defining hanging position name is relative to plaster line. Hanging positions downstage of plaster line are generically known as front of house (or FOH) positions. Although they may have many names, they're usually found in three locations. The position parallel to plaster line over the audience that provides the highest angle of light to the stage is often known by one of the terms for the architectural features in which its located; the

cove, the **catwalk**, the **beam**, or the **slot**, to name a few. Hanging positions on the sides of the audience providing diagonal frontlight are often named for their adjacency to the audience box seats. These positions are usually called **box booms**. The position providing the flattest angle to the stage is often found in front of the balcony closest to the stage. This hanging position is usually called the **balcony rail**.

Hanging positions upstage of plaster line above the stage may be known as **electrics**, **overhead pipes**, **catwalks**, or, in large theatres with moving catwalks, **overhead bridges**. The electric closest to plaster line is the **first electric**. The farther away from plaster line, the higher the position number. Likewise, if there is more than one FOH hanging position from approximately the same angle, the hanging position of each type closest to the plaster line is listed first.

The hanging positions on either side of the stage are identified by their degree of permanence, their appearance, or their function. Hanging positions permanently accessible by architectural catwalks on either side of the stage are often called **galleries**. Structural frameworks temporarily suspended from the grid in that same approximate location may be referred to as **ladders**, since their typical appearance resembles that device. Permanent vertical hanging positions built into or adjacent to the proscenium are often called **torms**. Temporary structures that sit on the stage providing vertical hanging positions are often referred to as **booms**. Individual lighting instruments mounted on movable structures that sit on the stage are known as **stands**, **rovers**, or **floor mounts**. Lighting instruments attached to pieces of scenery are often referred to as **set mounts**. Positions contained in the deck, creating a gap in the stage, are often known as **troughs**. A trough in the stage running parallel to the downstage edge of the apron is often referred to as a **footlight trough**, while the same gap upstage containing instruments used to illuminate backdrops is often called a **cyc trough**.

Theatrical Lighting Numbering Systems

All hanging locations not intersecting centerline are often sub-named by their location relative to centerline. Ladders, booms, and such are divided between stage left and stage right. The hanging locations are then numbered by their relative proximity to plaster line. The stage left boom closest to plaster line, for example, is known as 1 Boom Left. Each boom on that side of the stage, farther from plaster line, receives the next higher whole number.

A numbering system is employed to identify the instruments at each hanging position. Each instrument is given a unique whole number to speed identification.

The first instrument at each position is usually labeled as unit number 1, and continues in whole numbers to the end of the position. Over time, the terms have become interchangeable; instruments are often referred to as units. The act of "counting the instruments" has historically been performed while standing on stage, facing the audience. Because of that, the numbering of the instruments starts from the left orientation, and runs from stage left to stage right. When instruments are stacked vertically, unit numbering is related to height and proximity to plaster line. The typical convention is to number the units from top to bottom. When pairs of instruments are on the same level, the numbering starts with the downstage instrument and proceeds upstage. Paired units stacked in box booms are often numbered starting from centerline and proceed offstage. Units hung on FOH positions parallel to centerline start numbering from upstage and proceed downstage, away from the plaster line.

Hanging locations in non-proscenium venues require a different set of nomenclature tactics. Pipe grid positions suspended as a gridwork are typically labeled as hanging locations on one axis with numbers, and alphabetical letters on the other. When the hanging positions are asymmetric, designating them by compass point, or numbering from a clockwise manner, is sometimes employed. Hanging locations that repeat, such as bays, usually number from a consistent starting point. When the hanging location defies a simple name assignment, leave it to the electricians. Numbering methods, though, should conform to other compatible hanging locations on the plot, or everyone will be confused.

Additional electrical devices are often represented in a light plot, which may or may not be controlled by the lighting console. To avoid confusion, each separate device requiring line voltage or a control signal receives a unique unit number. A strobe light hung in the middle of an overhead electric, for example, would be assigned its own whole unit number in sequence with the rest of the lighting instruments. The numbering methodology for electrical devices that are accessories affecting the beam of an instrument, on the other hand, has recently changed. In the past, the host instrument's number coupled with an alphabetical letter would identify the device. For example, a color scroller mounted to unit 22 would be named "22A." While this provided unique identification, it could just as easily become the source of confusion, since alphabetical letters are also used to identify instruments added after the initial position numbering. The additional instrument hung between unit 22 and unit 23 would also be labeled as unit 22A. These days the technique is to replicate the host's whole number to any additional electrical accessories; regardless of how many devices may be associated with unit 22, they are all identified as unit 22 as well. The information listed in the "type" field of the database identifies the host unit as a lighting instrument, and thus eliminates any potential confusion.

Since counting instruments and keeping numbers and letters organized in a large light plot can quickly become confusing, updating unit numbering at each hanging position is one of the final tasks performed before the light plot is distributed, or "published." Leaving numbering until late in the game gives the best hope that the number of additions (and additional letters) will be minimal, and each unit will have a whole number.

When moving lights are a part of the light plot, they receive whole numbers too. In this case, though, the single moving light contains many devices, or functions, that affect that instrument's beam, such as pan, tilt, color, and so on. For these types of instruments, the numbering methodology is to assign each function the host number with a numeric point number, in the order they are addressed within the unit. In the past, separate sequential control channels controlled each function. Nowadays, console software assigns those functions as "**attributes**" to the single host channel number.

Focus and Function Nomenclature

When lighting instruments are focused for a production, a set of terms is used to describe the characteristics of the light beams. A different set of terms describes the function that each instrument is assigned to perform in a lighting design.

Almost every lighting instrument produces a **beam** (or pool, or cone) of light containing several characteristics that are referred to when a lighting design is being constructed, and when an instrument is being focused. Figure 1.5 shows a side view of an instrument's beam targeted at a designer. The overall size of the light beam is called the **beam spread** and is usually measured in degrees. The beam spread created by some units is broken down into three distinct areas. The outside portion of the beam spread is called the **field angle**, which is technically defined as the outer cone where the light diminishes to 10% of the center intensity. Approximately the middle half of the beam spread is the **beam angle**, which is defined as the internal cone where the light is 50% of the center intensity. The center intensity, which is the brightest portion of the beam spread, is commonly referred to as the **hot spot**.

The hot spot is the portion of the light beam usually targeted at a specific location. The location on the stage where the lighting designer stands to act as

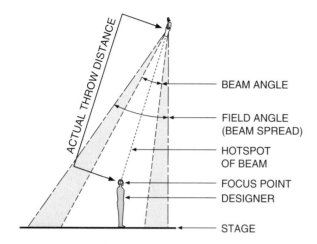

Figure 1.5 The Different Portions of a Light Beam

a target is often referred to as a focus point. When the designer stands on that point, this term is also used to refer to the targeted space occupied by the designer's head. In general, however, a **focus point** is defined as the location on the stage, scenery, or in space where the instrument's hot spot is pointed. The amount of light that's produced by any instrument increases in size and decreases in intensity the farther the light has to travel. The **actual throw distance** is the measured distance between the instrument's bulb and the focus point, which is used to calculate the size and intensity of light beams.

When a single instrument is focused to either a specific location or purpose, that instrument is typically labeled as a **special**. Multiple instruments, equipped with the same color filter, may be focused to cover more than one area of a stage. When they are activated and used together, they can be collectively referred to as either specials, or a **system**. A system is often comprised of at least two instruments that are used together, focused to different or adjacent areas of the stage. When multiple instruments of matching color are focused so that their overlapping beams create a consistent hue and intensity over a portion or all of a performance area, they're collectively referred to as a **wash**. The two terms are often used interchangeably, but while a system may be composed of several instruments focused to different areas of the stage, a wash implies a smooth blend of instruments in a matching color.

Systems and washes of light are often the fundamental tools used in a light plot to create lighting on the stage. They're often hung and focused in such a way that multiple bands of light are created across the width of a stage. A single band of light aimed at focus points equidistant from plaster line, so that the overlapping beams create a consistent intensity across the width of a stage, is called a

zone. Overlapping zones are then combined to create a wash. A frontlight wash, for example, may be comprised of several zones allowing a performer's face to remain a consistent intensity beyond the depth of a single light beam while moving up- or downstage.

System Direction Nomenclature and Analysis

In a theatrical setting, the primary systems of light are typically constructed to illuminate the performers. These systems are generally called **area light**, or **performer light**. They're often identified by their **direction of origin** relative to a person standing on the stage, facing the audience. In many cases, that means by the degree of angle from centerline, but it can also include their relative height to a person's head.

Frontlight

Light striking the front of a person's body is often referred to as **frontlight**. Frontlight is a system, instrument, or light beam originating above and "in front" of a person standing on a stage. The primary goals of frontlight are to provide visibility, allow performers, faces to be seen by the audience, and to help direct the audience's stage focus. Frontlight is often plotted to every anticipated performer location. Coverage may be broken into areas of control, depending on the type of performance, the size of the performance space, the parameters of the lighting package, and the amount of scenery involved.

A typical frontlight wash starts with an even blend of several instruments into a single zone. Often several zones are plotted, to provide overlapping coverage for the entire depth of stage. If frontlight visibility isn't required upstage, on the other hand, the wash may be limited to a single zone downstage. In almost every case, if frontlight is used, the first zone will begin at the portion of the stage closest to the audience.

In a proscenium open-stage setting, the overall depth of a frontlight wash may be directly linked to the presence or absence of a scenic stack upstage of it. Sidelight can provide focus point coverage for someone standing next to a masking leg; the light can hit the edge of masking goods and harmlessly spill into the wings. Frontlight is a completely different matter. If there are goods upstage, one unwritten commandment that's almost always applied in this scenario is to construct and focus the system to keep frontlight (and performer's shadows) off the scenic stack. Since upstage frontlight is usually placed in the overhead electrics, keeping light off those goods usually results in the system's coverage stopping prematurely—usually the upstage opening has a reduced amount of frontlight, or none at all.

When the scenic design includes upstage walls for plays, on the other hand, maintaining consistent visibility on the performers' faces often overrides the commandment to eliminate shadows. In that situation shadows are embraced; the more systems that can splash light onto the walls, the better. While the top shutters control the height, and the beam edges are softened, additional light hitting the walls from other directional systems helps fill in the shadows caused by frontlight. While scenic "interiors" may seem simpler to light, that's often deceiving. The number of specific sectional views and the amount of careful planning on the part of the lighting designer often multiply for each interior setting in a show.

In the same vein, productions with walls often call for the the addition of ceilings to the scenic design as well. When the overhead electrics are all covered by ceilings, the remaining options left to provide basic illumination in the upstage nooks and crannies, may be reduced to low flat frontlight. Collaboration and communication are the best tools to overcome this challenge and come to a mutually beneficial decision; often this results in the ceiling somehow being divided to allow some light in from the overhead. In most cases, scenic designers realize that lovely renderings may never be realized if the scenery can't be adequately lit. Likewise, lighting designers know that they can't have instruments in every location since this may then potentially destroy a lovely scenic design. Successfully negotiating the relative placement between ceilings and hanging positions in an interior setting can often be a painstaking process involving both designers, the director, and numerous members of the production staff. In almost every case, the sooner that these discussions begin, the better.

The construction and focus of a frontlight wash can also be linked to the amount of control assigned to it. If a single channel is assigned to control a frontlight wash, the overall number of instruments required to provide the wash may be reduced. If portions of the wash need to be turned off or brightened, though, that can quickly translate into the need for more instruments. Likewise, the amount of control can affect the frontlight focus; if one channel controls an entire zone, the need to carefully blend shutter cuts between beams is reduced, since the individual beam edges won't be isolated and seen. If the zone is divided into several control channels, on the other hand, the individual beam edges will probably need to be softened, so that the audience's attention isn't drawn to the edges of sharply focused frontlight beams.

In a proscenium configuration, a **straight frontlight** system consists of instruments positioned directly downstage of each focus point, so that their focused beams travel parallel with centerline. Light striking a person's body from approximately a 45°

angle from centerline is often called **diagonal frontlight**. A pair of instruments hung at this matching angle from either side of centerline, and then focused back towards each focus point, is often referred to as **area frontlight**. Area frontlight instruments are often evenly distributed at matching angles across a cover or batten, for example. If a diagonal frontlight wash originates from the box boom position, on the other hand, the system can be called a **box boom wash**. Frontlight originating from below eye level is called **low frontlight**. Sources sitting on the stage producing this type of light are often referred to as "foots."

When straight frontlight is the sole source of facial illumination, it is sometimes perceived as creating a relatively "flat" appearance from the audience. The performer's face is solely shaped by the shadows that are created, relative to the vertical height between the instrument and the performer's head. The successful use of straight frontlight may depend upon supplemental box boom, or area frontlight, to help provide more dimensional shapes and shadows to the performer's face and figure. On the other hand, since straight frontlight is directly downstage of the focus point, it creates a "narrower" pool of light. The single unit is often more successful isolating a performer, than a pair of area frontlights.

If a light plot contains no area light systems, instruments in the box booms can help provide downstage facial visibility and dimensionality from the Front of House. A successful box boom focus is typically perceived as a wash of light which provides even coverage across some portion of the stage. The coverage usually begins at the downstage edge of the playing area. Sometimes this system is continued upstage using instruments in the overhead electrics, hung at matching diagonal frontlight angles. The colors used in the system can also be reinforced, with varying degrees of success, using instruments mounted on sidelight booms.

The box boom location can also be useful for washes other than facial light. Depending on the location, low-hung instruments can be useful illuminating scenic legs or downstage drops. The position is also useful for any specials required to focus on architectural elements in the house, specials on musicians, or the conductor in the orchestra pit.

Sidelight

Light striking a person's body from approximately a 90° angle on either side of centerline is called **sidelight**. In a proscenium configuration, these are instruments positioned on either side of a focus point, so that their focused beams travel perpendicular to centerline. If the instrument is hung above the person, it can be referred to as **overhead sidelight** (or high sidelight, or **high sides**). Instruments lower to the stage, on the other hand, can be referred to as low sidelight, or referred to by their hanging position as **boom sidelight**.

Overhead Sidelight

Sidelight systems are often used to provide dimensionality on performers' bodies, and three-dimensional scenery. When walls are involved in the scenic design, overhead sidelight can gain even more importance. If other systems behind the person can't reach particular areas of the stage, the overhead sidelight may be the only system that can prevent an area from looking "flat" (the result of being illuminated only with frontlight). In many situations, overhead sidelights are often plotted like another system of area frontlight, with a pair of instruments, one from each side, focusing to the same focus point.

When the stage is more open and has less scenery, several overhead sidelights can be plotted to provide a single-zone full stage wash from either side. An even sidelight blend in a single zone is often achieved using only three instruments focused to the far quarterline, centerline, and the near quarterline. With careful beam spread choices and hanging placement, these three instruments provide an even blend of sidelight coverage from one side of the stage to the other.

When the batten isn't long enough for the near quarter instrument to match the focus angle of the other two, the far and center instruments may remain hung on the overhead electric, while the near instrument is shifted to a sidelight boom in the same opening. The boom unit's vertical location on the boom is measured to the proper height in order to duplicate the focus angle of the other two overhead units; the same angle of light is projected onto the near quarter line of the stage.

Another style of overhead sidelight plots only a single instrument at the end of a batten to create a single light wash only onto the opposite side of the stage. Instead of plotting additional overhead instruments to complete the wash from the near side, this manner of plotting relies on boom sidelight to "fill in" the coverage from the near side instead.

When overhead sidelights are used in scenic designs involving side walls, providing coverage at head height invariably implies that the beam will also be splashing onto the opposite wall. Though a top shutter cut can reduce the amount of light on the wall, the beam is usually softened, so that the edge of the beam "fades out," rather than abruptly stopping with a barrel focused to a sharp edge. A stage without scenery, however, presents a different challenge.

The instrument focused to the far quarter line also splashes light onto the black masking legs. To reduce halation and retain as much light as possible, the barrel is often focused so that the shutter edge is sharp. To reduce the amount of light hitting the legs, the upstage shutter is then cut off of the black masking leg that defines the upstage side of the opening containing the overhead sidelight.

Producing a high angle sidelight from an overhead electric often results in the instruments being hung as far offstage as possible at the end of the batten. This common hanging location has become another name for the system. Overhead sidelights hung at the end of a batten are also referred to as **pipe ends**.

Boom Sidelight

Adding formalized sidelight booms to light plots is generally credited to a woman named Jean Rosenthal. While reviewers of the day had little appreciation for the look low sidelight produced on performers (making them look more dimensional or "plastic"), the angle and placement of the lighting system has become recognized as one of her many contributions to the craft of lighting. Low sidelight is now a cornerstone of every major North American dance company's light plot, and used in countless productions around the world. A boom sidelight system is typically comprised of a series of instruments, one in each opening, that are mounted at matching heights, equipped with matching colors, and focused in matching ways. A successful boom sidelight system is generally viewed as an even wash of sidelight that covers the entire depth of a performance space and illuminates the sides of performers' bodies (or dimensional objects) from the audience's perspective.

While the instrument type and focus designation assigned to boom sidelights are unique to every show, there are some general guidelines. Usually, the farther the actual throw distance, the smaller the beam spread and the higher the mounting location on the boom. For example, instruments mounted at the top of a 21'-0" boom are often assigned to focus points between the centerline and the opposite black masking leg. Since the actual throw distance to their focus points is the greatest, their beam spreads are comparably the smallest, often having beam spreads of 12 to 30°. Instruments mounted between 10'-0" and 15'-0" above the deck are often assigned to focus points between the two quarter lines. Their beam spreads usually range between 30 and 40°. Units mounted below 10 feet are often assigned to focus points between the near black masking leg and centerline. The beam spread chosen is often selected to fill the depth of each near opening, so that the performer passing up- or downstage next to the near black leg remains in as much light as possible. Most units assigned to this function have beam spreads ranging between 30 and 90°.

Combining the available instrumentation and the needs of the production makes these kinds of general height distinctions somewhat fuzzy. Any number of instrument types and focuses can be specified for each design. Most designers follow the guideline stating that instruments mounted at the top of the boom focus to the far side, while lower-mounted instruments focus to the near side. The focused beams don't "cross," reducing the possibility of having too much intensity between two overlapped light beams in the same system.

Almost any instrument type can be used for boom sidelight. When the light beams need to be shaped with a sharp edge, ellipsoidal lighting instruments are often the first choice. While other instrument types are just as useful to produce sidelight, their beams often require additional accessories to shape the beams. This often translates into more time and effort spent preparing or focusing them. In addition, the combined weight of several accessories can alter the boom's center of balance, and may increase the overall footprint of the sidelight position. If alternate instruments are chosen for the job, then the amount of scheduled time or space may need to be increased in order to use them.

The successful boom sidelight system begins with symmetry between positions. Regardless of what instrument is used for each system, the unit type should be the same and be mounted at the same vertical height on each boom. Matching the unit type means that kind of light will be the same throughout the system. Matching the mounting height insures that the focus angle will be duplicated in each opening. Not only does this mean that the light source will be consistent throughout the system; it also means the performers will contend with the same vertical instrument arrangement while running around the booms.

Next, successful boom sidelight instruments attempt to be as compact as possible. Often this translates into all the instruments being hung in the same horizontal plane, one directly above, or below the other. While some booms mount the instruments directly upstage or downstage of the vertical supporting pipe, the even more compact booms reduce this "thickness" by hanging the instruments onstage of the vertical support. Not only does this often facilitate focus, but it also translates into more space between the boom and either of the masking legs for performers or other objects to pass around it. Sometimes the instruments are double-hung, both sticking out on either side. The phrase "double-hung" implies a pair of instruments, both vertically mounted at the same

height. Obviously their combined width makes the overall boom width "thicker." In tight quarters, a typical plotting tactic is to restrict mounting double-hung instruments to only above head height; single-hung units are mounted from the floor to approximately 8'-0", in order to provide as much passage space as possible for performers or moving props between the sidelight booms and masking legs.

Downlight

Downlight, or **toplight**, is generally defined as a system, instrument, or light beam originating directly above a person standing on a stage. The visual epitome of downlight are shafts of light pointing straight down, so that light covers the head and shoulders of the person. The combined light beams form symmetrical pools, equidistantly overlapping left to right, and up- and downstage. A full stage single-color downlight wash typically covers the entire performance area, from side to side, and from the upstage scenic stack to head height at the downstage light line.

In reality, downlights rarely point straight down. An overhead hanging position rarely gets placed directly above each zone of focus points. In many cases, the instruments end up on electrics that are located in the up- or downstage side of an opening. In order for the focused pools to *appear* properly overlapped up- and downstage, the downlights are slightly tipped during the focus to produce that effect. Since this is one of the systems that is more obvious to the audience's angle of observation, however, care must be taken during the plotting, the hang, and the focus to create the illusion that the instruments are focused "straight" down.

While the focus points for downlights in the first zone can be centered in the middle of the opening, they may just as easily be shifted upstage, so that the downstage beam edges land close to the downstage light line. The focus points for downlights in the final zone, on the other hand, are often shifted downstage so that the upstage beam edges land at the upstage light line. If the section is drawn so that accurate trims and beam spreads of the instruments are shown, it will be clearly seen where the beam edges and focus points of intermediate zones will need to be located, so that the pools symmetrically overlap.

The number of downlight zones, and the number of instruments used in each zone, are unique for every show. When a production is presented on an open stage, however, the focus and symmetry of a downlight system will be much more apparent to the audience's angle of observation. Depending on the overhead electric trim heights and the beam sizes used for the system, the number of zones is often equal to or less than the number of openings on the stage. The same criteria also determine a rough number of downlights across each zone. To provide proper beam overlap, the most basic downlight system for one zone is usually considered to be as few as three pools across, focused on the centerline and the two quarterlines.

Typically, the appearance of downlights on an open stage is a series of round beam pools. In that scenario, shutter cuts or sharp beam edges from barndoors are avoided unless necessary. The key to a successful downlight system begins when the instruments are plotted. The beam spreads drawn in the sectional view will inform the viewer if there's any chance that the light beam edges will hit scenery in the air. Sometimes entire electrics are shifted up or downstage to be certain that the downlight beam edges won't catch adjacent borders, and thus force the downlight to receive a straight-edged shutter cut. If that's unavoidable, the cuts are often matched on all of the beams in that zone. If a zone of downlights needs to potentially tip upstage in order to produce equidistantly spaced pools between zones, it's ill advised to hang the instruments on an electric that has an adjacent border on the upstage side.

The second key to producing successful downlight systems relates to the instrument's hanging location on the electric. Units on one side of centerline should be equidistant to each other and should match their counterparts on the other side of centerline. Though they may not end up pointing straight down, their on- and offstage hanging locations should be directly "in line" with each of the focus points. When that's not possible, the distances should be "mirrored" from one side to the other and matched between electrics.

The third key to the downlight system's success is to match the focused barrel softness, so that one beam doesn't stand out. If the production involves an atmospheric haze, the hanging positions and the beam edges will stand out even more. Care must be taken while plotting and focusing to ensure that the appearance of the light shafts is symmetrical.

Finally, the success of a downlight system can be seen in the way in which it is controlled. If each instrument is assigned to an independent channel, the units can be used as a series of specials, isolating each portion of the stage. When dimmers or channels become scarce, attention should be paid to the blocking of the production. If there's little need for one side of the stage to be isolated, adjacent instruments in a zone may be combined. Another approach may be to combine the offstage channels of the second and third zones of downlight. Usually, the center instruments of each zone are jealously guarded to remain separate, since they can isolate different portions of the most important area of the stage.

Backlight

Backlight is generally defined as a system, instrument, or light beam originating above and "behind" a person standing on a stage. This often means that backlight is pointed downstage towards the audience, so that light covers the head and shoulders of the person. A full stage single-color backlight wash typically covers the entire performance area, from side to side, and from the upstage scenic stack to head height at the downstage light line. In order to provide coverage at the downstage light line, backlight usually spills onto the apron, into the orchestra pit, and sometimes into the first row of the audience. In a proscenium configuration, this coverage is more successfully achieved when the backlight electric is located in the upstage side of its opening between the borders. In that way, the instruments can tip as far downstage as possible, under the next border closer to the audience, without being in view. This will be illustrated in detail in Chapter Five.

Backlight systems can be plotted in several different variations. In a proscenium configuration, **straight backlight** is plotted so that the focused beams travel directly downstage to each focus point. The focused beams travel parallel to centerline, but the light is 180° from straight frontlight. Focused backlight striking a person's body from approximately a 45° angle from centerline is often called **diagonal backlight**, but almost any backlight between straight back and straight side is often assigned that same directional label. Another style of backlight clusters instruments together at centerline, and then "fan focuses" the units out from center to the sides of the stage to evenly cover the zone. Since each style of system incorporates a different number of instruments to provide coverage, each system creates different amounts of intensity on the performance surface.

Regardless of their plotted style, the number of backlight zones and the number of instruments used in each zone are specific to each situation. The width of the stage opening, the height of the overhead electrics, and the beam spread of the selected instruments are the main parameters that define the number of instruments required for each light zone.

The first key to a successful full stage backlight system is to properly place the instruments during the plotting process. Scaled sectional views, drawn from the front viewing plane, help determine the number of instruments required to adequately overlap the beams and provide an evenly-spaced blended zone of light. If the system is a straight back focus, then the instruments should be placed on the electrics so that the instruments are directly upstage of their respective focus point. If the system is planned to be a diagonal focus, the instruments should be plotted to be the same consistent angle on either side of the focus points.

The second key to a successful full stage backlight system is to provide adequate up- and downstage coverage. The sectional view drawn from the centerline viewing plane helps determine the number of zones required to provide coverage for the depth of the performance space.

The third key to a successful full stage backlight system is symmetry in focus. Like downlight systems, focused instruments that don't match in size, beam edge, or beam shape can be seen from the audience's angle of observation. Usually, shutter cuts or sharp beam edges from barndoors are avoided, unless necessary to eliminate light off of masking. If a straight edge is required, it's usually matched for the entire zone.

Finally, the success of a backlight system can be seen in how it's controlled. If each instrument is assigned to an independent channel, the units can be used as a series of specials, isolating each area of the stage. When dimmers or channels become scarce, the production's blocking should be reviewed. Depending on the locations requiring isolation during the show, it may be possible to join control of the sides of the upstage zones together. Other times a single channel may control the entire upstage zone. The amount of control required by a backlight system can also be affected by the color of the light. For example, a backlight system equipped with a cool or saturated color may require fewer control channels. A second backlight system, in the same light plot, may contain warmer or more desaturated color. Since that color may provide more visual punch, the second system may be assigned more control channels, and assume the task of providing isolation.

From the audience's angle of observation, an even blend of a single color on the floor eliminates the possibility of distractions caused by seeing bright or dark spots on the performance surface.

Other Lighting Systems

In a theatrical setting, other systems of light have their own nomenclature. One category are lighting systems whose primary responsibility is to illuminate the scenery, rather than performers. Predictably, this category is generally referred to as **scenery light**, or **scenic toners**. While those terms may refer to systems focused onto legs, borders, or other scenic pieces or units, a **backdrop wash** always refers to the instruments used to illuminate the backdrops, translucencies, scrims, or bounce drops at the back of the stage.

Backdrop Wash

Lighting backdrops, cycs, and translucencies are often considered by many observers to be an art form unto themselves. Painted backdrops may require specials, or special systems to "pop out" parts of a backdrop, but often the real challenge posed by goods in the scenic stack is creating an even wash of light.

That's the epitome of a successful backdrop wash; an even wash of light, without hot spots, dark spots, or horizontal bands of lower intensity, that completely covers the piece of goods, horizontally from leg to leg, and vertically starting at the bottom where the goods touch the floor all the way up to where the black border visually cuts off the top. For the purists, the black masking is a black portal—there's no light on either the black legs or the black border; there's no "shadow line" across the top of the goods (caused by the black border being in between the lighting and the goods; and there are no "scallops" of light across the top of the goods (from striplights being too close to the goods or trimmed too low).

Sometimes, an even wash of light on the backdrop is not the visual goal. If the drop is a mix of fabric, or contains some abstract design, or if the show is a *film noir* or cinematic realization, then an even wash might be the furthest thing from the designer's objective. In a majority of situations, however, ranging from miniature cycs seen through interior windows, to exterior wraparounds, to romantic painted backdrops, to sky cycs and translucencies, the objective is to at least start with an even wash. For scenically painted goods, it's often a sign of respect to just provide even light and allow the design to speak for itself.

Most drops can be lit with some kind of **striplight, box cyc light**, or multi-circuit sources, which are often placed in any available space on either side of the drop where they might fit in. Striplights are designed to project bands of light, and typically contain multiple circuits. A single instrument automatically provides the ability to mix colors of light onto the goods. Box cyc lights are also multiple-circuit instruments, but they require more distance from the goods in order to properly spread their light beams.

For translucencies or seamless drops, the first choice is to place lights low, behind the goods. In most theatrical situations, if there's any room upstage of the goods, striplights quickly come into play. A long row of these instruments is often placed upstage of a translucency on the deck, butting into each other. This typical configuration is called a **striplight groundrow**. If there's room in the air, another row of the same kinds of instruments is hung across a batten to create an **overhead striplight electric**. Striplights can also be mounted on vertical booms, adjacent to the sides of the goods. In that arrangement, the same instruments are then collectively called **vertical toning strips**, or **VTS's**.

If the goods consist of an opaque painted drop, the entire overhead striplight electric and the striplight groundrow are shifted to the downstage side of the goods, in order to light the face of the drop. Sometimes a short constructed flat, called a **scenic groundrow**, is placed immediately downstage of a drop to hide the silhouettes of the striplight groundrow and their light leaks. If no adjacent room for striplights exists downstage of a drop, illumination must come from other sources.

Generally speaking, the remaining choices are either low, medium, or high. Low positions include cyc troughs, footlights, or lighting positions in the orchestra pit. Medium hanging possibilities include instruments on stands in the downstage leg openings or the FOH balcony rail. And high choices include overhead electrics, or FOH hanging positions. Almost all of these hanging positions aren't close to the drops, so the lighting instruments used are no longer striplights, they're other types of lighting instruments.

Lighting downstage drops means the goods are closer to plaster line, and therefore they might be lit by more hanging locations in the FOH. In most cases, lighting drops from the house usually translates into instruments hung on the balcony rail or somewhere that shoot "straight in" to the drop. Since there is no need to provide three-dimensionality, the instruments are usually positioned so that they focus straight into the goods. While frontlight positions might be considered, the lower the position, the easier it is to provide light as high as possible on the drop, up under the borders.

In many cases, regardless of their hanging position, any instruments primarily assigned to provide illumination onto a backdrop or goods is still often called a **drop wash**.

Overhead Template Wash

Other systems are named using a direction and a modifier. A **template wash** refers to a system of light that, rather than a smooth blended wash, is "broken up" or textured. A template wash can be focused towards a piece of scenery or a backdrop and assigned that name: the "mountain template wash," or the "sky temps," for example. It might also be assigned to sidelight booms or the balcony rail. But an **overhead template wash** almost always implies a wash designed to focus down and cover the performance surface.

These days the word "template" refers to many objects and devices that can be inserted into the optics of an ellipsoidal lighting instrument. For many old-school designers, the term still refers back to the original object, a thin piece of metal with holes. Once inserted into an ellipsoidal, the light beam is reshaped to mimic the design of the holes. Since templates "break up" the light coming out of an ellipsoidal, they're perceived as producing "textured" light. Depending on the angle, direction, color, intensity, and movement, templated light can define a location, provide dimensionality, establish a time of day, or evoke a feeling. They're usually used in four main applications.

First, templates can be focused from overhead positions to produce textured light on horizontal surfaces, like a stage. A templated ellipsoidal, equipped with a window template, produces that pattern of light on the floor, and can define the scene's location as an interior. If, instead, the window gobo is exchanged for a tree branch template, that pattern will be projected onto the floor, re-establishing the scene as an exterior. An abstract "breakup" pattern, on the other hand, might project mere blobs of light onto the stage, and affect the audience's perception of the scene, rather than the placement.

Second, templates can be used to add texture and dimensionality onto vertical scenery. If a lake is painted onto a backdrop, a templated instrument can be focused onto the water. After being shuttered to the boundaries of the water in a soft-edged focus, the mottled spots of light will add texture to the lake. The movement of a film loop (inserted into the same instrument) in the same focus can increase the illusion. If a scenic design consists of several walls, on the other hand, a system of templated instruments can be focused high on the walls. At a reduced intensity, the breakup pattern can visually add texture and subtle interest to the flat surfaces.

Third, templates can be used to supply texture and dimensionality to animate or inanimate objects on the stage. One example of this is templates inserted in low-hung sidelights. When focused as part of a typical boom sidelight wash, the "mottled" light can be seen on the sides of performers' bodies as they move about the stage. Another example is when templates are projected onto a unit set centered on the stage. When templated light is projected onto the scenery, it adds dimension to the otherwise flat surfaces.

Finally, templates can be used to apply texture to the air. When haze is used in a show, it's often not seen until light beams strike the particles in the air. Light beams, otherwise unnoticed, can change the look and perception of an entire scene, shaped by the different shafts of light now seen by the introduction of the haze. The number of beams (defined by the number of holes) from a templated unit can give the appearance of multiple sources of light produced by a single source. When this tactic is employed, the symmetric hanging locations for template systems may be as important a choice as the kind of ellipsoidal or the particular template used. Instruments hung on overhead electrics, for example, are often located at specific distances from centerline, so that their beams will produce symmetrical shafts in the air.

Templated light often combines these applications. They may be included in a plot to light both the stage and the performers moving through the space, or they may be designed to project light that is both seen in the air and striking objects on the stage.

Occasionally, templates will be used to provide a breakup pattern over an entire backdrop. To produce this effect, initial choices are made to define the hanging position, the beam spread, and the number of ellipsoidals. To maintain a consistent focus for the beam edge of each "hole" in the template, the instruments are often placed so that the templates focus straight into the backdrop. As a result of this choice, the instruments are often placed either on the first electric or the balcony rail. Drawing a section from either position shows the actual throw distance and the potential coverage using various-sized beam spreads. Choosing the proper beam spread is directly related to the number of instruments needed to cover the entire backdrop. One formula used to determine the total number of instruments needed is based on the cautious assumption that a typical template will cut the overall diameter of an instrument's beam by about 50%. Based on that assumption, the number of instruments of any particular beam spread can be determined.

When template systems are used to "break up" an entire performance surface, they are often designed so that they produce as much patterned light as possible, while requiring the fewest instruments to achieve that coverage. To achieve the maximum actual throw distance for each instrument, the units are often plotted into side galleries, ladders, or overhead pipe end hanging positions. The farther the actual throw distance, the larger the eventual gobo projection.

Templated instruments are also combined with many other devices to provide visual movement while only using conventional ellipsoidal instruments. Gobo rotators, film loops, and other devices expand the ways that templates can be used to create a more diverse visual environment.

Creating all of these systems is achieved by understanding the different concepts and components of theatrical light. This understanding begins by examining the properties and control of electricity, the form of energy that allows theatrical lighting to exist.

ELECTRICITY AND DISTRIBUTION

Electricity is a fundamental form of energy that is created by the movement of atomic particles called electrons. The combination of technological devices that manipulate electricity, coupled with the desire to control the visual environment, has helped propel the lighting designer's role in theatre. From the artistic point of view, the lighting designer visually reinforces the director's interpretation of the production. From a technical point of view, the lighting designer controls the amount of electricity to each lighting source. While the lighting designer is typically not required to have a detailed knowledge of electricity, he or she should have a basic grasp of this form of energy. The designer must have a comprehension of how to control electricity, if for no other reason than safety.

Basic Electricity

A basic electrical circuit is comprised of three components: a **source** of electricity, a **load** using the electricity, and **circuitry** providing a path between the two. There are two basic types of electricity: **direct** and **alternating current**. Every electrical system uses one of these two types. A demonstration of direct current can be seen in a typical flashlight. The electrical flow moves in a single direction of polarity from the positive terminal of the battery (the source), through the bulb (the load), and back to the negative terminal of the battery to complete the circuit. In today's world, low-powered direct current is seen in batteries, and is used to internally power computer devices.

Most electrical power provided to the consumer, ranging from entire nations to household outlets, is alternating current. This type of electricity is created by large generators, which essentially consist of fixed magnets surrounding a rotating shaft carrying three coils of insulated wire. The rotation of the shaft within the magnetic field generates pulsing electrical current in each of the three coils. The pulsing current reverses direction, or alternates polarity, 60 times a second, thus the term **60-cycle alternating current**. The individual current produced by each of the three coils is called a **phase** (or a "hot"). Three-phase 60-cycle alternating current is the standard distributed throughout the United States, but the actual number of phases installed in any building or performing facility may vary. Regardless of the number of phases, an additional wire is present which completes the circuit back to the generator, called the **neutral**. In many installations, another wire is also included as a safety precaution, called a **ground**.

Electricity has three related electrical attributes: amperage, wattage, and voltage, which are measured in amps, watts, and volts. An **amp** is the unit of measurement for electron flow from one point to another in a circuit, often interpreted as the amount of electrical flow possible through a wire. A **watt** is defined as a unit of measurement expressing the amount of electrical energy consumed by a device or a load. A **volt** is a unit of measurement expressing electrical pressure to form a current, or the electrical "force" of current through a wire. 220 volts "pushes" twice as "hard" as 110 volts. (Although typical U.S. voltage is 117 volts, the number is often "rounded off" to 110 volts.) One analogy used to explain the three attributes uses the image of a water hose and a pump. Amperage is the amount of water (or electricity) available to pass through the hose to the pump. Wattage is the amount of water (or electricity) that must be pulled through the hose to power the pump. Voltage is the pressure at which the water (or electricity) is pushed through the hose.

Two primary types of circuits are used to distribute electricity from the source to the load. An example of a **parallel** circuit is demonstrated by several clip lights plugged into a plugging strip. Two wires, a hot and a neutral, run to each bulb. Although all of the loads are connected to a single source, if one of the clip lights burn out, the rest of the lights will still continue to operate. This is the type of circuit commonly found in households and theatrical lighting installations.

A **series** circuit, on the other hand, is wired so that electricity "daisy-chains" and follows a single path through each of the lights to each other and the source. Like some common strings of Christmas tree lights, when one of the lamps burns out, the circuit is broken, and the other lights in the string no longer function. Although this type of circuitry isn't commonly used in theatres, an example can be seen in striplights using low voltage MR-16 lamps. Each lamp is designed to require only 12 volts of electricity, but the combined voltage of 10 lamps wired in a series circuit is 120 volts. The voltage is equally divided between the lamps. Just like the Christmas tree lights, however, a single burned out lamp results in the loss of the entire circuit.

The Control Path

To manipulate light in a theatrical setting, the lighting designer separately controls the voltage supplied to each electrical device. To provide this separation, each device has its own **control path.**

Figure 1.6 is an example of the four points in the control path for an instrument in a computer lighting system. The four points are the device, the circuit, the source, and the control.

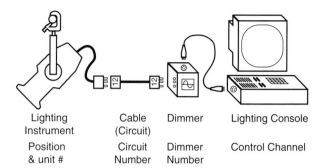

| Lighting Instrument | Cable (Circuit) | Dimmer | Lighting Console |
| Position & unit # | Circuit Number | Dimmer Number | Control Channel |

Figure 1.6 The Control Path

Electricity is supplied to a device, in this case, a **lighting instrument.** The electrical source is a **dimmer**, which regulates the amount of 110-volt current conducted to the lighting instrument. The dimmer is connected to the lighting instrument using a circuit, which usually refers to a **cable.** The cable contains wires that bridge the electrical gap between the dimmer and the instrument. The dimmer allows the instrument's light output to become more or less intense. In this example, the computer lighting console controls the dimmer with low voltage current. For our purposes, the word **control** can be used not only as a verb, but also as a noun. Control can refer to any generic device that controls a dimmer, and is a requirement for every electronic dimming system.

The electrical path must remain unbroken in order for the lighting instrument to receive controlled voltage and function correctly. Understanding each point in the path allows the lighting designer to properly control the electricity supplied to each device or lighting source.

Dimmers

Historically, direct current was the first type of electricity installed in theatres. The **resistance** dimmer, powered by this current, was the standard device used to control the voltage fed to lighting instruments. Dimmers were assembled in mechanical groups called **piano boards,** so named because their appearance resembled an upright piano. A piano board was mechanically constructed so that its individual dimmers could be collectively interlocked and controlled by a single handle, called a **grand master.** These dimmers were bulky, hot, and hazardous. The number of dimmers required for a light plot directly translated into the same number of individual moving handles, which in turn defined the number of light board operators. The amount of control available to a light plot was often determined by labor cost or the amount of backstage space available for the piano boards.

The **autotransformer** dimmer was introduced as alternating current became more available for theatrical use. Although these light boards were comparably more compact and generated less heat, each dimmer was still manually manipulated by a separate handle.

Other types of dimming systems were introduced, but they failed to gain wide acceptance. Eventually, the electronic silicon-controlled rectifier, or **SCR**, proved to be the innovative device that eventually replaced both resistance and autotransformer dimmers. Rather than direct mechanical control provided by a handle, a separate control device sent low-voltage direct current to the SCR, which in turn controlled the amount of alternating current sent to the lighting instrument. These dimmers were more compact and generated much less heat, allowing more of them to fit into the same space. Not only that, but since they could be controlled remotely in smaller groups, a greater number of dimmers could be controlled by significantly fewer light board operators. The SCR dimmer was originally controlled by manual preset light boards, which will be examined later in this chapter.

The components of modern dimmers still consist of an SCR, an "amperage rise controlling device," some electronic controls, and a circuit breaker. Beyond that, however, today's dimmers are quieter, faster, smarter, and more compact. Several dimmers are typically packaged into a single unit containing specific shelves (or racks) and internal wiring called a **dimmer rack**. Figure 1.7 is known as a portable (or touring) dimmer rack, because it's mounted on rolling casters. It's a self-contained unit requiring only an electrical source to distribute power to the individual dimmers. Thick **feeder cables** are often used to supply power from **a power distribution** box, or **PD**, to the dimmer rack. Cables or wires then run from the dimmers to the individual units. Large circuit breakers or fuses protect the "line" side, while individual circuit breakers or fuses protect each dimmer on the "load" side.

Sometimes a dimmer rack is assigned to control electrical devices that can't be dimmed; doing so can damage the device's internal electronic components.

Figure 1.7 A Portable Dimmer Rack

In these situations, some dimmer racks can be equipped with a device called a **non-dim**. Swapped out in place of a dimmer, while still being controlled by the console, the unit is essentially a switch. Any device circuited to the non-dim either receives full voltage or no voltage at all. Non-dims are often used to control motors, transformers, or electronics.

Improvements in technology have reduced the size of individual dimmers while inversely increasing the complexity of these devices. Although a single light board can now control numerous dimmers, additional devices may also be required. "**D to A's**" (short for digital to analog converters) are devices that translate the control signal from modern lighting consoles to older dimmers. An **opto-isolator** is a device that's inserted into the control signal's path, in order to split the digital signal or act as a safeguard for the electronic components inside lighting consoles. These additional devices should be treated carefully, since their omission or failure can result in nonfunctioning dimmer racks.

Likewise, the control signal connecting the light board to these devices or the dimmers usually runs through relatively small cables. If the cables don't work, the dimmers don't function either. As such, these small **control cables**, and their connectors, should also be treated with extra respect.

When constructing a light plot, attention must be paid to the number of dimmers that will be used and the amount of amperage they can handle. When the number of existing dimmers doesn't provide the amount of flexibility required to produce a lighting design, one solution is to replug (or **repatch**) cables during the performance. Repatching will be examined in Chapter 9. Other solutions may include installing additional dimmer racks (sometimes called **road racks** or **rental racks**) in the performance space for the show. Before any installation is considered, a knowledgeable electrician familiar with the space should be consulted.

Since electricity is required for any dimming to occur, and thereby most lighting designs to take place, protective devices are often installed in order to protect against the possible loss of power to the lighting console. Having a battery backup for an entire dimmer rack is often not a financial possibility. So when the dimmer power is cut off, limited solutions include running feeder cable to a different PD, or quickly installing a compatible generator. When the control power is turned off, even if the dimmers are functional, they might as well be dead. Protecting relatively small amounts of control power is not only financially feasible, but often now a typical part of any installation.

Devices such as **line tamers** "smooth" the voltage feeding computer lighting consoles, and prevent voltage spikes or dips to interrupt the electrical flow within those delicate electronics. An uninterruptible power supply (**UPS**) is essentially a large battery coupled with an electric sensing device. When control power is lost, the battery immediately kicks on to supply power for a period of time. Since the output of a UPS is often limited to only two female connections, the temptation is to plug both of them with **plugging strips**. At the time of this writing, many manufacturers quietly recommend that if power strips are used in this fashion, they should not be equipped with any surge protection. UPS battery power is notoriously "dirty"; even though lighting consoles can handle that, the plugging strip might not, and it might then be the plugging strip that blows the power to the console.

Circuitry

Although instruments, dimmers, or electrical devices can be mounted anywhere, an electrical route must be provided to conduct electricity between them to complete the circuit. This electrical route is collectively called **circuitry**, and each separate route is often referred to as a single **circuit**. Circuitry usually consists of three elements: **Wires** conduct the electricity, **insulators** cover each wire to contain and separate electrical flow, and **plugs** installed on both ends of the wires make certain that the electricity in the wires is connected in the proper arrangement. The construction and diameter of the wire determine the amount of current it can safely carry, which must be larger than the current required by the load. If this basic rule is not followed, an overload will occur, and the circuit will be disrupted. While only two wires are required to complete the circuit, most circuitry and cables consist of three separately insulated wires, enclosed in a single rubber skin or jacket with plugs at both ends.

Plugs are constructed to either be male (conductors sticking out of the plug), or female (conductors concealed inside the plug). To reduce the possibility of confusion or electrocution, the established standard is to always have the female contain the source of electricity. In practical terms this means that instruments are always wired with male plugs, while dimmers are always wired with female sockets.

Circuitry is often broken into two categories, either preinstalled or added. **Preinstalled circuitry**, part of the permanent electrical infrastructure of a performance facility, is often contained in a conduit and terminates at metal enclosures known as **raceways, plugging strips, plugging boxes, floor pockets,** or **drop boxes**. Some facilities are equipped with an intermediate point between permanent dimmer racks and pre-installed circuitry. These **circuitry transfer panels** allow the circuit's path to the dimmers to be interrupted and routed instead to road racks.

Since the hanging positions for the instruments may vary between productions, **added circuitry** may be installed. It often consists of cables that are plugged between the instruments and the preinstalled circuitry or dimmers. Several forms of cables may be employed to rapidly install additional circuitry in performance facilities. Initially, the path and total distance from each hanging position to the dimmers is determined (the "**run**"). If added circuitry is used exclusively to route electricity from an instrument to the dimmers, that cable is often referred to as a **home run**.

If the electrical path between the dimmer and the instrument is broken, the instrument will not work. To reduce the opportunities for that type of separation, additional circuitry is usually assembled to include as few plugs as possible. Old-school circuitry additions consist of groups of cable tied or taped together, typically referred to as a **bundle**. Usually the cables in a bundle are all the same length, with the plugs labeled at both ends. Using bundles during installation means that the same amount of effort required to install a single circuit will instead result in the installation of several. The modern form of added circuitry employs several groups of wires enclosed in a single jacket, known as **multicable**, or **mults**. Mults can terminate either in several plugs at each end, or with a single connector. The plugs are then contained in a separate modular unit with a matching connector, called a **breakout**. Since mults employ a single outer jacket, the overall size and weight of a length of mult is much less than a comparable bundle, which makes it easier to transport, handle, and install.

In many cases the cable wire size is large enough to supply electricity to more than one instrument. When two instruments are assigned to share the same circuit, a **two-fer** can be used to complete the connections. A two-fer usually consists of two female plugs connected to cables that join into a single male connector. When three instruments can be safely connected to a single circuit, a **three-fer** can be used.

It is worth noting that several different types of plugs are available for theatrical use. Although plugs allow for rapid connection of wires, they must be compatible with one another. If the plugs of additional circuitry don't match the existing plugs of the preinstalled circuitry, **adapters** must be utilized to bridge the gap.

The overall bulk of cable installed during a load-in can quickly increase the overall weight and dimension of any hanging position. As such, additional cable is often installed by initially being attached to the instruments at the hanging position. As the cable is installed, it's tied out of the way as much as possible. Following this method results in any extra lengths of cable being collected out of the way near the dimmers.

If there's any possibility that the placement of the instruments or the hanging position may need to be adjusted, though, an additional portion of the cable should be initially allocated to the hanging position. Otherwise, any movement on the part of the instruments or the hanging position may result in the addition of short cables to complete the circuit and introduce additional plugs to those routes. And as every electrician knows, every additional plug in a circuit is a place where the circuit can fail.

Determining the paths, and amounts of cable required, for an installation is just one of the many responsibilities delegated to the production electrician, since he or she is ultimately responsible for the installation, maintenance, and functionality of the lighting package. In many cases, enough circuitry exists so that there is no need to know the number of available circuits at each hanging position. Other situations may require the lighting designer to be acutely aware of the existing circuitry inventory, since he or she will ultimately decide the final distribution of units at each hanging position, and have to live with the potential repercussions.

Load Calculations

It has been said that all electrical devices require some amount of amperage to operate. If a device such as an instrument draws more amperage than a cable can handle, the result will be an **overloaded circuit**. When that occurs, the protective device, such as a **fuse** or a **circuit breaker**, should break the continuity of the circuit. If the total number of instruments plugged into a dimmer pulls more amperage than is supplied to the dimmer, the result will be the same, but the entire dimmer will shut off. Although the production electrician hypothetically double-checks all of the electrical demands required by the light plot, lack of time or knowledge may result in power problems that can result in lost time.

To ensure that scenario doesn't occur, **load calculations** are performed before a light plot is mounted. These calculations determine the overall amount of electricity required by the plot when every instrument is at its highest intensity. They are often performed as the light plot is being designed. Otherwise, one may discover that the amount of amperage required by a completed plot may exceed the amount of electricity available in the performance space. Although many different formulas and charts can be used to express electrical relationships, the power formula and a wire gauge chart are the two pieces of information typically utilized by the lighting designer to perform load calculations.

The **power formula** (or the "West Virginia" formula) is based on the three related attributes of electricity: amperage, wattage, and voltage. The formula, usually displayed in three variations, shows the relationship between these three attributes:

$W = V \times A$ — Wattage equals voltage multiplied by amperage. This arrangement is how the formula is often memorized (W. Va).

$A = \dfrac{W}{V}$ — Amperage equals wattage divided by voltage.

$V = \dfrac{W}{A}$ — Voltage equals wattage divided by amperage.

If two of the factors are known, the third attribute can be determined by using these formulas.

The second piece of information is a **standard lamp and extension cord current capacity chart**. The American Wire Gauge (AWG) system assigns a number to each size of wire and establishes the amount of current that each wire size can safely carry. Most cable used for temporary theatrical circuitry is either #12 or #14 wire gauge. The identification number is often marked on the cable.

Wire Gauge	10	12	14	16	18
Amp Capacity	25	20	15	10	7

Although the rated current capacity for any wire gauge can vary greatly due to the type of metal in the wire or the number of wires in the cable, this small chart shows a generic sampling of wire gauges and capacities. A #12 (or 12-gauge) wire can safely carry 20 amps, while a #14 wire can only carry 15 amps. The specific wire gauges and capacities for each cable type employed should be determined prior to load-in.

In practical terms, the power formula and the current capacity chart are two tools used by the lighting designer and the production electrician to make certain that no circuits, dimmers, or PD's can be possibly overloaded. Here are two examples of how the two pieces of information are used to perform basic load calculations.

Example 1: Is it possible to plug three 1000-watt instruments (or 3 kilowatts, or 3 kw) simultaneously into a single #12 cable? Multiplying the individual wattage by 3 results in the total wattage being considered (1000 × 3 = 3000 watts). Since the voltage is a given (110 volts), the second version of the power formula is used. Divide 3000 watts by 110 volts, resulting in 27.27 amps, much more than the 20-amp rating assigned to the #12 cable. The answer is no; three 1000-watt instruments should not be plugged into a single #12 cable. Two 1000-watt instruments, on the other hand, equal 18.18 amps, and could be plugged into the #12 cable without exceeding its amperage rating.

Example 2: The dimmer is rated to handle 30 amps. How many 750-watt instruments can be plugged into that dimmer? This question could be determined in two ways. The first method would use the second version of the power formula to convert 750 watts into amperage, and then divide the 30 amps by that result: 750 watts divided by 110 volts equals 6.8 amps. Thirty amps divided by 6.8 equals 4.4 instruments. In theory, the dimmer could safely carry 4.4 instruments, but practically, it can only carry four 750-watt instruments. The second method would use the first version of the power formula to convert the 30-amp dimmer into wattage. Thirty amps multiplied by 110 volts equals 3300 watts. If that result is divided by 750 watts, the result is again 4.4 instruments. Either method arrives at the same result.

One rough rule of thumb used is that each 1000-watt instrument is roughly equivalent to 10 amps. (In reality, it's just above 9 amps.) Using that rough yard stick, how many 1000-watt instruments can be plugged into a 12-pack of 20-amp dimmers? 12 times 20-amp dimmers equals 240 amps. So, using the 10 amp rule of thumb, the rough answer? 24-1000-watt instruments should not overload the dimmer pack. (In reality, 24 × 1000-watt instruments, divided by 110 volts, equals 218 amps. Safely under the 240 amp limit of the dimmer pack.)

Rule of thumb two: How many amps are needed to power 15-1000-watt instruments? Rough answer: 15-1000-watt instruments equals 15 × 10 amps each, or 150 amps. (In reality, 15,000 watts, divided by 110 volts, equals 136 amps. Safely under the rough 150-amp calculation.)

When possible, the production electrician's load calculations on a dimmer system should be a double-check of prior calculations made by the lighting designer. On larger shows involving multiple dimmer racks and power sources, however, load calculations become an exclusive part of the production electrician's domain. If the lighting designer possesses a basic knowledge of electricity, though, he or she will be able to make certain that the designed light plot can be physically realized without on-site power limitations imposing last minute restrictions to the design.

Since electricity is the element that allows theatrical lighting design to occur, the lighting designer and all members of the lighting department must be aware of its attributes, and the fact that it's dangerous. Electricity can easily cause injury or death. Knowledge, caution, and common sense are the basic tools that should always be practiced during any time spent on a stage. And that is doubly true when electricity is involved. This text presents some of the basic laws and principles about electricity, but other texts more closely analyzing this topic are worthy of examination. A sampling of them can be found in the bibliography.

CONTROL

Two general terms are applied in theatrical situations where dimmers control voltage to lighting instruments or devices. **Manual control** implies physical movement of a handle, lever, dial, fader, or slider to affect a dimmer. An autotransformer light board is an example of this control type. Moving the single physical handle up or down, directly affects the voltage supplied to an instrument, and makes the light brighter or darker. "Handle" has now been adapted as a generic term, referring to anything that affects an instrument's intensity. **Computer control**, on the other hand, implies an electronic interface with the dimmer rather than a physical one. In most cases the dimmers are affected by commands issued from a remote device with keypads called a computer light board or a computer lighting console.

The term "control" is also used to describe the numerical arrangement of the channels or dimmers that regulate instrument intensity. When a light plot is constructed, the lighting designer decides which instruments will operate together, which separately, and how they will numerically relate to each other. Their arrangement is documented in a form called a **hookup**. The word "hookup" is an anachronism carried over from the days of manual road boards. The physical action of plugging cables into the dimmers meant the cables were being "hooked up" or "patched" to the dimmer boards. The word is still used today, but when used in conjunction with lighting systems controlled by computer boards, the word "hookup" also refers to the action of electronically assigning dimmers to control channels. This action is also referred to as **softpatching**.

That has resulted in a linguistic back construction for the older system of physically plugging the cables into the dimmers, in order to provide control to a lighting instrument. That's now called **hardpatching**. If an instrument is plugged into a cable or circuit that's hardpatched into dimmer 1, then the instrument will turn on when the handle or fader for dimmer 1 is manually brought up.

With a computer lighting console, on the other hand, no matter what dimmer the instrument has been plugged into, the dimmer can be assigned to any channel by softpatching the dimmer. In this example, the cable is plugged into dimmer 2. The computer is then programmed so that dimmer 2 is softpatched (assigned) to channel 1. Now, when the computer light board is instructed to bring up channel 1, channel 1 will instruct dimmer 2 to activate, and that same instrument turns on.

Since computerized lighting systems electronically control dimmers, it's possible for a single channel to control more than one dimmer. Returning to the same example, the same instrument is still hardpatched into dimmer 2. Another instrument is plugged into dimmer 3. The computer light board is now programmed to softpatch both dimmer 2 and dimmer 3 to be controlled by channel 1. Bringing up channel 1 now activates both dimmers, and both instruments will be brought up together. On most modern computer light boards, it's possible for any number of dimmers or instruments to be controlled by any single channel. For the ultimate flexibility, every instrument is hardpatched into a separate dimmer, and then the dimmers can be softpatched into any combination of control channels.

Manual Control

Two kinds of manual light boards are still used in today's theatre. Autotransformer boards contain levers, each of which directly attaches to a single dimmer. Manually moving each lever directly affects the amount of voltage passing through that dimmer to the instruments.

A **preset light board**, on the other hand, contains rows of sliders, knobs, or levers that electronically control the voltage passing through the dimmers to the instruments. Instead of a direct mechanical connection, the preset light board is remotely connected to the dimmers by an electronic cable. Although the dimmers aren't directly controlled, this type of light board is still considered a manual device, since controlling the voltage to an instrument's light can only be accomplished by manually moving some mechanism on the board. Usually each slider in one row controls a single dimmer. Each row (or **preset**, or **bank**, or **scene**) of sliders duplicates control to the same dimmer. Slider 1 in the top row controls the same dimmer as slider 1 in the subsequent rows. While the top row is "active" (controlling the dimmers), the sliders in the following rows are manually "preset" by an operator for subsequent lighting **states** (or **looks**, or **cues**).

Movement from one row to another, illustrated by de-activating row 1 while simultaneously activating row 2, is accomplished by "cross-fading" from one row to another. An **X-Y cross-fader**, or some mechanical variation, serves this function. It's often

designed as two handles, which can move together as one. When the board is designed with more than two banks, additional switches adjacent to the cross-fader assign any bank to either handle. Most preset light boards also possess a **scene master** that also controls each bank. Some preset light boards possess an additional row of switches above each slider, allowing the dimmer to be separated from the X, Y, or scene masters to an **independent master**. Almost all preset light boards, however, contain a grand master, which overrides all other controls.

Computer Control

Computer lighting consoles often activate channels through individual sliders or knobs, or by using keypads and software commands.

Figure 1.8 is a computer lighting console designed to control and observe channels and other information about the light cues. In many cases, the information is often displayed on the monitors. While those are differences, what sets computer control apart from manual control is "cue storage" and "playback." On a manual preset board, the active light cue may be one of many arranged banks of sliders, for example. Once the cross-fade has been performed to activate the next cue, the first row of sliders is physically reset. Each cue is "stored" on a document, the written numbers indicating the level intensity for each slider in that particular cue. In a computer console, on the other hand, the light cue's intensity levels are stored in recorded software units called **memories** or **cues**.

Rather than cross-fading from one scene to another, the computer lighting console "plays back" different memories by loading them into a **fader**. One basic method to load a new memory (and to cross-fade to a new cue) is to press a single button, often labeled

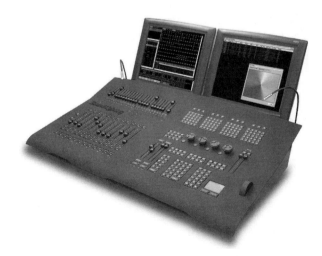

Figure 1.8 A Computer Lighting Console

as the "Go" button. Consoles are usually designed so that each memory can be assigned a predetermined length of time. This **time duration** is the amount of time between the moment when the Go button is pressed, and the moment the memory is completely loaded into a fader (and the cross-fade is complete). Many consoles are designed with several faders, so that several memories can be simultaneously loaded. Instead of independent masters, most computer lighting consoles have physical handles called **submasters** that control assigned channels. Software "handles" are designed into many consoles in the form of **groups**, which control assigned channels. Most current console software assigns repetitive keystroke combinations to simple keystroke shortcuts called **macros**. All of these functions are discussed more thoroughly in Chapter 9, but the online or printed manual for most consoles is the most accurate source of information describing the capabilities of that particular light board.

Many computer lighting consoles can be equipped with additional devices to increase their functionality. **Alphanumeric keyboards** can be connected to several consoles, allowing typed identification labels to be assigned to cues or other functions. A **remote focus unit** (or RFU, pronounced "ar-foo") is a small device that either connects directly to the console or operates through a wireless network, allowing basic console tasks to be performed solely using that device. **Printers** are often seen as a necessity to provide printed reports of the information programmed into the console. Some consoles are now equipped with touch screens, bypassing the need for keypad entry. External backup devices can store some number of memories as "snapshots" from the main console. In case of catastrophic console interruption (or failure), the backup device can assume the role of providing intensity information to the dimmers, regenerating some of the show's "looks", in lieu of the disabled console.

Computer Control Protocols

When computer control was first introduced into theatre lighting, its initial objective was to communicate intensity information to dimmers and other devices using a form of digital language or "protocol." **DMX512** was the first nationally recognized standard in this form of communication, and it's served well for many years. It acquired its name because it could send out control signal information to 512 channels, a number designated as a single **universe**.

The complexity of today's theatrical devices, however, has required more sophisticated protocols. **DMX512-A** has updated the protocol to include international text packet transmissions. **RDM** (remote device management) is a bi-directional protocol that can send out "inquiries" and receive responses from smart electrical devices. **ACN** (Architecture for Control Networks) is now being used in large installations, since it can be distributed via an Ethernet-based system using an Internet-based "star" network of switches. ACN works with other protocols to form networked audio, lighting, or other control systems. **Art-Net** is another Ethernet-based protocol. Though it's relatively simple, and easy to implement, some consider it a "bandwidth hog." While all of these new protocols have their own strengths and weaknesses, most devices on the market still also speak the original DMX512 standard. While lighting designers aren't expected to completely understand these newer technical languages, they should strive to grasp the implications when using or combining any protocols.

Another form of dimming control is "wireless DMX," which is basically sophisticated radio transmitters and receivers exchanging entire universes of DMX or other protocol information packets over airwaves utilizing proprietary message formats. Using different methods to ensure high levels of data fidelity, these systems co-exist with Wi-Fi technology in the currently-unlicensed 2.4-GHz band. At the time of this writing, though, these forms of control are still in flux, and no doubt will remain so for some time until new standards are adapted.

Computer Memory Storage

Computer lighting consoles are designed to store information about the memories and other lighting functions on storage media. Initially that included microfloppy and floppy disks. Nowadays, storage includes hard drives and USB devices. To utilize the capabilities of a computer lighting console, the lighting designer must have a basic understanding of how computer information is stored. Like every basic modern computer, there are two basic elements involved in computer memory storage. The first element is **random access memory** (RAM), where information can be changed, like thoughts in a brain. The second element is the **storage media**, ranging from a floppy disk to a hard drive, where information can be written down, like a book.

To change information in a book, the book must first be read. Reading the book transfers all of the information from the book to the brain. Then thoughts about the book can be altered and changed in the brain. Afterwards, all of the thoughts, both old and new, can be written back into the book. If changes are made in the brain, but the brain sleeps before writing the changes back into the book, then all contents of the book will be forgotten. The brain must read the book again before the thoughts can be changed.

The RAM in a computer lighting console is much like that brain. To be able to change information in a computer console, the information must be transferred from the floppy disk or hard drive into the RAM of the console. Once the information is in RAM, the information can be changed or altered. After the information is changed it can be written back onto the floppy or the hard drive. If the RAM of the computer reboots, in some cases, it's the same as the brain going to sleep. All of the altered information may have been forgotten. Whatever information has been changed in the RAM since the last transfer back to the floppy disk or hard drive may have been lost. For information to be written (or stored), it must be transferred back to the storage media. This topic is discussed further in Chapter 8.

Computer Lighting Console Control Philosophies

Understanding the basic logic employed by modern computer lighting consoles can be assisted by examining the methods and reasoning used to execute light cues on manual light boards. A piano or autotransformer light board, for example, typically consists of six handles, each handle mechanically controlling one dimmer. All six handles can be mechanically "interlocked" and controlled by a seventh, **master** handle. When the grand master moves up or down, the other affected handles move with it. The term "grand master" is now commonly applied to any fader or handle that overrides all other intensity output in a light board.

Each light cue on an autotransformer board is achieved by manually grasping the handles and moving them at a predefined speed. Figure 1.9 shows two written cues and their actions on two different light boards. Figure 1.9A shows the written shorthand for light cue 1; dimmer 1 and 2 fade up to full in 7 counts. Next to that is a sketch showing the handles for dimmers 1 and 2 moving in the direction of their 7-count fade up to full. If a light cue requires several handles to move simultaneously in different directions to different levels, it may require more than one person. If the light plot is controlled by many autotransformer boards arranged in the same area, the light cue's timing is typically coordinated by one of the senior board operators. After the stage manager says the magic "G" word*, the senior board op counts the seconds in reverse out loud to the rest of the operators, in order

---

*The magic "G" word is "GO", but it's never spoken on headset (especially by the stage manager) unless used to give a command. Otherwise, when folks hear the word out of context, if they're not paying attention, they can jump the gun, and perform a cue at the wrong moment in the show.

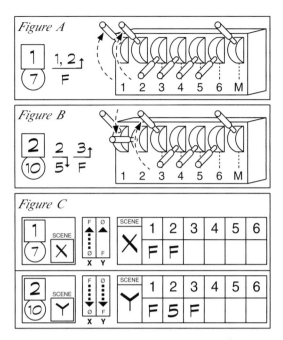

Figure 1.9 *Manual Light Board Written Cues and Moves; A) Autotransformer LQ1, B) Autotransformer LQ2, and C) Preset for LQ1 and LQ2*

to keep everyone in the same rhythm. SM: "Light cue 1, GO!" Board Op: "6, 5, 4, 3, 2, 1, complete!"

Once light cue 1 is complete, the board operators then refer to their individual cue sheets to prepare for light cue 2. Figure 1.9B shows the written shorthand for light cue 2; dimmer 2 fades down to 5, while dimmer 3 fades up to full, all in 10 counts. In this cue, while the other two dimmers **cross-fade**, dimmer 1 remains stationary. Since it doesn't move, dimmer 1 doesn't get listed; these manual cue sheets only list the dimmers that move and change intensity. When the stage manager calls "Light cue 2 GO," the affected dimmers move to their new levels in 10 seconds, again counted down by the leader. Dimmer 1 remains untouched, "tracking" through the light cue.

Manual preset light boards, with multiple rows of dimmers, introduced a new way of cross-fading between light cues and required a new method for the cues to be recorded. A basic preset light board has two scenes. Figure 1.9C shows the operator sheet for the same cue sequence. Both scene X and scene Y are preset with the same levels that were shown on the autotransformer board. When the call is made for Light Q1, the board op moves the Scene X fader handle up in 7 seconds, and the sliders for dimmer 1 and 2 fade up to Full. When the stage manager calls for Light Q2, the board op cross-fades to Scene Y.

Once complete, the sliders for Scene X are completely deactivated, and can be re-set for Light Q3. The common operator tactic is to first move all the sliders in Scene X to zero. Performing this action means there's then no chance that an errant slider will be accidentally left active at any level from the previous cue (light cue 1). Yes, it's rather embarrassing. After all the sliders are "zeroed," then the operator presets the sliders to the intensities written on the preset sheets for Light Q3. The preset sheets list each slider's intensity. Once the scene is set, the operator visually checks to make certain that the physically preset sliders match the written paperwork.

The thought processes shown in these examples provide the basis for the two types of logic used in today's computer lighting consoles. As an interesting note, the original code name assigned to the original Strand Palette computer lighting console was the "4PB6E," shorthand for "4 piano boards, 6 electricians." The logic employed in the console design was an emulation of the actions and logic used to run either earlier light board. Both logics are based on the fundamental fact that "looks," or "light cues," or "states" can be recorded as memories and assigned a numeric label. When the GO button is pressed, a command is sent to the light board, which "loads" the memory into a fader. After the memory has been loaded, the handle of the fader may be used like a grand master. One memory could be loaded into a fader at one time. Today's lighting consoles are designed with multiple fades, allowing several separate memories with different levels and time durations to be simultaneously executed.

Each memory or lighting state in a **computer preset console** is recorded as an individual snapshot, like the manual 2-scene preset board. The intensity level of each channel is individually addressed in every memory. The **computer tracking console**, on the other hand, sees light cues like the autotransformer board. It records the same memories, but only alters channel intensities that are different from the previous memory. Unaddressed channels "track through" that memory. For further explanation, consider this next example.

Figure 1.10A shows a grid, with memory numbers listed down the left-hand row, and channel 1 listed at the top of the column. Five memories are created on both types of light boards. Channel 1 is brought up to Full in memory 1, and then recorded at that intensity through memory 5. After all five memories have been recorded, the decision is made to reduce channel 1's intensity to 50%, in all five memories. Figure 1.10B shows that process on the computer preset console; each of the five memories must be accessed, channel 1's intensity is reduced to 50%, and then each memory is re-recorded.

The computer tracking console has initially programmed channel 1's intensities the same way. Figure 1.10C shows channel 1 brought to Full in

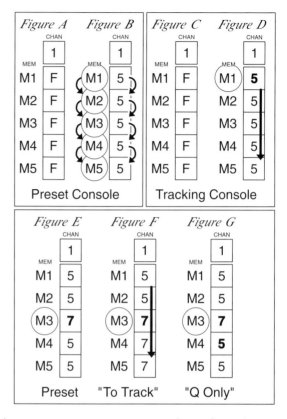

Figure 1.10 Computer "Cue Only" and "Tracking" Screens

memory 1, and then recorded at that level into the five memories. Since channel 1 has been unaddressed after memory 1, and remained at the same intensity in memories 2 through 5, however, the console has automatically assigned the channel's non-movement in those memories as "**tracking**." Figure 1.10D illustrates the process employed to make the same change in channel 1's intensity in all five memories. Memory 1 is accessed, the intensity for channel 1 is reduced to 50%, and memory 1 is then re-recorded "**to track**." Since the computer tracking console has now recorded a new initial (or hard) command for channel 1, it will track that reduced intensity through the following four memories. The single record instruction changes the level in all five memories.

There's a second function in a computer tracking console that separates it from the computer preset console. Using the five-memory example, the decision is now made to increase channel 1's intensity up to 70%, but record that only in memory 3. Figure 1.10E illustrates processing that change in the computer preset console: Access memory 3, keystroke channel 1 to up to 7, and re-record memory 3.

That could be the same keystroke sequence typed into the computer tracking console, but Figure 1.10F shows the result of re-recording memory 3 "to track."

Channel 1 then tracks at 70% through memory 4 and 5. To confine the intensity change solely to memory 3, the computer tracking console must be instructed to re-record the intensity change in memory 3 "**cue only.**" Figure 1.10G illustrates the result of this command. While the light board records channel 1 at 7 in memory 3, it also automatically reverts channel 1's intensity back to its previous level in the following memory. In this example, after re-recording memory 3 "cue only," memory 4 is assigned a hard command reverting channel 1's intensity back down to 50%. Memory 5 then follows that command, and tracks channel 1's intensity as 50% as well.

A **hard command**, or **hard level**, in this type of console is defined as an intensity change assigned to a channel, which establishes a point of tracking, as opposed to a matching intensity level from a previous memory that then merely tracks through that memory. The hard command given to channel 1 in memory 4 initiates a tracking change in channel intensity. Once the channel's intensity is changed and recorded into memory, the hard command forces the channel to remain at that intensity through all subsequent memories until another hard command is encountered to alter the intensity level. In this example, channel 1 will remain at 50% until a subsequent memory is loaded into the fader that has channel 1 changing to a different recorded intensity, a hard command.

To create memory 6 as a fade to black (FTB), all active channels from memory 5 would be programmed to 00% and recorded "to track" as memory 6, effectively stopping any tracking intensities. If memory 7 is then recorded without changing any other channel information, it will contain no active channel intensities, since no levels are tracking into the memory. The hard command zeros in memory 6 block the path of any intensity information that may be tracking from hard commands given in memories 1 through 5, and are known as "**blockers.**" To ensure that a memory designated as a "fade to black" doesn't later have intensity information track into it from prior memories, the FTB memory is often programmed with all pertinent channels containing hard command zeros. The FTB memory can then also be referred to as a **blocker cue**, since all tracking intensity information is being stopped at that memory.

Shelley's Notes: Know Your Console

This is a basic explanation of the logic used in the two primary types of computer light boards. Certainly, there is much more complexity regarding command structures than can be discussed in this text. Knowing the logic, command language, limitations, and work-arounds of a given computer lighting console can be critical to achieving a successful design. Understanding the differences can affect how the memories are constructed, stored, or manipulated. If there are any questions or unfamiliarity with a particular console, the advice is simple: Be prepared. Acquire information from every possible source, including manuals, downloaded cheat sheets, board operators, lighting rental shop technicians, or manufacturer reps, to name a few. Borrow time on a showroom demo model, if one can be found. Watch the board being programmed for another show. Acquire phone numbers of experienced operators who will tolerate late-night blithering phone calls of confusion. Don't presume that the board operator will have a full understanding of, or grasp the implications, of actions taken while programming the console. If the lighting designer doesn't have a complete understanding of functions or commands, hours of work can quickly be destroyed.

Cue and Memory Nomenclature

The word *cue* has two general meanings. A **called cue** is a command (usually given by a stage manager) at a specific moment to initiate a specific action. The spoken command given during a show results in an action, or the cue, being taken. ("Curtain, GO!") When combined with an adjective, however, the word *cue* is also defined as the specific desired effect predetermined to take place as a result of that command. Other types of cues may occur during a performance to affect scenery ("Fly Cue 14, GO!"), sound ("Sound Cue F, GO!"), or other facets of the production ("Banana Cue, GO!"), but a **light cue** usually implies a change in dimmer or channel intensities from one state or look to another. When manual light boards are used, a completed light cue usually refers to a completed static arrangement of dimmers or channels to produce a single visual image.

When computer light consoles are involved, the unit of RAM containing a recorded arrangement of channel intensities is called a **memory**. Strictly speaking, while a cue is a command that may activate a memory, it may instead imply the movement of a submaster, activation of a macro, or any other manual change in the overall electrical state of the production. As far as computer light consoles are concerned, however, the distinction between these two terms has blurred. While a memorized unit of RAM is indeed a memory, any memory may also be referred to as a cue.

When referring to light cues, nomenclature is used to identify the type of cue being discussed. Whereas called cues are initiated by the stage manager's spoken command, additional cues may be programmed to begin automatically without a second command. A stage manager's call book will list the called light cues, but there may be many uncalled follow cues programmed "in the background" to initiate additional lighting changes, preset moving light fixtures, activate special effects, or control other devices. A **follow cue** begins the instant that the first memory completes its fade; the second cue is referred to as an "**autofollow.**" Here are other names given to types of light cues:

- A **preset cue** often refers to the lighting state seen on stage prior to the beginning of a show, or the opening of the main curtain.
- A **fronts up cue** typically adds only frontlight to a preset cue. This term is often applied to the first light cue called after the main curtain has been removed to begin a performance.
- A **fronts out cue** typically subtracts only frontlight from the previous cue. This term is often applied to the final cue called before the curtain flies in at the end of an act or a performance.
- A **base cue** is the name given to the first cue in a scene, upon which other less substantial cue changes within the same scene are made.
- An **effect cue** involves a programmed series of actions typically involving a collection of channels, which activate in a sequential pattern.
- A **fade to black cue** fades all of the lights completely out, resulting in darkness.
- A **blackout** is the same action as a fade to black cue, but the fade typically happens in a zero count (a bump).
- A **bow cue** is the look used during curtain call when performers take their bows. Though it may be a copy or modification of a cue seen earlier in the show, its main intent is to make certain that the faces of the performers can be seen.
- A **bow preset cue** is often used when a closed main curtain prevents the audience from seeing the performers move to their position onstage prior to the bows. It's usually the same as the bow cue, but without any frontlight. When the cue is active, no light is seen on the curtain.
- A **bow ride cue** adds frontlight to the bow preset cue when the main curtain opens for bows. It often consists of intensities loaded into a submaster. Bringing the sub to full adds the frontlight onto the bow preset cue. The sub's intensities can then be removed or added as the curtain opens or closes. When the bow ride cue is removed, the bow preset cue remains on stage.
- A **restore cue** is a copy of a previously used cue. One example may be seen during bow sequences at the end of a show, when the stage quickly fades to black, followed by the lights fading back up and restoring to the same previous lighting state.
- A **postset cue** is the lighting state seen by the audience as they leave the theatre after the bows. This cue is often used when the main curtain is not closed and the stage is exposed to the audience's view.

There is also nomenclature for series of cues that occur close in time to one another:

- An opening sequence often begins with the house lights fading to 50% (or half) and ends with the lighting state that establishes the first "look" in the show.
- A **transition sequence** usually begins with the final cue of the first scene, and ends with the lighting state that establishes the second scene.
- A **final sequence** often begins with the first cue changing the last established look in the show, and ends with the bow preset cue.
- A **bow sequence** often begins when the curtain is raised for the bows. This sequence is often a combination of a fronts up cue and a series of blackouts and restores.

Computer Lighting Console Syntax

For many computer lighting consoles, spoken words or phrases are interpreted by a board operator and typed into a keypad to achieve the desired result. On many computer lighting consoles, a specific area of the computer monitor, known as the **command line**, reflects these programmed keystrokes as numerals or symbols as they are typed in (or "entered"). The command line provides a simple visual confirmation that the correct programming sequence of instructions has been executed. Although programming sequences, or **command structures**, may vary wildly between lighting console manufacturers to achieve the same result, many typographical symbols have been adopted as shorthand for English words. Many lighting designers write their notes and corrections using this shorthand, so that the symbology of the written notes match the command structure display to confirm accurate programming.

For example, the ">" and "@" characters are often employed, respectively, to display the selection of a continuous range of channels and their intensity activation. If channels 1 through 10 are simultaneously activated, the command line displays "1 > 10." If the same channels are set to a matching intensity of 50%, pressing the "at" "5" and "0" buttons can result in the command line displaying "1 > 10 @ 50." In another example, the "+" symbol is often used in place of the words "and" or "plus," while the "–" symbol is often employed to represent "minus" or "less." If channels 1 through 10 and channel 15 are set to a matching intensity of 25%, the command line might read "1 > 10 + 15 @ 25." If channels 1 through 5 and channels 7 through 10 are all set to 70%, the command line may read "1 > 10 – 6 @ 70." For the purposes of this text, the ">" symbol will indicate any continuous number series, the "@" symbol will replace the word "at," "+" will replace "and," and "–" will mean "minus."

Depending on the manufacturer and model of computer lighting console, some variation of this command structure may be successful and achieve the desired action. Or not. Some program languages are reversed and require the channels to be addressed after the intensities. Other languages, on the other hand, are completely touch-based interfaces. In order to understand and be assured that the proper programming is taking place, the lighting designer must undertake the effort to understand the programming structure employed by that particular lighting console. Some lighting designers write the console's name on their paperwork, in order to remind them which one they're working on at that moment.

Time Fades

Understanding time fades is fairly simple. On a manual light board, the time fade assigned to a cue indicates the amount of time that should occur between the stage manager's call and the moment the fade is complete. Dimmers assigned to move in a light cue can be divided into two categories: dimmers that move up (an **upfade**) and dimmers that move down (**downfade**).

One example of an upfade cue is the first cue to fade up into a scene from a black stage. A downfade cue, on the other hand, is the last one at the end of the scene, that fades the stage out to complete darkness, a fade to black.

When discussing a computer light board, a **time fade** is defined as the duration of time that occurs between the moment the GO button has been pressed (to load a memory into a fader) and the moment the fade is complete (the memory is completely loaded). In most computer lighting consoles, every memory used as a light cue can be assigned a single time fade, which determines the amount of time that will occur for all of the channels to complete their movement. If memory 1 is assigned a 5-second time fade, it could be illustrated with a time map, as shown in Figure 1.11.

The numbers across the top show the number of seconds. The time fade of memory 1 is shown as a line with a dot at each end. The 5-second time fade starts at zero, when the GO button is pushed, until the fade is complete.

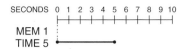

Figure 1.11   A Basic Time Fade

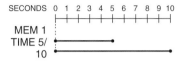

Figure 1.12   A Split Time Fade

Some light boards have the ability to "**split**" the time fade. All of the channels that move up can be assigned a different speed than all of the channels that move down. If memory 1 is assigned an upfade time of 5 seconds and a downfade time of 10 seconds, most consoles would display that time duration as "5/10." Figure 1.12 is a time map showing memory 1 with that split time fade assignment. Although the upfade channels still take 5 seconds to complete, the downfade channels in the same memory take 5 more seconds to complete the overall fade.

Waits and Delays

Understanding waits and delays can be a bit more involved. Both of these terms also refer to durations of time, but they are separate from a time fade, and the definition of the terms can interchange between manufacturers of different lighting consoles. These additional time durations can be assigned to most memories used as light cues. Consider two memories, memory 1 and memory 2, each assigned a time fade of 5 seconds. For our purposes, a **wait** is defined as the amount of time that occurs between the moment at which the GO button is pressed and when memory 1 actually *loads* into a fader. The wait affects only the memory to which it's assigned. Figure 1.13 is a time map that shows the effect of assigning a wait of 3 seconds to memory 1. After the GO button is pushed, 3 seconds will elapse before memory 1 begins its timed fade. The overall elapsed time is 8 seconds. The value of this function is discussed later in Chapter 13 when part cues are examined.

A delay, on the other hand, always implies a "link" to another memory, usually the next memory in sequence. For our purposes, a **delay** is defined as

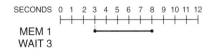

Figure 1.13   A Time Fade with an Assigned Wait

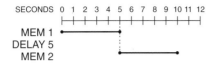

Figure 1.14 Two Time Fades with an Assigned Delay

the amount of time between the moment at which the GO button is pressed (loading memory 1 into a fader) and when the cue that it is linked to (in this case memory 2) automatically loads into a fader. The GO button is only pressed once to complete the two fades. Figure 1.14 is a time map that shows the effect of assigning a 5-second delay to memory 1. After the GO button is pushed, memory 1 immediately begins its timed fade. Five seconds later, memory 2 automatically begins its timed fade. The overall length of time for both cues to complete their fade is 10 seconds. In this example, the length of the delay is the same as memory 1's fade time. Since the second cue starts loading at the same moment that the first cue completes, this is a perfect example; memory 2 is an autofollow cue.

Figure 1.15 is a time map that shows the effect of assigning a 3-second delay to memory 1. After the GO button is pushed, memory 1 immediately begins its timed fade. Three seconds later, memory 2 automatically begins its timed fade. The overall length of time for both cues to complete their fade is 8 seconds.

The terms "time fade," "wait," and "delay" can vary in their meaning, depending on the manufacturer of the console. Not only can the terms imply different functions between manufacturers, the terms can also have unique implications for different lighting consoles created by the same manufacturer. Though the semantics may be interchangeable, or completely different, most computer light boards provide these functions. Since semantics can vary between consoles, the lighting designer must know which set of terms to use in order to properly program that particular lighting console. Smart (or cautious) lighting designers often write definitions of the terms directly on paperwork they keep close at hand while they create the light cues, in order to eliminate confusion.

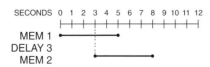

Figure 1.15 Two Time Fades with an Assigned Overlapping Delay

LIGHTING INSTRUMENTS

The lighting instrument is a device typically containing a lamp that receives electricity to produce light. Selecting the proper lighting instrument is a basic skill that a lighting designer must possess in order to provide designed illumination. That selection begins by knowing the different characteristics of each instrument type. The characteristics of the instruments are determined by a combination of their individual components.

Components of Lighting Instruments

Theatrical lighting instruments usually consist of three components contained within a housing. These components are lamps, reflectors, and lenses.

The Lamps

Most modern theatrical lighting instruments produce a beam of light using a lamp as a source. Different lamps create different colors, intensities, and types of light. Modern lamps contain a **filament** and an inert **gas**, both of which are enclosed in a transparent **bulb** or envelope mounted on a **base**. Electricity passing through the filament produces light. Not only does the base secure the lamp to the socket and conduct electricity to the filament, bases often pre-align the filament in the proper relationship to a reflector within an instrument.

The two main types of lamps used for modern theatrical stage lighting are **incandescent** and **tungsten-halogen** lamps. Both of these types of lamps are manufactured in a variety of wattages and produce a range of color temperatures.

Figure 1.16 shows an HPL lamp that contains the proprietary four-filament design branded as "Source Four." The HPL is the light engine for an entire product line of theatrical lighting instruments. While this lamp can be "burned" (or turned on) regardless of its physical position, some lamps must be turned upside down (or burned "base-up") to ensure proper lamp life.

Figure 1.16 HPL Lamp with Four Filaments

Distinctions between the types and wattages of most lamps are designated by three-letter codes assigned by the Accredited Standards Committee C78. This committee is one of many overseen by the American National Standards Institute (ANSI). The three-letter codes, typically referred to as the ANSI code, provide a system to assure compatibility among similarly coded lamps from various manufacturers. Among other attributes, the ANSI code identifies the type of base, the wattage, the rated length of life, and the physical dimensions of the filament and lamp. Other attributes typically listed for each lamp include its color, and the amount of light produced by that lamp. The measurement used to define the amount of light produced by a lamp is expressed in units called lumens. A **lumen** is roughly defined as the time rate flow of light emitted by the flame of a theoretical wax candle. A **foot-candle** is the level of illumination on a surface 1 foot away from the flame of that theoretical candle.

Often the design of a lamp is specific to a particular instrument. If the proper lamp isn't used, the light output may be hampered, the lamp may have a prematurely shortened life, or, in some cases, the lamp may explode. The proper lamp should be placed in the proper instrument.

In most cases, any oil, grease, or foreign matter left on the bulb can drastically reduce the life of the lamp. Any fingerprints or smudges on a bulb should be removed.

Black lights (UV) are used to visually "pop" chemically treated colors on stage, or to provide eerie visual effects. Since the source requires a ballast, "dimming" the source often translates into expensive dimmable ballasts, or the need for external dousing devices.

Other types of illumination sources have been adopted by the theatrical industry. Metal halide lamps (**HMI**) produce a high color temperature light. Once exclusively used in movies and television, these sources and fixtures have become mainstays when intense beams of light are required. Since the source requires a high voltage and a ballast, the source can't be dimmed. Instead, the housings also require external dousing devices. Regardless of their housing, HMI instruments require knowledge to safely mount the instrument, control the beam, and especially change the lamp.

The **LED**, acronym for Light Emitting Diode, was a source initially used for years in small devices, such as alarm clocks or calculators. In the late 90's, fixtures were introduced using LEDs in the primary colors of red, blue, and green (RBG). Today's lighting devices are powered by multiple-colored LED systems, achieve millions of color mixes, and are housed in a variety of instrument types. Applications for the source are in constant development, and manufacturing improvements consistently increase lamp life and intensity and significantly reduce power consumption. While the eventual niche of LED fixtures in entertainment lighting is still to be seen, it seems apparent that they will be a part of the industry. At the time of this writing, however, the color consistency of LED sources is still hard to maintain, their light output is still rather "spotty," and almost all of the fixtures are very expensive to rent or purchase.

One source that's only recently been displayed at trade shows is the **plasma** light source. In their current pill-sized shape, these sources claim to be 10 times more efficient than traditional incandescent light bulbs, twice as efficient as current high-end LEDs, and have eye-popping lamp life. How they will fit into the entertainment industry is, at the time of this writing, a source of massive speculation.

The Reflectors

The light that is created by most lamps is cast in all directions. Theatrical instruments are designed so that a lamp is typically contained within a mirrored reflector to direct as much of the light as possible toward the lens. Three different types of reflectors are most often used in theatrical lighting instruments. They are shown in sectional view in Figure 1.17.

The **spherical reflector** on the left-hand side of Figure 1.17 redirects rays of light that would otherwise be lost in the housing back through the source toward the lens. Though not all of the light is efficiently used, the reflector dramatically increases the amount of light coming out of the front of the instrument. This reflector is used mainly for Plano-convex and Fresnel instruments.

The **parabolic reflector** in the center of Figure 1.17 directs the rays of light in a more controlled fashion. When the source is placed at the proper location, the rays of light reflected from a parabolic reflector are essentially parallel. This reflector often uses no lens to concentrate or direct the light.

The **ellipsoidal reflector** on the right-hand side of Figure 1.17 is shaped like a football with one end cut off and a small hole for a lamp cut in the other. This reflector redirects more light towards the lens, and is

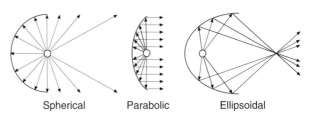

Spherical   Parabolic   Ellipsoidal

Figure 1.17 Spherical, Parabolic, and Ellipsoidal Reflectors

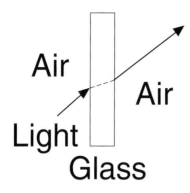

Figure 1.18 Refracted Light

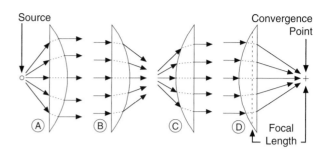

Figure 1.20 Light Passing Through a Plano-Convex Lens

often considered by many to be more efficient than the first two. The diagram shows that the beams of light cross in front of the reflector.

The Lenses

Figure 1.18 shows light refracted, or redirected, as it passes through glass. In theatrical lighting instruments, the amount of refraction is a result of two choices; the curvature and thickness molded into the lens, and the angle of the light source in relation to the lens. Some amount of light passing through a lens is transformed into heat. Because of that, thicker lenses absorb more heat and are more susceptible to heat fracture. Lenses in theatrical instruments are constructed from either glass or plastic to control the beam of light created by the lamp inside the housing.

Figure 1.19 shows three basic types of lens surfaces. The **convex** lens on the left-hand side bulges out, while a **concave** lens in the middle cuts in. A convex lens cut in half results in a Plano-convex lens ("Plano" means flat), shown on the right-hand side. This is the basic lens configuration employed in most theatrical lighting instruments.

By varying its position, in relation to the light source in a theatrical instrument, a convex-convex lens is used either to converge the light to a single point, or concentrate a spreading beam of light into

a tighter, more powerful beam. Figure 1.20A shows rays of light from a single source passing through the Plano side of a lens. The spreading light from the source is condensed to form a more powerful beam. Figure 1.20B shows parallel rays of light entering the Plano side of the lens and converging to a single point. Figure 1.20C shows rays of light from a single source passing through the convex side of a lens. The lens concentrates the beam to create parallel rays of light. Figure 1.20D shows parallel rays of light entering the lens and converging at a single point. The distance from that single point to the optical center of the lens (roughly the middle) is called **the focal length** of the lens.

The left-hand side of Figure 1.21 shows light from a source passing through a **step lens**. The shaded area represents the glass area that has been "cut away" from the Plano side of the lens. Although much of the glass has been removed, the effect of the lens has been retained. The elimination of the glass has reduced the weight and the amount of heat absorption.

The center illustration of Figure 1.21 shows parallel rays passing through a **Fresnel lens**. The shaded area represents the portion of glass that has been "cut away" from the convex side of the lens. This type of lens produces a more diffused, softer edged beam of light.

The right-hand illustration of Figure 1.21 shows rays of light from a source passing through a **double plano-convex** lens system. The distance between the

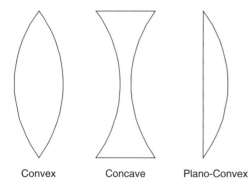

Figure 1.19 Convex, Concave, and Plano-Convex Lens

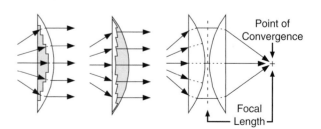

Figure 1.21 Step Lens, Fresnel Lens, and Double Plano-Convex Lens

optical center of the lens system (if the two lenses are identical, this is in the middle between them) to the convergence point where the rays cross, establishes the focal length for the lens system.

The Individual Instruments

Lamps, reflectors, and lenses combined in different housings, create theatrical lighting instruments. They are generally categorized by type, wattage, and the degree of beam spread that they produce.

This next section provides a brief description of today's current lighting instruments, accompanied by a small illustration. Almost every instrument shown is produced by multiple manufacturers. Due to space limitations, only one example is shown to illustrate each fixture type. While all of the equipment pictured in this section is of high quality, the manufacturer's name is included solely to provide clarity, not endorsement.

Figure 1.22: The **beam projector**, or **BP**, consists of a parabolic reflector mounted in a housing without a lens. The lamp and a small circular secondary reflector, which blocks direct light from escaping the housing, move together on a carriage relative to the static reflector. The carriage movement alters the size of the beam spread. If the beam is focused too wide, however, the secondary reflector blocks the center of the beam, creating a "doughnut" of light with a dark hole in the middle. BP light is often described as "shafty," and is typically used to create "sunlight." Controlling the edges of a BP beam can be very difficult.

Figure 1.23: The **Plano-Convex** instrument, or **PC**, is comprised of a housing containing a lamp and a spherical reflector. The beam spread is controlled by a single convex-convex lens mounted in the housing, with the flat side of the lens facing into the lamp. The lamp and reflector move together on a carriage closer or farther away from the lens, allowing the cone of light coming out of the instrument to become larger (or **flooded**) or smaller (or **spotted**). The edge of the beam can be shaped using external accessories such as barndoors. The beam edge of a PC is sharper than that of a Fresnel lens. This instrument has historically been one of the workhorses of European lighting.

Figure 1.24: For many manufacturers, the **Fresnel** instrument is the same as the PC, but equipped with a Fresnel lens. It's the same body, containing a lamp and spherical reflector mounted on a carriage in the same arrangement as the PC. Because of that, the Fresnel's beam spread can also get larger or smaller, and the edge of the beam can be shaped using barndoors. The main difference between the two

Figure 1.22 The Beam Projector

Figure 1.23 The Plano-Convex Instrument

Figure 1.24 The Fresnel Instrument

instruments is the lens; the Fresnel lens has a softer edge. Perhaps because the Fresnel lens is "cut-away," though, it can withstand greater heat. Current instruments equipped with Fresnel lenses can be lamped up to 18,000 watts.

Figure 1.25: The parabolic aluminized reflector, or **PAR**, is a sealed-beam lamp, like a car headlight. The filament, reflector, and lens are combined into a single, non-moving unit. The housing, or **PAR can**, merely holds the lamp, color, and any external hardware. The size and dispersion of the lamp's elliptical beam depends on the type, size, and number of facets that are molded into the lens. The light beam has "punch," but often retains a soft edge.

Figure 1.26: The **Ellipsoidal Reflector Spotlight**, also known as an **ellipsoidal**, an **ERS**, or a **profile**, combines the ellipsoidal reflector and a double convex-convex lens system. Some versions of ellipsoidals

Figure 1.25 The PAR Can Instrument

Figure 1.26 The Ellipsoidal Reflector Spotlight Instrument

use a single step lens, but no matter; they're generically named after the reflector. The lens system of the ellipsoidal directs the lamp's beam to invert, or "flip-flop". An opening in the middle of the instrument, known as the **gate**, is located close to this inversion point. This is where pieces of metal called **shutters** are shoved into the light beam to shape its edges. The beam can also be shaped with other devices, like a template or a film loop, which will be discussed later in this chapter. Those devices can shape the beam to project images ranging from a static pattern to moving projected flames. The lenses are contained in a tube, or **barrel**. Adjusting the tube, or "running the barrel," moves the lenses closer or farther away from the reflector, and the light beam changes focus, becoming sharper or softer. Since the ellipsoidal's design enables it to project concentrated light beams over extended distances, the instrument is often also chosen to perform long-range tasks in a light plot.

Figure 1.27: While lamps have become more efficient, the body designs have also become smaller and more lightweight. The **ETC Source Four Ellipsoidal** uses the HPL lamp, which is equipped with four filaments. The Source Four's beam output exceeds many comparable lamps of higher wattage while consuming less electricity. Between their economy and efficiency, the Source Four is the chosen workhorse for many lighting designers. Source Four's are now available in fixed beam spreads ranging from 5° to 90°.

Figure 1.28: While many ERS instruments possess only a single fixed beam spread, other versions have the ability to change the relationship between their lenses and the reflector. Generically known as **zoom ellipsoidals**, their beam spread can dramatically change in size, while retaining the ability to shape or alter the beam. Since their beam size can be easily altered, they're often selected for tasks where the unit's pool size may be undecided until the moment when they're focused. This **Selecon Pacific 14°-35° Zoomspot** exemplifies the unit type; the beam spread boundaries are part of its name. Though useful for a variety of tasks, zoom ellipsoidals contain more mechanical parts, so they're usually a little bulkier and heavier than their fixed-beam counterparts.

Figure 1.29: The HPL lamp has also been adapted to other bodies and reflectors. The **Source Four PAR** and **Source Four PARNel** have become compact alternatives to both the traditional PAR and Fresnel. Utilizing Source Four technology, both of these lighting instruments have established themselves as lighting instruments with their own set of strengths. While the Source Four PAR changes beam spreads by exchanging lenses, the PARNel can spot or flood the beam spread by rotating one of a pair of lenses contained in the housing.

Figure 1.27 A Source Four Ellipsoidal Instrument

Figure 1.28 A Zoom Ellipsoidal Instrument

Figure 1.29 A Source Four PAR or PARNel Instrument

Figure 1.30: Housings containing a row of multiple lamps are called **striplights**, whose main purpose is to create a smooth band of light. Striplights are usually internally wired to produce more than one wash of light from a single unit. Each wash, or **circuit**, is typically equipped with a matching color. Changing the intensities of the circuits allows the different washes of color to be mixed. While striplights are often hung in a row across a batten in order to light backdrops or areas of the stage, they can also be placed on the apron and used as footlights. A row of striplights placed on the deck to light backdrops is often referred to as a **groundrow**. The size, weight, number of circuits, and lamp types available in striplights are extensive.

Figure 1.31: A different striplight configuration is used specifically to project light onto backdrops or cycloramas. Since this is their designed intent, they're often referred to as **cyc lights**. This illustration shows a four-circuit (or four-cell) cyc light in a square configuration. When plotting these instruments, the general rule of thumb is to provide 1 foot of distance between the cyc light and the backdrop for every foot of side-to-side coverage desired on the backdrop.

Figure 1.30 A Striplight Instrument

Figure 1.31 A Four-Cell Cyc Light Instrument

Figure 1.32: Followspots are used to provide focus, highlighting a performer or an area of the stage. Their basic design is similar to that of an ellipsoidal. This Lycian Starklite Model 1271 is a one example of a well-made followspot. The housing contains a lamp, a reflector, and a series of lenses. In addition to those basic elements, followspots are typically equipped with additional manual controls, including an iris (to alter the beam size), a douser (to alter intensity), and the ability to easily change colors (color boomerang). The characteristics and methods of control are unique for every manufacturer. Since the light can move, followspots can be used to highlight any static or moving point of focus, but to be fully utilized, they almost always require an operator.

Figure 1.33: Strobelights can provide the flash in thunderstorms, the "pizzazz" in concerts, or the punch in climactic theatrical moments. One example of the "special effects" (or SFX) family of lighting fixtures, this High End Systems Dataflash AF1000 is one of the industry's strobelight workhorses. By merely changing the dip switch settings, the fixture can exhibit different "personalities." While SFX units are all excellent tools for a design, the lighting designer must understand the different configurations of each unit type in order to effectively use them.

Figure 1.34: A Scene Machine is a projector that can project numerous images. The housing is based on an ellipsoidal reflector design, so the light beam can be shaped. This is the GAM Scene Machine, which is designed as a modular system. Swapping out multiple lenses, accessories and devices, scene machines can project static gobos, spinning patterns, moving clouds, flame, rain, slides, and so on. Smaller, more compact accessories are now available for ellipsoidals, expanding the functionality of this type of projector into smaller, budget-conscious venues.

Figure 1.35: This non-moving fixture's sole property is to act as a **color changer**. There are no other motors to change the position of the lighting fixture. One control channel adjusts the intensity of the beam, while other associated channels or attributes change the color of the light beam. The design of this Ocean Optic SeaChanger Engine allows it to be inserted into the body of an ETC Source Four fixture, while other instruments are stand-alone fixtures complete with their own color-changing capability. Both of these systems can be seen in either ellipsoidal or fresnel-styled housings.

Figure 1.36: For situations that require a small number of moving or repositioned specials, **automated yokes** are comparably inexpensive alternatives to moving light fixtures. This City Theatrical Autoyoke® converts a conventional lighting fixture into a moving light. The yoke's sole function is to change the pan

Figure 1.32 A Followspot Instrument

Figure 1.33 A Strobelight Instrument

Figure 1.34 A Scene Machine Instrument

Figure 1.35 An Internal Color Changer Instrument

Figure 1.36 An Automated Yoke Device

Figure 1.37 A Simple Automated Light

and tilt of the attached unit, and consistently restore its beam to memorized positions programmed into the lighting console.

Fig e 1.37: Simple Automated Light. The next step up are automated yokes equipped with lighting fixtures outfitted with bays for gear. The • ETC

Revolution is currently the only fixture that fits into this category. It has three bays that can be fitted with different modules; a changeable iris, changeable static gobos, changeable rotating gobos, and shutters. Equipped with a color scroller on the front, this unit's strong selling point is it's low noise performance.

Figure 1.38: Automated Light. Originally used in rock concerts, automated lights (or **moving lights, movers,** or **wiggle lights**) have become established mainstream fixtures. They are now the convention rather than the exception, found in almost every form of theatre. Automated lights are in constant development; new manufacturers and improvements now seem so common that models often become obsolete in a remarkably short time. Originally, moving lights like this High End Systems Cyberlight were designed with a static body and a programmable mirror (now often generically referred to as a **scanner**). Over time fixture development has changed; a majority of moving lights now consist of a fixture body wrapped in some kind of programmable automated yoke.

While some early automated lights required only 12 control channels, the latest releases require dozens of control channels or attributes to refine movement, control iris size, change gobos, rotate gobos, mix color; the list can be extensive, and it's unique to just about every automated light. Each one has its own strengths, weaknesses, and particular quirks. For theatrical purposes, however, one of the biggest questions is fan noise. In many cases, the answer to that question is directly related to which bulb type powers the fixture. Regardless of the bulb type, though, most moving lights are now released as two flavors, either profile or wash. The main difference between the two fixtures is their lens system.

Figure 1.39: Profile Automated Light. The design of profile moving lights is based off an ellipsoidal lens system; they have sharp beam edges, so they can be equipped with numerous templates. This Martin Mac 250 Entour is one profile moving light. Like many of this type of instrument, the Entour can spin the templates, or be equipped with glass templates to provide half-tones, and provide strobe-like effects. Some profile movers can also be programmed to perform mechanical shutter cuts.

Figure 1.40: Wash Automated Light. This Martin Mac 250 Wash™ contains many of the same mechanics as the Entour, in order to provide the fixture's movement. The Wash's lens system uses a Fresnel lens, though, so it has a soft edge. Like most wash movers, it has the ability to change size, but it can't have a sharp beam edge. Because of this, wash movers usually have no shuttering, or the ability to project any templates. In essence, they're color wash instruments that can change size and move.

Figure 1.38 An Early Automated Light with a Moving Mirror

Figure 1.39 A Profile Automated Light

Figure 1.40 A Wash Automated Light

Figure 1.41 A Digital Light Projector

Figure 1.41: Digital Light Projector. This type of moving light fixture actually integrates a high output light "engine" with a media server containing video content. This High End Systems DL.3™ Digital Light is one example of this type of unit, which also contains a HAD sensor camera and an infrared illumination system. Not only can this unit project light in any variety of "shuttered" appearances, it can also project static images or any accessible video content. It accepts input ranging from personal computers to numerous media devices.

Although specialized lighting instruments can be viewed as increasing the flexibility of a light plot, the devices can also increase the complexity of a lighting package. While these instruments can produce exceptional visual effects, they can also become a time-consuming headache if they're not properly installed, maintained, or utilized. Trial setups and a thorough understanding of the components and their operation can speed the time required for setup and execution.

Likewise, moving lights can be viewed as a simple solution to limited resources, since these instruments can be remotely focused, colored, and sometimes patterned. The addition of these instruments to a light plot, however, can add extensive complexity to any lighting package configuration. Potential problems can be significantly more complex without an experienced moving light console operator. While they may initially be seen as a panacea for the lighting designer, the inclusion of moving lights to a light plot should be carefully considered. Moving lights may require a separate lighting console and a separate lighting console operator.

Another aspect to consider, before adding movers to a plot, is the amount of programming time available to cue moving lights into a show. As moving lights and consoles have improved, however, the tools available to pre-program or monitor the status of channels or fixtures have also been radically upgraded.

Lighting Console Support Software

Software applications can be used to pre-program the lighting for a production. **Off-line editing programs**, installed on personal computers, can emulate the console on a laptop screen. In some cases they don't show any 3D environments, but instead show rows of channel numbers, plus faders, buttons, encoders, and displays. Off-line editors can help reduce the time spent programming directly on a console. When connected to a console, some off-line editors allow the laptop to act as a remote monitor; the lighting designer can watch the programming without having to view the console's displays. In most cases, the purpose of these programs is to allow a show file to be created or updated. The file can then be transferred to the proper console, and reflect the new or updated programming changes.

Pre-visualization programs are separate software applications that can be installed on personal computers. These applications, such as **WYSIWYG, Capture Sweden, ESP Vision, LightCongress, Martin ShowDesigner**, and others, display a detailed 3D simulation of the light plot on the computer's screen. When connected to a console, it can be used to program a show. Alternately, an off-line editor can be used to program instead. Either way, once the visualization software is connected to a lighting console, programming changes made in the off-line editor or on the console change the static or moving lights in the physical light plot.

The same software can be used as an **on-line visualization program**. When connected to the lighting console, it can integrate with the console's software operating system, and allow the observer to see programming changes on the computer screen without viewing the physical lighting beams in the plot. This function is especially useful when the movers may be at the other end of the building, for example.

Other software is available for specific tasks. **FocusTrack** is software specifically designed to document how moving lights are used in theatrical productions. **Future Light** is pre-visualization software primarily designed to produce accurately colored stage pictures.

Computer lighting software is constantly changing and evolving. Keeping pace with any product requires a deeper examination to stay abreast of the latest updates. Other texts keep much better pace with this technology, and should be used as a more complete reference. Suffice it to say that the lighting designer who wants to invest time or money in any pre-visualization or off-line editing programs is strongly cautioned to consider the interchangeability and function of the current crop of software and software tools before making console and off-line choices.

Computer Lighting Design Software

Far from the days of hand-drafting, most light plots and drawings are now drafted and rendered on computers equipped with lighting design software. Sometimes it seems that the usefulness and possibilities of the applications are often reflected by the complexity of their learning curve and their relative cost. Basic computer drafting software produces drawings much like using rubber hand stamps for each instrument type. The basic drawing reflects the desired position of the lighting instruments. More advanced applications, such as **SoftPlot**, or **Microlux**, attach data to each instrument symbol, and can be viewed in both 2D and 3D environments. **LD Assistant, AutoCAD**, or **Vectorworks**, on the other hand, are beefier CAD applications that can render in 3D, as well as export and import data. Not only can data be changed in the applications, it can also be exported and updated in other external programs, such as **Lightwright, Filemaker Pro**, or **Microsoft Word** or **Excel**.

Housing and Hanging Hardware

The housing of most lighting instruments is designed to shape or alter the beam of light, and is usually equipped with hardware to secure the instrument.

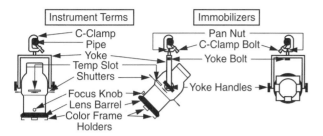

Figure 1.42 Hanging and Housing Hardware Terms

Figure 1.42 shows the different hanging and housing hardware terms for an ellipsoidal. Instruments are often mounted using a **c-clamp** assembly bolted to pipe.

The c-clamp assembly includes a c-clamp bolt, a yoke bolt, and a pan nut used to secure the instrument to a hanging position. The c-clamp is attached to a **yoke**, which is a U-shaped bracket that wraps around the instrument. The yoke is compressed to the sides of the instrument housing by two **locking handles**. Not shown is a piece of aircraft cable with a loop at one end and a snap hook at the other, commonly referred to as a **safety**. Safeties are often connected to create a loop around the yoke and the hanging position as a precautionary measure.

Ellipsoidals contain specific hardware to shape their beam. A **template slot** is a gap in the housing, which is adjacent to the internal gate. Devices inserted into the slot internally shape the beam of light. **Shutters** are also contained within the gate, and commonly consist of four pieces of metal that can be used to shape the beam.

The front of most instrument housings is equipped with metal brackets called **color frame holders**. While these are primarily used to hold color media mounted in **gel frames**, they're also used as a mounting position to hold other external accessories designed to slide into the brackets. Housings that are designed to alter the size or focus of the light beam are equipped with a **focus knob** for that purpose.

Accessory Hardware

Accessory hardware generally includes devices added to lighting instruments to alter or shape the beam of light. Back in the day, they were separated into two categories. One set of accessories were those that altered the beam of light after it had left the lens, while the other set were accessories that fit inside instruments to internally alter the beam.

Nowadays accessories are divided into different kinds of groups, but it depends on who's talking. As far as Vectorworks is concerned, there are two groups: Any device that fits on or in a lighting instrument, or a lighting system that requires its own power or

separate control channel is categorized as an **accessory**; and any doodad that *doesn't* require a separate control channel or voltage source, and basically just sits there, is categorized as a **static accessory**. Lightwright, on the other hand, divides the "accessory" category into more distinct sub-categories; **devices, practicals, special effects, power**, and so on. This semantic discussion has been going on for some time, and it can affect the way that data is exchanged between the two applications. For the purposes of this book, however, accessories will be presented as before: those that fit internally, and those that fit externally. After they're presented, their status will be reviewed. The internal accessories are typically limited to equipment that's designed to fit inside ellipsoidals, like irises, templates (or gobos), and gobo rotators.

The left-hand illustration of Figure 1.43 is an **iris**. When inserted into the template slot of an ellipsoidal, the handle extending above the device can be moved to contract the size of the hole. This reduces the diameter of a light beam while maintaining its circular shape. While many irises are built into ellipsoidals, other irises can be easily inserted into compatible instruments specifically designed to accept them.

Templates (or gobos, patterns) initially referred to thin pieces of metal with holes in them. When inserted into the gate of an ellipsoidal, light escaped through the lens of the instrument in the shape of the holes. Although templates can be made from aluminum pie plates purchased from a store, a wide range of designs in different sizes and shapes are available from several manufacturers. The center diagram of Figure 1.43 is an illustration of a Rosco Designer Pattern 77733 called Dense Leaves. Running the barrel of the ellipsoidal alters the edge of each hole to appear sharp or soft.

Today, "templates" now generically refers to light-shaping materials that fit into the gate of an ellipsoidal. While numerous metal templates are still available in a variety of sizes and shapes from manufacturers' stock, or created from custom artwork, the accessories have expanded and evolved. Templates now include half-tone and color images made from high temperature dichroic glass, allowing today's projected images to

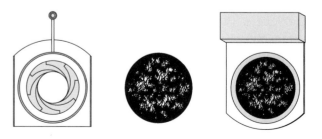

Figure 1.43 An Iris, a Template, and a Gobo Rotator

range from graphic linear artwork to photo-realistic images. In addition to that, separate "effects glass" pieces have been introduced that refract, diffuse, or bend light, and can be used separately or in combination with other templates in the same ellipsoidal.

Templates can be combined with another device that allows the patterned light to move. The right-hand illustration of Figure 1.43 shows a **gobo rotator**. When the device is equipped with a template and inserted into the template slot of an ellipsoidal, the patterned light from the instrument spins in a circular fashion. Some gobo rotators are designed to accept two templates, which can then be controlled to spin in opposite directions in a variety of speeds.

Mechanical devices that attach to the front of instruments to affect the light beam include tophats, halfhats, color extenders, barndoors, donuts, and scrollers. The left-hand illustration of Figure 1.44 is a **tophat**, which looks like a piece of stovepipe attached to a gel frame. It is used to reduce **halation**, or scattered light falling outside of the primary beam of light. Tophats are also used when the lenses of ellipsoidals are focused towards the eyes of the audience. If a border is not used to conceal a backlight electric, for example, the first rows of the audience may be able to see the inside of the barrels through the lenses of the instruments. Although the instruments may be shuttered so that no direct light is hitting the audience's eyes, the first row may be distracted by the glints of light bouncing off the inside of the barrel. If a tophat is inserted into the color frame holder, the stovepipe may mask the inside of the barrel from the audience's view, and eliminate that visual distraction.

Sometimes, however, a full tophat may not be a complete solution. Rather than looking at the barrel glint, the audience may instead be distracted by the portions of light bouncing off the inside of the tophat. The center illustration of Figure 1.44 is a **halfhat**, so named because half of the stovepipe has been removed. Once inserted in the color frame holder, the halfhat may block the barrel glint from the audience's view. The absence of the other half prevents any portion of the beam from being seen.

The right-hand illustration of Figure 1.44 is a **color extender**, which is essentially a color frame holder attached to the end of a tophat. The purpose of this device is to move the color away from the heat coming out of the instrument. Doing so attempts to retain the dye in the color media and reduce the need to replace burned-out color media.

The left-hand illustration of Figure 1.45 shows a four-door **barndoor**, which is often used to shape the light beams of Fresnels, PAR cans, or PCs. The design of many barndoors allows the entire assembly

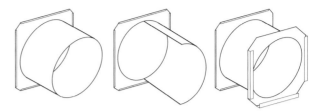

Figure 1.44 A Tophat, a Halfhat, and a Color Extender

to be rotated after being inserted in an instrument's color frame holder, so that the doors can "cut" the beam to a desired angle. Since a set of barndoors can occupy all of the space provided in an instrument's color frame holder, some versions include a slot for color media.

Sometimes the ambient light produced inside an ellipsoidal will produce unwanted light outside of the beam. One solution used to reduce this halation is a piece of metal known as a "**donut**," illustrated in the center of Figure 1.45. The outside shape of a donut is the same size as the color frame for an ellipsoidal. The centrally located hole in the middle of the donut is roughly the same size as the diameter of the gate inside the ellipsoidal. The donut is also used to "clean up" the beams of ellipsoidals that are equipped with templates.

The right-hand illustration of Figure 1.45 shows a **color scroller**, which is a digital color changer. When inserted into an instrument's color frame holder, this device allows a single instrument to project numerous colors. Colors are assembled into a long strip (a gel string) and inserted in the scroller. The scroller is then digitally assigned to a control channel in a computer lighting console, separate from the channel that controls the intensity of the instrument's lamp. Altering the "intensity" of the scroller's control channel directs the gel string to move to different positions, exposing different colors in the gel string to the instrument's beam. The number of colors, along with the power components, control constraints, and amount of cooling fan noise, varies between manufacturers. Although color scrollers can increase the flexibility of a light plot, the lighting designer should be well versed in the additional computer programming these devices require before including them in a lighting design.

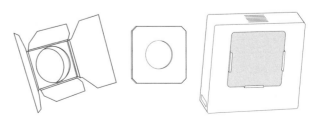

Figure 1.45 Barndoors, a Donut, and a Color Scroller

While all of these items fall under the heading of accessories, only the gobo rotator and the color scroller require a separate control channel or voltage. Using Vectorworks nomenclature, the rest of the collection are "static accessories," while the rotator and the scroller are "accessories." Using Lightwright nomenclature, those same two things are categorized as "devices." While the two software applications continue to negotiate a semantic agreement, what's valuable to remember is that the two "devices" are useful tools for the lighting designer, but he or she must be aware of their control and voltage needs, and what label any given software program assigns to them.

Atmospherics

One component of a light plot that's not a lighting instrument, but is often critical to the show's visual success, falls under the heading of "atmospherics." While they're referred to by any number of names, these devices are generally lumped into two categories: **hazers** and **foggers**.

Even as late as the 1970's special atmospheric effects were relatively primitive. Dry ice fog covered the stage with low-lying puffy clouds, often seen at the top of Act 2 in *Nutcracker*. That was typically achieved with a combination of a 50-gallon drum, dryer hose, hot water, an oven element, and dry ice. At one point Mole-Richardson distributed a heated reservoir that sprayed out oil that sort of turned into smoke. Or just made a mess on the deck. If the lighting designer called for some kind of "haze" in the air, it was often achieved using ceramic devices called **smoke cones** filled with sal ammoniac, and heated to produce a smoky haze. *Black and Blue* is credited as being one of the first Broadway shows to use non-smoke haze. It used "crackers," which consisted of compressed air nozzles submerged into 5-gallon buckets of mineral oil.

Thankfully, atmospherics have come a long way. Manufacturers now produce very specific DMX-controlled devices generically referred to as "droplet generators" or "particulate generators," which disperse fine droplets of oil, or glycol and water, or glycerin and water into the air to catch, reflect, or diffract beams of light.

Figure 1.46 is an Interesting Products Dry Fogger Mammoth LN2 fog machine, which uses liquid nitrogen to create the equivalent of the dry ice, low-lying fog. Other dispersal foggers can generate "cool" droplets for low-lying fog, or "hotter" droplets for a higher, less billowy fog.

Figure 1.47 is a LeMaitre Radiance, a hazer that disperses a thin spread of longer-lasting

Figure 1.46 Liquid Nitrogen Fog Machine

Figure 1.47 Thin Particulate Hazer

particulates higher in the air to create a uniform atmosphere. Well-made haze gives light beams substance; instead of merely illuminating focus points, they sometimes become part of the visual and emotional scene.

Quality modern atmospherics are carefully designed to stringent health and safety standards; Actor's Equity and ESTA have both conducted intensive studies providing information to protect performers, technicians, and the general public. And while health is a primary issue, fire detection is right behind it. Modern fire detection is now so sensitive that even a simple blast of haze or fog is sometimes enough to set off alarms. Before any foggers or hazers are specified or tested, check to see if there's an automated smoke detector system in the venue, or in the air handling system that serves it. If there is one, whoever is in charge of it should be consulted. Meetings with the facility's manager and the local fire marshal will help select appropriate equipment and design successful effects, without inviting un-planned visits from the local fire department.

COLOR

In most theatrical presentations, color media (commonly referred to as "**gel**") is placed in front of the lighting instruments to change the color of the light beams. To effectively use this property of light, the lighting designer must have an understanding of the concepts and physical elements of color. Understanding color begins by understanding the physical nature of light and how we see it.

Light is the very narrow portion of the **electromagnetic spectrum** that is visible to the human eye. Light possesses several characteristics; it travels in straight lines unless modified by reflection, refraction, or diffusion. Light waves pass through one another without alteration; a beam of red light will pass directly through a beam of green light unchanged in direction or color. Finally, light is invisible passing through space, unless a medium (such as dust or mist) scatters it in the direction of the eye.

Color is merely different wavelengths of light within the visible portion of the electromagnetic spectrum, measured in units called "nanometers." The span of the **visible spectrum** can be seen when white light is separated into colors by a prism. Relatively "slow" visible wavelengths start with red, and increase their speed through orange, yellow, green, and blue, finishing with violet. Wavelengths slower than red include infrared, television, and radio waves, while wavelengths faster than violet include ultraviolet, X-rays, gamma rays, and cosmic rays. The human eye contains two specialized nerve cells in the retina called rods and cones. While **rods** in the human eye perceive light and dark, the **cones** of the eye are divided into three groups of receptors that are sensitive to red, green, or blue wavelengths of light. The cones are the cells in the eye that actually perceive color.

Defining Color

Hue is the quality that differentiates one color from another. **Primary colors** are defined as hues that cannot be created from any other colors. While the primary colors of pigment are red, blue, and yellow, the primary colors of light are **red, blue,** and **green**.

Figure 1.48 shows a gray-scale representation of two **color wheels**. See the inside back cover to see these figures in color. The left-hand side shows the primary colors of light: red, green, and blue. The right-hand side shows the primary colors of pigment: red, yellow, and blue.

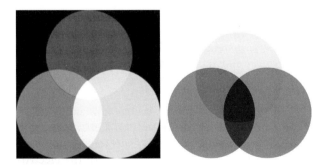

Figure 1.48 The Light Color Wheel and the Pigment Color Wheel. (See the inside back cover of this book to see these figures in color)

An equal combination of the three primary colors of light hypothetically results in white light. An equal mix of the three primary colors of pigment, on the other hand, results in the color black. The equal mix of two primary hues of light produces three **secondary** colors: Red equally mixed with green results in **amber** (or yellow); red equally mixed with blue creates **magenta**; and green equally mixed with blue results in **cyan** (or blue-green).

Complementary colors are often defined as being opposite each other on the color wheel. When two complementary colors of light are equally mixed together, the hypothetical result is white. When two complementary colors of pigment are equally mixed together, on the other hand, the result is black.

Color **saturation** refers to the amount of hue in a color mixture. A pale blue has much less saturation than a primary blue. The **value** of a hue is defined as the lightness or darkness of a color. The pale blue color has a much higher value than a dark green color. A **tint** is defined as a color of high value mixed either with white pigment or light, while a **shade** is a color of low value, mixed with black. A color mixed with both white and black simultaneously is known as a **tone**.

Color Temperature

Although **color temperature** can be confused with degrees of heat or cold, it only defines color, and is a comparative measurement of different wavelengths of light. A spectrometer is a device that produces these wavelength measurements in degrees of Kelvin (K). The color temperature of a household incandescent bulb, for example, is much lower than the color temperature of sunshine on a sunny day.

When mixing colors using theatrical instruments, the typical objective is to begin with beams of light that are equally white before adding color media. Although all standard theatrical instruments produce beams that can be considered "white," the comparative color value between two uncolored beams from different instruments can be distinctly unique between the two. The quality or type of lamp, lens, and reflector alters the actual wavelength, or color temperature, of the light produced.

Equipped with two different types or wattages of lamps, the color temperature of light beams between two otherwise identical instruments can also be wildly different. For that reason, inventories may separate the same kind of instrument into groups defined by different manufacturers, wattages, or lamp type. Provided with this information, lighting designers often allocate instrument groups of similar type and color temperature to the same system.

By making this assignment, they hope to achieve a uniform color temperature of light before any color media is added.

Color Perception

All people react to color, and each person's reaction to color may be unique. One person might find a particular green "comforting," while another person might find the same color "repulsive." Tests have shown that this reaction or perception may be either conscious or subconscious; people often have different emotional reactions to color without even being consciously aware of them. Color used in theatre often attempts to capitalize on conscious or subconscious reactions held by the majority of a viewing audience to help telegraph the production concept or transmit the emotion of a specific moment on stage.

Color perception is also based on comparison. A blue paint chip held next to a red wall might be perceived differently from that same blue chip held next to a green wall. Since color perception is variable, "warm" and "cool" light can refer to the tint and shade of colored hues relative to one another. It can also refer to the perception of that filtered light by an observer.

Light colored in the red and yellow hues is often perceived as "warm," possibly connected to a deep ancestral connection to firelight. Blues and greens, on the other hand, are often perceived as "cool," possibly connected to night or water. This basic perception is often employed as a guideline in theatrical productions. Comedy is warm and bright, while tragedy is cool or dark.

The color palette chosen for a lighting design can be affected by the genre of the production. While productions set in natural surroundings often employ a tinted or less saturated color scheme to reinforce the show's "natural" setting, the style of musical comedy or opera often uses a more saturated palette in keeping with the heightened nature of the performance.

Colors for light may be chosen to reinforce the color palettes employed by the scenic and costume designer. Filters can also enhance skin tone, subconsciously allowing the eye of the audience to watch an extended performance without growing tired. The colors chosen by the lighting designer can be emotional, symbolic, or iconographic, all selectively chosen to heighten the message being delivered to the audience by the action on the stage.

Color Mixing

Additive color mixing in light is the result of different individual hues being transmitted by the eye and interpreted (or "mixed") by the brain. The left side of Figure 1.48 illustrates a typical mix; where two colors overlap, additive mixing produces a secondary color. At the center point where the three beams overlap, additive mixing produces white light on the surface.

An example of additive color mixing uses a piece of red fabric placed on the surface. The red light will make the color of the fabric more pronounced, the blue light will alter the fabric to some shade of lavender, while the green light will subdue the value of the colored fabric. The color of the light additively mixes to change the value of the hue in the surface of the fabric.

Subtractive color mixing in light is typically demonstrated by the insertion of any colored filter in front of an uncolored beam of light. The physics of color filters allows only their own hue to pass through the filtered medium. The filter absorbs all other wavelengths of the visual spectrum. When a beam of light is colored with a primary blue filter, for example, all other colors in the visual spectrum are absorbed by the filter and physically transformed into heat. The only wavelength passing though the filter is the blue hue.

If a second lighting instrument is focused to the same surface colored in the complementary color of amber, the additive color mix between the two pools would result in white light. If the same amber color filter is placed in front of the first beam of light already containing the blue filter, however, the subtractive quality of the amber filter will stop the remaining blue wavelength. The combined filters will stop all wavelengths of light, and no light will come out of the instrument.

Color Media

Color media often refers to anything placed in front of an instrument's lens that changes the properties of its light beam. In the past, color media primarily referred to thin translucent sheets, manufactured from animal gelatin or acetate and colored with dyes, that were used to color light. Today's color media, in addition to changing the color, can also diffuse, shape, or alter the color temperature of a light beam. Instead of a gelatinous base, the "body" of current color media can be made of glass, polyvinyl chlorides, polycarbonates, polyesters, Mylar, or "spun" filters.

The creation of plastic media falls into one of three manufacturing processes. In the first process, the hue (contained in a dye) is "surface coated" (like paint) onto a clear base. In the second process, the hue is "co-extruded" (or mass-dyed), which means that the hue is essentially sandwiched in between two clear bases. In the third process, called "deep-dyed," the chemical containing the hue is molecularly linked with the clear base. This means that the clear base is heated to open molecular pores in its surface, and then the dye is applied, so that the hue is "stained" into the clear base. Although many different materials are used for the base in colored filters, they're still often generically referred to as "**gel**." When color media is inserted in front of an instrument's lens, it is often kept rigid by being packaged in a gel frame.

Because all wavelengths of the visual spectrum stopped by color filters transform into heat, a more saturated color filter will absorb a greater amount of heat. Under intense heat, dyes "move away" from the hot center, resulting in a faded gel. Since the saturated color will get hotter faster, the hue of the color will comparably fade more rapidly than a less saturated filter. Saturated greens and blues absorb the most infrared energy, so they're the colors most susceptible to lose their hue due to heat. Technological improvements in lamp design have increased the intensity and temperature output of instruments. This has resulted in numerous tactics being adopted to reduce the amount of heat absorbed by the color media in an effort to retain the hue.

One tactic begins with color selection. Some color manufacturers suggest choosing filters that transmit high amounts of light in the 700-nanometer wavelength range. The nanometer range is shown in the spectral energy distribution curves included in most color swatchbooks. Other color manufacturers suggest reducing the intensity of the hot spot in light beams by altering the relationship between the lamp and reflector of ellipsoidals, also known as aligning the instruments to a "flat field."

All color manufacturers recommend increasing the distance between the lens and the filter, or providing airflow between the two. Practical "distance" workarounds include taping the color onto the front of a tophat or barndoor, or adding a color extender between the two. Another tactic commonly employed involves adding a second piece of media between the lens and color media commonly known as "heat shield," which is constructed of Teflon™. Some manufacturers claim that "heat shield" has a higher melting temperature, so it absorbs much of the convected heat. Others contend that there's no significant drop in beam temperature on the color media when the material is added. If "heat shield" is added between lens and color media, air space between it and the gel must be maintained. Otherwise the two pieces become heat-welded together and the color is lost. Regardless of that debate, all agree that the most effective heat shield is a special dichroic glass filter. **Dichroic** glass products actually reflect infrared and ultraviolet energy away from the color filter, and protects the color filter from convected heat. Since this form of heat shield is very expensive, however, a combination of the other suggestions is often employed to reduce the loss of hue in the color filter instead.

One difficulty often encountered with many ellipsoidals is achieving a barrel focus that produces an equally soft edge on both the shuttered and unshuttered portions of the light beam. Although the barrel focus can be adjusted to many different positions, in many cases a soft edge on one side of the beam will result in a sharp edge on the opposite side. Many different diffusion materials known as "frosts" can be inserted in the color frame holder, which alters all edges of the beam to equal softness.

Technology and innovation are so swift in this facet of the industry that keeping track of the changes and improvements is a challenge. Although swatch books give some indication of the wide range of tasks that media can perform, experimentation by the lighting designer in the light lab or the lighting rental shop is the true test to determine accurate application and success.

This concludes a rudimentary review of various physical and conceptual elements that form a basic framework of practical knowledge required for a lighting design to begin to take place. The next step is to examine the artistic and technical hierarchy that exists in a typical North American theatrical production.

THE STAFF OF A PRODUCTION

The role of the lighting designer exists within an organization of other personnel, and the designer must understand his or her role within this group. Every production has a staff that executes specific tasks. Although the titles may change or the responsibilities may shift from one show to another, the tasks must still be accomplished.

The Management and Creative Staff

In professional for-profit productions, the management staff starts with a **producer**, who oversees the entire production, and initially recruits investors to provide the money to support the show. Everyone answers to the producer. The **general manager** oversees the collection, budgeting, and distribution of those monies. A **company manager** is typically the general manager's on-site representative in the theatre, overseeing many on-site expenditures, box office income, and addresses offstage needs for the performers or production staff. These responsibilities may be delegated to other members of the management staff.

The creative staff includes the **director, scenic designer, costume designer,** and **sound designer.** Teamed with the **lighting designer,** these people comprise the collaborative artistic core that creates and implements the production concept for the show. Depending on the origin or form of the production, other creators may be added to this core staff, depending on the type of piece being presented, and if it's the premiere. These folks may include the playwright, choreographer, writer, composer, or lyricist, to name a few.

The Production Staff

The following broad technical job descriptions indicate the general responsibilities and functions for each role within a production.

The **production manager,** who heads the production department, supervises all technical elements and stage personnel for the production. The production manager is often ultimately responsible for successfully mounting the production while adhering to the budget, so he or she must have a detailed knowledge of each facet of the concept, design, labor, and scheduling of the show. Because of that, he or she is usually responsible for the original creation and oversight of technical aspects of the production schedule.

The **stage manager** oversees the performers, and coordinates their interaction with the technical aspects of the production. Whenever performers are involved in rehearsals or performances on stage, the stage manager is in charge. While he or she is responsible for (at least initially) calling the show, the stage manager is also responsible for updating all paperwork that pertains to running the show.

The **technical director** is responsible for the overall on-site success of the production schedule. He or she oversees and coordinates all of the technical departments for each work call. To execute these responsibilities successfully, the technical director often works closely with the production manager to coordinate each element and the time framework involved.

The next five members of the production staff are "heads" of their respective departments. Not only do they oversee their specific area, on larger shows they're responsible for payroll and to make sure that enough people are present representing their department for every crew call.

The **production carpenter** oversees all aspects of the preparation, installation, and maintenance of the scenic package, and supervises the carpentry crew. If the overall design involves equipment suspended over the stage, a **head flyperson** may be assigned the task of making certain that all goods suspended in the air are safely secured, balanced, and functional. If pieces

of the scenic design or other elements require square footage on stage, the **deck carpenter** oversees the assemblage, movement, or placement of those pieces.

The **production electrician** oversees all aspects of the preparation, installation, and maintenance of the lighting package. Not only does this include the elements of the light plot, it may also include peripheral equipment requiring coordination of the overall use of electricity within the performance space. Other scenery or properties associated with the show that require electricity, may at least require his or her involvement. While the creative team is vital to the aesthetic success of the show, the production electrician is a crucial member of the lighting designer's support staff for any production.

A **production properties head** is often hired to facilitate numerous tasks, principally overseeing the preparation and use of any properties carried by performers during the production. He or she may also oversee preparation, installation, and maintenance of any covering that tops the stage. Other tasks may include installation of equipment into the orchestra pit and the wardrobe area.

The **production sound head** is responsible for preparation, installation, and maintenance of all aspects of the show involving sound. This includes installation of the sound console, playback devices, amplifiers, and speakers for producing sound to the audience and all other areas that need to monitor the show. The production sound head is also often responsible for headsets and any visual communication, including cameras and video monitors. If the production involves live sound, microphones specific to each task must also be installed and maintained.

The **wardrobe head** oversees the preparation, installation, maintenance, and execution of any elements that cover the performers' bodies during a production. This often includes all clothing parts and any head coverings, but may also include makeup and coordination of other elements used with costumes, including wireless microphone placement or hand prop storage.

The House Staff

Up until now the technical personnel have been referred to as members of the production, because in a commercial venture they are hired by the producer. When a commercial show is produced, or goes on tour, it either rents or gets booked into a theatre typically owned by someone else. The theatre owners often have their own staff in place to deal with any incoming shows. These professionals are collectively referred to as the **house staff.** In smaller venues, the house staff may be a lone technician possessing a ring of keys and the phone number of the theatre's manager. Larger venues, on the other hand, may have a staff representing each technical department. Collectively referred to as the **house heads**, they're often three technicians: the **house carpenter**, the **house electrician**, and the **house props person**. They all co-exist with the **house manager**, who deals with anything else in the theatre downstage of the plaster line.

Depending on the size of the show, or the contract with the theatre, the number of production staff members may change, but the number of house heads is never reduced. They're hired by and act in the stead of the theatre owner, so whenever a tenant is working in the theatre, the house heads are usually there too. In some venues, there may also be the person hired to be **house wardrobe**, but that role is often a case-by-case basis.

There may also be a regular list of technicians hired for events that take place in that venue. They're collectively known as **the house crew**, and on union calls, they're often departmentalized, and assigned to work for only one of the three department heads.

This basic distinction between house and production is important to understand; the house staff and crew is paid by, and owe their allegiance to, the theatre. The production staff is paid by, and owe their allegiance to, the producer. Understanding this fundamental employment difference is essential in order to grasp much of the finance and politics in today's commercial theatre.

The Lighting Department

On larger shows, the lighting designer leads the lighting department. On smaller shows, the lighting designer may *be* the lighting department. In between, there may be any mix of titles or responsibilities that help the lighting designer execute the design.

The Lighting Designer

The lighting designer is the artist who, in collaboration with the rest of the creative staff, bridges the gap between the director's vision and the technical creation of the lighting for a production. He or she is responsible for the design, implementation, execution, and documentation of all lighting and effects associated with the show. Along with the other designers, the lighting designer's responsible for the creation of the production's visual and visceral environment. While dealing with the realistic limitations of time, space, money, or labor, he or she strives to provide illumination, assist direction of stage focus, and reinforce the concepts of the production. To achieve these goals, the lighting designer draws on many talents to produce a well-lit show. He or she must have a passion for light, and be a combination of artist and realist, seeing what could be, while being aware of what will be required to produce it. The lighting designer often draws upon several skills:

- Collaborate on the production concept and conceptualize the part lighting will play in the performance.
- Analyze, direct, and realize concepts in light that reinforce the production concept.
- Visualize the images and colors based on the concept, and work with the other designers.
- Communicate; express lighting ideas using verbal and/or graphic skills. Listen, in order to understand ideas, and respond to them.
- Coordinate and orchestrate the lighting with the other production elements.
- Accomplish the goals of the lighting within the existing parameters.

The Associate Lighting Designer

The associate lighting designer (associate) is hired by and beholden to the lighting designer, and is the most trusted member of the lighting designer's team. When the lighting designer is present, the associate is there to listen, provide guidance, or support. When the lighting designer is absent, the associate acts in the lighting designer's stead, and speaks with the lighting designer's voice. The associate knows when to make judgment calls in the lighting designer's absence, and knows when it's better to wait. The associate is the lighting designer's backup, and acts as a communication conduit to the other associates. In the designer's absence, the associate provides information and delegates responsibilities to the assistant lighting designer.

The Assistant Lighting Designer

The assistant lighting designer (ALD) is also hired by and beholden to the lighting designer, and is the junior member of the lighting designer's team. When the lighting designer is present, the ALD is there to listen and take notes. When the lighting designer and associate are absent, the ALD listens, takes notes, placates, appeases, and promises to pass on all concerns without agreeing to a single demand. The assistant's role is to provide technical expertise, backup, and support; be a communication conduit and filter; attempt to fill in unanticipated problems or challenges; keep a sunny disposition and retain a cheerful attitude regardless of the bloodbath that's being witnessed; offer to buy coffee when the lighting designer's forgotten to get money from the bank.

Staff Summary

Depending on the level of complexity, detail, or the amount of time or money, the size of the production staff may increase or contract; in a larger production, individual responsibilities may be parceled out, while in smaller shows, the same responsibilities may be consolidated and distributed within a smaller group. The actual titles, assignments, and the amount of responsibility assigned to each role are typically unique to every production. Bottom line, the hat rack always remains the same; the number of hats you or anyone else gets to wear is often the only thing that changes.

The only thing that won't change is one date in the schedule, and that's opening night. All of the events that take place, in order for the show to occur, must be in a sequential order much like the storyboard for a film, which is another way of looking at a production schedule.

THE PRODUCTION SCHEDULE

The **production schedule** details the order and projected amount of time required for every onstage activity involved in producing a theatrical presentation. A typical production schedule may span months, include production meetings, offstage activities, and deadlines, and as the opening grows nearer, it may become more and more defined for each time increment.

This text will follow the timeline of a lighting design placed within the context of a production schedule. Stages of the design will be discussed before or after specific meetings or deadlines. Once the light plot has been prepared, however, this text will become principally concerned with the time period in the life of a production that begins when the show actually begins work on the stage, and ends with the first performance. This relatively small period of time between those two finite moments is defined as **stage time.**

The events that have to take place during stage time differ for every production. Although the name, sequence, and amount of time required for each activity can vary, in almost all cases the basic events that must take place to mount any production are universal. Stage time usually officially begins with the period of time solely devoted to unloading all of the technical equipment related to the production into the performance space. Although there are many titles given to this initial period of time, for the purposes of this text, it will be called the **load-in.** (When equipment is transported to the space from remote locations, it is "loaded in"). The load-in continues in periods of time known as **work calls** until all of the components are assembled and "preset" in the locations where they'll be used during the production.

The production schedule is often constructed so that initially any goods that will eventually live in the air above the stage are assembled, attached to the battens of the fly system, and "flown out" into the air and out of the way. While the carpentry department hangs these scenic goods, the electrics department mounts the instruments, electrical devices, and cable onto battens. This process is usually referred to as **hanging the plot** or just **the hang.** Once the instruments for an entire hanging position have been mounted and circuited, the functionality of each instrument's electrical path is checked or "**hot tested**" to determine and solve any problems.

At an appropriate time during or after the installation of the overhead equipment, the stage is usually cleared, swept, and then often topped with a deck, canvas, or vinyl covering generically referred to as **the performance surface.** Once the performance surface is in place, the stage is again used as a work area. Additional scenery and properties are assembled and stored. Through this entire process, the sound equipment is distributed to its proper locations throughout the theatre, after which it is connected and tested as well.

Once the overhead equipment is installed, a period of time is spent placing the goods and electrics in their performance positions. Each piece is either shifted to a predetermined height above the stage or visually sighted from a viewpoint in the audience, establishing its proper relationship to the other goods in the air. This positioning process is often referred to as "**setting the trims.**" For electricians, the "**trim height,**" or "**trim,**" is usually defined as the vertical height required for lighting instruments to produce the proper beam spread and focus range of the instruments, while for carpenters the trim often refers to the adjustment made to flying goods so that the audience views the desired stage picture. Often trim heights are established so that the masking prevents the audience from seeing the instruments in the overhead electrics. Once the proper performance trims are established, their locations are marked, or "**spiked,**" so they can be moved if need be and subsequently returned to their performance positions.

Once the overhead goods and electrics are trimmed and spiked, the **focus session** takes place. This period of time is dedicated to pointing the light beam of each instrument to a location on the stage or onto scenic elements. While the focus session occurs, scenery or properties involved in the focus may be placed on the performance surface and their locations marked (or spiked) as well. Offstage of the playing area, storage positions for scenery and properties are established, and the backstage area is cleaned.

After the instruments are focused, a separate period of time is dedicated to creating the light cues that will be used during the performance, often called the **light cue level setting session**. The lighting designer sits at the production table and constructs each "look" for the show. Once the light cues are created, the scenery placed, the performance surface installed, the sound cues set, the headsets and monitors operational, and the backstage area clean and clear, the space is deemed safe, and performers are introduced to the space.

During the **technical rehearsal**, or the **tech**, performers and production elements are added to the stage and the timing of every technical cue is established. Once the sequence and flow of the show have been determined, costumes, makeup, and wigs are added to complete the stage picture, a period of time known as **the dress rehearsal**, or the **dress**. Following the final dress rehearsal, the house is cleared of all equipment in preparation for the audience. Before the show, the preshow checks and presets are completed, and then the production is presented to an audience (the **performance**). In many cases, the initial performances are called **previews**, which allow the director and the designers an opportunity to view the completed production with an audience, and make adjustments to the show. Finally, a performance is given for an audience that includes invited critics who then review the show (the **opening**).

Though the amount of time and the sequence of these events may vary from show to show, some form of each of these fundamental activities is usually required to produce a theatrical presentation. In some cases, activities may overlap; it may be possible to set trims while the performance surface is being installed, for example. In other cases, the time and order of each activity must be discrete; the focus session must occur first, before the cue level setting session can take place.

Through all of this, the focus of this book will remain on the lighting design. The two core graphical documents that are created to illustrate the design are the light plot and the lighting section.

THE LIGHT PLOT AND LIGHTING SECTION

The **light plot** is a map that graphically presents the physical components of a lighting design, showing the position and electrical assignments of all the instruments and electrical devices used to provide illumination and visual effects for a production. Usually drawn in a groundplan viewpoint, it also shows their physical relationship with the other elements of the show, and any prominent architectural elements of the venue. Although the actual physical equipment that's represented on the light plot can also be referred to as the **lighting package**, it's often called the light plot as well.

In addition to identifying the type, wattage, and electrical assignment given to each instrument and device, the graphic light plot specifies their location in the performance space and allocates a unique identity to each unit.

The **lighting section** is the companion graphic document to the light plot. Rather than looking down onto the production, the document is drawn looking at the elements of the lighting, the scenery, and the rest of the architectural elements of the venue from the side. More accurately, the document's typical viewing plane is through centerline, viewing one side of the stage or the other.

Both of these documents, as well as numerous other reports and forms, are all based on the lighting design.

Creating and Constructing a Lighting Design

Creating and constructing a lighting design is a process that is unique to the personality of each lighting designer. While techniques and approaches may vary from project to project, and the final product may have absolutely nothing to do with the original plan, lighting designers generally agree that a structured methodology provides the best results and causes the least stress. One such method will be discussed in this book. That method begins with background preparations; the first stage is **research and analysis**, which is then followed by the **preliminary document** stage. Once the design has been reviewed and approved on a variety of levels, the third stage includes the preparation, installation, and realization of the final lighting design. The design is then deemed complete, and archived in the fourth stage.

While that may sound a little naive or passé, it's a bare bones overview of the method that will be discussed. And while the amount of complexity in any given production may threaten to become overwhelming, the basic steps are still the same. That first step begins with background preparations. From the beginning of the design process, the lighting designer's goal is to contribute and further the director's vision and realize the visual objectives of the production concept. Understanding and applying the properties and objectives of theatrical lighting is a fundamental step toward achieving that goal.

Properties of Light

Virtually all texts agree that light possesses four controllable properties: brightness, color, distribution, and movement. The **brightness** or intensity of a light is directly affected by the contrast between that light and the surrounding environment. The surroundings may range from beams of light from other instruments to the relative color and texture of the objects being lit. The **color** of light can change the emotional perception of a scene. It's been stated that warm colors are often associated with comedy, while cool colors are associated with tragedy. It's also been noted that desaturated colors are typically perceived as more realistic, while saturated colors are associated with more dramatic or stylized stage moments. The form, angle of origin, and coverage all refer to the **distribution** of the light. The speed at which any of these three properties of light changes from one moment to another is referred to as the **movement** of the light. The faster the change occurs, the more likely that it will be consciously perceived.

Objectives of Light

Most lighting texts also agree that stage lighting is said to have four objectives. The first is to **achieve visibility**. Since the eye is naturally drawn to the brightest point of a picture, a successful lighting design provides the proper visual focus for the viewing audience. It's often said that what can't be seen can't be heard, so the visual focus is often directed to the acoustic source, such as the speaking performer. Conversely, the lack of illumination in a lighting design deflects attention from areas or elements of the performance that should not concern the audience.

A single low-angle frontlight source can result in a flat perception of the stage. Since most of what might be shadows is "filled in," all objects often appear to be flattened against the backdrop, compressed onto a single visual plane. In contrast, a scene utilizing numerous sources from a variety of angles provides a plasticity, or a sense of form and mass, which sets the performer apart from surrounding scenery. This illustrates the second objective of lighting, **providing illumination in a three-dimensional form** of light and shadow.

Visually painting the stage with intensity, color, and distribution of light achieves **composition**, the third objective of light. Any number of paintings created by the great masters demonstrates successful composition. The successful integration of these objectives creates **mood**, the fourth objective.

SUMMARY

This concludes a basic review of the various organizational and conceptual elements that attempt to complete the basic framework of practical knowledge required for a lighting design to begin to take place. Coupled with the practical information outlined in the beginning of this chapter, this review is now complete. The rest of the text will apply this combined framework of knowledge towards creating and constructing the lighting design for an imaginary production. For our purposes, the name of that show is *Hokey: A Musical Myth*.

Before diving in, consider the amount of information that needs to be acquired in order to create a lighting design. In order to create a design, it must be part of a whole; a lighting design can not be created out of whole cloth; it's part of the director's vision, and one of the design elements of that production. In order to produce of that design element, the first step often taken is to produce two basic lists.

One list is all the information that needs to be gathered and analyzed to understand everything that may, in any way, contribute to, or affect the creation of, the lighting design. The second list includes every document that communicates what has to happen in order to create the lighting design. The more often you do it, the more you understand how many things need to be included on each list to make it work for you. And it's a good bet that the things included on each list will change for every show.

Chapter 2

Paperwork Overview

The first edition of this book focused on the paperwork and the process involved with installing and realizing a lighting design. This edition broadens that scope to examine the paperwork and process involved in the initial creation of a lighting design. This additional time period has resulted in expanding and re-compartmentalizing a spreadsheet called the Document Distribution Chart into different stages, detailing when documents are gathered, created, and distributed.

This chapter is an overview of that amended spreadsheet; examining the documents that will be discussed during the rest of this text. As a single collection, these documents can be viewed as a complete lighting paperwork package for a production. For the purposes of this edition, they're divided into the four chronological stages that trace the history of a lighting design. While the flow of every production is different, there are four finite stages that bracket the paperwork for a single lighting design:

1. First encounter, research, and analysis.
2. Preliminary design through approval.
3. Approved working design through opening night.
4. Archival records.

The first stage begins when the show is first encountered, and ends when the preliminary lighting design starts to be constructed. The second stage picks up at that point and continues until the preliminary lighting design is approved. Once this design is approved, the third stage begins, continuing through the production period of the lighting design, and ending when the show is frozen (or when there are no more changes). The fourth and final stage is archiving the show information so it can be used again in the future.

These four stages are merely being used as a way to segment the information. They're certainly not meant to replace the three finite moments of any lighting design:

1. The moment that you're hired or agree to design the show.
2. The moment that the show begins to load into the performance space.
3. Opening Night.

 Shelley's Notes:
The Production Book

As each lighting design gets under way, documents are acquired or created that are often then stored in a single location. Some folks like to throw all the information into a file folder or plastic string envelopes; if nothing else, all the information is in one place. I'm guilty of just making piles on my drafting table for each show. Inevitably, there comes a point when the information pile gets so tall that, even with careful sifting and re-stacking, I can no longer find anything. That's when I three-hole punch the entire caboodle of documents and sort them into a three-ring binder notebook. By doing so I not only categorize everything, I also discover what I'm missing.

To that end, the documents detailed in each of these stages reflect the contents of many of my old lighting production books, in much the same sort of order. When I'm simultaneously working on different shows, keeping track of what document has been sent out, versus which incoming document is being waited for, things can get confusing in no time flat. Add to that the fact that some shows are quick one-offs, while others take months of pre-planning, and the chance that details might fall through the cracks is no longer a case of "if," but "when."

Over the years I've developed charts that break down the documentation of a show into these four major stages. I now keep copies of these charts in the front of each book. By constantly updating the book's contents in the charts, I can open any book and quickly determine what's there, what's missing, and what's still being worked on. Updating the charts for each notebook can be a time-consuming chore, but I make myself do it when I leave the book for a period of time. The payoff is when I return; I can quickly analyze the state of the documents, the state of the process, and pick back up on the lighting design for that show.

THE DOCUMENT PRE-APPROVAL AND DISTRIBUTION CHARTS

The first stage of a lighting design often centers around gathering and privately exchanging information. Before any rational decisions can be made, there has to be a framework. After that the design can begin to be generated, and then properly distributed. While experience can provide some designers with the ability to "just know" which documents are needed or required for any given project, I've found that creating some kind of systematic lists can reduce guesswork, stress, and reliance on an increasingly faulty memory. On top of that, creating "to do" lists makes it simpler to chart a course of action. In the first edition, it was just a single list. Now that the steps and documents involved in design construction have been added to the spreadsheet, it's too long. So for the purposes of this text, it's been divided into two lists; documents that are involved in the process before the preliminary light plot is approved, and documents created after that point.

Document Pre-Approval Chart

A **Document Pre-Approval Chart** lists potential information that is created, acquired, or exchanged up until the preliminary design documents are approved, reflecting the first two stages of a lighting design.

Figure 2.1 shows the document pre-approval chart for *Hokey*, laid out in a spreadsheet format. The left-hand columns identifies Stage 1 as the **research**

and analysis containing both the artistic and the technical documents, and Stage 2 as the **preliminary documents**. The "Sched" and "Actual" (scheduled and actual) columns on the left side of the chart can merely be filled in with X's to track what information has come or gone, or to more closely notate when it's scheduled to arrive, and when it actually shows up. These columns can become important to keep track of scheduled overnight deliveries or promised email files that don't appear. As additional documents are added to the list, such as research resources, meeting documents, or updated versions of preliminary design documents, they can be added to rows on the bottom of the document.

The "Document" column identifies each piece or collection of information that might be involved in the first two stages. The adjacent grid matrix identifies who receives or shares each of the documents. The first two columns are the electrics department: the lighting designer and the production electrician. Next is the management office, followed by the rest of the creative team, and the rest of the production staff. The final column on the right-hand side "Total" shows the total number of copies that are needed for each document, while the total number of documents that are needed for each recipient is shown in the "Total" row at the bottom of the document.

Typically, for example, the first row shows that everyone gets a copy of the piece (or script, etc). The next rows show that the director and the rest of the creative staff share their research and preliminary designs with one another, but typically not with the management office. The preliminary cue master, on the other hand, is usually so basic that it's not distributed to anyone.

The initial artistic documents include the **piece**, the **research**, and the **preliminary core design documents**. The piece (script, score, treatment, etc.) always remains in an accessible portion of the book. The background information, including all the research and notes, is in constant use as the framework as the lighting design evolves. The design takes shape using the preliminary core design documents; the cue master, the systems and specials sheet, and the magic sheet.

As the design evolves, it has to adapt to the specific technical realities that exist for each production. The **parameters** are another part of the lighting design's framework, and are often integral parts of the production book while the lighting design is created. That includes the **contract**, the **production schedule**, the **lighting budget**, the **contact information**, and the rest of the information about the **performance space**.

The second stage consists of the **preliminary documents** involved in the lighting design's approval. That primarily includes the **preliminary light plot**

Hybrid Theatre 2010   **HOKEY DOCUMENT PRE-APPROVAL CHART**   Date: 2/13/10

				DOCUMENT	Electric		Man	Creative				Other Departments						Total
		Sched	Actual		LD	PE	GM	Dir	ScD	CD	SoD	SM	PM	TD	PC	Prop	Sound	
STAGE 1	Research and Analysis			Piece info (script, score, etc.)	1	1	1	1	1	1	1	1	1	1	1	1	1	13
				Research	1			1	1	1	1							5
				Meeting Notes	1													1
				Other Department's Designs	1			1	1	1	1	1	1					7
				Preliminary Cue Master	1													1
				Systems & Specials	1													1
				Preliminary Magic Sheet	1													1
				Contract	1		1											2
				Production Schedule	1	1	1	1	1	1	1	1	1	1	1	1	1	13
				Lighting Budget	1		1											2
				Production Contact Sheet	1	1	1	1	1	1	1	1	1	1	1	1	1	13
				Personal Contact Sheet	1													1
				Truck Groundplan	1	1							1	1				4
				Theatre Tech Specs	1	1		1	1	1	1	1						7
				Technical Drawings	1	1		1	1	1	1	1						7
				Theatre Measurements	1								1	1				3
				Theatres Photographs	1	1			1		1	1	1	1				7
				Theatre Video	1				1		1	1	1	1				6
STAGE 2	Preliminary Documents			Preliminary Light Plot & Section	1	1	1		1			1	1	1		1	1	10
				Instrument Spreadsheet	1	1												2
				Circuitry & Dim Spreadsheet	1	1												2
				Preliminary Hookup Worksheet	1	1												2
				Shop Order	1	1	1						1					4
				Perishables Order	1	1	1						1					4
				Labor Projections	1	1	1						1					4
				Quotes	1	1	1						1					4
			TOTAL		26	15	10	7	10	7	10	9	13	8	3	4	4	126

Lighting design by Steve Shelley 917.xxx.xxxx   Page 1 of 2

LD = Lighting Designer, PE = Production Electrician, GM = General Manager, Dir = Director, ScD = Scenic Designer, CD = Costume Designer, SoD = Sound Designer, SM = Stage Manager, PM = Production Manager, TD = Technical Director, PC = Production Carpenter, Prop = Props Head, Sound = Sound Head

Figure 2.1 The Document Pre-Approval Chart

and **lighting section**, created from the core design documents. Once the preliminary plot and section are complete and artistically approved, the gear shown in those documents is then counted and analyzed to confirm there's enough gear in the performance space to equip the light plot. On productions that need to rent lighting equipment, the plot is translated into a **shop order** and a **perishable order**. These are collectively sent out for quotes and approval.

Keeping this chart updated makes it possible to systematically keep track of what is anticipated, what has been delivered, and what is still missing before the process can move forward. For that matter, the chart may reflect additional preliminary lighting notes or research scheduled to be sent out. Adding information to this chart as additional rows, notes, or even just scribbles, centrally locates the incoming and outgoing flow of information, in order to reduce the chance of something falling through the cracks.

Document Distribution Chart

A **Document Distribution Chart** lists the documents created, or acquired, for the next two stages of the show. These start with the approved version of the lighting design drawings, and continue with the production packets created once the lighting design has received approval.

Figure 2.2 shows the document distribution chart for *Hokey*, detailing the list of documents that are created and distributed. The left-hand column identifies the next two stages. Once approved,

Hybrid Theatre 2010 · **HOKEY DOCUMENT DISTRIBUTION CHART** · Date: 2/13/10

Date	Rev	DOCUMENT	Electric		Man	Creative				Other Departments						Total
			LD	PE	GM	Dir	ScD	CD	SoD	SM	PM	TD	PC	Prop	Sound	
		Light Plot	1	3	1	1	1		1	1	1	2	2	1	1	16
		Section	1	3	1	1	1		1	1	1	1	1	1	1	14
		Instrument Schedule	1	1												2
		Hookup	1	1												2
		Dimmer Schedule	1	1												2
		Circuit Schedule	1	1												2
		Color Cut List	1	1												2
		Template List	1	1												2
		Color Cards	1	3				1		1	1	1	1	1		10
		Floor Cards	1	3			1	1	1	1	1	1	1	1		12
		Hang Plot	1	1			1		1	1	1	2	2	1	1	12
		Headset Layout Diagram	1	1		1			1	1	1	1		1	3	11
		Disk Master	1	1												2
		Infrastructure Cues	1	1												2
		Groups	1	1												2
		Submasters	1	1												2
		Focus Point Ground Plans	2							1	1	1		1	1	7
		Focus Document	1													1
		Focus Chart	1													1
		Magic Sheet	1							1						2
		Cheat Sheet	1							1						2
		Cue Master	1							1						2
		Light Cue Sheets	∞													∞
		Followspot Cue Sheets	∞													∞
		Console Operator Sheets	∞													∞
		Repatch Sheets	∞													∞
		Worknote Sheets	∞													∞
		Light Board Printout	1	1												2
		Digital Focus Photographs	1	1												2
		Excel Track Sheet	1	1												2
		TOTAL	26	27	2	3	4	2	5	10	7	9	7	7	7	116

Left-margin labels: STAGE 3 — Light Plot, Section, and Support Packet / Load-in and Focus Packet / Cue Construction Packet; STG 4 — Archive Packet.

Lighting design by Steve Shelley 917.xxx.xxxx — Page 2 of 2

LD = Lighting Designer, PE = Production Electrician, GM = General Manager, Dir = Director, ScD = Scenic Designer, CD = Costume Designer, SoD = Sound Designer, SM = Stage Manager, PM = Production Manager, TD = Technical Director, PC = Production Carpenter, Prop = Props Head, Sound = Sound Head, ∞ = Infinity

Figure 2.2 The Document Distribution Chart

the lighting design moves into the third stage, and expands into three separate packets of information. The initial packet is the **light plot, section,** and **support paperwork packet,** presenting the mechanical view of the design. Not only is it the primary source of information about the lighting package, it also helps define the amount of labor required to run the show. The **load-in and focus packet** includes the paperwork used to install and focus the light plot, in order to create an operational lighting package. The **cue construction packet** includes the paperwork used to create, record, and monitor the cues of the lighting design.

Though all of the packets are constructed prior to the load-in process, the final version of any of these documents won't exist until the production is "frozen," so that no other changes in the show will be made. Once frozen, the last updated version of the documents will comprise the **archival packet,** reflecting the fourth stage of the design.

While updating documents may not seem important to some lighting designers, it's often a contractual responsibility to provide accurate documentation once the show is open. In many cases, these records will also be stored in an archival file for future potential regeneration. It seems inevitable that whenever accurate documentation of the archival packet is skipped, it will later be required. While numerous documents may be added to the packet before the show is open, one document that can't truly exist until the show is frozen is a **final light board printout**, documenting the contents of the computer lighting console. The archival packet may also include copies of photographs taken at a pre-show light check.

In this chart, the left-hand tracking columns have been re-labeled "Date" and "Rev" (for date created and revision). They can be used to track the completion and initial revision dates of each document that gets published, or distributed. In order to accommodate additional revisions, additional blank columns can be added for more dates. The rows in the "Document" column list each piece of information that will be produced. The columns immediately to the right show their destinations within the electrics department, while the rest of the chart shows the destination and number of copies required for the rest of the creative and production staff. The final column on the right-hand side "Total" shows the total number of copies that will be needed for each document, while the total number of documents that need to be supplied to each individual is shown in the "total" row on the bottom of the document. The forms at the bottom of the cue construction packet are marked with ∞, a symbol meaning infinity. Why? The number of blank forms needed for light cues, followspot cues, board operator cues, repatch sheets, and work note sheets is a judgment call based on the anticipated complexity of the show—and often it seems like there's never enough of them.

The final composition of these two charts is unique to every production. They're included to show some of the sources, destinations, and the number of copies that may be required for each document. Some form of these two charts can act as a diary to track the arrival, the creation, and the proper distribution of original and revised paperwork. When these documents are created, they can also be used to determine who in the creative and production staff wants copies of which documents.

Not only does this clarify the total number of copies and their proper destinations (so no one feels left out), it might also reveal that someone else intends to produce and distribute their own version of the same document. The scenic department may take ownership of the hang plot, for example, or the sound department might lay claim to the headset layout diagram. In those cases, provide them with the lighting information and thank them for their help; any document's assimilation by another department is one less document the lighting department has to create, update, or distribute.

The Three Document Categories

Lighting paperwork usually falls into three categories. The first category includes graphic diagrams, which may be either public or private. Public documents, such as the light plot, provide information to other personnel. Like maps, in order to be understood, they include keys and legends. Magic sheets and other diagrams, on the other hand, are private documents. They're created by the lighting designer for his or her personal use. They're not meant to be shared outside of the electrics department, so there's no graphic explanation. To an outsider, they're cryptic.

The second paperwork category contains information in a spreadsheet format, usually sorted in many different ways so that information can be easily found. The search criteria is almost always assigned to the left-hand column of the documents, since that's the side of the page where an English-speaking eye naturally looks at first. The remaining columns are then often sorted in a specific order, so that logical comparisons can be made between them. These documents range from lists of data about the lighting instruments to inventories about the counterweight system. Sometimes columns containing related information are added, reducing the need to consult other information sources.

The third category of paperwork is made up of forms that get filled out to provide a record of actions taken. In most cases, these forms are designed to be easily understandable. That's because, in most cases, these documents are designed for speed—they have to be filled out *fast*. Because of that, they're designed so that all necessary reference information that might be needed is already there, included on each form. When they're filled out, the only marks written or drawn on the form are the information specific to that circumstance. These documents include focus charts, light cue sheets, and board operator sheets, to name a few. By including pertinent reference information in each document's layout, each filled-out form not only provides the information about that specific action, it can help explain additional information surrounding that action. Each document becomes an independent reference tool, reducing the need to consult separate documentation.

Document Analysis

The accusation is often made that the lighting department creates too much paperwork, but that statement is usually made by someone who's never acted as a lighting designer or an electrician. In the department's defense, a well-executed and archived lighting design usually needs a lot of different documents to retrieve, modify, and record the information about all of the aspects of the design. In addition to all of the data, the lighting package for any production physically exists in space; graphic documents are needed to show its relationships with all the other technical elements, and additional drawings are often needed to illustrate how tasks are performed.

Yes, it could be said there are a lot of documents. Because of that, while the primary goal of any paperwork package is to legibly communicate information, a secondary goal is to present the information for all relevant parties in the most compact possible form. Tidy record keeping practices aside, the potential amount of paperwork required to accurately chronicle the paper trail of a production can be heavy. Fewer documents mean less stuff to carry, and less strain on the back.

Deciding which documents are needed for any production is best done on a show-by-show basis, and this can change during the course of a tech period. Documents may need to be added or divided, in order to provide more information, or they may need to be organized in a better way. One exercise used to help determine document numbers for a show is to pose the question, "What information needs to be seen by whom, and when?" It may be possible to combine information from two documents into one. If that seems feasible, it should be considered; the fewer documents constructed, the fewer to update. And any time documents are updated, human error can occur; if the same updated information isn't corrected on all the documents, the now-conflicting information can cause problems.

Brilliantly designed paperwork is useless, if the people assigned to use it can't understand it. In many cases, the lighting designer initially constructs the layout of a document so that he or she can read it. After that document is distributed, however, the lighting designer may rarely refer to it again. If the document is the reference source for other people, the lighting designer needs to ignore his or her personal instinct or tastes. Discuss the layout and content of the paperwork with the people who will use it, and tailor the document's design to their preferences so they can read it.

In the ideal world, a complete lighting paperwork package is assembled and distributed (or published) long before the load-in. This means that as a complete package, all of the documents can be compared to one another at one time, all the better to spot anomalies. The sooner the package is published, the more time there is available for all involved to recognize, analyze, and address potential problems before the load-in starts. Documents may have to be updated and redistributed, but the sooner the updating cycle

starts, the greater the number of problems that can be solved before the load-in begins.

For public documents, many designers insist that some amount of "title block" information is included on every kind of document. This title block information often remains in the same spatial location on each page—for example, the title block on every graphic drawing in a series, placed in the lower right-hand corner. For database documents, the title block information translates into consistent header and footer information, with only the document's name changing for each document. Fill-in forms may adopt that same header and footer layout design, or adapt it to include different reference information.

Title Block Information

Regardless of document type or layout, the basic title block information should include:

- The name of the show.
- The creation or revision date, or the version number.
- The purpose or title of the document.
- This document's page number, and the total number in this group: "Page X of Y."

Other logistical information may include:

- The lighting designer and/or production electrician's name.
- Contact information: phone, email.
- Name of the performance facility or producing entity.
- Reference information specific to this document: console, channel and dimming configuration, for example.

When lighting designers consider what reference information might be relevant to a specific document's title block, many pretend to analyze a single page from the middle of that stack, separating it from the "herd" (the rest of the paperwork package.) Next they consider viewing the document as if they were completely disassociated from the production, the proverbial "Man from Mars." Is there enough information in this orphan's title block to understand where it came from, what it was for, and how to use it? Is enough information included in the title block, without searching for additional information in other documents? Finally, they take it one step further, and imagine viewing the document as an orphaned archive document twenty years from now. Does the title block still contain enough necessary information for the document to be identified and used as an independent reference? Bottom line, when in doubt, most lighting designers err on the side of including too much information in the title block, rather than too little.

Soft Copy Distribution

What the document acquisition and distribution charts don't address is the delivery format. Before the Internet, all of these documents were distributed as individual pieces of paper. In one sense, that made it easier to keep track of the document distribution. A single trip to the photocopier would result in stacks of paper, sorted FedEx envelopes and shipping bills, and so on. Not any more—nowadays, most of these documents are electronically sent via email as PDF attachments. In this way, they're essentially "snapshots;" recipient computers don't need matching applications or fonts, the documents retain their original look and layout, and the document can't easily be changed. If some folks want their documents as PDF's, while others prefer hard copy, two copies of the charts may be required, labeled "soft" and "hard," in order to keep straight who gets what when updates get sent out.

In some cases, in addition to the PDF's, the original documents are also sent to specific staff members so that they can alter, update, and exchange them. Documents sent to the production electrician are often emailed both as PDF's, and as soft copy in their native software formats. For production electricians who have matching CAD applications, sending them the light plot as a software document allows the PE to produce the specific graphic documents they want for their crew calls. Sending the matching PDF document gives the recipient something to compare the soft document to, in order to confirm the document's matching appearance.

These days it's typical to note when the lighting database changes hands. When the Lightwright file is sent from the lighting designer to the production electrician, for example, that moment is noted as the point when the "football is passed." Whoever is giving the file up, will not alter or update it again, until the "football" has been returned. In this case, that means the lighting designer won't make changes to the file until the production electrician has finished assigning dimmers to the lighting database and sent the file back.

Hard Copy Distribution

When the entire document distribution chart is distributed as collated collections of paperwork, the amount of copying, collating, and distribution shown on this chart can be very time consuming. Reproducing drawings may require special trips to a photocopy shop equipped with large format printers or copiers. And no matter how many times the number of requested copies is double-checked, it always seems like additional copies of any document are needed in the midst of a frenzied load-in. For all of those reasons, many designers make spare copies as they see fit.

After moving into the theatre, an area out of harm's way is often designated as "the library," where the originals and spare copies can be stored. Sometimes this can be as simple as an expandable file; other times it might require series of drafting tubes. Depending on the size of the show or the length of the tech, sometimes a copy of the document distribution chart is posted in a plastic sleeve protector, so that it can be updated as new documents are added to the library.

When updated documents are added to the library, the outdated versions are then hidden from the public view. Any copies taken from the library in the designer's absence will still match the current version in use. Retaining the outdated versions provides a record if the production reverts to that interpretation of the show.

On smaller shows, the library may fit into into a single three-ring notebook, which may then be referred to as "the show bible." On bigger shows, keeping archival, as well as updated, information close at hand may force the documents to be divided between several show bibles. All versions of the cue construction forms may fill a single binder, that's refilled with fresh information after each rehearsal. Other productions get so out of control each aspect of the cue construction process requires its own binder, or its own pile of paper on the production table.

Shelley's Notes: Keeping Paper in the Notebook

One last note about any primary documents, no matter what they may be. Many designers keep their private documents, such as the magic sheet, cheat sheet, or other production book front matter in separate plastic page protectors. Not only do they usually work as advertised (protect the paper), but they can also become individual storage containers to archive all previous versions of the same document in one pouch, or to keep extra copies tucked away.

Upon review, the reader may determine that some of the paperwork listed on these charts may seem unnecessary, while other forms may seem to be missing. That's to be expected; the documents examined in this book are specific to the production of *Hokey*. No one set of documents will be perfect for every production.

If nothing else, all of the paperwork in this text can be considered as templates, starting points to be adapted to individual circumstances. They also serve as reminders that good record keeping is part of the job. There's just too much; information has to be written down, and it's a good habit to record the relevant item somewhere in order for it to be found again later.

SUMMARY

Okay, so maybe the lighting department *does* create a lot of paperwork. Guilty as charged. Hey, there's a lot of information that needs to be collected or distributed. And almost all of that information starts by acquiring information about the show and the rest of the people involved in making it happen.

Stage 1

Research and Analysis

Chapter 3

Background Preparations and Preliminary Design Paperwork

INTRODUCTION

This chapter examines the background information, meeting notes, and preliminary paperwork that make up the artistic portion of the research and analysis stage of a lighting design.

BACKGROUND PREPARATIONS

The conventional process used to construct a lighting design and the light plot begins by a thorough study, research, and analysis of the **piece**, represented by a script (or score, or treatment) and any related matter. If this core document is a script, it's read, re-read, studied, and absorbed. If it's music, it's listened to time and time again. If it's movement, hopefully there is video that can be watched numerous times. The lighting designer gains an understanding of the piece, along with ideas regarding his or her contribution to the presentation. Throughout this process, the lighting designer creates and develops **core design documents** which provide a structure for the lighting of the piece; the **cue master, the systems and specials sheet,** and the **preliminary magic sheet.**

The lighting designer then joins with the rest of the creative team. Documents about the piece, images, or other material to inspire support or illustrate ideas are collectively referred to as **research** and shared between the group. As ideas develop, the creative staff may also provide **preliminary sketches** or **designs** to illustrate their visual contributions and proposals for the look of the show. Overseen by the director, the creative staff hammers out the key ideas and organizing principles that define and embody this particular production, the **production concept.**

Design and production meetings encompass larger numbers of the production team, during which logistical, tactical, and practical matters regarding the show are discussed. **One-on-one** meetings, between members of the creative team, focus on the abstract and practical integration of design elements to further the objectives of the production. **Notes** taken from all of those meetings are collated, absorbed into the core design documents, and become part of the lighting designer's reference material.

 ## Shelley's Notes: Background Preparations

While all of this may sound warm and fuzzy like a storybook dream, that's because often it is. While the real process attempts to sequentially emulate all of these steps, including background preparation—the research, the meetings, the concepts—sadly, they just don't often take place in that kind of structured format. In almost any realistic day-to-day scenario, these events overlap, or take place in a completely discombobulated order. Or, for that matter, not at all; there may be no discussion or production meetings, the production concept might instead be the director's edict: "make it pretty and romantic—I'll see you at tech." Or the producer: "we only got $300, make it look historical, don't screw up." The speed of getting hired, or accidentally being in the management's office at the right time to see things: "I was just about to FedEx this off to the set designer, would you like to see it?" Chatting with people: "Oh, you're doing the lights for that? I just got hired to do costumes!" Acquiring technical information: "Wow, the stage door's unlocked!" These occurrences often don't follow any cut and dry schedule. While all of these processes and steps are presented in an orderly structured fashion in this book, reality rarely provides that structure.

That's not to say that the opening idyllic scenario is completely jettisoned; much the opposite. If nothing else, the working lighting designer remembers these ideal scenarios; occasionally, something like them *does* happen. And in those rare instances, it's possible then to sit back, analyze what has happened, and think: "Oh yeah, this is the way it's really supposed to work. And it really can make a difference."

Because of the relative craziness surrounding the creation of any production, one key to collaboration and creative success is the designer's ability to recognize *when* information about the show is being presented, no matter what form it's in. Whether that information is ethereal, physical, or purely pragmatic, the lighting designer's ability to shift his or her mental state and understand, process, and properly react to that information can be fundamental in moving the process along. Whenever knowledge about a project is presented, a designer needs to recognize the opportunity to gain information, listen up, and take notes.

The Piece: Script, Score, or Treatment

In order for the creative team to work and communicate as a cohesive unit, they must all be familiar with the source material. When the first meeting about the production takes place between the lighting designer and the director, the director often has already researched and analyzed the piece. For that reason, as soon as the lighting designer receives the piece, he or she is well advised to absorb it as quickly as possible before any other meetings or conversations take place.

In this case, the piece is a simple musical entitled *Hokey: A Musical Myth*. *Hokey* is an imaginary musical theatre piece synthesizing movement, song, and dance. On one level, the production is a campy pseudo-children's musical based on the song *Hokey Pokey*. On another level, the show also examines the developing relationships of the performers playing the roles. Originally workshopped in a small downtown space, *Hokey* is now slated for production at the 499-seat Hybrid Theatre in New York City. It will be presented in three acts, consisting of three scenes in each act. Insider reaction to the workshop production was very positive. Anticipation runs high.

For the purposes of this text, the role of lighting designer for the fictional production of *Hokey: A Musical Myth* has been verbally awarded to our lighting designer. The treatment has just arrived along with the list of musical numbers (Figure 3.1). The work of the lighting designer can now begin.

Musical Numbers	Cast
Act 1 scene 1; Fairyland	
"Welcome to Our World"	Company
"A Very Fairy Wedding"	Wendella, Friar, & Fairies
"You're My Cookie"	Hokey and Pookie
Act 1 scene 2; The Storm	
"Dangerous Winds, Light a Match"	Fairies
"It's All About Me"	Tee-boo
Act 1 scene 3; The Aftermath	
"We're All Going to Die"	Fairies
"Lost My Pook, Now She's a Spook"	Hokey
"Choose a Path"	Wendella
"I Will Find You"	Hokey
Act 2 scene 1; The Scary Woods	
"Lost in the Weeds"	Hokey
"What's Knot to Like?"	Low-Raine & Piners
"Knots are Tight"	Piners & Hokey
"Alone With the Moon"	Hokey
Act 2 scene 2; The Beach	
"Save Me"	Pookie
"I Will Find You" (You're My Cookie)	Hokey
"The Love Dance"	Hokey and Pookie
Act 2 scene 3; The Beach	
"Rock Solid"	Rock & the Boulders
"Rescue from the Sandbox of Snakes"	Company
"Crankyland"	Tee-boo
Act 3 scene 1; Fairyland	
"Back at the Ranch"	Wendella & Fairies
"A Very Fairy Wedding"	Wendella, Friar, & Fairies
Act 3 scene 2; The Face Off	
"Everybody Loves a Winner and It's Me"	Tee-boo
"Heaven and Hell"	Hokey and Tee-boo
"The Precipice"	Hokey and Tee-boo
"The Love Dance"	Hokey and Tee-boo
Act 3 scene 3; The Finale	
"You're My Cookie"	Hokey and Pookie
"A Very Fairy Wedding"	Company

Figure 3.1 The Musical Numbers for *Hokey; A Musical Myth*

Hokey: The Treatment

Hokey: A Musical Myth is a pseudo-children's rock musical that is one part *Rocky Horror Show*, one part *Teletubbies*, and one part *Noises Off*. It's a love story, an epic tale of mythic struggle, and a comic backstage romp.

The Story

Hokey is a tongue-in-cheek satire of the fantasy world genre, loosely based on the song "Hokey Pokey." The story is billed as a timeless fictional tale that traces the travails of two fairies, Hokey and Pookie.

Act 1 begins with the cast assembling on stage singing "Welcome to Our World," in which characters introduce themselves to the audience. Hokey and Pookie are introduced in the song "A Very Fairy Wedding." As the ensemble prepares for the couple's wedding, they are surprised and honored by the arrival of the Oracle Wendella. Her reason for attending is two-fold, Wendella explains. Not only is she present to bless the union, but also to prevent the Knotty Piners, gnomes of suspicious character, from interrupting the ceremony. As final preparations for the wedding are made, Hokey and Pookie swear their love to one another in the duet "You're My Cookie."

The action seamlessly moves to Act 1 scene 2 when a storm suddenly forms over the proceedings, surprising everyone as they sing "Dangerous Winds, Light a Match." It has been conjured by the evil wizard Tee-boo, who enters singing, "It's All About Me." He kidnaps Pookie for his own nefarious purposes and disappears. Wendella then explains to Hokey the true seriousness of the situation. Her associates have foretold that Hokey's future heir will unite the kingdom. Unless the union between Hokey and Pookie takes place, the future of the kingdom is in doubt. Kidnapping Pookie is Tee-boo's first step in his plan to take over. Upon hearing this, the ensemble expresses their concern, singing "We're All Going to Die." Hokey is at a loss, singing "Lost My Pook, Now She's a Spook." Wendella explains that Hokey is at a crossroads of his destiny, singing "Choose a Path." Hokey makes his decision and sings "I Will Find You," before leaving on his quest to rescue his soul mate.

Act 2 begins with Hokey's search for Pookie deep in the Really Scary Forest. He comforts himself by singing "Lost in the Weeds," which is interrupted when he's confronted by threatening figures. His fears are unfounded; the group reveals themselves to be the Knotty Piners, led by Low-Raine, who are just mischievous gnomes out to have a good time. They explain their fun-loving nature in the song "What's Knot to Like?" and agree to help Hokey in his quest. This partnership is celebrated in the song "Knots Are Tight." The group then beds down for the night on a beach, and Hokey sings "Alone With the Moon."

Scene 2 begins as Hokey falls asleep. Pookie appears in his dreams where she's been confined by the evil Tee-boo, in the Sandbox of Snakes. Pookie sings "Save Me," and Hokey awakens in his dream and sings in counterpoint "I Will Find You (You're My Cookie)." Pookie then teaches her lover "The Love Dance of Hokey and Pookie," and he falls back to sleep.

Hokey and the Knotty Piners awaken at dawn, and discover the Rock O' Thought, who not only knows the location of anything on Earth, but also passes his time with riddles. Hokey wins the Rock's support by solving his riddles. The Rock agrees to help them in their quest with his song "Rock Solid," and tells them where to find Pookie. With this knowledge, Hokey and the Knotty Piners defeat the Snakes and rescue Pookie from her dungeon ("Rescue From the Sandbox of Snakes"). After the victors depart, Tee-boo arrives at the battle too late. Surrounded by his defeated snakes, Tee-boo swears revenge on Hokey and all his friends, singing "Crankyland."

Act 3 begins as the fairy world welcomes the Knotty Piners and celebrates Pookie's safe return, singing "Back at the Ranch." This song segues into a reprise of "A Very Fairy Wedding," as preparations for Hokey and Pookie's union resume.

Suddenly Tee-boo appears to reclaim his former prisoner and descend into Hell. After regaining control of Pookie, Tee-boo claims victory with his "Everybody Loves a Winner and It's Me." Hokey and Tee-boo engage in a furious battle. Their struggle takes them to the Precipice of Doom, in the song "Heaven and Hell." As Tee-boo is about to claim victory, Hokey challenges him to follow the Dance of Hokey and Pookie. Tee-boo attempts to follow the movements indicated in the song, but being dyspraxic, missteps ("right foot out—I mean in—whoops!"), and falls into the abyss. The lovers sing "You're My Cookie" as they're reunited, and the tale ends as the couple is married ("A Very Fairy Wedding").

The End.

Casting The cast is made up of 8 actors who can sing, and 8 dancers who can act. Each has specific roles, but when not identified as such, are members of the ensemble.

Scenery The script calls for an "open stage look." Not a lot of scenery.

Costumes The costumes are based on leotards and tights. Added pieces are used to identify the lead characters; Hokey, Pookie, Tee-boo, and the Knotty Piners. The Rock is up for discussion.

Lighting The lighting for *Hokey* will define the locations throughout the production. It will be presentational and colorful.

Sound will be live music provided by a small orchestra. Additional sound cues will be used to support a storm sequence and to establish other background sound.

Notes for *Hokey*

Even while reading this initial treatment for the show, the lighting designer can make many notes. In order to communicate on any level about the show and be able to view the theatre with any thought of how the production will relate to it, quick work must be made of both the research and preliminary paperwork.

During the interview process, *Hokey* has been described as a presentational ensemble production, combining puppetry and hand props to provide the illusions in the show. All of the technical elements will be simple. This low-tech approach is due to two reasons; conceptually, it's a simple show, and realistically, there's not enough money to provide expensive effects. Both concept and budget dictate that the lighting is going to be carrying a heavy part of the load to make this show work. The director has stated that the overall look of the production should feel "other-worldly" or "fantasy comic book-like," and that she wants the show to move rapidly, like a "will-'o'-the-wisp in a hurricane."

Core Design Documents

The process of creating a lighting design is different with each experience, but the basic methods typically result in the creation of three core design documents that become the basis for the lighting designer's creative course of action.

One document, culled from notes made studying the piece, often develops into a list that shows each moment when the lighting changes. This list often evolves into some variation of a **cue master**. As that document becomes more finite, and as the visual looks for each scene or group of cues becomes more visually defined, the color washes, directions of light, and visual focus points are sorted into lists, sometimes referred to as the **systems and specials sheet**. As both of those documents become more developed, the number of instruments needed for each color wash or group of specials becomes clearer. In addition to that, which lights need to turn off, stay on, or get added during each light change becomes defined. The graphic document that evolves and reflects this portion of the process often becomes adopted as the **preliminary magic sheet**.

Since all three of these processes reflect three aspects of a lighting design, simple shows may combine all of them onto a single piece of paper. Typically though, so much information is being processed, it makes sense to eventually separate them into three different documents. Updating one process doesn't then require copying the rest of the information from the other two processes. Once these three core documents have evolved to a level of familiarity and comfort, the lighting designer then uses them in conjunction with the preliminary drawings, facility information, and other parameters to create the preliminary lighting section and light plot.

Cue Master

The **cue master** is a document that highlights each moment that the lighting changes during a show. It's both a tool and a communication device that reflects the visual light changes over the course of an entire production. One analogy for this document is a movie storyboard. While a film storyboard sequentially outlines each shot in a movie, a cue master outlines each lighting change. The cue master allows (or forces) the lighting designer to define, on paper, a general sense of each moment in a show when the lighting should change.

Initially the cue master may note big obvious moments, like the beginning or end of a scene. Then there may be notes for smaller changes, like when curtains are opened as part of the stage action. Finally, there may be even more minute changes, to reinforce the slow shift of emotion within a scene. Each one of these "looks" or "snapshots" is recorded in sequential order, so they can be remembered, collated, and communicated. Often the method used to keep track of these looks is based on the medium of the piece.

If the medium is music, looks may be written into the margin of the score. If the medium is drama, ideas may be written into the script. If the piece is dance, quick sketches or miniature groundplans of the performance space might be drawn on a legal pad. Lines, arrows, and geometric shapes may be drawn to represent the movements shown on stage.

While it may include notes in the margin of the script, Post-its in a musical score, or a list on a separate piece of paper, all of these documents are some kind of cue master. While some designers resolutely keep the cue placement and timing in those original formats, others prefer to separate the listing into a separate spreadsheet. Doing so makes it easier to visually scan through multiple cues at one time, making it easier to change cue numbering and print out a fresh, updated copy of the document. Cue masters, no matter what format they're in, often get covered in hand-written notations during the course of any given tech rehearsal period.

When constructing a cue master as a separate spreadsheet document, the designer usually begins by first outlining the different acts, and the scenes in each act. Then, within each scene, the cue master is filled with a sequential list of each light change, indicating the placement, timing, purpose, and action for each change. The designer also starts to fill in light changes required as transitions between scenes. Initially it's not necessary to know each of these attributes for every look; in some cases, that clarity won't take place until after the show is open. Sometimes the only thing that's known is the instinctual sense that the lights need to change. While the lighting designer may not fully understand why, when the cue master is later reviewed, the purpose for the change may become immediately apparent.

Creating this document allows the lighting designer to mentally construct sequential changes

before he or she is sitting at the production table staring at a blank stage.

Cue Master for *Hokey;* Version 1

Figure 3.2 is the initial cue master for *Hokey,* based on the information gleaned from the scene breakdown and the story information, but at this point, no research or analysis has taken place. The entire

Hybrid Theatre 2010					HOKEY CUE MASTER V1				Date: 2/7/10
ACT	**SC**	**SEC**	**CUE**	**CNT**	**SONG**	**NOTES**	**ON**	**FOR**	**ACTION**
1	1	Open			Welcome	Company			
						Character intro			
					A Very Fairy Wedding	Hok/Pook intro			
						Wendella enter			Gnomes bad
					You're My Cookie	Love swear			
	2	Storm				Transition			
					Dangerous Winds. Lite Match	Fairies			
						Tee-boo enter			
					It's All About Me	Tee-boo			
						Kidnap Pook			
						Exit			
	3	After				Fortelling			
					We're All Gonna Die	Fairies			
					Lost My Pook	Hokey			
					Choose a Path	Etheria			
					I Will Find You	Hokey			
2	1	Forest			Lost in the Weeds	Hokey			threat
						Fun Knotties			fun-loving
					What's Knot to Like	Knotty Piners			
						Join Forces			
					Knots Are Tight	Knotty & Hokey			
					Alone With the Moon	Hokey			solo
	2	Dream			Save Me	Pookie			sandbox
					I Will Find You	Hokey			
					Love Dance of H & P	Hok/Pook			
	3	Beach			Knock, Knock, Who's a Rock?	Rock riddle			
					Rock Solid	Rock & Boulders			
					Rescue from Sandbox	All			
					CrankyLand	Tee-boo			
3	1	Wed			Back at the Ranch	Fairies			
					A Very Fairy Wedding	Hok/Pook set			
	2				Everybody Loves Winner	Tee-boo			
					Heaven & Hell	Tee-boo/Hok			
					Do the Hokey Pokey	Tee-boo/Hok			
					Love Dance	Hok/Pook			
					You're My Cookie	Hok/Pook			
					A Very Fairy Wedding	Company			

Lighting design by Steve Shelley 917.xxx.xxxx   Page 1 of 1

Figure 3.2   The Cue Master for *Hokey,* version 1

production is sequentially listed by row. The two left-hand columns list the act and scene. The next column, listed as "Sec," refers to a section or name of a scene. The next two columns labeled "Cue" and "Cnt" are reserved for future use when cues and counts will be assigned to each row. The "Song" column indicates the musical numbers, including dances, while the next column "Notes" is used to indicate not only who's singing songs, but the location of the presumed book scenes between the songs. At this early stage the "Cast," "Block," and "Action" columns are blank. Depending on the show, and the amount of information that can be categorized, column headings might also include location, time of day, imagery, or props, to name a few.

Shelley's Notes: Cue Master

For many productions, I often convert the light cue information into this condensed format. Being able to compress the cue information into a relatively small document means I can discuss cue sequences without constantly searching for the cue in the written text or score. Having the document in spreadsheet format allows me to copy and paste cues from one row to another. It also allows me to expand on the cell arrangement to include other information for other documents. Often, the cue master becomes the basic document given to the stage manager to write the cues in his or her call book before the tech rehearsals begin. Presuming I've properly prepared the cue master, when schedules conflict, the cues can still be written in the stage manager's book without my being present.

Some lighting designers keep this information as a word processing document. I applaud them, but I find a spreadsheet application simpler to use. Using a spreadsheet means that updating cue information, and reformatting text are reduced to only negotiating between cells. Then, any cell can have its formatting changed, without impacting the rest of the text in that line or paragraph.

Now that the basic structure of the cue master has been roughed in, any work on either of the other two core design documents is typically set aside until some amount of research has taken place.

Research

Before the Internet, research and ideas had to be exchanged in face-to-face meetings, or had to be delivered overnight in order to allow both parties to see the same visual images. Nowadays, much of that activity has been supplanted by scanners and email. Back then "doing research" often meant going to the library and photocopying pictures; now it means typing queries into search engines and forwarding links to the rest of the creative team. While the comparative speed and ease of pursuing and exchanging research has accelerated by leaps and bounds, there's still a place for face-to-face exchanges. Being able to sketch and doodle side by side with another member of the creative team is one of the fun things about working with other designers on a show.

The amount of research needed varies for any given show. Research can be categorized on two levels; first, there is research into the time period in which the piece is set; the social, economic, religious, and cultural conditions may be among the many things that may also need to be investigated. Two, the designer may also need to do research about previous productions of the piece. Research may be required regarding people who are characters in the piece, or the people surrounding the previous productions. The amount of available material about any production is unpredictable, and there's no telling where the research will lead the lighting designer. A cursory glance of this material is often viewed as a basic requirement if the lighting designer is to comprehend or appreciate the piece in question. Typical research may include investigations into the following:

- Time period of the original presentation.
- Time period of this presentation.
- Context for both: Social, economic, historic, and cultural.
- Different landscapes, locales, cultures in that geographic location.
- Artwork, sketches, photos. Work by artists and architects in that time and place.
- Times of day in the geographic locale. Times of year.
- Light sources in that place, time, and world.
- Audio: music, sounds from the relevant time.
- Why it was created? What was the point then? Now?
- Themes? Rhythms? Contrasts? Literary structures?
- If the piece is brand new, on the other hand, is there other source material or antecedents that should be identified and investigated?
- Write questions about the piece. Produce your own answers, and then write them down. Relate this to the director, in order to see if your questions are relevant, and to see if your answers match. If not, be corrected—then write the correction by your initial answer. In this way you create a diary, showing your initial instincts, and

how the director shaped them. This also provides a record of what choices were yours, and which were the director's.

- Create a written diary for moments in the piece. Define, refine, and create broad images. Emotions for each scene. Words that describe that scene, that moment. How it looks, how it feels. Visceral. Physical. Emotional.
- Look for contrasts, similarity in moments. Color swatches. Color images, or black and white.
- The Internet. Google. Yahoo.
- Books from the library; paintings, abstracts.
- Artists from the period, colors, collections.
- Written articles, passages, evocative writing.
- Visual images from film, television, image catalogs, printed matter.
- Clippings from the lighting designer's personal files. (I keep a large clippings file filled with images I've clipped out of magazines over the years.)
- Bios and other info about the creative team. In this day it's typical to use search engines to get a better idea about the folks you'll be working with for days on end during production.

Research for *Hokey*

Since *Hokey* is an original piece, research for it will be in the form and style of the production (comic books and fantasy), rather than anything historical. Other searches might be for illustrations of other fantasy productions, films, or presentations. Other research ideas include:

- Get a copy of the original song.
- Get copies of the other songs in the show. Any preliminary recordings?
- Fantasy sources: fairies, wizards.
- Icons, motifs, check template catalogs.
- Other shows with fairies, depictions of fairies.
- Pictures of fairy locales, fantasy locales.
- Snake pits, rock formations.
- Hell.
- Comic books.

All of this research must be done rather rapidly. The script arrives later tonight, and the meeting and site survey will take place tomorrow.

 ## Shelley's Notes: Doing Research

There are times when the process of creating a lighting design may be so harried that conducting research and analysis can become thought of as a luxury, rather than a necessity. In hindsight, this is often recognized as a mistake in judgment.

Not taking the time to acquire a sense of the piece's background, the history of the show, and placing it into a coherent context for the production means that the piece risks losing its integrity and a sense of a shared basis for the choices made by the creative team. At the very least, there's a two-part loss; one, the loss of what conceivably might be the trigger for many of the creative choices the designer needs to make, and two, the basic tools for effectively communicating those choices with the rest of the creative staff. Without research these basic individual and shared understandings about the piece slip away.

Systems and Specials Sheet

As research is being acquired and considered from the library and the Internet, the cue master can begin to be analyzed. There are several scenes that repeat, and visually repeating some of those "looks" means those systems may then be useful for other scenes in the show. This type of analysis can better take place in a separate document that compares the "recipes" used throughout a show, called the **systems and specials sheet**. As each of the broad visual looks imagined in the cue master becomes clearer, the systems and specials that will be required to create each overall look are then listed on this document like recipes in a cookbook. This is often broken into several columns: one column for systems and washes, and another for specials. Sometimes it's created as a series of color keys, showing the different washes and the angle direction used to create the overall look or special moments in each scene.

Once a series of scenes is defined and the systems filled in, along with the specials, they can then be compared between scenes. The warm backlight in Act 1, scene 1, for example, may be used for the second wedding scene in Act 3, scene 1. With that as a basis, perhaps it can also be used in some way for the beach scene in Act 2, scene 3. Once multiple scenes are imagined and listed, each system or special can be compared and considered in this way. At the same time, making these comparisons starts the process of defining the separation and number of control channels required for each wash. This document is a broader overview of the cue master, allowing more different scenes to be viewed at once, in order to see what systems or specials might be used in more than one scene. It shows the recipes used to create the big looks, but it lists the components in a "shopping list" format.

Systems and Specials Sheet for *Hokey*

Figure 3.3 is the first preliminary version of the systems and specials sheet for *Hokey*. Transferred from the cue master, this is the first breakdown of washes and specials for the first act. In this version, each row

Act & Scene	Systems	Specials	Backing
Act 1 scene 1 "Welcome" "Wedding" "Cookie"	Warm sunny day; wedding Amber backs Color floor	intros Haze wedding couple CC?	Cyc day Warmth Rainbows; stripes? Muppets?
Act 1 scene 2 "more evil"	Blue? Cloudy? More down-y? FOH shadows for chorus Tee-boo enter Blue sides?	Tee-boo enter? Lightning?	Cyc blue Tornado skies? Green porriage? Cyc get ugly Swirl; movement?
Act 1 scene 3 "Tee-boo gone"	Cool when Tee-boo gone Then warm to partial restore of A1sc1 Blue sides? Cool FOH	back to wedding CC but no pookie? a "hole" in her place	Cyc partial restore with Tee-boo depart Desolation bare trees Cemetery

Figure 3.3 The Systems & Specials Sheet for *Hokey*, version 1

comprises one scene. The "Act & Scene" column lists only abbreviated song titles, while the "Systems" and "Specials" columns list general images as well as specific washes. Once the look for each song or scene becomes clearer, it will then be possible to first list the specific washes and colors used for the big looks or changes for each scene. Then it will be possible to compare all of the colors and systems used over the course of the entire production. The final column for *Hokey* is "Backing," used to list the different colors that are, right now, imagined for the translucency. Once the looks needed on the translucency for the entire show are more defined, the number of color washes can be totaled up over the course of the show. In this version, the cyc appears to need blue, green, and "day."

At this point, these are the only two core design documents that exist. Until more information is provided, it is not possible to make more defined decisions about systems or colors. Until that information is coalesced, the preliminary magic sheet can't yet be constructed.

Meetings

Webster's dictionary defines the word **collaborate** as "the act of working or laboring together, or to act jointly in works of art." To be able to collaborate, however, requires communication and cooperation. Communication is certainly one topic; all members of the design team must "speak the same language," i.e., know the piece, the structure, the style, and the overall objective. Cooperation is another matter altogether and it can often be traced directly back to individual psychology. Sometimes egos and theatre don't make for the healthiest of combinations.

In theatre, meetings are organizational tools that, on paper, provide both those goals. In reality, like any other organization, they're often viewed as both a boon and a bane. They're useful to distribute information; instructions and directions are stated only once, and everyone hears the same thing. They're sometimes useful as a forum for exchanging ideas and making decisions. And sometimes they turn into private discussions held in a public forum that preclude the ability to get anything accomplished. Any meeting can easily turn into any or all three of these scenarios. Meetings that are quick, to the point, and allow mutual conclusions or decisions to be made, are the ones considered the most successful.

Meetings can be classified into three different types, based mainly on the number of participants or the agenda: **production meetings** with the entire production team, **conceptual meetings** with members of the creative staff, or individual **one-on-one** meetings, held only between two members of the team.

Most designers feel it's smart for the production stage manager to attend most of the meetings, while other designers insist that the stage manager attends every one of them. Most of the time, in professional situations, it's the stage manager who calls the meeting in the first place.

Production Meetings

At some point there's hopefully, at least, one production meeting when the entire production team convenes in order to be introduced, review the production schedule, coordinate or address potential outside conflicts, and address any cross-departmental issues. Ideally, there are many meetings to check that schedules are being met, and make sure that potential problems are addressed before they become issues. On the other hand, meetings about the show may be delayed until all of the creative team has been hired. If that doesn't happen until the last minute, there may be only one meeting, and its first order of business may be to quickly create a production schedule. In those cases, the initial production schedule presented at the

Hokey; A Musical Myth   Prod Schedule

Rehearsals begin	March 15, 2010
Load-in	April 5, 2010
1st Preview	April 13, 2010
Opening night (press)	April 20, 2010

Su	M	T	W	R	R	Sa
4 **A**	5 **Load-in**	6	7	8	9	10
11	12	13 **1st Pre**	14	15	16	17
18	19	20 **Open**	21	22	23	24

Figure 3.4   The Initial Production Calendar for *Hokey*

meeting may consist solely of the four dates included in the top written portion of Figure 3.4.

In this case, three of those dates are included as part of an otherwise-blank calendar, like the bottom portion of Figure 3.4. A larger version of this calendar may be passed out at the first production meeting. While the rehearsals are important, this meeting's main scope focuses on the three subsequent dates: the load-in, the first preview, and the opening night. All departments quickly exchange all known information about the scope of the piece, and their best guesstimates regarding the amount of time required to accomplish the large tasks. As each department agrees to time demarcations, the calendar begins to get filled in, and the production schedule begins to take shape.

Armed with only those three production dates on the calendar, the lighting designer can still start to make general assumptions, and provide input to the production schedule. In this case, there are only nine days between load-in and the first preview. Presuming that April 13, the preview day, will involve no meaningful tech work, and at least three or four days will deal solely with tech, that leaves four or five days to get the show's lighting up, focused, cued, and ready for the performers at the tech rehearsal. The rest of the departments in the show will be under the gun to match that same deadline. Presuming that the producer wants to limit work calls to eight-hour days until the cast gets onstage, that means that there will be only 32 to 40 hours of stage time to be ready for the tech process.

Second, there's only one week of previews; presuming there are two matinee days (usually Wednesday and Saturday), that means there will only be three or four day rehearsal sessions once the show is in previews. On those days there will presumably also be morning work calls. With afternoon tech and work note sessions, a plan will be required in order to quickly set up and strike the tech table in the middle of the house. Adhering to that plan will provide

the most possible time at the table to view and make corrections, and to watch rehearsals.

Initially, the schedule gets "talked through" once, and the team's initial challenges and concerns are discussed. Everyone takes their own notes on their own calendar as each relevant deadline and agreement is reached. After the meeting, the broad schedule is compiled by the production stage manager into a single updated document to be distributed, compared, reviewed, and discussed again at the next production meeting.

Because everyone's schedule may be in such flux, this first (and possibly only) production meeting may take place at any given time: prior to or immediately following the site survey, in the midst of the one-on-one meetings, or just before the load-in. While it seems out of sequence, (and it probably is), that may just be how it happens. If the meeting takes place before the lighting designer is fully versed about the demands of the production and the desires of the artistic staff (aka "up to speed"), some decisions may just have to be delayed. The process may get temporarily derailed. And when that's the case, determine the information required, schedule a time to reconvene with the relevant parties, and move on.

On the other hand, sometimes a fundamental decision must be made in order to move ahead. When that's the case, while everyone is aware that the decision in question may not be quite right, as long as they mutually agree to potential adjustments down the road, the choice can be made and the process can continue to proceed.

A typical way of beginning this type of meeting is to review each department's current status, examine how they relate to one other, followed by a discussion of the next set of challenges or collaborative teamwork deadlines. The schedule is often reviewed in two parts; the activities that take place up to load-in, and then through opening. Sometimes show elements or specific transitions are reviewed in order to convey decisions made in one-on-one meetings to the rest of the group. If there are large challenges that impact several departments, this is the opportunity to air those concerns. If the problem concerns solely negotiation with only one member at the meeting, most folks recommend saving that discussion for a future, smaller meeting.

Shelley's Notes: Tips for Production Meetings

Here's a list to consider before attending production meetings:

- Bring a pencil or pen and paper to take notes. Don't be the doofus who says "anybody got a pen?"

- If you're showing a document to be referenced in the meeting, bring copies.
- If you're unfamiliar with the staff, write their names down. Don't keep asking "what's your name?"
- If you've received the script, or other show-related material, read it before the meeting and come prepared with any questions you may have about the material.
- Be polite: Turn off your cell phone, PDA, etc. Don't talk when others have the floor.
- Don't eat during the meeting unless everyone else is as well. Coffee or other liquids are okay.
- Bring coffee or sit near the door to open it when it gets stuffy and you want a nap.
- If you have a topic you want discussed in the meeting, inform the meeting's organizer beforehand, so it can be scheduled into the agenda.
- Bring your production book, contact sheet, production schedule, or any logistical information that might be referenced.
- Don't agree to schedules or budgets if you don't know what's going on.
- Note other meetings or discussions that need to take place outside of this meeting.
- If a discussion is necessary with only one person, don't waste everyone else's time for your public exchange. Wait to speak to them after the meeting.
- Bring a thumb drive (or other storage media) so that folks can give you soft copy of a document from their computer on the spot.
- Don't let it get personal. Don't yell.
- If a deadline is requested, try to provide it. Or tell them when you'll be able to tell them.

Concept Meetings

Concept meetings, on the other hand, are often convened for the declared purpose of "bouncing ideas around," and "limited" to members of the creative team. By excluding the constraints of any parameters, the purpose of these meetings is to "bounce ideas around." With direction, ideas, and research to exchange, these meetings provide an open forum allowing everyone to hear, see, and state things at the same time. On the other hand, without direction, material, or clearly stated objectives, these kinds of meetings seem to have little value unless a free beverage or appetizer is at hand.

One-on-One Meetings

In the ideal world, all of the designers are simultaneously hired and begin their work at the same time.

In this scenario, the group and the director collectively create a production concept, or the director presents the production concept to the entire design team at the same time. The team then collectively reacts to that presentation, and mutually collaborates and supports each other to realize the production concept. More often than not, however, contracts, individual schedules, and politics don't allow this ideal scenario to happen. In many cases the lighting designer is the last collaborator joining the party; regardless of when he or she is added to the team, the faster the lighting designer can get prepared and up to speed, that much faster the process can move forward.

In the day-to-day world of freelance, juggling multiple productions often reduces face-to-face meetings to snippets of emails, text messages forwarding links to web sites, faxes, late night phone calls, or brief phone conversations that take place during breaks for completely different shows. While many things can be accomplished at a full production meeting, many production issues get resolved during smaller one-on-one encounters.

Meeting: The Director

Most lighting designers feel strongly that the director should be the first member of the creative team met in a one-on-one fashion. It's the best way to initially get the information "direct from the horse's mouth." It also allows the lighting designer to enter the meeting without any other pre-conceived notions or judgments.

Meetings with the director, like the rest of the creative staff, are opportunities for the lighting designer not only to receive information, but exchange and compare ideas. If there's only one scheduled meeting before the tech, on the other hand, the warm and fuzzy "getting to know you" chat might quickly go out the window. If this is going to be *the* meeting with the director, for example, many designers consider this one-on-one the lighting designer's sole opportunity to *get* information. Many designers believe it's more prudent to just listen, ask questions, and occasionally make suggestions; rather than make major declarations, act more like a sponge, absorbing and noting everything the director is expressing. When the meeting is limited to a single conversation, time can't be wasted on details, or off-topic war stories. If this is the only meeting with the director before the light cue level setting session, at least ask the director's favorite and most-despised color. There's no worse feeling than to load the first light cue and hear: "*Red? Why is it red? I hate red!*"

If it appears that there will be more than one chance to meet, on the other hand, then the meeting's dynamic shifts towards a more balanced and relaxed give-and-take. Certainly, the meeting's prime focus remains on the director to express her concept and visual objectives for the show. That said, this is also the opportunity for the lighting designer to present his own ideas, research, and perceptions about the piece and the production as well. When multiple meetings are anticipated, the first one-on-one is not only an exchange of ideas, but also a way for the two to establish communication, play "do you know so-and-so?," begin to work together, and hopefully begin another relationship in mutual artistic trust.

The first time that a director and a lighting designer work together, they often must begin the process of creating a semantic language that both can understand. In some cases, the phrase "romantic," when applied to lighting, can mean a host of choices. In that situation, the two attempt to find a common point of reference, referring to research material, or alternately suggesting a particular scene or moment from a film or TV, or a printed image, that illustrates the "romantic" look the director wishes to see on the stage.

Questions for the Director:

- What is the overall production concept? Any specific sources? Visual sources?
- What is the general look of the stage? Do we see the overhead electrics? The backstage?
- Audience perceptions, colors, images for an act? Scene? Location? Special moment?
- Audience perceptions, colors, images about each main character? Groups? Relationships?
- Any specific colors or other lighting elements that you like? Hate?
- What is the flow from scene to scene? Any special transitions in mind?
- Any special blocking? Special areas of the stage? Relationships to other performers?
- Any special casting choices? What skin tones need to be considered?

Information to share with the Director:

- Color palette (or color key) thoughts for major scenes. Swatch book pieces taped onto paper. (Or time with gelled instruments in the lighting studio.)
- Sketches or renderings of major moments in the show.
- Pictures of any conceptual inspirations.
- Any research or sources: movies, web sites, television, printed material, etc.

If the pair has worked together in the past, previous productions, moments, or evocations can also be used to provide a basic semantic framework to verbally exchange illustrations, feelings, or facilitate communication. Find a common base and work from there.

In many cases the light plot may need to be designed, if not hung, before any run-throughs take place. In that situation, it's necessary to define the broad use of the space and scenery for the show, where the blocking will and will not take place. Will the performers use every portion of the stage? Will they be in the house? In the orchestra boxes? Does anyone get elevated high in the air? Establishing broad ideas of where action happens sometimes helps the director focus on the blocking. It might also accidentally provide the director with new ideas of where to go in the theatre.

Director's Meeting Notes

For the purposes of this book, the director for *Hokey* is a woman. She wants the show placed in "nowhere, in a void"; each scene will be defined by the lighting. There won't be any scenic projections or scenic pieces used to define location. To reinforce "the void," she's requested the feeling of a "black surround," meaning that once the audience's vision reaches the onstage edge of the vertical or horizontal masking, there is no other visual intrusion. It's clear that this means she doesn't want to see any lighting instruments, either overhead or from the sides of the stage. The director wants to use as much of the width of the stage as the proscenium will allow, but realizes that she needs to give up some depth in order to have the translucency visually succeed.

The show will be somewhat presentational. At the top of the show, for example, the performers will step out of character, and speak directly to the audience. A phrase used by the director to describe the overall look of the show is "comic book-like." During the discussion it becomes clear that in the director's vision, this alludes to color saturation, both on the performers, bodies and the translucency. The director also made reference to potential "stark contrasts"; the example given includes scenes when the frontlight will be at a relatively low level, allowing light sources from other directions to provide a more dramatic feel to the visual image. Although the scenes will be blocked to provide stage focus, there will be times when followspots will be required to direct focus to specific performers.

The comic book reference also refers to the fade time of light changes. Just as comic books are edited to quickly change from panel to panel, the light changes from look to look will in most cases be very apparent. While this doesn't eliminate the use of slow-moving light cues, it does imply that many changes are going to be rapid, signaling the different beats in the script or song.

It's decided that the lighting color scheme will be reflected in the costumes as well. Hokey and Pookie's colors will be in the orange and peach range. The Knotty Piners will be blue and turquoise, while the Rock will be in the lavender range. Tee-boo will be green and purple, while the Snakes will be purple and reds.

Talking Through the Show

For the purposes of the book, this is the meeting in which the director and the lighting designer "talk through the show." At the top of the show, the director wants the stage to be "bathed in warm sunlight." This will help provide the contrast to the gathering storm, which will cool the atmosphere as the scene progresses. By the time Wendella enters, the stage should look like a "renaissance painting." After further discussion, it's determined that this phrase means the scene will be lit from a strong key angle with lots of shadows, as opposed to bathed in candlelight. The staging of the wedding scene will reinforce this.

The next scene is the storm. Because the piece is presentational, the director is ambivalent about strobe lights: "Let's see them. I might cut them." As a backup, the lighting designer will construct an effect that flashes conventional lighting instruments. At the height of the storm, the group (and all stage focus) will be up center or stage right. The edges of the stage, especially stage left, will be dark so that Tee-boo and the two assistants can sneak onstage and get preset in their positions downstage left. When Tee-boo is revealed, the director wants a light and sound "punctuation point." Not only will there be a light change, but as he turns and is revealed to the audience, the director wants a small pyrotechnic flashpot to go off at his feet.

In general, whenever Tee-boo is present, the director wants the whole stage, or some portion of the stage, to get "evil." One image is that the stage changes with his entrance, like blood spreading from a wound. For this production, in her mind, the color that subconsciously signals evil is green.

At the top of Act 2 when Hokey is searching for Pookie, the scene initially needs to appear "scary at night in the woods ." When the Knotty Piners enter, the lighting will "open out" and cover more of the stage in frontlight to see the Knotty Piners' faces during the book scene. When they sing their song "What's Knot to Like?" the scene can shift completely out of context and become very colorful. The song will have a reggae rhythm. As the group beds down for the night, the scene will fade down to specials or spots on Hokey and Low-Raine stage right so that Pookie and the Snakes can get preset upstage left.

In scene 2 Pookie appears to Hokey in his dream, surrounded by the Snakes. Initially the scene should be dreamlike. When she steps away from the Snakes to perform the Hokey and Pookie "Love Dance" duet, the entire stage can open out to cover the third and fourth opening, to retain the separation from Hokey downstage right. Before Pookie and the two dancers move downstage the rest of the stage can change to include Hokey in the same light.

Scene 3 should be a bright morning for the riddle scene with the Rock O' Thought. When the Rock sings "Rock Solid," the lighting should again be colorful and upbeat. The song will have a rock-and-roll beat. When Hokey and the Knotty Piners battle the Snakes to rescue Pookie, the director wants the lighting to become "murky." Specials will be needed to isolate small portions of the stage for individual battles. This might need to be another 4-followspot sequence to properly direct stage focus. After the rescue is complete, everybody leaves except for Tee-boo and his posse, when his song "Crankyland" will end with the antagonist center-center in a pool as the curtain falls. But the director asks that the curtain's descent be as fast as possible.

The third act will open with "Back to the Ranch," using the same type of look from Act 1 scene 1. The same warm and bright cues will essentially repeat as preparations are made for "The Very Fairy Wedding." Then there will be an abrupt change as Tee-boo enters and breaks up the ceremony. During "Everybody Loves a Winner and It's Me" the lighting will become more saturated. Then the lighting will become stark and red for the Battle. The director is very clear that she wants to see red light for Hell. The edge of the stage will become "The Precipice," which suggests uplights in the orchestra pit. While the director is aware that lights in the orchestra pit might be a problem, she will take responsibility for telling the musical director that he or she will have to share their space with a collection of lighting instruments. "It won't be a problem," she says assuredly.

After Tee-boo's demise, the stage needs to return to the wedding look, and then build to a bright cue for the end of the finale.

Director Meeting Notes Summary

The director has dictated very clear ideas for some aspects of the lighting and specific moments for the show. In general, when the audience watches the show, the director's objective is to make them subconsciously feel like they're watching a comic book. She wants to see lighting with high contrasts between light and dark, and high saturation in different colors.

She also wants to see naturalistic skin tones in addition to the saturates. The lighting will be more naturalistic during book scenes, and more color-saturated for the songs. The lighting will become less and less naturalistic as the conflict or tension gets higher; the most stylized lighting in the show will be during the final battle between Hokey and Tee-boo.

In terms of the overall stage "look," the director wants to create a void, a nowhere, a place where "magic may happen." Put into practical terms, the director doesn't want to see lighting instrument lenses from the overhead electrics or the side light booms. And the way that the director talks about the different moments in the show, it's apparent that she wants the stage to remain uncluttered. Slick, crisp. Not junky.

Other notes that have been jotted down: quick light changes, lots of color "bumps," fast lighting movement for the rapid musical numbers. Followspots for the leads. Yes, there will be scenes where three followspots will absolutely be needed. Moving lights or color changing instruments seem like they'll be needed as well.

After discussion, it's apparent that the color convention of green light representing evil and red light representing hell are a basic choice and very clear in her mind. The lighting designer would like to use an alternate color and break this convention. Or to discuss it in a future meeting, making a convincing case for an alternate choice and seeing if a consensus can be found. Ignoring this basic request and not informing the director prior to the tech, however, would be at the lighting designer's peril and could cost him his job. It could potentially cause a huge clash, break the director's trust in the lighting designer, and be interpreted as rude as well. Experience has shown that, in most cases, it's more prudent to provide the director with his or her desire and to see if the director's choice will actually work for the overall production concept, regardless of the lighting designer's opinion.

Meetings: The Creative Staff

After meeting with the director, the lighting designer now has a more specific grasp of the desired overall look and feel, some of the scenes, and some of the transitions in the show. Certainly the core design documents aren't complete but the lighting designer has a much better idea of the director's overall vision.

In the meetings with each of the creative staff, it will be wise to review the director's desires and make sure that everyone is on the same creative page. Checking in with the other designers about the director's likes and dislikes reduces the chance for miscommunication. If the lighting designer's ideas more closely agree with the other designers instead of the director, it may be that a particular phrase or idea was misunderstood. Double-checking with the rest of the team makes sure that conflicting ideas get clarified long before final decisions are made. Try to define the pattern or the misstep in communication so that you can avoid it in the future and not lose time, or the job.

Discussions with each of the other designers often involve two different levels of interaction: the conceptual and the practical. The conceptual level will concentrate on the collaboration between the lighting and the other design elements of the show. The practical discussions will consider the physical relationship of the lighting to other departments' elements in the venue. In each meeting the show will be talked through focusing on the interaction of the lighting with each of the other design elements for the show.

The agreements, language, and ideas expressed in these meetings form the basic conceptual and practical understandings and agreements for *Hokey* that might not be realized for months. Since it's possible that the these meetings may be taking place in the midst of several other productions, clear communication, accurate note-taking, and documentation reduce the amount of potential misunderstanding. Often, that translates into having a smart assistant with a note pad.

Meeting: Production Electrician

While meetings with the creative staff tend to focus on the design aspects of the production, meetings with the production electrician focus mainly on practical matters, ranging from the budget, scheduling, labor, and equipment, to basic topics such as the final scale for the light plot or where to install the tech table in the theatre.

In smaller situations, meetings with the production electrician, or the PE, often don't begin in earnest until the lighting designer has a full understanding of the show's needs, or a finished plot in his or her hand. While there might be brief conversations about special instruments that need researching, the infrastructure of the theatre, or practical ideas how to accomplish a special effect, the PE typically doesn't become heavily involved in a smaller production until a completed plot requires analysis in preparation for its implementation using house equipment, or being submitted to rental shops for a bid.

When a show is large, or complex, the production electrician may be much more involved in the overall process. He or she may be provided a copy of the script or the scene breakdown in order to become acquainted with the show's language. The LD and the

PE may be in frequent contact, before or after the creative one-on-one meetings with the rest of the creative staff. If nothing else, the lighting designer often defers to the production electrician when questions arise about the placement, makeup, or distribution of the physical components for the production (dimmer beach, routers, headsets, cue lights, tech table), and how they integrate with other departments (cable runs relative to the sound gear, hazer placement relative to other departments' electronics). While the lighting designer might offer ideas or insights, he or she is very unwise to not to defer or consult with the production electrician on these questions. On the other hand, the lighting designer may also have effects that need to be solved.

Meeting: Production Stage Manager

During initial concept meetings or one-on-ones, the interaction between the design team and the production stage manager is not on a conceptual level. In these meetings the stage manager's role is to observe, facilitate, and notate, rather than creatively participate. The stage manager should be included in any communication between any departments. When the final production concept is produced, the stage manager knows as much about the integration of the design elements as any of the designers.

During the rehearsal process, the stage manager's role is of key importance to the lighting designer. At the conclusion of each rehearsal, the stage manager prepares and distributes a **rehearsal report**, summarizing that day's changes and notes to the entire production team. Although a section is devoted to notes for each design department, the stage manager alerts all readers to any significant alterations, additions, or changes requested by the director in that day's rehearsal. This may range from the addition of a wall switch to motivate a light change, to a new moment created by the director where the light change will motivate the acting.

If the lighting designer isn't in the rehearsal studio, these daily reports may be the only link that alerts him or her to changes in the show made by the director that potentially may alter the plot, the hang, or the structure of the lighting cues. This is especially true in productions that don't have the comparative luxury of followspots.

While the production stage manager attends all the initial one-on-one meetings, a short amount of time should be allocated to speak with her separately to clarify practical decisions. One practical topic is to determine how the final light cue numbers and their placement will be transferred from the lighting designer to the stage manager. The methods typically employed may range from copying the light cue placement from the lighting designer's script, to handing the script over for a night, to a scheduled meeting between the two to "talk through" the cues, to the lighting designer providing the stage manager a prepared cue master document. If the pair can determine a method, and better yet, a time period to perform the exchange, it won't sneak up on both of them. If they fail to determine a course of action, they may both suddenly discover the only time available for the transfer will be during the light cue level setting session, or the tech rehearsal. On a complex show, this is a potential waste of stage time.

If there aren't any run-throughs before the focus, then the lighting designer may need to rely upon videotaped run-throughs or have the stage manager talk through the blocking for each scene. These methods may be the only recourse to help define the focus and the cue master before the technical rehearsals begin.

Stage Management Notes

On a conceptual level, the production stage manager can be used as a resource to double-check understandings or questions the lighting designer may have when it's not possible to speak directly to the other designers. For that matter, the stage manager may be able to provide clarity when the Director is unavailable for questions.

 Questions for the Production Stage Manager:

- Will the stage manager provide spike marks prior to the focus call?
- Will the stage manager be on site or available for consultation during the focus call?
- Where will the stage manager be located during the technical rehearsals?
- Which side of the tech table does the PSM wish to sit on?
- Where will the director be located?
- Will the PSM have a printer at the table? What kind?
- When will the stage manager move to the performance calling position?
- Will the stage manager need a cue light system?

Meetings Summary

If any of the meetings are spaced over a long period of time, notes made during each meeting become a critical source of reference. The subsequent production meeting is an opportunity for each designer to broadly review the results of the one-to-one meetings, and articulate his or her next steps. Doing so defines each designer and department's agenda, along with interaction and deadlines with the other departments.

Once the schedule is publicly reviewed, any other topics regarding cross-departmental communication or coordination is discussed. Presuming that everyone has a clear understanding of the tasks at hand, decisions are made, and the process can continue to move forward.

Hokey Re-Analysis

Now that all of the meetings have taken place, another layer of structure can be added to the collected information about *Hokey* that will be applied to the lighting design.

While there's a mid-stage painted scrim and a black traveler, there's no other flying scenery. This suggests that all of the overhead electrics will be able to be located to their best advantage (read as: the lighting designer can place them with the scenic designer's approval). The meeting with the scenic designer also indicated very little deck scenery, suggesting that sidelight booms should be included in the light plot. Presuming low sidelights can be added to the plot, they will provide dimensionality on the performer's bodies and color them differently, while the overhead systems can color the floor and isolate the areas.

The scenic stack will include the brand new translucency and a black scrim. The scenic designer may wish to be involved with the color schemes used for the trans, since that will be a major scenic element. The gray floor is potentially going to be a large reflective surface, which could be problematic. If there's any way to create a mock-up in order to see what the challenges may be, now's the time to figure that out.

Scene Breakdown and Analysis

There are three distinct scenes in each act. Act 1 will begin with a warm sunlight day look. This look will also repeat with much of Act 3, for the repeats of the wedding. Act 1, scene 2 will contrast with the transition to the storm sequence, when the lovers are separated. Since the storm also signals Tee-boo's first entrance, the storm colors may become the colors used to signal Tee-boo's presence every time he's seen. Detailed discussions should certainly take place to determine the look of the storm. The director was conceptually ambivalent about actual strobes. A test showing her the comparison between a strobe and the programmed flash of a conventional fixture should help clarify that visual moment. Anyway, after Pookie's kidnapping, the scene will restore to the initial look of the first scene, but with less warmth.

The first scene in Act 2 introduces the Knotty Piners. Since this is some kind of forest look with scary night connotations, a foliage (bare branches?) template system should be considered; haze should be added to the plot. The scene 2 "night on the beach" look will need to contrast with the internal dream sequence.

What kind of look will telegraph the "dreaminess" to the audience? Floor fog might be an initial choice, but it sounds as if the performers will be laying down on the floor. That choice may not be the best for the respiratory health. Aside from that, the cost for an additional floor fog unit should be considered. Dry ice fog is out; there's no question that the budget wouldn't be able to sustain the weekly cost for CO_2 dry ice blocks. How much time will there be from the end of the dream, until scene 3, with the Rock at sunrise? Attention to timing and traffic patterns around the Rock will need to be carefully observed during rehearsals.

Act 3 is a restore of Act 1, scene 1. Again, this will contrast the transition for Tee-boo's entrance. Maybe repeat the cues and make a "bit" out of it? Another area of discussion will be about the stairs and ways to show the entrance of Hell: floor fog again? Or some kind of smoke rising from the pit? Maybe other alternate units might be considered.

Hokey's battle with Tee-boo will certainly be dramatic. How will that be staged? The edge of the stage used for the dance challenge will need isolation, to define the Precipice of Doom. The precipice will need a different look; the number of people on stage during that sequence will be blocked to a different area of the stage in order to focus on Tee-boo and Hokey. Between the battle, the storm, the forest, and the "otherworldliness" of the show, the next conversation with the director should make inquiries to see if lights shafts would be acceptable. If that assumption is accurate, some sort of haze will definitely be required. One unit or two?

Between the cast size, the group scenes, and the artistic staff's directions, there will be a need for followspots, in addition to a number of specials. The director mentioned three, the choreographer mentioned four. That's big. Even if it's only two followspots, there's enough imagined activity that additional personnel will need to choreograph and call the followspots during the rehearsals. Presuming there are only enough assistant stage managers to run the deck, and that the production stage manager won't have time during the tech rehearsals, an assistant lighting designer will be required to act as followspot director. Aside from that, the overall running crew size should be checked to make sure there's enough in the weekly labor budget. All of the atmospherics, along with the addition of booms, begins to suggest a deck electrician being part of the running crew.

As production or creative staff meetings continue, the relationships between the lighting and other aspects of the production evolve. The wireless microphones, for example, will require pockets to be sewn into specific costume pieces to contain the base packs. The lighting and scenic designer will need to mutually choose the fabric used for the china silk, in order to make sure the right material works for both them. Maybe they can go to a fabric store together. On the other hand, there may be no time for anyone to collectively get together again until just before load-in.

Hokey Cue Master, Version 2

Throughout all of these meetings, the lighting designer has been absorbing and notating everyone's individual and collective input, recording the information on a legal pad or a laptop. For the time being, there are still only two core design documents, the cue master and the systems and specials sheet.

Figure 3.5 shows the results of the first updating of the cue master for *Hokey*. Several rows have been added so that all of the added beats and moments that were revealed in all the meetings can be added. To help make a distinction between the songs and any other action, the song titles have been bolded. The information in the columns on the right-hand side may not have everything in the right place, but the first priority is to collect all of the available information into a single document as rapidly as possible. Every new beat or moment, every blocking or staging notation, and every song style indication has been included. All of the scribbled notes from the other meetings have now been absorbed into this single document. Entering the information as soon as possible after the one-on-one meetings often calls up other verbal notes that happened so quickly they weren't written down. Assembling and viewing the notes allows the designer to compare fresh information. This might include notes on costume colors, which may become particularly useful when examining color choices for the translucency.

Obviously, not all of these lighting change ideas will survive into the light cue level setting session. At this point, however, this document is a repository for every conceivable lighting change, listed in a sequential format, with some sense of when and why it would take place.

One of the benefits of the cue master is that it allows the lighting designer to have a more global view of an entire scene, and place it in the context of the entire production. It makes it possible to begin comparing cues to one another—the lighting designer can see that Act 1, scene 1 looks like it may potentially repeat or restore to some degree during Act 3, scene 1.

As the cue master expands, it allows the designer to define cue placement choices for more subtle movement of light, as well as for obvious cue points. The

qualities and movements of light, now described in the cue master, can now be viewed by the lighting designer in much the manner that a composer would view a musical score. The lighting designer now has an overview of all of the scene names, characters, and song titles—the beginning of the language for the show. Since all of this information is collected on a few pages, it's possible to easily refer to almost any aspect or point of the production, and see adjacent scenes or songs, or see where they are relative to the rest of the show.

Hokey Systems and Specials, Version 2

Once the cue master has been updated, it's printed out and studied. Then, any applicable information about the systems or blocking notes gets transferred over to the systems and specials sheet.

Figure 3.6 shows the result of this first updating session, compared to Figure 3.3 at the beginning of the chapter on page 66. Already the amount of information and structural analysis have dramatically expanded. During this updating process, ideas about colors, angles, and cueing thoughts have begun to emerge. And now, that information may be turned around and re-entered back into the cue master.

At this point in the process, many of these thoughts may still end with question marks by them. But as the information gets more distilled, and as the big looks and recipes for each scene continue to be developed and honed, patterns and similarities of colors, angles, and mental pictures start to emerge.

As Figure 3.6 shows, not all of the information is strictly in the correct column. As a complex show grows and changes, it's common to see information overflow from one column to another, until another column is added. As new systems are decided, this type of document often increases in size, and can quickly require multiple pages with larger paper and smaller fonts. Sometimes lighting designers start by rotating the document to a landscape layout, expanding it onto legal-sized paper, and adding columns for each direction of light. In this way it can be easier to see repetitions and patterns emerge.

The important thing is to condense the looks of the show into the most compressed possible layout. Then it's possible to compare systems used in various scenes to one another, and then see how much any system is used throughout the show. As more information and more cue sequences are added to the cue master, the overall number, color, and purposes of each system or special series is expanded, contracted, or eliminated altogether. Each system is constantly reviewed, decisions made about the color and amount of coverage can then be

Hybrid Theatre 2010 — HOKEY CUE MASTER V2 — Date: 2/7/10

Act	Sc	Sec	Cue	Cnt	SONG	CAST	NOTES	BLOCK	ACTION
					Poolie USL				Pook USL
1	1	Open			Welcome to our world	Company			Warm sunlight
						Character intro		Circle @ CC	X DS to talk
					A Very Fairy Wedding	Hok/Pook intro		Plat @ CC	
						Friar US		Friar US	
						Wendella enter		SR in1	
					You're My Cookie	Love swear	4 spots		50's flavor
	2	Storm				Transition			Wendella; cool off
					Dangerous Winds	Fairies; candles	china silk	Silk poles	storm; Cool stage
						All US or SR			SL dark: Tee-boo + 2
				Ø		Tee-boo DSL		Green	Flashpot; strobe?
					It's All About Me	Tee-boo			
						Kidnap Pook DSL			
						Exit			
	3	After				Fortelling			Wend & Hokey DC
					We're All Gonna Die	Fairies			
					Lost My Pook	Hokey			50's doo-wap
					Choose a Path	Etheria			
					I Will Find You	Hokey			Exit SL @ end
2	1	Forest			Top of Act 2				Scary night; woods
					Lost in the Weeds	Hokey		Piners US; shadow	End DC
						Fun Knotties		book scene	Open; see faces
					What's Knot to Like	Knotty Piners		whole stage	Color; Reggae
						Join Forces			
					Knots Are Tight	Knotty & Hokey			Stick Dance
					ends song				End DSR; pools
					Alone With the Moon	Hokey	scrim reveal	US dark P preset	Pool/spot DSR
	2	Dream			Save Me	Pookie & snakes			US Pookie reveal
					I Will Find You	Hokey			counterpoint
					I'm Your Moon Love	Hok/Pook		Dance DC; neat pit?	Open DS
						add 2 dancers		more dance	
					I'm Your Moon Love	Hok/Pook		Dance DC; neat pit?	Open DS
						scrim conceal?			end; ftb
						rock preset			Rock & boulders
	1	Beach			Knock, Who's a Rock	Rock riddle			Color; R&R
					Rock Solid	Rock & Boulders			Tap number X USR
					Rescue from Sandbox	All		Pookie USL w/snakes	Murky fight
					CrankyLand	Tee-boo			
3	2	Wed			Back at the Ranch	Fairies		Pookie CC	Copy A1, sc 1
					A Very Fairy Wedding	Hok/Pook set		Friar US; Hokey 1SR	
					Wend/Hok/Lo-raine book				
					Start wedding				
	3	Battle		Ø	Everybody Loves Winner	Tee-boo DSL			Restore Tee-boo 1?
					Book; hell	Cast X US			
					Heaven & Hell	Tee-boo/Hok	DC		Red in Pit
					Do the Hokey Pokey	Tee-boo/Hok		Hokey DSR	
					Love Dance	Hok/Pook	Tee-boo DC		Restore A1, sc 1
					You're My Cookie	Hok/Pook		Wedding CC	
					A Very Fairy Wedding	Company			

Lighting design by Steve Shelley 917.xxx.xxxx — Page 1 of 1

Figure 3.5 The Cue Master for *Hokey*, version 2

Act & Scene	Systems	Specials	Backing
Act 1 scene 1 "warm sunny day" "Welcome" "Wedding" "Cookie"	NC Back wash R20 Back wash Skin tone HS Dance; shape sides Color BxBm "Welcome" Warm Sides	Special 1E to CC; Pool USL; follow her Front spec DSL, DC, DSR for intros Haze for shafts	Cyc day. 2 color top Blue bottom. Separate cntr/side? Rainbows groundrow; side to side transitions
Act 1 scene 2 "evil poof"	Dk Blue FOH wash Down/back-green? Lav follow Turquoise sides (evil) Blue sides later? Side Temps low Side Temps low Lav FOH; contrast Dk blue FOH for chorus? Or shadows?	Pool DSL ½ Tee-boo Strobe cannon down Then he X to DC; follow him; haze Segment green down/back; infection spreads w/his ent? Affects chorus/they droop?	Cyc blue top/Green bottom. Then Cyc total green for Tee-boo; evil, evil, spawn of devil Flash on background to silhouette? Cyc xfade with hand gesture?
Act 1 scene 3 "Tee-boo gone" Restore 1-1 only sad	Neutral FOH wash Cool when Tee-boo gone Then warm to partial restore of A1sc1 Blue sides? Dark blue FOH?	Wendella & Hokey special separate from rest of crowd	Cyc partial restore with Tee-boo depart; desolation, empty bare trees temps Cemetery-like Dusk?

Figure 3.6 The Systems and Specials Sheet for *Hokey* Act 1, version 2

considered, accepted, or rejected, as the cue master "score" for the entire show is reviewed with each new batch of information or inspiration.

Hokey **Preliminary Magic Sheet, Version 1**

Now that there is enough information to start mentally constructing visual images for the show, it's also possible to begin the process of figuring out how to control the different light beams and paint the mental pictures. Often this process starts by sketching small pictograms, separating the different colors and specials into systems, and then each pictogram is divided to represent how those systems will be constructed or controlled.

If the warm backlight wash envisioned at the beginning of the show will be turned on and off as a single channel, for example, then it might require only a single channel of control. Depending on variables like the stage size, the instrument types, and the dimmer capacities, the warm backlight wash for the entire stage might be one instrument in a single channel.

Figure 3.7 shows the first version of the **preliminary magic sheet** for *Hokey*. In the top left-hand corner is a small square with the text "Warm" above it. This pictogram is a miniature groundplan showing the current status for the proposed

warm backlight system. Underneath it is handwritten text "R23?"—one color being considered for the system. This drawing indicates that, with the present envisioned cues, controlling this warm backlight system would take three channels: one for the circular pool upstage left (marked "open" for "opening"), a second channel for the rectangular shape in the middle (labeled "wed" for "wedding"), and a third channel for everything else. When those three channels are turned on or off at the proper time, all of the cues presently imagined would properly look correct.

So how many lighting instruments would be required to make up this entire system of warm backlight? At this time, that doesn't have to be a consideration. That portion of the process will take place later. At this point, the goal is to mentally review all of the visual images that involve the warm backlight, and draw their separate pools of control into this small single groundplan. As the images for each visual moment in the show become more defined, the amount of separation required for this warm backlight system will be illustrated with additional internal circles or squares. Each one will represent individual light pools that need to be turned on or off, to make the different "looks" involving warm backlight, over the course of the entire show. In this

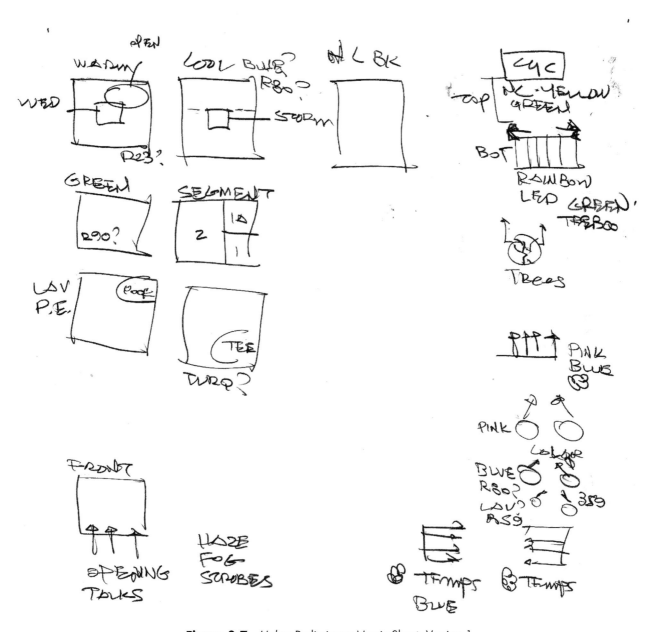

Figure 3.7 *Hokey* Preliminary Magic Sheet, Version 1

case, the separation is represented by small ovals, drawn and re-drawn, inside that system's miniature groundplan.

Along with all of the other systems, it's then possible to see the amount of separation required for each color system in the proposed light plot in a single glance. Each of the drawn squares potentially represents a different color system. Next to the "warm" square is a "cool" square, and an "NC Bk," for "No Color Back." Likewise, the current thoughts about the cyc lighting are drawn in the upper right-hand corner; the top systems in the cyc currently list NC (for the day look at the top of Act 1, scene 1) and green (for Tee-boo). The bottom striped rectangle

indicates "rainbow LED." This will refer to the LED striplights currently envisioned for the bottom of the translucency.

Core Design Document Review

As the lighting designer becomes more familiar with each act, scene, and moment in the show, he or she is able to write the lighting "score" in the cue master. The colors, directions, and specials used within a scene are then transferred to the systems and specials sheet. Each system or color indicated on that document is then transferred to the preliminary magic sheet, and a detailing of what needs to be turned on or off within each of the systems is indicated in each miniature pictogram.

Using these three core design documents, the lighting designer is able to oversee the choices of color, direction, and control in order to eventually construct the light plot and create the lighting cues.

As the cue master, the systems and specials sheet, and the preliminary magic sheet are now updated, they're reviewed and cross-checked against each other to make certain the information between all three documents is a match. The notes from the day's meetings are all reviewed one more time to be certain that all requests and ideas have been considered, and every meeting memory has been jogged. After the final review, the last version of the core documents, along with out-of-date notes are stored in the back of the production book. These three fresh core documents will go into plastic protective sleeves in the front of the book, so they're instantly accessible.

By constructing some element of these three core documents as a place to sketch ideas while working on any aspect of the show, the lighting designer has taken a huge step towards organizing and structuring the lighting score. From now on, when any conversation is had regarding this show, these core documents will be close at hand, both as references and as documents to record changes.

While these three documents are just lists, they're also an evolving repository of everyone's contribution to the production concept, bringing the lighting designer's thinking into focus on how to utilize the controllable properties and objectives of stage lighting design to further the production concept.

SUMMARY

Now that some grasp of all of the ethereal ideas for the production are at hand, the mental images have now started to be adapted and molded to the visual reality of the specific production. Systems and specials are being considered. Colors and templates are being bandied about. Everyone has been initially spoken to, and both conceptual and practical information has been exchanged.

In reality, some amount of time often passes after the second analysis of *Hokey*. For the purposes of our text, however, the notes have been absorbed, and now the second portion of the research and analysis stage will be examined: the practical parameters that surround this, or any, show. Many boundaries limit a lighting package and a lighting design, ranging from the number of instruments, the amount of control, the other design elements, or the venue's architecture. But that's not all. Many other parameters impact the final lighting design, and while they might range from logistics to the kind of show that's being presented, most of them are all based on a single common denominator: money.

Chapter 4

The Parameters

INTRODUCTION

In the creative timeline of any lighting design, there's a point when the concepts and aesthetic lists are set aside, and the lighting instruments begin to be selected and distributed on the groundplan. This is the point when the actual construction of the light plot begins. Before that point, however, there is value to take a moment, step back, and be certain that all of the parameters that surround any production have been considered.

Determining the physical, conceptual, and financial limits unique to any production or performing space, will prevent (or at least reduce) assumptions made that may later be realized as critical errors in judgment. Decisions based on ignorance can create compound problems that didn't need to exist in the first place. Determining the parameters of any given production recognizes its realities, and reduces the effort expended in redoing tasks that were planned or performed before the parameters were defined.

Another way of saying this is: Ask questions and listen before you act. If there's information that is unknown, don't patiently wait for the information to arrive. Ask. And when the answers arrive, listen, analyze, and react to the answers. If that means asking more questions, then do so as quickly as possible. More time can be spent trying to regain focus, as just responding to the question. It can be said that defining the parameters sets limitations on the artistic esthetics of a project. While that may very well be true, it also introduces structure and saves time. Knowledge and preparation are two basic tools that prevent on-site judgments from becoming erroneous snap decisions.

First, it is important to define the expectations and obligations of the lighting designer. In all cases, this is expressed in some form of a **contract**, which informs the lighting designer about the responsibilities that will be assigned, when they need to be completed, and what to expect in return.

The **production schedule** influences the lighting package and the production as a whole. Each time increment details or implies tasks that must be complete in order for the next step to be taken. And sometimes while the budget may seem unforgiving, the production schedule can become especially hostile, especially if the scope of the light plot hasn't been adequately tailored to match the amount of time provided.

The production is also defined by the **budget**, which outlines the overall size of the show, the production staff, and specifically the number of people employed in the electrics department to mount the lighting package and run the show. It often outlines the number of hours projected to complete the work, and defines the amounts spent on the rental and purchase of lighting equipment. If the production has to travel, the budget also states the costs to house, transport, and feed the production staff.

The **type** or **size** of the production affects the lighting package. The **origin** of the show, whether it is an original presentation or a remount of a prior production, can affect how the light plot is designed. The **movement** of the production, whether it's a tour or a transfer from a shop to a single theatre, affects the design and flexibility of the lighting package. The cubic limitations of the **mode of transport** may affect the size and preparation methods employed to create the lighting package.

The parameters provided by the **production facility** often constrain the size, preparation, or placement of the components of the light plot. An examination of the existing **house lighting system** helps define the amount of additional equipment that may be required or allowed. Information about the **house lighting console**, or **house light board**, allows the lighting designer to judge its suitability to accommodate the lighting package.

In many cases, when parameters are defined for a production, this often results in paperwork that becomes basic reference documents in the lighting production book. Having these documents at hand allows decisions to be made on fact, rather than on assumption.

Successfully creating a lighting design while acknowledging parameters is a constant challenge and a skill acquired by knowledge and experience. Knowing what questions to ask, how to ask them, and how to properly interpret the answers, are all developed talents that allow the primary focus to shift back to the ethereal aspects of the lighting design.

DEFINE THE CONTRACT

For the purposes of this book, the contract is presented as one of the many parameters that impact a lighting design. In cold reality, a discussion regarding contracts is lengthy and complex, and worthy of several chapters. While the importance of a contract can't be underrated, it's not the primary focus of this book. To that end, this book will provide a brief overview, and highlight specific clauses and contract points. A more thorough understanding, however, begins by reviewing other resources for more detail. At the time of this writing, the United Scenic Artists website (www.usa829.org) provides downloadable Standard Design Agreements, which are excellent reference documents containing contractual language for multiple design disciplines.

The contract should be the first piece of business addressed before any other activity takes place. United Scenic Artists, for example, requires a filed contract before their members can submit any work. Passing on any designed sketches, drawings, or renderings is a no-no until a mutual agreement has been hammered out between the two parties, and the signed documents are submitted to the union. While that stance is designed to protect the designer, it doesn't mean that the designer avoids any contact with the potential show. Much the opposite; once a verbal agreement has been reached, the designer works with all due haste as quickly as possible to create said sketches,

drawings, or renderings. That way, when the union office has received the signed contracts, the designer's work can be swiftly distributed.

In a small theatre, or a situation where the show's being created between a group of friends, this stance may seem harsh or extreme. In a "triage" situation, it may not seem wise to delay the matters at hand until the contract's been signed. Some other last-minute situation may be so rushed that it may seem more prudent to focus on the production and assume that contractual matters will fall into place.

In all of these situations, the contract can quickly become a nagging piece of business that "has to be done." And when things haven't been spelled out, concerns can grow that there may be unexpected contractual "by-the-ways." While that's valid, that's not the point. Until a contract is reached and written down, until two copies of the document are signed, and until the designer has one of those copies in his or her hand, he or she is *not protected*. Until that point, the designer should not give any design work, physically or electronically, to the producer or any producer's representatives.

Section One

A basic contract is usually divided into four sections. The first section identifies the parties and the logistics surrounding the agreement; the names of the designer and the producer, the name and scope of the show, the performance space, and the principle dates of employment. Typically, three dates are earmarked: the date the contract is signed, the date drawings and paperwork are submitted for bids or analysis, and the date declared as "opening night."

Employee versus Independent Contractor

While all of this information is important, one of the most important wordings in this first section is that the contract should define the lighting designer as an employee, rather than as an independent contractor. While this may seem of little consequence, at the time of this writing, this definition has massive implications regarding unemployment and disability insurance, on how much money actually appears on the paycheck, and who pays health expenses in a work-related accident.

The *employee's* paycheck will have local, state, and federal taxes taken out (resulting in a W-4 at the end of the year). One-half of the FICA tax (Federal Insurance Contributions Act) will also be withheld from the paycheck, but that sum is eventually returned to the employee. The *independent contractor's* paycheck, on the other hand, will be paid as the gross amount, with no taxes taken out (resulting in a 1099 instead). Not only will the independent contractor probably have to pay the taxes on that amount at the end of the year, he or she will also be stuck paying the FICA as well. Contemporary common wisdom states that it makes more financial sense to be defined as an employee, and have taxes taken out of the paycheck.

The "employee versus independent contractor" definition also has a huge impact on accidents and insurance. The *employee* injured on the job is covered by workman's comp. The *independent contractor* is not. If the lighting designer is hit by falling scenery while standing onstage during a focus call, this is obviously a work-related accident. Designated as an employee, the cost for ambulance transport, emergency room procedures, and any follow-up exams will all be paid for by workman's compensation insurance, which in turn is paid for by the employer. Also known as workman's comp, this is part of the agreement when taxes are taken out of the employee's paycheck. As an employee, taxes are deducted from the paycheck, but the employee is covered for work-related accidents by mandatory insurance paid for by the employer. If, instead, the lighting designer is designated as an independent contractor, the paycheck is paid as a single fee, with no taxes withheld. But the same accident won't be covered by the employer's workman's comp insurance. All of those previously mentioned costs would instead be billed to the lighting designer's personal insurance, or paid directly out of his or her pocket. For those of you who have not yet had to consider the cost of medical transport or procedures, God bless you. Your time will come.

Section Two

The second section of a contract explains the promises made in the agreement, who is responsible for what, and the details surrounding those promises. Typically, this section provides a list of things the producer is obligated to do for the designer; provide logistical information, coordinate production meetings, hire a crew, and deal with all copyright issues. On the other hand, most contracts contain language to the effect that "the lighting designer is responsible for the following" and then a list of services, which often includes:

- Provide full lighting equipment lists and a light plot drawn to scale from scenic design and theatre drawings provided by producer.

- Provide color, hook-up plots and instrument schedule including all information required for the realization of the design.
- Coordinate and plot special lighting effects.
- Supply specifications for competitive bids for lighting and special effects to suppliers mutually satisfactory to the producer and the lighting designer.
- Oversee focusing of the lighting equipment and setting of lighting cues.
- Attend rehearsals as necessary, in order to design the production and conduct the lighting rehearsals.
- Adhere to the lighting budget.

Section Three

The third section states the compensation (the money), and explains how and when it will be paid. While assistant or associate design contracts are typically negotiated as a weekly rate paid for some number of weeks, the lighting design contract for a single show is often listed as a single lump sum, known as "the fee." Union agreements often break the fee into thirds: One, when the contract is signed; two, when the plot and support paperwork are submitted to the producer (for review or for submission to lighting rental shops for bids; and three, opening night.

On smaller contracts, the fee is often broken into two payments spread over some amount of time, so that the lighting designer has some income while work on the show is being done. Worst case scenario, if the project is cancelled, at least the lighting designer has some compensation to show for his or her work. Regardless of the fee structure, historically speaking, the final payment has always been delivered before curtain on opening night. In an act of good faith, the lighting designer receives the final portion of compensation before the curtain goes up.

The third section also addresses other monetary issues. If the show opens in a city that is remote to the lighting designer's home, the topics of housing, transport, and per diem need to be addressed. Other negotiations on large shows address additional weekly compensation, also frequently referred to as "royalties." Designers on long-running hits usually get a weekly royalty check, but most shows can't afford to provide designers that luxury. Union contracts also include a clause regarding pension and welfare payments.

Another monetary topic included on almost every contract is petty cash, typically defined as "usual and customary expenses incurred by the lighting designer related to the production." Typical items that fall under the heading of petty cash include phone bills, fax bills, shipping and overnight delivery expenses, transport to and from meetings, printing costs (photocopy, plotting), and tools or perishables that will then belong to the production. While petty cash covers expenses related to creating the final product, it's merely a method to quickly compensate vendors for goods or services with relatively small amounts of cash, and be quickly reimbursed for out-of-pocket expenses. Petty cash should not be considered "the production budget," or a replacement for paying with checks, purchase orders, or other common accounting practices. At least a verbal agreement should be made to the lighting designer, outlining the method, speed of reimbursement, or advancement of those monies, before the production period begins.

Section Four

The fourth section of a contract lists all of the other points of agreement. Occasionally, assistants are a point of contract negotiation. A clause may state the length of their contract, their salary, and if they'll be placed on a union contract. On smaller shows, getting an assistant paid for by the producer, for any amount of time, can be perceived as a major contractual coup.

Other clauses in the fourth section are usually determined on a show-by-show basis. These address many "what if's"; what happens if the show is delayed or abandoned, what happens if the show is filmed, what happens when the production is produced by two organizations, or goes to two places, or goes on tour, or is sold to someone else; the list is extensive, but each clause should be reviewed as each contract is negotiated.

Four clauses are strongly recommended in any contract. The "dispute clause" provides legal recourse in case the two parties can't agree on something. A typical dispute clause reads something like "any adjudication of the contract shall be submitted to an independent arbitrator," meaning that a third party can make a final, binding decision. A "right of first refusal clause" is also highly recommended; if the show has a subsequent life after the present production closes, this clause guarantees that the lighting designer must be the first one called when the show is booked in the next incarnation. It is then the designer's choice if he or she decides to accept or decline the opportunity to design this show again. The third clause is the "ownership clause"; while the producer has the right to retain copies of the light plot and lighting records, the ownership of the design and all original drawings and records, paperwork and soft copy, belong solely to the designer.

Finally, due to recent legal rulings, the fourth clause is now a "must-have" in every contract, regardless of design discipline. For years it was thought that a liability disclaimer, printed directly on a light plot, was sufficient protection to legally absolve the lighting designer from any accident involving equipment in the lighting package. Every light plot had some variation of this disclaimer paragraph pasted somewhere in the drafting:

> "The lighting designer is unqualified to determine the structural or electrical appropriateness of this design, and will not assume responsibility for improper engineering, construction, handling, or use. All materials and construction must comply with the most stringent applicable Federal and Local Fire, Safely, Energy, and Environmental Codes."

Accepted wisdom was that, by including this disclaimer on the light plot, the lighting designer would avoid being personally sued. At the time of this writing, that's no longer true. So for the latest in legal protection, the union now includes the "insurance clause" on all of its contracts. Why? Just because the disclaimer's on the light plot, doesn't mean the producer has read it, agreed to it, and thus, legally, there is no contract. It also doesn't legally state two vitally important points; one, the lighting designer isn't the party that should require liability insurance, and two, it's the producer's responsibly to provide it. To make a long story short, this issue is still in flux. But as protection, the "insurance clause" should be included in every contract, and include language stating some variation of this paragraph:

> The Designer is responsible for the visual or aural aspects of the production only, and it is understood that all specifications relate solely to the appearance of the lighting and not to matters of the safety. The Designer agrees to make prompt correcting alterations to any specification found to be incompatible by Producer with proper safety precaution.

> Producer will indemnify, defend, save, and hold the Designer(s), his/her heirs, executors, administrators and assigns harmless from and against any and all liability, charges, costs, expenses, claims and/or other loss, including reasonable attorneys' fees, whatsoever which they may suffer by reason of the designs furnished hereunder.

> Producer agrees to carry comprehensive general liability insurance applicable to any claims that might arise due to any work performed under this Agreement.

Including some variation of this language in every contract is important. A shorter version of the clause on the light plot can't hurt but, by itself, is not enough. If there is any accident, heaven forbid, in these litigious days, this clause may save the lighting designer from ruin. In this collection of clauses, the two that are the most important are the dispute clause, and the insurance clause. And since the courts are always changing, check with your local attorney or legal representative to confirm the proper wording for any of these clauses to be properly included in any contracts or on any other documents. See the following:

> "The author is unqualified to determine the legal appropriateness of any writing within this text, and will not assume responsibility for any usage of any of phrases contained in this book inserted into any legal document."

Shelley's Notes: Contract Negotiation

Contract negotiation is a never-ending education. Negotiating is a skill based on experience, as much as the accumulated skill of designing light. That's why people retain agents.

People often ask: "What should I charge for this contract?" In many cases, determining this number starts with a projected number of hours/days/weeks that it will take to complete the project, multiplied by an estimate of what monetary value you place on your time. In this line of thought, then, the calculation starts with the ability to analyze a schedule and see how much work will be required both in the theatre and in preparation for it. The next step is an analysis of your value, depending on the task you're performing. What is your hourly rate? Your daily rate? Your weekly rate? How are those rates affected by the potential responsibility you might be assigned? Lighting design? Assisting? Drafting? Keeping track of the paper? Next, how to determine those rates? Check with your peers, your mentors. Check the rate books on web sites. Talk to other designers who have performed that role in that space. What was their fee? Make your calculations and take your best guess. Keep track of your hours and figure out how badly you misjudged the amount of time required to produce the design, learn from that, and adapt your formula for the next contract.

People state: "I'm not going to get paid the money I know I'm worth on this contract, and they'll never agree to the money I should justifiably earn. What do I do?" Sadly, the first response to that is "welcome to theatre." The next response is "welcome to design in theatre." Designers historically get paid worse than most of the crews, regardless of the level of the production. If you compare the weekly wages of most of the crew, you'll sadly come to realize that most of them, on hourly or weekly wages, usually earn more money than either the lighting designer or any assistant. So the third response can then be: "Since money can't be your motivation, what will make executing the job worth it to you? How badly do you want the show? How much are you willing to give up in order to design this piece? How little can you earn and not become resentful?"

People say: "I know this show is going to be exhausting/this director is crazy/this theatre is a snake pit. Do I really want to do it?" If you know going it that the situation is going to be a challenge, how do you make it worth your while? Money can't always be the motivation, or you're in the wrong business. Is it the chance to get your foot in the door of that theatre? The opportunity to work with that particular group of people? Is it the chance that you'll then be first considered for the big show, the one you *really* want to design in the first place? Is it the chance to work with that team of creative people whose work you've admired? Is it the chance to work with that director or designer that everyone's talking about, that you want to hitch your wagon to his or her star? Is it billing? Is it experience for your resume? Some guarantee that you will have assistance to get the show up? Free advertising for your other business? What is it about any contract that makes you want to be involved? Some amount of self-analysis must take place in order for you to recognize what boundary of any contract exceeds the breaking point.

A wise friend once told me: "When you sign the contract for a show, always say to yourself, 'I'm doing this show because _____', and then *write it down*. That way, when the wheels come off, or blamestorms seem to be looming on the horizon, you won't then waste precious time sitting there dazed, wondering "why did I agree to do this?" You'll *know*. You can read your statement of purpose, and get back to the task of fixing the disaster at hand."

Shelley's Notes: Contract Hints

While understanding contracts seems to be a never-ending life lesson, there are a few hints that can make the experience less nerve wracking:

- You don't have to sign the contract right there on the spot. It's your right to take some amount of time to read (and fully understand) each clause. If that means you take it home overnight, do so.

- Do not sign a contract that contains language that you don't fully understand. If you don't understand a clause, ask for an explanation. If you're not satisfied with the explanation, ask someone else.
- Keep a copy of your contract and know where it is.

Once the contract is signed and delivered, many designers keep a copy of it close at hand, in a private place in their bag or briefcase. They believe that if there's a need to review the contract, it should be immediately available. Other designers leave it at the home office, believing that once signed, the contract won't need to be referred to again. In any event, all designers with an eye towards business agree that all design contracts should be stored together in a single folder or binder. Having all of the contracts in one place, rather than separated by tax year, makes searching for or comparing old contracts a snap, rather than an extended parade through one's tax receipts in order to find the right one.

Shelley's Contracts for *Hokey*

Figure 4.1 is an imaginary non-union agreement between Steve Shelley and the Template Enterprises Company for the lighting design of *Hokey: A Musical Myth*. The show is currently being booked into The Hybrid Theatre for an open-ended run. This is the first time that the show will be fully mounted. The producer and the general manager are top-tier, and on the surface appear to have been hired with the purpose to get this show up on it's feet and move it to Broadway, or at least to a subsequent life. All of the clauses included in this contract have a basis in the United Scenic Artist 829 Standard Design Agreement Contract, so none of them should be perceived as odd or unique. At the present time, any thought of filming or video-taping the show has been vigorously denied. So while there's no specific filming or taping clauses, all of those "what if" clauses have been combined into a single "if anything happens, renegotiation will need to occur" in the preamble. While royalties were brought up in contract negotiations, they were abandoned; checking with the rest of the other designers, they weren't successful negotiating any AWC either. On a positive note, however, the company has agreed to pay for an assistant, albeit only for five weeks. If the technical rehearsal period, or the preview period, get extended, then either the assistant will be forced to start later in the process, the designer will have to pay for additional weeks out of his pocket, or renegotiation will have to take place.

Figure 4.2 is Shelley's Union Cover Sheet Contract for *Hokey: A Musical Myth*. It's a much simpler form to fill out. Under the designer's name are the relevant dates to be filled in. Under that is the area to fill in for the compensation thirds. It also includes a space for the AWC, and below that, a space to fill in the Pension and Welfare payment.

Below the regional offices are the two vital clauses, the insurance clause, and the dispute clause. The dates show that the representative of the company, Dr. George Spelvin, signed the contract the day before the designer. This is standard operating procedure; the designer should always sign the contract after the producer, before it's sent into the union office. That sequence should be true for every contract; the employee signs *after* the employer. And when that can't happen, for your own protection, photocopy the contract with your signature *before* you send it back.

DEFINE THE PRODUCTION SCHEDULE

The **production schedule** is the calendar constrained to show-related activities for a single production, or the monthly flow of a multi-show season. In general, the document's scope ranges from listing specific technical events, to activities that impact the production department. As the production meetings in Chapter 3 showed, while the production schedule may list task names for time periods or work calls, it starts by highlighting the dates for a production's load-in and opening night. The production schedule and the budget are often viewed as two of the most important parameters of any production. And in a way they are: *time* and *money*. So much so that, when many union lighting design contracts are submitted for approval, the budget and production schedule are included as support documents.

By the time the lighting designer is hired, a production schedule may range from being completely frozen to being completely liquid. At one end of the spectrum is the job where, once the lighting designer's been hired, he or she is provided with a rigid production schedule and advised to adapt to that established structure: "Nope, you only get 6 hours for focus. That's the way we've always done it." At the other extreme are "not yet decided" contracts, when the lighting designer arrives on the scene, and the schedule hasn't been touched. The only "times of knowledge" listed on the schedule may be the first day of the load-in, and the date of the opening. After getting the job, the lighting designer's first order of business may be to quickly help create a production schedule on the fly in a hastily-called production meeting: "Hi, you're hired. What do we do?"

Steve Shelley, Light Design   <u>Hokey: A Musical Myth</u>   Date: 24 January 2010

1. <u>Preamble</u>

A. This document details an agreement between Steven L. Shelley [the "Designer"] and Template Productions [the "Company"] wherein the Designer will provide the lighting design for the Company's theatrical production of <u>Hokey: A Musical Myth</u> [the "Production"], under the terms and conditions set forth below. When signed by both parties in the spaces provided below, this contract shall constitute a binding agreement between the two parties in regards to the Designer's artistic collaboration with respect to the Company.

B. The Scope of the work covered under this Agreement is focused on the Production, but includes still photography, television broadcasts, and still and motion picture images intended for viewing on a television, video, web-cast, pod-cast, or any other kind of viewing screen including images created on film, video tape or by any other mechanical, electronic, magnetic or digital means. Any reproduction in any electronic or internet-based viewing for any for-profit venture other than those covered in the "Uses in Other Media" clause will require separate negotiation and compensation for the Designer.

2. <u>General Provisions</u>

A. The Designer shall provide, according to the date mutually agreed upon in the Schedule, visual presentations, specifications, shop orders, and any special effects drawing for the execution of designs. The Designer shall be responsible for the completion and delivery to the Company of all designs and design specifications.

B. The Company will provide, in a timely manner, all necessary theatre dimensions, inventories, production schedules, and/or other information required by the Designer to fulfill his obligations to the production. The Company agrees that a reasonable design period of not less than 4 weeks is necessary prior to submission of the design for bid, or execution of the design.

C. The Company will inform the Designer of appropriate pre-production meetings connected with the production in a timely manner, and the Designer shall, at the request of the Company, attend such conferences.

D. The Designer shall be provided one assistant of his choice, for a period of 5 weeks, or a period of the time at the Designer's discretion. Said assistant shall be an employee of, and paid by, the Company.

E. The Designer shall not be required to perform the work of the production staff.

F. The Company agrees to engage adequate quality personnel for the proper realization, installation, running, and maintenance of the Production.

G. The Company shall assume the responsibility to secure all necessary copyright, publishing, and mechanical clearances required for the production.

H. All uses of the design, subsequent to the Production, shall be according to the terms of the Subsequent Use Clause of the Agreement.

I. Designer shall be offered the first opportunity to render Design Services for any future remounting or revivals of this production, produced by the Company or its licensee(s) subject to current USA rates and conditions.

3. <u>Services Provided</u>

A. The Designer shall design the lighting and render the following services, if required, and agrees:

1] To provide full lighting equipment lists and a light plot drawn to scale from Scenic Design and theatre drawings provided by the Company

2] To provide color, channel hookups, and instrument schedules including all information required for the realization of the design;

3] Coordinate all lighting records, i.e., the cue sheets, track sheets, control plots, floor plots, boom charts and front-of-house focus charts of the Production;

4] To coordinate and plot special lighting effects.

Contract-Hokey-LD-100109.doc   Page 1 of 5

Figure 4.1   Shelley's Non-Union Lighting Design Contract for *Hokey*

(Continued)

Steve Shelley, Light Design   <u>Hokey: A Musical Myth</u>   Date: 24 January 2010

5] To supply specifications for competitive bids for lighting and special effects suppliers mutually satisfactory to the Company and the Designer.

6] To attend the rehearsals as necessary to design the Production, and to conduct the lighting rehearsals.

4. <u>Design Fee and Payment Schedule</u>

A. In consideration of the services provided hereunder, the Company agrees to pay and the Designer agrees to accept as a Design Fee, Five Thousand [$5,000.00] Dollars. This fee is compensation accepted solely for the Production at the Hybrid Theatre. Designer accepts this Fee as an Employee, with all applicable city, state, federal, FICA, and social security taxes deducted from the gross amount.

B. The Company shall pay the compensation to the Designer according to the following schedule:
One-third (1/3) upon the signing of this contract by the Designer
One-third (1/3) on the date that drawings, specifications, and all preliminary paperwork are accepted
by the Company
One-third (1/3) upon the specified termination date, but no later than Opening Night.

C. The Designer shall not be required to furnish designs until the Company has executed the first third of the fee.

D. The Producer and the Designer agree that the termination date will be Opening Night. The Designer's services will not be required beyond the contracted termination date. If the Company requires the services of Designer for any time after opening night, because of changes related to staff, cast, Theatre request or theatre, Designer will be compensated for any such services at a daily rate of no less than One Hundred Fifty [$150.00] Dollars.

5. <u>Reimbursable Expenses</u>

A. The Company shall reimburse the Designer for expenses incurred directly related to the production including, but not limited to, the following: art and drafting materials, meals while in transit at the request of Company, research materials, telephone, fax, postage, shipping, and copying.

B. The Company agrees to make funds or forms of credit available, in advance, for production related expenditures. Best effort will be extended to use a legally executed Tax Exempt Form if provided by the Company. All cash expenditures will be accounted for to the Company in the form of receipts or other proofs of purchase, submitted to the Company no later than thirty (30) days after the official opening of the production. The Company shall reimburse the Designer for receipted expenses within fourteen (14) business days of submission.

C. The Company agrees to reimburse the Designer and/or the Assistants for all out-of-pocket expenses for local transportation when required for the purchase, coordination or assembly of items related to the production. It is understood that the Company, when practical, will supply these funds in advance or arrange for the transportation.

D. Receipted reimbursed expenses shall not be considered income to the Designer, nor reported as income for tax purposes.

6. <u>Property Rights and Subsequent Use</u>

A. The Company agrees that all rights in and to the design as conceived by the Designer in the course of his services hereunder shall be, upon its creation, and will remain, the sole and exclusive property of the Designer. The design includes all physical documentation, all printouts, and all forms of electronic storage media, including contents of disks, hard drives, flash drives, and the like, and as such, no subsequent use is permitted without compliance hereto.

B. The Company or its licensee(s) shall not use the designs for the lighting in any live stage production or electronic reproduction of the Production without the notification, written permission, and additional compensation to the Designer. Compensation for additional use or license of the design by the Company shall be subject to an additional and separate agreement between the Company and the Designer. Any compensation will be no less than the original fee, or the monetary compensation offered to any of the other Designers, whichever is greater.

Contract-Hokey-LD-100109.doc   Page 2 of 5

Figure 4.1 cont'd

Steve Shelley, Light Design	Hokey: A Musical Myth	Date: 24 January 2010

C. The Company shall notify in advance, in writing, the Designer of its intention to revive, extend, move, or tour the production, or its intention to transfer the production to another producer. The Company will supply the production schedule and dates of Performance.

D. The Company agrees not to alter, nor to permit anyone to alter or make substitutions, for any lighting or special visual effects as designed and approved by the Designer after the first public performance without the deliberate written consent and approval of the Designer.

E. All original drawings, elevations, and other specifications shall be returned to the Designer no later than thirty (30) days following the final public performance of the production. The Company shall have the right to retain copies of all of the foregoing. Design materials retained by the Company may be used by the Company for its promotional and public relations purposes, which are understood to include community, promotional, and similar non-commercial purposes.

7. Archival and Promotional Recording

A. Where any part of the lighting, or the design for same, are broadcast or recorded during rehearsal or performance by any means, or for use as a television or internet broadcast spot, commercial, educational, or promotional program about the production, and where the recorded segment is no longer than fifteen (15) minutes of air time, no additional compensation shall be due to the Designer.

B. For archival purposes of Theatre or other official library theatrical archive, the Company shall have the right to make a film, videotape, or make other visual record of the final dress rehearsal or of performances. Such record shall be labeled "for archival use only".

C. The Company shall not release any part of any promotional or archival recording, for any purpose, without the written consent of the Designer. In addition, the Producer must secure written agreement to the terms of use in the Subsequent Use Clause of this Agreement from the party seeking to use the recorded material.

8. Postponement and Abandonment

A. If the opening date is postponed, payments shall be made with the same force and effect as if the production had been carried out and opened on the originally named date so long as the Designer shall have completed the necessary plots, working drawings, and lighting records.

B. In the event the Production is abandoned prior to the first public performance and the Designer shall have completed the necessary plots, working drawings and lighting records, the Designer shall receive three quarters (3/4) of the originally agreed upon payment.

C. In the event the production is abandoned and the Designer has not completed the designs agreed upon, the Designer and the Company shall agree to negotiate remaining payment due, but in no event shall the Designer receive less than one-half (1/2) of the originally agreed upon payment.

9. Billing

A. The Designers shall receive billing in the program on the title page, cast page, or with placement substantially comparable to such, and on house-boards, in the customary order of Set, Costume, Lighting, and Sound Designer, in the same size, quality, and format , in substantially the following form:

Lighting Design by
Steven L. Shelley

In all cases where any Designer receives billing, all Designers shall receive billing.

B. Any video production or motion picture filming of a portion or all of the production originally designed by the Designer, shall include the name of the Designer in the applicable forms as indicated above.

C. In addition, best efforts shall be made to give billing to the Designers in printed newspaper advertisements, posters, cast recordings, internet advertisements, window cards, website or any other public acknowledgment,

Contract-Hokey-LD-100109.doc	Page 3 of 5

Figure 4.1 cont'd

(Continued)

| Steve Shelley, Light Design | <u>Hokey: A Musical Myth</u> | Date: 24 January 2010 |

excluding television and radio, where billing is given to more than two other creative participants in a production (director, choreographer, actors, etc.).

D. Where a biography, other than that of the author(s) appears, the Company shall include a biography of the Designer and Assistant Designer. The Designer shall have the right of approval of biographical material for the program and souvenir program. Approval must be in writing and shall not be unreasonably withheld. Biographical materials not approved within 48 hours of its submission to the Designer shall be considered approved.

10. <u>Safety and Liability</u>

A. The Designer is responsible for the visual or aural aspects of the production only, and it is understood that all specifications relate solely to the appearance of the lighting and not to matters of the safety. The Designer agrees to make prompt correcting alterations to any specification found to be incompatible by the Company with proper safety precaution.

B. The Company will indemnify, defend, save, and hold the Designer, his heirs, executors, administrators and assigns harmless from and against any and all liability, charges, costs, expenses, claims and/or other loss, including reasonable attorneys' fees, whatsoever which they may suffer by reason of the designs furnished hereunder.

C. The Company agrees to carry comprehensive general liability insurance applicable to any claims that might arise due to any work performed under this Agreement.

11. <u>Dispute</u>

A. In the event of a difference, dispute, or controversy between the parties hereto relating to this Agreement, which cannot be settled by the Designer and the Company, the matter shall be submitted to an arbitrator designated by the American Arbitration Association. The arbitration shall be conducted in accordance with the Voluntary Labor Arbitration rules of the American Arbitration Association.

B. The arbitration shall be by one Arbitrator whose fees and expenses, including expenses normally charged by the American Arbitration Association, shall be apportioned equally between the Company and the Designer. It is further understood that each party is responsible for and shall pay the cost of its own transcript, witnesses, representatives, etc. in the presentation of their case before the Arbitrator.

C. The arbitrator(s) shall not have the power to amend, modify, alter or subtract from this Agreement.

D. The decision of the arbitrator(s) shall be final and binding on all parties.

12. <u>Uses in Other Media</u>

A. In the event that any portion of any program is recorded, reproduced, or transmitted by TV camera, motion picture film, or by any other means of recording or reproduction for public or private viewing, Company agrees to pay Designer a fee of no less than Five Thousand [$5,000.00] Dollars, said fee shall be paid no later than the commencement of photography.

B. In addition to the above fee, in the event any program, or portion of any program, is recorded, or reproduced by any media other than motion picture film, Designer will be offered the first option to direct the lighting for such media production at compensation applicable for such additional services to be negotiated in good faith.

C. The foregoing notwithstanding, however, the Company shall have the absolute and irrevocable right to produce television commercials for use in promoting the Company, and Company-produced programs, with no compensation required to be paid to Designer therefore, provided that Company receives no compensation or profit except for reimbursement of actual out-of-pocket expenses.

D. The Company shall also have the absolute and irrevocable right to produce television commercials, print advertising and publicity displaying the lights, and to authorize the filming, videotaping, and/or sound recording any portions of any programs not to exceed ten [10] minutes in duration for purposes of publicizing and

| Contract-Hokey-LD-100109.doc | Page 4 of 5 |

Figure 4.1 cont'd

promoting the Company or its programs on news, magazine format, and interview type shows, with no compensation required to be paid to Designer therefore, provided that Company receives no compensation or profit except for reimbursement of actual out-of-pocket expenses.

13. <u>Force Majeure</u>

A. It is expressly understood that in the event of war, riot, rebellion, blackout, fire, flood, strike, labor action of any kind, force majeure or any similar or different causes beyond the control of the respective parties hereto, neither party shall be held liable for the delay or suspension of performance of services and employment occasioned thereby, but that this contract shall still be held intact.

14. <u>Entire Agreement</u>

A. This agreement sets forth the entire agreement between Designer and Company and supersedes any and all prior agreements, whether written or oral, between the two parties, with respect to the subject matter contained herein, and may only be modified, amended, waived, terminated or discharged by a written instrument signed by each party. Each party executing this Agreement warrant and represent to the other that they have the right and authority to enter into this Agreement on behalf of and legally bind the party for whom they are signing.

Agreed and accepted by:

Designer: Company:

_____   _____

Steven L. Shelley   Dr. George Spelvin
Lighting Designer   Template Enterprises

Date:_____   Date:_____

Figure 4.1   cont'd

Some see the production schedule as an untouchable sacred document that, once agreed upon in the meetings, must be adhered to. Most everyone else sees the production schedule as a guideline, one that is followed, but a document that is readdressed and adapted at the end of each day—especially when the show moves into the tech rehearsal portion of the process.

Production Schedule Analysis

In a broad sense, creating a production schedule that perfectly fits all the tasks involved in one particular show, and having that schedule remain unchanged throughout the technical process of the show, is a little like making a rope out of sand. In most cases, it's better left to others who are smarter than you. On the other hand, if you realize that you're supposed to be the smart one, you'd best be considering all of the options.

One method that's often used to initially structure a production schedule involves thinking backwards, starting with the first performance. Construct a list that catalogues all of the required activities needed to mount a specific production. Assign a time duration to each task, and then list those tasks in reverse order, beginning with opening night.

For the first performance to smoothly take place, dress rehearsals need to take place first. Each of those rehearsals requires its own time periods to add another layer of complexity for costumes, or in some cases, the orchestra. In order for the dress rehearsals to take place, technical rehearsals must then begin at a specific point prior to that. Working backwards, then, all work preparing for the initial technical rehearsal needs to be completed prior to that time. This process continues backwards to the date of the load-in.

Another way of approaching the production schedule (and define the light plot) is to start with the number of work hours available. How many hours of stage time exist between the beginning of the load-in and the time the space must be exclusively available for the performers? That amount of time, regardless of length, often has a direct impact on the size of the crew, and, as such, the size and scope of the plot.

Print Form	**UNITED SCENIC ARTISTS • LOCAL USA 829 • IATSE**

PROJECT ONLY AGREEMENT 2008-2009—DESIGNER / ARTIST

This Agreement must be signed by all parties in triplicate. Send all 3 copies to USA 829 for approval, along with checks for Pension and Welfare. The Designer will not furnish any designs until the Agreement has been executed by the Union.

AGREEMENT of Employment is made between **United Scenic Artists, Local USA 829** and:

THEATRE / PRODUCTION COMPANY: TEMPLATE PRODUCTIONS

hereinafter referred to as the **Employer**, for the Production / Project known as:

NAME OF PRODUCTION / PROJECT: HOKEY: A MUSICAL MYTH

TO BE PRESENTED AT (VENUE): THE HYBRID THEATRE

This Agreement is limited to the Production / Project known named above.

PROJECT SHALL COMMENCE ON OR ABOUT: 15 FEBRUARY 2010 **& SHALL TERMINATE ON:** 20 APRIL 2010 (the date of the Press Opening, if applicable.) **It is not precedential or citable** in any proceeding other than to enforce this Agreement, and does not bind or obligate the Employer in any way beyond the scope of this Project.

DESIGN CATEGORY: ☐ SCENIC ☐ COSTUME ☒ LIGHTING ☐ SOUND ☐ PROJECTION ☐ ASSISTANT ☐ ARTIST

NAME OF DESIGNER / ARTIST: STEVEN L. SHELLEY

DESIGNS ARE DUE: 1 MARCH 2010 **TECH PERIOD FROM:** 5 APRIL 2010 **TO:** 20 APRIL 2010 **CLOSING DATE:** 13 JUNE 2010

COMPENSATION — The Producer agrees to pay the Employee the following amounts, according to the listed schedule:

1/3 on Signing: $	$1,666.66	☐ Daily or ☐ Weekly: $	
1/3 on Design Approval: $	$1,666.67	Hourly: $	
1/3 on Opening: $	$1,666.67	OR Overtime: $	
TOTAL: $	$5,000.00	For ____ Work Days / Weeks	
		TOTAL: $	

ADDITIONAL WEEKLY COMPENSATION: DESIGNER WILL RECEIVE AN A.W.C. OF $ TBD PER WEEK, BEGINNING:

TRUST FUNDS: It is further understood that the Employer, in order to provide certain **Pension and Health Benefits,** shall make a contribution equivalent **Seventeen Percent (17%)** of the Gross Compensation, to the *United Scenic Artists Pension & Welfare Funds* which shall be allocated 10% to Welfare and 7% to Pension. *A check for the full amount of* $ **$350.00** *should be attached to this document and sent directly to the appropriate Regional office below:*

NEW YORK	**CHICAGO**	**LOS ANGELES**	**MIAMI**
29 WEST 38TH ST. • 15TH FL.	203 N. WABASH ST. • STE. #1210	5225 WILSHIRE BLVD. • STE. #506	10459 SW 78TH ST.
NEW YORK, NY 10018	CHICAGO, IL 60601	LOS ANGELES, CA 90036	MIAMI, FL 33173
212-581-0300	312-857-0829	323-965-0957	305-596-4772

INSURANCE: Employer will indemnify, defend, save and hold Designer, his or her agents, heirs, executors, administrators and assigns harmless from and against and any all liability, charges, costs, expense claims and/or other loss whatsoever, including reasonable attorney fees, which may suffer by reason of the designs furnished hereunder. Employer agrees to carry comprehensive general liability insurance applicable to any claims that might arise due to any work performed under this Agreement.

DISPUTE: In the Event of any dispute arising between the parties, relating to this Agreement or work relating to it, the matter shall be submitted to Arbitration in one of the above-named cities, as may be appropriate, or in such other location as may be agreed between the parties hereto, in writing, prior to the execution of this Agreement. Said Arbitration shall be pursuant to the then-existing voluntary labor arbitration rules of the American Arbitration Association. The Arbitrator's decision shall be final and binding.

NO CONFLICT: This Project Only Agreement may not be used for work covered by any United Scenic Artists Collectively Bargained Agreement.

RIDERS: Any rider or addendum mutually agreed to by the Employer and the Employee, and approved by the Union, shall be attached to and become part of this Agreement.

ACCEPTED: by Producer	**ACCEPTED: by Union**	**ACCEPTED: by Designer**
SIGN NAME *Rx Sp X*	SIGN NAME *Martha Detroit*	SIGN NAME *Steven L. Shelley*
PRINT NAME Dr. GEORGE SPELVIN	PRINT NAME MARTHA DETROIT	PRINT NAME STEVEN L. SHELLEY
DATE 1 FEBRUARY 2010	DATE 14 FEBRUARY 2010	DATE 2 FEBRUARY 2010
ADDRESS XXXX BROADWAY		ADDRESS XXX AMSTERDAM AVE.
SUITE 800, NYC, NY, 10036		APMNT 15, NYC, NY 10025
PHONE 212.555.1212		PHONE 212.XXX.XXXX
EMAIL Spelvin@fieldtemplate.com	IS A RIDER ATTACHED? ☒ YES ☐ NO	EMAIL MrTemplate@earthlink.net

Production Sched & Budget 2/1/10

Figure 4.2 Shelley's Union Cover Sheet Contract for *Hokey*

Some production managers compare the creation of a complex production schedule to fitting together individual pieces that create a finished jigsaw puzzle. Some pieces fit with each other; other pieces don't. Some pieces can only fit in one direction; other pieces can be attached to one another in a variety of combinations. Reflecting the needs of each show, a length of time and an objective are assigned to each separate activity, creating a puzzle piece. After analysis, the task's objective and time duration may be split into two separate units, creating two smaller pieces. Though additional pieces can be perceived as creating more confusion, it can also introduce more flexibility. More pieces mean more possible combinations. After all of the activities have been divided into their individual time-defined components, the total number of puzzle pieces becomes a known. The process then becomes one of comparing the pieces to one another, in search of a "fit," when two or more activities can simultaneously occur. Finding the proper fit to construct a complex production schedule is a time-consuming task that's discussed, published, analyzed, and discussed again.

No matter how it's constructed, once the load-in begins, the production schedule is often reshaped through the course of each day. At the end of the day, informal production meetings are typically held to define and prioritize the objectives of the following day's schedule. Successful execution of a production schedule depends on communication, coordination, and the ability to prioritize and cooperate to head off potential show-stopping problems. For some folks who spend their careers making shows happen, the successful collaboration of a production schedule can be viewed as much of a miraculous achievement as the successful integration of elements to create the overall design of a show.

The bottom line is that while every schedule attempts to utilize every available moment on stage, it becomes a daily negotiation to coordinate all of the different departments. The successful production schedule ensures everyone has the time required to achieve their specific goals, clearly states who has the priority for critical work sessions, ensures that all involved receive proper break and rest periods, no one goes into overtime, and everyone happily works together under budget. In my experience, I think that's happened twice.

Hokey's Production Schedule

Initially, the production schedule for *Hokey* consisted of only three or four lines. Figure 4.3 is the latest version, distributed after the production meetings in Chapter 3. As the most current schedule, it will be included as a rider to the lighting designer's contract, regardless of whether it's submitted to a union or not.

HOKEY: A MUSICAL MYTH — **PRODUCTION SCHEDULE APRIL 2010 V2** — Date: 1/20/10

	SUNDAY	MONDAY	TUESDAY	WEDNESDAY	THURSDAY	FRIDAY	SATURDAY
	4 APRIL	**5** LOAD-IN HYBRID THEATRE	**6**	**7**	**8**	**9**	**10**
		8:00A 12:00N LOAD-IN ELEC & RIG	8:00A 12:00N DECK LOAD FLOOR LOAD	8:00A 12:00N FOCUS W/WORKS	8:00A 12:00N LOAD-IN FOCUS/CUE	9:00A 1:00P SPACE CUE	8:00A 12:00N TECH
		12:00N 1:00P LUNCH	12:00N 1:00P LUNCH LAY FLOOR	12:00N 1:00P LUNCH	12:00N 1:00P LUNCH	1:00P 2:00P LUNCH TUNE PIANO	12:00N 1:00P LUNCH
		1:00P 5:00P ELEC FOH SCENERY IN	1:00P 5:00P TRIM FOCUS FOH	1:00P 5:00P LOAD-IN FOCUS	1:00P 5:00P LOAD-IN CUE	2:00P 6:00P TECH	1:00P 5:00P TECH
							6:00P 10:00P TECH
	11	**12**	**13** PREVIEW HYBRID THEATRE	**14**	**15**	**16**	**17**
	1:00P 1:30P HALF HOUR	1:00P 1:30P HALF HOUR	1:00P 1:30P HALF HOUR		1:00P 4:30P NOTES/TECH	1:00P 4:30P NOTES/TECH	
	1:30P 5:00P TECH	1:30P 5:00P TECH	1:30P 4:00P ORCH DRESS (INVITED) PHOTOG	1:30P 2:00P HOUSE OPEN PREVIEW 2			1:30P 2:00P HOUSE OPEN PREVIEW 6
	5:00P 6:00P DINNER	5:00P 6:00P DINNER	DINNER		DINNER	DINNER	DINNER
	6:00P 11:00P PIANO TECH	6:00P 11:00P PIANO DRESS	7:30P 8:00P HOUSE OPEN PREVIEW 1	7:30P 8:00P HOUSE OPEN PREVIEW 3	7:30P 8:00P HOUSE OPEN PREVIEW 4	7:30P 8:00P HOUSE OPEN PREVIEW 5	7:30P 8:00P HOUSE OPEN PREVIEW 7
	18	**19**	**20** PRESS OPENING HYBRID THEATRE	**21**	**22**	**23**	**24**
					TBA	TBA	
	1:30P 2:00P HALF HOUR PREVIEW 8	DAY OFF		1:30P 2:00P HOUSE OPEN PERF 2			1:30P 2:00P HOUSE OPEN PERF 6
			6:00P 6:30P HOUSE OPEN PERF 1	7:30P 8:00P HOUSE OPEN PERF 3	7:30P 8:00P HOUSE OPEN PERF 4	7:30P 8:00P HOUSE OPEN PERF 5	7:30P 8:00P HOUSE OPEN PERF 7

TEMPLATE PRODUCTIONS 212.555.1212   NEW YORK, NY 10025   www.fieldtemplate.com

Figure 4.3 The Production Schedule for *Hokey*, Version 2

In this second version of the schedule, the objectives in the initial work calls are now more clearly defined. The "house open" times before each preview or performance are also now included. If the stage preset is an open stage without a main curtain, the amount of seating time prior to the show may have an impact on the show call times for the running crew; they'll have to come in earlier to preset the stage without being seen by the audience. Depending on the collective agreement with the stagehands, earlier show call times could increase their overall number of hours, and as such, their weekly salary.

In order to adhere to the production schedule, the lighting designer has to compartmentalize the basic tasks, and have a sense of the time and people power necessary to complete each one: the hang, the focus, and the cueing session. In order to gauge that, though, the process typically requires three general groups of knowledge. First, there has to be (at least) a loose definition of the final product's appearance; that would be the show, or at least the light plot. Second, some knowledge about the performance space and its current state is absolutely needed. Third, an idea of the other design elements of the show, the budget, and the planned amount of labor, is essential in order to predict how the politics and personalities in the collective staffs will mesh together. While some of this is based on experience, it all begins by having a sense or understanding of the rest of the parameters surrounding any production. Understanding these other elements will allow the lighting designer to provide an informed opinion and be certain that there's enough time to prepare the lighting for the production.

DEFINE BY THE BUDGET

One of the primary factors that define the size and shape of the lighting package is the budget, which lists the amount of money allocated towards all things related to lighting the show. A typical lighting budget is often broken down into four line items: rental, perishables, transport, and labor. "Rental" refers to the cost paid to a lighting rental shop in exchange for using their equipment. Every lighting fixture, every piece of hardware, software—whatever is not part of the theatre inventory, and not something that is eventually thrown away, which is part of the lighting package—that's the rental.

Sometimes tight budgets eliminate any possibility of a rental. The lighting gear available to the show may be limited to the inventory existing in the performance facility. Sometimes, that's not a bad thing. If the house inventory is cared for, it can sometimes be perceived as more advantageous than having a rental in the first place. That's especially true if incoming rental gear is in crappy condition.

Other times there may be enough money to supplement the light plot with rental gear. In those cases, the lighting designer is forced to make tactical decisions about what to rent. Each light plot might be improved in any number of different ways, depending on the amount of money, the amount of load-in time, the existing house gear, and the equipment that's available for rental. The supplemental rental package is a fundamental choice made by the lighting designer's to improve the lighting for the show, and acquire the best bang for the show's buck.

If the budget allows for a lighting rental to supplement the existing house inventory, the lighting designer should make every attempt to incorporate the house equipment somewhere into the light plot. On-site preliminary visits that review the exact numbers and quality of the house inventory will allow the lighting designer to make informed choices as to its use. If a preemptive decision is made to exclude the house equipment from the light plot, the reasons leading to that choice should be reported to the lighting designer's employer. Ignoring a minimal or substandard inventory may seem minor to the lighting designer when compared to the overall scope of the project, but dismissing the use of existing equipment without investigation may taint the employer's perception of the lighting designer's ability and intent. If the reasons for this action aren't properly communicated, it may be interpreted that the lighting designer has no interest in adhering to the budget, and isn't striving as a "team player" to keep overall costs down for the production.

Sometimes the performance facility owns no lighting equipment whatsoever. In that situation, the budget has to include the monies to pay for the rental of the entire lighting package. This usually has a huge impact on the light plot. A supplemental rental often translates into additional lighting instruments, dimmers, or special devices. A four-wall rental, on the other hand, has to include the entire lighting package, soup to nuts; not only must it include every item required to plug the entire system together from the point that electricity comes out of the power distribution panel on the wall, it has to include every tool or device necessary to make the lighting package a working and functional light plot. That ranges from every ladder, stage cable, or extension cord, to the stapler and clip light.

The next budget line item is perishables. "Perishables" generally refers to anything that, once the wrapper's open or it's been used, can't be returned to a rental shop for credit. Perishables can also include printer cartridges or other items purchased from office supply stores, or consumables that will be used and then thrown away.

Two common lighting package perishables include gel and templates. Once the sheet of color has been cut, or the template burned inside the instrument, it belongs to the show. Perishables can also include film loops, fog fluid, tape, Sharpies, label tags, brads, or reams of paper. Depending on the shop's policies and imagination, perishables can also include clip lights, worklights, Littlites®, and any number of larger hardware items. While you may think these definitions are open to interpretation or seem a little skewed, the shop's policy usually trumps any designer's opinion. Knowing what falls under the category of "perishable" before getting the final bill can avoid awkward moments with the producer.

"Transport" usually refers to the number of trucks or other vehicles budgeted to get the lighting package from the lighting rental shop to the performance space. This figure is often part of a larger number (not in the lighting budget) that also then includes the trucking of scenery, costumes, properties, or other goods to or from the performance space. Obviously, the fewer times that a truck has to come or go containing lighting gear, the lower the cost. It's also worth noting that fewer deliveries or pickups translate into fewer disruptions to the crew's other activities. Less time spent unloading, unpacking, or inventorying gear (or the reverse to deal with a pickup), means more time getting the lighting package up on its feet.

"Labor" refers to the number of bodies estimated by the budget's creator and the production manager that actually refers to three separate sums. On a larger show, when the light plot substantially consists of a rental package, the first labor sum listed will be for "the prep." This money covers the amount of time spent by the production electrician to prepare his or her paperwork, hire the crew, and make arrangements for the show. That same money also covers the time it takes the production electrician and the crew on the show's payroll to assemble, prep, and pack the rental package in the shop. The second sum is the load-in money budgeted to pay the electricians to unload, install, and focus the lighting package. On larger shows the production electrician staffs and runs those crew calls. It's one part of his or her job to calculate the amount of labor required, and hire the right people to successfully achieve each crew call's goal.

The third sum is the weekly money allocated for the "running crew," or run crew, the electricians hired to tech and then run the show's lighting on a weekly basis. While the hiring of the electricians for the run crew is also part of the production electrician's domain, the size of the run crew can become critical to the design itself. If the director *must* have three followspots, for example, including three instruments in the rental order may have no significant impact on the weekly cost. If the budget doesn't include money to pay

for three followspot operators, however, it can quickly become a topic of discussion, and one that the lighting designer can and should become actively involved in.

On smaller shows, the labor budget is considerably simpler. If there's no rental, then the prep period may be limited to the production electrician spending time reviewing the house inventories and figuring out how to plug the plot. Aside from that, though, some number of electricians will still be required to get the plot up and focused, someone will be needed to program the lighting console, and someone will need to "baby-sit the rig," restore any focus, and replace any lamp or color burnouts.

The budget is usually in place long before the lighting designer gets hired. So, while an incredible light plot can be generated ignoring this parameter, the lighting budget will typically not be expanded to allow that plot to be realized. Additional time will be wasted in reanalyzing and regenerating an abridged version of the lighting design. The careful lighting designer analyzes the house inventory and all aspects of the budget to combine that with the ethereal images in order to create a viable plot and plan that will be cleanly installed the first time.

Figure 4.4 shows the basic lighting budget line items for *Hokey*. While it may seem worthy to find out who concocted these figures, in order to understand what plan or brilliant notion that person possessed in the midst of creation, the bottom line is that they are what they are. There's every chance the intern who created this budget left the organization months, or even years ago. What's important is that they were part of what was used as a part of the big number that investors paid money into, in the hopes that this show will somehow earn them money. At this point, while it may be possible to shift these sums a bit, trying to change any of these numbers (read as: increase) is going to be formidable, unless the lighting designer and the production electrician can show good reason why the budget should be deemed inadequate. *Really* good reason.

As far as labor is concerned, quickly calculating those into something conceivable can seem daunting. A good starting point is to begin by estimating a weekly salary. A rough gross number used for an

Hokey; A Musical Myth	Lighting
Rental (Weekly)	$3,500.00
Perishables	$1,500.00
Labor -- Prep & Load-in	$18,000.00
Labor -- Weekly	$6,000.00

Figure 4.4 The Initial Lighting Budget for *Hokey*

average off-Broadway electrician's salary is some-where around or under $1,000.00 a week. That's an average, before any taxes are taken out. The production electrician and assistant may make more, and the youngest electrician would probably earn less. The load-in weeks will be higher, the weeks running the show will be lower. But $1K a week, per electrician, is a reasonable place to start calculations. Using that formula, the load-in payroll is budgeted for about 25-person weeks, while the running crew will be limited to six or seven people at the most.

Since it appears to be 5 days in the theatre until the tech begins, and presuming that most of the lighting package will be rented, it's possible to bench-mark the "prep" period at approximately a week. If the prep/load-in/get-us-thru-focus crew includes the production electrician, an assistant, and another eight electricians, that roughly translates to $10,000.00 a week. If the "prep" period only refers to the period of time through focus, the $18K number seems high and might be able to be adjusted to other line items. If the "prep" instead is referring to the entire period of time through previews until opening, which is over 2 weeks, then the designer potentially there may be a problem.

The funny part about budgets is that often it seems like it's all about interpretation, depending on who's analyzing them. They're like the half glass of water; some say the glass is half empty, others say the glass is half full, and some say the glass is too big. Even though the budget's numbers don't change, their impact can often be radically different, depending on who's doing the talking. Here are some questions that might be posed to the person who's actually going to analyze the projected labor costs and the results of the rental cost estimates. In professional situations that will be either the general manager, or the producer:

- Will the crew be paid weekly or by the hour?
- When is the calendar break point between "load-in" and "weekly"?
- When is the break point between weeks? Sunday or Monday? During the tech there's no Monday off. Will the crew go into some kind of overtime?

Usually the lighting designer doesn't get involved in this facet of the show. For the purposes of this book, however, the issue of labor is going to be examined a few times, in order to see what takes place when money is tight and the show is too big.

As far as the weekly rental goes, looking at that number and having some sense of what it means is a little more difficult. Having worked in the Hybrid Theatre in the past, and having some

sense of the house inventory, a lot of the show will have to be rented. There aren't many instruments and there isn't much hardware stock in the venue. There are no boom bases, no pipe, and no side-arms. There's also very little cable and two-fers. If memory serves there's not much house circuitry, and the number of the functional house dimmers is questionable. Without a preliminary site survey, there's no telling how much house gear can really be used.

So how much gear does this budget actually translate into? Sadly, it depends on a lot of things; the city, the rental house, the quality of gear, what's available on the shelves, what's the latest expensive "gotta-have" toy, and so on. When you're the big-time lighting designer you can ask, or demand, that light shops cater to you, since you bring them a lot of business. When you're the small-time or the new-bie lighting designer, you rarely get those kinds of breaks, or that kind of treatment. There are many other ways to develop relationships with lighting rental shops. One method begins by familiarizing yourself with the shops and the rental account representatives and then finding the account rep that you get along with. Take him or her out for lunch, and ask questions: how to get the best rental bang for your buck, what's the best way to present them with rental requests, and so on. A different method is to make friends with the production electricians in that city, or the house elecs in town, and ask for their opinions about the lighting rental shops. Everyone has their own stories, and more often than not, is very willing to share them.

The amount of weekly rental money may not be substantial enough to cover both conventional and moving light fixtures. The rental will either consist of some number of conventional fixtures, or a lot fewer moving light fixtures. And that takes us to a discussion of moving lights.

Shelley's Notes: Movers or Not?

When confronted with having to choose between conventional and moving lights, there are two extremes and a lot of in betweens. Like the little devil on one shoulder, and the angel on the other, the devil says "Sure, the moving light fixtures provide you with more flexibility and pizzazz, they have movement, color, what's not to like?" But the angel says, "Yes, they are pretty, but they come at a price. They cost more money than the same number of conventional fixtures, and their replacement bulbs can be *very* expensive. Not only that, there are lots of extra pieces needed for the moving light: power supplies, special cables, special c-clamps, just for starters. All things that can break. You'll need spare units (no matter what anyone says, moving lights break—a lot). And when moving lights are in the performance space, you'll need some amount of storage space somewhere to store the travel cases, because they all need their (not so) little homes when they're not in the air."

Then there's the console; a basic decision is whether to control the moving lights from a separate console, or combine them with an existing console (which is also controlling conventional fixtures). If there aren't many movers, and the console has programming hardware built-in (like encoders, for starts), it might be possible to consider controlling both fixture types on the one board.

Next, there's time. If the existing console doesn't have the right additional hardware built-in to easily control some number of movers, so much time may be lost trying to inadequately program the movers that they're not worth the effort. The other half of that consideration is the brain; that is, the programmer's brain. If both fixture types are in one console, then only one fixture type will be able to be worked on at a time. It's impossible to program conventional lighting cues at the same time as moving light cues. Only one system can be addressed at a time. With two consoles and two separate operators, both needs can be addressed simultaneously: but now you're back to having two consoles and two operators, the potential headache to combine the two once the show's up and running.

There's also the programming time; moving lights are of no value unless time is built into the schedule to pre-program and establish focus points, color libraries, and template libraries. Without these basic components, trying to quickly write moving lights cues is like trying to write cues with conventional lights without the plot being focused or colored. The tools are not in place for the work to be efficiently completed.

Which then takes us to the issue of labor and skill. If moving lights are included as part of the light plot, then there will need to be someone who knows how to prep them, install them, replace them, program them, trouble-shoot them, and *maintain* them. (After a point, having moving lights in the plot is a little like having kids in the cast.)

When it comes to moving lights, whether the console is separate or combined with conventional fixtures, any moving light programmer is going to be a higher pay rate. Typical rates for good moving light programmers are sometimes equal or greater than the fees paid to lighting designers.

Now, just in case you think that getting a cheaper, less experienced programmer is a potential solution, the harsh specter of experience whispers from the back row: *fiasco*. Renting moving lights without having a competent programmer isn't a solution, but a recipe for disaster. When your new nervous programmer jokingly admits that, due to his lack of programming accuracy, his last lighting designer dubbed him "Mittens," it may be time to simplify the mover cues.

The moving light junkies, on the other hand, pooh-pooh the nay-sayers; see how the movers can change color, size, and focus? See how they can be used to quickly sculpt a scene? And you know what? They're right. Moving lights are fantastic pieces of gear that can become the additional character in the show. They can exponentially expand the possibilities of the production concept and the final product. They can make a crummy script look like a million bucks (or, in most cases, look like a really pretty crummy script).

While the flexibility of moving lights can be perceived as the perfect solution for liquid theatre (and in some cases they *are*), they must be carefully considered within the context of the surrounding parameters. If the money is built into the budget for them, they can be lifesavers and, with budget, support, and a programmer, make the lighting designer look like a genius. More often than not, they just need money.

For now, any decision regarding movers in the plot will be tabled. In order to make a clear decision, more information has to be acquired; the labor questions need some answers, the production schedule needs to be more closely examined, and the remaining big-picture parameters need to be examined. Is there power to run them? What's the venue? Is this a one-off? A tour? By considering all of the parameters, the lighting designer can make this major decision based on fact, not just "gut instinct."

Finally, one last thought regarding the topic of budgets: While it may seem obvious, it's worth remembering that all monies spent for rental, perishables, transportation, and labor, are all the financial responsibility of the producer, not the lighting designer.

DEFINE THE COMMUNICATION

Understanding the parameters is wholly dependent on exchanging information: asking questions and getting answers, and typically doing it fast. Those exchanges depend on the ability to communicate, and knowing how to get in touch with the folks who have the answers. To that end, contact sheets, search engines, email lists, and text messaging are now the primary tools that accelerate that communication. Knowing what questions need to be asked, and how to ask them are important skills, but grasping whom to ask the question from in order to quickly get that missing piece of accurate information, is just as important.

Getting passed from one contact to another, flailing to get the elusive answer, is time-consuming and can either delay a pressing decision or force a knee-jerk reaction that only has a 50 percent chance of being right. Determining who's the best person to provide the answer the first time is another skill developed with experience.

Occasionally projects start jumping into action before proper contact sheets can be constructed or distributed. Sometimes that just happens. The folks whose job it is to make the contact sheets aren't yet in place, or haven't had time to assemble one, or are being politically careful before releasing one. Whatever. Even if contact sheets aren't initially available to the lighting designer, their absence can't be used as an excuse for not making contact and moving the process along. When there's not a contact sheet, start your own. Collect the contact information on a single document, and write it down.

When the official production contact sheet does appear, most lighting designers absorb their preliminary contact information into it. While performing that activity, the lighting designer checks to confirm the correct contact information is listed for the entire lighting department: phone, cell, and fax numbers, their email and Internet VOIP accounts, and their snail mail addresses.

Sometimes the production contact sheet includes the theatre's house staff as well. If they're different from the staff for the production, though, it's smart to get a copy of the theatre's contact sheet as well. On top of all that, it's possible that additional numbers may need to be added that aren't listed or tied into the office phone answering system, like the pay phone in the basement or the lobby. The contact sheet should also include all phone and fax numbers, along with the mailing address, shipping address, and overnight delivery address for the theatre. Depending on the size of the facility, it's possible that there may be three distinct and separate addresses. Presumably, the theatre's contact sheet also lists all pertinent phone numbers for medical emergencies.

Another contact sheet in the lighting designer's arsenal is his or her personal phone book. While it may not be printed in the production book, it's a compilation of manufacturers, dealers, local vendors, and people who can provide backup, support, perishables, or equipment. If a lighting rental company is being used, it includes every office number, fax number, "inside" line, weekend emergency number, pager number, and home number that can possibly be acquired. Lighting designers often compile phone, fax, and e-mail information for light board operators and troubleshooters (who know the light console), dimmer manufacturers and troubleshooters

(who know the dimmers), or special effects specialists (for that weird new effect the show is using that seemed like a good idea at the time).

Depending on the scope, budget, or time constraint of a given project, it's wise to acquire any courier, overnight shipping account numbers, or local car service accounts that belong to the production. Many lighting designers also have their own accounts for times of extreme emergency.

One stress-saving facet of the personal contact sheet also includes some number of perishable vendor contact numbers in each time zone. Many have 800 phone numbers. With this list at hand, the "Yikes! We've *got* to have that by tomorrow" directive which becomes apparent after business hours on the East Coast, can still be fulfilled by vendors on the West Coast. This means the decision to order stuff can wait until as late as 7:45 P.M. Eastern time, be ordered before the end of the business day on the West Coast, and still be delivered on-site the next morning. If the possibility of late night rehearsals looms in the rehearsal schedule, consider acquiring vendors' phone numbers in Hawaii as well.

DEFINE BY TYPE AND SIZE OF PRODUCTION

The type of presentation can affect the size of the design, the lighting package, and the size of the staff. Knowing the size or type of presentation involved can provide a general grasp of the amount of lighting equipment that will be involved. Labels assigned to some productions immediately telegraph the scope of a project. For example, "Broadway," "Off-Broadway," "Concert Arena," or "Regional Theatre" are all labels that connote the physical size, the length of production schedule, the mode of transport, or the budget involved for each type of those productions. If nothing else, a short description of the size of the performance space can convey the amount and type of equipment that may be involved. If a production is defined as a 3-piece laid-back jazz concert on a 30-square-foot outdoor stage, seen by 200 people, the light plot's size is assumed to be clean, simple, and relatively spare, reflecting that intimacy. If the same jazz concert is described on an 80-square-foot stage viewed by an audience of 5000, the amount and type of equipment necessary to provide visibility for the performance space will be completely different.

A musical, for example, usually implies a larger cast of performers than a straight play. Directing the focus of the audience to the proper performers during group scenes immediately suggests followspots and the electricians to operate them. The musical form often involves representing several different locations, which requires additional lighting equipment that might not be needed in a less complex "static" presentation. A realistic drama, on the other hand, may not require the use of followspots to direct focus, but the scenic design may require more individual hanging positions, and requisite hardware, in order to provide illumination, or successfully reinforce the time of day. The complexity of the scenery may potentially increase the amount of time and money required for proper installation of the lighting package.

DEFINE BY ORIGIN

If the show is an original production, rather than a revival, the lighting package needs to be adaptable. Depending on the intangibles of the personalities involved, and the spontaneity of inspiration, entire productions may suddenly change direction in the course of a single post-rehearsal meeting. Being able to rapidly react to sudden requests may become essential when the process is being explored on the one-to-one scale model. Anticipating that possibility and adjusting the amount and flexibility of the gear is important to facilitate the exploration, and possibly the ultimate success of the production. With that in mind, savvy lighting designers construct the light plot with as much flexibility as possible. That flexibility may translate into extra gear, more dimmer distribution, or some amount of color changers or moving fixtures.

If a production's being remounted with the same design team, on the other hand, the need for rapid response in wild new directions will presumably not be as severe. While that may appear to be the case, wise lighting designers double-check who *exactly* is going to be in charge for the re-mounting. If it's the old crew who swear they just want to get the show up and go to the bar, the "simple remount" may be just that; a challenge to regenerate the "looks" of the production under different parameters to everyone's satisfaction. Other times, however, the "simple remount" by a bored artistic staff may open the door for "improvements": "But we've seen that before. Don't you have anything different?" Being asked to "improve" an existing show on the spot can imply many things. More often than not, it implies the need to turn to the producer and ask for more money. Reinventing the wheel, especially at the last minute, can be very expensive. Be certain that the director requests the change, inform him or her of the ramifications of that request, and

be certain the producer is involved in the decision to pay for the additional costs that will in all probability result.

Finally, if the show is an original with a subsequent life following its present incarnation, it may be changing faster than it takes to get ready to move to the next stop. In that case, it may take more time to produce accurate lighting documentation than the time available just to create the lighting. The archival packet may need to be created and evolved as the production is being mounted. If the show's getting mounted and then immediately moving onto a tour, the lighting designer may need to ask for an additional pair of hands with a brain, in order to assure that the lighting records are properly updated before the show leaves town.

DEFINE BY MOVEMENT

A production planning to load-in to a single venue is often tailored to fit into that specific theatre. If the show will be touring to several different locations, on the other hand, the flexibility of the lighting package may need to be more emphasized. The equipment assigned to different hanging positions may need to quickly shift or adapt to each performing facility; fixed-beam ellipsoidals may need to be converted to zoom units instead. The number of dimmers included in the lighting package may need to be greater than required by the light plot, so that existing circuitry within each performance facility can be incorporated into the lighting package. The lighting package will probably require more prep time in the shop, so that it's more clearly labeled for local folks unfamiliar with the setup. Depending on the complexity and the speed of installation, the package may be fitted so that the dimmer racks can fit on either side of the stage and the cabling will remain intact.

Touring with a package is a whole different magilla, and often requires an additional set of skills as both a designer and as an electrician. While it is an advanced education, and a remarkable way to see the world, it is not the focus of this book. Other texts speak in much more detail about this facet of the theatrical and entertainment industry.

DEFINE BY MODE OF TRANSPORT

If the lighting package is transported from a lighting shop or a warehouse to the performance facility, the type of transportation can affect the size or configuration of the light plot. If a small truck has been allocated to transport the entire plot, for example, its cubic size may determine the size and scope of the lighting package. If one truck is utilized for several loads of equipment, the package will need to be prioritized, so that the proper equipment arrives on site in the proper sequence. On the other hand, in order to maintain the production schedule, the time allowed for equipment transport, or snarled traffic, may force the size and scope of the lighting package to shrink.

If the production will be performed in several different venues, the cubic size of the transport may also constrain the lighting package. If the lighting package won't physically fit into the truck, for example, some portion of the design may be left sitting on the loading dock.

If the mode of transport will be a consistent element (or constraint), the obvious first step is to measure the confines, whether that be the interior of the truck, the sea container, the packing crate, the hamper, or the footlocker. Whatever packaging becomes the parameter, having a written schedule of the size, weight, or spatial limitations provides a structure so that knowledgeable packing decisions can be made. That's when you see the lighting designer, or a member of the staff with a measuring tape, carefully noting the inside dimensions of the truck.

On the other hand, if the show is traveling by plane and only using house gear, today's airline restrictions make lighting transport a whole new ball game. Checking airline web sites for the latest size and weight restrictions can quickly turn into a new hobby, and taking electronic gear overseas can often turn into an afternoon pastime. Folks who are touring by plane often carry their own color package and any other immediate necessities with them in their checked luggage or in their carry-on to insure that the equipment they need to do the job will always show up with them.

If the electrics package is coming from a lighting rental house, attention still needs to be paid to the overall amount of gear and how it will fit into the transport truck. Back when gas was cheap, the number of truck trips wasn't an issue. Nowadays it's usually a separate line item in any rental bid, and in some cases the trucking is split between "drop-offs" and "pickups." While coordinating the delivery of the lighting gear is part of the production electrician's domain, the lighting designer should have a say or at least be aware of when specific equipment is going to arrive on site. If the lighting designer has a load-in agenda and doesn't share it with the production electrician, the necessary gear may be missing until after all of the truck deliveries have been made.

DEFINE THE PERFORMANCE FACILITY

While the production is discussed, dissected, and conceptualized in the ethereal world, it will eventually have to be placed in the real world. Many purists feel that the conceptual process demands that initial discussions about the production should focus solely on the movement and growth of the piece with no regard to any physical limitations. Like it or not, however, the time must come at some point when the show has to come to terms with reality, and the limitations of the performance facility, no matter what they may be, have to butt into the conversation. When that time comes, whether for better or worse, the vision of the production begins to adapt to that particular space. Sometimes that's viewed as having to succumb to a realistic limitation. Other times the performance space is viewed as a source for new artistic ideas, ways to relate (or distance) the concept of the show to the audience. In any event, whether it's a boon or a bane, at some point it is absolutely necessary and healthy to explore the parameter presented by the performance facility. Many designers consider it one of the first activities to take place, after the ink has dried on the contract. As a scheduled activity, this can be referred to as a **"site survey," "advancing the venue,"** or **"fact-finding trip,"** and many consider it just as much research as any preliminary sketch or drawing.

The performance facility impacts a lighting package in many ways. The size, shape, and permanent features of the facility must be recognized and acknowledged, since it's, well, permanent. Inevitably it forces many adaptations to the design. Choosing to ignore the spatial limitations of a performance space, for example, could result in an attempt to fit 15 overhead electrics into a stage possessing only 20 feet of depth. This would be viewed by many as an example of overkill, a desire to be added to the quixotic lighting hall of fame, or just plain dumb. Acquiring the information about the spatial dimensions of any performing space, prior to the inception of a design, allows the lighting designer to make informed choices that won't require reevaluation.

If access from the street to the stage of a performing facility is a labyrinth, for example, that might directly impact the way the light plot is prepared. Though hanging individual instruments, one-by-one, may be seen as a slower means of hanging the plot, trying to do-si-do pre-hung units on bars or trusses through the maze may consume even more time. When that doesn't work, grappling the pre-hung bars through alternate windows or elevator shafts may confirm that the one-by-one hang was really the best idea. If these methods aren't considered, discussed, or reflected in the production schedule before the load-in, time constraints may ultimately affect the success of the lighting design.

In addition to successfully installing the equipment in the venue, attention must be paid to the electrical infrastructure in the space. The number of existing circuits and dimmers may truncate any light plot. To alleviate this, additional dimmers may be brought in as part of a lighting rental package. Before committing to that plan, however, research should first take place to confirm that there is available power for the dimmers in the first place.

Tech Specs and Drawings

Obtaining this data about the existing electrical infrastructure allows the designer to accurately determine the amount of existing equipment that can be used to complete the lighting package. Together, all this information is usually available in the form of the facility's **tech specifications**, or **tech specs**, and a set of **facility drawings**, or just **drawings**.

Presumably, the facts about the performance facility are all accurate, updated, and catalogued in the tech specs. Figure 4.5 shows a sample of the tech spec for the fictional Hybrid Theatre. Although most facilities attempt to update the information on a regular basis, there's always a chance that the data may be just a little out of date. Every piece of information, accepted on face value without confirmation, has the possibility of being the single item that may potentially hinder the success of any design, and make the designer ruefully wish he or she had double-checked that detail. If the lighting designer has questions, direct contact with the facility's technical representative will presumably provide clarity, and smooth the way for a lighting design to be constructed based on fact, not fiction.

Some form of groundplan usually accompanies the tech specs. These poor documents are instantly recognizable: teeny, tiny drawings scrunched onto a single letter-sized page, often showing all of the audience seating as well. These poor creatures are often the result of numerous photocopy reductions. While everything fits onto one page, they're worthless for either tracing in a scaled drafting, or making any kind of scaled measurements. The reason for this document's appearance is simple; in most cases, the initial purpose of technical specifications is for potential clients. The combined documents are designed to provide sufficient information about the facility so that producers and promoters can analyze the suitability of renting that space for their particular presentation. With that in mind, the reduced drawings are often included merely to give a general indication of the facility's dimensions. To reduce effort and cost, scaled drawings are often not included in the generic package of information. Acquiring scaled drawings of the space is typically accomplished by contacting the technical representative of the venue. Whether the drawings are accurate or not is another question that the lighting designer must either take on face value, or dig deeper to gain his or her own version of the information.

Taking the time to analyze scaled drawings of the performance space before drafting the light plot can pay unexpected dividends. Sometimes merely comparing the groundplan and section to one another can quickly illustrate basic discrepancies between them. Many designers start analyzing a new performance space by comparing the two "matching" lineset schedules. They simply fold the two drawings, creating an edge along each lineset schedule on the groundplan and the section, and then butt the two scaled lists together to compare the written and drawn distances from plaster line. It's amazing how often this simple exercise shows discrepancies between the drafted documents.

Further comparison between the two drawings may alert the lighting designer to other discrepancies between them or the written facts listed on the tech specs. Simply comparing the documents might quickly show circuitry differences between the tech specs and the groundplan, for example. More studied analysis might highlight the anomaly on the tech spec stating the batten length is much longer than what's shown on the drawing. It might be nothing, it could be huge. Without investigation, that simple mistake could be the only indication of massive potential pitfalls. If the wrong choice is taken, it might potentially disrupt the plot's installation during a tightly-scheduled load-in. Analysis and discovery of the error, before committing to a course of action, means that the design can be adjusted to the space. Or, for that matter, pipe extensions added to the battens can be delivered and installed prior to the load-in, rather than in the middle of it.

A **house lineset schedule**, or **hang plot**, is a fundamental document detailing the overall number, identity, measurements (distance from plaster line or smoke pocket), and possibly some characteristics of the fly system. Figure 4.6 is the Hybrid Theatre hang plot that is sent out with the tech specs. While there is a moderate chance that some amount of the information may be out of date, the number of battens and their general locations provide a starting point.

STAGE INFORMATION		
HYBRID THEATRE	Address	New York City, NY Zip
Telephone: (212) xxx-xxxx	Fax: (212) xxx-xxxx	Web Site: www.fieldtemp.com
SEATING CAPACITY:	A.	TOTAL: 499
	B.	Main Floor: 320
	C.	Balcony: 179
	D.	Orchestra: 10
	E.	Extreme sightlines: 9'-6" DS of plaster line, 21'-6" L & R from centerline, 3" above stage level
LOADING FACILITIES:	A.	Loading Door: (2) 9'-0"W x 12'-0"T
	B.	Loading Dock: 24'-0"W x 20'-0"D
STAGE DIMENSIONS:	A.	Proscenium opening: 38'-0"W x 25'-0"T
	B.	Curtain line to back wall: 31'-0"
	C.	Curtain line to DS edge of stage: 5'-0"
	D.	Height of DS edge of stage above house floor: 3'-2"
	E.	Centerline to SR wall: 35'-0"
	F.	Centerline to SL wall: 35'-0"
FLY SYSTEM:	A.	Counterweight, single purchase, 62 available linesets
	B.	Main curtain on line 1, 1'-0" US of plaster line
	C.	Battens: 42'-0" long, 1.5" I.D. pipe, all 6" centers
	D.	Stage deck to Grid: 62'-0"
	E.	Max pipe out trim: 59'-6"
	F	Arbors: Pipe weight 1200 lbs, 15,000 max. Lock rail SR
SOFT GOODS:	A.	Front curtain: Red with gold tassles, guillotine only, manual from SL deck
	B.	Legs: (3) sets, 8'W x 22'T, black, with 100% fullness
	C.	Borders: (2) 40'-0"W x 8'-0"T, black, with 100% fullness
WARDROBE:	A.	Washer and dryer: (1) each
	B.	Iron and iron board: (2) each
	C.	Steamer: (1)
LIGHTING DIM & CIRCUIT:	A.	ETC Expression 1, 36 x 2.4Kw dimmers, 24 x 4.0Kw dimmers
	B.	FOH Cove: (24) hardwired 20 amp circuits
	C.	Box Booms: (6) hardwired 20 amp circuits.
	D.	Stage: (8) x 6 circuit socapex multicable, moveable.
	E.	Deck: (6) x 6 circuit bundle, moveable.
LIGHTING INSTRUMENTS:	A.	(15) Altman 360Q 6 x 12 (1Kw)
	B.	(30) Altman 360Q 6 x 9 (750w)
	C.	(6) 6" Fresnel (500w, with barndoor)
	D.	(15) PAR 64 NSP (500w, no barndoor)
	E.	(6) R-40 3 circuit striplights, with some gel frames
LIGHTING MISCELLANEOUS	A.	Some stage cable
	B.	(10) Twofer
	C.	(1) A-frame ladder
	D.	Company switch: (2) 400 amp/3Ø, 120/208 DSL
	E.	(1) 100 amp/3Ø, 120/208 USL
	F.	(1) 100 amp/3Ø, 120/208 DSR
SOUND:	A.	(1) Teac Model 2A Mixer
	B.	(2) Cassette decks
	C.	(1) ¼" Reel to reel tape machine
	D.	(1) Crown DC300 amp
	E.	(2) Bose 802 speakers with processor
	F.	Clearcom:(1) 1 Channel system, (3) headset
SOUND PLATFORM:		Located back of house, orchestra level.

Figure 4.5 The Hybrid Theatre Tech Specs

Hybrid Theatre, NYC, NY
Proscenium: 38' wide x 25' tall
Steve Gonella, House Carp: 212.xxx.xxxx

6" centers; #1200 arbors, single purchase
Grid: 62', pipe travel 59'-6"
Batten Length: 42'-0"

Line	Footage		Goods	Trim
-	0'	0"	Plaster line	
-	0'	6"	Smoke Pocket	
1	1'	0"	Main Curtain	21'-0"
2	1'	6"	House Teaser	19'-0"
3	2'	0"	House Legs	
4	2'	6"		
5	3'	0"	1 Electric	
6	3'	6"		
7	4'	0"		
8	4'	6"		
9	5'	0"		
10	5'	6"		
11	6'	0"		
12	6'	6"		
13	7'	0"		
14	7'	6"		
15	8'	0"		
16	8'	6"	1 Blk Border	19'-0"
17	9'	0"	1 Blk Legs	
18	9'	6"		
19	10'	0"		
20	10'	6"		
21	11'	0"		
22	11'	6"		
23	12'	0"	2 Electric	25'-0"
24	12'	6"		
25	13'	0"		
26	13'	6"		
27	14'	0"		
28	14'	6"		
29	15'	0"		
30	15'	6"	2 Blk Border	19'-0"
31	16'	0"	2 Blk Legs	

Line	Footage		Goods	Trim
32	16'	6"		
33	17'	0"		
34	17'	6"		
35	18'	0"		
36	18'	6"		
37	19'	0"		
38	19'	6"	3 Electric	25'-0"
39	20'	0"		
40	20'	6"		
41	21'	0"		
42	21'	6"		
43	22'	0"		
44	22'	6"	3 Blk Border	19'-0"
45	23'	0"	3 Blk Legs	
46	23'	6"		
47	24'	0"		
48	24'	6"		
49	25'	0"		
50	25'	6"		
51	26'	0"		
52	26'	6"		
53	27'	0"		
54	27'	6"	4 Electric	27'-0"
55	28'	0"		
56	28'	6"		
57	29'	0"	4 Blk Border	
58	29'	6"	4 Blk Legs	
59	30'	0"	Black Traveller	
60	30'	6"		
61	31'	0"		
62	31'	6"		
	32'	0"	Back Wall	

Figure 4.6 The Hybrid Theatre Hang Plot

A Basic Checklist to Help Define the Performance Facility

In general, the objective of any site survey is to get as much accurate information as possible in a single trip, with the objective of answering any further questions without the need to return to the theatre a second time. The primary information to gather:

- The type of theatre: proscenium, thrust, arena, outdoors, or other. The number of seats may also assist understanding the scope of the facility.
- The height and width of the proscenium. For thrust or arena, the size of the playing area.
- If there's a main curtain, its location relative to plaster line. Does it part in the center as a draw

curtain, rise up as a guillotine curtain, or combine the movement, like a tableau curtain? What is the speed, in seconds, of the movement from full open to full close? If the main curtain's action is guillotine, does it have a split in the middle for performers to pass through during bows?

- The depth of the stage, from plaster line to the first lineset, the last lineset, to the back wall, to the front edge of the apron.
- The width of the stage, indicated as the measured distance from centerline to each side wall. Any interesting architectural challenges or obstructions, either on the stage or in the air. The location of any traps, floor pockets, or lighting troughs in the deck.
- The location of the sight lines in the audience (typically not indicated on the draftings of the facility; this information is required to determine accurate electric and border trims).
- The identity of all front of house lighting positions, and the number of balconies. The near and far sightline locations for each balcony.
- The type of fly system. The number, identity, length, and location of the battens. The load limit above batten weight (which will determine the number of instruments possible on each batten). Location of fly rail. Can the sheaves be kicked?
- If not a fly system, the pipe or catwalk layout over the stage, and the accessibility to, and the hanging methods for, those lighting positions.
- Height of the grid, pipe travel, loading rail.
- The size, numbers, and condition of the house soft goods: legs, borders, blackout drops, or backings. (If the show plans to use the house masking goods, it's critical to know the height of all of the legs. These dimensions typically have the greatest potential affect on all border trim heights.)
- Anything specific to the production: an alternate crossover other than the upstage portion of the stage, booms that require to be lagged into the deck, traps in the stage, to name a few.
- Existence, specifics, and locations of all power distribution panels included in, or close to, the stage.
- Existence, specifics, and locations of the headset system.
- Existence, specifics, and locations of any production tables.
- The size, access path, and adjacency of the loading door to the stage. Lighting on the loading dock for night deliveries.
- Names of other productions that have been presented there in the recent past. Names of the

lighting designers or production managers, who, when contacted, may provide additional insight to the facility or personnel.

Shelley's Notes: Advancing the Performance Facility

Whenever possible, a site survey of the performance facility should be part of the lighting designer's initial agenda. In a perfect world, the entire design and artistic team all simultaneously converge for a tour of the performance space. It's possible that major decisions can be made in short order, when the collective group required to make those decisions are all together seeing the same thing at the same time.

In some cases visiting the theatre is as simple as walking down the hall and opening the door. In other cases the theatre may be locked, and arrangements must be made to meet someone at the theatre with keys. When access is constrained, schedule conflicts by other members of the design or artistic team may delay the appointment when the group can collectively meet and tour the stage. Most designers believe that physically being present in the space, even for a moment, gives them a sense of the space. For many, having that sense is so important that, after a point, getting into the space, regardless of who else is available, is more important than standing upon ceremony. Waiting for a tour, so that the rest of the team can be present, sometimes becomes a courtesy that must be abandoned, in order to see the space at all. While it might be perceived as impolite to visit the performance facility without the rest of the members of the design team, it's an unwritten understanding between working professionals that sometimes schedules conflict, and you have to move on.

With luck, the lighting designer can then return for another viewing when the rest of the design team can also all convene. Sometimes this schedule works to the lighting designer's advantage. The first individual visit can strictly focus on assembling information and taking initial measurements about the space. When the entire team assembles at the space, it's then a return visit for the lighting designer, and his or her concentration can be on interaction with them, rather than splitting focus and simultaneously trying to acquire information about the space.

Shelley's Notes: Advancing Venues

Any time that you're provided with the opportunity to see a space before load-in, pinch yourself. In my experience, it doesn't happen all that often. And if you get to see the stage without some other show "in the way," consider yourself doubly blessed. Whether the load-in is tomorrow or a year from now, merely walking in and looking around gives you a sense of the space. For that matter, when the offer is made to go see a theatre that you have no connection to, consider taking a quick peek. You can always forget about a space. You can't remember what you've not seen.

Being in the performance facility allows the designer to actually see each lighting position. Whether it's overhead or FOH, having the opportunity to look at the stage from each position allows the lighting designer to take (if nothing else) a mental snapshot of the focus range from that hanging position. If there's not enough time for that luxury, then the opposite may be an alternate choice. Stand on the stage and look at each hanging position. Look at the followspot booth and walk to the extreme portion of the performance space. Is it still within the booth's focus range? Sit in the first row; how much of the stage surface can be seen from this perspective? Go to the last seat in the venue and sit there; how much stage surface can be seen now? While these quick exercises may not seem important at the time, they can impact how a show is lit. Knowing the general locations of the FOH hanging positions may impact the assignment of system washes. The focus range of the followspot may impact the border trims or the amount of depth to be considered if spots are involved. The amount of stage surface seen from the audience may change whether a light plot is designed to light the performer, the floor, or both.

When possible, bring someone with you for the advance. Another pair of hands can be invaluable, in any number of ways. Those hands can act as a scribe taking notes, or a photographer taking pictures. For that matter, that additional pair of eyes may see things in a completely different way, and provide you with another set of observations. Finally, that extra set of hands may come in very handy for no other reason than to hold the other end of the tape.

While a quick on-the-spot site survey is helpful, the more productive theatre advances begin with analysis prior to the event. Acquire and analyze the tech specs and drawings, and compose a list of questions or points that require clarification. With enough time prior to the advance, it may be possible to canvas colleagues and hear about others' experiences in the venue prior to your arrival.

Shelley's Notes: General Advance Questions

- Confirm performance dates.
- Confirm contact information with the electrician: phone, fax, email.
- Confirm work calls and tech prior to performance dates.

- Confirm the information received from the venue (GP, Sec, tech specs, number of pages).
- Confirm console information: type, software version.
- Confirm followspots or other special equipment.
- Confirm relevant details listed on the tech specs: number of dimmers, circuits, etc.
- Confirm any equipment missing from tech specs that are listed on the tech rider.
- Confirm the CAD applications you're using and what format or printed paper size the venue would like to receive it: Lightwright, Vectorworks, PDF, etc.
- Confirm what scale size of the drawings is acceptable: 1/4"? 3/8"? is ½" necessary?
- Confirm which documents will be sent to the local venue and when they should arrive. (This may actually be part of a larger set of drawings also including the scenic design. It might also be a contractual issue, so this question may be delayed until after initial discussions about the proper procedure are discussed.)

Hokey Advance Questions

- Distance from plaster line to back wall not listed on tech specs; instead it was shown as "main curtain" to back wall. Where is the plaster line relative to the main curtain?
- Distance to centerline to both side walls match; does that account for the locking rail stage right?
- How much HVAC equipment is attached to the back wall? Could this impact onstage crossovers?
- How big is the followspot booth? Is there room for all three spots, plus the lighting console?
- The battens are indicated as only 42"-0" long. Can they be extended for legs? Electrics?
- Cove circuits are indicated; use that for FOH frontlight?
- "Some" stage cable?
- Is there a ladder, and how high does it extend? Can we use it? Where does it store? Does it have casters? Is there an alternative?
- Company switches: size, location, and availability. Who gets what? For the install: dimmers, motors, no automation, right?

Shelley's Notes: Can't Get to the Advance?

When visiting the performance space is not geographically possible, extended conversations with the house electrician may clarify any potential misunderstandings that might be made regarding the facility. If needed, additional drawings, digital pictures, videotape recordings, or sketches may provide greater understanding about any complex relationships between elements in the space.

Sometimes the generic drawings and digital pictures are out of date, in shadowed light, or just plain wrong. If you suspect that things are not quite as they appear, either directly or through your production manager, ask for an updated copy of the lineset schedule, the tech specs, or possibly some fresh photos. It's also worth comparing the information that's been received with the rest of the creative team. Sometimes one member will receive information that no one has thought to forward to the rest of the designers involved.

If making contact with the venue becomes a challenge, the Internet may provide answers. Going to the facility's web site may provide programs from past years. That in turn may show who else has visited that facility in the past year or two. Send inquiries to technical chat rooms, or through the links pages on the USITT (usitt.org) or OISTAT (oistat.org) web sites.

Define the House Lighting System

Defining the size, attributes, and quality of the existing electrical infrastructure can have a direct effect on the construction of the lighting design. The technical specifications should include the **house inventory**, which lists the numbers and types of dimmers, the numbers and types of instruments, the light board, and any additional hardware or accessories included in the space. An accurate house inventory allows the lighting designer to make choices regarding the need or amount of additional equipment that may be necessary to produce the light plot.

 A Basic Checklist to Help Define the House Lighting System:

- The type, wattage, and number of all functional lighting instruments, along with any hardware accessories (such as gel frames or c-clamps).
- The manufacturer, type, wattage, location, and number of color frames in each functioning followspot.
- The number and location of all working circuits, including location, wattage capacity, and portability. The location, plug type, and circuit identity of any circuitry transfer panels.
- The actual throw distance to all front of house lighting locations, and the number of instruments that can be safely mounted at each position (top and bottom hung, if needed?).

- The current instrument inventory, if any, in the positions. Are the front of house instruments included in the first inventory?
- The number, physical location, and identity of functional dimmers: manufacturer, type, wattage, and numbers and types of inputs.
- A general sense of the amount, wire size, plug type, and length of functional stage cable.
- A general sense of the number of functional two-fers and three-fers, along with their wire size and plug type.
- The existence of lifts or ladders to focus the lighting instruments at each lighting position.
- The top height possible for the ladder used to focus overhead lighting positions.
- The location and characteristics of all company switches (power dedicated to additional dimmers), including amperage, phase, breakers, and any existing plugs mounted on the side of the box. The location and description of any other additional sources of power onstage, offstage, in the basement, or anywhere else in the building.
- The location for all DMX ports in the space. Where are the ports adjacent to any company switches? Where are the ports in the booth? The production table? Lighting positions?
- Any additional hardware: sidearms, pipe, boom stands, floor plates, or pipe construction or connection hardware.
- Solutions used for common problems in the past. Any history of unusual activity in the electrical power entering the facility.
- Names of other productions that have been presented there in the recent past. Names of the lighting designers or production electricians, who, when contacted, may provide additional insight to the facility and personnel.

Define the House Lighting Console

Initially, every piece of information gleaned about the type, identity, history, and condition of the **house lighting console**, or house board, is knowledge that may define its suitability for the overall lighting design. It's possible that the house electrician will know all of the parameters of the console in question. Any unknown console should be investigated by contacting manufacturers, lighting rental companies, production electricians, board operators, or other lighting designers. If the choice is made to use the console, knowing its capabilities, potentials, and limitations will allow the lighting designer to plan accordingly while preparing the lighting design.

A Basic Checklist to Help Define the House Lighting Console:

- The manufacturer, **model** name, and software version of the console.
- The actual condition of the console, including any history of problems and the last date the console was serviced.
- The largest number of dimmers that the console can address. The number of dimmer outputs located on the back of the console.
- The largest number of channels that can be controlled at any one time by the console.
- The largest number of cues contained within each RAM allocation (or disk).
- Is the light board a tracking or preset console or both? Can cues contain hard zeros?
- The ability of point cues to be inserted.
- The number of channels seen on each row of the channel intensity screen and the number of channels seen on each page of the channel intensity screen.
- The number of cues (listed with time durations) seen on the cue list screen.
- The number of split faders. The number of cues that can simultaneously occur.
- The number of physical submasters and their possible attributes. If the capability exists, the number of pages.
- The number of possible groups.
- Number of monitors required for fully functional system (showing channel intensity and cue list information).
- The existence and types of monitors for the production table (black and white, or color). The existence, condition, and length of monitor cable. Typical path and destination of monitor cable runs in recent past.
- The existence of a functioning alphanumeric keyboard to label the cues.
- The existence of a functional printer, and a printer cable to interconnect with the light board.
- The existence of a focus remote. Its typical location, condition, and history of problems.
- The typical location of the light board in the theatre. The distance to the stage, to typical rental dimmer rack locations, to the center of the house. The location of any DMX locations within the theatre. The existence of any DMX cable within the theatre.
- Any history of the console's use with any off-line editing programs. If so, can such a program be used?

- Names of other productions that have used the console in the recent past. Names of the lighting designers or production electricians, who, when contacted, may provide additional insight to the console or the personnel operating it.

A Basic Checklist to Help Define the House Manual Light Board

- The type, manufacturer, and model name of the light board.
- The actual condition of the light board, including any history of problems and the last date the board was serviced.
- Number of personnel required to operate the light board.
- The number of functional scenes. The number and identity of nonfunctioning sliders, handles, or knobs in each scene.
- The number of scene masters. The number of scenes that can be simultaneously active.
- The number of functional dimmers.
- Any specific switching requirements needed to allow for independent control of the scenes.
- The typical location of the light board in the theatre. The distance to the stage, to rental dimmer racks, to the center of the house. The type of plug connected to the cable controlling the dimmers.

If the condition or functions of the house lighting console initially seem inadequate to the needs of the production, the entire situation should be carefully analyzed before the choice is made to reject that console and replace it with a different board. If installing a replacement console is viewed as "breaking new ground," the issue of compatibility in every connection and protocol must be seriously reviewed. The apparent advantage of working with a more powerful console may not be worth the additional cost, effort, and potential time that may be lost making the replacement board function within the house system. If this seems to be a possibility, it may be prudent to consider the adage "if it ain't broke, don't fix it," and every work-around allowing the house lighting console to be used should be considered. The replacement console can easily become a disruptive element to a previously functional system.

Other situations may preclude this issue. When a production utilizing color scrollers is to be presented in a performance facility that has a two-scene preset light board, there's no question that the house board will be unable to control the scrollers and create the cues required. The performance will require the use of both the house board controlling the house dimmers and the board traveling with the company (the road board) controlling the scrollers. If the scrollers are critical to the success of the production, other options may require that the road board control the scrollers and also interface with the system to control the house dimmers as well.

Another common example may be found when productions, scheduled in several venues, involve extensive cueing. The amount of time and effort required to recreate the same cues on each house light board may be less painful than somehow adapting the signal from the road board to control each house system. The choices that need to be made regarding this issue are wholly dependent on the mutual judgment of the lighting designer and the production electrician.

Shelley's Notes: Measuring the Performance Space

When attending the advance, all drawings and copies of the tech specs should be on hand, in order to write relevant notes or questions directly onto the existing information. Likewise, all drafting notations can then be drawn or noted on the relevant portion of the drawing. One important piece of information is to check that every FOH lighting position is accurately placed and noted. Experience has also demonstrated that it's worthy to check and make certain that all of the FOH lighting positions are even shown in the drawings. With the drawings at hand, comparing them against the one-to-one scale model is that much simpler.

Even if current drawings exist for a performance space, many designers approach the performance facility as if the drawings did not exist. There's no telling if that one critical piece of information, specific to this particular show, has ever been needed or used prior to this production. This production might be the first that may install that new lighting position attached to the stage left wall, for example, and as such, may be the first time the (potentially) crucial distance from centerline to the stage left wall requires confirmation. For that matter, bitter experience has shown that even architectural drawings may not be updated to "as built" status after the completion of construction. Or it's possible that the new HVAC duct system has been added since the last drawing revision. In critical situations, having redundant measurements is better than relying on other's inaccuracies.

In addition to viewing and notating the current physical state of the space, many designers feel that the act of taking their own measurements provides them with a more tactile-memory grasp of the space. When questions arise about distances or physical relationships, they have a much better grasp of the physical space and feel better equipped to respond.

There's also the issue of responsibility. If an inaccuracy in the basic facility drawings results in a costly error down the line, most designers will assume responsibility for that mishap. If they're going to take that hit, however, they'll do it on their own terms. If they are going to be held accountable for an error, then it will be because of their misjudgments, not because they got lazy and relied on potentially out-of-date, inaccurate drawings. For that reason, most designers insist on basing their work solely on their own measurements and drawings.

Measuring the Performance Space Tactics

The basic intent during the measuring process is to record as much possible information in the shortest amount of time. In so doing, that means that every measured distance of importance to that designer is recorded. No matter how small, every distance is written down, along with any significant or insignificant relationships to other points. Doing so insures that it's been recorded by the designer's eyes, or the eyes of the designer's staff. In many cases, the person who acts as the draftsperson is the one who also writes and sketches the distances during the advance. While the amount of equipment and personnel involved in measuring a theatre can vary, everyone concerned with the project is well aware that the goal and the objective are to quickly accomplish the measuring tasks.

A Basic List of Gear Used to Document a Facility

- All relevant tech specs and drawings for the performance facility and the performance space.
- Relevant information, photographs, and any history downloaded from the Internet.
- Handheld distance laser.
- Transits (depending on the level of precision or detail required by the project).
- Chalk reel to snap straight lines on the stage.
- Rolls of 1/2" colored fabric spike tape. Used to secure measuring tapes, and also to mark things.
- Sharpies and paint markers to mark the tape or the space, when permissible.
- Pieces of chalk, to temporarily mark things that can then be wiped off.
- Four 100'-150' long tape measures. All based at groundplan zero-zero, they can then record

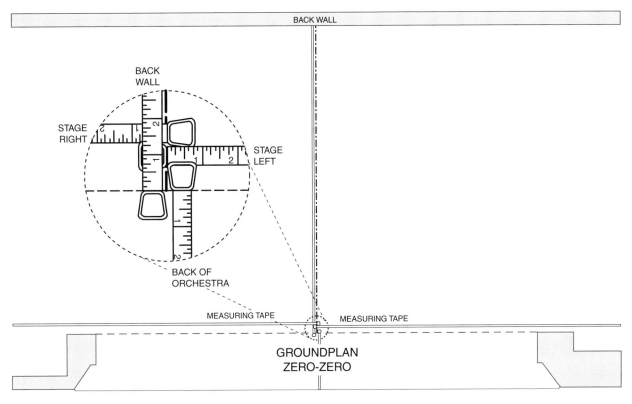

Figure 4.7 Four Measuring Tapes at Groundplan Zero-Zero

all relevant X and Y measurements at the same time, both up and downstage of the proscenium, and from centerline to either side wall.

- One 30′ long measuring tape, just to have around for measuring detail around the proscenium, for example.
- A clipboard with paper to write on.
- Gridded paper to draw scaled things.
- A fully-charged digital camera, disposable camera, or phone camera equipped with a working flash that can be turned off.
- A fully-charged video camera.
- Someone to stand in the frame and give the picture perspective.

Basic Performance Space Measuring Sequence

- Agree on placement of groundplan zero-zero with other departments; centerline and plaster line, or centerline and smoke pocket.
- Snap the plaster line (or upstage side of the smoke pocket).
- Measure across and divide by two; THAT is groundplan zero-zero.
- Define the up center location point.

- Lay the four tapes out and tack them down with pieces of tape so they can't be easily kicked out of position.

Figure 4.7 shows the four tape measures at groundplan zero-zero (the tacking tape is not shown since it would obscure the view). One tape is extended out to each side wall. The third tape is extended to the back wall, while the final (and longest) tap to the back of the orchestra seating. Note: make sure the measuring tapes are long enough. If the tape measures extended from centerline to the sides of the stage don't reach the side walls, for example, it may result in one set of measurements taken from centerline to the proscenium, and then a second set of measurements based from the proscenium to the side wall. Since the source point for the second set of measurements now has to be added to the first set of measurements, the chance for measured error has now been doubled.

Figure 4.8 is one list of measurements for a proscenium theatre. It can be used as a form to be filled in, which later can be used to create a groundplan and sectional view of the space. It should be mentioned that these measurements may already be reflected in existing drawings that haven't yet been seen. There's

SHELLEY'S SITE SURVEY MEASUREMENT TEMPLATE			
LEFT & RIGHT (Upstage of Plaster line):		**UPSTAGE TAPE (Plaster line to Back Wall)**	
Proscenium opening		Each approximate lineset location	
Smoke pocket		DS and US edge of lock rail	
Lift lines (Cables holding up batten)		Each door on either side of stage	
End of battens		Each window on either side of stage	
Circuitry Floor Pockets		Circuitry Floor Pockets	
On and offstage edge of loading rails		Obstructions in the air	
Onstage side of galleries		Beams left/right in the grid	
Onstage side of locking rail & crash bar		Each column on side wall	
Obstructions in the air		Last lineset	
Beams running up/down in the grid		Columns of back wall	
Side walls		Back wall	
Columns in back wall			
LEFT & RIGHT (Downstage of Plaster line):		**DOWNSTAGE TAPE (Plaster line to Rear Orchestra):**	
Edge of stage		Edge of stage; center & offstage	
DS Edge of orchestra pit		DS Edge of orchestra pit; center & offstage	
Near orchestra sightline		Near orchestra sightline; center & offstage	
Back orchestra sightline		Back orchestra sightline; center & offstage	
Back wall of orchestra seating		Back wall of orchestra seating	
FOH hanging points in house ceiling		FOH hanging points in house ceiling	
On & offstage edges of FOH positions		FOH lighting positions (up & downstage)	
Balcony Rail		Balcony Rail; center & offstage	
Aisles (orchestra and balcony)		Lighting Production Table	
Near balcony sightlines		Near Balcony sightline; center & offstage	
Back balcony sightlines		Back Balcony sightline; center & offstage	
Booth windows (followspots)		Booth	
Back of house side walls			
STAGE HEIGHTS (Stage deck to…):		**HOUSE HEIGHTS (Stage deck to…):**	
Batten working height		Bottom of orchestra pit	
Lock rail		Near sightlines	
Top of doors and windows		Lighting Production Table	
Lock rail crash bar		Back sightlines	
Each height change in the proscenium		Top & bottom of FOH Box Booms	
Each gallery lighting position		Top & bottomr of FOH overhead positions	
Loading rail		Lighting Production Table	
Top of pipe travel		Bottom of balcony	
Bottom of grid		Balcony rail	
Top of grid		Near balcony sightlines	
Height above grid		Back Balcony sightlines	
		Booth	

Figure 4.8 A List of Measurements Used to Define a Facility

also little doubt that there's a distance or measurement that has accidentally been forgotten. There always is.

Sometimes it's not possible to produce absolutely accurate measurements for height. There may not be a ladder at hand, or there may not be the personnel required to allow it. If a batten can be moved, it can be used as a rough yardstick. Select the batten closest to the proscenium. Bring the batten in to its lowest working height. Tape the end of the tape measure to the batten and read the measurement to the stage deck to determine the "batten working height" measurement. Slowly fly the batten out, stopping when the batten is eyeballed close to each element of interest, and record the distance. Using this system will produce no height taller than the top of pipe travel, but unless the measurements are critical, these rough approximations will be close enough for basic drawings.

Photographing the Performance Space

In addition to the measurements, photographs are a vital off-site reference. In general, photographs are invaluable to provide a visual reference for the overall shape of big-picture things, like all of the box boom lighting positions on one side of the theatre, for example. Or the entire width of a curved front of house lighting position, from one end to the other, in a single photograph.

Pictures are just as important to provide information about relationships. One set of relationships upstage of plaster line always seem to target on the distance from centerline to obstructions in the air on either side of the stage. The relationships downstage of plaster line seem to concentrate on how instruments hung in the FOH lighting positions relate to the proscenium opening, and more precisely, where their light can get around the proscenium (or portal masking) and get onto the stage. Where can those box boom lights be hung, and still hit the near the quarterline mark, before their beams are cut off by the near side of the proscenium? How far offstage can lighting instruments be hung on that curved FOH pipe, before their beams are cut off by the proscenium? How far upstage can the instruments on the FOH truss be focused, before they're cut off by the top of the proscenium?

Figure 4.9 is a list of potential photographs, and Figure 4.10 shows the matching groundplan reference points from which they would be taken. Obviously the way that a show relates to elements of the local architecture would dictate where additional angles and views would be required.

The list has been sequentially numbered and lettered in order to require the fewest movements before taking the next series of shots. Each series has been composed so the multiple photographs are listed in a clockwise direction. (Today's photo stitching software

PROSCENIUM THEATRE ADVANCE PHOTO LIST			
UPSTAGE OF PLASTER LINE		**DOWNSTAGE OF PLASTER LINE**	
1	GP Zero-Zero to SR Pros & Wall GP Zero-Zero to Back Wall GP Zero-Zero to SL Pros & Wall	1	GP Zero-Zero to SL House Wall GP Zero-Zero to Down Center GP Zero-Zero to SR House Wall
2	Center-Center to SR Wall Center-Center to US Wall Center-Center to SL Wall Center-Center to FOH positions	A	DC/Edge of Apron to SL House Wall DC/Edge of Apron to FOH Positions DC/Edge of Apron to Ceiling Rig Holes DC/Edge of Apron to SR House Wall
3	Up Center to SL Wall Up Center to DSL Pros & Wall Up Center to FOH Positions Up Center to DSR Pros & Wall Up Center to SR Wall	B	1st Row or Orch Pit to SL Pros 1st Row or Orch Pit to SL House 1st Row or Orch Pit to FOH Positions 1st Row or Orch Pit to SR House 1st Row or Orch Pit to SR Pros
3	Up Center looking up; distance between last batten and back wall	C	SL Sightline to SL Proscenium w/deck SL Sightline to SR Proscenium w/deck SL Sightline to SR House wall w/deck SL Sightline to SR FOH lighting
4	1 Leg line to middle of each aisle (include edge of stage/orch pit/bal rail)		
5	1 Leg line scrape pros to near Box Boom 1 Leg line scrape pros to near 2 BxBm 1 Leg line scrape pros to near 3 BxBm	D	SL Side Wall up to Ceiling Rig Holes
		E	SR Sightline to SR Proscenium w/stage SR Sightline to SL Proscenium w/stage SR Sightline to SL House wall w/stage SR Sightline to SL FOH lighting
6	1 Leg line to cutoff point of FOH positions 1 Leg line to cutoff point of Balcony Rails 1 Leg line to top > bot of Pros SL		
		F	SR Side Wall up to Ceiling Rig Holes
7	1 Leg line to top > bot of pros SR 1 Leg line up to loading rail & batten ends	G	Production table to House Left Production table across top of Pros Production table to Stage Production table to House Right
8	DS Plaster line looking up to batten ends; include proscenium DS Plaster line to back wall; include stage		
		H	Last center seat in orchestra
9	3 Leg line look up to load rail or galleries 3 Leg line to US side of Proscenium stage	J	First and last center seat in Balcony
		K	Last sightline seat in orchestra; balcony
10	1 Leg line SL to top > bot of pros SR 1 Leg line SL to SR Box Booms		

Figure 4.9 Proscenium Theatre Advance Photo List

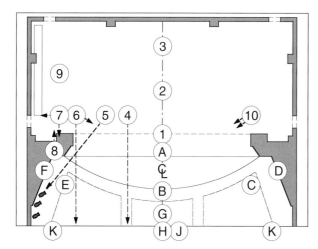

Figure 4.10 Proscenium Theatre Advance Photo Groundplan

often combines photographs from left to right.) If panorama or stitched photographs are being contemplated for a site survey, check the photography direction dictated by the camera or the software before taking the photos.

Disclaimers and notes: The shots indicated on centerline may have to be taken farther away from centerline in order to include more of the opposite wall. The shots indicated at 1 leg line may have to be taken farther upstage in order to include more lighting positions. Any shots showing vertical relationships may require the camera to be rotated to one side so that the stage surface is included in the same shot. This may require the photographer to kneel or sit on the stage, in order to get low enough to include both the stage surface and the subject of the photo. This list doesn't address cable paths or access doors. This list cannot include every need for every show. It's being provided as a template and to provide a starting point to think about what photographs might be required, prior to starting a hasty site survey.

Shelley's Notes: Advance Photography

Here are some quick thoughts about taking site survey photographs:

- Turn on every possible worklight. If possible, turn on applicable focused instruments.
- Know how to turn the camera's flash "on" and "off."
- Bring a big bright flashlight and some diffusion; it can help provide fill.
- The photographs will be dark; bring a small tripod or some way of steadying the camera.

- Fly out any masking. Reduce the cause of shadows.
- Be certain to take at least one photograph to each side of the stage and house with the curtain open, showing the relationship of backstage and plaster line to the architecture immediately downstage.
- Encourage people to be in the photographs to give the photos a sense of scale.
- Photographs showing front of house lighting positions may need to be photographed as multiple vertical panorama shots in order to show the architecture from the stage level up to the lighting position. Photographs of a lighting position without any information showing it's relative height to the rest of the architecture or the stage surface is not optimum information.
- Photographs showing vertical relationships need to somehow relate to the height of the stage surface. Without a relationship to sectional zero-zero the height information may be lost.
- All photographs showing horizontal placements need to somehow relate to the plaster line or the front edge of the stage, to relate to that half of the groundplan zero-zero.

Shelley's Notes: Not Enough Time

"Sure, you can come in, but I'm locking up in 15 minutes." Hearing that from the stage doorperson as you're trying to advance the theatre can give you pause. Now what? How much information can be acquired in that minuscule amount of time? Certainly some basic measurements can be taken, but in this case, having a second person (hopefully) who can run around like crazy and take reference photographs is just as important.

The photographer begins by standing down center. Starting at the stage left proscenium, photograph across the entire house in panorama format. Continue the stage right proscenium, and then continue to photograph in a panorama format across the entire stage area, finishing back at the stage left proscenium.

The photographer walks over to the locking rail. Standing next to the plaster line he or she photographs the locking rail close enough the batten numbers can be read. Take that photograph, and then pivot the camera directly up so the next photograph shows the pipes or battens above. Continue in this manner alternating a photo straight ahead, with a matching photo pointing straight up. In this manner the developed shots can be compared to see how much the sheaves have been kicked relative to the locking rail, after leaving the advance.

The photographer makes certain there's a photograph of every FOH position, and takes the picture so that the photo can be attached back to the first panorama sweep taken of the house.

Meanwhile, the scribe is first comparing both the groundplan and the section to be certain that every FOH position is properly listed on them. The scribe then places a tape measure on the ground next to the locking rail, and aligns the zero of the tape with the plaster line or the smoke pocket. The measuring tape is then laid out parallel to the locking rail to the back wall. The scribe's next step is to write the number or letter for each line set onto a legal pad. If there's an assignment from the last show, record that label as well. Then the photographer walks down the length of the locking rail reading the distances for each batten in the air, or from the lock on the rail.

No small amount of care should be focused on this final step; if the batten's positions have been moved (the sheaves have been kicked), their relationship to the plaster line will no longer match the measured distances sighted to each lock. On a regular basis, the photographer needs to visually confirm that the batten in the air still closely matches the position of that same lock on the rail. If it doesn't match, determine the true measured location of every tenth batten, for example, notate the projected distances as well as can be expected, and make plans for another more detailed visit in the future.

That easily takes up the 15 minutes. Thank the stage doorperson, and the pair can be on their way with basic visual and written up-to-date information.

Shelley's Notes: The *Hokey* Advance

Now that the Hybrid Theatre's site survey is complete, here are some of the notes that were made:

- The director and choreographer have agreed that the masking legs should be set for a 36'-0" opening. The portal legs may need to be set slightly wider for the near orchestra sightlines. They would like to be provided with at least 28'-0" of depth, but they realize this may become an issue.
- There doesn't seem to be enough room in the spot booth for 3 spots and the lighting console; 16'-6"W × 7'-3"D. window is centered, 12'-0" wide × 5'-0" tall. Need to check that against followspot cut sheets and see what the shops have available in stock. Spot focus range cannot

pickup anything in audience farther out than row D. See digital shots.

- Data path to backstage dimmers over the top of the ceiling; 2 runs of 5 pin XLR cable installed (1 backup), no Ethernet, no coax.
- The pass door to backstage is stage left; any cable must go over. No yellowjackets; all cable off deck.
- The battens are two pieces of schedule 40 pipe, 21'-0' each. They're welded on centerline, and are open at the ends.
- The house dimmers are questionable and if possible, skip using them.
- Company switches; DSL: 2-400 × 3Ø elec. USL, electric & motors. DSR, audio (isolation trans, share neutral with house dim).
- Haze was used in this house last year. According to the house electrician, it should not be a problem. Check to see what hazer was used in that show.
- There are house ladders to get to the box booms. Not drawn on the house section.
- The house instrument inventory appears to be in decent condition; keep them as backup.
- Very little other support gear. Treat this venue as a 4-wall house with instruments and cable.
- All house soft goods are old, some with fullness, not very large. Need to bring in all soft goods.
- The multicable is in good condition, recently purchased. The rest of the stage cable is crap and should all be burned. The 6 circuit bundles are designed for sidelight booms. Can also be used for electrics.
- The basement crossover is a labyrinth but well marked. Upstage may be necessary for quick crossovers.
- Side booms should be used but they need to be as thin as possible. Cable must go up, not on deck. How tall is everyone? Any spears? Tall sticks? Maybe supports from side walls instead of lines to grid? How will this relate to masking?
- Grid is clean; battens in good condition, recent renovation. Need pipe extensions for legs. Not possible for electrics. Tabs may be required for masking.
- Cove much too low; frontlight will spill on US scrim. Need FOH truss. How to focus? There's no second set of holes for a focus truss. Maybe invert triangle truss so electricians ride up with it for focus?
- House curtain red; recently purchased from RoseBrand; scene designer will get a swatch.
- There are no circuits to the balcony rail. Why are there no circuits to the balcony rail? Why did they bother installing a balcony rail? Check with production electrician about cable path; or drop circuits from box boom?

- There's a house lift, freshly serviced, with a fresh battery. Wasn't on the tech specs, but no matter; no longer needs to be part of the rental package. Needs apron with pockets inside the basket to contain gels and spare pieces.
- SR wall measurement doesn't account for locking rail for flies; may impact SR boom placement
- Sound will have front fill DS of plaster either side.
- Sound will use near points in ceiling for FOH high fill above orchestra.
- There's no circuitry in the pit for the Precipice uplights; can a hole be poked in a wall somewhere so the pit door can be closed?
- X101 & X102 will be the seats for preview; on aisle, close to center, but closest to exit to go backstage.
- Row G will be placement for tech table; hang downlights from balcony rail for worklights.
- Light racks SL; sound SR. Sound mix will be back of House Left. Not centerline. Sad for sound.

Shelley's Notes: After the Advance

Once the preliminary on-site theatre survey is complete, it may seem natural to check that task off the "to-do" list, and set the clipboard filled with measurements and notes aside—Don't! Experience has shown that every delay between the visit and the drafting process increases the probability that the identity, significance, or memory of any measurement (aka "chicken scratch") may be forgotten or misinterpreted, and require a duplicate measurement. Today's scribbled measurements quickly turn into tomorrow's incomprehensible gibberish. The lighting draftsperson should immediately use the measurements to draft the preliminary groundplan and section, and write up a written summation regarding the performance space. This way it's quickly discovered which measurements are confusing, require double-checking, or just need to be taken again.

SUMMARY

Now that the parameters are known for this hypothetical production of *Hokey: A Musical Myth*, the next steps can be taken toward the creation of the lighting design. One of the first steps is to interpret the advance notes, and draw the preliminary sectional and groundplan views of the Hybrid Theatre.

Stage 2

Preliminary Documents

Chapter 5

Create the Preliminaries and Send out the Shop Order

INTRODUCTION

This chapter examines the multiple phases and steps that are required to create a preliminary light plot, assemble the documentation for a shop order, and submit it to lighting rental shops.

Creating the preliminary light plot is a three-phase process. First, a **preliminary section, ground-plan,** and **front elevation** are created to define the performance space from the side, overhead, and front viewing planes. After the core documents of the preliminary lighting packet are reviewed, decisions and prioritizations are made about the colors, directions of origin, and control distribution. The lighting systems are then constructed, and their added information transforms the drawings into the **preliminary lighting section** and the **preliminary light plot.** As the plot takes shape, the amount of equipment is monitored using the **instrument spreadsheet** and the **dimmer and circuitry spreadsheet.**

Once the preliminary light plot is completed, final tabulations calculate equipment above and beyond the house inventories. This added gear is then compiled in an **equipment list,** while a **perishable list** itemizes the consumable supplies necessary for the plot. These two documents, along with a **cover letter,** are collectively submitted to lighting rental shops as the **shop order.**

Before this entire process takes place, basic decisions about the size, percentage, and use of the draftings need to be considered, along with a brief review of drafting guidelines.

CAD Drafting

In much of today's entertainment industry, hand drafting has been supplanted by computer-assisted drafting (CAD). Many valuable lessons can be gained by learning how to draft by hand: mentally laying out a complicated drafting onto paper, projecting the drafting within the finite confines of paper before it physically exists, or the kinesthetic calm that can come from drawing pristine lines with a lead holder. Likewise, there's no question that the initial learning curve of any CAD program often seems complex, bewildering, and time consuming. That said, acquiring the ability to change or move any drawn element after it's been created (instead of having to erase and re-trace it), or the ability to use any portion of a previously created document as the basis for another drawing (copy and paste), quickly makes the investment of time and energy seem well worth the effort, and the clear advantages provided by CAD drafting difficult to resist. Depending on the skill or discipline, there are many other advantages to CAD drafting; the ability to quickly change scales or print in different percentages, the ability to turn on or off different layers, or the ability to attach data to objects are just a few of the reasons CAD drafting continues to grow. Like it or not, CAD drafting is here to stay, and folks who want to get the higher paying jobs need to be well-versed in the latest graphic software.

That's not to say that all methodology used prior to computers should be abandoned. CAD drafting and computers are all marvelous tools, until there's no electricity and the battery goes dead. When that

113

happens, the laptop is a silent brick, and any drawings trapped inside will remain there. Having at least a fleeting grasp of how to draw, update, or distribute a non-computer-generated draft can eliminate delays in the process, or even save the day.

Scales

No matter if the drawings are hand-drafted or CAD-produced, one basic decision that has to be made about each drawing is its size, which is relative to its scale. In most cases the documents are produced in either 1/2″ = 1′-0″ or 1/4″ = 1′-0″ scale. Will both documents be drafted in the same scale? Or will the light plot be in ½″ scale, while the sectional view is published in ¼″ scale?

While an individual choice, in most cases the light plot doesn't need to match the scale used for the lighting section. Though both documents present graphics about the production that are in scale to the architectural space surrounding it, in almost all cases the amount of information presented on a light plot involves much more text than that shown on a section.

The light plot may include a unit number, a channel number, and a color number for each lighting fixture. All of the data must be readable in order for the document to be functional. Each additional piece of data shown for each instrument, however, increases its spatial footprint. If there's a lot of information that must be listed on the light plot, it may become so crowded that a larger scale may be necessary merely to accommodate all of the data. On the other hand, fewer bits of information means more room, which in turn then means the remaining text can increase to a larger font size, and the entire drawing can be produced on a smaller scale.

The section, on the other hand, typically only requires text to identify locations, hanging locations, goods, and individual measurements. As long as the smallest text is easily readable, it's often the first document considered to reduce to a smaller scale. On the other hand, if no real scenic section exists, the lighting section may be the only graphic document showing the relationship between lighting, scenery, and the surrounding architecture. If it's a complex affair, it only makes sense to produce the document in a large enough scale so that that all of these relationships can be clearly seen.

Document scale is often determined after considering several criteria:

- The overall spatial area being shown in scale on the drawing.
- Will the groundplan or light plot need to be physically compared to the section?

- What's the final desired paper size that will be used for the drawing?
- What's the application (for CAD drafting) that will be used for other departments?
- What's the final format that will be used to present the drawing?
- Will the drawing need to allow scaled measurements taken from it?
- How many lighting instruments (and individual data) will eventually be shown?
- In the case of hand-drafted light plots, what is the scale of available plastic lighting templates?

Printing Percentages

If a document can be accurately printed or duplicated at a percentage, it's possible to reduce the drawing's size and still maintain a measurable scale. Here are different scales that can be produced from a ½″ scale drawing:

- Print at 100% = 1/2″ scale.
- Change print percentage to 75% = 3/8″ scale.
- Change print percentage to 50% = 1/4″ scale.
- Change print percentage to 38% = 3/16″ scale.
- Change print percentage to 25% = 1/8″ scale.

The amount of reduction from an original ½″ scale drawing can impact the font size chosen for the document. While any number of formulas, or rules of thumb, can be proposed, the final font sizes chosen for any given percentage needs to be based on personal preference. Print examples to see if the reduced text is readable, before drafting the entire document.

Hard copy of drawings created in feet and inches can be slightly reduced and then measurable using metric rulers, but I struggled for years to remember which scale has to reduce or enlarge in order to make the proper transition to the other scale. Finally, I adopted the mnemonic phrase "Feets is bigger than meters" ("F" before "M") to remember the percentage relationships; if the drawing is imperial, it must be *reduced* to be measurable in the same approximate metric scale. If the drawing is in meters, it must be *enlarged* to be the same approximate imperial scale.

To convert a printed ½″ scale document to an approximate metric scale, use the following recipes:

- To convert a 1/2″ scale drawing to 1:25 metric scale = Reduce it to 96%.
- To convert a 1/2″ scale drawing to 1:50 metric scale = Reduce it to 48%.

To convert a printed 1:25 metric scale document to an approximate imperial scale, use the following recipes:

- To convert a 1:25 scale drawing to 1/2″ imperial scale = Enlarge it to 104%.
- To convert a 1:25 scale drawing to 1/4″ imperial scale = Reduce it to 52%.

Percentage printing can also be applied to A-sized paper. If a document has been designed to fit onto A1-sized paper:

- Change print percentage to 50% = fits onto A3-sized paper.
- Change print percentage to 35% = fits onto A4-sized paper.

Two notes: One, when any printing percentage has been changed, update the printed scale in the title block before distributing (publishing) the drawings. Two, after a drawing's percentage has been altered, any written distances or scale bar values shown in the drawing are probably wrong. Measured distances using a matching scale rule, however, should provide accurate measurements. Obviously, it goes without saying that both of these notes are based on sad experience. Overlooking and not notating these two seemingly innocent details can create *massive* confusion and be the source for extensive delays.

Departmental Coordination

The groundplan and sectional drawings for the show are not documents solely created or required by the lighting department. On most productions, the scene design department creates their collection of drawings first, and everyone else adds their own layer of gear or information on top of that. Stage management often reduces the groundplans to include them in blocking and call books. The sound department often works off both drawings to determine speaker and equipment distribution both on and off the stage. The lighting department usually adds its own layers to the scenic groundplan as well. While everyone seems to operate in his or her own sphere when it comes to the groundplan, the big debate that often looms before the load-in begins is: which department's sectional view will be used as the singular reference document for the load-in.

Sometimes everyone shares the same vision as to what the final product will look like. Other times each department seems like it has its own opinion as to the way things should turn out. While everyone is working for the common goal, each department typically focuses on its own domain. Scenic draftsfolk rarely employ the same attention to detail when drawing accurate electrical instrument outlines, for example. Their main concern is that the scenery won't bump into each other. Likewise, sectional drawings created by the projection or sound departments provide the most detail showing relationships that concern them. And lighting's no different, except that it's trying to make sure that its gear doesn't get whacked, or the equipment from other departments doesn't get in the way of the light beams.

Bottom line? Usually, each department draws its own section. And while it can be viewed as a duplication of effort, it also means that each department takes responsibility for itself. As long as everyone agrees on the same lineset schedule, then each department's interpretation of thickness will eventually work out during the load-in. Sometimes other departments will decline to provide any sectional drawing, deferring instead to the drafting produced by the electrics department. Accepting this responsibility may appear like it streamlines the process, but it comes with potential pitfalls; any errors on the drawing may then become the electrics draftsperson's fault. Any corrections for other departments' gear may now translate into time spent by the electrics draftsperson updating the drawing with non-electrical notes. Taking on the responsibility of being the production's *de facto* section is usually not a huge issue, but any department wishing to piggy-back on the electrics section should understand that any subsequent updates will be produced at the timing convenient for the electrics draftsperson.

Graphic Guidelines

The light plot is the basic document used to communicate spatial information and identify the attributes of each lighting instrument. If the outlines are too dark, the fonts are too cursive, or if the text is just illegible, then the document's purpose is doomed. No matter how "pretty" the plot may appear, unless it can be read, it's a practical failure. Providing guidelines for drafting light plots, the United States Institute for Theatre Technology (USITT) recently published RP-2, Recommended Practice for Theatrical Lighting Design Graphics. This document includes written descriptions, updated symbology, and methods to display information on the graphic document. At the time of this writing, the document is available at www.usitt.org.

Shelley's Notes: Drafting Hints

Although this text isn't a drafting primer, some basic elements of drafting etiquette are worthy of review, in order to provide fundamental clarity in the drafting process:

- Always include an indication of zero-zero when applicable.
- Include all possible accurate placement for all scenic and masking elements relative to electrics (showing the electrician possible locations for Zetex, scenery bumpers, or breasting lines).
- Indicate full and accurate lineset schedule information.
- Include relevant contact info: names, email, cell phone, etc.
- Leave an area to note the date of revisions. Number the revision so that it's simple to see which version of the document is being viewed.
- Cursive fonts should be avoided, especially for light plots that are continually reproduced, such as a repertory plan, or a touring document that may be faxed and re-faxed over the course of its lifetime. Imagine the fourth generation fax that can't be read because the text is too broken up. Now re-consider the font being considered.
- Colors should be reconsidered for documents that may be faxed.
- Include a scale bar drafted in the plan to demonstrate a default distance. That way when the fourth generation of faxing cuts off the scale dimension, or the faxing itself rescales the document, it will still be possible to measure that scaled distance, even with a pencil, and determine basic measured distances and relationships within the scaled drawing.

THE PRELIMINARY DRAWINGS

When lighting systems are graphically constructed, three drawings are typically used as the main reference documents. The **preliminary section** illustrates the side view of the performance space, and shows the height and depth relationships between the architectural and scenic elements drawn in the theatri the are made about position height and placement, **front elevations** illustrate side-to-side coverage and help determine which beam pool size is best suited to serve each lighting system. The **preliminary groundplan** shows the placement of the instruments in each lighting system and how they all relate to the scenery, the architecture, and the viewing audience.

In order to provide the broadest opportunity for learning, the scenic designer will provide general instructions, but the lighting designer will draw all of these documents.

Reference Information

Sometimes the architectural elements of the preliminary drawings can be traced or measured off the original architectural draftings that were used to construct the venue. Experience has shown that while these documents can be invaluable resources for general knowledge and shapes, they were often drawn before the building was constructed and are rarely a reflection of what was actually built. They're another set of reference documents, but should not be treated as sacrosanct. While drafting the preliminaries, other useful reference information to have on hand that may provide more detailed or up-to-date information includes:

- All technical specifications.
- Any facility drawings.
- All site survey information: pictures, videos, notes, measurements, and scribbles.
- A current lineset schedule showing relative distances from plaster line.
- A complete list of scenic elements and a sketch (or drafted groundplan) for each scene.
- A complete set of working drawings showing all relevant views of the scenic elements in the show.
- The dimensions of all masking goods.
- Number of openings required by the production.
- All contact information.

When preliminary drawings include drawing the architectural elements of a venue (for the first time), it's worthwhile to schedule on-site time to double-check any questions or details before publishing any drawings. For that matter, when I've been the first one to create draftings that include drawing the architecture, I've found it faster and simpler to get in the door and create the drawings while in the space. Being able to run to any corner of the facility with a tape measure to double-check a measurement can immediately answer any questions, save lots of time, and expedite an accurate drafting that contains no questions or assumptions.

While the existing architectural drawings for the Hybrid Theatre are accepted, for the purposes of this book, the measurements taken during the site survey will be used instead during the initial construction of each preliminary drawing. Both the section and the groundplan will be drafted in three steps.

The horizontal lines will be traced first, followed by the vertical marks. In reality, when these drawings are usually constructed, the horizontal and vertical measurements are often interwoven as they're drawn.

THE PRELIMINARY SECTION

The **preliminary section** is typically one of the first documents drawn in the preparation to create a lighting design. In its initial state, the document's purpose and appearance are to display the parameters that exist before lighting is added to the production. Usually this includes the main architectural features of the venue, the permanent hanging positions downstage and upstage of plaster line, and the extreme sightlines of the audience. The architectural features may not be detailed, all of the lines may not be finished or trimmed, and peripheral information may not yet be included.

Once scenery and masking are added to the drawing, it's then referred to as a **preliminary scenic section**. Presuming that discussions between the lighting designer and scenic designer have taken place, a complete preliminary scenic section may provide all of this information and indicate all of the temporary lighting positions specific to the show. On the other hand, there may be no communication between the two, and the scenic designer might include lighting positions in the section without any input, indicating them only in order to be polite. While lighting positions may be indicated by the scenic designer or other members of the technical staff, until the lighting designer starts working on the drawing, it's not a preliminary lighting section. Only after lighting information and decisions made by the lighting designer are added to the document, finalizing electric hanging positions and trim heights, can the document be called the **preliminary lighting section**.

The general orientation of almost any theatrical section is almost always absolute; the stage is drawn at the bottom of the document, while anything above the stage is located toward the top. In a proscenium theatre, the perspective of typical sections almost always uses the theatre's centerline as the **viewing plane**.

Decisions: Which Side?

While defining centerline as the viewing plane in a proscenium setting is almost always an automatic choice, deciding whether to draw the section looking stage left or stage right can be a little complex. While the decision can be based on several factors, the common choice is the side of the stage containing more complexity; more scenery, more height changes, or more electrical components. Complex productions involving non-symmetric scenery may need to see both sides of the stage, in which case two sections are drawn, one looking toward each side.

When all things are equal, many CAD-oriented designers prefer to draft the lighting section from the perspective of centerline looking stage left (or the stage left section). The back wall is then against the left edge of the printed (or drafted) page, and the majority of information is on the left side of the document. If the document is being printed or faxed, this means that the "meatier" portion of the section is processed first. When printing the stage and fly space of a reduced stage left section, it may not be necessary to show the entire auditorium every time the document is published. When details downstage of plaster line aren't vital to the drawing, that often translates into only having to print a single page showing the back wall to plaster line. Achieving this is possible by experimenting with reduction percentage and the page layout orientation.

If the section won't fit, and a second page needs to be printed, experimentation hopefully allows the page break to be placed somewhere other than the middle of the fly system. The two pages can be taped together, and relationships can still be seen without an obtrusive paper margin getting in the way. For many draftspeople, producing this two-page document as a stage right section always seems to result in somehow losing control of the page break's position, relative to either the plaster line or the back wall. Depending on the CAD program, producing only a portion of the full document can often also translate into the need to count which pages are printed ("page 5 of 6"), and in which direction, in order to achieve the same result.

For the purposes of this text, the preliminary section will be constructed from the perspective of centerline looking stage left.

Decisions: Sectional Perspective in Non-Proscenium Settings

It has been mentioned that the sectional viewing plane in proscenium settings is almost always based off the centerline. This choice is typically applied to thrust configurations as well. Arena stages, on the other hand, can sometimes be a case-by-case basis. The orientation of the overhead grid or any lineset system can often be the basis for the sectional view, but in situations where masking or scenic pieces are hung on matching diagonals, the sectional view may rotate in order to be perpendicular to that angle as well.

Doing so means the scenic goods are represented in the drafting by lines, not rectangles.

In some venues, the important sectional viewing plane is "in line" with actors' entrances to the performance space. At the Arena Stage in Washington D.C., performers access the stage through tunnels in the four corners of the stage, called "vomitories." Actors standing in these "voms" are seen from all sides of the audience—because they're so close to the audience, the voms are perceived as one of the most extreme and strongest locations in the performance area. Because of that, the voms are often treated as additional (and sometimes separate) acting areas. Drafting the sectional viewing plane, so it runs through a vom and its diagonal opposite, means the lighting designer can accurately plot low-hung lighting instruments from the opposite corner, lighting the performers' faces as they enter, without blinding the adjacent audience.

If the entrances aren't that important, common wisdom dictates that the sectional view chosen should be the one providing the clearest view of the hanging positions relative to the architecture, scenery, and the audience. If that's not enough criteria, a third sectional choice is to use the plane that provides the cleanest "side view" of the majority of lighting systems used in the show. In complex arena productions, there may be more than one viewing plane axis, and result in multiple section drawings.

Decisions: How Much Architecture?

Another sectional decision that needs to be made is the amount of surrounding architecture that needs to be shown. If elevators, traps, or steps leading to below the stage are part of the scenic design, the basement floor or the orchestra pit will probably need to be included in the drawing, in order to show information about sub-stage lighting positions. In proscenium settings with multiple scenic settings, it's typical to include the height of the entire fly system up to, and including the top pipe travel and the grid. Either of these distances may become important to confirm that flown scenery can be concealed when stored, and that any deadhung or chain-motor hung pieces provide the height or running length to match the heights indicated on the drawing.

Information Included on the Preliminary Section

The purpose of the finished preliminary section is to communicate spatial information and relationships between all elements to all departments (and selfishly, as they specifically relate to the lighting design). The following basic information should be represented on the section for a proscenium theatre to allow for rapid comprehension of the drawing by any observer:

- Stage floor, deck, or "vertical zero" location (indication of which one is being used as reference zero).
- Proscenium, smoke pocket, or the "horizontal zero" location.
- Back wall or upstage limitation of the performing space.
- Downstage edge of stage floor and/or edge of playing area.
- Height of grid, gallery, basement, and all other appropriate vertical offstage parameters.
- Trim heights for all gear and goods that change height.
- Pipe travel heights for all battens.
- Vertical and horizontal audience sightline points and/or sightlines.
- Architectural or scenic obstructions.
- Sectional views of all appropriate scenery (playing and storage positions).
- All masking (dimensioned).
- Title block (including a label stating which viewing plane is being used).
- Contact information for all relevant parties.
- Scaled human figure (or head height focus point plane).

 **Shelley's Soapbox: Sectional Need?**

Over the years, I've occasionally heard of lighting instructors who teach their students not to waste time on creating a lighting section. In my opinion, those instructors are just plain wrong. By making that statement they prove they don't understand the process of creating an accurate lighting design. Most lighting designers strongly agree that the lighting section must be constructed at the same time as the front elevations and the preliminary light plot, rather than after the fact. All three documents are often necessary, and the need for them overlaps during the plot construction process. Properly using them provides that much more insurance that the correct type of instrument with the proper beam spread will be selected to create the systems and specials. If you encounter a teacher who tells you that a lighting section is a waste of time, start looking for a new lighting instructor.

Tales from the Road: Why Bother with a New Section?

Obviously, I have strong opinions about lighting sections and their use. What's the big deal? Why construct a lighting section at all? In some cases this may seem entirely valid. The scenic designer may have produced such a complete drawing indicating all of the relative locations and elements that, to produce a lighting section will essentially be a retrace of the scenic section and a redundant waste of paper. While that may be true, it doesn't necessarily include accurate illustrations of beam pool overlaps or approaching angles of light. I believe it's always wise for the lighting designer to take the time and double-check the angles drawn on sections for beam spread and focus range. Here's why:

Years ago I was involved in a Broadway production called *A Christmas Carol*, starring Patrick Stewart. It was a one-man show, and Patrick played over thirty-five roles in each performance. We had originally produced the effort at the Richard Rogers Theatre, and the show was going to be remounted at the Broadhurst Theatre. The show was an official hit, and the plan was to merely reproduce the show in every way. The same scenery, the same lighting instruments, focused to the same areas—we intended to use the light cues on the disk on the same type of lighting console that had used the year before. Both theatres were Broadway houses, and both had the same lighting positions. Taking the time to draft a lighting section was a waste of time and effort.

Or so we thought. We hung the same lighting package and the schedule was going along smoothly. Only when we turned on the lights on the FOH truss did we notice that the pools of area light seem a little smaller. After some checking we determined that the FOH truss position at the Broadhurst was approximately 5'-0" closer to the plaster line than the same lighting position in the Rodgers. The solution at this time-constrained moment was to fly the truss out to a higher trim. Taking this action allowed the pools of light from the instruments to get large enough so that they provided adequate area coverage. Solved that problem, right?

Wrong. During the technical rehearsal, we discovered that the frontlight angle was now so high no light struck Mr. Stewart's eyelids. The shadows under Patrick's eyes were so pronounced that, when he looked straight to the back of the orchestra seating, there were black holes where his eyes should have been. As an actor, one of his main tools for communicating, his eyes, was lost.

Our first preview was that night. Our course was set. As they were clearing the tech table from the house, our suggestion to Patrick was to play the entire show a "little higher." That is, angle his head back so that he was looking straight up a little higher to the first row of the mezzanine, rather than the back of the house.

After the show we met in his dressing room, and Patrick commented that he was beginning to get a crick in his neck from angling his head back for the entire show. We noted this discomfort and considered the fact that we had a sold-out 5-week run featuring this one world-class performer, who now was feeling discomfort for our oversight. After meeting with the producer, jumping on our swords, and making some late night phone calls to people at home, we came in the next morning with the crew. New instruments with larger beam spreads arrived at the theatre, and we proceeded to re-hang the entire position, re-trim it to a lower height, re-focus it, and allowed Mr. Stewart to give his performances without any further neck adjustment.

Had we paid more attention and taken the time to draw a section, we would have seen the difference in the distance to the Broadhurst's FOH position, and presumably would have changed the instrumentation. That would have then avoided the additional cost, the inconvenience to Mr. Stewart, and the loss of confidence from the producer. My lesson was that, no matter how silly or time consuming it may seem at the time, always create or check the section for lighting. It's become one of my own personal Golden Rules.

The Preliminary Section: Basic Drawing

The preliminary section is created in three steps. Using all available information, horizontal and vertical coordinates are drawn, double-checked, and then joined to create the scaled drawing. For clarity, the illustrations will show these lines properly spaced in the three steps to quickly create the overall picture.

Step 1: Draft the Rough Outlines

The left-hand side of Figure 5.1 shows the horizontal placement of the vertical lines that will be used to create the preliminary section of the Hybrid Theatre. Draw the first vertical line and define that as plaster line, one-half of sectional zero-zero. Now draw the left-hand column of lines or tic marks relative to that line (negative to the algebraic left). When completed, those vertical lines will resemble Figure 5.2A.

Next, the horizontal lines will be added. The right-hand column of Figure 5.1 lists the vertical placement of the horizontal lines. Draw the first line and define that as the stage, the other half of sectional zero-zero. Now draw the next two lines below the stage (negative to the algebraic "under" or below), and the rest of the lines above the stage. When completed, those added lines resemble Figure 5.2B. Now some quick drafting and a little artistic license will clean this up.

- The lines are shortened, joined, and shaded to show the preliminary shape of the architecture.

HORIZONTAL PLACEMENT			VERTICAL PLACEMENT		
Distance		Measuring Point	Distance		Measuring Point
-32'	0"	Back Wall	-10'	3"	Floor of the Orchestra Pit
0'	**0"**	**Plaster Line**	-3'	2"	Floor of the Auditorium
		DS of PLASTER LINE	**0'**	**0"**	**Stage Level**
1'	6"	Downstage Side of the Proscenium			**Above Stage Level**
5'	0"	Front Edge of the Stage	0'	0"	Near Orchestra Sightline
8'	6"	Near Orchestra Sightline	2'	3"	Far Orchestra Sight Line
10'	3"	Balcony Rail to Side Wall	5'	6"	Head Height Focus Plane
11'	6"	Upstage Side of the Orchestra Wall	8'	8"	Ceiling Under the Balcony
11'	9"	Near Box Boom Vertical	11'	0"	Balcony Rail
19'	9"	Far Box Boom Vertical	11'	8"	Top of the Balcony Rail Wall
26'	6"	Truss Holes in the Ceiling	13'	6"	Near Balcony Sightline
34'	0"	Center of the Balcony Rail	25'	0"	Top of the Proscenium Arch
38'	6"	Balcony Rail Sightline	26'	3"	Lower Box Boom Hanging Position
47'	9"	Ceiling Cove	27'	6"	Rear Balcony Sightline
51'	9"	Rear Orchestra Sightline	28'	3"	Upper Box Boom Hanging Position
65'	0"	Spot Booth	30'	0"	Spot Booth
66'	0"	Rear Balcony Sightline	32'	0"	Hypothetical Truss Hang Height
			36'	6"	Auditorium Ceiling
			59'	6"	Pipe Travel
			62'	0"	Bottom of Grid

Figure 5.1 Preliminary Section Measurements

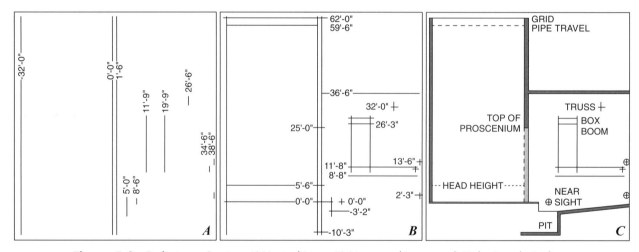

Figure 5.2 Preliminary Section: A) Vertical Lines, B) Horizontal Lines, and C) the Rough Outlines

• The sightlines are given circle outlines so they can be seen.
• The front edge of the stage is shaped.

The result is the general shapes and outlines in Figure 5.2C. The basic outlines and shapes required to provide sectional information are now complete.

Step 2: Fill in Information Upstage of Plaster line

The next step is to draft the framework showing the linesets and the relative height and depth information about the fly system. First, a 2'-6" dashed vertical line is drawn 1'-0" upstage of plaster line between the pipe travel horizontal (59'-6" above stage level) and the grid (62'-0"), with a centered circle underneath it. This represents the system cable and sectional view of the batten for lineset 1. As shown in Figure 5.3A, those two objects are then duplicated 61 times on 6" centers to illustrate the lineset schedule described in the house hang of the tech specs.

Above that, a lineset schedule box is drawn, showing the lineset number and distance from plaster line, and providing a placeholder for goods identification and trim height. These rectangles will be used to fill in the identity and height of each batten. Figure 5.3B shows a portion of the lineset schedule box.

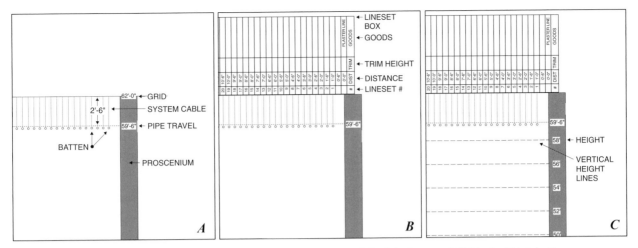

Figure 5.3 Preliminary Section: A) Linesets, B) Lineset Schedule Box, and C) Vertical Height Lines

Finally, vertical height information is drawn as horizontal dashed lines, extending from plaster line to the back wall. Adjacent to the lines are numerical labels indicating their height, starting at 14'-0" above the stage. Figure 5.3C shows the result of vertically duplicating this arrangement on 2'-0" centers.

Step 3: The Scenic Masking

During the site survey, the director and choreographer stated that they wanted the performance space to be "about 28'-0" deep by about 36'-0" wide." The scene designer agreed with this assessment, and added that the borders should be "around 20'-0" above the stage." With that information, the lighting designer will now design the masking for the show without any further assistance or feedback. In reality, the lighting designer would be reacting to or collaborating on preliminary plans provided by the scenic designer. There might also be constant conferences, sketches, and drafting exchanges between them and the director and the choreographer.

Typically, masking design for an open stage starts by placing the "perimeter scenery," starting with the downstage portal masking and main curtain. The term "portal" merely defines its location—the masking often consists of the same black border and leg materials used elsewhere in the performance space. Placing these portal goods not only helps define the downstage light line, it also establishes the shape of the portal opening. The house main curtain is 28'-0" tall, while the proscenium is 25'-0" tall. Presuming the main is tied to a batten close to the proscenium, there's no need for a black border downstage of it to hide the curtain's system batten.

Creating a classic "black surround" look, however, means that no portion of the red curtain is seen when it's flown out and not in use. Since the pipe travel

is 59'-6", the curtain can fly completely out of sight above the top of the proscenium and be concealed by it when the curtain is not needed. In order to mask overhead lighting positions in the first opening, however, a black portal border will be required. Not only will the portal border hide the electrics in the first opening, it will also hide the batten pipe of the portal legs. The legs will frame the sides of the proscenium opening, and prevent the audience close to the stage from seeing the first sidelight booms and the backstage.

All of this is leading to the first decision, choosing which soft goods will be hung on lineset #1. While it may not seem that important, for shows that need a "fast curtain," what gets hung on lineset #1 can have a huge impact. Figure 5.4A shows a closeup of the top of the proscenium and the first three linesets, looking stage left. The lighter-shaded rectangle is the top of the proscenium opening; the darker-shaded rectangle is the solid thickness of the top of the proscenium arch. The right-hand vertical line is the black portal border, hung on lineset #1 and trimmed to 20'-0". The main curtain is hung on lineset #2, and the portal legs are hung on lineset #3. The dotted diagonal lines are sightlines. In this configuration, when the main curtain flies out, it's bottom will "disappear" above sightlines, when it clears above 21'-8". If the goods on the first two linesets are switched, the impact is potentially dramatic.

Figure 5.4B shows the main curtain hung on lineset #1 and the portal border hung on lineset #2. The main will be visible as soon as it descends below the top of the proscenium; it will then have to lower an additional 8'-4" from that moment until it actually begins to vertically cut off the visual view of the stage. Since the director asked for a fast curtain at the end of "Crankyland" in Act 2, the hang plot will be arranged so that the portal border is on lineset #1, while the main curtain is moved to lineset #2.

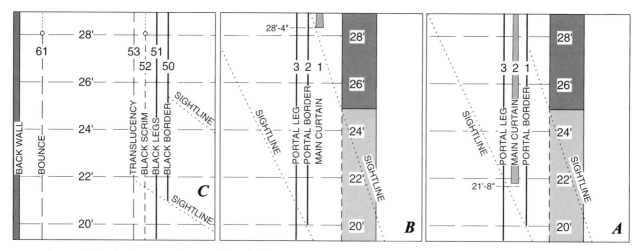

Figure 5.4 Preliminary Section: A) and B) Perimeter Scenery Downstage, and C) Perimeter Scenery Upstage

Now that the downstage portal and main curtain have been temporarily designated, the next step is to define the upstage edge and light line of the performance space by assigning the soft goods that fall under the heading of the **scenic stack**. In this case that will include the black scrim, the white translucency, and the bounce. For some, it also includes the masking that conceals the edges of these goods. In any event, a scenic stack using a trans and a bounce typically requires at least 3 feet between the two goods in order for the light projected in between to diffuse enough and cover the back surface of the trans with a universal intensity. Some designers feel that, depending on the instrumentation used, 3 feet may still be an insufficient gap between the two. If the distance between the goods isn't sufficient, the light can't "break up" enough. The result is often a hot streak across the bottom and top of the goods, and a darker area that then runs across the middle of the trans or the cyc. This horizontal dark streak is known as "the black band." Lighting designers strive to avoid the black band for several reasons: one, if the bottom horizontal stripe is too bright, the contrast between it and the performers adjacent to it can make it difficult to focus on the performers. Two, if the top horizontal stripe is too bright, the audience's eye will be subconsciously drawn up to it, and away from the performers down on the stage. Three, the visual and conceptual objective of a translucency is to create a uniformly-lit glowing rectangle, a "living presence" in the performance space. When properly focused, that even distribution of light, making the entire surface a shadowbox, is consistent no matter how dim or bright the intensity upstage of it.

When young designers first encounter the black band, their initial reaction to eliminate it is to brighten the light intensity between the goods. Typically the only thing this "quick-fix" achieves is make the hot streaks of light at the top and the bottom of the goods brighter and more distracting. The real solutions to eliminating the black band include refocusing the striplights, altering the light output with additional diffusions, increasing the distance between the two sets of goods, or adding additional rows of lights focused into the middle of the bounce. Inevitably, all these solutions take some amount of experimentation, time, and resources.

When the overall depth needs of the scenic stack are pondered, another factor to consider is the need for onstage performers' crossover. In order for a performer to enter from either side of the stage, he or she must have a path somewhere in the theatre in order to do so. Some venues are designed with a hallway immediately upstage of the back wall. More confined theatres are designed with a staircase on either side of the stage, and passage through the trap room underneath. For quick exits and entrances, either of these arrangements can result in scenarios involving wild offstage sprints by performers matched with choreography by the backstage crew to keep their passage absolutely clear. To keep passage time to a minimum, the best solution is to provide performers space upstage of the bounce drop, so they don't have to leave the stage in order to get to the other side.

How much space? Performer thickness aside, the bounce usually has to be placed at least 1'-6" to 2'-0" downstage of the back wall. If there are quick crossovers, the wind current caused by one person running behind the bounce is still enough to see the "light ripple" on the translucency. When that can't be avoided, one solution is to install another piece of soft goods on a separate batten immediately upstage of the bounce. Usually, this is a heavy set of soft goods, like a black velour drop. Once in place, it's then added to the lineset schedule as the "windbreak" lineset.

In the case of *Hokey* at the Hybrid Theatre, the problem is depth. If the 3'-0" depth required for the scenic stack goods is placed 2'-0" from the back wall, the black legs framing the downstage side of the goods will be approximately 25'-0" upstage of plaster line. Since the portal leg is at 2'-0", that reduces the playing depth down to 23'-0", which is significantly less than the 28'-0" the director and choreographer requested. In order to get the process moving, the decision is to made to place the translucency on lineset #53 at 27'-0". The black scrim will then be placed on the next line downstage, lineset #52, and the black legs will be hung on #51, 26'-0" from plaster line. Figure 5.4C shows this initial, temporary placement of the scenic stack.

In this configuration, the playing depth is only 24'-0". While this doesn't fulfill the artistic team's depth request, following this path will hopefully lead to one plan that will work. Once a working plan is developed, it can be analyzed, adjusted, or adapted. An onstage meeting to view the taped-out groundplan might be in order so that everyone can see the challenges involved. The next step toward creating that potential working plan is to place the intermediate black masking legs. Their addition will then define the number of openings to the stage, and provide a more complete picture about the entire scenic and masking arrangement.

Leg Analysis

The process of placing the legs and borders during the masking design process is a delicate balance. On the one hand, the concept is to hide the backstage area and create room to conceal overhead electrics and unused scenic goods. At the same time, the spatial design must include enough room on the deck for all of the equipment, and still allow performers and everything else to get on or off the stage.

While the borders can be placed in any number of different arrangements, their main purpose is to hide the overhead electrics, the leg battens, and any remaining battens for flying scenery. While that's important, their placement doesn't directly impact the flow of the show. The placement of the legs is what really defines the traffic patterns on and off the stage. The number and depth of each opening directly affects the choreography or blocking—not so much specific onstage movements, but instead the broader concept of how performers, props, or scenery enter and exit the performance area. The leg placement can also influence the number of electrics, the speed of transitions, and the general safety on the stage, especially during a hectic production.

If there are not enough openings, sightlines looking offstage may see lighting booms and the entire backstage area. If there are too many, they may be too "thin," and performers can accidentally run into each other or gear that's then in the way. Too many openings can also cause performer confusion, resulting in other collisions caused by choosing the wrong opening during the course of a show. If sidelight booms are part of the lighting design, each one can easily become a traffic impediment. The boom usually doesn't move, so the performer traffic pattern, and the boom placement, must be carefully negotiated in each opening.

There's also the question of equality: does each opening need to be the same depth? Some dance companies, for example, firmly enforce that the first and last leg opening depth be 8', for example, while the intermediary openings can be an equal division of whatever is left over. The leg openings reflect the needs of the choreography and performance patterns for those particular companies—they have more people and scenery designed to get on and off the stage in the four corners of the performance area, rather than in the middle of each side. Other dance companies strive to make all of their leg opening depths equidistant, so that the performers have the same spatial sense of their surroundings, regardless of which opening is being used for passage. Other situations call for the downstage leg openings to get progressively thinner; this acknowledges the near audience sightlines and attempts to place the legs so that additional masking isn't required.

From an electrical point of view, the number of leg openings is another case of delicate balance. More leg openings often translate into the need for more overhead electrics to provide smooth upstage-downstage lighting system coverage. When low sidelight washes need to be consistent over the depth of the stage, each opening usually demands a separate sidelight boom, with a matching instrument for each system on each one. As a general rule of thumb, fewer leg openings translate to fewer sidelight booms. If there are too few booms, however, the light beams may not be able to spread wide enough, resulting in upstage-downstage gaps in the coverage.

Finally, from the scenic point of view, having less masking and electrics in the air means there's more room for the scenery. In this Hybrid Theatre fly system, a portal, consisting of a pair of legs and a border on two adjacent linesets, requires 6" of depth. An overhead electric typically requires at least 18" of depth and, if accessories like barndoors are used, may need additional air space on either side of it. An average performance space designed with four openings and six electrics, then, roughly requires 14'-0" of overall depth just for the electrics and masking (6 elec × 2'-0″ deep + 4 portals × 6″ deep). In a proscenium production, that leaves about 10'-0″ of available depth which translates to about 21 linesets. If scenic legs are considered as part of the design, standard operating procedure is to assign a pair downstage of each set of masking legs. In a four opening setup, three sets of scenic legs then translates into 6'-0″ of depth (3 sets = 1'-6″ deep × 4 sets). If any hard flying scenery is thicker than 6″, it may invalidate the adjacent lineset. The amount of available space in the air can get quickly eaten up, and while budgets play a role defining the amount of masking, scenery, or electrics available to any production, the available depth in any venue must eventually be taken into account.

In this case, both the choreographer and the director requested that the opening depths be equal. Based on that, if the overall depth is approximately 24'-0″, then a three-opening arrangement would imply 8'-0″ deep openings. A four-opening setup would translate to 6'-0″ deep openings, and a five-opening setup would mean the legs would be hung on 4'-6″ or 5'-0″ centers. While these potential leg arrangements can be compared in sectional view, grasping the spatial repercussions of these choices can only be fully understood by also looking at the groundplan. Only then is it possible to understand how the relative opening depths relate to the near orchestra sightlines, and what impact that has on the need for any additional masking, the on- and offstage traffic patterns, and any other relationships. The next step is to construct the preliminary groundplan.

THE PRELIMINARY GROUNDPLAN

The preliminary groundplan is the other primary document drawn in the preparation to create a lighting design. Its intent is to provide a basic framework of spatial information, and display the parameters that exist before scenery or lighting is added to the production. Like the preliminary section, this includes the main architectural features of the venue, the permanent hanging locations downstage and upstage of plaster line, the lineset placements, and the extreme sightlines of the audience.

The groundplan for a proscenium theatre is almost always drawn from a viewing plane above the theatre while facing the stage. This orientation often matches the same viewpoint used by the scenic designer to show the spatial placement of the scenery. The bottom of the document typically represents the audience, while the top of the document indicates the back wall or the farthest applicable upstage area away from the proscenium. This orientation is typically used for thrust configurations as well. Arena groundplans are another thing altogether, and are often based on previous drawings of the space or placement of the tech table.

While the preliminary section focused mainly on the relative heights involved in the production, the groundplan's focus is targeted on relative footprints. Once initial scenery and masking have been added to the document, it's often referred to as the **preliminary scenic groundplan** (or groundplans for multi-scene shows). Once any production elements start getting added to the document, notes containing the acronym "TBA" (To Be Announced) start being added as well, which is designer-speak for "we don't know yet."

In some cases, coordination between the lighting and scene designer may result in a preliminary scenic groundplan that indicates not only all of the scenic and masking information, but temporary lighting positions as well. Without the lighting designer's involvement or approval, however, that information isn't taken in earnest. Once the lighting designer has added or approved the lighting decisions and information that has been added to the document, it then begins to take shape as the **preliminary light plot**.

Information Included on a Preliminary Groundplan

The purpose of the preliminary groundplan is to communicate spatial information and relationships of all other elements to all departments from an overhead viewpoint (and once again, selfishly, as they'll relate to the lighting design.) The following basic information should be represented on the groundplan for a proscenium theatre to allow for rapid comprehension of the drawing by any observer:

- The clearly-marked intersection between centerline and plaster line (or whatever is being used instead of plaster line).
- Lineset schedule with relative distances from plaster line.
- FOH notations and/or measurements for edge of stage, sightlines, all lighting positions.
- Depth and width measurements to back wall and all other protuberances surrounding the performance space.
- Centerline to both sides: proscenium, end of battens, side wall.
- Dimensioned masking goods.
- Scenic groundplan information for each scene.
- Title block (with scene-identification labels).
- Contact information for all relevant parties.

The Preliminary Groundplan: Basic Drawing

The preliminary groundplan is created in three steps. Using all available information, horizontal and vertical coordinates are drawn, double-checked, and then joined to create the scaled drawing. For clarity, the illustrations will show these lines properly spaced in the three steps to quickly create the overall picture.

Step 1: Draft the Rough Outlines

The left-hand side of Figure 5.5 shows the horizontal placement of the vertical lines that will be used to create the preliminary groundplan of the Hybrid Theatre: stage right and stage left. Draw the first vertical line in the middle of the drafting surface and define that as centerline, one half of groundplan zero-zero. Now draw the left-hand column of lines or tic marks relative to centerline, on the left-hand side (stage right) of the page. Next the second column of lines or tic marks can be made relative to centerline, on the right-hand (stage left) side of the page. When completed, those vertical lines will resemble Figure 5.6A.

Next, the horizontal lines will be added. The right-hand column of Figure 5.5 lists the vertical placement of the horizontal lines: stage right, center, and stage left. Draw the first line and define that as plaster line, the other half of groundplan zero-zero.

Now draw the following lines or tic marks relative to that line (positive to the algebraic "over" or above, negative to the algebraic "under" or below). When completed, those added lines resemble Figure 5.6B. Now some quick drafting and a little artistic license will clean this up.

- The lines are shortened, joined, and shaded to show the preliminary shape of the architecture.
- The sightlines are given circle outlines so they can be seen.
- The front edge of the stage and the orchestra pit is shaped.

The result is the general shapes and outlines shown in Figure 5.6C. The basic outlines and shapes for the groundplan are now complete.

Step 2: Fill in Information Upstage of Plaster line

The next step is to draw the current masking positions upstage of plaster line. First, this means drafting the location of each lineset relative to plaster line. This is one moment when CAD drafting can be an advantage; copy the lineset schedule box from the section, and paste that into the groundplan. The box then includes the lineset number, the distance from plaster line, and a placeholder for the trim height and the goods. After rotation, the box is aligned so that

HORIZONTAL PLACEMENT of VERTICAL LINES				VERTICAL PLACEMENT of HORIZONTAL LINES				
SR	SL	Distance	Measuring Point	SR	C	SL	Distance	Measuring Point
		0' 0"	**Centerline**	x		x	32' 0"	Back Wall
x	x	19' 0"	Proscenium Opening	x			30' 3"	US Side of Lock Rail
x		20' 4"	USR Onstage Door			x	30' 6"	USL US Side of Door
x	x	21' 0"	Batten Ends			x	27' 6"	USL DS Side of Door
x	x	22' 6"	Offstage Side Pros Opening	x		x	16' 5"	US Side of Side Wall Columns
x		28' 0"	USR Offstage Door	x		x	14' 5"	DS Side of Side Wall Columns
x		28' 0"	Locking Rail			x	3' 9"	DSL US Door
x		32' 6"	SR Onstage Columns	x			1' 6"	DS side of Lock Rail
x		33' 4"	SR Offstage Columns (SR Wall)			x	1' 3"	DSL DS Door
	x	26' 9"	SL Onstage Columns	x	x	x	0' 0"	**Plaster line**
	x	28' 0"	SL Offstage Column (SL Wall)			**DS of PLASTER LINE**		
		DS of PLASTER LINE				x	-1' 6"	SL Back of Proscenium
x	x	18' 3"	Near Orchestra Sightline	x		x	-1' 6"	Downstage Side of Pros
x	x	21' 0"	Offstage Edge Butts into DS Pros	x			-3' 4"	SR Back of Proscenium
x	x	21' 10"	Offstage Edge of Orchestra Wall		x		-5' 0"	Front Edge of the Stage
x	x	6' 0"	Onstage Truss Holes	x		x	-8' 6"	Near Orchestra Sightline
x	x	14' 0"	Offstage Truss Holes		x		-11' 6"	Upstage Side of Orchestra Wall
x	x	20' 6"	Box boom Near Vertical	x		x	-11' 9"	Box Boom Near Vertical
x	x	25' 6"	Box Boom Far Vertical	x		x	-19' 9"	Box Boom Far Vertical
x	x	29' 6"	Balcony @ Side Wall Architecture		x		-26' 6"	Truss Holes in the Ceiling
x	x	27' 0"	Ceiling Cove		x		-34' 0"	Center of the Balcony Rail
x	x	6' 0"	Spot Booth	x	x	x	-47' 9"	Ceiling Cove
					x		-65' 0"	Spot Booth

Figure 5.5 Preliminary Groundplan Measurements

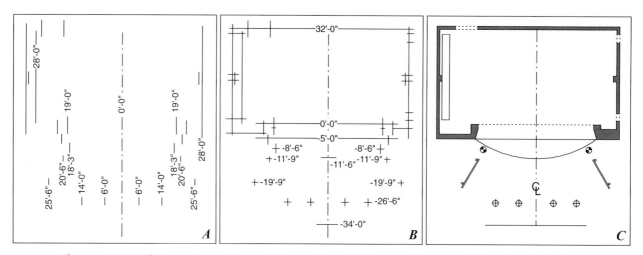

Figure 5.6 Preliminary Groundplan: A) Vertical Lines, B) Horizontal Lines, and C) the Rough Outlines

the middle of the "plaster line" rectangle is vertically bisected by the dashed plaster line, and the onstage side of the box is aligned with the 28'-0" measurement for the onstage edge of the locking rail, illustrated by Figure 5.7A. The onstage placement of the lineset schedule box is a relatively standard drafting procedure. In addition to listing information closer to the battens, the box also then acts as a visual boundary, spatially reinforcing the fact that the stage level stops at that point in the physical groundplan.

The next step is to indicate the left-to-right information relative to centerline. The battens are 42'-0" long, so Figure 5.7B shows one of two vertical dashed lines drawn 21'-0" on either side of centerline as a yardstick, indicating the end of the battens. A dotted vertical line is also drawn 18'-0" on either side of centerline to indicate the onstage edge of the masking legs (that will create the 36'-0" wide leg opening). Tracing these two lines, it becomes apparent that the battens are short—on one side of center-

line, they're only 2' longer than the proscenium is wide. While the black legs reduce the opening width to 36'-0", that's still leaves only 3' of batten available to tie the soft goods on before the end of the pipe. In order to use black masking legs that are wider than 3', the solution chosen is to add pipe extensions onto the ends of the battens. During the site survey it was confirmed that the battens are pipes without plugs at the ends. Additional pieces of 1½" pipe with sleeved pieces of 1¼" pipe welded into them are one common method used to extend the battens farther offstage. The house carpenter confirms that 3' pipe extensions have been safely installed and rigged in the past, so the legs will be drawn 6'-0" long.

With that in mind, the downstage perimeter scenic information is traced in. For the time being, the black portal border on line 1 and the main curtain on line 2 will not be traced, in order to focus on the horizontal masking. Instead, the 6'-0" long stage right portal leg is drawn

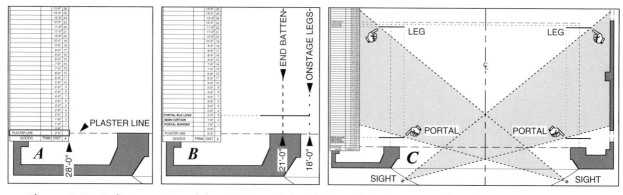

Figure 5.7 Preliminary Groundplan: A) Lineset Schedule Box, B) the Batten Length and Leg Opening Lines, and C) Perimeter Scenic Goods Placement

2'-0' upstage of plaster line, starting at 18'-0" from centerline. The leg is drawn offstage of the 18'-0" batten end line because the fabric will be tied to the sleeved pipe extensions. A short dashed "leader line" connects the offstage end of the leg to the lineset schedule box. (Leader lines are a theatrical drafting standard visually connecting two things, in this case the offstage ends of goods to their respective lineset.)

Figure 5.7C shows the entire stage, with the upstage pair of black legs and the rest of the scenic stack drawn in. Two lightweight-dashed sightlines are drawn from each of the near orchestra sightline points to the opposite wall. The shaded triangle, between each pair of lines, illustrates that sightline's horizontal field of view. Currently each one is seeing an unencumbered view of the opposite backstage wall, cut off only by the black legs (highlighted by the pointing fingers); the *onstage* edge of the portal leg and the *offstage* edge of the final black leg. The purpose of side masking is to stop either sightline from seeing *any* portion of the backstage wall on the opposite side. The groundplan is now ready to analyze different ways and methods to achieve that.

Step 3: Define Scenic Masking

Figure 5.8 highlights the stage left side of potential masking. The proscenium is at the bottom of the illustration, while the offstage edges of the black scrim and the translucency can be seen at the top of the drawing. The top of Figure 5.8A shows the basic "straight-leg" technique to construct horizontal masking, starting with the fifth black leg. A dotted sightline (1) is drawn from the sightline point to the fifth black leg's offstage edge. The point where the sightline crosses the vertical 18'-0" leg opening line (pointed finger) marks the onstage edge of the fourth leg (2). After that leg is placed, another dotted sightline is drawn to the offstage edge of the fourth leg (3), and the third leg is placed (4). This process is repeated for the entire depth of the stage, with adjustments later being made so that the leg actually "lands" on the measured placement of an overhead batten.

One variation to this technique is demonstrated at the bottom of Figure 5.8A, using the first and second leg. This "angle-leg" technique twists the offstage edge of the legs almost perpendicular to the sightlines. A dotted sightline (5) is drawn from the sightline point to the third black leg's offstage edge. The point where the sightline crosses the vertical 18'-0" leg opening line marks the onstage edge of the second leg (6). After that leg is placed, another dotted sightline is drawn to the offstage edge of the second leg (7), and the first leg is placed (8). While this technique uses fewer legs, there are also some downsides; only a few 42'-0" battens (and

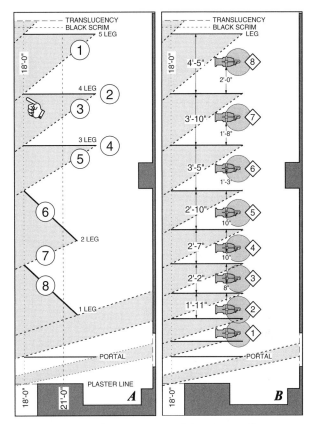

Figure 5.8 Preliminary Groundplan: Two Different Masking Techniques

borders) will be able to easily fly in around these angled legs, and hiding the angled leg battens can be very difficult. In addition, there's very little passage room for rapid performer access, there's very little room for sidelight booms, and any low sidelight splashing onto the legs will clearly be seen from the audience, along with any performers' shadows.

In order to use any low-mounted sidelight boom instruments on an open stage and *not* clearly see performers' shadows on the opposite side, the straight-leg technique is the usual choice. That's the leg masking technique that will be used for *Hokey*. The next step is to determine how many legs will be required to fully mask the depth of the stage.

Figure 5.8B fully applies the initial "straight-leg" masking technique to this situation. Starting upstage, the intersection of each sightline to the 18'-0" leg opening line has defined the onstage placement for each successive leg. As a result, the sides of the stage have been successfully masked; the side view looking backstage is completely blocked except for a small gap downstage of the portal leg. This plan requires ten pairs of legs that are spaced closer together downstage (the leg opening gets thinner) in order to account for the angle change from the sightline.

A basic sidelight boom, concealed from the audience, has also been included in each opening. Each boom is drawn as an instrument attached to a vertical piece of pipe with a sidearm. The large circle under the instrument represents a 50-pound boom base. While there's 2'-10" of clearance on either side of the eighth boom in the final opening, there are only 8" on either side of the boom in the third opening. For a typical open stage design, almost any lighting designer would pronounce that this plan uses too many legs, has too many openings, and has inadequate offstage traffic space.

Since *Hokey* is planned to have constant activity in the wings, other masking alternatives need to be considered. After checking the one-on-one meeting notes with the director and choreographer, there doesn't seem to be a clear sense of one set of openings having more traffic, and requiring more depth, than any other. In lieu of a clear-cut direction saying otherwise, leg configurations with equal depth will be considered.

Figure 5.9A shows two intermediate black masking legs, equally spaced to create three 8'-0" deep openings. The diagonal sightlines highlight the shaded fields of view, which are now reduced to

unencumbered views of the backstage area. Sidelight booms are shown in each opening.

Figure 5.9A show that while 1 boom left is in partial view from the sightline, 2 boom left, 3 boom left, and the backstage wall are in clear view by a large portion of the audience. While most observers would declare these sightlines fairly abysmal, there's almost 6'-0" of room around the booms tucked into the corners of the openings, and over 3'-0" of room on either side of the 2 boom placed in the middle of an opening.

Figure 5.9B shows another version of masking using four intermediate black masking legs. This creates five 5'-0" deep openings (ok, the fifth opening is only 4'-0" deep). While the third, fourth, and fifth booms are relatively concealed from the opposite sightline, the 1 and 2 booms are still fairly well in view. The amount of traffic space around the first and fifth booms has been reduced to less than 3'-0", and the amount of room on either side of the intermediate booms is down to 1'-3". With clearance that tight, typical performance conditions strongly suggest that the side shutters on almost any low-hung boom instrument will get smacked. For that matter, any low-hung instrument on any boom runs the risk of becoming a performer's safety hazard.

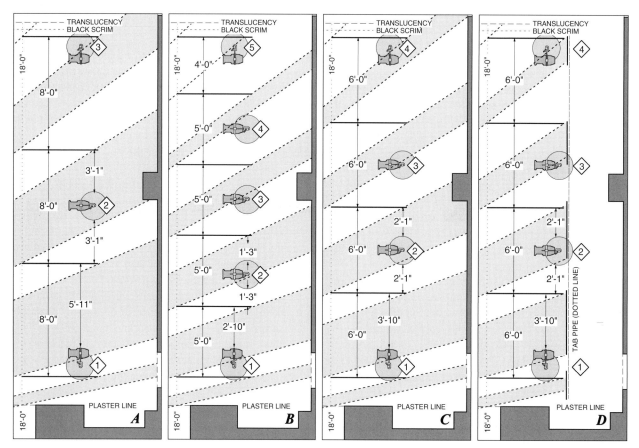

Figure 5.9 Preliminary Groundplan: A) Three Leg Opening, B) Five Leg Opening, C) Four Leg Opening, and D) Four Leg Opening with Tabs

Figure 5.9C shows the stage left wings with three intermediate black masking legs, creating four 6'-0" deep openings. The sightlines show that the backstage wall and the 1 and 2 booms are still fairly exposed. But the traffic space around the first and fourth booms has been increased to almost 4'-0", while the amount of room on either side of the two intermediate booms is now over 2'-0". Presuming that there are not huge amounts of scenery or costumes passing through these openings, the 6'-0" deep version appears to be the best solution. In order to keep the backstage concealed, however, one solution is to hang a **tab pipe** offstage of the batten extensions. Figure 5.9D illustrates the position of five tab curtains hung from this offstage pipe, which then stops the sightline's ability to see the backstage wall. When this tab-pipe method is chosen to visually "seal off" the backstage area from the audience, it's more quickly installed when the legs tied onto the tab pipe are all the same height.

While none of these proposals provides perfect masking, Figure 5.9D conceals the backstage area, provides for some amount of performer traffic on- and offstage, along with performer traffic backstage. Installing the batten extensions and the tab pipes will require some amount of additional time, materials, and labor. Once installed, however, *Hokey* will be adequately masked.

Step 4: Transfer Leg Locations to Section

Now that the final leg positions have been determined, their locations can be transferred back to the preliminary section. Figure 5.10A shows the legs drawn in on lines 15, 27, and 39. In order to make sure that both the legs and tabs are tall enough to extend above any vertical sightlines, 30'-0" tall goods have been spec'd.

Standard masking procedure is to assign a black masking border on the first lineset immediately downstage of each leg batten. Doing so insures that, no matter what other scenic or masking issues take place, the leg system pipes will always be concealed. If painted legs are part of the scenic design, those are often installed on their own linesets immediately downstage of the black masking legs and the black border is bumped to the next lineset downstage, shown in Figure 5.10B.

Sometimes assigning black borders downstage of each set of legs may seem excessive, but they can always be flown out or removed later. At this preliminary stage, before everything is known, it's wise to assign a black border to the adjacent lineset immediately downstage of each leg batten. To maintain flexibility, a common tactic is to specify all of the borders with a matching height. Borders are manufactured at a variety of heights, and some are tall enough to be used as full blackout drops. In this case, all of the borders will be spec'd at 10'-0" tall until the final section has been approved. When they're ordered from the rental house, the borders will be spec'd with three additional conditions: they'll be flat (without fullness sewn in), they'll have a pipe pocket (to allow them to be weighted), and they'll extend the full width of the masked performance space (in this case from the offstage edge of one leg to the other, around 47'-0"). Rounding up, the goods will be ordered 50'-0" long. Since they're longer than

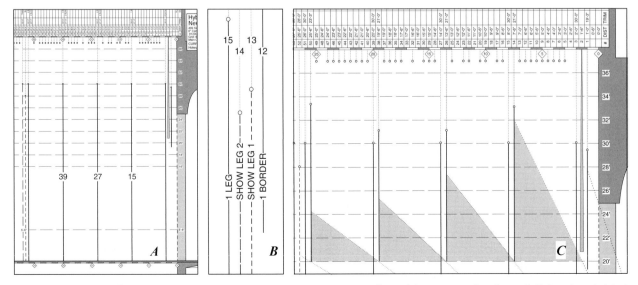

Figure 5.10 Preliminary Section: A) Four Leg Opening, B) Hypothecial Scenic Leg Stack, and C) Borders Added to the Four Legs

the system battens, additional pipe extensions will be needed from the scene shop. Based on the scenic designer's note, all of the borders will initially be drawn in the section with the bottom trimming at 20'-0" above the stage. Figure 5.10C shows the borders added in, sightlines added, and shaded triangles to initially show the viewing area seen from the audience.

Now that the preliminary masking has been designed and drawn into both the section and groundplan, the next step is to create the third graphic drawing that will become a primary reference document used to construct the lighting systems: the front elevation.

THE FRONT ELEVATION

When the preliminary section and groundplan are being created, the draftsperson typically pays a little more attention to both their layout and arrangement. For good reason: in their final form, they both become core documents in the paperwork packets, and vital visual references throughout the installation of the lighting package. For that reason, as both documents are created, some attention is paid to be certain they don't ultimately appear sloppy, and to make certain they're not missing any important information.

The **front elevation**, on the other hand, is the "ugly step child" of the trio. The front elevation is the preliminary document (or series of documents) that never needs to worry about looking presentable in any way (other than possibly at a union exam). It's usually a series of quick sketches that will rarely, if ever, be seen by any other eyes other than the lighting designer's, or at best by the lighting designer's internal staff. No title block, no keys, no legend. Its sole purpose is to quickly provide information.

Reference Information for a Front Elevation

The measurement information required to draft an accurate front elevation includes:

- The stage level.
- The relative vertical height of the focus point (+5'-6"), the border trim (+20'-0"), and the proscenium (+25'-0").
- The horizontal width of the leg opening (36'-0") and the proscenium (38'-0").

The Front Elevation: Basic Drawing

For the purposes of this book, the front elevation will be drawn with the lines properly spaced to quickly create the overall picture. First, the horizontal lines will be drawn.

Figure 5.11A shows the vertical placement of the horizontal lines that will be used to create the front elevation. Draw the first horizontal line and define that as the stage, half of the sectional zero-zero. Now draw the dashed line at 5'-6" and the other two lines to define the border trim and the proscenium height.

Figure 5.11B shows the horizontal placement of the vertical lines; the centerline is drawn first. Then the leg lines and proscenium lines are drawn at 18'-0" and 19'-0" on either side of centerline, respectively. Now some quick drafting and a little artistic license will clean this up.

- The lines are shortened, joined, and shaded to show the preliminary shape of the architecture.
- The internal lines are shortened, joined, and shaded to show the shape of the masking.

The result is shown in Figure 5.11C. The basic outlines and shapes required to provide front elevation information are now complete.

Now that the front elevation has been constructed, the preliminary draftings are complete, and the next steps can be taken toward constructing the lighting systems for the *Hokey* light plot.

DEFINE THE *HOKEY* LIGHTING SYSTEMS

Now that all of the research is complete, the parameters known, and an understanding of the final appearance and objectives of the production at hand,

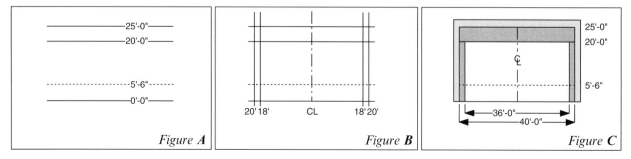

Figure 5.11 The Front Elevation: A) Horizontal Lines, B) Vertical Lines, and C) the Rough Outlines

the lighting systems for *Hokey* can be defined. This fundamental phase of the design process is usually accomplished in three steps.

For many designers, the first step started with the construction of the **cue master**, which provided a list of sequential lighting changes and individual pictures during the course of the show. The summation of the visual components needed to create those pictures has then been compiled into the **systems and specials sheet**, listing the recipes of colors, systems, directions of origin, and ideas used to visually construct each scene. As the research, meetings, and collaboration have refined this production, both of these documents have been constantly updated, scrutinized, and compared to see which colors, systems, or specials are used in different scenes. While updating these documents takes time, they're both different visual diaries, reflecting both the specific and the general overall plans that will be used to construct the light plot.

The second step in this phase adjusts the focus to the big picture, the systems and specials sheet. Since it provides the global view of all the washes and specials used in the entire production, the completed systems and specials sheet is distilled and condensed, so that all of the recipes currently envisioned for the entire show can be seen in one place. This sheet is used to keep track of the systems, as they're constructed. When constraints appear during the plotting process (instruments, dimmers, circuits, etc.), this document allows the designer to prioritize and make choices about what needs to be retained, amended, or cut to create the strongest and most functional light plot for the show.

The third step adds the third core design document, the **preliminary magic sheet**. As the recipes of the systems and specials have developed, this document has graphically reflected the amount of control separation required by each one of them. A color wash covering the entire stage may require only a single channel of control, for example. It may be possible to achieve that coverage using only three instruments controlled by one dimmer. A second color wash, covering the same amount of stage space, may require the stage to be broken into six areas to achieve the pictures in the recipes. That wash will then require at least six instruments in order to provide the proper separation of control. These numeric combinations and labels are the **channel hookup**, which can be arranged and analyzed in rough spreadsheets that eventually become the **cheat sheet**.

Step 1: Systems and Specials Analysis

Based on the meetings, everyone agrees that the overall lighting for *Hokey* is going to be "cartoon-ish," colorful, and not completely realistic. But there has to be skin tone, some amount of naturalism; lead performer's faces cannot be bright pink or green. Based on that statement, the performers in *Hokey* will be lit with a combination of pastels and saturated colors. The pastels will be facial tints coming from the front at a higher angle so they produce natural-angled area light. High sidelight will also have pastel tints, possibly slightly different, to provide color variation. Mid- and low sidelight will reiterate those skin tint colors.

Saturates will originate from high-angle systems in the overhead, pointing down to color the floor. Low saturates will originate from side booms and color in the shadows in the performer's costumes. Saturates will be plotted from the angled box boom positions, which are also lower than the truss position used for the frontlight.

Figure 5.12 shows the condensed systems and specials sheet, which has now been distilled to list only the color systems used to create the light plot. It's divided into broad categories of frontlight, sidelight, overhead light, and cyc light.

FRONT	COLOR	SIDE	COLOR	OVER	COLOR	CYC	COLOR
Warm Front	R33	Hi Sd Warm	R51	Warm	R20	Top 1	NC
Cool Front	L161	Hi Sd Cool	R64	Cool	G850	Top 2	R20
Autoyoke	Scroll	Color Scroller	8	Rock	Lav	Top 3	G850
		Template	L201	Red	R26?		
BxBm 1	R51			Tee-boo	Green	Bottom 1	Red
BxBm 2	R64	Head Hi Warm	R51	NC Tops	NC	Bottom 2	Blue
BxBm 3	L116	Head Hi Cool	R64			Bottom 3	Green
BxBm 4	R44	Blue Mid	G850	Specials DS	NC		
BxBm 5	Temp	Green Mid	L116	Specials CC	3-NC		
						Pit 1	L201
Bal Rail Drp 1	G945	Color Scroller	8			Pit 2	R73
Bal Rail Drp 2	G850	Template	R60	Strobes		Pit 3	R26
Bal Rail Drp 3	Temp	Pyro	DSL	Hazer			

Figure 5.12 The Condensed Systems and Specials Sheet for *Hokey*

The drawings for the Hybrid Theatre and the site survey confirmed that there's some amount of rake in the orchestra seating. Everyone in both the balcony and the orchestra is going to see the floor. The best bet to color it will be using overhead backlight and downlight systems: warm for the wedding and the dawn (R20), cool for the night scenes (Gam 850), green for Tee-boo (Lee 124), and lavender for the Rock (Gam 945). In order to desaturate all of those colors, and provide a system of special pools, a No Color system will also be included, presumably as one of the downlight systems.

The cue master shows that the performance will begin with Pookie in 4 Left. While her placement might seem ideal in a down pool, I suspect her final placement will change once we get into the theatre. I also get the feeling that she won't remain static all that long. A high sidelight pipe end special will provide a more side-to-side coverage, without seeing the source of light as strongly bounce off the floor. For that matter, I'm inclined to expand that focus and create an entire high side pipe end system; it's a good stage wash that provides dimensionality using relatively few lighting instruments. It can be initially used as the rest of the company enters and joins Pookie. Since there's so much skin exposed outside of the costumes, and so much action upstage of any frontlight cutoff points, the pipe ends will be colored in a light lavender tint, Roscolux 51. Because of the number of night scenes I intend to match the pipe end system with a desaturated blue, covering the entire stage in Roscolux 64. Those colors will be repeated in the head high instruments on the boom, at least for the first act of the show. In addition to those two systems, a third system of high sidelights will be plotted with color scrollers. They can be used to provide saturated punch from the high side as well.

Presuming that the high side systems work later in the plotting process, the same position could also be used for a template system. Templates will be needed for the night scenes, and can also be used to provide dimensionality and break up the light in other scenes.

While the skin tone from the high side will be the light lavender, the frontlight will be a light pink tint, Roscolux 33, to provide a color contrast between the two systems. Likewise, the cool frontlight will be a slightly different tint of blue, Lee 161. Both of these colors appear to work well with the costume swatches. Mainly due to the director's request to keep the lighting clean and maintain the black surround, the frontlight will be plotted as straight frontlight. Any angled frontlight runs more of a risk of causing performer's shadows on the black masking legs. In addition to followspots, there will be three frontlight specials on Autoyokes hung on the truss to provide frontlight specials. They'll also be equipped with a color scroller.

The box boom position is a little lower than the frontlight truss. Some skin tone pastel systems will be included, along with some saturated colors for Tee-boo (Lee 116), the Knotty Piners (Roscolux 44), and a general template breakup to provide more dimensionality. There will be a two-color drop wash on the balcony rail, along with a template breakup system, for the rock drop. The orchestra pit will also contain color systems used to illuminate the Precipice of Doom in Act 3.

The trans will be lit by LED striplights on the bottom, so that conceivably any color can be created. The overhead strip lights will fill in day, night, and a neutral No Color wash.

Special gear will also include strobe lights and pyro, used mainly for Tee-boo's entrance and the kidnap scene. Haze will become very important during the night scenes and the battle. If there's enough room on the overhead electrics, a system of moving lights from either the back or down positions will help provide additional color, punch, and flash.

Step 2: Preliminary Magic Sheet

From an abstract perspective, the ebb or flow of a lighting system's growth can be a compelling personal observation. For example, the center-center front special, noted in the Act 1, scene 1 wedding, is presently listed as a high-angle frontlight from the 1st Electric. As the systems and specials sheet for the entire show is reviewed, it may become apparent that the high-angle frontlight, or that color, may be called for in similar specials around other areas of the stage. Eventually that color or angle may spawn an entirely new multi-instrument system covering the first zone, which might conceivably expand to the entire performance area. Comparing the complete sheet allows the designer to remember how the system came to be, and how each component's function will perform.

Consider another example: the green stage wash originally earmarked for Tee-boo (Figure 5.13A) any time he's onstage, is then noted as possibly being "segmented" and "infection spreads w/his entrance?" with his entrance in Act 1, scene 2. As Tee-boo enters, the warm color of the floor might slowly cross-fade into green from one side of the stage to the other, spreading across the stage after his entrance (Figure 5.13B). That system, which initially had been considered a single-channel stage wash, might slowly be broken apart and assigned to upstage/downstage stripes of control, in order to cross-fade in that manner. Channel 1 is assigned to his entrance, then 1A

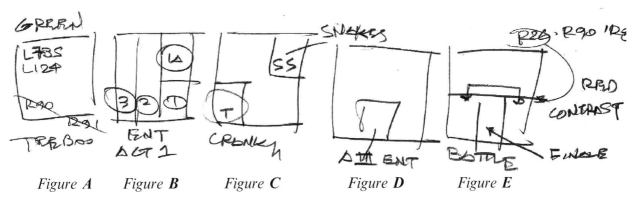

Figure A   Figure B   Figure C   Figure D   Figure E

Figure 5.13 The Development of Tee-boo's Green Wash

cross-fades upstage of him, then the channel 2 stripe, and finally the channel 3 stripe to complete the stage wash's color change to green. In order to realize this series of light changes, the warm backlight system, in place before this transition, may then need to match the segmentation control pattern.

If there are other scenes where single areas of the stage highlight Tee-boo's location on stage—if everywhere he goes, in any scene, that portion of the stage goes green (Figure 5.13C for "Crankyland" and 5.13D for his entrance in Act 3)—that might be more reason to separate control between more of the instruments in the green wash. Finally, as Tee-boo and Hokey face off in the Battle, the downstage half of the stage might change to green while the upstage half remains a different color for the chorus (Figure 5.13E). Eventually the green wash might be assigned a dimmer for each instrument in the system. Observing the single-channel wash transform into individual channels of control starts by comparing the system's use in the systems and specials sheet to the preliminary magic sheet.

The amount of coverage and control detailed in the preliminary magic sheet may be illustrated as a historical progression, drawn as side-to-side panels like Figure 5.13, or it might be a single square, erased numerous times with different lines of division. Some designers will outline a stage area and label segments of separation with leading arrows: "End A2," "Finale," and "Cranky," for example.

Figure 5.14 shows the current state of the preliminary magic sheet as plotting is about to begin. As the designer's personal document, it's not designed to be quickly comprehended by outsiders.

Figure 5.15 shows the same document with lines drawn in to make it easier to read. The top two rows show the current thoughts for the backlight systems; the top row includes the warm system on the left, and then progresses through the cool, the lavender for the Rock scenes, and the red for the Snakes and the Battle. The upper-right-hand corner includes thoughts

about the cyc. The second row details the progression of control for Tee-boo's green wash. The third row shows ideas for the two pipe end systems. To their right is the control breakdown for the template wash, next to thoughts about the box boom systems. Finally, the bottom left corner shows initial ideas for the specials, the special effects, the lights in the pit for the Battle, and the boom sidelight.

As each system is defined, by both it's overall size and separation of control, the preliminary magic sheet allows the designer to recognize the comparative need for control in a duplicate system (like the warm system cross-fading to the green), or merely consider the number of instruments necessary to provide the punch and coverage originally described in the cue master.

Whether they're expressed in three separate documents, or mashed together into a single piece of paper, the three thought processes exemplified by the cue master, the systems and specials sheet, and the preliminary magic sheet enable the lighting designer to envision, record, and construct the lighting for the show. Updating some form of these documents means the designer then has an idea of when the lights will change, what they'll look like when they change, and what needs to be turned on or off in order for each cue to look right. Along with all of the research, analysis, and meetings, these core documents reflect the state of the lighting that is part of the collaborative design conceived with the rest of the creative team.

Step 3: Preliminary Hookup

In addition to all the decisions about color, placement, and unit type, another design aspect that requires consideration is the sequential numeric order that identifies the systems and specials in the light plot. Whether they're numbers that relate to dimmers, channels, or some other hardware handle or software activator, that arrangement of the numeric labels that activate instruments in the light plot is

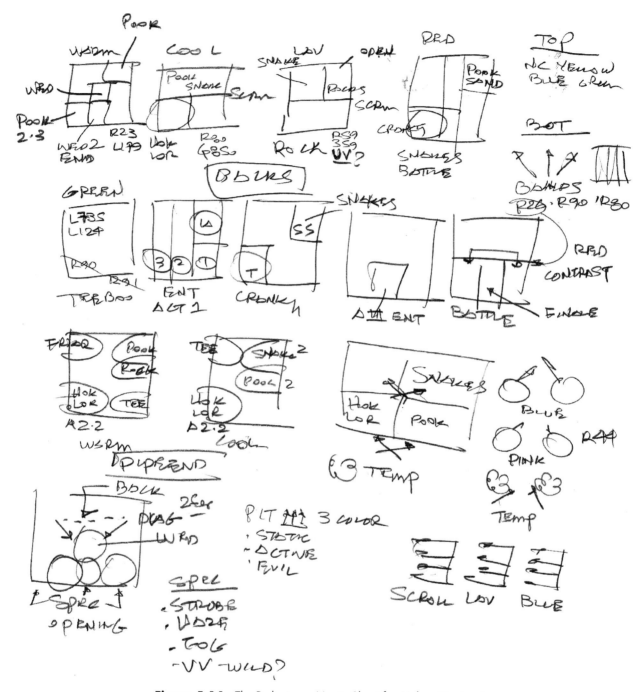

Figure 5.14 The Preliminary Magic Sheet for *Hokey*, Version 1

collectively called the **hookup**. For manual boards, it's usually called the dimmer hookup. When computer consoles are involved, the term is usually specific and called the **channel hookup**—the channels are the identifying numbers directly called for when activating the instruments. When a computer console is used, the number of electronic ways to identify and control channels dramatically increase. That will be examined later in Chapter 8.

The hookup is being discussed at this point in the text since (for some designers) it is an important aspect of defining a light plot. But the point that it becomes important is different for every lighting designer. For some designers, assigning groups of numbers starts at the beginning of the process, when the systems and specials sheet begins to take shape. For others, it's when the preliminary magic sheet starts to coalesce. Some designers don't worry about the hookup until

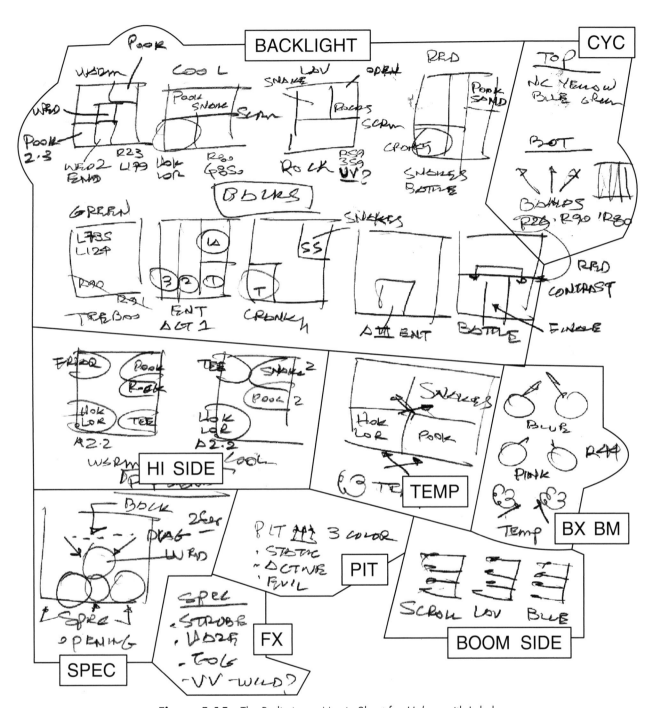

Figure 5.15 The Preliminary Magic Sheet for *Hokey*, with Labels

the plot has been completely drafted. But for most designers, at some point in the process, the numeric arrangement of the systems and their relation to one another becomes important.

Then there are the lighting designers who don't care how the identifying numbers are arranged or called for over headset. They literally start the numbering (or **channeling**) on the light plot with the first instrument in the FOH and end it with the final instrument against the back wall. Other designers find this approach abhorrent. They consider the hookup a crucial tool and an integral part of the light plot; each number has significance relative to the rest of the channels, and what they're controlling. For those lighting designers, the overall and individual numerical sequence of channels is a large mnemonic, and many members of the lighting department have memorized most of the hookup by the time the production opens.

Who cares? Why is number recognition so important? For one thing, many designers believe that having a sense of the numeric arrangement makes it faster to call for channels over headset. Some designers maintain that the channel arrangement patterns on the monitor makes it easier for them to interpret and compare intensity and other information between channels focused to the same area. Other designers believe that a well-constructed hookup makes it easier to read printed-out cue information and mentally envision the visual appearance of the cue on stage. For all of these reasons, most designers pay extra attention to the numeric sequences, and attempt to make them easy to understand.

In many cases, keeping track of the numbers is much more than just how they're arranged; it's about running out of them. The hookup is often part of a parameter, and represents the finite number of dimmers. When manual boards are used, the *highest* dimmer number is also the *last* dimmer number. When that number is reached, that's the end of the hookup. If there are still many instruments that need to be plugged, then the systems and specials sheet needs to be reconsidered, choices need to be made, and control needs to be consolidated. Computer consoles can soft patch the dimmers to channels, so keeping track of limited dimmers in that situation is a little trickier. While the total number of dimmers used must be constantly monitored, the channel numbers can be sorted and assigned in any number of ways to help the lighting designer remember or view the system, color, and purpose of the instruments in the light plot.

Hookup Arrangements

For a long running show, the lighting designer may only need to remember the numbers through the production period, while the crew may use those numbers as part of their lexicon for months. Creating numeric sequences helps lighting designers remember where washes or specials are located, but hookups are also often built so that everyone who understands the system can quickly remember the numeric location for a specific light. Basic hookup arrangements are typically based on some kind of numeric pattern that repeats in a logical manner.

In most cases, this starts by dividing a hookup into four main categories: system light, scenery light, specials, and everything else (channels that don't need to be constantly viewed on the screen). Usually, starting with channel 1, the system lights are listed first; in a typical light plot, they're the primary instruments that will be used to make the cues for the show. Usually, the systems are arranged relative to the lighting designer's working location in the audience. For a proscenium theatre, this means that a typical hookup will start with frontlight, then sidelight, downlight, and backlight, and any low sides. Once divided into systems, the hookup is then sorted by the color washes in each system. Traditionally, when there are multiple color washes from a single direction, the warmer colors are listed first.

The overall number of channels, and the number of instruments controlled by each channel in each color wash, is information that was initially sketched and then transferred from the preliminary magic sheet. In many cases the control separation indicated for any system is as much based on what lights need to be turned off, as opposed to which lights need to be left on during each given moment of the show. For systems with multiple color washes in the same direction, standard operating procedure is to mirror the division and distribution of control channels between washes. That way it's possible to control the color blend between two washes at any location on the stage, regardless of the channel separation.

One typical hookup technique is to assign the same "starting point" for each system in the same stage location, and trace the same directional pattern while counting through the channels of each system. In a proscenium situation, many designers start numbering each system downstage right. Visually counting the channels across the stage then mimics the eye's direction of movement while reading the channels on the computer display, left to right.

Once the area light systems have all been accounted for, scenery washes are also the next collected group of channels. Leg washes, drop washes, scenic stack treatments, and specials focused toward scenic units are all sequentially assigned channel numbers close to one another. This allows the lighting designer to see and compare, on the cue screen, which channels are active and their relative intensity in the group illuminating the same scenic area. Specials are often the next cluster of specialty-focused instruments assigned adjacent channel numbers. That way the designer can see and compare which channels are active in that group. There may be several specials at center, for example. Following the same sequential pattern of organization, the first special channel would be frontlight, the second channel a downlight, and the third channel backlight.

Hookups and Cue Screens

The introduction of computer monitors to lighting design has made a major impact on how hookups are constructed. Before computer lighting consoles, manual light boards had no monitor displays. If the lighting designer wasn't sitting next to the board operator, the only way to compare intensity information between two instruments in different dimmers focused to the same area of the stage was to ask the board operator, or look at the track sheet being filled out at the production table by an assistant (this will be discussed in Chapter 9). Once the remote CRT monitor became an addition to the tech table, the lighting designer could then visually compare the intensity of those same two instruments, or any instruments, without asking the console operator for that information or looking at another piece of paper. Being able to view the channel content of any cue on the monitor, live or in blind, was a welcome change for all lighting designers. With the increased number of channels in a typical light plot, though, the limitation on most of today's console monitors is now the number of channels shown on a single cue screen.

On many consoles, the cue screen is the label given to a monitor display showing the intensity and attribute levels for each channel in a single cue. While a console may be able to control hundreds of channels, it can typically only display one portion (or "page") of them at any time. The usual number of channels seen on one page is typically somewhere between 100 and 125. Most current console design is such that the only way to look at the next sequential group of channels is to press the "next page" button. If a designer sees that the warm down center frontlight in channel 3 is at 50%, for example, and wants to compare that with the intensity of the cool down center frontlight focused in the same location, he or she merely needs to look at the other channel. If the channel is 13, it's a simple visual comparison. If the same instrument is assigned to channel 413, on the other hand, the console operator has to press the "next page" button some number of times to arrive at the 400 cue screen, just to see that channel.

Once the initial lighting looks are recorded into the individual memories, no small amount of the lighting designer's activities during the rehearsals is spent comparing channel intensity information. If multiple monitors aren't available at the tech table, so several cue screen pages can be simultaneously viewed, then the channels for a single light cue can only be seen one cue screen at a time. In that case, most designers agree that instruments in the same system, focused to the same area, or in the same color, need to be grouped together in some kind of numeric pattern, and ideally on the same page of the hookup, so that faster comparisons can be made during the techs. For that matter, the fewer the cue screens, the less times the "next page" button will have to be pressed over the course of the production period.

Some console manufacturers have responded to the "channel 413" scenario by introducing a display software feature that hides any channels from the display screen that haven't been recorded in any cues or other software library packets. Skipping unused channels can condense channel numbers from many different hundreds of pages onto a single cue screen page. The only problem with this solution concerns folks who then memorize channel numbers by their location on the display. If a new channel is activated and recorded to any cue or library, that number then appears on the condensed monitor display and all the subsequent numbers are shifted from their old positions. Looking for channel numbers then often takes some amount of visual searching until the new channel layout is memorized.

Hookups and Monitor Rows

Several hookup tactics have evolved over the years to visually utilize the rows on the cue screen to expedite channel comparison. In some cases, however, these tactics are wholly dependent on the number of channels displayed on each row.

Figure 5.16 shows several views of a cue screen made up of twenty channels on each row. Figure 5.16A illustrates the numeric assignments of two matching eight channel frontlight washes, soft patched so that the two systems are numerically adjacent to one another. The third channel in the warm frontlight wash is focused down center (DC) and soft patched to channel 3, while the third channel in the cool frontlight wash, also focused down center, is soft patched to channel 11. Comparing the cue screen intensities of these two instruments means visually comparing two channel numbers that have no real relation.

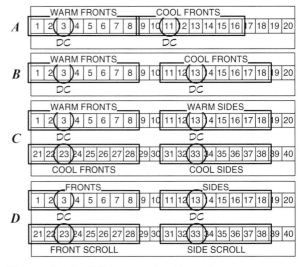

Figure 5.16 Different Hookup Examples

Figure 5.16B has shifted the cool frontlight channels so that the second integers match. The cool DC frontlight is now in channel 13, matching the same focus as the warm DC frontlight in channel 3. Channels 9 and 10 are currently unassigned, but comparing intensity information between the two color washes is now simpler to see on the cue screen. The eye moves horizontally between the channel numbers and compares the two that end with the number "3."

Figure 5.16C utilizes that numeric recognition system but applies it vertically in a columnar format. It shows two rows of twenty channels each, and lists two systems, each with two color washes. The warm frontlight is still soft patched to channels 1 > 8, but the cool frontlight wash has been shifted to channels 21 > 28. Warm and cool sidelight has been added in the 11 > 18 sequence, and the 31 > 38 sequence, respectively. Comparing the warm and cool frontlight channels is now an even shorter distance; the eye moves vertically from the "3" on the top row to the "23" on the second row. Likewise, the sidelight washes are hooked up so that they match each other. The instrument focused to down center in each wash is assigned to the third channel in it's system. The eye can see the warm and cool side intensities focused to the same area of the stage by comparing channels 13 and 33.

Visually matching channel numbers for comparison isn't limited to intensity. Figure 5.16D shows the same 2 row × 20 channel format. This time channels 1 > 8 are the frontlights, while channels 21 > 28 are the single-channel color scrollers mounted in the color frame holder of each frontlight. While channel 3 indicates the intensity of the instrument, channel 23 indicates the color position for that same instrument.

With these techniques, the lighting designer uses the spatial layout of the hookup on the cue screen to reduce the number of times his or her eye needs to refer to another piece of paper (the magic sheet or the cheat sheet) to determine the focus location of instruments in the light plot.

The software on some lighting consoles displays 20 channels on a single row, while others show 25. Some consoles can change between the two layouts, while others can to change to completely fluid layouts. And don't forget about the display options that skip unused channels as well. The impact of these different layouts will be discussed in more detail in Chapter 9.

 ## Shelley's Notes: Hookups

While the appearance on the cue screen can be one goal for a hookup, most designers agree that the numeric systems used for a hookup are primarily

to help remember sought-for instrument numbers. Creating a hookup that is a mnemonic can make it easier for everyone using the light plot to call up channel numbers no matter where they are or what paperwork they may have on hand.

Designers have their own "hookup habits." Some start their hookup from the sidelight, some from the back, while others assign channel 1 to a different system altogether. I usually start my hookups with the frontlight, and try to keep the fronts all clustered together in one chunk. That way, when I look at a screen in preview, I can quickly tell if all frontlight is turned off when the front curtain is closed. (That may be a habit leftover from my years working in dance.)

With small shows, number patterns that remain confined to a single page make it easier to "count off" the system and then the color wash. On larger shows, numbering schemes can be thought of in a more global context. All frontlight may be on the 100's page, all sidelight assigned to the 200's, and so on. All of the warm washes may then be assigned to start in the 20's, while all the blue washes start in the 40's. Based on those broad numeric specifications, the number 243 might then translate to the down center blue sidelight.

Hookup for *Hokey*

The preliminary hookup for *Hokey* is based on the control separation detailed on the preliminary magic sheet, but the preliminary light plot is being constructed long before rehearsals have begun. While numerous meetings and conversations have occurred regarding the blocking, the light changes within each scene, and the transitions between scenes, the cue master still lists many light changes that are blank placeholders on the page. In a perfect world, a run-through of the entire show would take place that would give the lighting designer a sense of the changes that will be required before the plot was drawn. That's possible on shows that are remounts, but for original productions, that rarely (if ever) happens. The lighting designer must assemble all available information and then make his or her best guesstimates.

At the present time there's no constraint about the number of dimmers or channels for *Hokey*—the entire system is going to be pulled from a lighting rental shop. While general ideas about control separation can be seen on the preliminary magic sheet, the final number of channels required for any wash may not be revealed until that system is constructed. In order to retain as much flexibility as possible, the final numbers assigned to each system will then be dictated by the number of instruments used to produce each system wash. The entire plot will be assembled as a dimmer-per-channel style of hookup.

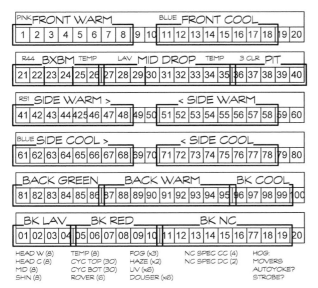

Figure 5.17 Preliminary Hookup Worksheet for *Hokey*

In the meantime, systems can be assigned groups of channels and kept in a sequential order. The final number of channels will be assigned once the systems are constructed. Figure 5.17 shows a preliminary hookup worksheet for *Hokey* based on the current preliminary magic sheet. The two front washes will be assigned to the first 20 channels, followed by the box boom washes and the mid-stage drop systems. The two sidelight washes will be separated by color, warm and cool, and by direction of origin. The instruments focused toward stage left will be listed first, followed by the instruments on the opposite side. They will match their second-integer control label, so that channel 41 will be focused to the same area as 61. Likewise, 51 and 71 will also be focused to the same area of the stage.

The backlight channel sequence is still under construction. The preliminary magic sheet indicates that the No Color and warm washes will each require nine channels of control (three instruments × three zones), while the green and the red appear to be penciled in for six channel systems (two instruments × two zones). Right now they're listed in the order that they appeared in the prelim magic sheet. If the completed control systems are successfully constructed in these ways, then the hookup may be reorganized, so that the No Color and warm systems match their second-integer control label either on the same row, or on adjacent rows. Same for the red and green washes, since they're currently both at the same channel count and appear to need the same control separation.

Under the backlight, the remaining systems and their current anticipated control channel totals are listed, starting with the low sidelight, the scenic stack, and the rest of the current system needs. As the

systems are constructed, this entire worksheet will be changed numerous times to reflect each choice that's made as the preliminary plot takes shape.

Now that the hookup worksheet has been examined, attention can return to the cue master, systems and specials sheet, and the preliminary magic sheet. As these three core documents are reviewed, analyzed, and codified to the lighting designer's satisfaction, preparation can continue toward beginning the construction of the lighting systems. One useful step in that preparation is a review of general plotting practices and guidelines.

PLOTTING GUIDELINES AND THE SLINKY METHOD

Constructing lighting systems (or "plotting") refers to creating stage washes. A more clinical definition might be "determining the most appropriate instrument types that provide the proper beam spread and the right number of pools for each system, in order to create a single color wash that provides the desired coverage."

While the methods used to produce the washes, the light plot, and all of the support paperwork are again individual to each lighting designer, there are fundamental guidelines that most lighting designs employ in order to create stage washes and to place instruments so they better relate with the scenic environment around them.

Basic Plotting Guidelines

Constructing systems of theatrical light is typically one of the first tasks completed when a light plot is being created. There are four basic guidelines that are generally followed to successfully create washes of light:

- The lighting instruments in the wash should all be the same instrument type and wattage.
- The lighting instruments in the wash should all be approximately the same actual throw distance to the focus points.
- The lighting instruments in each zone of the wash should all be approximately the same approaching angle of light (or the Angle of Incidence, or AOI) relative to the focus points in the system.
- The pools of the lighting instruments in the wash should all overlap, by some amount, in order to create a consistent intensity. They should overlap left-to-right in order to create a smooth blend of light in a single zone. The zones should overlap with one another in multiple zones, to create a smooth upstage-downstage blend of light.

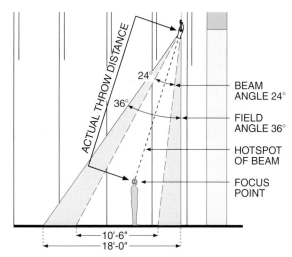

Figure 5.18 Field and Beam Angles of a Source Four-36° Ellipsoidal Hung in the First Opening

A more complete understanding of overlapping beams begins with a more detailed analysis of a theatrical light beam.

The Slinky Formula and Method

Chapter 1 stated that a typical theatrical lighting instrument produces a cone of light, which consists of three parts: the field angle, the beam angle, and the hot spot.

Figure 5.18 shows the cone of light from a Source Four-36° ellipsoidal hung in the first opening. The overall field angle of the cone is 36°, creating a light

pool on the stage floor 18'-0" in diameter. The beam angle is 24°, creating a brighter internal light pool 10'-6" in diameter. The bright center of the beam is the hot spot. Most theatrical lighting instruments are optically designed in such a way that the degree spread of the beam angle is almost always at least 50% of the overall field angle. This can be expressed in an equation known as the **slinky formula**:

$$\frac{\text{field angle}}{2} = \text{beam angle}°$$

The **slinky formula** states that if the field angle of any instrument is known, dividing that number by two results in a rough number that can be used as an approximate beam angle. Chapter 1 defined a lighting wash (or system) as a consistent intensity of light wider than the width of a single beam angle. With that in mind, consider this next illustration.

Figure 5.19 is a groundplan showing three instruments hung in the first opening and focused as straight frontlight in a single zone. The dashed lines coming from each instrument trace the beam edges of each cone to the pool on the floor. Each pool of light (pool A, B, and C) is shown as two circles, one inside the other. The larger shaded circles represent the field angle (edge of the cone) for each light, whereas the white internal circles represent the brighter beam angle within each cone. Three performers (A, B, and C) are standing at their matching focus point within each pool, creating shadows

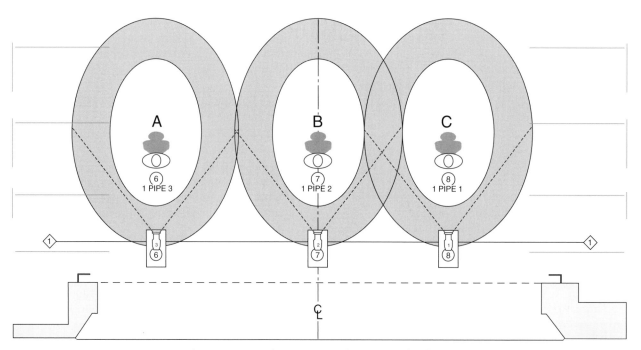

Figure 5.19 Three Non-Overlapping Pools of Light

directly upstage on the floor. The field angles of pools A and B are barely touching, while the field angles of pools B and C are overlapping to the edge of each pool's beam angle.

When performer A walks stage left toward performer B at centerline, he will become dark midway when he walks between the A and B pools of light. If performer B walks stage left toward performer C, she will merely grow darker as she crosses through the overlapping field angles between pools B and C, but there will still be a visual "dip" of intensity as she walks towards performer C. To prevent darkness or any visual dip between two pools of light, the pools must be focused so that the *beam angles* are touching or slightly overlapping.

Figure 5.20 shows the result of hanging and focusing the instruments to achieve a blended system. (For visual clarity, the performers' shadows have now been eliminated.) The hanging positions of the three instruments have been shifted so that the cones are still focused as straight frontlight. The field angles are overlapping, but the internal beam angles of the three pools are touching. Performer A can cross stage left to performer C without any visual dip in intensity. A consistent level of illumination has been created that is larger than the beam angle of a single instrument. The three instruments have now created a partial straight frontlight system for a single zone.

It is important to note that two relationships have been created by this successful straight frontlight system. First, the edge of pool A overlaps into the *middle* of pool B, bisecting pool B's beam. Second, the edge of pool A is almost *touching* the edge of pool C.

Figure 5.21 shows a complete zone of straight frontlight focused across the stage. To allow the beam angles to touch or overlap, the field edge of pool A is landing in the middle of pool B. As important, however, is the fact that the edge of *every other field pool* is touching, illustrated by the edges of pools A, C, and E. As a rule of thumb, when every other pool's edge is touching, the combined pools should result in an even wash of light.

Looking at the sharpened focus of a blended system or wash, it's possible to see the overlap of the pools in relation to each other. This is called the **slinky configuration** because of the way the overlapping pools can be drawn with a single line, as shown in Figure 5.22.

The slinky configuration illustrates the formula that presumes the beam angle is half of the field angle, the overall pool of light. Successfully plotting or focusing instruments into an even wash can be achieved by using the observations illustrated in Figure 5.21:

- *Every other* pool at least touches each other's edge.
- Each pool at least *bisects* the adjacent pool of light.

Based on these two guidelines, it's possible to calculate the overall zone width or depth of a system once the field pool width of a single instrument is known.

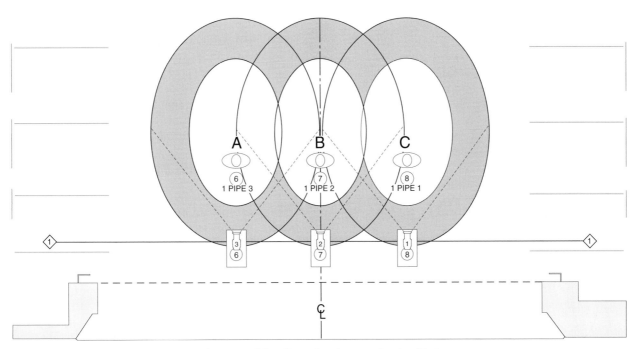

Figure 5.20 Three Overlapping Pools of Light

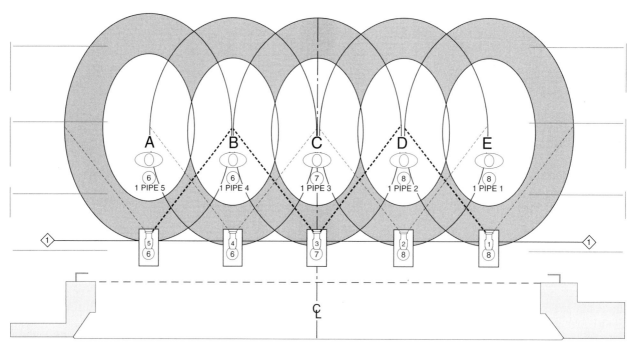

Figure 5.21 Five Overlapping Pools of Light

While everyone agrees on the basic plotting guidelines and the basic concept of the overlapping technique, there are always discussions about the amount of overlap required to insure an even blend of light. Some designers insist that the pools should be placed so that only the internal beam angles touch. Others question whether those beam angles should touch at floor level, or at the head height focus point plane. Over the years I've developed these fundamental observations into a system that works for me. These interrelated guidelines are collectively part of the **slinky method**:

- To provide proper overlap between two lights and achieve a smooth blend, the edge of the second beam should land in the *middle* of the first beam.
- To properly plot straight washes, the ideal distance between each hung instrument should be approximately *half* of one beam pool width, either side-to-side for zones, or upstage-downstage, between zones.
- If a symmetric straight wash consists of an odd number of units, the middle one should be placed on centerline. If the symmetric wash consists of an

even number of units, the middle two should "split center," (which will be demonstrated).
- Using the first two guidelines, the overall beam pool width of any zone can be calculated by multiplying the half beam pool width by the number of instruments (plus one).

Some designers think this amount of overlap is overkill, and combines too much intensity between the internal beam angles. Depending on the lighting instruments in question, that may be true. But in my experience, using this method, I have rarely (if ever) created a system wash with intensity dips. And in my experience I have found that it's always easier to spread systems of light out to even a blend, instead of adding an instrument to fill a visual dip. The interrelated guidelines proposed by the slinky method will be the basis for the systems constructed during the rest of this chapter.

Overhead Electric Placement

The overlapping example placed instruments focused as straight frontlight in the downstage side of the first opening. From a sectional viewpoint that makes perfect sense—by being placed in that location, these instruments then have the most focus range possible for their purpose. In the downstage side, they're more hidden from view, and they can tip frontlight farther upstage than instruments hung in the upstage side of the same opening. But that's only one zone of frontlight. A review of the reasoning, and the choices made about where to place lighting systems, relative to

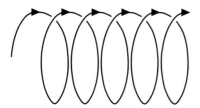

Figure 5.22 The Slinky Configuration

overhead masking in a proscenium theatre, is worth-while. That review begins with a general unwritten rule. When plotting or focusing overhead lighting systems that hide the instruments behind masking, the unwritten rule that is almost always followed is:

- Light beams should not splash onto the face of the masking.

Even small portions of light beams, hitting the edges of masking, are almost always perceived as careless plotting or a sloppy focus job. The unwritten rule is typically extended to include the upstage side of masking as well. Focused light beams that hit the back of masking can reflect back upstage as scattered light and cause unwanted shadows. Even light striking the bottom edge of a border downstage of it is usually perceived as visually distracting from the audience's point of view. This topic will be discussed further in Chapter 12.

Figure 5.23 shows four stage left sections, each illustrating the same three overhead electrics. They're all masked from the shaded vertical field of view by having successively higher trims behind the 1 border. In this configuration, the first electric is lowest in the downstage portion of the opening, while the third electric is highest, in the upstage side of the opening. Figure 5.23A shows 36° instruments on all three electrics focused as backlight. While the third electric stays off the 1 border, the second electric's beam would either have to tip upstage or receive a shutter cut to stay off that same border. In order to hit the same focus point, the first electric beam is significantly smacking the 1 border. If that light beam isn't tipped upstage, the top shutter would have to cut into the middle of it in order to keep light off the border.

Figure 5.23B shows the same three instruments, this time focused as downlight. While the light beams from the first and second electric both clear the 1 border, the third electric's beam is now splashing all over the downstage side of the 2 border. The third electric's beam would have to either tip downstage (and shift the focus point), or the upstage shutter would have to significantly cut into the beam in order to keep the light off the face of the goods.

Figure 5.23C shows the same three instruments, now focused as frontlight. The first electric's beam, being downstage in the opening and lower than the other two, is ideal for shooting light upstage. The second electric's beam has some success reaching the same focus point, but due to its raised trim, will require a top shutter cut. The third electric's beam is a failure. It might as well be turned off.

Figure 5.23D shows the same three instruments, now focused in an idyllic combination of lighting systems in a single opening. While this is pretty, having more than two electrics in any given opening doesn't happen that often; flying scenery, flying performers, constrained opening depth, lack of circuitry, snowbags—any one of these conditions can preclude the possibility of having more than two electrics in a typical opening, and shove the existing ones into the up- and downstage portions of the space. Faced with that, frontlight is often kept to the downstage side, backlight is usually stashed to the upstage side, and downlight (or sidelight) is placed on the electric best suited to hit its focus points and splash the least amount of masking. When electrics are placed close to borders, standard operating procedure is to keep the electric at least 1'-6" away from any soft

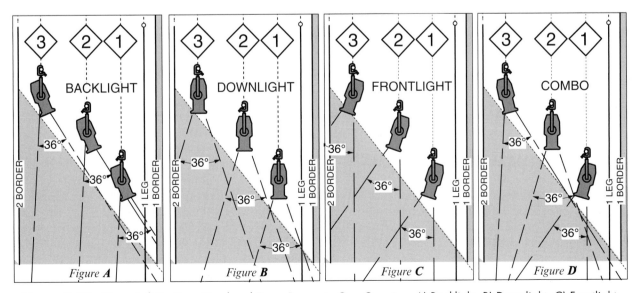

Figure 5.23 Stage Left Section: Overhead Focus Range in One Opening; A) Backlight, B) Downlight, C) Frontlight, and D) All Three Combined

goods upstage of them. An electric in the downstage side of an opening, on the other hand is often placed only 1'-0" away from the legs downstage of it. While a border runs all the way across a batten, a set of legs is only close to the downstage batten if there are high side pipe end systems on the end of the electrics batten.

Shelley's Soapbox: Electrics Placement

In many cases, the preliminary section provided to the lighting designer includes the masking, which then defines the number of openings and the leg opening depth. This masking is often specified and placed by the scenic designer, or by the director. Sometimes overhead electric placements, along with suggested trims, will be included in the drawing. To an outsider, it may be thought that the preliminary scenic section has completed both tasks, and the lighting designer's sectional work is complete. But the savvy lighting designer knows that electrical information included on the preliminary scenic section should only be taken at face value, and be considered only a basic starting point in the process.

The usage, placement, and trim of each electric hanging location should be double-checked and approved by the lighting designer. No matter how complete the drawing may appear, it may not be accurate. Or it may only be drawn in as a suggestion. In any event, the final placement and trim of the electric hanging positions are not the scenic designer's responsibility or domain. Any errors in lighting position placement cannot be attributed to him or her. The lighting designer must take responsibility for his or her own actions, and take ownership of all matters relating to electrical placement of goods for the show.

Now that basic plotting guidelines and formulas have been reviewed, the next step is to construct the lighting systems.

CONSTRUCT THE LIGHTING SYSTEMS

The third phase toward creating the preliminary light plot is to construct the lighting systems. From a conceptual point of view, "designing several systems of light is achieved by combining the proper number of instruments necessary to provide the intensity, coverage, and control required to realize all of the lighting designer's mental images for the use of light in the production."

From a practical point of view, constructing lighting systems is basically a repeated two-step process: first, the decision is made about which instrument type and beam spread should be used for each system; and second, the instruments are then distributed to the proper locations in order to provide the optimal coverage. This is a very nebulous step in the process, and often depends on a host of considerations: the amount of scenery, the angle of the wash, what it's trying to avoid, what it's trying to hit, how much of the wash will be seen on the floor, the overall coverage area, or the overall intensity in comparison with the rest of the plot, to name a few. A full explanation of all of those considerations and how they relate to one another involves judgments made over the course of careers, often on a case-by-case basis. This text will instead focus solely on the technical methods used to achieve those two steps, relying on **cut sheets** and **preliminary draftings** as the prime documents used to determine the layout and construction of the lighting systems.

Basic Construction Techniques

Creating full stage washes on an open proscenium stage typically relies on two standard conventions: one, focus points for a single zone in a basic system are equidistantly spaced across the width of the stage; and two, a single batten (or other hanging positions parallel to plaster line) is used as a lighting position for an entire zone of focus points. Hanging multiple instruments along a single batten achieves two of the four plotting guidelines; the instruments are all the same actual throw distance to their respective focus points, and they're all the same approaching angle of light. Using instruments of matching type and wattage fulfills the third guideline. Equidistantly spacing them across the batten to create overlapping beam pools across the width of a stage completes the fourth guideline. The result is a single row, or zone, of light. Creating overlapping zones that cover the entire stage then creates a full stage light system.

Building a zone starts by measuring the actual throw distance from a single instrument placed at a hanging location to either the focus point or to the stage. Consulting the manufacturer's cut sheet about the instrument confirms both its field angle and the multiplier number. Once the field angle is known, there are two different methods used to determine the beam pool size. The first method draws the field angle lines from the instrument to the actual throw distance, and then measures the width of the beam pool. The second method multiplies the actual throw distance by the multiplier number to produce the same beam pool size.

Once the beam pool size is determined, it's compared to the size and intensity produced by other instruments' beam pools from the same throw distance, using formulas or graphics. Once the decision is reached about which beam pool is more suitable for that situation, the instrument is then distributed across the lighting position to create a zone. As the multiple zones of each system are added to the groundplan, the preliminary light plot takes shape.

Reference Worksheets While Plotting

As the systems are being created, another pair of worksheets becomes useful to keep track of the equipment. The **instrument spreadsheet** keeps a tally as to how many instruments have been used, while the **circuitry and dimmer spreadsheet** keeps track of how many dimmers, circuits, and even cables may be needed to plug up the light plot and make it work.

Sometimes these two documents are used only to keep a tally of how much equipment is going to be needed. Sometimes it's the other way around—there's a finite inventory of instruments, dimmers, or whatever—and the sheets become vital to keep track of how much gear is *left* as the light plot takes shape. Inventories can quickly escalate in importance as reference documents if any portion of the equipment used in the plot is a parameter. In that situation, it's very simple. When the equipment runs out, the process must return to the core documents in order to review the priorities for the show, and a modification then takes place.

Instrument Spreadsheet

As each lighting system is constructed, some number of instruments will be added to the list that are acquired from another source, or allocated from the house inventory. In either situation, the lists are carefully checked and rechecked as each system is placed. While there are situations when the amount of instrumentation is unlimited, those are few and far between. For the rest of the situations, the initial goal is to create all of the desired lighting systems before running out of instruments. Once the instruments have run out, either more need to be acquired, or some portion of the light plot will require modification. Experience has shown that, sometimes even seemingly minor modifications can ultimately result in a re-think of the entire light plot, forcing the process to start over from scratch.

Figure 5.24 is the first version of the instrument spreadsheet for *Hokey*. The instrument types are listed across the top rows, while the positions are generally listed down the left-hand column. The Subtotal row consists of formulated cells that automatically total all

HOKEY INSTRUMENT SPREADSHEET V1

POSITION	Source Four 575w 19°	Source Four 575w 26°	Source Four 575w 36°	14" 1k Scp	Mini 500 10	LED Strp 3Cir	Spot 1.2k Spot	Pos Total	POSITION
Truss								0	Truss
SL Box								0	SL Box
SR Box								0	SR Box
1 Elec								0	1 Elec
2 Elec								0	2 Elec
3 Elec								0	3 Elec
4 Elec								0	4 Elec
5 Elec								0	5 Elec
6 Elec								0	6 Elec
Pit								0	Pit
Booms L								0	Booms L
Rovers L								0	Rovers L
Booms R								0	Booms R
Rovers R								0	Rovers R
Groundrow								0	Groundrow
SubTotal	0	0	0	0	0	0	0	0	**Subtotal**
Spare								0	**Spare**
Rental	0	0	0	0	0	0	0	0	**Rental**
								0	**Total**

Figure 5.24 The Instrument Spreadsheet for *Hokey*, Version 1

of the cells directly above them, one subtotal for each instrument type. The right-hand "Pos Total" (Position Total) column consists of formulated cells totaling all of the contents for the position in that row.

As the systems are constructed, this worksheet is updated. If any instruments are finite, then that may be entered in another cell underneath the "Rental" row, so that any potential overage can be seen.

Circuitry and Dimmer Spreadsheet

In many situations, one aspect of lighting design is to know the parameter, and to stay inside that line. For that reason, many lighting designers believe keeping running totals of circuits and dimmers is as much a part of the plotting process as performing instrument counts or constructing the systems. Sometimes this is done to keep track of how much gear will need to be ordered; other times it's to be wary of whatever will become the first parameter as the plot takes shape. The circuitry and dimmer spreadsheet is useful in both of these situations. When using house circuitry, the updated spreadsheet informs the lighting designer when a position has run out of circuits, and will instead require additional cables run from a remote location. When a plot is being constructed using only rental equipment, the same document will display the number of circuits, multicable runs, and dimmers that will be necessary at each hanging position, and for the show.

HOKEY CIRCUITRY & DIMMER SPREADSHEET V1

POSITION	Circuits in light plot			Dim 192 48		NOTES
	575	1.2K	TOTAL	1.2K	2.4K	
Truss			0			
SL Bx Bm			0			
SR Bx Bm			0			
1 Electric			0			
2 Electric			0			
3 Electric			0			
4 Electric			0			
5 Electric			0			
6 Electric			0			
Pit			0			
Booms L			0			
Rover L			0			
Booms R			0			
Rovers R			0			
Groundrow			0			
Total circuits plot:			0	0	0	

Company switch is DSL.   1.2K 2.4K

Figure 5.25 The Circuitry and Dimmer Spreadsheet for *Hokey*, Version 1

Figure 5.25 shows the circuitry and dimmer spreadsheet for *Hokey*. No house circuits or dimmers are going to be used, so this spreadsheet is relatively simple. This version of the document has been constructed to monitor the amount of circuitry and dimming that will be required for the rental lighting package. The circuits and dimmers are listed across the top rows of the document, while the positions are generally shown down the left-hand column. The next two columns of circuitry listed for each position will result in cable runs to each hanging position. The first column will indicate the number of single *575* watt circuitry runs, while the next column shows any 1200 watt circuitry runs (if any two-fering is required). The right-hand columns should reflect the circuitry totals, but will show anomalies if any circuits are combined at the dimmer racks. At the present time, in order to provide some kind of structure, 192-1200 watt dimmers are shown, along with a backup rack of 48-2400 watt dimmers. While the overall size of the light plot isn't yet known, this should address the needs of the show and still stay within the power distribution provided in the theatre. One the plot gets more defined, the number, size, or distribution of the dimmers may change in order to make the plot more compact, less expensive, or easier to install.

Armed with these worksheets and the core design documents, the system construction can now take place. When questions or constraints surface during the plotting process, this collection of documents should ideally provide enough information to allow informed negotiation to take place, and clear decisions can be made. As the systems are defined and applied to different hanging locations, for example, it may become apparent that there's not enough room for six colors of backlight on one electrical batten. One of the colors may need to be a mix of the other two, converted to a different overhead system, reduced to a single special, or eliminated altogether. Which one needs to stay or move? Check the systems and specials sheet. Can one system be controlled with fewer channels or does it need to be more "broken apart," in order to have the right amount of light turned off in that particular cue? Refer to the preliminary magic sheet. Are there enough plugs on that raceway to separate control of each light in the system? Better take a look at the circuitry and dimmer spreadsheet. This part of the process is inevitable, and it's part of the job. It will also take place later, once the final preliminary light plot is taking shape.

At the present time, concentration will now be directed to the construction of the lighting systems. The worksheets will be discussed in more detail later in this chapter and the next.

Reference Documents While Plotting

In addition to the worksheets and the core design documents, when the lighting systems are constructed, everything regarding the show should be available. Experience has shown that, no matter what unnecessary piece of information is neglected while the systems are being created, *that* will be the piece of information that potentially stalls the process. That said, the above documents are the most closely monitored, referenced, and updated throughout the process. After that, the list is about what would be expected:

- All show-related research and preliminary material.
- Any preexisting groundplans of the space (regardless of scale).
- Any preexisting sections of the space (regardless of scale).
- Any photographs or video of the space.
- The measurements and notes from the advance visits.
- The tech specs.

Illustration Notes

In order to provide visual clarity, the construction of the backlight system will be shown without any other instruments on the drawing. Doing so allows the viewer to see the system in its "pure" state, producing the optimal approach angle. For many lighting designers, the physical placement of the lighting systems, and their resulting beams and angles, can be as important as the choices made about instrument type, color, or the hookup for any light plot.

What also won't be shown in this exercise is the accumulated jostling that takes place as each system is added to the light plot. As lighting systems are constructed, the need for parallel beams or adjacency to centerline can sometimes make one system shift in order to give spatial priority to another. As each system gets added, the other systems already drawn may need to be nudged in order to make room for one another. All of this is a case-by-case basis and unique for each show.

The process to determine appropriate instrumentation and properly position instruments to create systems of light is another process that's individual to every lighting designer. Most methods are based on calculating the intensity or size of an individual beam of light from a given hanging position. This method will use backlight as an example.

Construction of the Backlight System

The backlight system for *Hokey* will now be placed into the drawings. The third pair of columns on the condensed systems and specials sheet (Figure 5.12) shows the planned usage for six overhead washes. While it's optimistic to think that all six of them will be backlight, that issue can be set aside until the components of a single wash can be successfully created and analyzed.

The notes on the preliminary magic sheet indicate that at least the warm, red, and the green backlight system will require at least three or five separate control areas for the cues currently envisioned in the cue master. Regardless of the final number, the center area of both systems will need control separation, so that the side pools can be dimmed, while the stage action at center can be brighter.

Using the illustrations in Figure 5.23D as an example, Figure 5.26 is a stage left section showing an instrument placed at a hanging position out of sightlines, in the upstage side of the final opening. The horizontal height lines, and gray vertical field of view triangles, have been removed in order to provide visual clarity. A figure containing a focus point is drawn in the third opening. The ATD (actual throw distance) between the instrument and the stage following the angle through that focus point is 26′-0″.

Backlight: Cut Sheet Analysis

The next step begins by consulting the manufacturer's cut sheets representing the proposed instrument inventory. In this case, it's been determined that the

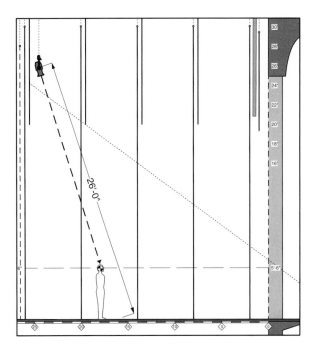

Figure 5.26 Stage Left Section of Initial Backlight Placement

instrumentation will mainly consist of ellipsoidals. So the question is: What size beam pool will best be suited for the proposed backlight system with an actual throw distance of 26′-0″ to the stage? Figure 5.27 shows a combined cut sheet for six different sizes of fixed-beam ellipsoidals. For the purposes of this text, these will be the six lens sizes considered for the *Hokey* systems. The top rectangle provides information about the Source Four-50° Ellipsoidal. Across the top of the rectangle are three rows of information: the top row indicates a **distance range** for the instrument, and the next two rows indicate the beam pool diameters and foot-candle measurements at each of those distances. Below those rows is a pictogram indicating the beam and field degree angle spreads for the instrument. Under the drawing of the instrument, there are two written **multipliers**. These are mathematical percentages that, when multiplied to the ATD, provide the approximate beam pool width at that distance.

This compilation of cut sheets provides a graphic indication of which beam spreads to consider for each distance. In this example, the 50° shows the 25-30′ distance in the "medium-long" end of it's range, while the 36° includes the 25-35′ distance more in its "medium" range. Neither the 14° nor the 10° even include 25′-0″ as a referenced distance.

Why? To determine the 14° beam pool size at 26′-0″, multiply 26 feet by the 14° field diameter multiplier of .26. The result is 6.76, or about 6′-9″ (potentially too small of a beam pool). The medium

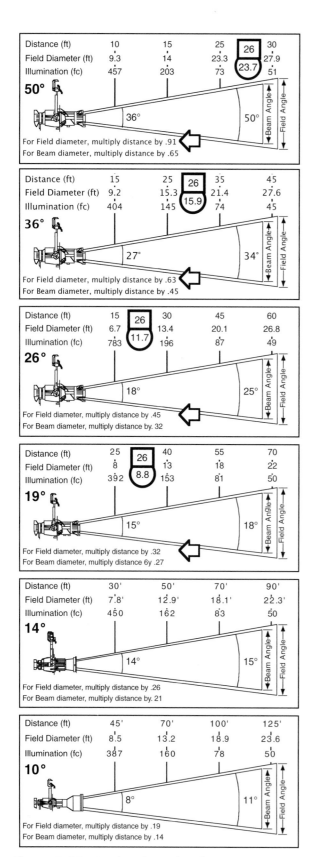

Figure 5.27 Combined Cut Sheet for 10°, 14°, 19°, 26°, 36°, and 50° Ellipsoidals

range of the 14° ellipsoidal is listed as 50 to 70 feet in diameter; as we'll see later, 26'-0" is too short of a throw, producing too small of a beam pool, for this situation. And the 10° beam pool? Multiply 26 feet by the 10° field diameter multiplier of .19, for a result of 4.94. That's less than 5'-0" in diameter (smaller still).

Generally speaking, cut sheets usually display the designed distance range for each lens size. If an instrument is being considered for a specific throw distance, and that distance isn't included in the instrument's distance range, it may be the wrong lens size.

Backlight: Front Elevations and Calculations

In this situation, the choices for the proposed backlight beam pool are now reduced to the 50°, 36°, 26°, and the 19° ellipsoidals. To simplify matters, the beam pool diameters have been calculated for each lens size. The 26'-0" distance (in each bold rectangle) is the constant for each lens size, while the field multipliers (adjacent to the arrows) have been used to calculate the beam pool size for each lens (in the bold circle).

Based on the first guideline of the slinky method, the number of beam pools needed to create a single zone wash can be determined by knowing the beam pool size and the overall leg-to-leg width of the zone:

- To provide proper overlap between two lights and achieve a smooth blend, the edge of the second beam should land in the *middle* of the first beam.

This can now be graphically examined. While overlapping beam pools can be seen in groundplan view, their relative side-to-side beam spreads can be more clearly seen in front elevations. Figure 5.28 shows four front elevations in a column. Figure 5.28A shows a single 19° instrument placed at 26'-0" above the stage. Under the stage, a dimensioned measurement shows that the leg opening is 36'-0". Above that measurement, the dimensioned beam pool for the 19° is 8'-8" wide. For clarity, the instrument (and its beam) is shown "in front" of the masking and the proscenium. Using the slinky method, since the second pool's edge lands in the middle of the first pool, each additional pool will extend the zone's overall width another *half* a pool, or 4'-4".

Figure 5.28B shows the rest of the 19° instruments added to create a single zone. To provide straight-angled overlapping backlight, this illustration shows the instruments placed at matching 4'-4" intervals. The dimensions are shown above the proscenium. Since it's an even number of instruments, the middle pair would "split center," i.e., each one would be placed at half the 4'-4" distance from centerline.

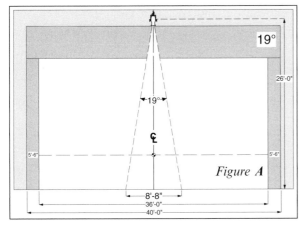

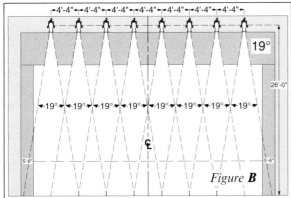

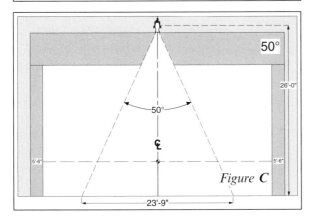

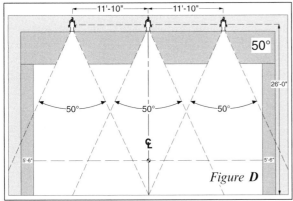

Figure 5.28 Front Elevations of 19° and 50° Backlight Systems

This illustration shows that covering this zone leg-to-leg would require 8 19° instruments (36'-0" divided by 4'-4"). That's a lot of instruments for one zone. Since the current performance area measures 24'-0" deep, using 19° instruments could potentially turn into a five-zone system (24'-0" divided by 4'-4"), requiring 40 instruments in order to create a single smooth backlight blend. This is a good time to remember the old adage, "the fewer lights to focus, the faster to make the cues." If nothing else, this confirms that there's no need to draw a front elevation for any lens system with a smaller beam spread.

How about the 50° instrument? Figure 5.28C shows a single beam providing a 23'-9" beam pool width from the same hanging location. Using the slinky method, Figure 5.25D shows the zone covered leg-to-leg using only three instruments placed on 12'-0" centers. The calculations:

- Space between instruments = beam pool width (23'-9") divided by 2 = roughly 12'-0".
- Number of instruments per zone = leg opening (36'-0") divided by ½ beam pool (12'-0") = 3.
- Odd number of instruments, so the middle one is placed on centerline.

Following the method and these calculations, Figure 5.28D shows that only three pools of light are required to provide complete coverage for the zone, and washing the stage could be accomplished with only two zones (24'-0" deep divided by 12'-0"). These calculations suggest that the full stage wash could be achieved using only six instruments, which might be perfect for both the red and green wash. Due to the actual throw distance, the lens optics, and the saturation, however, the overall intensity may be significantly lower. With the 50° lens system considered and temporarily set aside, compare the beam pools of the 26° and the 36° lenses.

Figure 5.29A shows a 26° instrument hung at this same hanging location creating a beam pool dimensioned at 11'-6" wide, noted under the stage. Following the slinky method, the calculations:

- Space between instruments = beam pool width (11'-6") divided by 2 = 5'-9".
- Number of instruments per zone = leg opening (36'-0") divided by ½ beam pool (5.75) = 6.
- Even number of instruments; middle pair splits centerline (2'-10½" each side of center).
- And what was that about calculating the overall beam pool coverage? To determine overall width of beam pool coverage in this zone, multiply ½ beam pool width (5'-9") × 7 instruments (6 instruments *plus one*) = 40'-3".

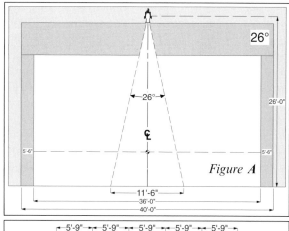

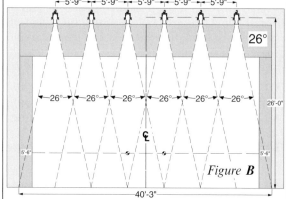

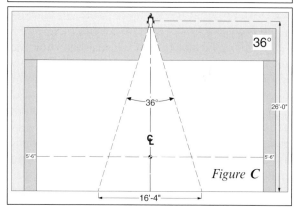

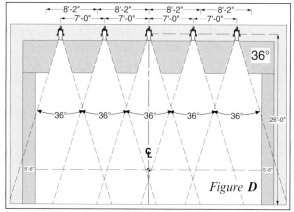

Figure 5.29 Front Elevations of 26° and 36° Backlight Systems

(Why the "plus one?" I envision each ½ beam pool starting from the center of each instrument going to "one side." In order to get an accurate width, another ½ beam pool must be added to the total number of multipliers. Rather than trying to remember and recalculate this every time, I just "add one"—ss.)

Figure 5.29B illustrates these calculations and positioning, showing the 26° instruments and their pools, spaced on 5'-9" centers. This straight backlight system zone achieves side-to-side coverage with six instruments. Since this zone consists of an even number of instruments, though, providing control separation on centerline can no longer be achieved with a single beam pool. At best the two overlapping center instruments will have to function together in order to make the center area brighter. How wide will the beam pool be for those two combined units? Multiply ½ beam pool width (5.75) × three instruments (two instruments *plus one*) = 17'-3". For a 36'-0" wide leg opening, that's a fairly wide center area—that's almost quarterline to quarterline.

While considering these zone width calculations, it's also worth considering zone depth, and the number of zones required to cover the stage. This 26° configuration, at this benchmark 26'-0" trim, will require some number of zones. How many? The calculation:

- Performance depth (24'-0") divided by ½ beam pool (5.75) = roughly 4 zones.

Using the slinky method, a straight backlight system using 26° lenses in this manner will then potentially require 24 instruments, and that's just one color. While that's a lot of control, that's still a lot of instruments—and there's not that much separation of control to centerline. Alternatives to consider might include increasing the trim height to increase the beam pool size (and possibly reduce the number of zones, or reduce each zone to 5 instruments across), or shifting the entire system across the batten to one side or the other (to create diagonal backs, and also increase the ATD). The 26° lens system wash requires some number of instruments, which will also increase the amount of control, circuitry, and dimmers required. Next up, the 36° lens system.

Figure 5.29C replaces the initial backlight instrument with a 36° unit. The dimensioned beam pool is now 16'-4" wide. The calculations:

- Space between instruments = 8'-2".
- Number of instruments per zone = 36'-0" divided by 8.16 = 4.4.

- Since that's almost another half an instrument greater than four, round it up to the next highest number.
- An odd number of instruments: the middle unit gets placed on centerline.
- Overall beam pool width = 8.16 × 6 (5 *plus one*) = 48'-10".

Figure 5.29D illustrates these calculations, but shows the extra amount of beam pool overlap. Actually, the initial 8'-2" spacings are shown above the proscenium, but placing the instruments at 8'-2" intervals meant that both offstage instruments were 16'-4" from centerline. Keeping focused light off the masking legs would result in the shutters cutting almost through the hot spot of the beam. When there's more than adequate beam pool overlap (resulting in the outside instruments being positioned too far offstage), a variation of the slinky method can be calculated instead:

- Space between instruments = leg opening (36'-0") divided by number of instruments (5) = 7'-2".

Round the distance down to 7'-0", and this zone of the straight backlight system achieves the side-to-side coverage with five instruments. Since it's an odd number, centerline separation will be possible with only a single beam pool. While there's potentially too much beam pool overlap, there's sufficient overage so that side shuttering between the five pools can take place and the side-to-side intensity coverage will not suffer. On the other hand, if the visual objective is to produce a series of circular, un-shuttered backlight pools, replacing the instruments with zoom ellipsoidals or Fresnels if they're in stock. If neither of those choices is appealing, it might be possible to add an iris accessory into each 36° ellipsoidal instead, thereby slightly reducing each instrument's overall beam size. Before making any final choices, however, it's prudent to complete the task. The rest of the full stage wash will now be constructed.

Backlight: Downstage Zone Construction

Rather than calculations, the additional downstage zones will be added to the section, in order to view the available choices to create a full stage wash of blended light using 36° elllipsoidals. Following the slinky method, the next zone of backlight should be at a matching angle relative to the next set of focus points. Where? That will be achieved by establishing hanging positions in the upstage side of the next openings downstage.

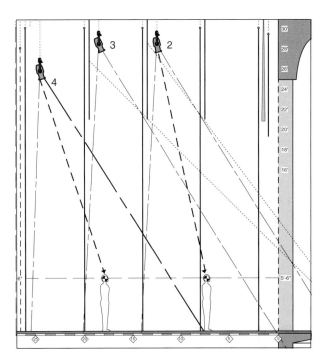

Figure 5.30 Sectional View Adding Downstage Backlight Zones

Figure 5.30 shows the next two downstage electric hanging positions in the second and third openings, both drawn with the 36° beam spread. Initially, this seems like a clear solution, but it's then realized that this plan will require 15 instruments for each backlight color (five instruments × three zones). If this system is replicated to create the desired six backlight color washes, that will result in 90 instruments—just for backlight. That still seems like a lot.

Can one of the two proposed downstage zones be cut? Further graphic review reveals that the second electric provides head height coverage all the way downstage to plaster line, but it can't tip upstage without splashing onto the face of the black border just upstage of it. The beams from the backlight on the third electric can't cover head height downstage to plaster line without striking the upstage side of that same border. The only way for the third electric to cover that far downstage is to lower its trim. Lowering it to achieve that coverage then results in the third electric instruments dropping into sightlines and being revealed to the audience. The third electric can't be lowered, so the second electric backlight must be retained.

Time for a quick review: while retaining the third electric backlight makes perfect sense from a beam-overlap point of view, an additional third zone translates into five additional instruments. With the six-color scenario, that multiplies into 30 additional instruments. Even assigning only 60 seconds of focus time to each instrument (a relatively brisk pace), that quickly turns into an additional 30 minutes of focus time for the third zone, wherever it might be.

Further pondering reveals another graphic fact—the downstage beam edge from the fourth opening electric lands almost perfectly in the middle of the beam pool cast from the instrument in the second opening. Another teaching from the slinky method.

The quandary is complex, but the choice is simple: plot the backlight with three zones, insure overall coverage, and accept five more lights in each backlight system? Or cut the backlight position in the third opening and somehow make do with only two zones? After making adjustments to the section and groundplan, a review of the cue master and the preliminary magic sheet shows that the lighting designer has visually broken the backlight into a downstage-upstage configuration. That tips the balance. The fourth opening electric trim is slightly raised (so the beams can spread a little more) and those instruments are slightly tipped downstage (to get downstage a little bit more). The decision is then made to eliminate the electric in the third opening, and establish the backlight for *Hokey* as a two-zone system.

Since the side-to-side leg opening width and the stage shape aren't different in the downstage portion of the performance surface, creating the second zone of backlight is relatively simple. Copy the five instruments and their associated pools and shift them downstage into the second opening. The top half of Figure 5.31 illustrates this action in groundplan view, showing the two overlapping zones of backlight pools. Even from this perspective, it's apparent that there's not as much overlap between the two zones of pools as stated in the slinky method. Ideally, the downstage portion of the upstage beams would be in the middle of the downstage zone pools. Well, that's why they call them guidelines, and not rules.

The bottom half of Figure 5.31 shows the two-zone backlight system in wireframe view, with the borders and the proscenium removed. While this isn't the perfect wash, each five-instrument 36° zone will provide an even focus point coverage and an even blend of intensity for the width of the performance area. Since it's built on an odd number of instruments, the symmetric wash includes an instrument placed on centerline, so center control separation is still a possibility. And with only two zones, washing the entire stage is accomplished using only ten instruments.

Completing the Preliminary Drafting

Now that the backlight system has been created, the process will be repeated for each of the other proposed systems shown in the *Hokey* systems and specials sheet:

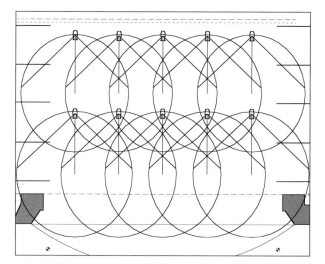

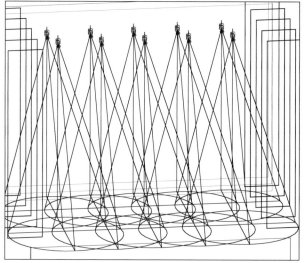

Figure 5.31 Groundplan and Wireframe View of Two-Zone Backlight Pools

downlight, overhead sidelight, boom sidelight, frontlight, box boom light, and the scenic stack. The basic preliminary systems for the *Hokey* light plot have now been constructed. The rest of the plot is then roughly drawn out to indicate instrument placement:

- Ten Source Four PARs are specified to be placed in the orchestra pit for the Precipice.
- Three Autoyokes are added to the truss on centerline and quarterline.
- Eight moving lights are added to the overhead electrics, two in each opening. Each instrument is tentatively placed on quarterline.
- Blacklight fresnels and dousers are drawn on the balcony rail.
- Foggers are indicated to be placed on the deck on either side of the stage.
- Hazers are indicated to be placed in the grid on either side of the stage.

- Six strobes are drawn in the overhead electrics, and two are drawn for the FOH.
- Three followspots are drawn and specified for the spot booth.

Figure 5.32 shows the result of these additions to the constructed systems on the preliminary light plot. While many of the instruments have not yet been assigned channel numbers, the basic components of the light plot are now included in the groundplan. Once the instruments are on the document, their placement can be shifted around in order to provide the best distribution and matching angles for all the systems and specials in the plot.

Peripheral Lighting

While the Hybrid Theatre has some amount of equipment, the site survey notes indicate that it's not a fully equipped facility. As a matter of fact, the diary said "treat this venue as a four-wall house with instruments and cable." Loosely translated, that means: Don't presume that anything will exist in the space.

Any additional equipment required for the show will need to be brought in.

As the preliminary light plot is being constructed, all of the notes and shopping lists are checked and rechecked to make sure that all peripheral lighting needs are included in either the drawings or on notes that will be included in the rental requests. In addition to all of the instruments and devices that will be used to create a lighting design, the lighting package often includes several peripheral systems or devices that may not directly appear on the preliminary plot. While they may not be drawn, they can often be just as important to the show. More than that, they're additional gear that should be included as part of the original package, rather than an addition once rental agreements have been made. Here's a short list of gear to make sure it's included in the plot, on the rental, or in the venue.

One system that's almost always part of a lighting package are the **worklights**. Their objective is to light the stage and eliminate as many shadows as possible. Usually that translates to one system of instruments hung in the overhead (one pair downstage, one pair

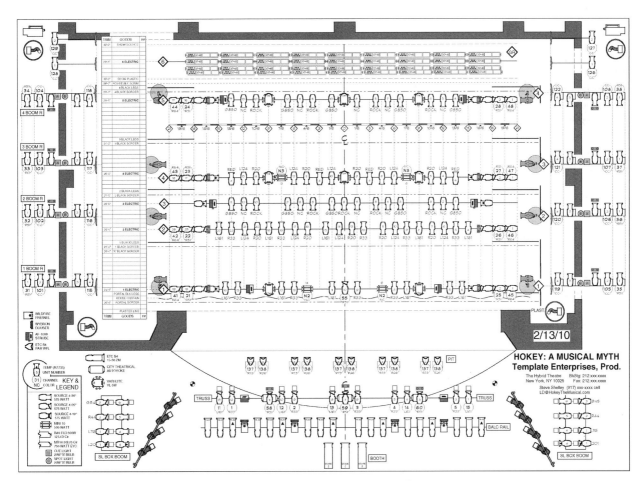

Figure 5.32   The Preliminary Light Plot for *Hokey*

upstage), and another set hung in the front of house locations (in order to prevent facial shadows). While not everyone draws them into the light plot, savvy designers and production electricians make sure they're not forgotten. Typically, worklight control is a switchbox on the stage manager's console or breakers on an electrical panel, powered completely separate from the show's dimmers. This means they can be switched on, regardless of whether the dimmers are working or not. In union situations, having the worklights completely separated from the lighting system also means that they can usually be turned on or off without requiring additional personnel.

If there's a possibility that the show will have blackouts or any involved offstage activity during the course of a show, **running lights**, and any necessary extension cords or adaptors are often included in the lighting package. The term applies to any offstage lights used during performance to provide visibility backstage, and may range from clip lights to lighting instruments dedicated to this function. If sidelight booms are part of the light plot, small colored "golf ball" lamps may be attached to each boom and circuited to remain on throughout the performance. This means that the sidelight boom positions can then always be seen, even in blackouts.

If the performance includes dance or the need for performers to know the location of centerline or other reference points without referring to tape marks on the deck, **spotting lights** may be part of the light plot. These small lights are often placed on the balcony rail, at the back of the audience, or wherever performers need to "spot" their dance turns or orient themselves while facing the audience. To prevent confusion, spotting lights are often assigned a different color than the exit lights in the theatre. Spotting lights that use LEDs are also now available as battery-powered alternatives to 120-volt sources. These are often taped to the front edge of the performance surface.

An involved production may have cued actions that take place without a headset being involved, or that need the reinforcement of a visual signal. **Cue light systems** often use small colored bulbs circuited to a main switchbox at the stage manager's console. If there are several different types of cues, cue lights in different colors may be used at the different locations to identify the action.

Productions with involved blackouts that include critical choreography or timing often provide the stage manager and other members of the tech staff with special monitors so they can see what's happening in the dark. These are **infrared systems**, and they consist of three components: the light source, the camera, and the monitor. In many cases, the audio department provides the infrared monitor and camera, but the lighting department often provides the light sources. **Infrared light sources** (or IR sources) typically consist of a PAR-can type of enclosure and a special (and expensive) IR bulb.

Shelley's Notes: Avoid the Box

As the light plot construction process is nearing completion, experienced lighting designers build in a cushion to avoid constraint and provide flexibility. Assigning spare instrumentation and channels addresses these concerns within the plotting process, but allocating spare circuitry and dimming in a light plot should also be considered to allow some "room for growth." Discovering a lack of "reserves" in the middle of the rehearsal process forces reanalysis of priorities, taking time away from the actual realization of the design. Retaining a reserve avoids being "boxed in," forcing the lighting designer to constrain the design during the rehearsal process sooner than necessary. Having reserves means that when the need for another special is suddenly discovered, the structure is in place to add the special, rather than spending time reviewing the plot in search of equipment or a channel that can be stolen from another assignment.

Shelley's Notes: Preliminary Plotting Tactics

The other side to that coin is when there are insufficient instruments available for the light plot. Reviewing the system and specials sheet can quickly point out a questionable system that's used for only one look or scene, or one that may not need to cover the entire state. Unless this is the climax of the show and it makes the audience stand on their feet, it may be decided that using ten instruments for a special system seen for less than 10 seconds might be a waste of resources. Here are a few thoughts to consider:

- Use an alternate system instead, not yet seen that much in the show.
- Use the questionable system in place of the similar one, so it's being used more, to justify its existence. Dedicate more control channels to segment the questionable system more.
- Use the questionable system in place of the similar system, and cut the similar system instead.
- Allocate more control channels to the similar system, providing the questionable system's desired isolation.

Shelley's Notes: Plotting Observations

While it may sound like a logical progression of simple steps to create a light plot, in almost every case it's a give-and-take struggle, a constant checking and rechecking between documents as the systems and light plot take form. For many designers, it often seems like it's a circuitous process; start with a choice, cross-reference information between documents, make a decision, execute that decision. Consider a new choice. Rinse. Repeat. As the choices get fewer and fewer, the circle gets smaller and smaller, until the choices are all made, or the remainder are set aside to be dealt with at a later time.

After some time working in the business, it may seem like the key to success is to make all of the choices and all the allowances for everything at one time, eliminating the need for additional time spent making any subsequent or adaptive changes before load-in. While this is a great idea, quite frankly, it's never going to happen like that. Theatre's too fluid and too goofy—people change their minds, egos erupt, lovers quarrel, budgets bottom out, schedules change; the chance that a single lighting plot and plan will remain unchanged between its inception and the load-in are somewhere between zip and nada.

The best that anyone in the business can do is create a plan and a method that work for him or her, and then maintain the ability to roll with the punches.

COMPLETING THE PRELIMINARY LIGHT PLOT

Once the preliminary light plot and lighting section are completed, the drawings will then be distributed to the management and the show's staff for comments and reactions. The management office usually has no official comment about the content of the drawings until the costs are known. The scenic designer, sound designer, or other members of the tech staff, though, may have questions or concerns once they see the specific preliminary plans. Addressing those reactions may take some amount of time, and could potentially slow the approval process.

Prior to Completion

To avoid that situation, most designers make the effort to collectively or privately communicate some form of their general plans to the rest of the creative and production team before the preliminary light plot is complete. Collective communication may be

to update everyone to the present status of that day. Private contact is not for any form of secrecy, but rather to address any individual concerns. In either case, communication often takes the form of phone calls, memos, emails, or copies of the current state of the light plot. Taking this action provides information, invites responses, or confirms that the overall plan still remains on course. This way everyone has some sense of the light plot, and continues to work together as a team. When the preliminary lighting drawings are then published, the information doesn't catch other staff members by surprise.

On larger shows with a long pre-production period, so much information may be involved that there's no question that some information is destined to fall through the cracks. In that situation, the purpose for the first set of preliminary drawings is to level the informational playing surface. When the drawings are published, everyone may be surprised here or there, just because the drawings are communicating so much information to everyone involved. In addition to the light plot and lighting section, there may be many additional drawing plates detailing how the lighting interacts with scenery, props, costumes, or other departments, and who's responsible for all the different elements. After these kinds of preliminaries are published (along with preliminaries from the other departments), a production meeting may be called for, in order to clear the informational air. That way everyone has an opportunity to respond, and the entire team can come to a consensus. Once all of the information is gathered and distilled, a second set of preliminary drawings may then be circulated for approval.

Smaller shows often barely have time in the schedule to produce one set of preliminaries, much less gather responses and produce a second set. In that situation, the preliminaries aren't intended to present initial ideas, they're to show a product that's been pre-approved by everyone who may have something to say about the lighting. When these prelims are published, they're hopefully confirming all of the individual agreements. That way, no one has any significant comments about them, so that management can then say: "Looks great, send it out to get bids."

To achieve this, lighting designers will often have quick individual meetings or privately send out "current state of the plot" drawings (or pre-preliminaries) to selected folks in order to get their separate input or approval. Sometimes that may be as simple as casually reviewing drawings with the sound designer and getting input, approval, or suggested changes that might facilitate the load-in for both parties. Other times may involve sending full copies of the pre-prelims to the scenic studio to make sure the agreements made between the two designers actually made it into print.

Pre-prelim PDF's may be emailed to the production manager or the technical director to get their input, opinion, or approval for highlighted questions or elements indicated in the drawings. All of this effort pays off when the preliminaries are published in time-sensitive situations, and the phone doesn't ring off the hook from folks demanding explanations or last-minute changes.

Regardless of the amount of communication with other staff members about practical aspects of the show, the primary contact for the lighting designer during the preliminary process is the production electrician. In the ideal world, the production electrician has been involved in the process long before this point. In the realistic world of freelance, it may be difficult to exchange more information than a broad logistical synopsis of the show until a preliminary is close to completion. If nothing else, enough mutual time is hopefully set aside before distribution in order to conduct a complete review of the preliminary lighting package, and get practical feedback or receive tacit approval. The production electrician may have any number of ideas how to approach specific mechanical challenges, how to more easily or quickly electrically adapt to the space, or how to specify equipment to speed up the load-in. The production electrician may also be able to provide the latest detailed tips regarding specific gear, lighting rental shops, personnel, or politics.

From a tactical point of view, it also makes sense to make certain the production electrician is fully aware of each aspect of the light plot. As the coordinator of the electricity and the labor, he or she is vital to the success of the lighting package, and the production electrician is the last person who should be surprised by any element shown on the preliminary lighting drawings.

Depending on the situation and the staffing, offering copies of the light plot's current state to other members of the tech staff may make perfect sense, but should be approached on a case-by-case basis. While some folks appreciate the opportunity to provide feedback or point out problems before the preliminaries are distributed, other folks view any pre-prelims as extra clutter in their lives—all they want are the real published preliminaries.

In the case of *Hokey*, time is so precious that as soon as preliminary drawings have been close to being finished, they've been collectively and privately sent to the rest of the creative team for initial reactions and response. The drawings have then been updated to reflect their collective and individual input.

The production electrician has had time for a one-hour session while his apartment was being cleaned to examine all of the pre-prelim information. Once everyone has had opportunity to comment on

the pre-prelim status of the drawings after a quick analysis, the preliminary light plot and lighting section are quickly finished, declared complete, and sent out so that everyone can publicly approve it and the process can proceed toward tabulating the equipment list in order to send it out to the lighting rental shops as a shop order.

After the Completion

Once the preliminary light plot has been completed, it's distributed to the creative and production staffs and the management office for their individual and collective approval. In educational settings, approval may be granted once instrument exchanges from one venue or college to another have successfully been arranged. In community theatres approval may take place after quiet in-kind loans from one theatre to another have been agreed upon. In situations where some portion, or the entire lighting package, must be rented, the approval process can potentially take more time, introduce more politics, cause more anxiety, and have as much of an impact as any conceptual consideration.

Sometimes on larger shows the management office takes charge of the drawings. Once in their possession, copies are then distributed to all relevant parties. More often than not, though, an agreed-upon number of drawing sets may be sent to the management office, but often the lighting designer distributes the drawings, based on the numbers agreed to in the document distribution chart. Back in the days of hand-drafting, prudent designers would retain the original documents, to make sure that changes didn't accidentally take place to the drawings while they weren't in the designer's possession. Nowadays drawings are often exchanged as PDF files. The greatest concern is often making sure that everyone is working from the same revision version of the documents at any given time.

 ## Shelley's Notes: Distributing the Preliminaries

While these published preliminaries may be close (if not exact duplicates) of documents that have already been received by the creative and production team members, it's still important that they are all delivered—One, to make sure they're all operating from the same matching copy, and two, to acknowledge receipt. Including everything on the document pre-approval chart and keeping the recipient list updated insures that no one is accidentally forgotten. No one is left out of the information loop.

Likewise, everything that is scheduled to arrive has shown up. In some studios, the person who originally receives the delivery signs his or her initials, in order to keep track of who got what. While each of the documents is important to the process, confirming that each of the documents has arrived or departed is just as important. Not only does it reduce the amount of potential information that can fall through the cracks, it insures that responsibility is left at the proper location.

While the Internet and email have accelerated information exchange in every aspect of modern life, there are still times when delivered hard copies have their place. For example, to reduce costs, contracts are often made between productions and theatres to use the house equipment either as part of the theatre rental agreement, or at a lower fee. The preliminary light plot then often shows the distribution of house instruments. In order to prevent any misunderstandings, lighting designers often include a copy of the house lighting inventory in the preliminary drawings packet sent to all appropriate representatives of the house, not to mention the management office. If the actual house lighting equipment totals are less than what is shown on the inventory, discussions regarding who pays for the additional rental will be much more quickly resolved, and out of the lighting designer's hands. In those situations, some lighting designers send hard copies that require a signature to prove acceptance. In case of misunderstanding, this document can then be used to show that the drawings were sent and arrived in good faith.

In the case of *Hokey*, that situation won't come up, since the production isn't using any house gear. It will all be part of the rental package that will come from the lighting rental shop. Once the preliminary lighting documents have been distributed to the management office, the creative team, and the production team, work can immediately begin to tabulate the equipment in order to send it out to the lighting rental shops as a shop order.

THE SHOP ORDER

For the purposes of this text, the **shop order** refers to a set of documents that detail lighting equipment that is rented from a vendor. It usually consists of two documents, the **cover letter**, and the actual list of requested gear, the **equipment list**.

Vendors that specifically rent lighting equipment are generically known as **lighting rental shops, or rental houses**. Once equipment rented from a lighting rental shop is loaded into the venue and combined with the existing house gear, the complete lighting package is created. When the theatre is a **four-wall rental** (i.e., the only thing the theatre provides in the rental agreement is the four walls), most lighting designers first carefully check the tech specs to see exactly what, if anything, may be useful or available for the show. In many commercial theatre rentals, the amount of house gear is limited, which in a way makes the job easier. Merely list everything that might conceivably be needed to install the light plot. That's the idea on paper. The reality, of course, is completely different.

Since the total amount of equipment required to produce a lighting design is often unknown until the preliminary lighting design is created on paper, the shop order is typically one of the last documents created in the preliminary plotting process. If a theatre owns equipment, the combination of the house inventory and the rental should result in the lighting package. If it's a four-wall theatre, the shop order will list every piece of equipment, gel frame, and piece of tie line that will be needed to install the light plot.

Once created and checked, the shop order is then usually sent to at least two lighting rental shops, so that their prices can be compared. Once each rental company analyzes the dates, logistics, and their own gear availability, they respond with a **bid** (or **quote**, or **estimate**). A typical bid is a sum of three basic numbers; the **rental price** for everything associated with the equipment list, the cost of all **perishables**, and the **trucking**. A fourth price may be added for any **truss rental**; many production companies now break that into a separate figure so it can be charged to a separate line item associated with carpentry or rigging costs.

After the quotes have been analyzed, some amount of negotiation often takes place between management and the leading candidates. Once a decision is made, a shop is selected as the vendor to supply gear for the show, and the public declaration is made that the shop has been **awarded the bid**.

Sometimes the light plot's design isn't finished by the deadline required to submit the shop order, in which case the best guesstimate is made. Once the bid has been awarded and a rental price is agreed upon, the shop order becomes a portion of the binding contract that is made between a lighting rental shop and the production, so anything specific that is needed should be included in this document. While the rental package may slightly change while being prepared and packed, the hope is that no major changes will occur, which could radically alter the amount of gear and force the vendor to change the overall price. If items aren't included in the shop order, adding them later may change the rental price. That's usually not perceived as a good thing.

As the preliminary light plot approaches completion, discussions take place about which shops to use, and preparations are made to submit the shop order. The lighting designer may be tempted to continue working on the paperwork and generate more documents for the load-in. This is a really good time to take pause, and NOT work on any other elements of the paperwork packets until the plot has passed this demarcation line. If the quotes returned from all the shops are too high, it'll be necessary to completely chop the light plot in order for it to fall inside the budget's limits. As soon as that step is taken, any documents created looking too far ahead will be seen as "jumping the gun." Those documents will all become contributions to the recycling pile, and the time spent constructing them will have to be repeated.

Once the preliminary light plot has been distributed for approval, producing the documents for the shop order is the next step in the process. While this is the first time that lighting rental shops will be discussed in this text, they've been a topic of discussion that started back around the time the lighting designer's contract was signed.

Selecting the Lighting Rental Shop

Conversations about which lighting rental shops to consider as potential vendors take place between the lighting designer and the management office, and may often include the production electrician as well. Often this is one of the first topics of discussion after the designer has signed the contract. Sometimes, it's even a point of conversation during the interview. While the lighting designer may have his or her own preferences, the smart question to ask first is if the producer or the management office has any preferences about which rental shops should receive the bid. Are there lighting rental shops that should be avoided, or shops with established relationships? Should the bidding process be bypassed altogether and the show's needs merely funneled to a single rental shop? While it may seem odd to ask the management office these questions and defer to their wishes, the bottom line is that most vendors, producers, and management offices have all been in the business for some amount of time. Unless they're just starting out, it's probable that everyone knows everyone. The lighting designer may be the comparable newbie to pre-existing relationships that may go back for years.

Shelley's Golden Rule: Selecting Vendors

This is one good lesson that should be quickly learned by anyone starting out in any business. The producer pays the bills and your salary. For every type of expense, always allow the producer the first opportunity to select who he or she wants to pay money to. Check with the producer or the management office to insure that for each new type of expenditure, they don't have a preferred vendor. If there is none, then the designer's free to contact his or her personal list of preferred vendors. But taking this pro-active stance avoids awkward (and possibly defining) moments when, after the bids have been awarded, the producer expresses disappointment because no one asked him or her about vendor preference.

Sometimes defining vendor preference is as simple as inquiring if the producer has a special rental shop, or if the general manager has established accounts with specific perishable vendors. Either may welcome fresh applicants to the pool of potential shops. Inquiry may also reveal old bad blood between the producer and a particular shop. Finding out about that beforehand saves the embarrassment of innocently asking for a bid from the producer's bitter nemesis.

Not asking for vendor preference is a potential mindfield; there's no telling which teeny, seemingly innocuous purchase may be the producer or general manager's personal white whale. Moving lights? Color? Fog juice? Paper color frames? When a new expenditure requires the addition of a new vendor, it's always wise to check with the people who have the money before negotiating any kind of billing or invoice that they will then have to pay for. It's their money. Let it be their prerogative and their first choice.

Lighting Rental Shop Analysis

On the surface, lighting rental shops seem like a lucrative business. The shop buys lighting equipment for a sum from each of the manufacturers, and then rents it out to customers. Once the initial investment has paid off, any money coming in after that is pure profit. Right?

Wrong. As soon as the gear has been purchased, just like driving the new car off the lot, its overall value is automatically decreased. Add to that the fact that the purchased gear now all has to be checked every time before it goes out on a job, checked every time it comes back from a job, identified so it can be monitored about when it'll next be available, and fixed in the shop or shipped back to its home planet if it's a delicate device.

A staff needs to be in place to fulfill all of these functions, a large enough space to store and test all this gear, loading docks to load and unload this equipment, marketing, advertising, transportation, technical support, shipping—and suddenly this business doesn't look like quite the gold mine it did two minutes ago. Today's lighting shops have to be aggressive and smart, and not only rent gear but they often have to get heavily involved in permanent installations and any other way to generate income and stay afloat.

As far as rentals go, light shops are sometimes perceived as banks. They exchange the rented gear for a fee, but in essence, they're the ones walking the financial high wire. If the rented gear is stolen or destroyed, the cost of the rental often doesn't even begin to cover the cost of replacement. Recent legal rulings have driven the point home, and most rental shops won't allow gear to leave their dock without proper documents of guarantee called certificates of insurance in hand. This will be discussed in more detail in Chapter 10.

In order to have all of the different pieces and parts available to assemble into lighting systems, most lighting rental houses have to form alliances with different manufacturers. While they're somewhat stuck when it comes to lighting instruments (everybody wants access to every kind of ellipsoidal for specific reasons, it seems) the rental house will purchase dimming equipment from one manufacturer out of the three or four powerhouses to choose from in the industry. From a business viewpoint, this makes perfect sense; loyalty breeds trust, not to mention discounts and long-term financing along the way. The same can be said for control, accessories, and every other category of entertainment lighting gear.

As the rental houses get more shows, it has to buy more equipment. The point of renting the gear is to get income when it's out on the job. The high wire act comes when the shelves are fairly clear, and a fat shop order comes in the door. Does the rental shop buy more gear so it can rent it? Or does the shop call up a friendly competitor and sub-rent the needed pieces from them? And how does all of this fit in with insurance for the business, the building, and the gear. Now this rental business is starting to sound like a headache.

Add to that the trucking, the liability, the payroll—and there's a good start to the explanation why there aren't dozens of lighting rental shops in every city. The current financial structure for each shop also goes a long way to reflect how they do business and structure their rental agreements. One significant difference is when the rental actually begins; some shops don't start the rental clock until the gear pulls away from the loading dock, while others wait until the show has actually opened. While that's mainly on big shows, it illustrates the fact that while lighting shops all have gear, that may be where the similarities between them peter out. Here's a quick list of differences between today's lighting rental shops:

- How is the rental fee structured? On short-term shows, there's usually just a single price. On longer running or open-end shows, the rental is usually loaded "up front"; a relatively hefty fee (to make up for the bulk of the preparation and return costs) and then after some number of weeks, it drops down to a smaller weekly amount. This way, if the show opens and bombs, the shop can still recoup its basic operating costs.
- Does the quote include perishables or not? Some shops will quote a price that includes everything on the plot: color, templates, etc. When the production electrician comes in the door and adds all the other tapes and consumables needed to get the show installed, that then often becomes a second, potentially unplanned-for invoice. Other shops just exclude perishables altogether, and inform you flat out that a separate invoice will be issued once the gear is packed and the consumables have all been totaled.
- What are the trucking rates? Some shops charge for one way, some for round trip.
- Is there a list defining a perishable? Some shops consider clip lights, worklights, even running lights a purchase. Sometimes even un opened fog fluid may be a permanent charge to the customer.

When the final list of potential lighting rental shops is tabulated, there may be out-of-state vendors, or vendors suggested by the producer that the designer has never heard of. While the lighting designer may have some input as to which lighting rental shops receive the shop order, he or she usually has very little say about the final financial negotiations and which shop is selected to get the bid for the lighting package. Many lighting designers consider that a blessing.

Once the list of lighting rental shops has been defined, the next step is to see if anyone has a contact in any of the shops. While each shop has an owner and general manager, the folks that are the direct contact with the lighting designer and the production electrician are the account representatives (or the rental agents) for each shop.

Lighting Rental Account Rep

A typical lighting rental shop account representative (or **account rep**), like a lot of folks in the business, is often still an active lighting designer, electrician, or somewhere in between. While an account rep needs to have a brain for business, his or her "active knowledge" resume often needs to include the following:

- A fairly intimate knowledge of all the lighting instruments, current and not-so-current.
- The relative attributes for each kind and size of conventional lighting instruments.

- The relative attributes for each kind and size of moving light instruments, not only in the shop's inventory but throughout the industry.
- A full knowledge about all of the different accessories, devices, and data control.
- A knowledge of color, color temperature, color filters, and all the latest whiz-bang products.
- A full knowledge about all the different lighting consoles and their different attributes.
- A knowledge about dimming, and all of the different makes and models of dimmers.
- A knowledge about electricity, load calculations, and ohm's law.
- A knowledge about power and the hardware needed to adequately distribute it.

Possessing the knowledge about lighting instruments and their relationships to each other makes sense. Having this knowledge allows the account rep to intelligently propose alternate instruments when substitutions need to be made, or communicate the benefits or different price structures applied to different lighting instruments. But why does the account rep need to have the all the electrical knowledge about dimming and power distribution? Mainly because, when it comes to electricity, many of the customers the account rep has to deal with on a daily basis have no idea what they're talking about.

Some of these customers are lighting designers. When they hear the phrase "load calculations," it makes them as jittery as hearing "budget deficiencies"; it's not part of the art, so they exclude themselves from knowing or understanding these basic elements of a lighting rental: "I just want it *here*. You figure it out." When the client gives up responsibility understanding the gear, then the account rep can only provide as much knowledge as he or she has been provided. When the designer can't, or won't, specify the exact components for the lighting package, if the final product delivered doesn't live up to the designer's expectations, there is really no one to blame but him- or herself.

The review information in Chapter 1 showed that the theatrical world has an entire language of theatre-speak for instruments, system design, and ways to assemble instruments and accessories. If the rental shop supplies gear to the TV or film industry, communicating with either of those clients over the phone means the account rep has to know both of those languages as well. And yes, they are very different.

On top of that, most account reps need to have some knowledge about rigging, an idea about the general cable lengths and paths of different venues in the rental shop's territory, and awareness of all the latest blazingly-fast changes in technology. The

account rep is all these things rolled into one. He or she is the interface between the lighting designer and the entire shop; the rep can be an invaluable resource, both for the specific lighting rental, and for general knowledge about lighting gear.

With all that said, sometimes the account rep can be someone who is not Superman. Everyone has his or her own set of strengths and weaknesses. When getting familiar with someone, the best way is to be open; say when you're on shaky ground knowledge-wise, and likewise, ask when the answers you receive lead you to believe that you may know more than he or she does. Account reps are like any other business relationship; you must treat them with trust and openness, but you must also remember that their job is to provide you with a service.

In any lighting rental house, there will be at least one account rep, or someone acting in that stead. In larger rental houses, there may be a dozen. But rather than just blindly sending the shop order to anyone, do some research and find out who might be the best contact. If nothing else, addressing initial correspondence to a specific name, rather than just "to whom this may concern," makes the shop start to consider you as a person, not just a blank slate. And while commercial theatre is show *business*, it's still a very small world, based more on relationships than anything else. Determine how to reach the account rep or reps, find their names, numbers, and emails on the web. Or just call on the phone and ask for a list of names. If you're calling blind, then ask the receptionist for the account rep who specializes in theatrical rentals. That way you'll at least speak to someone who can understand your theatrical language.

The Cover Letter

The **cover letter** provides the basic logistical information and summaries about the production. Back in the day, the cover letter started as a "title page" politely providing introductions and information. Not any more. The information included in the cover letter may critically impact the overall presentation or acceptance of the shop order as a viable customer. Nowadays, the cover letter has become an absolute logistical necessity.

Figure 5.33 shows the shop order cover letter for *Hokey*, which includes the following:

- The name of the show, and the name and address of the theatre. If the shop has installed other lighting packages in the space, they may know about problems, workarounds, or additional equipment that may be required.

| **SHOP ORDER for** *Hokey: A Musical Myth* | **Version 1** | **2/14/10** |

Bid distributed:	2/14/10	Shop Prep: Thursday, April 1, 2010
Quote Deadline:	2/24/10	Load-in: Monday, April 5, 2010
Bid Awarded:	2/28/10	Opening Night: Tuesday, April 20, 2010

PRODUCER:	Dr. George Spelvin 212.xxx.xxxx Office 917.xxx.xxxx Cell No1@YouTalkin.org	Template Enterprises xxx Amsterdam Avenue NYC, NY 10025
GENERAL MANAGEMENT:	Dr. Erika Feldman 212.xxx.xxxx Office 917.xxx.xxxx Cell Ericka@Ruler.org	Insulso Insilias Management xxx Columbus Ave. # NYC, NY 10036
PRODUCTION MANAGER:	Rhys Williams 843.xxx.xxxx Office 843.xxx.xxxx Cell Rhys@spoletousa.org	TTS xxx George Street Charleston, SC 20402
LIGHTING DESIGNER:	Steve Shelley 212.xxx.xxxx Home 917.xxx.xxxx Cell MrTemplate@earthlink.net	xxx Amsterdam Ave. NYC, NY 10025
ASSOCIATE LD:	Ruth Blenderella 843.xxx.xxxx Home 512.xxx.xxxx Cell	xxx Folly Road Savannah, GA 31405
PRODUCTION ELECTRICIAN:	Mike Carne-Pup 212.xxx.xxxx Home 703.xxx.xxxx Cell 703.xxx.xxxx Cell	xxx W. 95th Street NYC, NY 10026
THEATRE:	The Hybrid Theatre 212.xxx.xxxx Office 212.xxx.xxxx Stage Door	xxxx Columbus Ave. NYC, NY 10036

ALL MATERIALS AND CIRCUITING MUST COMPLY WITH THE MOST STRINGENT APPLICABLE NATIONAL AND LOCAL FIRE AND SAFETY CODES. ALL DRAWINGS AND THESE SPECIFICATIONS REPRESENT VISUAL CONCEPTS AND CIRUITING SUGGESTIONS ONLY.THE DESIGNER IS UNQUALIFIED TO DETERMINE THE ELECTRICAL APPROPRIATENESS OF THIS DESIGN AND WILL NOT ASSUME RESPONSIBILITY FOR IMPROPER ENGINEERING, CIRCUITING, OR USE OF ELECTRIFIED SCENERY AS PERTAINS TO THESE SPECIFICATIONS.

- **No substitutions without the written approval of Steve Shelley.**
- Entire package to be made ready by shop and to include all lamps, connections, cables, c-clamps, side arms, pipe bases, controls, interfaces, color frames, iron, ladders, cable, multicable, feeder, distribution panels, plugging boxes, worklights, pattern holders, donuts, and zetex, etc. for a complete working system.
- All cabling and connectors, controllers, power distribution, and rigging elements for a complete working system to be specified by Production Electrician. All methods and techniques of electrification subject to approval by Production Electrician.
- All electronics are to have the latest software unless otherwise specified.
- All ellipsoidals shall be ETC SOURCE FOUR of the latest generation available; all will be aligned in the shop.
- All equipment, including rigging hardware and accessories, shall be a uniform flat black (front and back).
- All Automated Fixtures to have NEW lamps.
- All Automated Fixtures available to be turned on and checked by the Designer and Programmer one week prior to shop load-out.
- All Scrollers shall be loaded and calibrated by shop prior to delivery to Production Electrician.
- Any modifications to accessories and or units to be done in shop to ensure proper fit and operation.
- All equipment should be available on first day of shop prep unless alternate plans have been discussed with Production Electrician.

- *HOKEY* IS AN OPEN-ENDED PRODUCTION. ACTOR'S EQUITY, USA 829, OFF-BROADWAY CONTRACT.
- SPARES ARE INCLUDED IN THIS ORDER.
- THE BID SHOULD BE BROKEN INTO 3 SUBTOTALS: RENTAL, TRUCKING, AND PERISHABLES.
- THE SHOW WILL PROVIDE PRODUCTION ELECTRICIAN + 5 FOR SHOP PREP.

Do not pull equipment from this list. This list is for BID PURPOSES ONLY. Final shop order to follow.

Figure 5.33 The Shop Order Cover Letter for *Hokey*

- The contact name and billing address, which is typically not the same address as the theatre.
- Contact information for the producer or employer (including street addresses, phone numbers, and email), the lighting designer, the production electrician, and the production manager. When questions arise, the shops know whom to contact and how to get in touch with them.
- Schedule information, including the date and time that the package gets assembled, loads out of the shop, or loads into the theatre, or both.
- The anticipated date that the package will return to the shop (presuming it's a limited run). The dates are important because the length of time the lighting package is out of the shop, coupled with the size of the package, determines the rental price.
- The date and time that the resulting bids, based on this shop order, must be returned to the producer or employer.
- A sentence saying whether or not the lighting rental shop will be responsible for trucking. Some shops include the delivery and pickup of the equipment in the rental price. Others add it as an additional cost once the final price has been determined.
- The amount of labor, if any, supplied by the production to assemble the package in the shop. If no one from the show is present to oversee the assemblage of the rental order, some shops charge additional monies for their personnel to perform in that capacity.
- A version number on every page, usually the date the shop order was created. If there's more than one published version of the shop order, the version number or date confirms that everyone's working with the same document.
- Any general notes regarding gear: These usually include broad topics, giving the lighting shops an idea of the standards that the show will accept. Examples include "all instruments painted black" (or whatever color if they're to be exposed), "all instruments equipped with lamp, c-clamp, and safety cable," or "each instrument type to have spare lamps," or "all ellipsoidals are to be aligned" to name a few.
- Other notes are specific about how the show expects to be treated in the shop: Examples of this include "All equipment should be available on first day of shop prep unless alternate plans have been discussed with production electrician," or "No substitution of equipment without written consent of lighting designer."

One important statement that should be included can be interpreted as redundant, since it's stating a basic fact that should be assumed. That said, since it's usually not a stated part of the contract between the two, the note often reads:

> "The entire lighting package is to be made ready by the shop and is to include all components, including instruments, hardware, connectors, cables, controls, frames, etc., so as to comprise a complete working system."

This basically states that whatever the lighting shop eventually produces in the form of the lighting package will indeed all plug together to make the complete working light plot. After receiving an incomplete package, hearing the telephone explanation of "but it wasn't on the order" can be very disappointing. Not only is it incredibly irritating, this situation can also delay the schedule and waste time.

The Shop Order

After the shop order cover page comes the substance of the document. While the information included in the cover letter is important, the document must contain the lists that are the basis for the numbers generated in each shop's quote. While some folks create the shop order as a Word-style document, others prefer to keep it in a spreadsheet format. That way it's simpler to identify each row with a unique number in order to provide a quick numeric reference. This portion of the document is usually broken into two parts, the rental and the perishables.

- The first part is the **equipment list**, which is a summary of the requested instrumentation, control, dimmers, cable, hardware, special effects, and any specially built devices constructed by the shop. These numbers are what the lighting shops analyze, along with the length of the rental period, to determine the weekly or total rental cost.
- The second part is the **perishables**, (if it's part of the lighting package). Sometimes perishables aren't included in the shop order, but they're purchased from a separate vendor. If the color isn't included in the shop order, however, it won't be cut and framed with the rest of the order, and may then need separate preparation time during the load-in.

The Equipment List

Figure 5.34 shows the compressed equipment list for *Hokey*. For the purposes of this text, the entries have been compressed into two series of columns. In reality, each item would be on a single row extending across the page.

The left-hand column is the italicized identification number, followed by the quantity, and then the actual name of the item. Italicizing the ID number

Hybrid Theatre 2010   **HOKEY EQUIPMENT LIST V1**   Date: 2/13/10

#	QTY	ITEM	#	QTY	ITEM
		INSTRUMENTS (all with c-clamp, saftie, gel frame, and bulb)	114	6	1 1/2" couplers
1	6	ETC Source Four-19° 750w	115	38	Hanging irons for LED Strips-matching
2	45	ETC Source Four-26° 575w	116	38	Groundow trunions for LED Strips-matching
3	130	ETC Source Four-36° 575w	117	16	6.25" Source 4 Half Hats (Eyelash)
4	20	ETC Source Four-25>50 Zoom 575w	118	30	6.25" Source Four Top Hats
5	12	Source 4 Pars WFL 575w	119	24	Source Four template holders
6	7	Mini-10's 300w	120	20	7.5" Source Par barndoors
7	3	14" Scoops 500w	121	2	PD 120volt 20A x 24 Soco/Edison
8	7	6" Fresnel 750 watt			**DATA CABLE**
9	38	LED Striplights (4' long, 7 color or equiv.-discuss)	151	2	6 pin RFU cable 250' X 2
10		LED Striplight power supplies (as required)	152	15	5 pin cable 10'
11	3	1.2kw Medium Lycian Starklite 1272 (w/ballast & stand)	153	15	5 pin cable 25'
12	1	Spare HMI Lycian spot ballast	154	5	5 pin cable 50'
13	10	Vari-Lite VL5 Tungsten (Hog 2; matching personalities)	155	2	5 pin cable 2 x 50'
14	10	VL-5 Lens Kit	156	4	5 pin cable 100'
15	10	All with NEW1200w lamps	157	6	5 pin cable 2 x 100'
16	6	VL-Smart Repeater Boxes (w/120v Edison Male)	158	5	3 pinM/5 pinF adapters
			159	5	3 pinF/5 pinM adapters
		FX			**FEEDER CABLE**
31	8	AF-1000 Strobelights (or equiv.-discuss)	171	3	Sets #1 camlock 10'
32	4	City Theatrical Autoyokes (16 bit DMX, matching software)	172	1	Set #1 feeder tails
33	4	City Theatrical Auto Iris (include power cords)	173	1	Sets #1 camlock 50'
34	21	Wybron ColoRam II Scrollers (with 6.25" plate)	174	1	4Ø feeder set 10'
35	1	Wybron 12 x color brain (include power cord)	175	2	4Ø feeder set 25'
36	1	Wybron 24 x color brain (include power cord)	176	2	Sets camlock Tee's
37	4	50 Gallon Dry Ice Foggers (or equiv.-discuss) with hose	177	2	Sets 4Ø feeder tails
38	2	MDG Atmosphere Haze Machine (w/DMX interface)			**MOVER CABLE**
39	4	Blacklight Fresnels 250w (Wildfire or equiv.-discuss)	191	10	25' VL Series 300 Lamp Cable
40	4	Blacklight Fresnels Dousers (Wildfire or equiv.-discuss)	192	5	50' VL Series 300 Lamp Cable
		CONTROL			**120V CABLE**
51	1	ETC Ion 2000 (2048 outputs)	201	10	25'-6 CCT mult
52	4	Ion Flatscreen Monitors (2 return after opening)	202	10	50'-6 CCT mult
53	2	Net 3 Remote Video Interface (include power cord)	203	20	75'-6 CCT mult
54	1	Ion RFU	204	18	100'-6 CCT mult
55	2	Net 3 Gateway	205	28	Female 2P/G breakout 6 CCT 11'
56	4	Ethernet Switches	206	3	Male 2P/G breakout 6 CCT 11'
57	2	Ethernet cable 2 x 200' (Dim > console, dim > table)	207	30	5' jumpers
58	5	Sets of ethernet jumpers (5', 10', & 25')	208	40	10' jumpers
59	1	Reflection (include power cord)	209	20	25' jumpers
60	1	Whole Hog 2 (latest Hog 2 software)	210	15	50' jumpers
61	4	Flatscreen Monitors (2 return after opening)	211	12	100' jumpers
62	3	UPS (1 return after opening)	212	15	100' Edison
63	1	Deskjet printer + cables to consoles + power	213	20	Twofers
64	2	Keyboards (1-Ion, 1-Hog)	214	10	Threefers 20 amp male/20 amp female
		DIMMER (Dimmer Beach will be DSL in "Betty")	215	25	Med adaptors
71	4	12 x 2.4k sensor pack w/pass thru	216	25	Fed adaptors
72	2	96 x 2.4kw sensor rack (CEM Plus) w/pass thru			**OTHER**
73		Spare non-dim cards, dim cards, CEM Module	231	10	Waber plugging strip
74	2	Opto-isolators (per Production Electrician)	232	6	6 x 20 switch boxes (cue & worklights)
75	4	City Theatrical WDS Transmitter	233	15	Basket (2) S10 Blue Bulbs (Spotting lights)
76	10	City Theatrical WDS Receiver	234	30	Basket (2) S10 R/Y/G Bulbs (Cue lights)
77	10	City Theatrical WDS Dimmer	235	12	Quad boxes and adaptors
		HARDWARE	236	12	Black Sandbags
101	40	12" single Tee sidearm	237	2	8' fiberglass ladder
102	30	18" single Tee sidearm	238	4	10'-0" x 18" triangle truss
103	35	30" Pipe Stiffeners	239	5	18" walkboards for truss (black)
104	6	Mega-claw for Autoyokes	240	24	Sets hardened truss bolts/washers/nuts
105	20	1.5" cheeseboro rigid	241	8	6' spanset
106	8	1.5" cheeseboro swivel	242	5	5/8" shackle
107	12	Pigeon plates (Source Four PAR in pit)	243	4	Steel 12' x 3/8" (safety for span set)
108	6	35 pound bases (Rovers)	244	1	Paper cutter
109	16	50 pound bases (booms & dimmer)	245	15	Music Stand Lights (40w, black, matching)
110	16	1.5" Sched 40 pipe 5'	246		Spare bulbs for each instrument type
111	12	1.5" Sched 40 pipe 8'	247		Spare end caps for Source Four ellipsoidals
112	10	1.5" Sched 40 pipe 12' (sidelight booms)	248		Spare barrels for Source Four ellipsoidals
113	3	1.5" Sched 40 pipe 21' (thread both ends)			

Ion; 420 chan, 240 dim   Lighting design by Steve Shelley 917.xxx.xxxx   Page 2 of 3

Figure 5.34 The Compressed Equipment List for *Hokey*

reduces the chances of confusing it with the actual quantity amount for each item in this compressed format. The italicized ID number is unique to that listing; there's only one item #1. The italicized ID numbers for the perishables in Figure 5.53 start in the 300 series. Keeping each line item unique eliminates confusion otherwise brought on by trying to refer to two different item #1's. If there's a chance that the shop order will be modified, categories are often assigned their own blocks of numbers; instruments start with ID#1, the FX units start with ID#31, the control starts with ID#51, and so on. That way, as the shop order changes and shifts while the show is being processed, gear can be added to each category without the need to re-number the entire ID column.

The categories shown on the equipment list may be sorted into any number of arrangements, depending on the lighting rental shops involved. Since every shop is slightly different, the information will look different by the time it's processed into each shop's rental software. So the category sorting on this document is for the benefit of the lighting designer and the production electrician.

- The first category covered in most rentals is the instrumentation. Instruments are sorted into groups, usually starting with the greatest number of one type first. In the case of *Hokey*, that's the ellipsoidals. Wattages and beam spreads are included where applicable in order to make a distinction between each type. If one instrument type includes groups lamped with different wattages, they're usually listed as two separate rows.
- The instruments often include any moving lights. Moving lights often require more information to specify all their different qualities. In some cases it's often necessary to specify the hanging hardware. Usually there's either specific cable lengths, or at least a mention to supply all necessary control and distribution cables, along with all interface components to once again "create a full working system." The control console that'll be used is mentioned (if it's also part of the rental, it will be listed separately under the control listing), along with any special instructions about turning the lights on, notes about their internal software, their templates, colors, and if they require brand new lamps.
- FX items (short for special effects) may actually be distributed between different departments, depending on the shop. In this case the electronics include the strobes, the scrollers, the atmospherics, the UV instruments, and the dousers. While specific manufacturers have been

listed to indicate a preference, the parentheses indicate that if reasonable substitutes can be found, substitution can be discussed. The cover letter, however, is specific that no substitutions can take place without permission. The designer needs to be made aware of, and approve, any potential substitutions.

- The control portion of the equipment list includes specific information about the lighting console and it's monitors; the type of lighting console, the software version if applicable, and the number of monitors needed for the console and the production table. In addition to that, for many shops, the control category also includes all of the hardware components that must be interconnected in order to make the control portion of the system work. That often includes the video nodes, the opto-isolators, and any "snapshot" type of backup devices. Other ancillary gear is also included in this category of the equipment list; the printer, the uninterruptible power supply (UPS), the RFU, and any keyboards.
- Dimmers are often the next category on the equipment list, since the department is often adjacent to control in many shops. The equipment list should indicate the number, wattage, and rack configuration, along with feeder cable. Nowadays, this category also includes any components involved in any wireless dimming.
- Hardware generally includes static accessories that don't require power or control data. That includes mounting or accessory items such as truss, pipe, base plates, sidearms, c-clamps, pipe stiffeners, scenery bumpers, tophats, barn doors, and template holders.
- Depending on the shop, cable sometimes gets sub-divided into data, feeder, and 120-volt, but it's all listed by length, and in some cases the number of circuits: 120-volt cable includes multicable or bundles, individual jumpers, two-fers, three-fers, and breakouts. Feeder cable, for power distribution, usually lists the runs as "sets" (3 hots, 1 neutral, 1 ground). Often only power runs outside that 5-wire norm get individually listed, but again, that's often a case-by-case basis. When in doubt, there's never any penalty for providing too much information.

The data cable sub-category adds a critical piece of information to the cable listings specific for its genre: the number of pins in the XLR plug. In most cases, DMX signal cable uses 5-pin connectors, but beyond that, there's no established standard. RFU's have historically used 6-pin connectors, and many devices (such as scrollers, for example) use 4-pin connectors.

While it would seem that everyone would play nice and pick the right pin numbers for the right jobs, that's not always the case. Every so often stories are told about the right pinned-XLR getting plugged into the wrong device, and then poof! All the smoke gets out. When new gear gets added to the lighting package, the savvy production electrician immediately checks the data connectors, notes the number of pins, and checks the cable runs potentially impacted by any pin number change. As this text is being written, standard operating procedure is to label all data cable in the shop to indicate that it belongs to the electrics department. With any luck this will be sorted out in the future.

In the meantime, the Ethernet is expanding and becoming the next phase for data transmission. There's no doubt that cables and hardware will soon expand to include more varieties of RJ-45 connectors, routers, nodes, and repeaters. It will be an interesting transition as those protocols continue to expand with the new DMX protocols that will soon be more commonly used in the entertainment workplace.

The final category on the equipment list is often referred to as "other," but it might as well be listed as "the kitchen sink." While this category may include cue lights, quad boxes, and rigging, it can just as easily include tables, chairs, and workboxes. (Sometimes the theatre has no production table, or the light booth is a bare room.)

Shop Order Tips

The more information provided to a rental shop, the faster an accurate estimate can be returned. Many designers often say "cable per production electrician." Savvy designers will at least include a copy of the plot, allowing the shop to more quickly estimate about how much cable that will really be.

If every instrument is going to have a lamp, a c-clamp, a safety cable, a pin connector, and a color frame, that can be listed as part of the header above the list. Obviously, though, each item needs to be included. Even if some number of instruments will be hung on sidearms, or have scrollers, and not use the c-clamp or the color frame, the hardware is often included to make counting simpler.

While the designer's basic instinct may be to include every backup and contingency on the shop order, moderation has to be taken into consideration. Granted, if the shop is not in the city where the production will be produced, some overage needs to be included. On the other hand, it's a bit unreasonable to request massive numbers of spare instruments, duplicate consoles, or backup dimmer racks. Some of these requests also depend on how far away the shop is from the performance venue. If it's across

town, dealing with equipment failure may require an after-hours phone call and a quick trip to the shop for replacement gear. If it's across the country, that's another matter altogether.

A list of possible spare gear to include in an equipment list:

- For every rented fixture type that doesn't match the house inventory, rent a spare.
- Consider how many spares will be required. There is no formula. Some electricians call for one spare every 20 units. Others say it depends on the fixture's upkeep in that particular light shop.
- Some electricians build in a cable cushion of 15%, depending on how little house cable may exist. A very wise production electrician once told me: "It sucks to run out of cable."
- Spare two-fers, three-fers, MED's, and FED's. (Male and Female EDison-to-stage pin adaptors).
- Make sure there is at least one spare bulb for every unit type.
- Depending on the manufacturer and the lamp, many electricians build in spare end caps for ellipsoidals. The heat buildup is such that, in many cases, the cap (and the tips of the lamps) are the first to go.
- Spare lens barrels, especially for instruments with universal bodies.
- Spare cards and brains for the dimmer racks.
- Spare electronics like opto-isolators, when possible.
- Spare video node, if possible.
- Spare non-dim cards for the dimmers.
- Spare barndoors, especially if the hardware from that shop is a bit beat up.
- Make sure the hanging irons for the striplights match.
- Make sure the trunions on the groundrow match.
- Consider a spare ballast for any followspots, or for any HMI units.

Shop Order Analysis

The shop order documents need to be properly prepared, for several reasons. One, it becomes part of the contract between the lighting shop and the producer. Two, by presenting it in the proper format, it allows the account rep to enter the information into the inventory database more quickly, produce a more rapid quote, and then go get lunch. Just sending a list without proper presentation shows a lack of thought and respect, will take the account reps longer to prepare, and make them irritated since they've now missed lunch.

Points to consider while assembling the equipment list:

- Boil the shop order down to the shortest possible list; one line for each different item. Not broken apart by hanging position. That really drives account reps nuts.
- Rental shops are not your mother. They will not put your socks away, and they will not pretend to think for you. They will do what you say, and nothing more. You must be specific, or you will get whatever they think you mean. If you know what you want for dimming, put it on the list. If you don't specify, they'll make their best guess. But it may not be what you really wanted. Is this making sense yet?
- If you know what you need for cable, list it. If you don't, shops will do a quick count and guess that you'll only use four or five circuits out of the six-circuit mult. If that means you pay for more mult, too bad you didn't take the time to count it out yourself.
- If feeder cable isn't listed, at least indicate the dimmer rack's location, or distance to the company switch. Otherwise there may be extra feeder, or not enough.
- If you don't know exactly what you need, but you're dealing with constraints, discuss this with the account rep. Don't just list the need for generic "dimmers" if they have to fit into a very specific area. If the designer doesn't list the specific dimmer rack that will fit in that area, the shop may substitute the generic request with another rack, which may not fit into the space.
- If you purchase some lighting instruments with plugs, but don't specify that you want the plugs installed, be prepared to receive the instruments with bare end wires and a box of plugs. It costs more for the labor to install them; if you want the plugs on the purchased units, you need to specify that. Shops that think for you and add the cost of the plug installation then don't get the order.
- Don't blithely state "add 10% spares" to the bottom of the shop order. Some shops will take you at your word, and provide 10% of *every* item on the shop order. And basically add 10% more to your total cost.
- Don't forget to at least mention infrastructure gear that may not exist on the light plot: cue light systems, repatch systems, worklight systems. While these may seem like minor expenses, they may ultimately get added to the final invoice, which will then be greater than the price the producer agreed upon when the contract was drawn up.
- Don't forget to at least mention special effects gear that may not yet exist on the light plot– (hazers, strobes, and the like). Final invoice with higher price = irritated producer.
- The production electrician must be a part of this process. No matter what any lighting designer thinks, the production electrician has a better idea of how the shop works, what the gear is, and what it's like to work in that theatre.

The Perishable List

The term "perishables" can extend to include just about anything that gets consumed during the course of a production. Over the years, lighting rental shops have stocked many of these consumable items for a small (or not so small) additional fee, but in these days of cutthroat economics, the Internet has completely leveled the playing surface. Shows are now much more wary about blithely agreeing to purchase all their perishables from the same shop that wins the bid; sometimes, the additional perishable invoice makes any perceived savings quickly disappear. Instead, many shows now shop out the perishables as a separate line item, and as such, the lighting rental shops have had to be much more careful about their overage charges.

The perishables list is typically broken down into three categories: color, templates, and everything else. The color category often starts by counting the cut pieces of color and the templates in the hookup. Different unit types define different color cut sizes, which are then combined and fitted onto different sheet sizes. While most color manufacturers produce sheets of color that are approximately 20″ × 24″ (50 cm × 61 cm), they are all slightly different. Likewise, many colors are also produced in large rolls. With that information in hand, the cut colors are tabulated and calculated in order to determine the overall number of sheets required for the light plot. The total number of each sheet is then listed on a separate row. Depending on the run of the show and the color saturation chosen by the designer, additional sheets may be automatically added. Sheets of diffusions are also added as a backup for softening ellipsoidal shutter cuts, blending striplights on backdrops, and providing followspots with a fuzzy edge. The templates are totaled and listed, with a different line for each number, and subdivided by outside size, gate size, or format.

Hybrid Theatre 2010   **HOKEY PERISHABLES LIST V1**   Date: 2/13/10

#	SHT	ID	ITEM	#	SHT	ID	ITEM	#	QTY	ITEM
		COLOR				COLOR & TEMPLATE				HARDWARE
301	2	R02	Bastard Amber	313	7	R132	1/4 Hamburg Frost	361	2	Roll of Tieline #4 Black 600'
302	3	R20	Medium Amber	314	3	G250	Medium Red	362	2	Rolls Blackwrap 12"
303	1	R23	Orange	315	4	G850	Blue Primary	363	1	Roll Blackwrap 24"
304	2	R26	Light Red	316	2	G945	Royal Purple	364	2	Rolls Blacktak 2" wide
305	3	R33	Blush Pink	317	1	L116	Medium Blue Green	365	3	Rolls Black Gaff Tape 2"
306	1	R39	Skelton Exotic Sangria	318	4	L124	Dark Green	366	3	Rolls White Gaff Tape 2"
307	1	R44	Middle Rose	319	4	L161	Slate Blue	367	16	Sharpies
308	4	R51	Surprise Pink	320	2	L201	Full C.T. Blue	368	1	Roll of Heat Tape
309	4	R60	No Color Bllue	341	8	R77722	Breakup (Large)	369	5	Rolls of Electrical Tape
310	4	R64	Light Steel Blue	342	8	43802	Prismatics	370	12	Paint Pens
311	2	R76	Light Green Blue	343	9	R77733	A Size Source Four	371	12	Cliplights (w/40w bulbs)
312	7	R119	Light Hamburg Frost	344	2	R77780	A Size Source Four	372	10	PS-12180 Batteries (Wireless)

Ion; 420 chan, 240 dim   Lighting design by Steve Shelley 917.xxx.xxxx   Page 3 of 3

Figure 5.35 The Compressed Perishable List for *Hokey*

Figure 5.35 shows a compressed perishable list for *Hokey*. For the purposes of this text, these entries have been compressed into three series of columns. In reality, each item would be on a single row extending across the page. While the left and the middle columns list color and templates, the right-hand columns list other consumables.

The left-hand column again starts with a unique identification number, the one referred to during the discussion of the shop order. In this arrangement, the next column indicates the number of sheets for each color, while the ID column refers to the identification number for each color. In the case of *Hokey*, the "R" colors refer to a manufacturer named Rosco, the "G" refers to Great American Market, and the "L" refers to Lee. Every color also has a unique name; when the numbers can't be read, the text is there to act as backup.

Items 221 through 224 in the second series of columns refer to templates instead of color. The R77722 Breakup template will be used in conjunction with the 43802 Prismatic to create a multicolored dichroic breakup on the mid-stage scrim. One of each of these pieces will be placed into each zoom ellipsoidal on the balcony rail to be focused onto the painted scrim. The R77733 will be used in the overhead template system, while the R77780 will be used in a sidelight system during Act 2's night scene.

The third column lists some of the items that are commonly part of a perishables package for a load-in. The black tieline will be cut into short pieces, in order to tie cables to the battens or other hanging positions. The blackwrap and blacktak will become invaluable during the focus session to cover light leaks or control errant light beams. The gaff tape will be used, along with the Sharpies and the paint pens, to mark innumerable items in the shop and during the load-in. The tape also comes in handy for keeping things attached to each other. The heat tape will be used to keep the templates immobile in their template holders, while the electrical tape will be used to label the feeder cable while the dimmers are being installed. The clip lights will be used for backstage running lights, while the batteries will be part of the wireless dimming system in the costume pieces.

This list only scratches the surface of items commonly used during a load-in. Other items include; colored spike tape, clear dance floor tape, and friction tape. The use of office supplies has surged as office supply stores have provided more diverse labels, label makers, highlighters, and marking utensils.

Perishable Notes

Depending on the lighting rental house, the perishable label often extends to include worklights, clip lights, and other smaller fixtures. In a long-term rental, the more small doodads that are defined as "perishables," the better the chances are that the weekly rental price for the lighting package will be a little lower. In a short run situation, the overall price tag of the bid may be the same, no matter whether said doodads are perishables or rentals. The challenge is often figuring out what the small stuff in the lighting rental is before the load-out; if it's been purchased as a "perishable," make sure it's not returning as a "rental." If nothing else, some amount of credit should be applied to the final settlement between the production and the lighting rental shop for any purchased items that were never used and returned.

Rental Shop Rudeness

Some folks have differing opinions about different shops. Some have personal relationships and go golfing with upper management. Others submit shop orders to potential vendors with less respect than they deserve, and they can often reap what they sow. Shops typically consist of a bunch of theatre people, who collectively have their own feelings and loyalty to their employer. If a designer treats a shop like hired help existing only to service his or her artistic vision, the shop may quickly feel abused. One account rep related this story: "We got a shop order for 45 moving lights and cable as 'specified by the production electrician.' No dates, not even a theatre name. We had no idea what the cable routing path's might be, how long they needed to be, how the lights would be hung. We had no idea if we had available gear on the shelf that would be matching what wasn't even specified in the equipment list. We took a pass, and haven't quoted for him since." Sometimes, no matter what the money or enticement, the designer or the production electrician can quickly be perceived as not being worth the effort, and the shop will start refusing to provide a quote, wholly based on the personalities involved. Be nice.

Smart lighting designers never divulge the quoted numbers from one shop to another. This advantage allows one shop to undercut another's estimate and get the bid. While some designers don't see this as bad practice, shops are smart and quickly figure out what's going on. In turn, the losing shops may accurately feel abused; in their eyes, the only reason you submit a shop order to them is to provide the other shop with a number to undercut. If you work for a producer who only wants to use a specific shop that you've been burning in this manner, you might find a cooler reception than you think.

Shelley's Notes:
Rental Order Thoughts

As the shop order is being prepared, there are ways to proactively keep the rental number to a minimum. Here are a few ideas that may pay off:

- Go to the lighting rental shop and see what's on the back shelves; every shop has the dead bone area of gear that never gets rented. If it's in decent shape, it could potentially be big savings.
- Find out what brand of instruments, dimmers, or consoles the shop has the most of. That rents the cheapest.
- Find out what cabling costs are based on: the type? the length? bundles? old multicable?

- What's *not* the latest, but before that, decent version of dimmers? Presumably they're still in shape. Are they loud? Where do they need to be installed in the venue?
- What manufacturers does the shop represent? If they just rent it out, but they don't have the staff to maintain it, keep looking in their stock.
- What are the latest whiz-bang conventional lighting consoles? Great; set them aside. What do you need to do with this particular show? In many cases, the basic nuts and bolts conventional console will do most, if not all, that your show is going to need. Its not as *sexy*, but it's a lot *cheaper*.
- What's the latest moving-light console? Great; what's the earliest one in stock that you or your friend knows how to program? Maybe you can get two, one for backup?
- What's considered a perishable and what is the rental? I ran into one shop that charged $15 for a clip light that I could buy at the hardware store for $6. Hey, if you want it, they'll sell it to you.
- What's the cost of the perishables? Sometimes you can get a break on the rental price if you agree to pay their exorbitant perishable rates. On the other hand, these days, online perishable sales are cutthroat. If you can separate the line item and only get the rental from the lighting shop, you might save some money.
- That said, tread carefully. Deciding not to purchase perishables from a rental shop may be interpreted as an act of rudeness. Perishables can be a delicate topic. Be wary.

Shelley's Notes:
The *Hokey* Shop Order

For the purposes of this text, the *Hokey* shop order was created as three separate compressed illustrations. Regardless of the actual number of pages, it's usually sent out to the lighting rental shops as a single document.

The *Hokey* equipment list is a mix of technologies and potential negotiations. The Ion control console is relatively new at the time of this writing, so its weekly rental price may be a little more expensive. While the Ion has the hardware to program both the moving lights and the conventional instruments, the Hog has been included as a second control console to deal solely with the VL-5's. The present schedule already appears constrained for programming time. Assigning the responsibility of programming both the conventional and the moving lights to one console could potentially slow the process. The plan is to program the movers on the

Hog, and then transfer their control to the Ion after opening. This is still a plan in flux.

There are many more up-to-date moving lights currently on the market, but almost all of the local shops have some stock of VL-5's on the shelves, and everyone knows how to maintain them. Since they're no longer the "must-have" mover, the weekly rental price is going to be substantially lower. For that matter, the same can be said about the Hog lighting console. The only bad thing about the Hog is that it implies that a second console programmer will be required for the production period.

While the long runs of cable have all been spec'd as multi, some of that could be swapped out for bundles. Other things to consider if the quotes from the shop don't come under the numbers in the budgets:

- Keep one or both of the consoles at the tech table until just before previews. While it would get a little more crowded, it would reduce the number of flatscreen monitors and other hardware in the order.
- If need be, cut one of the 12-pack dimmer racks, which would also reduce the amount of feeder. It means there's that much less dimming flexibility. If need be, it could be possible to repatch a dimmer or two.
- If hard pressed, consider swapping out some of the Source Fours for some of the house gear. But only in dire conditions. The house equipment is old and won't be as bright, no matter where it's used.
- Cut the foggers down to two. The transition to the Precipice should fill the stage with fog as quickly as possible. If the budget gets tight, it might be possible to only have dry ice fog filling downstage first for that moment in the show.
- Cut the number of strobelights. While almost all of Tee-boo's entrances and scenes seem to be developing the visual need for strobes, there are currently eight in the plot. If needed, two might be cut without significantly hampering the moments.
- The color scrollers in the plot don't have to match color strings with each other. It would be nice, and it would make it simpler, but they don't necessarily have to match each other. The eight in the booms need to match, and all eight in the overheads need to match among themselves as well. If hard pressed, the shops may have sets of eight matching strings from other shows that might be available for a discount or as a loan.

While other effects might be cut, doing so will significantly impact the show and require some amount of rethinking to provide alternative solutions and create the same visual pictures.

The Shop Order Complete

Once the cover letter, equipment list, and the perishable list has been assembled, and at least reviewed by the production electrician, it's then ready to be submitted to the management office. They may not care about it, or they may only want to receive a copy for their files. Regardless, it makes good sense for them to have one on hand, if questions arise regarding financial information about the plot. Once the producer has approved the shop order, along with its presentation and its list of destinations, it can then be emailed, faxed, or overnighted to the chosen or requested lighting vendors.

Once the shop order has been sent out to the shops, the savvy lighting designer (or the production electrician) calls each shop to confirm that they've received the document. Just because information has left your hands, post office, fax machine, or email account, doesn't automatically imply that it's been immediately received. That same call can also briefly review contact information, and the scheduled deadline for the quote submission. Once all of the shops have acknowledged that they've received the information, the preparation and distribution of the shop orders are complete.

THE LABOR

In addition to working on the shop order, the production electrician has also studied the preliminary light plot and the production schedule. Combining those two pieces of information with previous knowledge about the performance facility, he or she can produce a preliminary labor projection to submit to management's office. On larger shows labor projections don't always seem to be as critical to the process. For smaller shows with finite funding, labor projections often receive more scrutiny.

Figure 5.36 shows the initial Electrics Labor Projection for *Hokey*. The document is broken down into approximately 4 weeks, one per large rectangle. The end of each work week, and each pay period, is Sunday. That said, the top rectangle combines the 2 days of prep (April 1 and 2) and the first week of load-in (April 5 through April 12) into a single pay period. The top row shows the date, the second row the day of the week, and the third row the scheduled activity. The left-hand column identifies the week, and then breaks down the members of the electrics crew. There's the production electrician, the assistant, and a total of 12 electricians. In reality the largest number of electricians working

HOKEY @ THE HYBRID   **ELECTRICS LABOR PROJECTION: V1**   Date: 2/13/10

HOKEY	Prep	1-Apr	2-Apr	5-Apr	6-Apr	7-Apr	8-Apr	9-Apr	10-Apr	11-Apr	12-Apr			
		THURS	FRI	MON	TUES	WED	THURS	FRI	SAT	SUN	MON			
WEEK 1+		Shop	Shop	Load-in	Load-in	Focus	Cue	Cue/Dry	Tech	Tech	Tech	TOTAL	RATE	TOTAL $$
PE	8	10	10	10	10	10	10	10	12	12	12	114	$35.00	$3,990.00
Asst		10	10	10	10	10	10	10	12	12	12	106	$30.00	$3,180.00
Crew#1		10	10	10	10							40	$25.00	$1,000.00
Crew#2		10	10	10	10							40	$25.00	$1,000.00
Crew#3		10	10	10	10							40	$25.00	$1,000.00
Crew#4		10	10	10	10	10						50	$25.00	$1,250.00
Crew#5				10	10	10						30	$25.00	$750.00
Crew#6				10	10	10						30	$25.00	$750.00
Console				10	10	10	10	10	12	12	12	86	$25.00	$2,150.00
Deck						10	10	10	12	12	12	66	$25.00	$1,650.00
Deck						10	10	10	12	12	12	66	$25.00	$1,650.00
Follow 1							10	10	12	12	12	56	$25.00	$1,400.00
Follow 2							10	10	12	12	12	56	$25.00	$1,400.00
Follow 3							10	10	12	12	12	56	$25.00	$1,400.00
												836		
Total HRS	8	60	60	90	90	80	80	80	96	96	96	836		$22,570.00

HOKEY	13-Apr	13-Apr	14-Apr	15-Apr	15-Apr	16-Apr	16-Apr	17-Apr	18-Apr			
	TUES	TUES	WED	THURS	THURS	FRI	FRI	SAT	SUN			
WEEK 2	Tech	Show	Show (2)	Tech	Show	Tech	Show	Show (2)	Show	TOTAL	RATE	TOTAL $$
PE	8	4	8	8	4	8	4	8	4	56	$35.00	$1,960.00
Asst	8	4	8	8	4	8	4	8	4	56	$30.00	$1,680.00
Console	8	4	8	8	4	8	4	8	4	56	$25.00	$1,400.00
Deck	8	4	8	8	4	8	4	8	4	56	$25.00	$1,400.00
Follow 1	8	4	8	8	4	8	4	8	4	56	$25.00	$1,400.00
Follow 2	8	4	8	8	4	8	4	8	4	56	$25.00	$1,400.00
Follow 3	8	4	8	8	4	8	4	8	4	56	$25.00	$1,400.00
										392		
Total HRS	56	28	56	56	28	56	28	56	28	392		$10,640.00

HOKEY	20-Apr	20-Apr	21-Apr	22-Apr	23-Apr	24-Apr	25-Apr			
	TUES	TUES	WED	THURS	FRI	SAT	SUN			
WEEK 3	Tech	Show	Show (2)	Show	Show	Show (2)	Show	TOTAL	RATE	TOTAL $$
PE	8	4	8	4	4	8	4	40	$35.00	$1,400.00
Asst	8	4	8	4	4	8	4	40	$30.00	$1,200.00
Console	8	4	8	4	4	8	4	40	$25.00	$1,000.00
Deck	8	4	8	4	4	8	4	40	$25.00	$1,000.00
Follow 1	8	4	8	4	4	8	4	40	$25.00	$1,000.00
Follow 2	8	4	8	4	4	8	4	40	$25.00	$1,000.00
Follow 3	8	4	8	4	4	8	4	40	$25.00	$1,000.00
								280		
Total HRS	56	28	56	28	28	56	28	280		$7,600.00

HOKEY	27-Apr	28-Apr	29-Apr	30-Apr	1-May	2-May			
	TUES	WED	THURS	FRI	SAT	SUN			
WEEK 4	Show	Show (2)	Show	Show	Show (2)	Show	TOTAL	RATE	TOTAL $$
PE	4	8	4	4	8	4	32	$35.00	$1,120.00
Asst	4	8	4	4	8	4	32	$30.00	$960.00
Console	4	8	4	4	8	4	32	$25.00	$800.00
Deck	4	8	4	4	8	4	32	$25.00	$800.00
Follow 1	4	8	4	4	8	4	32	$25.00	$800.00
Follow 2	4	8	4	4	8	4	32	$25.00	$800.00
Follow 3	4	8	4	4	8	4	32	$25.00	$800.00
							224		
Total HRS	28	56	28	28	56	28	224		$6,080.00

Figure 5.36 The First Labor Projection for *Hokey*

on any given day is nine, including the production electrician and the assistant. The running crew will not become available until later in the first week, as the show is getting focused and cued. By Thursday, April 8, the show crew is on payroll for the cueing session, and remains so through the end of that week.

The second rectangle details the second week, starting on Tuesday, April 13. The schedule starts on Tuesday because after opening, Monday will be the dark day. The columns in the second rectangle show fewer hours, but part of that is due to the fact that there's a division between a work call and a show call. On Tuesday, April 13 there are actually two columns; the 8-hour work call during the day, and the show call that night. Wednesday, April 14, shows only 8 hours, since that will only be two 4-hour show calls. There will be no work call during that morning; between the preview on Tuesday night, and the two shows on Wednesday the 14th, a work call would have very little value, and could potentially invoke overtime rates.

Thursday the 15th, on the other hand, there will be 8 hours of work and tech, followed by another 4-hour show call. The same schedule will hold for Friday the 16th as well, but Saturday the 17th will be only two show calls. No work or rehearsal in the morning for the cast. Finally on Sunday the 18th, there will be only the show call for the matinee, and then, by the grace of all that is holy, there will finally be a night off on Sunday night, and a day off on Monday, April 19.

The remaining rows within each rectangle show each crew person's role with the show, and the number of hours they'll be working for each session and each day. The right-hand columns shows the sum of each row of hours, the rates, and the final column shows the estimated amount of gross pay that each stagehand will receive.

Glancing at the bottom right-hand corner of each rectangle, it's then possible to see the total amount that will be spent for the electrics department for each of the first 4 weeks. The first pay period is comparably high, because of the overall number of hours, and the fact that it also includes two days of prep from the week before. As the weeks progress, however, this labor projection chart shows that, by the time the show is in performance-only mode, the weekly cost for the electrics crew has dropped down to only $6,080.00.

While the load-in, second, and third weeks are higher than what was originally budgeted, the weekly total after that is only $80.00 more than the original budget projection. The production electrician is comfortable with the amount of labor indicated on the labor projection to get all of the work done for the show. The document is submitted to the management office for approval.

THE MASKING AND SCENIC RENTAL ORDER

The soft goods order that has been submitted to the soft goods rental shops requesting quotes is as follows:

- Five pairs of black legs 30'-0" tall × 10'-0" wide.
- Four pair black legs 30'-0" tall × 6'-0" wide (tabs).
- Five black borders 12'-0" tall × 50'-0" long.
- One black traveler, consisting of (2) 30'-0" tall × 30'-0" wide panels (with track, hardware, and black rope).
- One black scrim 30'-0" tall × 50'-0" wide.
- One white translucency 30'-0" tall × 50'-0" wide (PURCHASE).
- One bounce drop 30'-0" tall × 50'-0" wide.
- 20 3'-0" long batten extensions.

After some amount of study this all seems to make sense. The black traveler is going to take the most time being installed in the middle of the stage, and potentially get in the way of everything else. The schedule should be reviewed to see if a time period could be set aside for the traveler's installation. The traveler also presumably means that the rental shop will have to deliver the rental in a longer truck in order to deliver the pieces of the track, along with the carriers, and the rest of the hardware.

SUMMARY

The shop order has been sent off to lighting rental shops for their quotes, which will be submitted to the management office. The preliminary labor projections have been compiled by the production electrician and submitted to the management's office. The management office has also sent off copies of the masking and scenic goods rental to soft goods vendors.

Now that the light plot's been approved and the shop orders have been sent out, the next step is to receive the quotes and negotiate an agreement with a lighting rental shop. After that, the drafting and the paperwork for the light plot can begin in earnest. This is now a moment that the lighting designer can sit back and take a breath.

Chapter 6

Cuts and Changes

INTRODUCTION

This chapter examines some of the events that take place after the shop order has been sent to the lighting rental shops. In some cases, changes are sometimes necessary to a preliminary light plot in order to make it fit within predetermined budgetary constraints and receive the producer's approval.

When the shop order is sent out, each lighting rental shop responds by producing a **quote**, or a **bid**. Once the quotes are sent **back** to management for consideration, each one is analyzed and compared to the original shop order and each other.

If all of the bids are too high, either the producer has to increase the size of the electrics budget, or the light plot has to cost less. In order to cut costs, the equipment specified in the rental needs to be exchanged (or swapped) for alternate brands, older gear, or removed altogether from the order; the light plot gets cut. Cutting the plot usually involves downsizing the equipment list and perishable list, and then resubmitting the shop order. When the producer accepts a shop's adjusted quote, based on those changes, the two come to an agreement. The producer then **awards the bid** to the shop, publicly declaring it to be the vendor supplying the equipment and perishables for the lighting package. While there will be numerous changes as the light plot is finalized, the lighting rental shop that received the bid will now be the exclusive resource for lighting or electrical components for *Hokey*.

THE BIDDING PROCESS

Preparing, researching, and selecting a bid are time-consuming processes. Choosing the best lighting rental shop, and finding the right fit for the show takes attention to detail, and a knowledge of lighting equipment. In some situations the lighting designer may not be directly involved in this portion of the process. Other times, if no one else is representing the lighting designer's interests, he or she may be drawn into active participation based solely on the instinct of self-preservation and defending the integrity of his or her design.

This next section is a quick overview of the typical events that take place between sending out the shop order and awarding the bid. All too often, these events take place in less time than one would prefer. Timeliness is desirable, and late is expensive. Understanding the process, and knowing the capabilities of similar types and brands of equipment, are two tools that can help the lighting designer successfully negotiate the best possible lighting package in spite of cuts or changes.

The Shop Order Arrives at the Shops

When the shop order arrives at each lighting rental shop, it's then assigned to an account rep. For that matter, preliminary phone calls with the lighting designer or production electrician may have already allowed the shop to decide which account rep to assign to the anticipated show. All the information listed in the shop order is then re-entered into each shop's rental software system. In most cases this procedure is performed for two reasons: one, to determine how much of the requested equipment will actually be on hand during the time period specified in the shop order, and two, to use the software's pricing formulas to calculate the rental prices.

If specific brands of gear requested in the shop order aren't carried by the shop, most lighting shops feel obligated to inform the designer of the swap, even if it's the same instrument type. If the equipment list requests Strand SL-10° ellipsoidals, for example, but the shop only has ETC Source Four-10° ellipsoidals instead, standard business practices dictate that the shop should still inform the lighting designer of the change.

Likewise, if the gear requested in the equipment list isn't available during the rental period, the account rep's first step is to check the "in-house" inventory (on the company's shelves). Comparisons are made to see if something in-house can be suggested that the lighting designer will accept as a substitution. Successful substitutions mean the shop can still provide something like the item in question, without having to pay money to sub-rent the gear from other competing shops. Accepting a reasonable equipment substitution helps keep the final price down, but the lighting designer may in turn feel that the light plot is being compromised. If the substitution is refused, then the sub-rental takes place. That additional cost, though, is then added to the quote, and the final bid number escalates. This process is often a delicate series of negotiations; everyone wants to produce an affordable package that achieves the lighting designer's vision, but without angering anyone and jeopardizing potential future work.

While discussing substitutions makes good business sense, it's also a contractual necessity. The typical shop order cover page contains the clause stating "no substitutions without permission." Over time, negotiating changes or substitutions within a show has become standard operating procedure. Typically an account rep compiles a list of questions, anomalies, absent gear, and possible substitutions. The rep then calls and discusses all of the issues at once with the lighting designer or the production electrician. Decisions are reached or temporarily tabled, so that the process can move along.

Once the logistics and the equipment totals are fed into the shop's rental software, built-in formulas help tabulate the rental price. The different formulas, discounts, and fee structures are often radically different between shops and software. Usually they're based on the number of weeks, the value of the gear involved, and the rental fee structure (off-Broadway, Broadway, Industrial, TV, and so forth). Some portion of the rental price is also based on the calculated cost of the shop's staff, to both maintain and assemble the lighting package before it leaves the shop (the **prep**), and to restore the equipment back to the shop's shelves once the package is delivered back to the shop after load-out (the **return**).

If a live-stage production is submitted as a limited-run engagement, those costs might be part of a weekly rental fee, multiplied by the number of weeks, to produce the rental price. In this case, the show has been presented as an open-ended run. Since there's no telling if the show will be a hit and run for years, or a flop that closes the day after the reviews come out, the fee structure is loaded up front. The first three weekly payments might be $12,000.00, for example, and then the weekly fee after that might drop down to $3,500.00 a week. By structuring the initial payments higher, even if the show flops the shop will still be covered for the time incurred by the staff for the prep and the return.

After the gear availability and substitutions are considered and addressed, the next question considered is transport. How many trucks will be required to transport the gear from the lighting rental shop to the performance space? Each truck will cost some amount of money for the fuel, not to mention the driver. Although the shop order that has been received has attempted to list every item that will be required, the lighting rental shop still gets stuck estimating how many trips in which sized truck will get the rented lighting package from Point A to Point B. On top of that, somewhere in the price a cushion has to be built to cover the additional trips for the trucks to pick up the empty containers, and the "Whoops we forgot this little doodad" or the "Oh, the one thing we didn't get a spare of just broke, we must have a replacement as soon as possible" trips.

While the size and number of trucks are one set of issues to ponder, another set is the delivery schedule. If delivery dates and times aren't clearly stated on the shop order cover letter, making the wrong assumption can have a big impact on the shipping price. Deliveries after business hours usually cost more than deliveries during the day. Deliveries during the weekend are often even more costly. In addition to that, the speed in which equipment needs to be on site may make a significant difference as well. If a single truckload provides enough gear to work for the first work call, the same truck loaded with the second load may be able to avoid the need for a second rented truck altogether. The late night weekend delivery will probably cost more, taking a larger portion of the overall bid. In turn that will reduce the amount of money left to rent the lighting equipment in the first place.

Finally, the perishables portion of the bid is relatively simple to produce, presuming that it's based on facts, not just general description. Statements on a shop order that include "color as needed" merely indicate the plot isn't complete, and most shops won't even submit a number. While a young account rep might assume that any instrument will only require one piece of color, they'll be mortified when the designer later adds an extra piece of diffusion to every instrument and doubles the color cost.

Constructing a competitive bid is not a simple process. The more finite the shop order, the more likely the bids will reflect an accurate cost for the package. The more general the shop order, the more likely the shop will "pad" against what they perceive as hidden potential costs. By protecting their interests (and their bottom line), the final bid will reflect that uncertainty and may be higher than it really needs to be.

Constructing a competitive bid is also not a quick process. It takes some amount of time to enter the information, check the stock, make substitution choices, and negotiate an accurate and complete lighting package. Allowing some amount of time between sending out a shop order and requesting a quote allows the account rep and the shop time to consider all the permutations and put together a reasonable order. Sending out a shop order with little time to process it almost always results in higher quotes. While everyone wants work and the chance to make money, no one wants to get caught short and submit a bid that doesn't allow some amount of overhead for the unknown. The shop will cover its financial back and pad the numbers where needed. If they're not given a proper amount of time, the quotes will consistently be higher.

Finally, constructing a competitive bid is not an easy process. The account rep has to produce final numbers that are comparable to the competition, provide a quality service to the client, but also provide some amount of profit to the shop. On top of that, the bid ideally is somehow more attractive to the client; the lower price always gets the first attention.

Sometimes it's not possible to provide the shop with all of the information. Sometimes the shop order is missing critical information and the lighting designer isn't aware of it. In either scenario, account reps may reach out to the lighting designer to ask questions, define the needs, and make the bid more accurate. To that end, during the time between when the shop orders are sent out and when the bids are due, the lighting designer must be available and ready to answer any questions, or consider substitutions. For that matter, some designers are more pro-active and call to "check in" with the account reps at a mid-point during the bid preparation period, as a point of courtesy and to provide the account rep with an opportunity to make any nagging inquiries and resolve any issues that might otherwise be missed.

The Quotes Arrive at the Management Office

When all of the negotiations and questions and substitutions are complete, the final numbers are totaled, put down on paper, and sent back to the show. Once the bid has been sent back, that's a line in the sand. Any changes, negotiations, or decisions are then based upon that set of numbers, and how they compare to the numbers from the other competing lighting rental shops.

In this case, all of the bids are emailed to the manager's office. Each lighting rental shop's quote is often a multi-page document made up of three parts. The first part restates logistics: the billing, contact, and destination information, followed by the relevant dates and method of delivery. Finally, some shops attach elements of their boilerplate contract to the bid. That often includes details about the shipping, labor, insurance, and payment information. One important label that each shop adds to their quote is an internal reference order number. This number is often the name of the document in their computer system. For most shops, using this reference number is the fastest way for anyone at that shop to access information about any aspect of this bid.

In addition to the logistical pro forma business information, the bid also usually includes a reiteration of the original equipment list translated into each rental shop's software. In order to keep track of the inventory, the relatively simple equipment list sent to any shop can turn into multiple pages of detailed, and often very confusing, inventory information. In some cases it may have been entered into the rental software in the same order as it was shown on the shop order, but it can still be seemingly gibberish by the time it gets back in the form of a quote. The reason for this is to streamline the process and have fewer mistakes in the shop. The inventory software breaks down each piece of equipment into its separate components, so that once the order is successfully selected for the bid, the same document can then be used for the prep. Any changes to the order, either during the bidding process, or during the assembly of the lighting package, are then updated in one document. Regardless of the appearance, this list usually only includes gear, and does not include pricing. After the equipment list is the perishables list. This is a reflection of what was originally sent to the shop, and may have a few substitutions as well. Again, it likely won't include individual line-by-line prices.

The final portion of the quote is the summation, initially separated into the three major line items, each with its own sub-total: the rental, the transportation, the perishables, and then any applicable taxes.

Once the bids have been submitted to the show management's office, they're individually reviewed and compared to one to another. After an initial review, the management of the show provides copies of all the quotes to the lighting designer and production manager. At some point during that time, a lighting rental shop is awarded the bid. The sequential order in which these actions take place is varied and usually produces a variety of results. Experience has shown that it's valuable to analyze the quotes before making a final decision. Usually the only people who can analyze and compare the bids with any speed or accuracy are the people who prepared the original shop order. In this case, those people are the lighting designer and the production electrician.

Reviewing each bid against the original shop order ensures that all of the gear initially listed on the shop order has actually been included in the bid. Errors entering information into the lighting rental software don't happen very often, but they do happen. Folks get interrupted, writing can't be read, assumptions are made; there are any number of ways that mistakes can take place. If the bid has been awarded and errors, or missing gear, are then discovered after the fact, it may be brushed aside as a minor honest mistake. If it's a big-ticket item that dropped through the cracks, on the other hand, the shop might want to adjust the bid. While the producer can say that the rental shop needs to provide what was on the shop order, the shop can argue that the producer awarded the bid based on the errant equipment list included in the quote. It can quickly turn into a "he said, she said" situation, and while it somehow always seems to work out, no one is happy, and it can quickly sour a budding professional relationship.

Other times, the price may be lower because gear has just been excluded due to changes in policy: "We don't rent printers any more." That's obvious to them in the shop, because they work there, or the policy change may have taken place so far in their past that it's now taken for granted. While it may be irritating to discover that the quote doesn't include everything that was originally requested, it's even more frustrating to make this discovery in the middle of the load-in after the trucks have dropped off the gear and departed. Carefully analyzing the quotes and asking questions cannot be stressed enough.

There are also instances when the bid may include accidental substitutions. Sometimes shops just don't have that particular doodad in stock, and the substitution isn't deemed important enough to notify

the lighting designer about the change. Sometimes lighting rental shop software works like a pharmacy. While the lighting designer specifies a brand-name device, the shop's computer may spit out the generic version of the same kind of product instead. Sometimes gear is swapped without the account rep being made aware of it; it can take place in his or her absence, and the colleague doesn't know the plot. It's rare that it will be discovered as an intentional act, but in any event, it's sloppy. Being surprised by an equipment swap on a quote sheet makes most designers' or production electricians' antenna start to quiver, and the rest of the entire quote is re-examined with a fine tooth comb.

Sometimes the shop just runs out of time to call the designer or production electrician in order to interpret what was asked for on the original shop order. What may seem clearly obvious to those who created the document may make no sense to those who are frantically trying to interpret it, in order to submit the quote before the deadline.

In any event, the lowest bid may not be the best one. Or it might be lower for a specific reason. It might have a better price because it's missing a dimmer rack, or all the automated fixtures. The total price may not include the perishables; that shop's policy may be to ignore them in the bidding process and treat them as a separate invoice after the fact. The bid may have completely misunderstood the delivery times, thinking that the trucks arrive at noon, rather than midnight. For all of these reasons, double-checking any quote is rarely seen as a bad idea. In order to check the bids, one common technique is to make as many copies of the shop order as there are incoming quotes. Pair off one copy to each bid, and then cross-check each one separately, line by line. Make up a list of questions or notes next to each one, and when the crosschecking is complete, label and staple the two documents together. When time allows, complete this cross-comparison before taking any other action.

Once all the bids are compared against the initial shop order, phone calls to each of the account reps may be necessary to answer any of those cross-checking questions, and to make sure that additional information won't lower the price of the submitted bid. If nothing else, taking this step ensures that when the bids are being compared to one another, they're being done so on a level-playing surface. At this point mistakes on both sides in the documentation or interpretation have been discovered and corrected. After this point, the bids are all considered hard numbers.

A meeting is typically held with the management of the show in order to share the comparisons and analysis. In addition to the question of money, the final decision may also rest on past experiences, reports from other shows, quality of the gear, speed of service, flexibility, and attention to detail. In addition to that, the management office may also be checking the fine print and comparing each shop's insurance policies, billing policies, and methods of accepting payment. And last, but certainly not least, is the issue of personal relationships between the show's management and the shops: who knows who, shared histories, financial scrutiny, desperation level, and so forth.

All of this is a complex process potentially involving significant sums of money. Proper research and analysis choosing the right bid take time. Because of that, standard operating practice is to build a day or two into the schedule between the submission deadline and the time the bid is awarded. While some of these events seem to take place in less time than one would prefer, it's certainly preferable to situations when suddenly the show seems to be on the brink of disaster, and serious choices must be made quickly in order to keep the production on course.

THE BUDGET GETS SLASHED

When the quotes from the lighting rental shops return to the management's office, sometimes everything moves according to plan. At least one of the quotes is found acceptable, the lighting rental shop is chosen, the contract is signed, and the lighting designer can begin producing the final light plot and support paperwork in preparation for the rehearsals, the shop prep, and the load-in.

Other times there may be a bit of a bump in the flow, as some amount of negotiation must take place. In most cases, this includes private negotiations held between the show's producer or management office and the lighting rental company's owner or business manager behind closed doors. In many cases the lighting designer isn't requested to attend or, in most cases, is politely asked to be absent while these meetings take place.

Finally, there are the times when the lighting designer is dragged into tension-filled meetings or conference calls, where he or she may then have to quickly respond to hard questions that have nothing to do with the art and all to do with the dollar. Sometimes those meetings take on the immediacy of triage surgery; in those rapid-fire situations, the lighting designer needs to remain calm and be very careful about what he or she says. Whatever statements or agreements are made in the heat of those meetings are likely to become part of newly created verbal agreements that significantly impact the lighting for the show.

For the purposes of this text, the remainder of this chapter will deal with the repercussions of that third type of meeting, and the dose of stinging reality that all lighting designers know too well. The quotes have returned, and what was the reassuring happy-go-lucky "Don't worry, we'll see, let's just get the numbers back" has now turned into the grim "The show may not survive, what are you going to do?"

Sometimes shows lose investors, agreements are broken, or financing falls through. While any number of stories can be told about productions that have ran into financial shoals, the end result is often the same: in order to survive, the show has to make some significant artistic cutbacks. The lighting designer (presumably along with the rest of the design and technical departments) must make practical compromises in order for the production to move ahead, albeit not with the originally conceived financial firepower.

In the case of *Hokey*, the producer has issued a series of edicts in order to save the show:

- The pyro won't pass local fire code. It was going to require more folks with a license. It's cut.
- The mid-stage painted scrim and blackout drop are cut. The sprung floor is cut.
- The vinyl floor will be rented. Thankfully, the white translucency has been saved.
- The custom-made boots and footwear have been cut. The costume budget has been slashed. The number of dressers is going to be cut.
- The second assistant stage manager has been cut. The first assistant stage manager will have to run the entire deck.
- The stage manager will no longer call the show from the back of the house next to the sound console. The seats that would have been removed in order for that to happen are now desperately needed. The stage manager's calling position will now move to the followspot booth.
- The lighting console operator will no longer be in the back of the house either. Those seats are also required. The lighting console will also have to move to the booth.
- The sound console is going to be downsized; smaller footprint, fewer house seats lost. But it will remain at the back of the house. But no longer on centerline; it's going to move into a back corner of the orchestra.
- The producer has "made a deal" with a friend who will now provide all of the masking soft goods.
- Each department must make massive cuts in their respective budgets. Lighting is no different— massive cuts must take place in both the budgeted amounts for the gear, and for the labor involved to produce and maintain the show.

This is yet another time that the lighting designer may not be involved in this portion of the process. Meetings with the management team may provide enough information so that the lighting designer many not have to become involved in this level of negotiation or deal with these kinds of changes. For the purposes of this text, however, that's not the case, and the lighting designer and production electrician have been given the task to do whatever it takes, without the intervention or support of the management office, to get what's needed for the show but still come in under the newly reduced number.

In addition to all of those announcements, Figure 6.1 shows the new production schedule being distributed. Thursday, April 10, which had been originally scheduled for the completion of focus and cueing time, has now turned into a dry tech starting at 10:00. Friday, April 11, which had been an afternoon tech, has now turned into a full "10 out of 12"; that means the performers can rehearse 10 hours in a 12-hour period. Basically, the overall amount of preparation time available before performers are added to the stage has been reduced by 12 hours. An already tight production schedule just got tighter. Obviously, this news dramatically impacts the load-in and labor for the installation of the light plot. While the lighting designer might initially be considering tactics to use in order to be ready for the technical rehearsals, there's no doubt that it's going to impact every work call before that as well.

Initial Analysis

Receiving either one of these announcements is a shock. Every carefully projected scenario or plan has been thrown into the air like a handful of Pick-up Sticks. Being presented with both announcements back-to-back on the heels of one another can double the shock. While it's easy to feel daunted or overwhelmed, having both of these incidents simultaneously take place is a hidden blessing. Dealing with either a budget cut or the compression of the production schedule is an extreme challenge. But reacting to one of them, making a plan, and *then*

		PRODUCTION SCHEDULE APRIL 2010 v3			
HOKEY: A MUSICAL MYTH — Date: 2/20/10

Week 1

SUNDAY 4 — APRIL

MONDAY 5 — LOAD-IN / HYBRID THEATRE
- 8:00A 1:00P LOAD-IN ELEC & RIG
- 1:00P 2:00P LUNCH
- 2:00P 7:00P ELEC FOH / RIG AS NEED / SCENERY IN

TUESDAY 6
- 8:00A 1:00P DECK LOAD / FLOOR LOAD
- 1:00P 2:00P LUNCH / LAY FLOOR
- 2:00P 7:00P TRIM / FOCUS FOH

WEDNESDAY 7
- 8:00A 1:00P FOCUS W/WORKS
- 1:00P 2:00P LUNCH / TUNE PIANO
- 2:00P 7:00P FOCUS DONE / CUE LIGHTS / WALKERS

THURSDAY 8
- 8:00A 10:00A CUE LIGHTS / WALKERS
- 10:00A 1:00P DRY TECH
- 1:00P 2:00P LUNCH
- 2:00P 7:00P DRY TECH

FRIDAY 9
- 8:00A 9:00A WALK THRU
- 9:00N 1:00P Q2Q-SPACE / PROPS LOAD
- 12:00N 1:00P LUNCH
- 1:00P HALF HOUR
- 1:30P 5:00P TECH A1 / STOP & GO
- 5:00P 6:00P DINNER
- 6:30P 10:00P TECH A/A2 / STOP & GO
- 10:00P 11:00P NOTES
- 11:00P END OF DAY

SATURDAY 10
- 8:00A 12:00N TECH TBA
- 12:00N 1:00P LUNCH
- 1:00P HALF HOUR
- 1:30P 5:00P TECH A2 / STOP & GO
- 5:00P 6:00P DINNER
- 6:30P 10:00P RUN
- 10:00P 11:00P NOTES
- 11:00P END OF DAY

Week 2

SUNDAY 11
- 8:00A 12:00N TECH TBA
- 12:00N 1:00P LUNCH
- 1:00P HALF HOUR
- 1:30P 5:00P PIANO TECH
- 5:00P 6:00P DINNER
- 6:00P 6:30P HALF HOUR
- 6:30P 10:30P DRESS TECH
- 10:30P 11:00P NOTES
- 11:00P END OF DAY

MONDAY 12
- 8:00A 12:00N TECH TBA
- 12:00N 1:00P SET PIT SOUND
- 12:00N 1:00P LUNCH
- 1:00P 5:00P ORCH SITZ
- 5:00P 6:00P DINNER
- 6:00P 6:30P HALF HOUR
- 6:30P 10:30P PIANO DRESS
- 10:30P 11:00P NOTES
- 11:00P END OF DAY

TUESDAY 13 — PREVIEW / HYBRID THEATRE
- 8:00A 12:00N TECH TBA
- 12:00N 1:00P LUNCH
- 1:00P HALF HOUR
- 1:30P 4:00P ORCH DRESS (INVITED) / PHOTOG
- 4:00P 4:30P NOTES
- 4:30P 5:00P NOTES/CLR
- 5:00P 6:30P DINNER
- 6:30P SHOW CALL
- 7:30P HOUSE OPEN
- 8:00P **PREVIEW 1**

WEDNESDAY 14
- NO MORNING CALL
- 12:30P SHOW CALL
- 1:30P HOUSE OPEN
- 2:00P PREVIEW 2
- 6:30P SHOW CALL
- 7:30P HOUSE OPEN
- 8:00P PREVIEW 3

THURSDAY 15
- 8:00A 12:00N TECH TBA
- 12:00N 1:00P LUNCH
- 1:00P 4:30P NOTES/TECH
- 4:30P 5:00P NOTES/CLR
- 5:00P 6:30P DINNER
- 6:30P SHOW CALL
- 7:30P HOUSE OPEN
- 8:00P PREVIEW 4

FRIDAY 16
- 8:00A 12:00N TECH TBA
- 12:00N 1:00P LUNCH
- 1:00P 4:30P NOTES/TECH
- 4:30P 5:00P NOTES/CLR
- 5:00P 6:30P DINNER
- 6:30P SHOW CALL
- 7:30P HOUSE OPEN
- 8:00P PREVIEW 5

SATURDAY 17
- 12:30P SHOW CALL
- 1:30P HOUSE OPEN
- 2:00P PREVIEW 6
- 6:30P SHOW CALL
- 7:30P HOUSE OPEN
- 8:00P PREVIEW 7

Week 3

SUNDAY 18
- 12:30P SHOW CALL
- 1:30P HOUSE OPEN
- 2:00P PREVIEW 8

MONDAY 19
- DAY OFF

TUESDAY 20 — PRESS OPENING / HYBRID THEATRE
- 8:00A 11:00A TBA
- 11:00A 12:00N LUNCH
- 12:00N 3:30P NOTES/TECH
- 3:30P 4:00P NOTES/CLR
- 4:00P 5:00P DINNER
- 5:00P SHOW CALL
- 6:00P HOUSE OPEN
- 6:30P **PERF 1**

WEDNESDAY 21
- NO MORNING CALL
- 12:30P SHOW CALL
- 1:30P HOUSE OPEN
- 2:00P PERF 2
- 6:30P SHOW CALL
- 7:30P HOUSE OPEN
- 8:00P PERF 3

THURSDAY 22
- 6:30P SHOW CALL
- 7:30P HOUSE OPEN
- 8:00P PERF 4

FRIDAY 23
- 6:30P SHOW CALL
- 7:30P HOUSE OPEN
- 8:00P PERF 5

SATURDAY 24
- 12:30P SHOW CALL
- 1:30P HOUSE OPEN
- 2:00P PERF 6
- 6:30P SHOW CALL
- 7:30P HOUSE OPEN
- 8:00P PERF 7

TEMPLATE PRODUCTIONS 212.555.1212   NEW YORK, NY 10025   www.fieldtemplate.com

Figure 6.1 The *Hokey* Production Schedule, Version 3

getting hit with the second situation, can be even more deflating. Making decisions and proceeding half-way through one set of changes, only to have the *second* one blow up in your face, can set you right back to square one. All of the initial changes now have to be reviewed and potentially altered to address the second new parameter.

While either situation is a challenge (and there is no question of that), having the opportunity to address both of them at one time has to be viewed as a tactical advantage. Figuring out the problems and solving the puzzles once will require only one set of decisions that can then be simultaneously applied to provide a single solution to both problems.

A General Plan

Approaching these challenges can be conducted in any number of ways. Here's one list of steps assembled as a general plan. As a caveat, I don't presume that this list is composed in the best sequence to make it useful for all of these kinds of situations. For that matter, these may not even be the right steps. Experience has shown, though, that some sense of these steps will advance the process toward a successful solution.

- Determine the amount of time available, and when final decisions need to be made.
- Make sure that everyone involved who needs to be notified of the situation is.
- Define the parameters: Determine the final target budget number for the bid, the final hours for the production schedule, the final size of the crew to install and run the show.
- Acquire information: get copies of every potential quote.
- Analyze and compare each potential bid for accuracy against the original shop order. If time is limited, use broad strokes.
- Determine if more than one shop will be involved. The selected shops are then labeled "relevant."
- Speak with each relevant shop to clarify anomalies in the bids, clarify big-ticket items, and identify all potential options and substitutions.
- Analyze the show and define what can be exchanged, altered, or cut.
- Ensure that the director and management are aware of the current situation.
- Negotiate an agreement about an altered lighting package with the relevant shops.
- Notify everyone involved, relevant or not, when agreements have been made.

- Instigate the changes, have them double-checked, and then distribute the updated information as rapidly as possible.

Although many of these steps may overlap or take place in a different order than what's shown here, they can all be distilled down to three basic guidelines:

- Make sure that everyone is aware of what is going on, especially the producer and the director.
- Whenever possible, make rational decisions based on facts, instead of knee-jerk reactions.
- Keep a detailed diary of everything that takes place. Keep all documents in archive for reference. When possible, have information double-checked before publication.

Determine a Timeline

Define a timeline to determine how quickly any actions and decisions need to take place. In almost any case, it's not possible to do much of anything in the next 10 minutes; merely getting a single account rep on the phone at any of the shops can conceivably take longer than that. In order to adequately analyze the situation, speak to all of the relevant lighting shops about changes in the shop order, make decisions, resubmit the shop order, and get new quotes—most lighting designers would agree that process would take some number of hours. Depending on variables, such as the complexity of the show or the monies involved, it may take a day or more to create the second version of the shop order. On the other hand, if an answer is needed immediately, presuming the lighting designer has the show fresh in his or her head, making quick decisions based on assumptions without a lot of analysis can always be made. In that situation, getting the information from the shops can take the most time. Sadly, however, if any of those quick assumptions turns out to be errant or off base, it's the lighting designer who will be stuck with the consequences.

Depending on the day of the week, or the time of day the announcements were made, getting new numbers may not be possible until at least the next day. While that may delay other decisions from being made, it may take an overnight session just to sort out what the alternatives, substitutions, or cuts need to be.

Notify All Concerned

If the lighting budget is getting cut, it only makes sense that the rest of the creative team should be quickly consulted before any decisive action is taken.

Presuming there is any available time, a production meeting of any sort can be extremely important and helpful for everyone to hear the same information, discuss possible solutions and alternatives, and as a team chart the new plan for the show.

The producer and management can provide a financial overview of the current status, answer questions, and provide a direction. Presumably the director and choreographer will be present, in order to react and adapt to the changes. They can also then hear the same limitations be placed on the rest of the design team. The rest of the design team or their associates can attend in person or by phone as well. No doubt each has a list of potential actions and decisions that may be made, along with questions for the lighting designer about shared elements and moments of the show.

In addition to the creative team, the technical staff should be alerted and join the production meeting as well. It goes without saying that the stage manager, production manager, and technical director's attendance is important. For the lighting designer, having the production electrician attend the meeting is just as important.

After a point, though, the number of folks invited to the meeting may be limited, if nothing else, by the size of the room. Completely outside of the realm of the technical aspects of the production, information and directives may need to include company management, the box office, advertising, casting, and group sales. While a financial hit like this is significant for everyone concerned with the technical aspects of the show, they are often by no means the most expensive elements of producing a for-profit theatrical venture.

There may be so many pending decisions that the first meeting may be more of a review of the current status, rather than a time for making any final declarations. A second meeting may be required after each department has more clarity regarding its new course in the adapted show.

Then there are the times of crisis when it seems no one can collectively get together for a cohesive conversation. Everyone is scattered to the wind, swallowed up by rehearsals or production periods for other shows. Although folks might not be immediately available to react to these types of drastic developments, most folks will agree that situations like these quickly must take precedence, even briefly, in order for the process to proceed, and more important, for the show to be saved. Regardless of whether the "circling of the wagons" takes the form of a full midnight production meeting after rehearsals, or limited by time zones to a series of emailed or texted responses, folks will stay in touch. When the meetings become scattered fragmentary instances,

however, most designers agree that keeping detailed notes and some form of diary provides the lighting designer with better odds to remember the flood of decisions, actions, and questions, while the production and the light plot gets any kind of significant "makeover."

While some amount of subsequent communication breakdowns and confusion will take place, this is one time that Internet communication really comes into play as a communication tool. Sending email or text blasts of decisions, choices, or even assumptions to the relevant team can quickly put everyone on the same page and establish a basis for dialogue. Web sites with downloadable FTP links can be used to quickly distribute new drawing versions to all parties. Web services such as gotomeeting.com allow several participants to not only discuss documents in a conference call, they can also all view the same document and add their own drawn or typed notes on screen at the same time.

In the case of *Hokey*, the scenery, costumes, and sound are all about to undergo significant changes. While it may be impossible to fully understand how each design element is going to integrate with one other, the basic framework often starts by talking (or writing) through the entire piece. While that may not be completely possible until clear decisions about the light plot are made, any decisions can only help provide clarity and the ability to make choices down the road.

In the meantime, emails, text messages, or brief phone calls should be sent to all of the account reps. Inform them that there has been a delay, and that the stated time scheduled in the shop order cover letter may be delayed. Let them know that you will be contacting them soon. This alerts everyone that any delay should not be construed as a dismissal. When your call comes in, it's not social, and you should not be put "on hold."

Define the Parameters

In this situation, the show has been presented to the shops as an open-ended run, so all of the bids have come back front-loaded. The price for the first 3 or 4 weeks of rental is much higher, and then after that drops down to a lower weekly price. The producer has given the lighting designer a target number that is less than a third of any of the bids for these first weeks. The producer has also cut the subsequent weekly rental fees in half.

The labor to mount the show is also now too high. While the projected weekly amount to run the show after it has opened only needs to be reduced to fit within the original budget, the labor cost to prep, install, and mount the lighting package cannot remain at the levels on the labor projection sheet. The producer has told the lighting designer and production electrician to reduce those labor projections by at least 35%.

Since the amount of time scheduled to prepare the stage prior to the beginning of the technical rehearsals has been truncated, however, the producer has approved extending the length of the work calls to 10 hours. This means that over the course of the first 3 days of load-in, there will be an additional 6 hours of stage time. But the amount of time to load light cues into the console between the end of focus and the beginning of the tech period with performers is still very short. It's apparent that a plan is needed in order to have some kind of light cues ready for the beginning of the technical rehearsals.

Acquire Information

Get complete copies of the quotes from the management office. If there's any question, make sure they're the same version of the documents that were originally received at the management office, to verify that everyone is operating from the same starting point. Sometimes it's faster, and makes more sense, to just go to the management office and photocopy all of the incoming documents.

Analyze and Compare the Bids

Check each quote for the dates of delivery, the contact information, and the billing information. Compare the quotes to one another for the number and size of the transport vehicles involved. Compare the quotes for any additional drop-off or pick-up costs.

Check each quote for the major components listed in the shop order. Large numbers to check include the overall number of conventional instruments, the number and manufacturer of moving lights, truss, consoles, and the number and make of the specialty instruments. Compare the overall number of dimmers, and the configuration of the dimmer racks. Check the overall number and lengths of the multicable, and the feeder cable. After the large numbers, then the smaller lengths of cable, iron, and so on. If time is an issue, assign some amount of time to each quote.

Make certain that what is being quoted closely matches what was originally submitted on the shop order. While some amount of substitution should be anticipated, sometimes miscommunication can occur. For example, dimming can be a point of interpretation between shop orders and quotes. Instead of the four 12×2.4-kw dimmer packs, the quote may instead list a third high-density 96×2.4-kw dimmer rack. Maybe the shop didn't have any 12 packs. Maybe the 12 packs weren't listed clearly enough in the proper manner, on the proper page, in the way that the person entering the information into the rental system preferred. If something sticks out, it may only be the tip of the miscommunicated iceberg.

It may turn out that the shop didn't have the LED striplights and so was going to sub-rent them from another vendor. Doing so added another percentage to the rental for the instruments.

Decide on the Number of Shops

A quick meeting or conversation should take place at least between the producer, management, and the lighting designer to define the first major decision: Is there enough time to send out a second reduced shop order and request a second set of quotes? More to the point, does it politically make sense to take this step? Will any (or all) of the lighting rental shops still want to be involved?

Once a shop has submitted a bid, they've done their job. The account rep has spent some amount of time assembling the numbers, negotiating the substitutions, and preparing the documents for the quote. At this point, all of this work has been done without any compensation whatsoever. When a shop doesn't get the bid, their account reps are being paid without generating any income. So after submitting the bid, all the shop wants to hear is either yes, no, or maybe. Upon hearing instead that the production needs to "cut down the design" sounds suspiciously like the show is clue-free, and wasn't properly funded in the first place. The "cuts" may merely be a decision by management that, after seeing everyone's bids, they didn't capitalize enough money for the technical aspects of the production. They're now announcing the cuts to get all of the shops to come down in price to match what was originally budgeted. After spending no small amount of time compiling the first submitted quote, some shops may see the cuts as a sign of poor management that may lead to unpaid bills. A second series of bids could be viewed as chasing a dead end.

If the decision is made at this point to ask all of the shops for a second series of bids, then each shop should be individually contacted in order to explain the situation, reassure them of the show's financing, and ask if they still wish to participate in the process. Those reassuring calls may need to come from someone with a little more financial "oomph" in the show management's office, rather than merely the lighting designer or the production electrician.

In this same meeting it may be valuable to double-check that no one has an unused contact, history, or new opinion about any of the rental shops that might be a useful resource. While initial inquiries for this kind of information were made long before the shops were chosen, it's worthwhile to bring this topic up again. Contacts or relationships may have changed since this topic was first broached, and it's another opportunity to ensure that all current courses of action being considered by the lighting department are approved by the producer or the show management's office.

In some situations, there may be time to speak with each of the account reps to repeat the same information and judge their individual responses. If time is constrained then it may be necessary to constrain the decision and choose a single shop, and a single account rep. That decision may be based on the price, or the document's presentation, or the shop's relationship with the producer, the management office, the lighting designer, or the production electrician. With all things being equal, the account rep chosen may be the one who will provide the additional background, reasoning, history, or insight that translate into the information, special deals, or inside tips specific to that shop which may in turn save the quote. Once decisions have been made, anyone in management not present in the meeting should be made aware of the course of action.

In the case of *Hokey*, the producer, the lighting designer, and the production electrician have discussed the amount of time required in order to prepare a reduced plot and make a second shop order. While the lighting designer can quickly react, make adjustments, and reduce the overall scope of the light plot, there's no telling if the reductions will be sufficient to stay within the new constrained budget. Likewise, this second request is going to come as a surprise to all of the lighting rental shops; the account reps may not have time available to devote to the construction of a second bid. The decision is made to target a single lighting rental shop that the producer has a prior relationship with. Presuming the producer makes the first call to the shop, the lighting designer will then be able to speak freely with the account rep.

Talk to the Shops

Call the account representative. Some folks believe that this phone call should remain private between the lighting designer and the account rep, while others think the production electrician or other members of management or the tech staff should be involved. If that's the choice, then speakerphones or conference-calling software can assist communication so that everyone involved all gets to hear the same thing at the same time. Experience has shown that if many folks are listening to the call, they should all identify themselves to the account rep at the beginning of the conversation.

Typically, the purpose of this first conversation is to review the current situation, define the schedule, and examine all potential substitution, replacement, or elimination possibilities in order to provide every feasible choice to the lighting designer. That way all possible options can be considered so that the best decisions can be made the first (and usually only) time. If there's any confusion about the equipment choices or the way that the original bid was constructed, this is the time to clarify any questions and remove them as future topics.

The meat of the conversation is to define what items in the quote represent the big-ticket expenditures. If there's been hesitation to discuss this topic before, this is the time to dispense with diplomacy and just ask. The show is in trouble, and presuming that the shop wants to be involved in the production, the account rep will be open to providing information regarding the reason for the high bid, and what might be exchanged, or cut, to quickly reduce the overall number.

When the possible choices for substitutions have been reviewed, a time should be scheduled for the next meeting to discuss cuts, or when the adjusted shop order should be sent to the account rep.

In some cases it may be very easy to determine what needs to be exchanged, or cut, from the shop order so that the final numbers that are returned as quotes are less than the new reduced budget demands. Sometimes it's only a single large change to make the monies balance out. Other times it's necessary to have a multi-step plan in place. In this case, there are three main big-ticket items.

- Moving lights, special effect lights, and LED striplights: While not top of the line, the moving lights are still not cheap. Including them, the Wholehog 2 lighting controller, and all the specialty hardware and cable combine to create a sum that is not insignificant. The special effect units, such as the strobes, the blacklights, and the Autoyokes, combine to create another sum that is not insubstantial. The LED striplights, at the time of this rental, is still relatively expensive. The fact that the plot is doubling up both the overhead electric and the groundrow means there are twice as many instruments included in the rental.

- Dimmers: The high-density racks and the small racks that have been specified on the original shop order are quieter, more efficient, and more compact. As such, they cost more to rent. If the show can find space for older, larger dimmers, the overall price would be less. If the choice is made to switch all of the dimmers to older models, they will take up more room, have louder fan noise, and potentially be more problematic. If the decision is to mix some old and some new dimmers, any fade curve difference between the two different kinds of dimmers may be noticeable from the audience. The two also have different inputs; the older racks only have stage pin plugs to each dimmer. The new dimmers have both stage pin plugs and multicable connectors.

- Cable: The original shop order asked for a substantial amount of multicable, rather than bundles. Since multicable is more compact and easier to handle, it's also more expensive. Multicable also terminates in compact connectors, while bundles are basically taped-together stage cables of matching lengths. Mixing and matching between the two dimmer systems will be more involved, and potentially require more adaptors.

With this information in hand, it is now possible to take a look at the shop order and make the adjustments necessary to satisfy the producer's requests. In other words, cut the plot. Hopefully, some amount of the show will still be left, once the cuts to the plot are complete.

Show Analysis

If the lighting package needs to be changed, or cut, most lighting designers agree "the sooner the better." The sooner the procedure takes place after the preliminary light plot and shop order are created, the fresher the light plot and core design documents are in the lighting designer's mind. In some situations, the lighting designer may able to rattle off which gear is expendable without thinking twice. Even while creating the light plot, many designers will mentally assign an internal prioritization to different equipment or effects: "This will create an incredible series of looks for the show, but if anything has to be cut, this would be one of the first things to go." Other than specific moments, however, having a solid sense about the amount of time or scenes that any system in the plot will be used can seem like a daunting task. But all of that information has already been decided and detailed in the systems and specials sheet.

Systems and Specials Sheet

The recipes listed in each scene or transition on the document details each system slated to play some part in that portion of the cues. The fewer recipes that systems are included in, the more likely they're not as essential to the overall look for the show. More often than not, the systems that are involved in relatively few cue sequences are often the first deemed expendable. They're often the first systems nominated for elimination.

Before any system is terminated, however, most designers first consider how to use the remaining systems to replace the nominee's functions throughout the show. For example, the red downlight system might only be mentioned in only a few recipes for scenes in the show. It's included in the recipes for the Sandbox or Snakes scene, Pookie's Escape, and the Precipice sequence, but in the current prelim systems and specials sheet, not much more than that. It can't merely be cut and mixed by others; the red color is an important visual contribution to all of those scenes. And since red is a primary color, it can't be an additive mix using other colors in the plot. Could it be one of the colors in the overhead scrollers instead? Or perhaps both the overhead and the sidelight scrollers? Do the scrollers need to be used in another color during that sequence? Worst case, the red might be shifted to being a boom sidelight color. While it would be a completely different angle of origin, the change would get the color on the stage, and the overhead system could be eliminated. On the other hand, if the red has to be included, has to originate from the overhead, and can't be in the scrollers, the system may need to be retained in its present configuration.

Once all nominated systems are determined, all of these options are considered and mulled over before reaching any final decisions regarding any system in the light plot. In addition to that, once initial decisions are made for cuts to the plot, subsequent decisions and replacements may result in reinstatement of instruments once earmarked for elimination. Again, case-by-case.

The systems and specials sheet is the starting point in this process, making it possible to scan and see how much any system is used over the course of the production. Obviously, the more columns in the document, the more separations listed between systems, and the easier it is to see what systems are integral for each scene, transition, or series of cues. If the systems and specials sheet is divided into numerous columns, comparing the activity between columns quickly shows which systems are fundamental visual tools to the overall look of the show, and which systems are only used for occasional moments.

The Cuts and Changes

Sometimes there's enough advance notice to properly analyze the impact that cuts will have using the systems and specials sheet and the cue master. Other times, there is no time for any sort of analysis, decisions must be made quickly, and the repercussions just have to be addressed at a later time. In the case of *Hokey*, there's been enough time to allow the lighting designer to consider and distribute the potential cuts into three phases.

Figure 6.2 shows the cuts and changes document for *Hokey*, arranged in the three phases. Each phase

Hybrid Theatre 2010		**HOKEY CUT & CHANGE V5**		Date: 2/25/10	
PHASE ONE					
	ACTION		**LABOR**		**CONSEQUENCE**
1	Cut the Balcony Rail Zoom ERS	1		1	Cut Prismatics from perishables
2	Cut Pit Source Four PARs	2		2	Use House PAR's; purchase WFL
3	Cut costume wireless dimming	3		3	Cut batteries from perishables
4	Cut blacklights & douser	4		4	Add Lav Front Fill from Box Boom
5	Cut four strobes	5		5	Less FOH and overhead flash
6	Cut the LED Striplights	6		6	Add MR-16 striplights to the order
					Add dimmers for incandescent strips
7	Cut one Followspot	7	Cut one Spot Operator	7	Redo Followspot Cue Sheet
8	Move SM & console to booth	8		8	Add cable for cue lights backstage
					Move remaining spots to Box Booms
9	Move spots to Box Booms	9		9	Add spot baskets and hardware
					Cut one set of Box Boom washes
10	Cut the Hog moving light Console	10	Cut the Moving Light Programmer	10	Use rented Ion Console
					The Ion Programmer will cost more
11		11	Cut 2 electricians out of prep	11	
12		12	Cut 2 electricians out of install	12	
13		13	Cut 1 deck electrician off show call	13	
PHASE TWO					
	ACTION		**LABOR**		**CONSEQUENCE**
21	Cut the 8 Moving Lights	21		21	More dependent on color scrollers
					Add NC backlight specials
22	Cut two strobelights; leave two	22		22	One FOH & one overhead left
23	Cut two fog machines	23		23	Only have two DS for precipice
24	Cut 2.4kw x 96 rack	24		24	Use more house circduitry
					Rehook show
					More Space DSL
25	Cut eight sidelight scrollers	25	More dependent on deck electrician	25	Cut gel strings from perishables
					Use color changes in sidelight more
26	Cut the rented Ion console	26	the Ion Programmer will cost less	26	Use the House Expression 3 console
PHASE THREE					
	ACTION		**LABOR**		**CONSEQUENCE**
31	Cut all 3 Autoyokes	31		31	Add 3 conventional Truss specials
					Have to rely on followspots & spec
32	Swap 96 x 2.4kw rack for 48	32		32	Use House dimmers & 4kw racks
					Add switchboxes for repatch
33	Cut 1-12 x 2.4kw dimmer rack	33		33	Use House dimmers & 4kw loaner
34	Cut 50-60 Source Fours	34		34	Use House Altman 360Q, cut plot
35	Cut red downlight	35		35	Add red in low sidelight
36	Cut lav backlight	36		36	Use Lav Box Boom
37	Cut final two strobelights	37		37	Extensive cueing with conventionals
38	Cut eight overhead scrollers	38		38	Cut gel strings from perishables
39	Check personal stock for color	39		39	
40	Check personal stock for templates	40		40	
41		41	Cut 1 electrician from prep	41	
42		42	Cut 1 electrician out of install	42	
43		43	Cut console electrician after tech	43	
Lighting design by Steve Shelley 917.xxx.xxxx				Page 1 of 1	

Figure 6.2 Cuts & Changes for *Hokey*, Version 5

includes cuts or changes that combine what can most easily be given up, along with the most expensive line items in the quote. Each phase is designed to leave some reduced amount of specialty gear to retain the most important looks or systems, and assign the tasks from instruments that are cut to alternate systems. While this list is an attempt at prioritization, it's actually the result after five attempts, and frankly none of them has been satisfactory. This list is the least offensive. No one likes to cut his or her plot, and when it has to be done under these conditions, and this close to the bone, the order of the choices and what is included in which phase is an attempt to keep the most flexible, less expensive things for the last cut, if it's absolutely required.

Each phase is separated to show both reductions between the shop order and the labor. While some of the cuts or changes impact only one or the other, some modifications impact both. Each of these phases may be presented as single line item offerings one at a time. For that matter, an entire phase may need to be offered as a package. Or it may become quickly apparent that, in order to survive, the show has to take the hit and slice through Phase Three.

The left-hand column lists each cost-cutting "Action" that can be taken regarding the lighting package. The middle column lists all the changes in "Labor," while the right-hand column is titled "Consequence," the direct result of the actions or labor. Sometimes the labor choices are completely separate from the actions affecting the light plot; in the first phase, items 11 through 13 itemize three labor cuts that aren't directly related to the light plot. Item 7 in the labor column, on the other hand, is a direct result of cutting the third followspot from the light plot.

Changes and Cuts: Phase One

- Cut the balcony rail zoom ellipsoidals that were placed for the now-cut painted scrim.
- Cut the templates and prismatics from the perishables list.
- Cut the 10 Source Four PARs. Use the house PARs and buy cheap bulbs to make them 1000w WFL.
- After checking with the costume designer, cut the wireless dimming for the costume specials. Cut the batteries from the perishables order.
- Cut the blacklights and dousers; they were going to be used mainly in the Rock scene, the "saving Pookie from the Snakes" sequence, and the Act 2 night scene.
- Cut four of the strobes. While the director hasn't seen them yet, leaving four of them in the overhead will still potentially help Tee-boo's

scenes, kidnapping Pookie, the "saving Pookie" sequence, and the Precipice sequence in Act 3.
- Cut the LED striplights. At the time of this writing, they're still expensive to rent, and their wattage didn't have enough punch to be used without doubling them up. That said, losing the color mixing ability on the translucency and the plan for vertical stripes is sad. Replace them with two sets of MR-16 striplights. This should reduce the prices significantly, but more dimmers will be required to account for swapping the striplights back to incandescent fixtures. Because of the massive reduction of channels, the hookup will be consolidated. To retain some of the original looks from the cue master, the striplights will be channeled with stage left, center, and stage right separation for each color. With three channels for each color, in both the groundrow and the overhead, the scenic stack will require 18 channels. It may be possible to rehook the plot onto fewer cue screens.
- Cut one of the followspots and one followspot operator. The weekly labor bill was too high and needed to be reduced. Sadly the most expendable show crew labor appeared to be one of the followspots. While this is sad, there are still the three Autoyokes to cover preset FOH specials.
- The stage manager is moving to the followspot booth, along with the light console operator. More cable will need to be added to move the cue lights from the back of the orchestra to the booth.
- There's not enough room for the stage manager, the lighting console operator, and the two remaining followspots in the booth. The followspots will be divided and move to the top of each box boom. Two followspot baskets and some hardware will be added to the equipment list. This movement will also require cutting one of the four box boom washes; there's not enough focus range room to squeeze in all eight instruments and the followspots.
- Cut the Hog moving light console. Cut the Hog moving light programmer. Control of the moving lights will be shifted over to the rented Ion lighting console. The lighting designer and the Ion console operator will program the moving light libraries off-line and check them in the shop before the load-in. With the limited time, the skill of the Ion console operator will need to be higher, since he or she will also be programming the moving lights. The cost of that contract will increase.

- The production electrician has agreed to cut two electricians out of the prep period in the shop.
- Two electricians have also been cut out of the install until the focus call.
- One deck electrician has been cut from the tech period. The assistant production electrician will cover any deck activities without a second person.

Changes and Cuts: Phase Two

It is hoped that the cuts from phase one will be enough so that the weekly rental is low enough and no more cuts are required. If that's not the case, here is the next phase of cuts.

- Cut the eight moving lights and hardware. Cut the moving light console. These are two big-ticket items that will hopefully reduce the weekly rental fees to an acceptable level. Additional conventional specials may be required to replace main looks assigned to the movers in different portions of the stage. The high side color scrollers will be used more in place of color washes formerly provided by movers.
- Cut two more strobe lights, leaving only one pair for Tee-boo's scenes.
- Cut two fog machines, leaving only one pair downstage on either side for the Love Dance in Act 2, and the Precipice in Act 3.
- Cut one of the high-density dimmer racks. Use house circuitry and dimmers in the overhead and the box boom. That will provide more space downstage left.
- Cut the eight sidelight color scrollers and the instruments. Plan on having many more color changes in the sidelight. The deck electricians will be more active than originally thought.
- Cut the rented Ion lighting console. Use the old house Expression 3 console instead. The show will definitely now need to be rechanneled; the channel screens are now completely different. The programmer will no longer have to program automated lights. The programmer no longer needs to be as expensive.

Changes and Cuts: Phase Three

There is now very little left of the original plot except conventional instruments. If another phase of cuts is required, though, here is a list. All of these changes or cuts will impact the look of the light plot. Then again, for the audience who has never seen the show, that won't make any difference:

- Cut the three Autoyokes. Convert them to non-moving conventional specials. Cut the Auto Irises. Lose the ability to highlight portions of the stage with frontlight specials. Will have to transfer Autoyoke cues to box boom followspots.
- Convert the remaining high-density 96 × 2.4-kw dimmer rack to a high-density 48 × 2.4-kw rack. Add four old sets of 12 × 4-kw dimmers to make up the difference.
- Cut one of the 12 × 2.4-kw dimmer packs. Use more house dimmers instead.
- Cut the lavender rock backlight, and the red snake and precipice downlight. Shift the lavender into the box booms, and the red into the low sidelight color change instruments for Act 3.
- Cut the final two strobe lights. Conventional lights will be used instead. It may require more programming time, but the effects that are created will be able to be stored and used in several places in the show.
- Cut the eight remaining color scrollers in the overhead pipe ends. Cut the gel strings from the perishables list.
- Cut 50-60 Source Fours out of the weekly rental; replace the instruments with house Altman 360Q ellipsoidals. Speak to the house about a possible maintenance call to clean and align those instruments before the load-in.
- Reanalyze the cable portion of the equipment order in detail. While the cable order has been mentally downsized with each phase of cuts, a reanalysis counting each piece of cable may allow for a significant reduction in the overall amount needed for the show.
- Check the rolls of old gel under the drafting table at home to see if anything can be used to reduce the perishables list.
- Check the shoebox of old templates in the file cabinet at home to see if anything can be used to reduce the perishables list.
- Cut another electrician from the prep in the shop.
- Cut another electrician out of the installation, up to the focus.
- Cut the lighting console operator after the tech period. Once the show goes into previews, either the production electrician or the assistant will take over console duties, and the other will oversee any problems in any part of the theatre. The production electrician isn't completely certain how to handle this assignment right now, but doesn't need to make a final decision until after the complexity of the show starts becoming clearer during the tech process.

Negotiations and Decisions

Once the lighting designer has constructed a plan about how much equipment can be cut from the show, and in what sequential order those cuts should be made, the next step is to speak to the account rep to negotiate a middle ground for the light plot. The lighting designer wants to keep as much equipment as he or she possibly can, in order to provide the maximum amount of flexibility for the plot. The account rep wants to provide the lighting designer with as much gear as possible to make the designer happy, but has to get a fair price for the gear rental and the shop support, in order to make the shop bosses happy. While both parties are striving for the same goal, they each have their own priorities. The challenge in finding the middle ground in these kinds of negotiations is the fact that the numbers that are discussed are for the whole package, rather than for individual items.

As an example, when a lighting rental shop talks about long-term rental costs, standard operating procedure is to not state (or write) any hard numbers for rental amounts. Even a simple statement such as "$25 a week" can be perceived as giving the lighting designer the edge; some lighting rental shops think even that single number could be used as a comparison point against the shop in many ways. It could be used to compare prices against other gear or rental fee structures from the shop. Worse yet, that number could be supplied to other rental shops as the number to beat in order to get the bid.

Other shops see the rental costs as fluid numbers that reflect the quality of the gear coupled with the skill and efficiency of the shop. For them, providing line-item rental pricing serves no purpose. It merely adds one more layer of issues to haggle about, without taking those other intangibles into account.

If the lighting designer reveals any hard overall target numbers for the budgeted rental costs to the account rep, some folks perceive that act as giving the account rep the edge. If lighting designers are forced to provide hard numbers, some protect themselves by supplying numbers that are slightly lower than what's declared on the budget, or merely ask for different options in order to reduce the current total.

While these are only two potential ways that rental packages are negotiated, neither one is very clear-cut. Usually most negotiations start with the overall package price, and go from there. Sometimes the negotiation can involve the transportation, insurance, and payment plan. If that becomes part of the discussion, most lighting designers ask that someone from management discuss those finer points of the contract.

The different layers and nuances of negotiating with any light shop is one matter. Adding personal relationships, competition between shops, who gets the "last look," and who "sharpens the pencils" to the mix takes the discussion of shop negotiation to a whole new level. Shop negotiation is often based on experience, both good and bad. The bottom line is that it's almost always a bit of a tussle; the shop wants a happy lighting designer, production electrician, and show management, but they also want to get a reasonable price for the rental of the gear.

While the negotiation is taking place, some designers merely make individual notes about the cuts or changes on a legal pad. Other designers will have some form of the cuts and changes document at hand to keep track of what's agreed to. Regardless of the record keeping, a preliminary version of the light plot is often kept nearby, so as each change or cut is agreed to, it's then crossed off or notated (in pencil) on the light plot. When negotiations get involved (which they usually do), noting the changes or cuts in pencil allows any action to be quickly undone. During the process, gear that gets cut may later be restored.

After extensive negotiation, it's determined that *Hokey* has so little money, the only way the show can afford any lighting package is to apply all three phases of the proposed cuts and changes. On top of that, the amount of cable also has to be significantly reduced.

Reaction

Sadly most of the rental has to go. The LED striplights, rental control consoles, scrollers, moving lights, one of the followspots; all gone. All the special effects gear had to be cut from the plot as well, along with the Autoyokes. Fortunately the haze was saved. MR-16's will be used for the overhead striplights, and the house R-40's will be used for the groundrow. The shop found two colors of glass roundels that they'll send as part of the package for no additional charge. But now that a tentative agreement has been reached, the plot needs to be quickly updated to make sure the cuts and changes can actually be achieved. After updating, the components can be retotaled to create a second version of the shop order. Since a verbal agreement was reached, a resubmitted shop order might be perceived as a formality that can be sent in without a time constraint, but usually that's not so. A shop order detailing the new needs for the show still has to be submitted for review. Once approved, final negotiations between the management office and the lighting rental shop can then take place, and a final agreement can be reached. Usually that can't happen without the documentation; the shop order is a pivotal portion of what will become that signed agreement.

Making the Changes to the Preliminary Light Plot

It was sad to cut "50 or more" Source Fours out of the equipment list. Cutting and swapping the function of the red and lavender overhead systems was painful, but determining which instruments can be swapped for house ellipsoidals without significantly impacting the overall look of the plot requires a different kind of analysis. Keeping track of the swaps will involve a more detailed version of the instrument spreadsheet.

It was also sad to cut and replace a major portion of the dimmers. The shop has offered some ancient 4000 watt dimmer racks for a reduced rate, but since so many rental dimmers have been cut, the equally ancient house dimmers will still have to be used as well. Updating and analyzing all these changes will require a more detailed version of the circuitry and dimmer spreadsheet.

For many designers, though, the first step is to double-check the notes made during the negotiations, and update the cue master.

The Cue Master, Versions 2.6 and 2.7

On the surface, shifting the usage of large design components is relatively simple. Analyzing or reacting to those changes in detail, on the other hand, is a bit more involved. While it's simple to decide that the moving lights are cut, understanding and interpreting the full implications of that action may not be so simple.

Figure 6.3 shows two versions the cue master for *Hokey*. The top half is version 2.6 (before), and the bottom half is version 2.7, after the three phases of cuts and changes have taken place. In the top half, the cue master includes columns for three followspots (SP1, SP2, and SP3) and a separate column for the moving lights (Movers). With cue 101, the four pipe end moving lights on the fourth and fifth electrics fade up as No Color instruments, pre-focused to center-center. They remain at center-center and only increase in intensity over the course of the next two cues. As Judy starts her cross to downstage left, cue 105 fades up the first electric stage left mover, already preset on the downstage left spike mark.

In the bottom half of Figure 6.3, the movers and SP 3 columns have been replaced by "Spec" (Specials) and "Cyc" columns. Actions taken by the movers or spot 3 have been reassigned to either new specials or the other two followspots.

Since the automated fixtures have been cut, the action of the No Color movers fading up in cue 101 could be assigned to the centerline No Color

instrument in the backlight system. The warm centerline downlight instrument might be added in this sequence as well. After consideration, however, using either of those instruments for this action is rejected. It's decided that the focus point for either of those two systems might not be in the middle of the stage. For that matter, until the cast is onstage, it's impossible to predict where the exact spike mark for the group's choreography around center will be placed. It's also decided that the non-shuttered 36° beam pool size may be too large. For all of those reasons, it's decided to add a 26° ellipsoidal placed on centerline, on the fifth electric. While this single special won't provide the same intensity, dimensionality shape, or the same number of beams as the four moving lights, it will still provide the sense of brightening and visually pull focus to the center of the stage.

In the top half of Figure 6.3, spot 3 (stage right side of booth) faded up on Judy as she moved toward center-center with cue 101. In the bottom half, that action has been shifted to spot 2 (now located on the stage right box boom). Since Judy is moving from upstage left to center-center, spot 2's beam will more likely catch her face than spot 1, located in the stage left box boom.

In the next action (at this point still un-numbered) Judy puts on her ears and "becomes" Pookie. When the plot had movers, the top cue master shows that the first electric stage left mover changed color. In the bottom cue master, that action has been reassigned to spot 1, which will roll into a different color to achieve the same visual color change on the performer.

By working through the entire cue master, it's then possible to reassign actions and movements from equipment that will no longer be part of the plot, to remaining gear that's then designated additional tasks. It's also possible to see when and where additional specials may be required in order to achieve the same visual product while missing more expensive gear. On the other hand, reanalysis may determine that without a specific piece of equipment, that specific moment no longer requires a lighting change, and that row can then be eliminated from the cue master.

Reviewing the cue master gives the lighting designer a sense of what needs to happen in order to make the remainder of the plot still work. There may now be chunks in the show that are missing looks, but at least those problem points are known. While keeping those points in mind, it's possible to review all of the diary and negotiation notes, and start making adjustments to the preliminary light plot and the instrument spreadsheet.

HOKEY CUE MASTER v2.6 BEFORE CUTS & CHANGES											
P	SEC	Cue	Cnt	ON	FOR	ACTION	Movers	SP3	SP2	SP1	SPOT NOTES
1	Open		3			Blocker					
		100.7	3		Preset	Pool in 4 L; blue bk					
			5	curtain out	Judy	SP3 pickup in wing					
		101	7	Judy arm back	Move to center	Center up	4P/5P NC to C		Judy		Tight; scrim
			7	2nd spin	1/2 group nter	Lav side/R20 back	Brighter		Ø		Lag out
			10	End music phrase	Rest group nter	Bright; add NC back	Brighter				
	Pook	105	5	Judy start X DL	Judy speak	DL up	1P SL to DL			Judy	
				Judy X SL 1/4	Judy	Add ears	change color				Color change
				Judy finish speak		DL down	1P SL Ø			Ø	
	Tee-boo	110	5	Mitch X DC	Mitch speak	DC up	1P SL/SR	Mitch		Mitch	
				Put on crown			change color				Color change
		114	3	Mitch finish speak		DC down	1P SL/SR Ø	Ø		Ø	
	Pine	115	5	Lorraine X DR	Lorraine speak	DR Spec up	1P SR to DR	Lor			

HOKEY CUE MASTER v2.7 AFTER CUTS & CHANGES											
P	SEC	Cue	Cnt	ON	FOR	ACTION	Spec	Cyc	SP2	SP1	SPOT NOTES
1	Open		3			Blocker					
		100.7	3		Preset	Pool in 4 L; blue bk		Blue low			
			5	curtain out	Judy	SP3 pickup in wing					
		101	7	Judy arm back	Move to center	Center up	5P NC bk up	Blue high	Judy		Tight; scrim
			7	2nd spin	1/2 group nter	Lav side/R20 back			Ø		Lag out
			10	End music phrase	Rest group nter	Bright; add NC back	NC Brighter	Brighter			
	Pook	105	5	Judy start X DL	Judy speak	DL Spec up	DSL truss up			Judy	
				Judy X SL 1/4	Judy	Add ears	change color			Roll	Color change
				Judy finish speak		DL down	DSL Ø			Ø	
	Tee-boo	110	5	Mitch X DC	Mitch speak	DC up	DC truss up		Mitch		
				Put on crown			change color			Roll	Color change
		114	3	Mitch finish speak		DC down	DC down			Ø	
	Pine	115	5	Lorraine X DR	Lorraine speak	DR Spec up	DR truss up			Lor	

Figure 6.3 The Cue Master for *Hokey*, Versions 2.6 & 2.7

The Instrument Spreadsheet, Version 2

While the preliminary light plot was being created, the instrument spreadsheet (Figure 5.24) was used to keep track of the amount of instrumentation used, and where it was distributed. After the preliminary light plot was completed, some spares were added for each instrument type, and then the totals were copied into the equipment list that was submitted with the rest of the original shop order.

The instrument spreadsheet is no longer just a reflection of the light plot. It's now a fundamental document showing how the house inventory has been used, and how much is left. In situations without a rental budget, the house inventory may be *the* parameter that defines the boundaries of the lighting design. In these cases, the instrument spreadsheet turns into a vital lifeline, keeping track of how much gear remains as each system is created.

In the case of *Hokey*, the site survey confirmed the numbers and wattage of the house inventory, which the diary noted as being in good condition. Figure 6.4 shows the instrument spreadsheet expanded to include the house equipment. As before, the grid of cells is laid out so that each row identifies a hanging position, while each column identifies a separate instrument type. In this case, the house instrumentation is separated from the rental units by the central shaded vertical line. While the left-hand column still lists the positions in a sort order that will reflect the instrument schedule, the next five columns are set aside for each category of the house equipment that was listed in the technical specifications. The "House Sub Total" column adds up the amount of house equipment for each position.

On the other side of the central shaded vertical line, the columns duplicate the instrument types that made up the original shop order. The "Rental Sub

Hybrid Theatre 2010 — **HOKEY INSTRUMENT SPREADSHEET V2** — Date: 2/13/10

	House 1kw X12	750 X9	PAR 64 NSP	6" Fres	R40 300w 3 cir	House Sub Total	Source Four 575w 19°	26°	36°	14" 1kW Scp	Mini 500w 10	MR16 750w 3 Cir	Stark 1200w Spot	Rental Sub Total	Total	
Truss	5					5	3	5						8	13	Truss
SL Box		3				3		3	1				1	5	8	SL Box
SR Box		3				3		3	1				1	5	8	SR Box
Pit			10			10								0	10	Pit
1 Elec		5				5		5	7	2				14	19	1 Elec
2 Elec		5				5		4	17					21	26	2 Elec
3 Elec						0		1	10					11	11	3 Elec
4 Elec						0		4	12	2				18	18	4 Elec
5 Elec						0		5	12					17	17	5 Elec
6 Elec						0						6		6	6	6 Elec
1 Bm L		1				1			4					4	5	1 Bm L
1 Bm L		1				1			4					4	5	1 Bm L
3 Bm L		1				1			4					4	5	3 Bm L
4 Bm L		1				1			4					4	5	4 Bm L
Rovers L						0			2					2	2	Rovers L
1 Bm R		1				1			4					4	5	1 Bm R
2 Bm R		1				1			4					4	5	2 Bm R
3 Bm R		1				1			4					4	5	3 Bm R
4 Bm R		1				1			4					4	5	4 Bm R
Rovers R						0			2					2	2	Rovers R
Groundrow					6	6								0	6	Groundrow
Total Used	5	24	10	0	6	45	3	30	94	2	4	6	2	**141**	186	**SubPlot**
Double Check						45								**141**	186	Double Check
House Stock	15	30	15	6	6	72										
Remaining	10	6	5	6	0	27	2	3	6	1	1	1	1	15	42	**Spares**
							5	33	100	3	5	7	3	**156**		**Total Rent**
														156		Double Check

Expression 3; 150 chan, 174 dim — Lighting design by Steve Shelley 917.xxx.xxxx — Page 1 of 1

Figure 6.4 The Instrument Spreadsheet for *Hokey*, Version 2

Total" column adds up all of the rented gear for each position, while the final right-hand "Total" column combines the two subtotals to produce the total number of instruments for each position.

At the bottom of the document, sums and formulas keep a running tally of the equipment used, and the remaining amount of house gear. On the left-hand side of the shaded line, the "Total Used" row of cells each combine the numbers for each instrument type above them. The "House Stock" row is the fixed amount of house gear listed from the tech specs. The "Remaining" row consists of formula cells that subtract the subtotal from the fixed inventory, resulting in the amount of each instrument type still available.

It's worth nothing that the right-hand cell in the "Total Used" row says "45." That's a formula cell adding the entire column of numbers above it. Under that cell is a cell in the "Double Check" row that also shows the number "45." That cell is a formula, adding the five cells in the "Total Used" row above and to the left of it (the black triangle is a visual reminder of this relationship). Having two formula cells adjacent to each other, totaling the same block of information, is one way to double-check that formulated information is being properly added up. Inserting row or column information can sometimes disrupt the formulas contained in the cells. If the two formulated cells don't display matching numbers, a formula is broken somewhere and needs to be fixed.

On the right-hand side of the central shaded line, the "SubPlot" row of cells adds up the cells for each instrument type above them. The "Rental Sub Total" cell in that row adds up all of the sums above it, while the "Total" cell in that row combines all of the total instruments in each hanging position above it as well. The two cells in the "Double Check" row sum up the same block of information, again from the horizontal formulated cells. The lower "141" is a sum of the rest of the "SubPlot" cells, and the lower "186" is a sum of the two lower "Double Check" cells.

The next row is the fixed amount of spares allocated for each instrument type, which is added up in the "Rental Sub Total" column (15), and added to the remaining house stock in the "Total" column (42). The "Total Rent" row consists of cells that add each spare cell and the "SubPlot" addition above it. The right-hand "Total Rent" cell (156) is a sum of the "SubPlot Sub Total" cell (141) and the "Spares" (15) below it. The "Double Check" cell (also 156) is the sum of the horizontal "Total Rent" cells. Each of the major additions has a double-check formulated cell to insure accuracy.

While all of the information on this document is worthwhile, the big-picture numbers include the number of rented instruments used in the plot (146), the total number of rented instruments in the equipment list (156), and the amount of remaining house equipment (27).

The Preliminary Light Plot, Version 2

In this current status of the light plot, the house Altman 360Q's have replaced rented Source Fours for the cool frontlight wash. After some thought, it has been decided that the cool fronts are the system that could be slightly less bright and not damage the overall plot; changing all of them swaps out 15 instruments. The 360Q's have also been swapped for the near throw instruments in the box booms, and the mids in the sidelight booms. In order to reduce the overall total of Source Fours in the rental, the red downlight and the lavender backlight systems were cut. Ten house PAR 64 cans replaced the Source Four PARs in the pit. The house R-40 striplights will be used for the groundrow to reduce the number of MR16 striplights that will need to be rented.

Figure 6.5 shows the result from all three phases of cuts and changes made to the preliminary light plot. A lot of gear has been cut (indicated by the "X's"), while other house equipment has been swapped out (shaded instruments). Another series of vertical dashed lines have been drawn in scaled 5-foot increments, starting from the stage left end of the battens. These lines will be used to help define the cable lengths needed to plug the overhead electrics.

Circuitry and Dimmer Spreadsheet

When the preliminary light plot was constructed solely using rental equipment, creating the cable and dimming lists was a relatively simple exercise; different cable lengths running from the instruments all plugged into one type of dimmer in one location (Figure 5.25). That has now turned into a much more intricate puzzle. Figuring out where to plug each position using the house dimmers and circuitry means that all of the circuitry will require reexamination. A more detailed version of the circuitry and dimmer spreadsheet will be used to oversee the circuitry, cable length, and dimming assignment for every instrument in the light plot.

All of the rented dimmers will be located downstage left, in the backstage area known as "Betty." While some of the overhead electrics will be plugged into pre-installed house circuitry, any added circuits will run to the stage left end of the batten, and then drop down following a specific path to the dimmers. In some cases, those circuits will be house multi-cable with breakouts. The rest of the runs, though, will consist of rented bundles. The rough distance

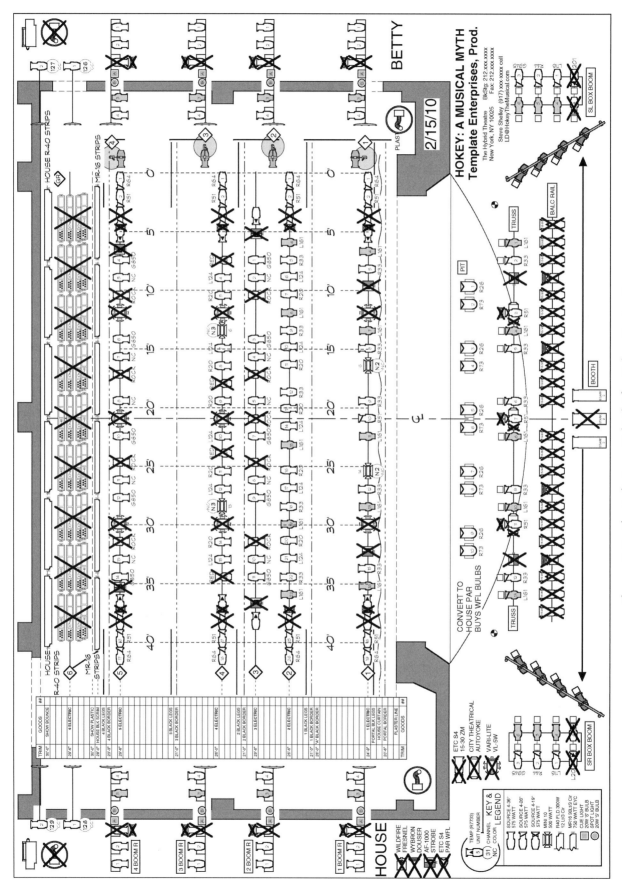

Figure 6.5 The Preliminary Light Plot for *Hokey*, Version 2

of the path from the dimmers to the downstage batten ends measures approximately 75 feet, while the same run to the upstage batten ends is roughly calculated as 100 feet. Using the vertical dashed lines on the preliminary light plot, it's then possible to quickly add the distance from the end of the batten to each instrument, or list it as a separate piece of cable. If the mult breaks at the end of the batten, for example, the added cables start at the termination point of the six female stage plugs. If the choice is made for the circuitry to consist of a single uninterrupted piece of cable, the distance from the stage left batten is then added to the rough distance to the dimmers. When a circuit runs from the instrument to the dimmer without going through house circuitry, the piece of cable is usually referred to as a **home run**.

In this case, the house mult listed in the tech specs will be assigned to the stage left sidelight booms, the third and fourth electrics, the pit, and the groundrow. All of the rented multicable will be swapped out for bundles.

Figure 6.6 shows the second version of the circuitry and dimmer spreadsheet for the cut-down version of the *Hokey* light plot. Now that the plot is going to use both rental and house electrical distribution, the document has significantly expanded. The initial expansion of this document starts with a detailed analysis of the location and capacities of the preinstalled circuits and dimmers in the tech specs. After studying the house drawings and other circuitry information, each circuit and dimmer is listed by location.

Hybrid Theatre 2010 **HOKEY CIRCUITRY & DIMMER V2** Date: 2/16/10

POS	Circuits in light plot 575	1K	1.2K	2K	TOT	Circuits exist	add	ExistDim 36 2.4K	24 4K	Add Dim 48 2.4K	36 1.2K	48 4K	NOTES
Truss	13				13		14			5		8	Home run
SL Bx		1		4	5	6		4					Pros L: 19 > 24
SR Bx		1		4	5	6			4				Pros R: 25 > 30
Pit			5		5							5	Home run to house
1 Elec	7	1	5		13	12	3	7	5				1 Elec: 1 > 12
2 Elec	16		5		21		21			21			Home run to rack
3 Elec	11				11	12		11					SL Flr Pockets
4 Elec	14	1	1		16		17			15			Home run to rack
5 Elec	15		1		16		17					16	Home run to rack
6 Elec				9	9	15						9	3 Elec: 31 > 45
1 Bm L	4	2			6			4			4		Run to rack DL
2 Bm L	4	2			6			4			4		Run to rack DL
3 Bm L	4	2			6			4			4		Run to rack DL
4 Bm L	4	2			6	6						4	UL Pocket: 43 >48
Rover L	2				2	2		2					UL Pock: 49 >54
1 Bm R	4	2			6			4	4				Home run house
2 Bm R	4	2			6			4			4		Run to rack DL
3 Bm R	4	2			6			4			4		Run to rack DL
4 Bm R	4	2			6	6					4		Run to rack DL
Rover R	2				2	2		2					UR Pock: 73 > 78
G'row	9				9	9						9	US Pockets

POS	Hse mult	125	100	75	50	35	20	10	5	2F	TOT
Truss		5	4	5							14
SL Bx								1	4	3	5
SR Bx								1	4	3	5
Pit	1x100					2	4	4	4		10
1E			3			1		4	8	5	16
2E		7	9	5	1				4	5	26
3E	4x50							4	4		8
4E	3x100					1		6	6	1	13
5E			4	5	5	1				1	15
6E			3	4	3					9	10
1L	1x75				2			2	2		6
2L	1x75				2			2	2		6
3L	1x75				2			2	2		6
4L	1x75				2			2	2		6
Rov						2	2				4
1R				6	6				2	2	16
2R				6	6				2	2	16
3R				6	6				2	2	16
4R				6	6				2	2	16
Rov						2	2				4
G'row	2x100							9	9		18

Total circuits required by plot: **175**
Total number of existing circuits used: **76**
Total circuits added: **96** | 36 | 24
Total existing dimmers used: **30** | **18**
Total added dimmers used: **41** | **24** | **42**

Company switch is DSL.
House dimmers are DSR.

Note: All overhead 1kw circuits are works;
Note: All boom 1kw circuits are cue or run;
run all to SM switchbox

	2.4K	1.2K	4K
Total need to add	41	24	42
Total 48 x 2.4KW	48		
Total 24 x 2.4KW		30	
Total 32 x 4KW			48
Extra dimmers	**7**	**6**	**6**

	125	100	75	50	35	20	10	5	2F	TOT
subtotal	43	49	26	4	8	2	45	59	31	236
										236
spare	8	10	8	8	6	10	15	20	15	85
total	51	59	34	12	14	12	60	79	46	321

Expression 3; 150 chan, 174 dim   Lighting design by Steve Shelley 917.xxx.xxxx   Page 1 of 1

Figure 6.6 The Circuitry and Dimmer Spreadsheet for *Hokey*, Version 2

Like the instrument spreadsheet, the left-hand column lists each hanging position. Next to that are six vertical blocks providing detailed information in the document. Starting on the left side, the first block consists of five columns. Four columns list the total number of each circuit size in the plot, while the fifth column is a formulated total for each row.

The next two-column block examines the circuitry that will be required for the light plot. The left-hand column of the pair shows hanging positions where circuits currently exist in the Hybrid Theatre. When the totals from the "existing" circuits column are subtracted from the "total circuits in the light plot" column, the result is the number of additional circuits required at each hanging position in the "add" circuits column. The notes column identifies the house circuits that will be used, or indicates the path for the added cable.

The remaining five columns analyze how the circuits in the light plot will be assigned to the house and rental dimmers. The left-hand pair shows circuits assigned to the 36-2.4kW and 24-4kW dimmers existing in the theatre, while the following three columns show the assignment of remaining circuits to the rental dimmers.

On the other side of the truncated position column is the largest vertical block in the document, detailing the breakdown of the cabling to plug the instruments in the plot. The first column shows where the house multicable will be installed, running to either house circuitry or rental racks. The next eight columns are labeled by footage, starting with 125 feet, and ending with 5-foot jumpers. The "2F" column is a label for two-fers. Since that column is different from cable, it's not included in the far right "Tot" (Total) column. The bottom cable subtotal row reflects the addition of the columns above each cell. The lower "236" is a double-check cell, reflecting the sum of the subtotal row (without the two-fer cell). The "spare" row underneath is a fixed calculation of the amount of spare pieces of cable for that length. The "total" row is a formulated cell combining the subtotal and the spare cell above it. The lower "321" is another double-check cell.

This version of the document shows in detail how rental bundles and dimmers will be added to preexisting house circuits and dimmers to create the electrical infrastructure of the light plot. The cable block provides an initial idea about the amount of rental cable that will be required for each hanging position. As the adjusted lighting design takes shape, seeing the amount and location of circuitry and the number of dimmers used allows the lighting designer to make informed choices and adjust the usage of circuits and dimmers. Having the combined electrical paths displayed on a single document allows the lighting designer can see where and how much additional cable will be required, and if any replugging will be needed to retain the amount of control desired. It also allows the designer to insure that the proper adapters are included to hardpatch house circuits to rental dimmers, or added circuits to house dimmers.

Once the instrument spreadsheet and the dimmer and circuitry spreadsheet have been adjusted and adapted to the satisfaction of both the lighting designer and the production electrician, the numbers are tallied once again and computed into a second shop order. Once the production electrician has seen that equipment list and perishables list, they're submitted to the lighting rental shop preferred by the producer.

The Labor Spreadsheet

Figure 6.7 shows the electrics labor projection for the *Hokey* load-in with reductions made in both the installation labor and the running crew. Cutting the number of electricians prepping and installing the lighting package, as well as cutting the third followspot and the moving light programmer, reduced the first pay period over 35%. The cuts in the second week dropped that pay period even more (with fervent hope there will be no overtime incurred). The running crew for the third and fourth pay period is under the $6,000.00 budget limit set by the producer.

SUMMARY

After numerous phone calls and adaptations to the plot and the labor projections, the third phase of cuts and changes to the light plot has reduced the projected installation and weekly costs to budgetary levels that are acceptable to the producer. By instituting all three phases of electrics crew labor reductions, the projected labor has also been reduced to meet the producer's requests. The producer awards the bid to the lighting rental shop, and approves the labor projections so that the crew can start to be hired.

The other lighting rental shops are contacted and thanked for their participation in the bidding process. This is only one show; the relationships established with the account reps representing the other shops will extend long beyond this single bidding situation.

There's no question that moments will occur when it will become painfully apparent there are not

HOKEY	Prep	1-Apr	2-Apr	5-Apr	6-Apr	7-Apr	8-Apr	9-Apr	10-Apr	11-Apr	12-Apr		
		THURS	FRI	MON	TUES	WED	THURS	FRI	SAT	SUN	MON		
WEEK 1+		Shop	Shop	Load-in	Load-in	Focus	Cue/DT	Tech	Tech	Dress	Dress	TOTAL	$$$
PE	8	10	10	10	10	10	10	10	12	12	12	114	$3,990.00
Asst		10	10	10	10	10	10	10	12	12	12	106	$3,180.00
Crew#1		10	10	10	10							40	$1,000.00
Crew#2		~~10~~	~~10~~	10	10							20	$500.00
Crew#3		~~10~~	~~10~~	10	10							20	$500.00
Crew#4		~~10~~	~~10~~	10	10	10						30	$750.00
Crew#5				10	10	10						10	$250.00
Crew#6				10	10	10						10	$250.00
Console				10	10	10	10	10	12	12	12	66	$1,650.00
~~Deck~~						10	10	10	12	12	12	0	$0.00
Deck						10	10	10	12	12	12	66	$1,650.00
Follow 1							10	10	12	12	12	56	$1,400.00
Follow 2							10	10	12	12	12	56	$1,400.00
~~Follow 3~~							10	10	12	12	12	0	$0.00
												594	
	8	30	30	60	60	70	60	60	72	72	72	594	$16,520.00

HOKEY	13-Apr	13-Apr	14-Apr	15-Apr	15-Apr	16-Apr	16-Apr	17-Apr	18-Apr		
	TUES	TUES	WED	THURS	THURS	FRI	FRI	SAT	SUN		
WEEK 2	Preview	Show	Show (2)	Tech	Show	Tech	Show	Show (2)	Show	TOTAL	$$$
PE	8	4	8	8	4	8	4	8	4	56	$1,960.00
Asst	8	4	8	8	4	8	4	8	4	56	$1,680.00
~~Console~~	8	4	8	8	4	8	4	8	4	0	$0.00
Deck	8	4	8	8	4	8	4	8	4	56	$1,400.00
Follow 1	8	4	8	8	4	8	4	8	4	56	$1,400.00
Follow 2	8	4	8	8	4	8	4	8	4	56	$1,400.00
~~Follow 3~~	8	4	8	8	4	8	4	8	4	0	$0.00
										280	
	40	20	40	40	20	40	20	40	20	280	$7,840.00

HOKEY	20-Apr	20-Apr	21-Apr	22-Apr	23-Apr	24-Apr	25-Apr		
	TUES	TUES	WED	THURS	FRI	SAT	SUN		
WEEK 3	Tech	Show	Show (2)	Show	Show	Show (2)	Show	TOTAL	$$$
PE	8	4	8	4	4	8	4	40	$1,400.00
Asst	8	4	8	4	4	8	4	40	$1,200.00
~~Console~~	8	4	8	4	4	8	4	0	$0.00
Deck	8	4	8	4	4	8	4	40	$1,000.00
Follow 1	8	4	8	4	4	8	4	40	$1,000.00
Follow 2	8	4	8	4	4	8	4	40	$1,000.00
~~Follow 3~~	8	4	8	4	4	8	4	0	$0.00
								200	
	40	20	40	20	20	40	20	200	$5,600.00

HOKEY	27-Apr	28-Apr	29-Apr	30-Apr	1-May	2-May		
	TUES	WED	THURS	FRI	SAT	SUN		
WEEK 4	Show	Show (2)	Show	Show	Show (2)	Show	TOTAL	$$$
PE	4	8	4	4	8	4	32	$1,120.00
Asst	4	8	4	4	8	4	32	$960.00
Console	4	8	4	4	8	4	32	$800.00
Deck	4	8	4	4	8	4	32	$800.00
Follow 1	4	8	4	4	8	4	32	$800.00
Follow 2	4	8	4	4	8	4	32	$800.00
~~Follow 3~~	4	8	4	4	8	4	0	$0.00
							192	
	24	48	24	24	48	24	192	$5,280.00

Figure 6.7 The *Hokey* Labor Budget, Version 2

enough bodies to accomplish the task at hand. There will also be moments when the lighting designer will be unable to produce the visual look or effect originally envisioned by the creative team. However, the show can still happen. The commitment, ingenuity, and resourcefulness of the lighting designer and production electrician, along with the rest of the creative and technical staff, will be utilized to maintain the original focus of the production, and produce the best possible product under duress. This is the reason they get hired; they can make it happen even when everything isn't perfect.

The light plot is approved and all work can now move forward toward preparing for the load-in and the production period to produce *Hokey*. That work will start by updating the light plot, section, and the initial support paperwork packet, and getting that information to the production electrician as quickly as possible.

Stage 3: Preparation

The Production Packets

Chapter 7

The Light Plot, Section, and Support Paperwork Packet

INTRODUCTION

The basic document of almost every lighting design, and the basis for the initial paperwork packet, is the completed **light plot**. Without the visualized graphic of a plot, it's almost impossible to define a basis for the remaining information. The finished **lighting section** is usually the companion document to the plot, graphically showing how many of the lighting systems relate to one another, and how the components of the light plot relate to the surrounding production elements and the performance facility.

The graphic representation of the instruments in the light plot often displays only a portion of the information about each instrument. The detailed data about all of the instruments comprise the lighting database, which can be sorted into different reports, collectively known as **support paperwork**. These reports almost always include the **instrument schedule** and the **channel hookup**, and may also include the **circuitry schedule** and the **dimmer schedule**.

If elements on the stage change focus, color, or channel identity during the production, **color cards** and **floor cards** are created to direct and document the progression of those changes.

The components of the light plot often need to be reduced to a list of raw numbers defining the elements required to install the lighting package. The **cut color sheet** lists the number of gels required at each hanging location, for each color frame size in the light plot. The **template sheet** lists the templates required at each hanging location, for each template holder size in the light plot. Manufacturer's **cut sheets** that were used while the systems were constructed are still included in the back of the production notebook, along with any **manuals** detailing information about the use and configuration of the different electrical devices and components of the lighting package.

THE LIGHT PLOT

The finished **light plot** is the map showing all of the lighting instruments and electrical devices, their control assignments, as well as their relative hanging locations in the performance space. This version of the plot serves to graphically communicate the number, location, and types of lighting instruments used in the production. It may also furnish information about the color, circuitry, and focus of each instrument. Though it doesn't need to be as detailed as the scenic designer's groundplan, the light plot often includes the spatial information about the architecture, masking, scenery in the air, where (and when) important scenery or properties are located on the stage, and the numbers and types of backdrops.

As the document's creator, the lighting designer has a choice about the amount of information that is shown on this published version of the light plot. The map can provide as much, or as little, information as he or she sees fit. Some designers insist that the less basic information shown on the plot directly translates into the greater number of questions that require an answer during the load-in. Others believe that the graphic outline of the instrument, and its unit number, is enough data to include on the plot; more text makes the plot look messy, and the rest of the data can be found in the support paperwork.

Although there are guidelines, the amount of data shown for each lighting instrument is still an individual choice made by the lighting designer. Before computer drafting, anyone who wanted to include more data on the plot was forced to write the information on the plot by hand.

With the current crop of CAD programs, however, it's now possible to change the amount of data shown for each lighting device in the same document. Data panes (or data fields) associated with each lighting instrument can be made visible or turned "off" with a few mouse clicks. In this way, the single document can reveal otherwise-hidden data information about each instrument needed only by the production electrician. With a few more clicks, the same data can be turned off and made invisible when the lighting designer works with the same document.

Figure 7.1 shows the lighting designer's version of the light plot for *Hokey: A Musical Myth*. The "unit number," "color," and "channel" data fields are turned on in the instrument symbols. Some instruments can also be seen with text filled into their "special purpose" and "template" data fields as well. This next section will examine and identify the finished *Hokey* light plot. A clean version of this light plot, without identifying circles, can be found on pages xviii–xix.

An Overview of the *Hokey* Light Plot

Figure 7.1 shows the *Hokey* light plot, drawn like most proscenium light plots from a perspective above the theatre while facing the stage. Alphabetic letters contained in large white circles identify drawing components and elements of the architectural space. The **front of house** (or **FOH**) hanging positions above the audience are at the bottom of the plot (A), while the back wall of the theatre is at the top (B). The stage right wall is shown on the left-hand side of the document (C), while the stage left wall is on the opposite side (D). In order to fit this plot onto two pages in this text, this version of the plot has been reduced. Light plots are typically drawn in either 1/2″ = 1′-0″ or 1/4″ = 1′-0″ scale. The scale is often chosen after considering the size of the architectural space, the overall size of the available paper, the number of individual instruments, and the number of their data fields that need to be seen. Sometimes decisions about the published scale are also affected when plastic drafting templates are used to make scaled on-site corrections.

There are two basic "road markers" in this light plot: the **centerline** (E) bisects the distance between the proscenium walls (F), while the **plaster line** (G) defines the upstage edge of the proscenium arch. The point where these two lines intersect is the **ground-plan zero-zero point** (H). All stage left, stage right, upstage, or downstage measurements are taken from this point, or from these two lines.

Two scales on the *Hokey* light plot provide distance information from the groundplan zero-zero point. The **up-and-downstage scale** (I), tucked against the stage right wall, illustrates the distance between plaster line and the electrics, the masking, or any flying scenic pieces. The **left-and-right scale** (J) between the first and second electrics, indicates distances on either side of centerline. A duplication of this scale also appears between the fourth and fifth electrics, in order to make it simpler to use as a point of reference during the hang. At that point in the load-in, the left-and-right scales typically become the main reference to ensure that the instruments end up in the right place on each batten. Even though the scale appears in two locations on this plot, the map is often accordion-folded, so that the scales then appear adjacent to each electric as the measurements are made on the batten. The marked measurements then establish the physical placement for each instrument's c-clamp.

The **lineset schedule** (K), shown against the stage right wall, identifies all of the objects hung in the air. Usually, that starts with the lineset number and the scaled distance from plaster line for all battens in a fly system. For battens used in the show, it also includes the trim height for those goods. In fixed-grid theatres, on the other hand, the lineset schedule may only list the name of the goods and their relative distance from a common origin point. Regardless of the theatre type, for any electric or scenic goods hung at unique heights, it's common practice to include the trim height information in a common area of the drawing.

In this light plot, the lineset schedule is drawn on stage right, matching the physical location of the locking rail in the theatre. While non-show related goods are often not drawn in the light plot (such as cable crossovers, or unused movie screens stored in the air, etc.), the lineset schedule lists anything hung on a batten. Even though it may not be relevant to the show, at least you know it's there. In the *Hokey* plot, the lineset schedule lists all of the masking and backdrops that will be used for the piece, as well as their lineset number, distance from plaster line, and trim height. Those trim heights will be graphically shown on the lighting section. Following standard drafting conventions, solid lines indicate where the masking will touch the stage, while dashed lines indicate the position of goods trimmed in the air.

The **key and legend** (L) identifies the type, beam angle, wattage, and anything unique about each lighting or device symbol used in the plot. It also translates the unit and channel numbers, along with any accessories associated with each lighting symbol. In the *Hokey* light plot, the channel assignment is located inside the circle adjacent to the instrument, and the color is noted immediately underneath the channel.

The **sightline points** (M and N) are the two scaled points drawn to indicate the most extreme seat positions in the house. They're the visual barometers used to confirm that the masking is adequate. If the occupants sitting at these points can't see the side backstage walls, any rigging hardware above the stage, or any other areas that are intended to be out of sight, then the masking is considered a success.

The **title block** (O) provides the basic logistical information about the light plot. It communicates the title of the show, the name of the theatre, the plate number of the drawing, and informs the viewer of the document's title and intent. It may also list the identities and contact information for the director and the designers, as well as the scale being used, the date that the light plot was published (released for public consumption), and the name of the person who created the document. When a paperwork package is sent ahead to either a remote theatre, or a lighting rental shop, the light plot may be the only document that filters down to the people who need further information. The title block is one location to list contact information, providing a conduit for questions. Simple answers provided prior to a hang can eliminate assumptions, hours of miscommunication, and lost stage time.

The **notes block** (P) between the stage left side of the truss and the orchestra pit, lists information about the light plot best communicated as text. This includes general notes that affect large portions of the plot, anything out of the ordinary, specifies standards required, and can include what's not yet decided. The **revision block** (Q), on the other side of centerline, is a placeholder to indicate what's changed with each new publication of the plot. It prevents the confusion caused when viewing two unidentified, yet different, versions of the same light plot. The **disclaimer block** (R), between the stage right box boom and the proscenium, is half of the current legal "recipe" that presumably protects the lighting designer in catastrophic situations. The other half is the language contained in the lighting designer's contract.

Considering the litigious nature and volatile changes in today's courts, the reader is warned not to accept any of this information at face value. Proper research and investigation are the best tools of defense; any legal information provided in this text could conceivably be out of date before this book is in print.

An Examination of the *Hokey* Lighting Systems

Numbers contained in shaded circles identify the general hanging positions in the light plot. Each hanging position is labeled with text in a rectangle, or a number in a diamond. Adjacent to each hanging position is a **position summary** (S), which lists the instrument inventory and the number of circuits that will be required. These lists are shown for each position, and are often referenced before and during the hang.

The *Hokey* Straight Frontlight Systems

The *Hokey* light plot shows three FOH lighting positions (A). The **truss** (1) contains the **two straight frontlight** washes, each consisting of five instruments, along with three specials. The warm wash, channels 1 > 5, is colored in Roscolux 33, while the cool wash, channels 11 > 15, is colored in Lee 161. The five light beams in each wash will create the downstage zone of straight frontlight. A smaller version of the left-and-right scale is drawn adjacent to the truss to simplify measurements during the hang.

The light plot shows six **overhead electrics** (3), or **electrics**, upstage of plaster line. In this plot, those electrics are battens hanging above the stage, labeled with large numbered diamonds at the end of each batten (any batten that has at least one instrument or electrical device hung from it can be considered an electric). Dashed horizontal leader lines then extend from the diamonds to the lineset schedule (K) in order to graphically confirm the number, distance, and trim for each electric. The first electric has five pairs of instruments equipped with the same matching colors as the truss frontlights, Roscolux 33 and Lee 161. They'll be focused as the mid-stage zones of the straight frontlight systems. The warm frontlights are channels 6 > 8, while the cool frontlights are channels 16 > 18. The center pair of instruments has been nudged aside to provide room for unit 10, assigned to channel 55. This unit will be focused as a frontlight special to center-center. The second electric has a duplication of 10 instruments in the same relationship to centerline, providing the upstage and final zone of frontlight coverage. The warm frontlights are again colored in Roscolux 33, and assigned to channels 9 and 10. The cool frontlights, colored in Lee 161, are softpatched to channels 19 and 20.

The *Hokey* Box Boom Systems

On the *Hokey* light plot, the two **box boom positions** (2) are drawn on either side of the truss. Each position contains three color washes: Lee 116, Roscolux 44,

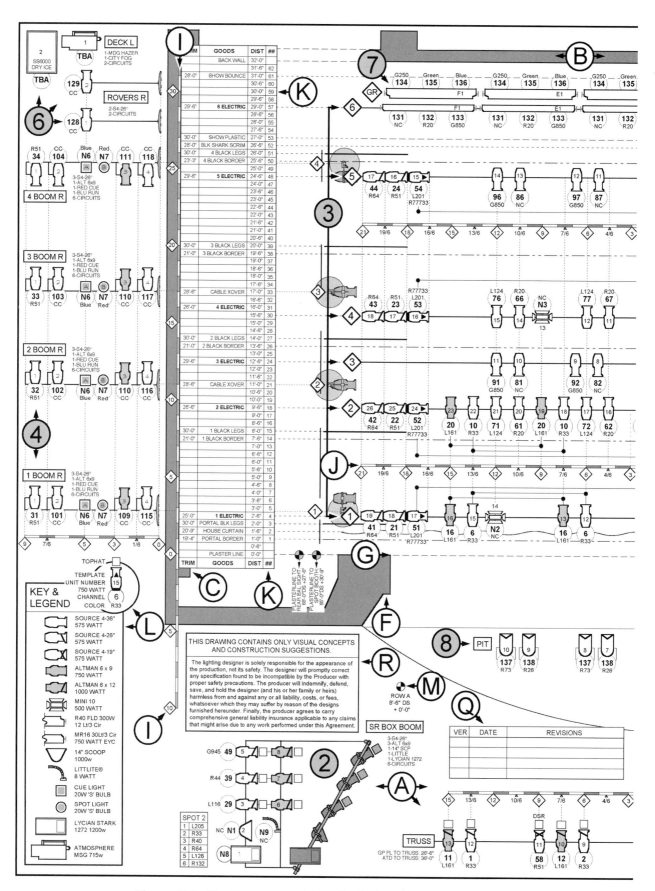

Figure 7.1 The Components of the Light Plot for *Hokey: A Musical Myth*

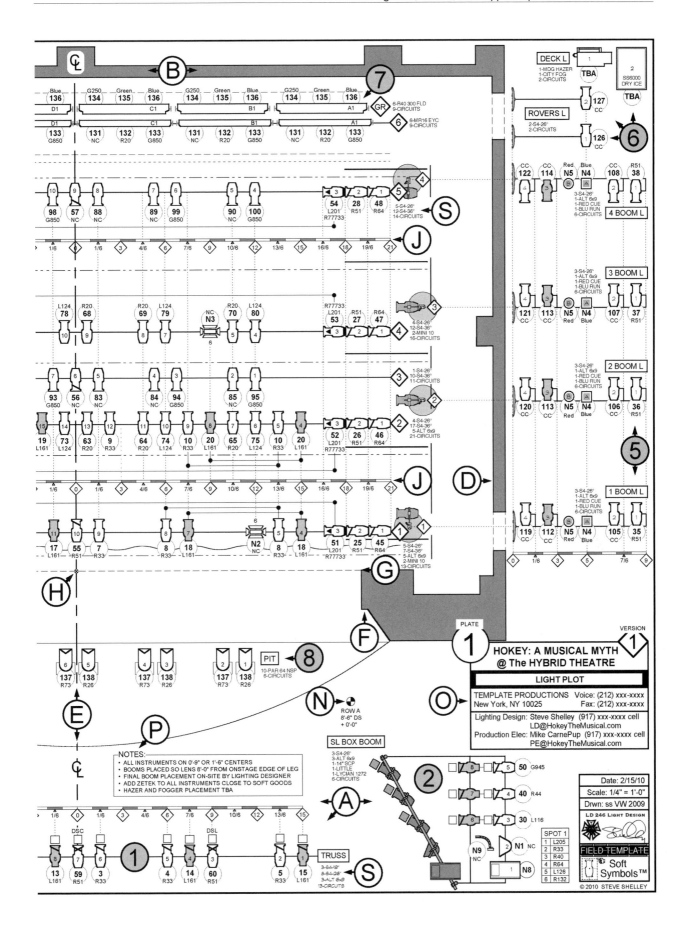

and Gam 945. Each wash is made up of a pair of instruments. There's also a worklight, a follow-spot, and a running light. The stage right washes are assigned to channels 29, 39, and 49, while the stage left washes are assigned to channels 30, 40, and 50.

The *Hokey* Downlight Systems

The second and fourth electrics in the *Hokey* light plot are home to the two **downlight systems**. As constructed in the preliminary light plot, each system consists of five instruments in a zone × two zones. The warm downlights are colored in Roscolux 20 and assigned to channels 61 > 70. The green downlights are colored in Lee 124 and assigned to channels 71 > 80. Since the second electric also contains the upstage zone of the frontlight system, it's not easy to recognize the downlights among the rest of the instruments on the electric without referring to the channels or colors. The systems are easier to see on the fourth electric.

The *Hokey* Backlight Systems

The third and fifth electrics in the *Hokey* light plot contain two of the **backlight systems** that were constructed in the preliminary phase of plotting. The warm backlight is uncolored (NC usually means "no color") and assigned to channels 81 > 90, while the Gam 850 cool backlight is assigned to channels 91 > 100. Again, the center pair of units is nudged aside to make room for specials focused to center-center.

The *Hokey* Sidelight Pipe End Systems

The first, second, fourth, and fifth electrics in the *Hokey* light plot have a pair of Source Four-26° instruments at each end of those battens that comprise the four-zone **pipe end systems**. The warm system is channels 21 > 28 and colored in Roscolux 51. The cool system is channels 41 > 48 and colored in Roscolux 64. As constructed in the preliminary light plot, these instruments will all be focused to the opposite quarterline.

The *Hokey* Template System

Onstage of those instruments, the Source Four-36° instruments make up the **pipe end template system**. All of the instruments contain a steel template called Dense Leaves #77733. This system will be primarily used in the first scene in Act 2, Hokey' nighttime forest encounter with the Knotty Piners. Using the preliminary focus layout, this system's design will cover the entire performance surface with this leafy pattern.

The instruments in this system have been boosted to 750-watt lamps to increase the template's beam intensity. Doing so means other systems' intensities in their cues can be brighter, and the textured light will still be seen on the performers and the stage. All eight of these instruments are assigned to channels 51 > 54.

The *Hokey* Sidelight Boom Systems

Upstage of the proscenium, the *Hokey* light plot indicates four **sidelight booms** (4 and 5) on either side of the stage. Though the detailed components of each boom are drawn offstage of the side walls of the theatre, dashed leader lines connect the individual positions to their actual location in the groundplan. The instruments on the booms combine to create four sidelight washes. In this plot, the two instrument systems mounted above eye level are called **head highs**. The eight instruments in the **top head high** sidelight system are colored in Roscolux 51, and controlled by channels 31 > 38. The **low head high** sidelight system is directly below the tops, colored in Roscolux 64 and controlled by channels 101 > 108. The instruments closest to the deck are the **shinbusters**, noted as "color change" instruments (C/C). Controlled by channels 115 > 122, they're earmarked to have different colors during the course of the show. The instruments above them are called **mids**. They're controlled in channels 109 > 114, and they too will have their colors changed. On either side of the stage, upstage of the booms, pairs of rovers (6) are mounted on adjustable stands, controlled in channels 126 > 129. Enough stage cable is coiled for each of these units, so they can be placed anywhere on their side of the stage. This allows the instruments to be used as deck specials, which can move, recolor, or refocus at different times in the show. There's also a dry ice fogger and a hazer drawn in that same area of the stage, but since their final positions and control channels have not yet been defined, they're all channeled as TBA (To Be Announced).

The *Hokey* Scenic Stack Systems

The sixth electric on the *Hokey* plot contains 3-circuit MR-16 **striplights**, assigned to channels 131 > 133, that will light the top of the translucency and the bounce drop. The plot also shows a row of R-40 striplights close to the back wall, "above" the sixth electric. Instead of a horizontal line drawn between each instrument (a batten), a small vertical line on either side of each striplight indicates that the units will sit on the deck. These instruments are **groundrow** (7), controlled by channels 134 > 136. This system will combine with the sixth electric, also located between the translucency and the bounce drop, to illuminate the upstage side of the translucency and make it glow like a shadowbox.

Finally, light plot shows the PAR 64 instruments placed in the **orchestra pit** (8). Mounted on square pieces of plywood, they will be used to illuminate the precipice during Hokey and Tee-boo's final battle. They're assigned to channels 137 and 138.

THE LIGHTING SECTION

Figure 7.2 shows an overall view of the lighting section drawn for the production of *Hokey: A Musical Myth*. Once again, alphabetic letters contained in large white circles will identify elements of the drawing and the architectural space, while numbers in large shaded circles will identify the different hanging positions. A clean version of this section, without identifying circles, can be found on pages xx–xxi.

The finished **lighting section** is one of the two primary graphic documents in the paperwork package. In this version, the document displays the side view of finalized relationships between the lighting fixtures, scenic goods, architecture, and the viewing audience. In addition to that, it provides three basic functions:

1. It illustrates the masking placement in the performance space.
2. It shows the full potential focus range from each hanging position.
3. It illustrates the planned beam pool overlap and upstage-downstage blend between zones.

One advantage to drawing the section on centerline is that the surrounding venue can be traced from architectural drawings. It was also demonstrated that constructing the preliminary drawing from this viewing plane was ideal to see spatial information about the lighting systems parallel to plaster line: frontlight, downlight, and backlight. The centerline sectional view made it possible to measure the actual throw distance for those systems. Now that the section is finished, the overlapping beams are drawn as points of reference.

In multi-scene productions involving different scenery or goods changing trims, several lighting sections may be required, one drafting or **plate** for each scene.

The Objectives of a Lighting Section

Regardless of which side is viewed or the number of plates, the finished lighting section has several objectives:

- Show the accurate size, shape, and relative position of lighting instruments in each hanging position to the sectional zero-zero.
- Show the accurate size, shape, and relative position of the architecture, masking, scenery, sightlines, and other scenic and production elements, as they relate to the hanging positions and to the sectional zero.
- Show all height locations for any production elements that possess more than one trim.
- Illustrate the typical appearance of the stage to the audience; are the overhead electrics to be exposed or concealed from the audience's view?
- Show the focus coverage and focus range of the different lighting systems and selected specials.

An Overview of the *Hokey* Lighting Section

Figure 7.2 shows the finished *Hokey* section, which is drawn looking from centerline to stage left. **The back wall** of the theatre (A) is on the left-hand side of the page, defining the architectural depth of the performance space, and the audience is drawn on the right. In a case of clarity winning the battle against accuracy, the full fly system of the Hybrid Theatre isn't shown so that the text in the drawing can be readable in this reduced view. If height measurements are necessary, the scaled distances can be measured using information from **the general information box** (Q), which has been copied from the tech specs.

There are two basic "road markers" in this lighting section. The **plaster line** (B), which is the upstage side of the proscenium, defines the horizontal axis, while the **stage** or **deck** (C) defines the vertical axis. The point where the plaster line touches the stage is the **sectional zero-zero point** (D). All height and depth measurements are based on this point, or on these two planes.

Some visual elements are duplicated between the light plot and the section. These include the **proscenium** (E), which is "cut in half" to show its thickness and illustrate the height of the proscenium opening. Since the battens are hung from the grid, the **lineset schedule** (F) has moved to the top of the document. The distances between the contents of the lineset schedule and the plaster line in the lighting section should match their counterparts in the groundplan view. It's common practice to place a section sideways to a light plot for the same production, and align the lineset schedules between the two documents. This double-check visually confirms that the measured distances and listed contents shown on both lineset schedules match between the two documents.

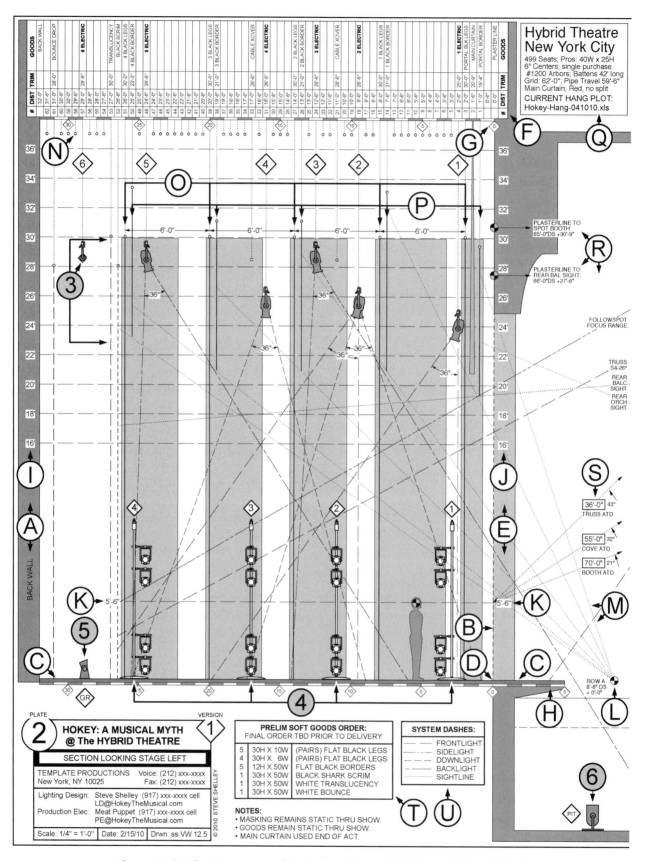

Figure 7.2 The Components of the Lighting Section for *Hokey: A Musical Myth*

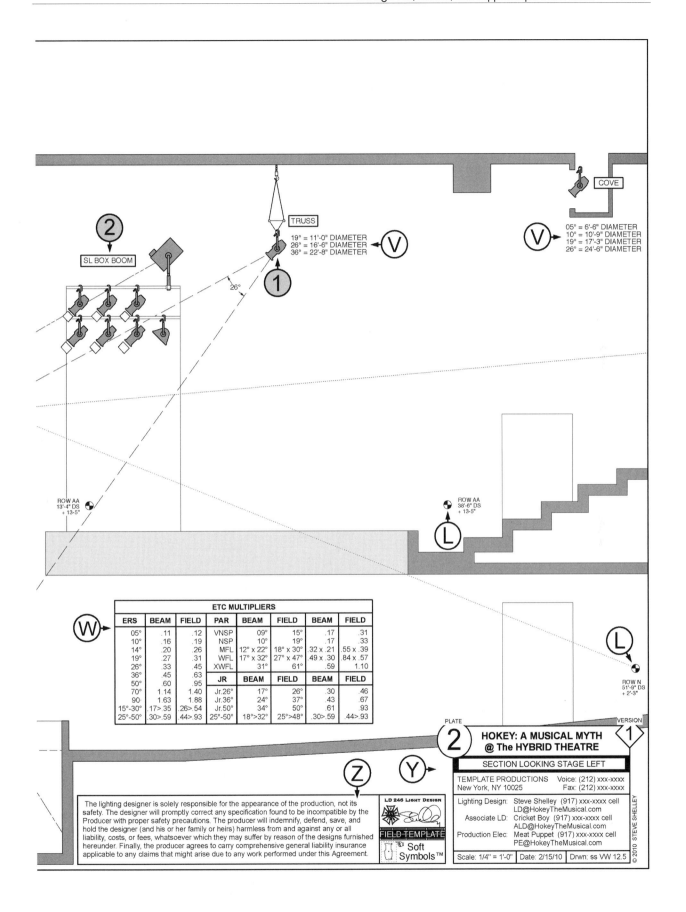

COVE

TRUSS

19° = 11'-0" DIAMETER
26° = 16'-6" DIAMETER
36° = 22'-8" DIAMETER

05° = 6'-6" DIAMETER
10° = 10'-9" DIAMETER
19° = 17'-3" DIAMETER
26° = 24'-6" DIAMETER

SL BOX BOOM

26°

ROW AA
13'-4" DS
+ 13-5"

ROW AA
38'-6" DS
+ 13-5"

ROW N
51'-9" DS
+ 2'-3"

ETC MULTIPLIERS							
ERS	**BEAM**	**FIELD**	**PAR**	**BEAM**	**FIELD**	**BEAM**	**FIELD**
05°	.11	.12	VNSP	09°	15°	.17	.31
10°	.16	.19	NSP	10°	19°	.17	.33
14°	.20	.26	MFL	12° x 22°	18° x 30°	.32 x .21	.55 x .39
19°	.27	.31	WFL	17° x 32°	27° x 47°	.49 x .30	.84 x .57
26°	.33	.45	XWFL	31°	61°	.59	1.10
36°	.45	.63	**JR**	**BEAM**	**FIELD**	**BEAM**	**FIELD**
50°	.60	.95					
70°	1.14	1.40	Jr.26°	17°	26°	.30	.46
90°	1.63	1.88	Jr.36°	24°	37°	.43	.67
15°-30°	.17>.35	.26>.54	Jr.50°	34°	50°	.61	.93
25°-50°	.30>.59	.44>.93	25°-50°	18°>32°	25°>48°	.30>.59	.44>.93

PLATE
2

VERSION
1

HOKEY: A MUSICAL MYTH
@ The HYBRID THEATRE

SECTION LOOKING STAGE LEFT

TEMPLATE PRODUCTIONS   Voice: (212) xxx-xxxx
New York, NY 10025   Fax: (212) xxx-xxxx

Lighting Design: Steve Shelley (917) xxx-xxxx cell
                          LD@HokeyTheMusical.com
Associate LD: Cricket Boy (917) xxx-xxxx cell
                        ALD@HokeyTheMusical.com
Production Elec: Meat Puppet (917) xxx-xxxx cell
                         PE@HokeyTheMusical.com

Scale: 1/4" = 1'-0" | Date: 2/15/10 | Drwn: ss VW 12.5

© 2010 STEVE SHELLEY

LD 246 LIGHT DESIGN

FIELD TEMPLATE
Soft
Symbols™

Two scales on the *Hokey* section provide distance information from the sectional zero-zero point. The **up-and-downstage scale**, providing depth distances, is duplicated both above (G) and below (H) the stage. The **vertical scales** on the back wall and the proscenium (I and J), along with their dashed lines in between, demarcate the vertical space. The lowest dashed line drawn between the vertical scales is the **head height line** (K) drawn at 5′-6″ above the stage. This arbitrary height measurement indicates an "average" eye (or top of head) level, and is used to define the vertical placement of focus points.

Another carryover from the groundplan is the side view of a **sightline point** (L), representing the eye level of the extreme audience member. While the pair of sightlines in the groundplan view defined the parameters of the side masking, this singular point may be placed at a different distance from plaster line, and used to define the relative trim heights of any scenery, masking borders, and overhead electrics. The **sightlines** (M) drawn from the sightline point up into the flies over the stage illustrate the limits of vertical visibility. When scenery or electrics are meant to be vertically hidden by borders from the audience, sightlines often help define their trim heights to remain concealed.

The **battens, pipes,** or **linesets** (N) are drawn in this section as small circles under dotted lines to represent the end view of pipe hanging from system cables. While only the active linesets are drawn as lines in the groundplan, many designers prefer to show all of the battens in the section even if they're empty. This way, available linesets can be visually considered and selected. In productions that mask the backstage from the audience, the battens and their system cables are concealed. Drawing the batten's vertical placement above the stage establishes the trim height of each pipe used in the show. A second batten location that may be important to include on the drawing, either graphically or as text, is the distance from the stage to the top limit of the batten's **out trim**, when the batten is **gridded**. This highest "out" location, also known as the batten's **pipe travel**, can become an important measurement. If the fly system is "short," or scenic units are too tall, the bottom of gridded scenic units attempting to fly out (and disappear) may instead remain exposed under the borders. In theatres with tall fly systems, pipe travel may never be an issue, but many designers consider it an important parameter to include somewhere on the drawing. The pipe travel information for the Hybrid Theatre is included with other basic information in the **general information box** (Q), which has been copied from the tech specs.

The **masking legs** and **borders** (O and P), which were dotted and shaded lines in the groundplan, are presented in this view as thick solid lines. Being drawn with these attributes makes it easier to see

the distances between legs and the depth of each leg opening. (The leg depths are also dimensioned above the leg battens.) Keeping the border lines thick makes them stand out and easier to read, relative to the sight lines and the instruments' focus range.

Below the theatre notes are heights and distances to **off-the-map-points** (R) that don't fit on this drawing. If the points are required, they can be measured out from these points. Below that are **actual throw distances** (S) to locations in the theatre. While the lines can be extended to their hanging locations in the full-scaled version of the drawing, the distance and angle info are compactly listed close to the proscenium. That way, the information is still included, even if this section is sent out as a single-page PDF.

The **soft goods order** (T) is included under the stage for handy reference. The **system dashes** (U) next to it are shown as a kind of legend, to help define the identity of each beam angle line. This can be especially helpful when all of the beam spreads are shown in the drawing.

Next to the truss and the cove, **beam pool sizes** are listed (V), showing the rough size of different beam pools from that position to plaster line. When an instrument needs to be quickly added to the position, consulting this list allows more informed decisions to be made.

Under the balcony is a **multiplier block** (W), an information table culled from several cut sheets. In order to determine a more exact pool size for either beam or field angle, the actual throw distance is multiplied by a value shown in the block. This table includes a beam and field multiplier value for the latest ETC Source Four Ellipsoidals, PARs, and Juniors.

The **title block** (Y) is sometimes a copy-and-paste of the title block from the light plot. The only difference is the plate number and the title informing the viewer of the document's function. Finally, the **disclaimer block** repeats the language from the groundplan, which is also included as part of the lighting designer's contract.

The Layout of the *Hokey* Lighting Section

In order to fit into the format of this book, the *Hokey* lighting section has been condensed and customized. First, it's been truncated; while the back wall of the theatre is included on the left-hand side of the page, the back of the balcony on the opposite side has been cut off. For large venues with remote reference points, this isn't uncommon. In order to keep the overall size of a drawing from becoming a bed sheet, "chopping off" a chunk of otherwise empty space is not unheard of. When only two or three rarely used reference points are lost due to drawing truncation, the drafting technique is to use "off the map points" (R) measured from a reference plane. In this case they're based off the plaster line, and located at their proper height above the top of the proscenium arch.

The drawing's height has also been chopped off. In reality, there's another 24'-0" of fly space not shown in this drawing, including the grid above the stage supporting the fly system. When the full-sized print of this drawing is created, the additional height may be shown. Cutting that space off for this version of the drawing, however, allows the entire document to be shown in a larger percentage, and allows readability without a magnifying glass.

Since this drawing has been created in a CAD program, it can be printed out in several size formats. Drafted in ½" scale and printed at 100%, the landscape drawing measures roughly 44" × 28". Reduced to 50%, in order to print out at ¼" scale, the same document produces a drawing measuring 22" × 14". If the document is reduced to 30% scale, the same drawing fits neatly into these two pages. That was the driving force to draft the document in this size. And while there are times when seeing the FOH truss or the rear balcony sight line is important, in many cases the meat of the section is between the sightline and the back wall. Sending out two pages makes little difference to the sender, but that means that the recipients are forced to print both pages and tape them together in order to see the assembled drawing. In the initial stages of developing or publishing a section, that's a lot of work, and in many cases it's not necessary.

For that reason, not only has this drawing been designed to comfortably fit onto two pages for this book, it's also arranged in such a way that most of the design information is contained on the left-hand page. A majority of the information has been "squished" into the left-hand page so that it can be sent as a single-page email PDF attachment. While the 30% size means it's no longer presented in a measurable scale, the inclusion of the drawn scale bars and distances allows information on the page to be understood (for the most part) without the need of a scale rule. The distances in the lineset schedule also become written signposts to gauge relative proximity of drawing elements to one another. At 30%, all of the text, including the 12-point Arial font used in the lineset information, is still readable to most observers.

When a section is drawn using this method, the left-hand page (and the show's sectional design) can then be developed and distributed between the creative staff, requiring only a single page to be emailed and viewed as a PDF attachment.

The trade-off may become apparent when the document is later plotted at 100%. At that scale, some of the fonts may appear too large, but often that becomes a question of visual preference. It's also worth noting that this section has two title blocks; in many cases, title blocks are assigned to appear in the lower right-hand corner of the drawing. For that reason, the title block is repeated on both pages. When the final drawing is printed in either ½" or ¼" scale, the title block under the stage can be "turned off" or eliminated.

The *Hokey* Lighting Systems in Section

In this section, the FOH hanging positions include the **truss** (1) and the stage left **box boom** position (2). The **overhead electrics** (3) are shown as instruments hung from battens, with a diamond indicating the numeric name assigned to each electric. This section also shows the four stage left **sidelight booms** (4) sitting on the stage. They too are labeled with small diamonds, their numbering relative to plaster line. The furthest upstage lighting position in this section is the **groundrow** (5), positioned on the deck upstage between the translucency and the bounce. The final lighting position shown in this section is the PARs in the **orchestra pit** (6).

Figure 7.3 separates the three main systems that were constructed in the preliminary section. Figure 7.3A shows the hanging positions, the focus points, and the un-shuttered beam edges of the instruments that will provide the two color-three zone **frontlight** washes (channels 1 > 20). (The truss position is not shown, only the resulting beam edges.) Although the angles of origin don't match, the beam overlaps will ensure even coverage from plaster line up through the middle of the fourth opening. The two overhead electrics (1 and 2) ended up very close to the same trim, meaning that their beam spreads and intensities should equal between the two upstage zones. The three small figures indicate the focus points for each zone. The dashed lines indicate the hot spot for each beam.

From this section it's apparent that the top edge of the truss frontlight zone will require a shutter cut, so the stage isn't illuminated with frontlight far upstage during moments of downstage isolation. The frontlight on the second electric will also need a top shutter cut to eliminate light that will otherwise splash the face of the scenic stack.

Although the box boom instruments are shown in the lighting section, their lighting beams aren't. Their beams are on a diagonal, not in line with the centerline section, so their intended section will remain on a separate beam section document. Drawing beam

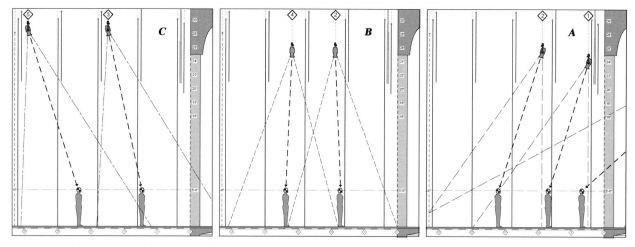

Figure 7.3 The A) Frontlight, B) Downlight, and C) Backlight Beam Sections for the *Hokey* Light Plot

edge lines for diagonal box booms is rarely seen on centerline sections, except for special situations. In Figure 7.2, for example, the top beam edge line is drawn from the followspot to the black scrim to illustrate its limited upstage coverage. The followspot can't cover anything above head height in the fourth opening, because the black portal border on lineset #1 cuts off the top of its beam. In this section, the rest of the box booms are shown in the lighting section so the viewers can see their relative location to the rest of the stage and the audience.

Figure 7.3B shows the hanging positions and the un-shuttered beam edges of the instruments that will provide the two color-two zone **downlight** washes (channels 61 > 80). The placement of these systems worked out very closely to what had been constructed in the preliminary section. The beams properly overlap to ensure an even blend of downlight over the depth of the entire stage. The beam edges illustrate, however, that the systems provide only floor coverage at the perimeters of the performance space. There's no head high coverage downstage of plaster line or upstage in the fourth opening. Since both electrics ended up at approximately the same trim, the beam pools and intensities will be equal between the two zones.

Figure 7.3C shows the hanging positions and the beam edges of the instruments that will be used to provide the two color-two zone **backlight** washes (channels 81 > 100). The fifth electric has been raised higher than necessary to be hidden from the upstage sightline. This has been done for two reasons; to match the beam pool size of the instruments on the third electric, and to help ensure the beam pool overlap between the two zones of backlight. Since both electrics are close to the same trim, the beam pools and intensity levels will be close between

the two zones. During focus, it may become apparent that the downstage zone on the third electric may require a top shutter cut, to keep light out of the audience's eyes.

Figure 7.4D shows the un-shuttered beam pools and hot spots for the two color-four zone **pipe end sidelight** washes (channels 21 > 28 and 41 > 48). The beam overlap ensures an even blend in sidelight coverage over the depth of the entire stage. Ideally, all of the overhead electrics are at approximately the same trim, so that the beam spread and intensity will be equal through the four zones. From this section, it's apparent that the sidelight on the fifth electric will probably require slightly higher intensities to make up for the fact it's actual throw distance is more than the rest of the instruments in the system. The instruments on the fifth electric will also require an upstage cut to eliminate the light otherwise splashing onto the scenic stack.

Combining the beam edges for all the systems into a single document can be confusing, but it can be important during the load-in process. If the electrics change trim height, or shift to different batten locations, the lighting designer can check the lighting section to see what impact any of those changes may have on the focus range of any affected systems.

In order to show the blend of the different systems in a single document, the beams of each system shown in the *Hokey* section have been drawn with a different series of dashes. Figure 7.4E shows the combined systems and focus points for *Hokey*. Long dashed lines represent the frontlight beams, short dashed lines show the downlight beams, dash-and-one-dot lines are used for the backlight beams, and dash-with-two-dot lines illustrate the sidelight beams. The legend illustrating their identities is shown under the proscenium (U) in Figure 7.2.

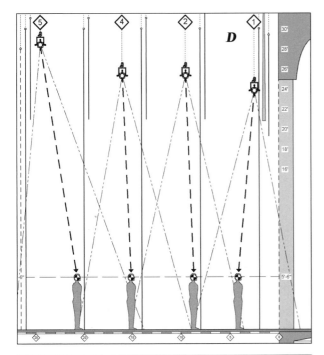

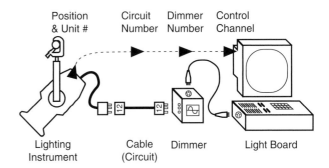

Figure 7.5 The Control Path in a Computer Lighting System

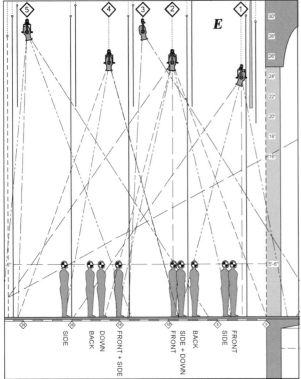

Figure 7.4 The D) Pipe End Sidelight, and E) Combined Beam Sections for the *Hokey* Light Plot

THE SUPPORT PAPERWORK

Although a lot of information is displayed on a light plot, it's been said that the graphic map often doesn't visually present all of the information about every

lighting instrument. Each instrument has its own **control path**, which can be traced from the instrument to the handle or channel that controls its intensity.

Figure 7.5 traces the control path for a computer lighting system, showing the four points of intersection, which translate into four data information fields:

- The position and unit number of the instrument.
- The circuit number (the identity of the cable connecting the instrument to the dimmer).
- The dimmer number (that the circuit is plugged into).
- The channel number (assigned to control the dimmer).

All of this information is part of the **lighting database**, the collection of facts about each of the instruments or electrical devices in a light plot. The lighting database can be sorted by the four different fields in the control path and viewed in different forms. Although each form contains the same information, it's sorted by different criteria.

The Instrument Schedule

The **instrument schedule** sorts the lighting database by the hanging position and unit number, mirroring the same sequential arrangement of the instruments and electrical devices drawn on the light plot (Figure 7.8).

Figure 7.6 highlights the instrument's location in the electrical path. If the unit's position is known, the instrument schedule is the document used to search for additional information. Additionally, visual searches for blank spaces in this paperwork can reveal instruments that have not been assigned a purpose or a focus, and may be available for use as a new special.

The formula used to sort the hanging positions in the instrument schedule use the four general guidelines that were mentioned in the review

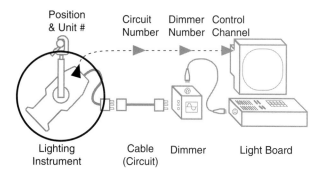

Figure 7.6 The Control Path Highlighting the Instrument's Position

chapter; they're sorted from the perspective of the lighting designer sitting in the audience, by their relation to plaster line, by their relative height above the stage (with the highest positions appearing first), and finally by their position relative to centerline. Figure 7.7 shows the basic instrument schedule position sort for the *Hokey* light plot. The first positions shown are the overhead front of house positions, sorted "backwards" so that the FOH position farthest from plaster line and highest above the stage appears first, followed by the next closest FOH position, and so on (Cove, Truss). Once the overhead FOH position closest to plaster line has been listed, the box boom positions are next. When there are matching positions on either side of centerline, the question may arise as to which side to list first. Since the starting point for unit numbering on the overhead electrics begins on stage left, standard practice is to list the stage left side of matching positions first (SL Box Boom, then SR Box Boom). The box boom farthest from plaster line would be listed first, and the stage right box boom closest to plaster line listed last. The lowest position closest to the plaster line would be the final FOH position listed (Pit).

After the front of house positions, the overhead electrics are usually listed next, starting with the position closest to plaster line (1 Electric). After the electric closest to the back wall is listed, the next

highest positions are addressed. Often this consists of the galleries and the ladders. Again, the stage left position closest to plaster line would be listed first, concluding with the farthest upstage right position listed last. The final hanging positions are those that sit on the deck, which usually include the booms and the groundrow. The boom closest to plaster line on stage left would be listed first (1 Boom Left), the boom farthest upstage right would be listed last (4 Boom Right), and the instrument schedule would conclude with the lowest position farthest from plaster line (Groundrow).

When information about two adjacent hanging positions can both fit on a single page of an instrument schedule, the two positions are often combined, with spaces in between. When the hanging location includes enough instruments that the position will be split between two pages, that practice is amended; the instrument schedule is divided so that only a complete position will appear on each page. This tactic visually separates positions within a multi-page document, and allows for one single position to be viewed by itself. It also means a single page (position) can be removed while hanging the plot, but the rest of the light plot's information stays complete in the notebook. Ideally, some amount of white space is left on each page where added instruments or notes specific to the hanging position can be written.

Figure 7.8 shows a combination of the first three hanging positions of the *Hokey* light plot. Columns containing the position and unit number are listed on the left-hand side in bold type, to confirm the sort order and the identity of the document. The next three columns are sorted in a logical progression, following the path of each instrument to its control channel. The instrument is plugged into a circuit, which is then plugged into a dimmer, which is then softpatched to a channel. Visually comparing two pieces of relevant information is simplified when the columns follow the control path. In this case, the male connector from truss unit #1 is plugged into the female connector of a cable marked "A-1." The male plug on the other end of that cable is plugged into dimmer 175. In the patch screen of the lighting console, dimmer 175 is then softpatched into channel 15.

The rest of the columns provide more information about truss unit #1. The instrument type is identified, along with the wattage of the lamp. The purpose or focus of the instrument is followed by the color it will receive. The final column lists any notes. In this case, the instrument is earmarked to receive a top hat.

While the instruments are being hung and circuited, the instrument schedule is often the document used to record circuitry or dimmer information.

Front of House	Overhead	Stage Left	Stage Right
Cove	1 Electric	1 Boom Left	1 Boom Right
Truss	2 Electric	2 Boom Left	2 Boom Right
SL Box Boom	3 Electric	3 Boom Left	3 Boom Right
SR Box Boom	4 Electric	4 Boom Left	4 Boom Right
Balcony Rail	5 Electric	Rovers Left	Rovers Right
Pit	6 Electric	Deck Left	Deck Right
			Groundrow

Figure 7.7 A Position Sort List for the *Hokey* Light Plot

Hybrid Theatre 2010 | **HOKEY INSTRUMENT SCHEDULE** | Date: 2/13/10

Position	#	Cir	Dim	Chan	Type	Watt	Purpose	Color	Notes
Truss	1	A-1	175	15	Alt 6 x 12	1kw	Cool Area 5	L161	Tophat
Truss	2	A-2	174	5	Source 4-26°	575w	Warm Area 5	R33	Tophat
Truss	3	A-3	173	60	Source 4-19°	575w	DL Special	NC	Tophat
Truss	4	A-4	172	14	Alt 6 x 12	1kw	Cool Area 4	L161	Tophat
Truss	5	A-5	171	4	Source 4-26°	575w	Warm Area 4	R33	Tophat
Truss	6	B-1	170	3	Source 4-26°	575w	Warm Area 3	R33	Tophat
Truss	7	B-2	169	59	Source 4-19°	575w	DC Special	NC	Tophat
Truss	8	B-3	168	13	Alt 6 x 12	1kw	Cool Area 3	L161	Tophat
Truss	9	B-4	167	2	Source 4-26°	575w	Warm Area 2	R33	Tophat
Truss	10	B-5	166	12	Alt 6 x 12	1kw	Cool Area 2	L161	Tophat
Truss	11	C-1	165	58	Source 4-19°	575w	DR Special	NC	Tophat
Truss	12	C-2	164	1	Source 4-26°	575w	Warm Area 1	R33	Tophat
Truss	13	C-3	163	11	Alt 6 x 12	1kw	Cool Area 1	L161	Tophat
SL Bx Boom	1	BBL-1	19	N8	Starklight	1200w	SL Box Boom Followspot		See plot for color
SL Bx Boom	1A	BBL-2	20	N9	Littlite®	8w	SL Box Boom Run light	NC	For music stand
SL Bx Boom	2	BBL-3		N1	14" Scoop	1kw	House Left Work	NC	
SL Bx Boom	3	BBL-4	22	30	Source 4-26°	575w	SL Box Boom Med-BG Far	L116	Tophat
SL Bx Boom	4	BBL-5	23	40	Source 4-36°	575w	SL Box Boom Rose Far	R44	Tophat
SL Bx Boom	5	BBL-6	24	50	Source 4-26°	575w	SL Box Boom Dk Lav Far	G945	Tophat
SL Bx Boom	6	BBL-7	22	30	Alt 6 x 9	1kw	SL Box Boom Med-BG Near	L116	Tophat
SL Bx Boom	7	BBL-8	23	40	Alt 6 x 9	1kw	SL Box Boom Rose Near	R44	Tophat
SL Bx Boom	8	BBL-9	24	50	Alt 6 x 9	1kw	SL Box Boom Dk Lav Near	G945	Tophat
		BBL-10					Spare		
		BBL-11					Spare		
SR Bx Boom	1	BBR-1	25	N7	Starklight	1200w	SR Box Boom Followspot		See plot for color
SR Bx Boom	1A	BBR-2	26	N9	Littlite®	8w	SR Box Boom Run light	NC	For music stand
SR Bx Boom	2	BBR-3		N1	14" Scoop	1kw	House Right Work	NC	
SR Bx Boom	3	BBR-4	27	29	Source 4-26°	575w	SR Box Boom Med-BG Far	L116	Tophat
SR Bx Boom	4	BBR-5	28	39	Source 4-26°	575w	SR Box Boom Rose Far	R44	Tophat
SR Bx Boom	5	BBR-6	29	49	Source 4-26°	575w	SR Box Boom Dk Lav Far	G945	Tophat
SR Bx Boom	6	BBR-7	27	29	Alt 6 x 9	1kw	SR Box Boom Med-BG Near	L116	Tophat
SR Bx Boom	7	BBR-8	28	39	Alt 6 x 9	1kw	SR Box Boom Rose Near	R44	Tophat
SR Bx Boom	8	BBR-9	29	49	Alt 6 x 9	1kw	SR Box Boom Dk Lav Near	G945	Tophat
		BBR-10					Spare		
		BBR-11					Spare		

Expression 3; 150 chan, 174 dim | Lighting design by Steve Shelley 917.xxx.xxxx | Page 1 of 11

Figure 7.8 The First Three Hanging Positions in the *Hokey* Instrument Schedule

It can also be used to double-check other attributes of the instrument, such as color or accessories. Finally, the instrument schedule is often the document used while circuits are plugged into dimmers, or when dimmers are softpatched to channels.

The Channel Hookup

The second form sorts the lighting database by its "handle" or control channel. This is the **channel hookup**, which displays the data in the same numerical order as the handles on the manual light board or the channels displayed on a computer lighting monitor (Figure 7.10).

Figure 7.9 highlights the control channel's location in the control path. The first row of a channel hookup for a light plot using computer control lists the soft patched contents of the first channel (usually channel 1), while the final row in the document lists the contents of the highest channel number used in the plot. When questions arise about the contents of a channel, the channel hookup is usually the form used to search for information.

In the case of the *Hokey* hookup, the channel numbers are assigned so that systems of focused instruments are numbered from stage right to stage left. This convention is based on the fact that English text runs left to right on the printed page, and as such, the natural inclination of the English eye is to view the left side of a document first. In this same manner, when the English-speaking lighting designer views the stage from the audience, it can be said that his or her eye looks at the left side of the stage picture first, so the channels are numbered in this manner. Numbering the channels in the opposite direction is a preference of the lighting designer, but whatever side of the stage is chosen to begin the numbering of each system, that "starting point" is often retained while assigning the channel numbers for the entire plot.

The rows in an instrument schedule can be single-spaced; an added instrument can be noted at the bottom of that position's page. Inserting an instrument into a single-spaced hookup, however, can quickly result in paper surgery involving scissors and tape. For that reason, the hookup is often produced with blank rows between each channel number. Not only does this visually separate the channel numbers on the document from one another, it also provides space for any additional instruments.

Figure 7.10 shows the hookup for the first 10 channels of the *Hokey* light plot. The control channel is listed in bold text in the left-hand column to confirm the sort order and the identity of the document. The next three columns continue the control path, but in reverse order from the instrument schedule. This is because the control path is also reversed. The channel is controlling a dimmer, which has a circuit or cable plugged into it. The other end of the cable is plugged into an instrument at a remote lighting position. The arrangements of the columns provide a logical method to visually compare the intersections in the control path. Presuming the light plot has been properly soft- and hardpatched, the patch screen of the computer light board will confirm that channel 1 controls dimmer 164. An inspection of the output for dimmer 164 will confirm that a cable with a male plug marked C-2 is plugged into it. Tracing the cable to the truss, the female end of the cable will terminate with a plug marked C-2, which is plugged to truss unit #12.

The rest of the columns reiterate the same information as the instrument schedule, identifying the type, wattage, and purpose of truss unit #12. Finally, the notes column states that the instrument will receive a tophat. After the light plot has been assembled, the channel hookup is the document used while performing a channel check.

The Circuitry Schedule

The third form uses an intermediate intersection in the control path to sort the lighting database in another way. This list is called the **circuitry schedule** (Figure 7.12). The information is displayed in the numerical order of the circuitry used to connect the instruments to the dimmers. To prevent confusion, every circuit is assigned a unique label.

Figure 7.11 highlights the circuit number's location in the control path. The circuitry schedule usually lists every available circuit in the house electrical infrastructure, along with every circuit added for that particular lighting package. Usually, there's some number of open (or unused) circuits. When it is necessary to find alternative or additional paths from a hanging position to the dimmers, the circuitry schedule is the form consulted to check for possibilities.

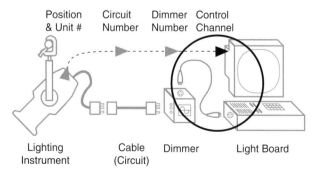

Figure 7.9 The Control Path Highlighting the Control Channel

HOKEY CHANNEL HOOKUP

Chan	Dim	Cir	Position	#	Type	Watt	Purpose	Color	Notes
1	164	C-2	Truss	12	Source 4-26°	575w	Warm Area 1	R33	Tophat
2	167	B-4	Truss	9	Source 4-26°	575w	Warm Area 2	R33	Tophat
3	170	B-1	Truss	6	Source 4-26°	575w	Warm Area 3	R33	Tophat
4	171	A-5	Truss	5	Source 4-26°	575w	Warm Area 4	R33	Tophat
5	174	A-2	Truss	2	Source 4-26°	575w	Warm Area 5	R33	Tophat
6	7	7	1 Electric	15	Source 4-36°	575w	Warm Area 6	R33	
6	7	7	1 Electric	12	Source 4-36°	575w	Warm Area 7	R33	
7	4	4	1 Electric	9	Source 4-36°	575w	Warm Area 8	R33	
8	3	3	1 Electric	8	Source 4-36°	575w	Warm Area 9	R33	
8	3	3	1 Electric	5	Source 4-36°	575w	Warm Area 10	R33	
9	84	E-4	2 Electric	12	Source 4-36°	575w	Warm Area 13	R33	
10	94	F-5	2 Electric	22	Source 4-36°	575w	Warm Area 11	R33	
10	90	F-5	2 Electric	18	Source 4-36°	575w	Warm Area 12	R33	
10	81	D-5	2 Electric	9	Source 4-36°	575w	Warm Area 14	R33	
10	77	D-5	2 Electric	5	Source 4-36°	575w	Warm Area 15	R33	

Expression 3; 150 chan, 174 dimLighting design by Steve Shelley 917.xxx.xxxx Page 1 of 13

Figure 7.10 The First 10 Control Channels of the *Hokey* Channel Hookup

Figure 7.12 shows the circuitry schedule for the first 10 circuits of the *Hokey* light plot. It shows that circuit 1 is currently unused, and that 1 Electric #4 and #7 are plugged into circuit 2. Since there's only one female plug labeled "circuit 2," that implies that the units are two-fered into the circuit.

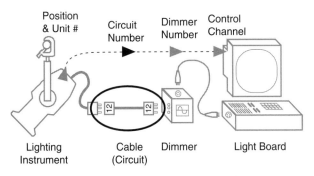

Figure 7.11 The Control Path Highlighting the Circuit

The circuitry schedule also shows that circuit 3 is connected to 1 Electric #5 and #8 (again a two-fer situation), but it's necessary to visually "skip over" the dimmer and channel column to reach that conclusion. Aside from that, the columns are again logically arranged to follow the control path. Circuit 3 is plugged into dimmer 3, which is then soft patched to channel 8. The rest of the columns reiterate the rest of the information regarding the instruments plugged into circuit 3. The type, wattage, and purpose of the instrument is identified, along with a column for additional notes.

During the load-in circuits are often swapped or changed in order to accelerate the installation and plugging of the instruments. A final version of the circuitry schedule may not be practical until the entire lighting package has been mounted, hot tested, and deemed operational. For this reason, printing an updated circuit schedule is often delayed until after the focus session has concluded.

Hybrid Theatre 2010   **HOKEY CIRCUITRY SCHEDULE**   Date: 2/13/10

Cir	Dim	Chan	Position	#	Type	Watt	Purpose	Color	Notes
1									
2	2	18	1 Electric	4	Alt 6 x 9	1kw	Cool Area 10	L161	
2	2	18	1 Electric	7	Alt 6 x 9	1kw	Cool Area 9	L161	
3	3	8	1 Electric	5	Source 4-36°	575w	Warm Area 10	R33	
3	3	8	1 Electric	8	Source 4-36°	575w	Warm Area 9	R33	
4	4	7	1 Electric	9	Source 4-36°	575w	Warm Area 8	R33	
5	5	55	1 Electric	10	Source 4-26°	575w	CC Front Special	NC	
6	6	17	1 Electric	11	Alt 6 x 9	1kw	Cool Area 8	L161	
7	7	6	1 Electric	12	Source 4-36°	575w	Warm Area 7	R33	
7	7	6	1 Electric	15	Source 4-36°	575w	Warm Area 6	R33	
8	8	16	1 Electric	13	Alt 6 x 9	1kw	Cool Area 7	L161	
8	8	16	1 Electric	16	Alt 6 x 9	1kw	Cool Area 6	L161	
9	9	51	1 Electric	3	Source 4-36°	750w	Temp DS Center	NC	T: R77733
9	9	51	1 Electric	17	Source 4-36°	750w	Temp DS Center	NC	T: R77733
10	10	21	1 Electric	18	Source 4-26°	575w	in 1 SL Far 1/4 Lav	R51	

Expression 3; 150 chan, 174 dimLighting design by Steve Shelley 917.xxx.xxxx   Page 1 of 15

Figure 7.12 The First 10 Circuits of the *Hokey* Circuitry Schedule

If there are only so many circuits available in an existing lighting package, or if adding circuitry is not an option, the overall number of circuits may become a parameter. Long-running shows with added circuitry have a higher probability of plug burnouts or wire breaks within cable runs. Instruments many need to switch to different functional circuits. All of these scenarios describe situations when the circuit schedule may become the reference document searched in order to find alternate electrical routes from the lighting instruments to the dimmers.

The Dimmer Schedule

The fourth form uses the final intersection in the control path as the basis to sort the lighting database. This list is called the **dimmer schedule** (Figure 7.14). The information is displayed in the same numerical order as the patch display in most computer light boards. To prevent electronic confusion, every dimmer has a unique number.

Figure 7.13 highlights the dimmer's location in the control path. The dimmer schedule typically lists all of the dimmers that exist in a lighting package. That way it's relatively simple to spot any open spare dimmers available for use. The first rows of a dimmer schedule list all of the circuits that are hard patched into dimmer 1, along with the identity number of any assigned control. The final dimmer entry is the highest dimmer number in the lighting system. When questions arise about the contents of a given dimmer, this document is the one consulted for answers. This form is usually produced with blank rows between each different number, allowing for handwritten circuitry notations to any dimmer.

Figure 7.14 shows the dimmer schedule for the first 10 dimmers of the *Hokey* light plot. This form is often produced with the dimmers listed in bold type in the left-hand column to confirm the sort order and the identity of the document. The next two columns again present the rest of the control path, but since the dimmer is an intermediate intersection in the

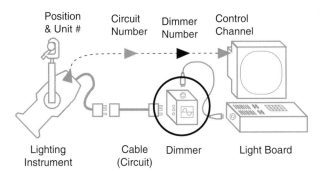

Figure 7.13 The Control Path Highlighting the Dimmer

path, it is necessary to visually "skip" over columns to confirm relationships that exist for each row.

The dimmer schedule for *Hokey* shows that dimmer 1 is "open" at this time, or available for use. Since the dimmer number matches the circuit number, it's possible to infer that dimmer 2 is hardwired to circuit 2. To check the channel assignment, however, it is necessary to visually skip over the circuit column

to see that dimmer 2 is soft patched to channel 18. Likewise, determining the position and unit number at the other end of the circuit, requires visually "skipping" over the channel column to see that dimmer 2 is powering 1 Electric #4 and #7. To the right of the position and unit columns are the rest of the logistical information: the type, wattage, purpose, color, and notes about each instrument.

The primary function of the dimmer schedule is to identify the circuits that are hard patched into the dimmer and then to identify the control channel to which the dimmer has been assigned. This form is consulted when a search for additional control to the lighting system is taking place. A visual gap in the list may indicate an open or unassigned dimmer that can receive a circuit.

In many cases, the circuitry and the specific dimmers are unknown until the hang is finished and the installation of the lighting package is complete. Because of that, printing an updated circuit schedule is also often delayed until after the focus session has concluded.

Hybrid Theatre 2010   **HOKEY DIMMER SCHEDULE**   Date: 2/13/10

Dim	Cir	Chan	Position	#	Type	Watt	Purpose	Color	Notes
1									
2	2	18	1 Electric	4	Alt 6 x 9	1kw	Cool Area 10	L161	
2	2	18	1 Electric	7	Alt 6 x 9	1kw	Cool Area 9	L161	
3	3	8	1 Electric	5	Source 4-36°	575w	Warm Area 10	R33	
3	3	8	1 Electric	8	Source 4-36°	575w	Warm Area 9	R33	
4	4	7	1 Electric	9	Source 4-36°	575w	Warm Area 8	R33	
5	5	55	1 Electric	10	Source 4-26°	575w	CC Front Special	NC	
6	6	17	1 Electric	11	Alt 6 x 9	1kw	Cool Area 8	L161	
7	7	6	1 Electric	12	Source 4-36°	575w	Warm Area 7	R33	
7	7	6	1 Electric	15	Source 4-36°	575w	Warm Area 6	R33	
8	8	16	1 Electric	13	Alt 6 x 9	1kw	Cool Area 7	L161	
8	8	16	1 Electric	16	Alt 6 x 9	1kw	Cool Area 6	L161	
9	9	51	1 Electric	3	Source 4-36°	750w	Temp DS Center	NC	T: R77733
9	9	51	1 Electric	17	Source 4-36°	750w	Temp DS Center	NC	T: R77733
10	10	21	1 Electric	18	Source 4-26°	575w	in 1 SL 1/4 Lav	R51	

Expression 3; 150 chan, 174 dimLighting design by Steve Shelley 917.xxx.xxxx   Page 1 of 14

Figure 7.14 • The First 10 Dimmers in the *Hokey* Dimmer Schedule

Color Cards and Floor Cards

One area of a light plot that often changes through the course of a performance is equipment that's accessible from the deck. This often translates into changes in the sidelight booms, rovers, the ground-row, or practicals specific to an act or a portion of a show. **Color cards** and **floor cards** are reference documents created to direct changes in color, focus, or circuitry that occur in one portion of a light plot during the course of a performance. When sidelight is concerned, this often results in two color cards—one for each side of the stage. The floor card provides focus information for instruments on both sides of the stage, and lists any other information specific to a particular act.

In addition to what may be indicated on the light plot, the color and floor cards clarify the amount of color and templates that the lighting designer intends to use in the sidelight booms. Before load-in, these documents give the production electrician a preliminary idea of the amount of electrical work that will take place on stage during breaks in the performance.

The truth be told, these documents could just as easily be included as part of the Cue Construction Packet, discussed in Chapter 6. They don't really become active until the lighting system is focused and the cues are being recorded for the show. Since their components were part of the shop order and the perishable bid, though, it was decided to include them in this portion of the text.

The Color Cards

Color cards are documents showing changes in the instruments of one portion of the light plot over the course of a multi-scene performance. In most cases involving sidelight, this means that the documents show the color and accessories that will be required for each of the boom sidelight instruments for each act of a show. Prior to each act, the deck electrician refers to a color card to complete three actions. First, change the colors in the sidelights. Second, preset the position, circuit, and color of any additional instruments on floor stands, or any other devices specific to that portion of the show. Finally, plug any special practicals, effects, or other sources into the circuitry on that side of the stage. When the changes are complete, the status of the physical color, circuitry, and instrumentation for that side of the stage should match the card.

Ideally, the color card shows all of the changes on one side of the stage for an entire performance, allowing the production electrician to see the total amount of color and accessories that will be required for that entire area in a single document. From a different perspective, it allows the lighting designer to trace the usage of a single instrument or an entire system through the course of an entire performance. Sometimes the number of changes between acts in any given location may be so extensive that a separate color card is required for each act. While this increases the number of documents, color cards quickly answer any questions about color media, templates, or special gear through the course of a show.

Enough copies of the color cards are distributed so that all electricians assigned to work on the stage (or **deck electricians**) can complete their tasks with a minimum of direction. One approach is to attach a card to each sidelight boom, highlighting only that position. A second approach is to supply one card showing all of the positions to each deck electrician. The method of distribution should be defined, since there's always the possibility that the cards will need to be updated. If the distribution method isn't clearly defined, deck electricians may unknowingly use outdated versions of the document to perform incorrect actions.

Figure 7.15 shows the Stage Left Color Card for *Hokey*. The card is divided into two main areas: the **footer** includes the title block information and the legend, while the **boom area** shows the channel and color for each instrument, for each act. The title block information in the footer includes the name of the show, the theatre, the version (the date), the lighting designer, and the side of the stage being presented. The legend under the title block explains how to read the symbols on the card.

The boom area of this color card is drawn from the perspective of an electrician standing on centerline and looking into the lenses and the colors inserted into the instruments on stage left. The numbered diamonds above each of the four booms on the card match the identity of the four booms on the stage. Boom 1 Left, for example, is drawn on the right-hand side of the card. When viewed from the proper perspective on centerline, Boom 1 Left is farthest downstage, the farthest boom "to the right." By arranging the card to match the actual configuration on stage, information can easily be compared between the graphic information on the card and the physical instruments.

The boom area is divided into three blocks. Each block represents the status of the same instruments during each act of the show. The name and length of the act are listed in the double squares, just downstage of the first boom in each block. Tall lines represent the vertical pipe supporting the booms, while squares represent each of the lighting instruments. The shaded lines represent the masking legs, to assist general orientation and rover placement. Each channel is

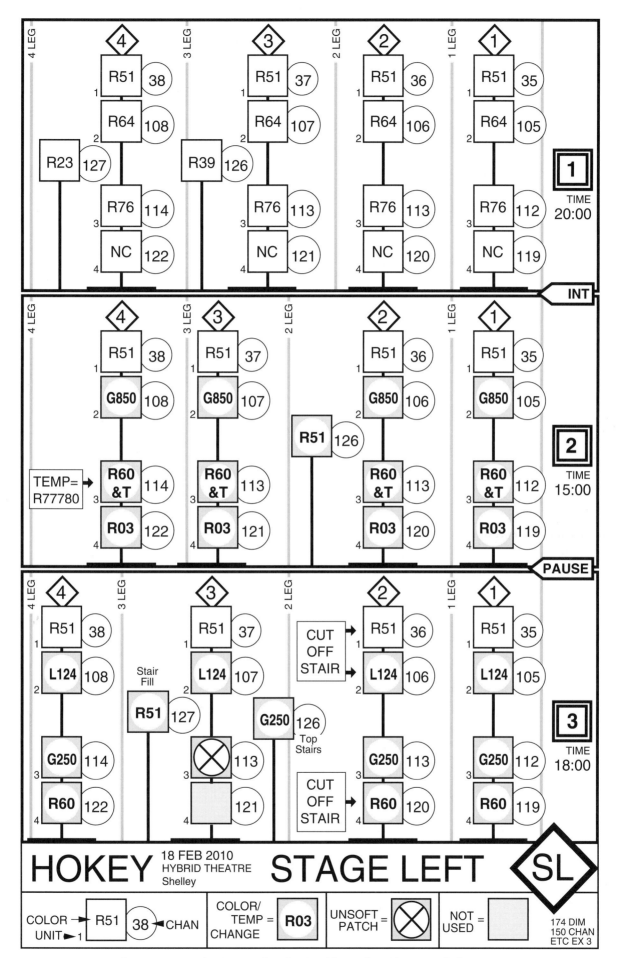

Figure 7.15 The Stage Left Color Card for *Hokey*, Showing All Three Acts

listed in a circle adjacent to each instrument, providing the channel hookup information for that side of the stage. Anyone looking at the card can call out for any channel and check its circuitry or color without the need to refer to an additional document.

The Floor Card

The companion to the color card is the **floor card**, which is a miniature groundplan of the stage. It graphically shows any special instrument focus and any preset checklists to be performed before each act. It's the document used for the second portion of presetting that portion of the plot, or that side of the stage. One technique involves inserting a color card and a floor card together into a plastic page protector, with the printed sides facing out. The combination of the two documents into a single package provides the deck electrician with all of the information required in order to preset that act.

Once the deck electrician has completed the color change prior to each act, he or she then refers to the floor card to complete four actions:

1. Alter any focus in the system sidelights.
2. Focus any additional floor stands or special units.
3. Check the focus and function of any crucial overhead specials required for that act of the show.
4. Perform any preset checklists prior to each act.

When the change is complete, the focus and function of the equipment on the stage should match the card. If there is room available on the document, it can be a repository for other information regarding the act, including memory numbers, the length of scenes or acts, or the timing of any deck cues.

Figure 7.16 shows the floor card for *Hokey*, Act 1. The document is divided into three components: the **footer** displays the title block and legend information, the **notes** are located above the footer, and the groundplan of the stage occupies the rest of the document. The title block information includes the name and act of the show, the length of time for the act, along with the version (the date) of the document. The legend in the middle of the footer shows how to read the symbols and the focus shorthand, while the right-hand side lists other archival information.

The notes area on the *Hokey* floor card indicates memory preset numbers, along with times for each act. The rest of the card is a groundplan showing the information about each additional unit, and indicating any special scenery involved in the act. The top of the page shows the channels and colors for the lights contained in the scenic stack. This information isn't necessary unless something about that area changes for that act. If the color in the instruments or the scenic backing changes, the channels should be checked for color consistency or to be certain that no light is bleeding under the bottom of the translucency. Overhead specials specific to the act are shown as dashed pools so that they can be included in the pre-act check as well. The rovers are shown on the sides of the color card in their relative position to the sidelight booms. The card reiterates any special circuitry that needs to be plugged, reducing the need to flip the plastic page protector and re-check information from the color card on the opposite side. The text in front of the instrument identifies the focus point and barrel focus of the instrument. The card is designed from this perspective based on the assumption that the electrician will stand behind the instrument or look away from the light while performing the focus. Based on that, the focus details are shown from the perspective of standing behind the beam of the instrument, rather than looking into it. The typical objective is for the system to be consistent, and work for the deck electricians who are performing the work.

Figure 7.17 shows a close-up of the focus diagram used to locate the focus point and indicate any shutter cuts. The circle indicates the beam pool. The text inside the circle indicates the location of the hot spot. Each line crossing through the circle indicates a shutter cut. The adjacent text gives a written description of the cut. This written focus format will be used throughout the rest of this text to indicate focus information for all remaining instruments.

In this example, then, the SR Rover, called up in channel 128 and colored in Roscolux 39, will be horizontally positioned to center-center. The hot spot will be locked off approximately 10 feet above the deck. The shutter cuts will be sharp. The upstage side cut will be off the #3 leg stage left, while the downstage cut will be into the smoke pocket. The top cut will be off the black borders, while the bottom cut will be to centerline—presumably following centerline.

The Combined Color and Floor Card

Depending on the complexity of the show or the preference of the production electrician, the color card and floor card may be combined into a single document. If all of the information can be included in this format, combining the two documents into one means one less piece of paper to update.

Figure 7.18 shows the same information as the previous floor and color card for *Hokey*, Act 1, produced in a different layout. The color

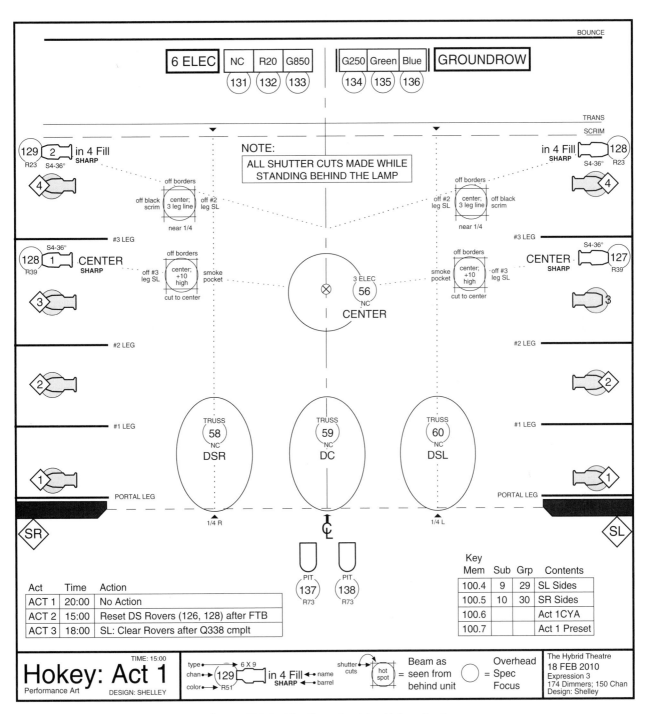

Figure 7.16 The Floor Card for *Hokey*, Act 1

and focus information is combined into a single document. In this layout, the rovers are located upstage of the booms, but each rover has its own

Figure 7.17 A Close-Up of a Focus Diagram

groundplan showing the placement and focus of the unit. A rectangle above each rover identifies its name. The groundplan under the rectangle shows the placement and groundplan focus for the instrument. The front view underneath shows the height placement of the instrument and the focus point, along with the top and bottom shutter cuts. Although this version is more compact, it doesn't include any additional channels or preset checklist information.

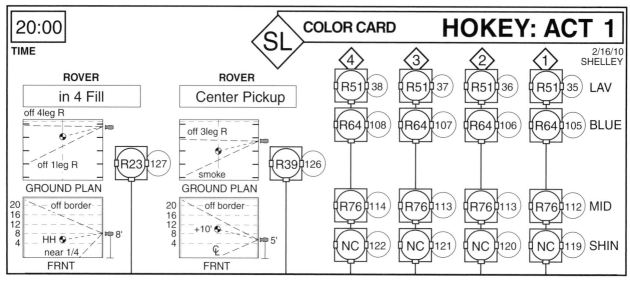

Figure 7.18 A Combined Color and Floor Card for *Hokey*, Act 1

Cut Color Spreadsheet

The task of cutting sheets of color into the proper sized pieces, placed into color frames, and then sorted into bundles matching the instrument schedule ("boxing the color") is one job that always seems to take longer than expected. For large shows, the typical tactic is to box the color before it leaves the rental shop. On smaller shows, the color may have to be cut while the show is being loaded-in and hung. And on the humbling shows, the lighting designer is cutting the color on the drafting table in his or her office the night before the load-in.

Regardless of the show's size, having the color properly prepared is important. Typically it needs to be done before the load-in, and just as important, it has to be right the first time. For all of these reasons, any paperwork that allows the color to be properly ordered and quickly boxed up can be a great time-saver. While the instrument schedule lists the color assigned to each instrument, and frame size can often be determined by familiarity with the instrument type, some amount of sub-sorting is required to create a list showing the total number of cuts for each size, in each color, for each position. Lightwright provides worksheet summaries that do just this; they list the colors and sizes needed for each position. The program also produces a worksheet that totals the complete color order if so desired.

Some lighting designers and production electricians want additional paperwork that tells them how many cuts of each color are needed for the entire show, rather than just one position. Structuring the color cut list by size in a spreadsheet format is another way of looking at the information, and for some it speeds

the color cutting process. It's then possible to see the total number of color cuts needed for each size, for each color, for the entire light plot.

Figure 7.19 shows a partial **cut color spreadsheet** for the *Hokey* light plot, focusing on two instrument sizes seen horizontally in the left-hand column: the Source Four-sized cuts (6.25″ × 6.25″) and the Altman cuts (7.5″ × 7.5″). Each row then lists each hanging position, matching the same sort order as the instrument schedule, while each column is assigned to a separate color. At the bottom of each instrument block, a row labeled "Subtotal" lists the total number of cuts, in that color, in that size. At the bottom of the document, a row titled "Sheets" lists the total number of sheets required to provide the proper number of cuts, while the "Spare" row indicates the number of projected spare sheets that will be needed in order to provide a safety net. The "Total" row provides the sum, and the total number of sheets that will be listed on the perishable order.

When the color is actually cut, each size can be cut for the entire lighting plot. Once all the colors for an entire size have been cut and boxed, they can then be combined in the right-hand "Cuts" column, or assembled in order using the instrument schedule. This cut color sheet's incomplete, since it doesn't include the cuts for the MR-16 striplights, the PARs, or the R-40 groundrow. Those are different sizes, so they'd be listed on another page of the document. It does, however, include back-up cuts of diffusion (Rosco 119 and Rosco 132, in this example) cut in both size formats.

Regardless of the show's size, standard operating procedure is to cut any partial sheets of left-over color into the most predictable size, storing it as pre-cut

Hybrid Theatre 2010   **HOKEY COLOR CUT LIST**   Date: 2/17/10

SOURCE 4 (6.25" x 6.25") 9 CUTS A SHT

	R03	R20	R23	R33	R39	R44	R51	R60	R64	R76	R119	R132	G250	G850	G945	L116	L124	L161	L201	CUTS	
Truss				5			3													8	Truss
SL Box Boom						1										1	1			3	SL Box Boom
SR Box Boom						1										1	1			3	SR Box Boom
Spots																					Spots
Pit																				0	Pit
1 Electric				5			2		2										2	11	1 Electric
2 Electric		5		5			2		2									5	2	21	2 Electric
3 Electric														5						5	3 Electric
4 Electric		5					2		2									5	2	16	4 Electric
5 Electric							2		2					5					2	11	5 Electric
6 Electric																					6 Electric
1 Boom L	1						1	1	1	1		1					1			6	1 Boom L
2 Boom L	1						1	1	1	1		1					1			6	2 Boom L
3 Boom L	1						1		1	1		1					1			5	3 Boom L
4 Boom L	1						1	1	1	1		1					1			6	4 Boom L
Rovers L			1		1		1													3	Rovers L
1 Boom R	1						1	1	1	1		1					1			6	1 Boom R
2 Boom R	1						1	1	1	1		1					1			6	2 Boom R
3 Boom R	1						1	1	1	1		1					1			6	3 Boom R
4 Boom R	1						1	1	1	1		1					1			6	4 Boom R
Rovers R			1		1		1													3	Rovers R
SUBTOTAL	8	10	2	15	2	2	21	7	16	8	20	20	0	18	2	2	18	0	8		**SUBTOTAL**

ALTMAN (7.5" x 7.5") 6 CUTS A SHEET

	R03	R20	R23	R33	R39	R44	R51	R60	R64	R76	R119	R132	G250	G850	G945	L116	L124	L161	L201	CUTS	
Truss																		5		5	Truss
SL Box Boom						1										1	1			3	SL Box Boom
SR Box Boom						1										1	1			3	SR Box Boom
Pit																				0	Pit
1 Electric																		5		5	1 Electric
2 Electric																		5		5	2 Electric
1 Boom L								1				1								2	1 Boom L
2 Boom L								1				1								2	2 Boom L
3 Boom L								1												1	3 Boom L
4 Boom L								1				1								2	4 Boom L
Rovers L												1								1	Rovers L
1 Boom R								1				1								2	1 Boom R
2 Boom R								1				1								2	2 Boom R
3 Boom R								1				1								2	3 Boom R
4 Boom R								1				1								2	4 Boom R
Rovers R												1								1	Rovers R
Groundrow																				0	Groundrow
SUBTOTAL	0	0	0	0	0	2	0	8	0	0	10	10	9	0	2	2	0	15	0		**SUBTOTAL**

	R03	R20	R23	R33	R39	R44	R51	R60	R64	R76	R119	R132	G250	G850	G945	L116	L124	L161	L201
SHEETS	1	2	1	2	1	1	3	3	2	1	5	5	2	2	1	1	2	3	1
SPARE	1	1	0	1	0	0	1	1	2	1	2	2	1	2	1	0	2	1	1
TOTAL	2	3	1	3	1	1	4	4	4	2	7	7	3	4	2	1	4	4	2

Expression 3; 150 chan, 174 dim Lighting design by Steve Shelley 917.xxx.xxxx   Page 1 of 3

Figure 7.19   A Partial Color Cut Spreadsheet for the *Hokey* Light Plot

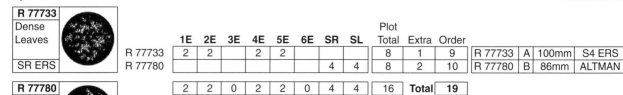

Expression 3; 150 chan, 174 dim · Lighting design by Steve Shelley 917.xxx.xxxx · Page 1 of 1

Figure 7.20 A Template Spreadsheet for the *Hokey* Light Plot

spare color in an expandable file. Certainly, much of the diffusion will also be pre-cut, labeled, and stored in the file, ready for the focus session.

Template Sheets

Another set of perishables that require advance preparation are templates. Depending on the manufacturer, the template holder size, and the number of templates called for in the plot, ordering templates can be a time-consuming process. As this book is being written, an extensive array of different sizes and formats are available, and that only includes the steel-cut types of templates. The number of designs, formats, and kinds of templates seems to increase on a yearly basis, and constant attention needs to be paid to the latest developments. Because of the diversity, however, ordering templates requires three notes of caution. First, just because it's seen in a catalog, doesn't mean that it will be at every local dealer. Some templates require no small amount of time to get shipped, and may not be immediately available without overnight shipping charges. Second, just because it's seen in a catalog, doesn't always mean that it's available in the size that's desired. These two notes of caution basically boil down to thinking ahead and checking before ordering. The third note? Take extra care to order the templates with knowledge, a catalog, and time available so that the order is clear, concise, and properly made. It's very common for last-minute, rush-order templates to arrive on-site as the wrong template, or in the wrong size, or in the wrong format. It can't be repeated often enough that extra care should be taken the original template order is made.

Once the templates are in hand, time should be set aside to prep them. For steel templates, that means trimming the extra bits of steel on the edges of the template so that they fit into the template holder and into the ellipsoidal of choice. While many folks just trim and prep the

templates into holders at the shop, superstitious lighting designers and production electricians take the templates and holders home with them and trim the accessories themselves. When they trim them at home, they then have the security knowing the templates will absolutely fit into the ellipsoidals of choice during the load-in.

Figure 7.20 is the template spreadsheet for the *Hokey* light plot. On the left-hand side, labeled images have been downloaded and pasted into the Excel document to provide a snapshot in case the identification numbers on the steel gobos accidentally get cut off while the templates are being prepped. The name of the template is included as well. On the right side, the format size, and the millimeter size and the ellipsoidal planned to receive the accessory are listed as well. In between, the spreadsheet shows, by column, which lighting position will receive the templates. Each row indicates one of the templates. The bottom row of the spreadsheet shows the totals for each position, and the right-hand columns indicate the plot total, any spares, and the amount to be included in the perishable order. The R77780 template is assigned for use in the sidelight; the color cards show that it will be inserted and removed in the mid instrument for Act 2 as part of the sidelight color change. As such, an extra spare is being ordered, since it's presumed that the repeated "in-out" during the color change will cause that template to fail more quickly than the templates permanently inserted in the overhead template pipe end system.

Manuals and Cut Sheets

The possibility always exists that equipment used in a light plot won't perform properly. Following Murphy's law, if there is any chance that equipment will fail, it will, and if unknown or untested equipment can exhibit unexpected behavior, it will. With that in mind, the amount of information needed for any piece of equipment is determined on a case-by-case basis. The newer or less familiar the equipment, the farther from a point of service, or the less troubleshooting time allowed in the schedule, then the greater the need to acquire as much contact, assembly, and troubleshooting information as possible. Any equipment provided to the lighting designer that includes the phrase "beta-test" should set off alarm bells, signaling the amount of caution with which it should be approached. The old adage "if you want to be on the cutting edge, you'd best be prepared to bleed a little" comes to mind.

For these reasons, it's wise to have manufacturers' cut sheets and a manual for every device whose complexity or failure might become a time-consuming problem. Instrument cut sheets were used when the systems were constructed for the preliminary light plot, but **cut sheets** for almost any device in a lighting package is rarely a bad idea. Usually the sheet consists of a single page of paper providing basic information about a piece of equipment. While the page may not provide complete details about the product, it often includes contact names and numbers of people who represent the equipment. While the sheets may not be able to answer every question, they're often miniature contact sheets, providing the names and numbers of people who can.

Sometimes folks go a little overboard with cut sheets; it's rare that a cut sheet for a c-clamp is going to be required. Collecting a **manual** for any devices used in the lighting package, on the other hand, is a very smart idea. While they may never be used as a reference, having the documents on hand allows new gear to be more fully understood before high-pressure situations have a chance to develop. With any luck neither of these documents will be needed, but they may provide the keys to finding a solution in urgent moments.

If a manual exists for an unfamiliar electrical device, many designers and production electricians agree a copy of that manual should be on site wherever the electrical device is going to be used. When the console operator isn't intimately familiar with the console, for example, a manual should be acquired with the light board. Discovering that no one knows how to program the suddenly needed software function at 2 A.M. can be the true test of friendship, since the situation may ultimately require waking up a colleague to determine the programming sequence. If the shop

is kind enough to supply a console manual, the document is returned as part of the rental. Keeping a stock of manuals on hand can quickly become an expensive and time-consuming proposition. When the console manual doesn't get returned with the rental order, it's becoming common to see its cost added to the final invoice.

If it's a new lighting console, gather whatever preliminary manuals, notes, or information you can. Ask for phone, text, Skype, email, or any other contact numbers of anyone representing the new console, and anyone who will admit to having used the console. If the production is utilizing a new kind of atmospheric generator, make sure that copies of the Material Safety Data Sheet are on hand. They may be requested at any time by the theatre's management, the performer's representative, or the fire marshal.

The case can be made that gathering this information is the domain and responsibility of the production electrician or the house electrician. That's all very well and good, but if the production electrician's time is being consumed getting the light package out of the rental shop, someone else had best get the information. The lighting department must be a team, and if time and personnel are short, the lighting designer and production electrician need to check to make sure that someone takes care of these innocent chores. Otherwise problems can suddenly erupt at the worst possible times, and if information is not close at hand, lack of knowledge about the gear can quickly become a parameter. Blamestorming at 11 P.M. on a Friday night in front of the newly dead dimmer rack does no one any good, and the lack of foresight and documentation may delay, and ultimately jeopardize, the lighting for the production.

Knowledge is the key that will ultimately allow the best decisions to be made for the production in times of human or equipment failure.

SUMMARY

Once the light plot, section, and support paperwork packet is created, attention can turn to the packet of paperwork that will provide additional information during the load-in.

Chapter 8

The Load-In and Focus Packet

INTRODUCTION

The load-in and focus packet includes documents used to install, program, and focus a light plot. Their design and intent is to help accomplish these steps in the process in the quickest possible time. A **hang plot** lists the placement of the masking and the scenery, and shows how they fit in with the overhead electrics. A **headset layout diagram** graphically defines the communication channels that will be used. **Focus cues, infrastructure cues, submasters,** and **groups** are designed to be programmed into the lighting console and speed up activities using that computer. **Spike groundplans** and **focus documents** can be used to facilitate the focus session, while a variety of **focus charts** can be used to quickly record the focus.

THE HANG PLOT

The **hang plot** is a more expanded view of the lineset schedule seen in both the light plot and the lighting section. But while the lineset schedule on those documents identifies and locates the goods on each batten, the hang plot provides a more comprehensive and detailed picture of the entire fly system for the show. Ideally, it's the product of a coordinated effort between the scenic and lighting departments, and may also include elements from the sound and other departments as well. If nothing else, the hang plot specifies the placement and trim for the overhead hanging positions that will be used for the lighting package.

Figure 8.1 shows the *Hokey* hang plot, which is separated into two series of columns, the lineset schedule and the spot line schedule. The **lineset schedule** details the relevant information about each batten: label number, distance from plaster line, and the name and trim height of the goods or electrics. The "Apx Weight" column provides an approximate weight, while the "Dist. CL" indicates distances from centerline where the legs or scenic pieces will be hung. The notes column lists other notes regarding pipe extensions or added cable runs. The **spot line schedule** refers to any hanging points or additions in the air other than the counterweight system. This may range from rope running through single sheaves "spotted" at specific points in the grid, to chain motors, to aircraft cable directly attached to the grid.

The hang plot is a communal reference document for many departments, and is often one of the first documents used during the load-in. The production electrician may use the information supplied on the hang plot to calculate lengths of suspended cable, while the props department might refer to it to determine the sidelight boom's location in relation to the performance surface. The carpentry staff uses the hang plot, along with other scenic drawings, to install the scenery.

THE HEADSET LAYOUT GROUNDPLAN

The production table (or "tech table") is usually placed on centerline somewhere in the house during load-in. The table's optimal placement is the most centralized viewing perspective in the house, the

		LINESET SCHEDULE						SPOT LINE SCHEDULE		
LINE	DIST.	GOODS	TRIM	APX WEIGHT	DIST. CL	NOTES Battens 42'-0" Long	LINE	DIST.	DIST. CL	SPOT LINES
	0'-0"	Plaster line								Plaster line
	0'-6"									
1	1'-0"	Main Curtain		250 lbs.			1			
2	1'-6"	Portal Border	20'-0"	150 lbs.		3'-0" extensions each end (10'H X 50'W)	2			
3	2'-0"	Portal Legs	30'-0"	100 lbs.	20'-0"	3'-0" extensions each end (30'H X 8'W)	3		26'-0"	
4	2'-6"	1 Electric	25'-0"			19-S 4's, house circ: trim to pipe	4			
	2'-9"							2'-9"	26'-9"	#1 Boom L & R
5	3'-0"						5			
6	3'-6"						6			
7	4'-0"						7			
8	4'-6"						8			
9	5'-0"						9			
10	5'-6"						10			
11	6'-0"						11			
12	6'-6"						12			
13	7'-0"						13			
14	7'-6"	#1 Black Border	21'-0"	150 lbs.		3'-0" extensions each end (10'H X 50'W)	14			
15	8'-0"	#1 Black Legs	30'-0"	100 lbs.	18'-0"	2'-0" extensions each end (30'H X 8'W)	15		26'-0"	
16	8'-6"						16			
17	9'-0"						17			
18	9'-6"	2 Electric	26'-6"			26-S 4's, bundles to SL side; trim to pipe	18			
19	10'-0"						19			
20	10'-6"						20			
21	11'-0"	Cable Xover	28'-6"			5 circuit bundle; 2 Boom R to SL dim	21	11'-0"	27'-9"	#2 Boom L & R
22	11'-6"						22			
23	12'-0"						23			
24	12'-6"	3 Electric	29'-6"			11-S 4's, bundles to SL floor; trim to lens	24			
25	13'-0"						25			
26	13'-6"	#2 Black Border	21'-0"	150 lbs.		3'-0" extensions each end (10'H X 50'W)	26			
27	14'-0"	#2 Black Legs	30'-0"	100 lbs.	18'-0"	2'-0" extensions each end (30'H X 8'W)	27		26'-0"	
28	14'-6"						28			
29	15'-0"						29			
30	15'-6"						30			
31	16'-0"	4 Electric	26'-6"			18-S 4's, bundles to SL; trim to pipe	31			
32	16'-6"						32			
33	17'-0"	Cable Xover	28'-6"			5 circuit bundle; 3 Boom R to SL dim	33	17'-0"	27'-9"	#3 Boom L & R
34	17'-6"						34			
35	18'-0"						35			
36	18'-6"						36			
37	19'-0"						37			
38	19'-6"	#3 Black Border	21'-0"	150 lbs.		3'-0" extensions each end (10'H X 50'W)	38			
39	20'-0"	#3 Black Legs	30'-0"	100 lbs.	18'-0"	2'-0" extensions each end (30'H X 8'W)	39		26'-0"	
40	20'-6"						40			
41	21'-0"						41			
42	21'-6"						42			
43	22'-0"						43			
44	22'-6"						44			
45	23'-0"						45			
46	23'-6"						46			
47	24'-0"						47			
48	24'-6"	5 Electric	29'-6"			17-Source 4's, bundles to SL; trim to lens	48			
49	25'-0"						49			
	25'-3"							25'-3"	26'-9"	#4 Boom L & R
50	25'-6"	#4 Black Border	23'-3"	150 lbs.		3'-0" extensions each end (10'H X 50'W)	50			
51	26'-0"	#4 Black Legs	30'-0"	100 lbs.	18'-0"	2'-0" extensions each end (30'H X 8'W)	51		26'-0"	
52	26'-6"	Black Scrim	28'-0"			28'-0" tall X 48'-0" wide	52			
53	27'-0"	Translucency	30'-0"	200 lbs.		30'-0" tall X 48'-0" wide	53			
54	27'-6"						54			
55	28'-0"						55			
56	28'-6"						56			Groundrow
57	29'-0"	6 Electric	29'-6"			6-MR-16 strips, bundles to SL; trim to pipe	57			Groundrow
58	29'-6"						58			
59	30'-0"						59			
60	30'-6"						60			
61	31'-0"	Bounce Drop	28'-0"			28'-0" tall X 48'-0" wide	61			
62	31'-6"						62			
	32'-0"	Back Wall								

Grid: 62'-0"; Pipe travel: 59'-6"   Lighting design by Steve Shelley 917.xxx.xxxx   Page 1 of 1

Figure 8.1 The *Hokey* Hang Plot

most "typical" audience view. From that location, almost all directorial and design choices are made. During the cue level setting sessions and the technical rehearsals, the tech table is usually considered the domain of anyone who has a seat there. Usually that includes the lighting designer, the stage manager, the director, and other members of the production staff. In thrust or arena theatres, it's not uncommon for the production table to be moved to different locations during the tech period, allowing the design elements of the show to be created and viewed from several visual perspectives.

For the lighting designer, the production table often becomes his or her office from the beginning of the cue level setting session through the end of the final rehearsal. Trying to simultaneously see the stage, the monitors, and the paperwork while communicating on headset during rehearsals often means that the lighting designer is essentially "tied" to the production table. If the stage manager and light board operator aren't present at the production table throughout the entire rehearsal process, the most essential item that must be present at the table is a headset. If followspots are involved, that need is even greater.

Being able to communicate to the correct personnel, while not having to listen to other departments, is one reason to construct a **headset layout diagram**. Headset systems are often equipped with more than one channel or line of communication. The headset layout diagram attempts to provide the sound department with the lighting designer's desires and his or her preferences as to who should be on which channel. Typically, the lighting designer needs to communicate with the stage manager (to listen and discuss cue placement and timings), the board operator (to make cue adjustments), and any assistants (giving direction and listening for information). The followspots are often assigned to a different channel when they're coordinated either by an assistant or a stage manager. When the number of headset channels is limited, everyone usually works together and shares a channel. But if there are at least two channels, electrics is often assigned to one of them. Why? In most situations, other departments don't want to listen to the numerous instructions made by the lighting designer to the console operator on headset. At the same time, in the midst of a complex tech rehearsal, the lighting designer doesn't want to hear about anything other than lighting over headset.

Figure 8.2 shows the preliminary headset and cue light layout diagram for *Hokey*, assigned to a much more comfortable 4-channel system. This non-scaled ground-plan sketch details the location and channel assignments for the different headset positions, along with the cue light locations. It's laid out much like the light plot with the production table in the house at the bottom of the

document, and the stage locations are at the top of the page. Channel A is usually designated as the general communication stage manager's channel; other channels are usually assigned by the general amount of predicted chatter. In this layout, electrics is assigned to channel B, the followspots are assigned to channel C, and sound is assigned to channel D. In more complex productions, carpentry, automation, projection, and any number of other departments may need their own exclusive channel. If there's a shortage, multiple departments may have to share a channel, or walkie-talkies may be included as well. This diagram also shows the cue light locations, providing the production electrician with a general idea about the circuitry that will be required for that system.

COMPUTER LIGHT BOARD INFORMATION

It is often heard that there's no reason to program anything into the light board until the focus is complete. That statement may very well be accurate if the light board in question is a manual light board. If the light board for the show is a computer lighting console, however, prefocus programming can make the console a much more efficient timesaving tool.

Every computer lighting console has memory components, including the memories that are used to play back light cues. A system that assigns memory block partitions for specific tasks can be mapped out using a **disk master chart**. Many current lighting consoles use alphanumeric keyboards to label memories, but if the keyboards are absent or broken, the memory's number may be the only means of providing identification. **Cue information and identification** systems can be used to identify memory chunks and entire disks filled with cues. **Infrastructure cues** are memories programmed to do much more than just play back cues for a show. Programming memories onto physical and electronic handles makes them simpler and faster to use. Programming **submasters** on a lighting console gives the operator physical handles to grasp, while **groups** give the operator and the lighting designer a more diverse selection of "electronic handles."

The nature and design of today's computer lighting consoles allow them to be much more than just "channel activators." Prior thought about the light board contents can help expedite the entire technical process by speeding the load-in, facilitating the focus, expediting cue construction, and rapidly performing preshow checks. Pre-programming can also provide an additional element of safety. In order to take advantage and provide all of these features, however, the lighting designer must first understand how computer light board memory works.

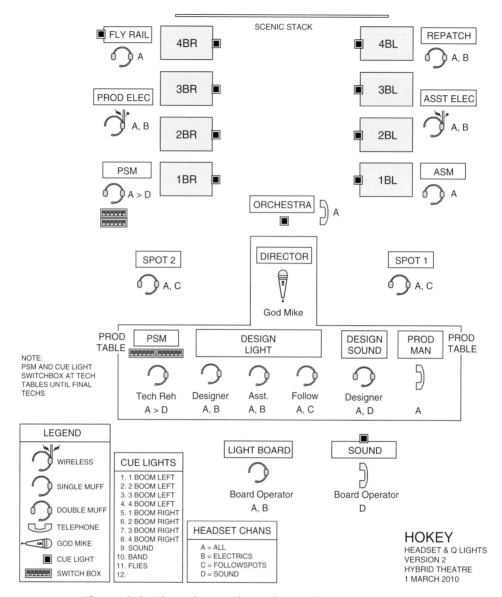

Figure 8.2 The *Hokey* Headset and Cue Light Layout Diagram

Memory Review

The main purpose of most computer lighting consoles is to record memories that will be played back during the show. Since almost all computer consoles automatically play back memories in numerical succession, cues are usually recorded in sequence. "Running the show" is then reduced to pressing the GO button every time the stage manager gives the command to do so. Since any "look" can be recorded in any memory, memories could be randomly recorded with no attention paid to their purpose or identity. Obviously, if those memories needed to occur quickly one after the other, out-of-sequence memory numbers could easily spell disaster. Consider this scenario: if a production's first act takes place in "moonlight," while the second act takes place during a "sunrise," for example, what would be the simplest way to record those memories in such a way to make it simple to identify each cue? A quick light board memory review will help provide solution ideas to this situation.

Most current computer lighting consoles are built with the capability to record memories labeled with whole numbers (1, 2, 3, and so on) numbered up to 999, along with nine "point" memories in between each whole number (1.1, 1.2, and so on). In these consoles, therefore, the highest possible memory number is 999.9. Since any lighting "look" can be recorded to any memory, establishing a structure to identify sections of cues can be helpful. On more complex shows, it can become a necessity.

If point cues are temporarily set aside, a total of 999 whole numbers remain that can be assigned to different memories. To reduce that sea of numbers into something manageable, visualize a large roll of film that's been removed from a camera. Instead of 24 exposures, this roll of film has 999 pictures. After the film is developed, the frame numbers start with 1 and end with 999. Imagine cutting the film into 10 lengths. Each of the 10 filmstrips now consists of 100 pictures (except the last strip, which only has 99). Set nine of the strips aside, and consider only the first strip.

In Figure 8.3, the first strip of 100 pictures includes pictures taken at night. The left-hand picture in Figure 8.3 is an obscured view of the moon at night; the moon's outline can barely be seen because of the cloud. Label that picture number 101, since it's the first picture on the first strip of film. The center picture, taken with the moon clearly in view, is labeled number 102. The right-hand picture has been taken after a bank of clouds has obscured the moon, and is labeled number 103. The rest of the pictures on the strip of film weren't used, so they're black. Set the first strip aside, and examine the second strip of film.

The second strip of 100 pictures was taken at dawn. The left-hand picture in this strip of film, shown in Figure 8.4, is on a beach, just before sunrise. Label that picture as number 201. The center picture shows the sunrise, and is labeled number 202. The right-hand picture shows the sunrise after a bank of clouds has obscured the sun. That picture is labeled number 203. The remaining 97 pictures on the second strip are also black. The two strips of film will now be

edited and combined. After cutting away the unused excess, the exposed pictures are taped together. Their numerical sequence is now 101, 102, 103, 201, 202, and 203.

Each of those strips of film is the same as 100 whole-numbered memories. Each picture is the equivalent of a recorded memory. The first picture (101) is the equivalent of the preset for the first act; it was obscured, as if the curtain was closed and the full image couldn't be seen. The second picture of the moon (102) is the equivalent of the curtain opening to be viewed by the audience. The third picture was again obscured (103) like the image left on stage after the curtain has been closed. Although the remaining 97 pictures or memories could be created, they were black (or unused). In computer light board memory, if the memories aren't created, then no label numbers for the individual memories exist. Those nonexistent numbers are "skipped over" to the next recorded memory. The next sequential number after memory 103 is memory 201, the first picture (or memory) for the second act. The sun has not yet appeared; it's like the preset for the act. The sun appears in the second picture (202) as the scene begins, and the clouds obscure the scene in the third and final picture (203), like the curtain closing for a second time.

The left-hand side of Figure 8.5 shows the list of all of those pictures together with a label as they would appear on a lighting computer monitor display. Each memory or cue number now has a time unit assigned to it. When the GO button is initially pressed on the computer, it will take 3 seconds for the 101 "picture"

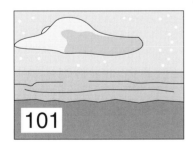 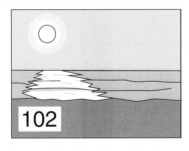 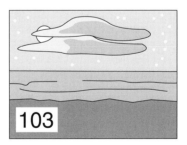

Figure 8.3 The Moonlight Pictures

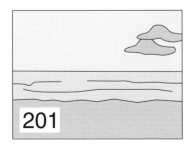 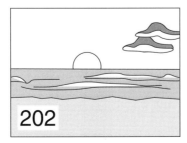 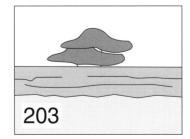

Figure 8.4 The Dawn Pictures

Q	Cnt	Label
101	3	Night
102	10	Moon Appear
103	5	Cloud Cover
201	3	Pre-dawn
202	10	Sun
203	5	Clouds

Q	Cnt	Label
101	3	Night
102	10	Moon Appear
102.5	2	Torch
103	5	Cloud Cover
201	3	Pre-dawn
202	10	Sun
203	5	Clouds

Figure 8.5 The Monitor Display Before and After the Torch Cue is Added

or *memory* to be "developed" or *loaded* into an active fader, allowing it to be seen on stage. When the same button is pressed again, 10 seconds will elapse while memory 102 is loaded into an active fader. In that same 10 seconds, all of the elements that make memory 101 will disappear. Time of almost any length can be assigned to most memories, including tenths of a second.

In the first strip of film, picture 102 showed the moon without clouds, while picture 103 was the analogy used "when the curtain closed." In the course of rehearsal, however, a stage action is added. Someone lights a torch. A new "picture" needs to be added and inserted between two existing pictures. One way to create this would be to relabel (or re-record) memory 103 to become memory 104. Then the torch cue could be created, and labeled (recorded) with the old label, memory 103. The memories would then remain in sequence. Instead of reprogramming, however, most computer lighting consoles allow any of those nine **point cues** (.1, .2, .3, and so on) to be created (or **inserted**) between each whole-numbered memory. The torch cue could be recorded anywhere from cue 102.1 to 102.9 and, when recorded, still be in sequence between memories 102 and 103. The right-hand side of Figure 8.5 shows that the torch cue has been inserted as memory 102.5, with a time of 2 seconds. Memory 103 has remained untouched.

Understanding memory numbers is like imagining a long roll of pictures. "Developed" pictures have a recorded memory number. Black portions (or unrecorded numbers) are skipped over to the next sequential memory number. Memories can be inserted in sequence between other memories. (Most consoles provide nine single-digit point cues between each whole-numbered cue, but newer consoles have now expanded to 100 double-digit point cues.)

Numerical Mnemonics

In the picture analogy, the pictures for Act 1 were numbered in the 100's, while Act 2's pictures were numbered in the 200's. When recording memories into computer lighting consoles, many lighting designers use this same numbering scheme. Knowing the memory number allows the lighting designer, the board operator, and the stage manager to be aware of their current location within the context of the show. This is an example of **numerical mnemonics**. The phrase means that the numerical digit assigned to the memory is assisting the brain to remember something else. In this case, if the memory number is a 100, then it's a cue for Act 1. If a memory is a 200, it's a cue for Act 2.

The concept of numerical mnemonics can be used to structure the memory blocks (or RAM) of the lighting console. Specific numbers can be assigned to cues and other board functions, which then informs the lighting designer of the memory unit's identity, location, or function. Since there are typically 999 whole memory numbers contained in the RAM of a computer light board, partitioning the acts into 100's means that any other memories not associated with cues for the show can be recorded using numbers other than 100 or 200. This means that memories 1 > 99 and memories 300 > 999 are available for other tasks. Partitioning the cues into acts is the first step towards designing a disk master chart.

Disk Master Chart

Blocks of memories not used as light cues can be partitioned as locations to expedite a focus, store other "looks," or speed pre-show checks. Assigning these functions to memory blocks can be illustrated with **a disk master chart**, which can be constructed once the identity and parameters of the console are determined. That information includes the following:

- The name of the manufacturer, the lighting console, and the software version number.
- The storage medium of the console: floppy disk, hard drive, server, flash drive, etc.
- The total number of memories that can be stored at any one time in the computer's RAM.
- The highest memory number allowed on that console.
- Confirmation that the console can record point cues. Single digit? Double digit?

Once these parameters of the lighting console are known, a disk master can be constructed.

Figure 8.6 shows the disk master for *Hokey*, which partitions the memory into blocks of 100's and 50's. The "Function" column identifies the assignment for each "Block" of memory. The first memory of each block is a "blocker" cue, stopping all tracking information from previous memories. The "Pre" or Preset column shows what memory number will contain the preset or the first memory for each act or block.

Hybrid Theatre 2010   **HOKEY DISK MASTER CHART**   Date: 2/13/10

MEM	FUNCTION	BLOCK	PRE	TIME	DELAY	NOTES	MEM
0	Focus Cues		0.7			Can be deleted after focus	0
100	Hokey Act 1	100	100.7				100
200	Hokey Act 2	200	200.7				200
300	Hokey Act 2 continued					No blocker; cues track from 200's	300
400	Hokey Act 3	400	400.7				400
500	Library Act 1	500	500.7				500
600	Library Act 2	600	600.7				600
700	Library Act 2 continued					No blocker; cues track from 600's	700
800	Library Act 3	800	800				800
900	Light Check; Position	900	900.7	5	20	Filament warmer	900
950	Light Checks; System	950	950.7	5	20	Filament warmer	950

Expression 3; 150 chan, 174 dim   Lighting design by Steve Shelley 917.xxx.xxxx   Page 1 of 1

Figure 8.6 The *Hokey* Disk Master Chart

Focus Cue Block

The first 100 cues in the *Hokey* disk will contain channel information that may be used during the focus session. As we now know, most light plots (and certainly *Hokey's*) are comprised of several systems. In some cases, while the instruments comprising those systems are located in different hanging positions, the focus points or beam edges are often focused in relationship to one another. Some systems focus so that their beams all land the same distance from centerline (sidelight), while other systems focus so that their beams are matching distances from plaster line (frontlight). After the first channel in a system is focused, it may be turned back on with the next channel in the same system, so that an aspect of the focus from the first instrument can be matched while focusing the next one. The first focused light beam becomes a reference point while focusing the second instrument.

Focus cues can be preprogrammed to achieve much the same effect. Instead of constantly activating two channels, the only button that's used is the GO button. Programming these cues also defines the choreography of the focus, since the cues activate channels in a specific sequence "across" a hanging position. In this case, the disk master shows that the focus cues will be allocated to the zero block, so the focus cues begin with cue 1.

Figure 8.7 shows a partial focus cue list for the *Hokey* plot. To keep the focus in sequence with the cues, unit 1 on the first electric will be the first instrument activated. The focus would proceed toward stage right. Each memory brings up the next instrument to be focused.

When 1 electric #9 is focused, cue 8 activates both channels 7 and 8. Channel 8 has already been focused in cue 5, so unit #9 can be matched to the

HOKEY FOCUS CUES

Q	Position & Unit	CHAN		Q	Position & Unit	CHAN	
1	1P1	45		21	2P23	16	20
2	1P2	25		22	2P22	6	10
3	1P3	51		23	2P21	71	
4	1P4	18		24	2P20	61	
5	1P5	8		25	2P19	20	
6	1P7	18		26	2P18	10	
7	1P8	8		27	2P17	71	72
8	1P9	7	8	28	2P16	61	62
9	1P10	55		29	2P15	19	20
10	1P11	17	18	30	2P14	72	73
11	1P12	6	7	31	2P13	62	63
12	1P13	16	17	32	2P12	9	10
13	1P15	6		33	2P11	63	64
14	1P16	16		34	2P10	73	74
15	1P17	51		35	2P9	9	10
16	1P18	21	25	36	2P8	19	20
17	1P19	41	45	37	2P7	64	65
18	2P26	41	42	38	2P6	74	75
19	2P25	21	22	39	2P5	10	
20	2P24	51	52	40	2P4	20	

Figure 8.7 The Partial Focus Cue List for *Hokey*

beam edge of unit #8. When 2 electric unit #26 is focused (channel 42), cue 18 will activate it and 1 electric #19 (channel 41). Since channel 41 has been focused, the beam edge of 2 electric #26 can be matched to channel 41.

Focus cues can minimize time spent waiting for matching pairs of channels to be determined or activated. Only the GO button is required to progress through the focus. Many productions traveling with their own lighting console create a focus disk that contains more sophisticated focus cues. Additional memories can be programmed that activate entire color systems, rather than just pairs of instruments.

While focus cues can shorten the time between instruments being activated, they are often created in a specific choreographic order. Unless the focus cue stack is carefully programmed, focusing out of order, for example, can quickly bring a focus session using this style of light cues to a halt. Depending on the complexity of the focus, and the number of channels activated in each focus cue, going out of order may create chaos, rather than eliminate it. Likewise, attempting to focus from the reverse end of the electric (starting the focus with cue 17 and 1 Electric #19, for example) may also seem tempting. To move across the electric, it may seem that merely pressing the console's Back button may provide the same results. Flash through the cues and see what is activated (and more important, what is not) before committing to this reverse course of action.

Act Cue Blocks

The disk master for *Hokey* indicates that Act 1 will occupy less than 100 whole-numbered memories, so it will be assigned to the 100's block. It's anticipated that the second act, however, may require more than 100 whole-numbered memories, so both the 200's and 300's will be allocated to the Act 2 cues. While this means that Act 3 will begin in the 400s, this numerical identity shouldn't become a source of confusion once the lighting designer, console programmer, and stage manager become familiar with the system.

Allocating blocks of cues doesn't have to be limited to acts; each block of 100's can be sub-partitioned and assigned to individual scenes. For example, the first act of *Hokey*, allocated to the 100's block, will have three scenes. If it's anticipated that the first scene will have some amount of light cues, those cues may be assigned to memories 101 > 124. The second scene might be allocated to memories 130 > 155, while the third scene may be allocated to memories 160 > 192. As long as the lighting designer remembers the cue block structure, he or she can identify memory 142 as a cue in the second scene of the first act.

Communicating in three-digit numbers through the course of a show can become exhausting for everyone involved. One work-around is to initially establish the memory number loaded into the console, and then truncate the rest of the memory numbers for that act. As an example, as the show is about to begin, the stage manager confirms the complete preset memory number: "Jim, we're in memory 100.7 for the top of the show, correct?" Once Jim confirms that the memory loaded into the active fader is 100.7, the stage manager then calls the rest of the Act 1 cue numbers eliminating the "100" digit, asking only for the remaining two integers. Rather than "cue 101," the next cue is "cue 1." As Act 2 is about to begin, the stage manager again

confirms the complete preset number: "Jim, we're now in cue 200.7 for Act 2, correct?" Once confirmed, the rest of the cues for Act 2 will be called starting with cue 1 as well.

Once the full memory number is confirmed prior to the beginning of a sequence, truncating memory numbers usually creates no problems. Since the memory numbers are sequentially recorded, this reduces the amount of speech on headset, and allows the stage manager to concentrate on other matters.

Library Blocks

During the course of technical rehearsals or previews, entire cue sequences may change in one rehearsal, only to be restored in the next. When the rehearsal process begins to adopt that amount of liquidity, then it's time to set aside a memory block in the Disk Master Chart to store and archive lighting memories.

In the midst of a technical rehearsal, for example, the transition sequence from Scene 1 to Scene 2 may be completely changed. Memories 122, 123, and 124 may no longer seem to have application to the show. The lighting designer's first instinct might be to delete these now-obsolete memories and record new looks labeled with those same memory numbers. That way the stage manager doesn't need to change any numbers in the call book. This, however, may be the moment for the shrewd designer to consider the larger picture. If this is a new production (check), there's no telling if the new transition sequence will be the final version. It's never been done before (check). Indeed, the lighting designer could delete the old memories, create a new sequence, tech the new sequence, and then be told that "the first way really was the best; let's go back and try that again now." And then the lighting designer would be sad. (But only on the inside!)

If there's a printout of the original transition cues, then restoring them won't take much time. The old sequence, once discarded, can be quickly read back into the old memory numbers. If there's no written record, and the original cues have been deleted, however, time will be wasted as the lighting designer tries to reconstruct the old sequence. Worse yet, if the transition in question is still not settled in the director's mind, it may be necessary to tech each version of the sequence several times until the final version is determined.

One way to avoid wasted time and preserve several versions of sequences, or store "currently unused" light cues, is to allocate memory blocks as storage areas. The cues still exist, but are "hidden" from active show use until called for. **Library blocks** refer to areas of the RAM used to store this dormant cue information. The disk master for *Hokey* has enough 100's room that a library block can be allocated

Q	Cnt	Label		Store	Active
121	10	H/P x CC	Link	→	
122	7\10	Final Warm	=>	522	**532**
123	Ø	Button	=>	523	**533**
124	5	Restore	=>	524	**534**
130	5	sc2; STORM	Link	←	

Figure 8.8 Library Storage and Linking for M122 > M124 Sequence

to each act. The 500 block will contain stored cues for Act 1, 600 for Act 2, and 700 for Act 3. In the perfect world, the same number of whole-numbered memories are set aside in the library to match each act's cue block. That way the memory numbers can easily be transferred.

Figure 8.8 illustrates this storage sequence. Rather than delete memory 122, it's instead recorded as memory 522 (which can be written as M122⇒ M522). The other two memories would also be transferred: M123 ⇒ M523, and M124 ⇒ M524. Then the original 127 > 129 memories could be deleted, and fresh programming could take place. If the two cue sequences were to be run alternately so that the creative staff could make their choice between the two versions, the new cues could be seen in the 120's sequence, while the old cues could still be used, stored in the 520's. Once the final version was chosen, the chosen memories would be recorded (or "moved back") as memories 122 > 124.

When a third sequence is required, it might be possible to record that series into the 622 > 624 block, but that's currently assigned as the library block for Act 2. Instead, it might be more prudent to record it into the 532 > 534 sequence (same last digit, if nothing else). On some lighting consoles, there's also the ability to **link** memories completely out of sequence. While this drives stage managers and console operators batty, one link could then be programmed from M121 to M532, and a second link from M534 back to M130. The two arrows illustrate this sequence. This way the console operator still performs the five-cue sequence by merely pressing the GO button but bypasses the currently out-of-date memories 122 > 124. When liquid theatre approaches this level, the lighting designer must religiously maintain the cue master or whatever document informs him or her of the current cue status and their relationship to one another. At the first possible opportunity, once "final" decisions have been made, the unused cues should be moved to an appropriate archive memory block, active cues should be moved back to sequential numbers in the original Act block, and the links should be removed.

Cue Information and Identification

Ideally, labeling each memory used in the show with an alphanumeric name makes it simpler for the lighting designer to rapidly scan a cue list printout for information, which is very handy, until the purpose of the cue changes five times but the number remains the same and there's been no time to grab the keyboard. For whatever reason, when it's not possible to properly "name" each memory on the disk, several systems can be used to identify different types of cues.

Act Preset Check Cues

If changes are made to the lighting package before an act (sidelight color change, rover refocus, and so on), preset checks performed behind the main curtain can confirm that the lighting package is correctly colored, focused, and functional. The intent of a preset check, and a preset checklist, is to view all elements of the lighting package used to be seen prior to curtain. Viewed another way, it's also the best method to prevent incorrect or otherwise unnoticed details from being seen *after* the curtain goes out. **Preset check cues** are a systematic method used to see an instrument that's no longer correctly focused, a unit that's received the wrong color, or a lamp that's burned out.

The key to constructing an expedient preset check is to define the largest number of channels that can be turned on at one time without losing the ability to see the beam edges of the individual instruments. Rather than a time-consuming check of individual channels, a sequence of recorded preset cues can confirm the ready status of the lighting package used in that act. A typical preset sequence might consist of the following:

- All of the stage left sidelights and deck specials, that are used only in the act, brought up to 50% so they can be seen. (Instruments activated in other acts aren't applicable and can be confusing.)
- All of the stage right sidelights and deck specials that are used only in the act brought up to 50% so they can be seen.
- A combination of all of the cues for the entire act (upstage of the curtain) combined into a single cue. This "super cue" contains the highest recorded level for each channel used in that act.

In almost all cases, the light cues will be different for each act. One set of preset check cues may be performed before the show. While the same sequence may be repeated during each intermission, the memory contents are different for each sequence. Identifying these cue sets, and keeping them in sequence with the rest of the memories used in the show, can become

Q	Cnt	Label
400	2.5	Fade Final Act 2 memory to black
400.4	2.5	Stage Left Sides and Deck Specials
400.5	2.5	Stage Right Sides and Deck Specials
400.6	2.5	Super Cue
400.7	7	Preset for Act 3
401	5	First Cue Called after Curtain flown out

Figure 8.9 Cue Sequence Between Acts 2 and 3

problematic. One method is to record each preset check cue sequence, using the same last digit point cues. Since each 100's memory in the act cue blocks is designated as a blocker (stopping all tracking), each set of preset check cues can be recorded between them and the first cues for each act. One way to identify the preset check cues at the beginning of an act is to consistently record them in a point cue numeric sequence. Here's one that's been successfully used for years:

100's cues = stopper cues (containing all hard zeros, stopping any channels tracking from the previous act)
.4 cues = stage left sidelights and deck specials
.5 cues = stage right sidelights and deck specials
.6 cues = the highest recorded level for every channel used in the cues for that particular act, the "super cue"
.7 cues = preset cue for that act
Cue "1" = the first cue called after the curtain has gone out.

To further distinguish the preset check cues from the "body" of the act cues, unique times can be assigned to the cues. Using the structure of a preset check sequence, a cue list monitor display might look like Figure 8.9.

Regardless of the act or the series of 100's, seeing that numeric point sequence of cues and times on the monitor display informs the lighting designer of the identity and function of each cue. The final preset cue for the act could be a point 9 memory (400.9). If a second preset cue is required to initiate an effect memory or some other autofollow sequence, however, there's no numeric location to place that cue without violating the preset structure.

Autofollows

Autofollow memories are linked to other cues. They begin without a separate press of the GO button. On manual light boards, autofollow cues are typically initiated without a separate spoken command from the stage manager. As soon as the prior light cue is complete, the autofollow cue is immediately taken. While autofollow cues aren't called, they can instead be identified by being labeled as an odd-numbered point cue. When the lighting designer looks at the cue list monitor screen and sees a separate point 5 (.5) memory in the middle of other whole-numbered memories, then it can be discerned that the memory in question is an autofollow cue. For this system to retain accuracy, added cues that are called by the stage manager are then often given an even point number (.2, .4, etc.).

Ghost Channels

Channels without assigned dimmers can be viewed as spare control or as unwanted clutter on the monitor display. If there's a chance that the channels will never be assigned, however, they can still have a purpose as **ghost channels** and provide the lighting designer with information. Many computer light console printouts include channel and level information detailing the contents of each cue, but there's often no date or time information included anywhere on the page. In many cases, if a date is indicated, it's usually a time stamp stuck on the printout from the time clock chip inside the computer. The result is a time noting the moment when the printout command was received, not the last time the memories were altered. Although it's certainly valuable to know when the printout was produced, it may not be enough. Knowing the date that the memories were last altered may be the needed piece to complete a puzzle.

Time Stamp Channels

Three unassigned channels adjacent to each other can be assigned as **time stamp** channels, providing a "version number" for that printout and the memories in the computer. By assigning the first channel as the day, the second as the month, and the third as the year, the time stamp channels will always show the last alteration date of the cues. Of course, the channels have to be constantly updated every time the cues are altered, or the system has no value. When the system is kept intact, however, the time stamp channels will clearly show when the memories were last altered.

If there are several different disks of different versions of the same cues, the time stamp channels will show which version was last altered in the RAM of the light board. In *Hokey's* hookup, the time stamp channels are assigned to the final three channels on the first monitor screen. Channel 123 is the month, channel 124 is the day, and channel 125 is the year. Care should be taken on a tracking light board not to assign any hard commands to the channels in any internal cues. If the channels are kept "clean," the change in date can be made in the first memory and given the command to track, resulting in every cue reflecting the date change.

Blackout Cues

Some light boards don't automatically display a cue list on the monitor. If a cue contains no channel intensity information, it may take moments to determine if the cue is a blackout, or if errant programming has taken place and channel intensity information lost.

One work-around for this dilemma is to designate a block of unassigned channels as **ghost blackout channels** to identify an "empty cue." In the *Hokey* hookup, channels 139 and 140, containing no dimmer assignments, have been designated as ghost blackout channels. They are activated to a unique level only in cues that are black on stage. In the *Hokey* memories, if channels 139 and 140 are displayed at an intensity of 11% (a unique level), then that memory is a blackout cue. Any channel intensities other than time stamp channels are suspect, and should be checked.

Shelley's Notes: Key Memory Numbers

This is every lighting designer's nightmare scenario: the cues for a production are contained on several disks and a disk containing memories for some portion of the show have been loaded into the computer light board's RAM; the disk has been removed, and then the board operator disappears. The lighting designer is left staring at the computer monitor. Which act is loaded into the board? Is this the right version of the act? Which disk was loaded into the board?

Every lighting designer has been there. Pre-programming disks with **key memory numbers**, however, provides a structure that identifies which memories are currently loaded into the lighting console. The memories "carry" a unique identity by numeric sequences in their ghost channels.

David K. H. Elliott introduced me to the concept of disk management and key memory numbers when he was the resident lighting designer at American Ballet Theatre. At that time, ABT produced an active repertory of 20 repertory (or one-act) and five full-length ballets that would change on a yearly basis. Although the company traveled with its own lighting package and a computer console controlling 72 dimmers, the local house light board was used as well to control FOH instruments and striplights.

At that time, disk storage was limited to floppy disk. Not only was it impossible for all of the memories to fit onto a single computer disk, the size of the repertory was so large that disks were changed at each intermission. Using David's method, however, it was still possible to view the monitor of either

lighting console to confirm that the proper memories were loaded for the correct ballet. This was accomplished using ghost channels and David's system.

Each repertory ballet, or act of a full-length ballet, typically had no more than 100 cues. Based on that assumption, the cues had been allocated into blocks of 100's. Each ballet started with a different series of 100's, so a disk contained nine sets of cues for nine different repertory ballets. The 100 series of cues were for the ballet titled *Murder*, the 200 series of cues were for the ballet called *Requiem*, and so on. There were a total of eight show disks in the ABT repertory ballet library, which, multiplied by the nine ballets on each disk, resulted in a total of 72 ballets.

That being the case, although every ballet had its own block of cues on its own disk, by looking at the computer screen alone, it would still be impossible to tell which disk had been loaded. Granted, the screen might display light cues starting in the 100's, but unless the board operator was present to confirm which disk had been loaded, it might be *Murder*, or it might be the 100 series of cues from another disk.

To eliminate that confusion, David had created a labeling system that assigned a unique four-digit number to each repertory ballet or full-length act. This four-digit key memory number was split between the first and the final three digits. The first digit was the ghost label channel identifying the number of the disk, and the next three digits identified the block of 100's cues on that disk. The key memory number for *Murder* was 7100, meaning that on Repertory Disk 7, all of the cues in the 100's belonged to *Murder*.

At that point, the highest channel number used in the ABT hookup was 72. Since the screen displayed 100 channels, channel 100 was assigned as the ghost channel labeling the disk number. The floppy disk containing *Murder* along with nine other rep ballets was labeled Disk 7. When that disk was loaded into the light board, no matter which ballet was chosen, channel 100 had a recorded intensity of 07%. Therefore, if the computer monitor showed that memory 101 was the next cue and that channel 100 was at 07%, the combination of the numbers identified the memory and the disk that had been loaded into RAM. The board had to be loaded for *Murder*.

System Size

When most computer light boards are turned on so that no information is contained in their memory, the system size is reset to default values. The **system size** refers to the number of dimmers that the board will recognize and the number of channels that appear on the monitor screen. On modern moderate consoles, the number of dimmers is often a single universe of

512 dimmers while the number of channels may be more than 1000.

Most lighting consoles display 100 or 125 channels per page. If the screen shows channels 1 > 100 and the designer needs to see the level of channel 150, pressing the "page" button flips to the second page of numbers on the display. In most cases, console screens can't usually page back; they can only cycle through the entire list of channels. If the second page is showing on the monitor screen, and the channel number is still set at 1000, necessary to press the page button eight more times to flip through the rest of the screens and eventually come back to the first page of channels. Likewise, the default number of dimmers is usually much more than the average situation will warrant. Since most lighting consoles address every dimmer in every memory regardless of channel assignment, a cue-intensive disk can slow the reaction time of some older light boards to a crawl.

Because of these awkward limitations, one of the first operations performed when programming a disk from scratch is to change the system size to a more "designer-friendly" configuration. All modern lighting consoles allow this modification. The number of dimmers is reduced to a size reflecting the actual number of dimmers that will be controlled, while the number of channels is reduced to reflect a number slightly higher than the number of channels indicated in the hookup. If the highest channel number in the hookup is 180, for example, the number of channels in the system might be reduced to 200. This allows 20 channels that may be assigned to additional dimmers or ghost channels, and the page button will only need to be pressed once to show the alternate channel screen.

The reason to be aware of this limitation is the lighting console. On some older computer light boards, the system size is an absolute given.

Once memories have been recorded, the system size can no longer be altered. If the number of dimmers or channels is altered, all information regarding memories will be erased from the RAM of the console.

Because of this fact, a cue-intensive production scheduled for a tour that doesn't carry its own lighting console should be viewed with particular attention. The identity of each house light board should be ascertained as soon as possible before any other decisions are made. If any of the venues has a console with these limitations, determining the manufacturer, software version, and the house dimmer configuration for that particular facility should be used to help define the system size of the lighting package for the entire tour. Doing so will maintain system size and channel hookup consistency throughout the tour, and will make certain that the same memory information can be used in all theatres possessing that same lighting console.

Infrastructure Cues

Although the computer lighting console has many advanced functions, the fundamental method used to turn on lights often requires a series of keystrokes. Repeatedly activating even sequential channels during the cueing process can quickly add time to the process. In addition to that, the computer lighting console may be the single electronic device controlling running lights, spotting lights, special effects, color scrollers, or triggering numerous other devices. Preprogramming handles that reduce the number of keystrokes needed to activate or control any of these devices can save time during the cue construction process.

Aside from the aspect of time management, the lighting console is often the only device controlling light on the stage. Almost every lighting designer agrees that, when it comes to safety, knowing how to get light on the stage quickly is one of the first responsibilities. There may be moments when worklight is needed immediately on stage and no one will be near the worklight switch. Regardless of the memory loaded into the faders, instruments controlled by the console may be the only alternative to get light on the stage. Systems should be in place to be able to rapidly react, provide basic illumination, and avoid moments of crisis.

Memories and other functions programmed in the "background" can be used to expedite all these situations. Generically referred to as **infrastructure cues**, this programming is often completed before the console is used for any scheduled task. Infrastructure cues are created to provide access to the basic framework of a lighting package. Once created, the cues can be assigned to alternate handles, allowing several channels to be activated in fundamental ways, using relatively few actions or keystrokes.

There are two main types of infrastructure cues. One series of memories activates entire **system washes**, while the second series activates all of the instruments at each **hanging position**. These two series of memories can be assigned to handles used to manipulate channels in a light plot in two distinct ways.

System Wash Memories

System wash memories are collections of channels that are programmed to turn on entire washes of light. Once they're programmed they can be converted to other functions within the lighting console and used as building blocks in the creation of light cues, preshow checks, or as worklight.

Figure 8.10 shows the system wash memory list for *Hokey*. Each row shows the memory number, time fade (or count, shortened to "Cnt"), channel intensity, and the channels involved. Memory 951 is the third memory listed for the *Hokey* light plot, for example, which has channels 1 > 10 recorded at Full. The rest of the memories are collections of channels arranged by color wash and following the same sequence as the channel hookup: frontlight, overhead sidelight, downlight, backlight, and boom sidelight. The time assignments and delays will be examined when preshow light checks are discussed in Chapter 14.

Hanging Position Memories

Hanging position memories are collections of channels that are programmed to turn on all of the instruments at a single hanging position. Once they're programmed they can be converted to other functions

---

Hybrid Theatre 2010   **HOKEY SYSTEM WASH MEMORIES**   Date: 2/13/10

Cue	Cnt	Dly	Lvl	System	CHANNELS	Cue
950	3		0	Blocker	1 > 122 126 > 138 @ 0	950
950.7	10	30	30	Warmup	1 > 122 126 > 138 @ 30	950.7
951	5	20	Full	R33 Front	1 > 10	951
952	5	20	Full	L161 Front	11 > 20	952
953	5	20	Full	R51 Bx Bm	29 30	953
954	5	20	Full	R44 Bx Bm	39 40	954
955	5	20	Full	G945 Bx Bm	49 50	955
956	5	20	Full	Pit	137 138	956
957	5	20	Full	SR R51>>	21 > 24	957
958	5	20	Full	SL R51<<	25 > 28	958
959	5	20	Full	SR R64>>	41 > 44	959
960	5	20	Full	SL R64<<	45 > 48	960
961	5	20	Full	R20 Down	61 > 70	961
962	5	20	Full	L124 Down	71 > 80	962
963	5	20	Full	NC Back	81 > 90	963
964	5	20	Full	G850 Back	91 > 100	964
965	5	20	Full	Lav Boom	31 > 38	965
966	5	20	Full	Blue Boom	101 > 108	966
967	5	20	Full	Mids	109 > 114	967
968	5	20	Full	Shins	115 > 122	968
969	5	20	Full	Templates	51 > 54	969
970	5	20	Full	Specials	55 > 60	970
971	5	20	Full	All Cyc	131 > 136	971
972	5	30	50	Foh INHIB	1 > 5 11 > 15 29 30 39 40 49 50 58 59 60 137 138	972
973	5	60	50	US INHIB	6 > 10 16 > 20 21 > 28 31 > 38	973
					41 > 48 51 > 57 61 > 122 126 > 136	
974	3		0	Blocker	1 > 122 126 > 138 @ 0	974

Expression 3; 150 chan, 174 dim   Lighting by Steve Shelley 917.xxx.xxxx   Page 1 of 1

Figure 8.10 The System Wash Memories for *Hokey*

Hybrid Theatre 2010 **HOKEY HANGING POSITION MEMORIES** Date: 2/13/10

Cue	Cnt	Dly	Lvl	System	CHANNELS																				Cue
900	3		0	Blocker	1	>	122		126	>	138	@	0												900
900.7	10	30	30	Warmup	1	>	122		126	>	138	@	30												900.7
901	5	20	30	Truss	1	>	5		11	>	15		58	59	60										901
902	5	20	30	SL Bx Bm	30	40	50																		902
903	5	20	30	SR Bx Bm	29	39	49																		903
904	5	20	30	Pit	137	138																			904
905	5	20	30	1 Elec	6	7	8	16	17	18	21	25	41	45	51	55									905
906	5	20	30	2 Elec	9	10	19	20	22	26	42	46	52		61	>	65		71	>	75				906
907	5	20	30	3 Elec	81	>	85		91	>	95														907
908	5	20	30	4 Elec	23	27	43	47	53		66	>	70		76	>	80								908
909	5	20	30	5 Elec	24	28	44	48	54	57	86	>	90		96	>	100								909
910	5	20	30	6 E/Grndrw	131	>	136																		910
911	5	20	30	SL Sides	35	>	38		105	>	108		112	>	114		119	>	122						911
912	5	20	30	SR Sides	31	>	34		101	>	104		109	>	111		115	>	118						912
913	5	30	50	Foh INHIB	1	>	5		11	>	15		29	30	39	40	49	50	58	59	60	137	138		913
914	5	60	50	US INHIB	6	>	10		16		20		21	>		31	>	38							913
					41	>	48		51	>	57		61	>	122		126	>	135						
920	3		0	Blocker	1	>	122		126	>	138	@	0												920

Expression 3; 150 chan, 174 dim   Lighting by Steve Shelley 917.xxx.xxxx   Page 1 of 1

Figure 8.11 The Hanging Position Memories for *Hokey*

within the lighting console and used as handles during load-in, during preshow checks, as general illumination, or to turn off an entire hanging position.

Figure 8.11 shows the hanging position memories for *Hokey*. Each row shows the memory number, the time fade, the channel intensity, and the channels involved. The delays will be examined when preshow light checks are discussed in Chapter 14.

Submasters

Autotransformer light boards contain a grand master handle whose only function is to control the rest of the dimmers in that rack. Rotating the handle of each "slave" dimmer allows it to "click in" mechanically and be controlled by the grand master. In this way, moving the single grand master handle then moves all of the dimmers. This function has been adopted into most manual light boards using "grand," "scene," or "independent" masters physically manipulated by small handles or sliders.

This same function has also been built into lighting computer consoles. The physical handles are often sliders and are called **submasters**, or **subs**. Rather

than physical handles mechanically controlling individual dimmers, subs instead control channels by a series of keystroke commands. While some earlier consoles limited a channel to be controlled by only one submaster at a time, others provide subs that could only control a single channel. Most modern lighting consoles are now packed with submasters that can contain any number of channels, and usually have three different "personalities" or attributes: inhibitive, pile-on, or timed.

Understanding these three submaster attributes is important; not only does it then allow the lighting designer to take advantage of their features, but the

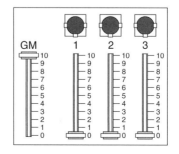

Figure 8.12 A Manual Light Board with a Grand Master and Three Dimmer Sliders

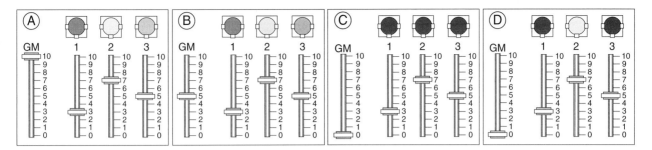

Figure 8.13 Illustration of Inhibitive Submasters

functions are applied to other functions of modern lighting consoles. To begin understanding submaster attributes, imagine a simple manual light board that has one grand master and three sliders.

Each slider controls one dimmer and one lighting instrument. The grand master is a common concept; it controls no lights, its only function is to override all of the other sliders. An **inhibitive submaster** acts just like the grand master. In this example, the grand master is "fixed" (or permanent). On most manual light boards, that's often the case: the grand master always controls all of the sliders, while the inhibitive submaster overrides all of the hardwired sliders, knobs, or handles assigned to it.

Figure 8.12 shows the grand master (GM) on the left at 100% (or Full). Above each slider is a front view of each instrument, showing the lens and the light coming out of the unit. The three sliders are set at zero. Even though the GM is at Full, each of the three lighting instruments is dark. No light is coming out of the lens of the instruments.

Figure 8.13A shows that while the GM remains at Full, the three sliders have been brought up to different levels. Dimmer 1 is at 30%, dimmer 2 is at 70%, and dimmer 3 is at 50%. The light from the three instruments reflects the levels of their respective sliders.

Figure 8.13B shows the sliders unchanged from their previous settings, but the GM has been reduced to 50%. The GM has "overridden" the individual sliders. Although the sliders haven't been touched, dimmer 1 is now reading at 15%, dimmer 2 is at 35%, and dimmer 3 is at 25%, half of their slider intensity.

The third illustration, Figure 8.13C, shows the sliders unchanged from their settings, but the GM has been taken down to zero. Again, the GM has "overridden" the individual sliders. Although the sliders haven't been touched, no light is coming out of the instruments.

No matter what level sliders 1 > 3 are placed at, the GM will override their levels, and the instruments will remain at zero. For any of the sliders and their instruments to be able to function, the GM must be brought up above a level of zero. The GM is inhibiting the other three sliders. Now imagine if the GM only controlled sliders 1 and 3.

Figure 8.13D shows the three sliders unchanged from their settings, with the GM still at zero. Since slider 2 is not controlled by the inhibitive action of the grand master, the light from the second instrument is reading at 70%. If an inhibitive submaster doesn't control a dimmer, it will function normally, regardless of the submaster's intensity.

The personality of a **pile-on submaster** overrides the sliders in the opposite manner. Any slider assigned to the submaster can have its own individual level at any time without the submaster being activated. When the submaster is brought to Full, however, all of the lights will also come up to Full, regardless of their slider position. Imagine the same manual light board as in Figure 8.13, except the grand master has been replaced with a pile-on submaster. The grand master again controls all three sliders.

Figure 8.14A shows the three sliders unchanged from their previous settings, with the pile-on submaster at zero. Since the pile-on submaster is

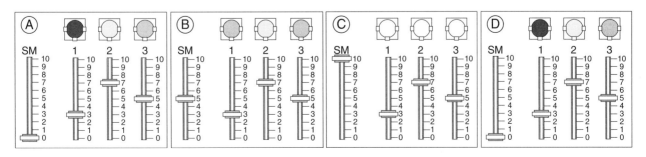

Figure 8.14 Illustration of Pile-On Submasters

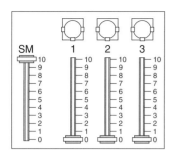

Figure 8.15 The Final Pile-On Submaster Position

dormant, the intensities of light from the three instruments match the level of their respective sliders.

In Figure 8.14B, the three sliders are unchanged from their previous settings, but the pile-on submaster has been brought up to 50%. Although slider 1 remained unchanged at 30%, the pile-on submaster has overridden its level, and the light from instrument 1 is at 50%.

In the next illustration (Figure 8.14C), the three sliders are unchanged from their previous settings, but the pile-on submaster has been brought up to Full. The pile-on submaster has overridden all three sliders. The light from all three instruments is reading at Full.

In the final illustration (Figure 8.14D), the three sliders remain unchanged. The pile-on submaster has been taken down to zero. The pile-on submaster no longer has any control over the three instruments. The light from all three instruments has returned to their original intensities, matching the levels of their respective sliders.

Figure 8.15 shows the three sliders taken down to zero. The pile-on submaster, though, has been taken to Full. The light from all three instruments is at Full. The pile-on submaster has overridden the level of the sliders.

Any channels assigned to a pile-on submaster can have their own individual levels at any time. When the pile-on submaster is taken to a level *higher* than the level of the slider, the level of the submaster will override the level of the slider.

The last usual personality is that of a **timed submaster**, which acts like a pile-on submaster, but adds three time elements to the sub: up, duration, and down. Imagine the manual light board. Both the pile-on sub and the grand master have been eliminated. Now imagine that a light cue is required that activates all three sliders from zero to different levels in 5 seconds, waits for 10 seconds, and then fades all three sliders back down to zero in 7 seconds.

To accomplish the two fades, Figure 8.16A shows the sliders preset at zero. No light is coming out of the instruments.

In Figure 8.16B, the sliders have faded up to their respective levels in 5 seconds.

After 10 seconds have passed, Figure 8.16C shows that the three sliders have faded back down to zero in 7 counts.

Channels recorded to a timed submaster can be used in any other memory or cue. When the timed submaster is activated, however, the submaster is programmed to fade the assigned channels up to their respective levels in a length of time, wait for a time duration, and then fade the channels back down to their previous levels in an assigned time.

Inhibitive and pile-on attributes will be assigned to the submasters programmed for *Hokey*. For this production, however, timed submasters will not be used.

The Submaster List

There are 24 submasters on the lighting console, and *Hokey* will use all of them. On this lighting console, the submasters are laid out in two rows of 12 submasters each. Figure 8.17 is the **submaster list**, which uses a combination of the two types of infrastructure cues. When these contents are programmed, the physical handles may be used to activate channels while creating cues, performing preshow checks, or rapidly supplying illumination for worklight. Since submasters have a physical handle, any electrician can be called upon to operate them.

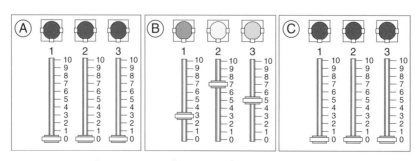

Figure 8.16 Illustration of a Timed Submaster

Hybrid Theatre 2010 — **HOKEY SUBMASTER LIST** — Date: 2/13/10

Sub	Lvl	System																				Sub
									CHANNELS													
1	Full	Truss	1	>	5		11	>	15		58	59	60									1
2	Full	SL Bx Bm	30	40	50																	2
3	Full	SR Bx Bm	29	39	49																	3
4	Full	1 Elec	6	7	8	16	17	18	21	25	41	45	51	55								4
5	Full	2 Elec	9	10	19	20	22	26	42	46	52		61	>	65		71	>	75			5
6	Full	3 Elec	81	>	85		91	>	95													6
7	Full	4 Elec	23	27	43	47	53		66	>	70		76	>	80							7
8	Full	5 Elec	24	28	44	48	54	57	86	>	90		96	>	100							8
9	Full	6 E/Grndrw	131	>	136																	9
10	Full	SL Sides	35	>	38		105	>	108		112	>	114		119	>	122					10
11	Full	SR Sides	31	>	34		101	>	104		109	>	111		115	>	118					11
12	Full	US INHIB	6	>	10		16	>	20		21	>	28		31	>	38					12
12	Full		41	>	48		51	>	57		61	>	122		126	>	136					12
13	Full	R33 Front	1	>	10																	13
14	Full	L161 Front	11	>	20																	14
15	Full	SR R51>>	21	>	24																	15
15	Full	SL R51<<	25	>	28																	15
16	Full	SR R64>>	41	>	44																	16
16	Full	SL R64<<	45	>	48																	16
17	Full	R20 Down	61	>	70																	17
18	Full	L124 Down	71	>	80																	18
19	Full	NC Back	81	>	90																	19
20	Full	R68 Back	91	>	100																	20
21	Full	Lav Boom	31	>	38																	21
22	Full	Blue Boom	101	>	108																	22
23	Full	Templates	51	>	54																	23
24	Full	Foh INHIB	1	>	5		11	>	15		29	30	39	40	49	50	58	59	60	137	138	24

Expression 3; 150 chan, 174 dim   Lighting by Steve Shelley 917.xxx.xxxx   Page 1 of 1

Figure 8.17 The Submaster List for *Hokey*

Submasters 12 and 24 have been assigned as inhibitive submasters. Submaster 12 controls every instrument upstage of the main curtain, while Submaster 24 controls every instrument downstage of the curtain. If a blackout check must be performed behind the main curtain after the audience has entered the theatre, Submaster 12 can be pulled down without affecting any channels being used as curtain warmers. When the main curtain has to close quickly, Submaster 24 can be pulled down, eliminating any light from the front of house that might otherwise splash onto the curtain. Unless they are needed, however, both handles will remain at Full through the entire show.

If the light plot includes channels containing house-lights, curtain warmers, page bow lights, or conductor specials, those channels are often not included in the FOH inhibitive sub (Submaster 24) since it's possible those channels may be needed while the submaster is pulled down. This will be examined more closely in Chapter 14. For the same reason, channels controlling running lights, spotting lights, or other devices that should remain constant shouldn't be included in the upstage inhibitive sub (Submaster 12).

Since the topic of lights being turned off or inhibited is being discussed, now's a good time to mention that, if music stand lights don't need to be dimmed, the lighting console should not control them.

When the light board crashes, the music stand lights will turn off, and the orchestra will stop playing music. While the show may still be performed with only worklight on stage, it won't matter if the musicians can't see their music. The show may be lost.

Submaster Notes

In addition to controlling systems or positions, submasters can be adapted for other functions as well. Here's a short list of other functions that submasters can perform:

- If atmospheric effects and fans are assigned to submasters, assign the atmospheric effect and the fans onto two separate submasters. This often provides more overall control. If enough submasters are available, consider splitting the sources from each other to separate subs to provide even more atmospheric control.
- If the light plot has scrollers or other devices, consider assigning all of the scroller or device channels to one submaster, and all of the instruments to an adjacent submaster. This speeds up preshow checks of the devices.
- Strobe lights can often require several channels of control. These channels can be assigned to separate submasters and adjusted manually to determine levels of control, which can then be programmed into the appropriate memory.
- Moving light fixtures have numerous attributes, which require several channels of control. Attributes that will often be universal, such as color, may be assigned to submasters to manually adjust the color of all of the fixtures at one time.
- Consider assigning any series of channels that commonly move together or require an extensive keystroking to a sub.
- Any channel or device that needs to activate like a switch may seem prudent to assign to a submaster, including worklights, systems that can be used like worklights, or emergency lights.
- Consider assigning infrastructure channels that may always need to be active, but may otherwise be forgotten in the cue construction process: spotting lights, running lights, or cue lights, for example.

While many modern consoles are built with a finite number of physical submaster handles, they're often also designed with a variation of the "page" software function that multiplies what the handles can control. Instead of flipping through monitor screens, the submaster **page** function replaces the recorded channel contents for an entire bank of physical submaster handles, typically with a single keystroke. Using this function, channel levels can be stored on subs that are not currently associated with the hardware; as they're being recorded, they're assigned to a different *page* of subs. While this expands the number of subs available to the lighting designer, understanding how to quickly access non-active pages is paramount in order to take advantage of this function. The lighting console should be carefully studied before heavily investing in this feature.

Groups

While submasters refer to actual physical handles, **groups** refer to a function, button, or software feature that acts like a software handle. On most computer lighting consoles, a group can contain any number of channels at any collection of levels, and more than one group can typically control a single channel. Most current lighting consoles provide at least 100 groups.

One reason to consider the group function is that a group can eliminate repetitive keystroking of the same channels by the board operator. Although constructing a group can be time consuming, once the group exists, it's a handle that can access numerous channels with a minimum of keystrokes.

Another reason to use groups is that they can act in both directions. While a submaster can be assigned as either pile-on or inhibitive, the channels included in the sub can't be controlled both ways. The contents of a group, on the other hand, can be activated and override any recorded information in either direction. A group can bring entire collections of channels to Full or take the same clump of channels to zero.

A third reason to use groups is that, on most modern lighting consoles, more than one group can be activated at the same time. On most consoles, attempting to key in "sub 1 + sub 2" produces an error alert; no more than one sub can be keystroked at one time. Keystroking "group 3 + group 4 @ Full" on the other hand will typically activate both groups at one time to Full.

And yet another reason to use groups is that most computer lighting consoles don't allow memories to be used as handles within other memories. Since groups can be activated within cues, they can be used in that function as a cue storage device. For example, if the combination of channels has been balanced to create the perfect sunset in the midst of an otherwise complex cue, the channels involved in creating the sunset can be activated and then recorded into a group. The sunrise cue in another scene can be constructed more quickly by activating that group and piling it onto any other memory in the show.

Groups can be programmed to copy the system wash memories. These groups can then be used as building blocks to activate entire systems while creating cues. When groups are used in this way, however, close attention should be paid to the recording process. Errant channels recorded in the wrong group may then be incorrectly recorded into memories. For example, an errant channel, accidentally assigned to the cool backlight group, may not be seen when the cool backlight is activated on top of other systems. Unfortunately, every time the cool backlight group is activated, the errant channel will then be accidentally programmed into every memory. Not only can it confuse the lighting designer to no end until the discovery is made, but since the errant channel has been recorded in several cues, eliminating the error will waste precious board time.

Groups can be built that duplicate the hanging position memories (position groups). Sometimes the flexibility to turn an entire electric on or off can be useful. When an overhead electric is flying out to trim, for example, turning on every instrument on the entire electric with one set of keystrokes allows all of the lenses to be seen from the sightline point. Not only does the position group expedite the trimming process; it confirms that the border conceals all of the lenses on that electric.

Position groups are also useful as a means of eliminating the contents of an entire hanging position. For example, when a midstage drop flies in during a cueing session, light from overhead instruments may splash onto the face of the drop. Time can be wasted while the errant instruments are located and turned off. On the other hand, position groups can be used to deactivate all relevant overhead electrics to zero. Individual channels can then be activated to build the cue, and errant channels can immediately be seen.

Figure 8.18 is a portion of the **group list** for *Hokey*, showing the programmed contents for groups 1 > 31. This series of groups includes both system wash and hanging position memories.

Note that the channels in the *Hokey* groups are all recorded at Full. The contents of a group must be recorded at a level above 00% for the group to function as a software pile-on submaster. If channels 1 > 10 @ 00% are recorded as group 1, activating that group to any percentage (Group 1 @ Full) will still result in the channels reading at zero. Since the groups for *Hokey* are all recorded at Full, each group can be activated at any intensity range. Group 1 can either be used as an inhibitive submaster (Group 1 @ 00%) or as a pile-on submaster (Group 1 @ Full).

FOCUS INFORMATION

During a focus session, the lighting designer instructs an electrician where to point and how to shape the beam of each instrument in the light plot. Typically, each instrument is turned on one at a time, so that the beam can be seen. The instrument is targeted to a designated focus point and immobilized (or "locked off"). The beam is then sized, softened or sharpened, and the edge of the light may be shaped with shutters or barndoors.

In an ideal world, each instrument in a system would be pointed to its individual focus point. After all of the instruments in that system were focused, the entire system would then be activated and visually checked for symmetry. While this idealized focus process makes perfect sense, it takes too much time. Moving ladders to different hanging positions in order to get to each instrument in the system may take more time than just focusing the instruments. Rather than choreographing the focus so that lights are pointed system-by-system, the need for speed forces most focus sessions to be choreographed instead by ladder movement. The typical objective is to gain access to and point the most number of lights while keeping the number of ladder "moves" to a minimum. After all of the instruments in one position have been focused, the ladder is moved to the next hanging position. The need to return to a hanging position a second time can be seen as a waste of time.

Conducting a focus session based on hanging position means that completed systems can't be viewed until every hanging position possessing instruments in that particular system has been focused. Using this method, once a position is accessed, each instrument is rapidly focused one after another. As an example, focusing a sequential series of instruments on an overhead electric may result in focusing a downlight, followed by a backlight, then a frontlight, then a special, and so on. Since each instrument is focused "out of context," overall decisions about the individual focus and the shape of each instrument in a system have to be determined before the focus begins. Consider the process that occurs to focus a single instrument:

1. The instrument's unit number (position identity) is determined.
2. Referencing that unit number to the instrument schedule, the corresponding channel number is identified and communicated to the console operator.
3. The channel number is activated, and the instrument turned on.
4. The assigned purpose of the instrument is communicated to the lighting designer.

Hybrid Theatre 2010   **HOKEY GROUP LIST**   Date: 2/13/10

Grp	Lvl	System	CHANNELS																		Grp
1	Full	R33 Front	1	>	10																1
2	Full	L161 Front	11	>	20																2
3	Full	SR R51>>	21	>	24																3
4	Full	SL R51<<	25	>	28																4
5	Full	SR R64>>	41	>	44																5
6	Full	SL R64<<	45	>	48																6
7	Full	R20 Down	61	>	70																7
8	Full	L124 Down	71	>	80																8
9	Full	NC Back	81	>	90																9
10	Full	R68 Back	91	>	100																10
11	Full	Lav Boom	31	>	38																11
12	Full	Blue Boom	101	>	108																12
13	Full	Mids	109	>	114																13
14	Full	Shins	115	>	122																14
15	Full	Templates	51	>	54																15
16	Full	Specials	55	>	60																16
17	Full	All Cyc	130	>	135																17
18	Full	All FOH	1	>	5	11	>	15	29	30	39	40	49	50	58	59	60	137	138	18
19	Full	All US	6	>	10	16	>	20	21	>	28	31	>	38						19
			41	>	48	51	>	57	61	>	122	126	>	136						
20	30	Warmup	1	>	122	126	>	138	@	30										20
21	Full	Truss	1	>	5	11	>	15	58	59	60									21
22	Full	SL Bx Bm	30	40	50															22
23	Full	SR Bx Bm	29	39	49															23
24	Full	1 Elec	6	7	8	16	17	18	21	25	41	45	51	55						24
25	Full	2 Elec	9	10	19	20	22	26	42	46	52	61	>	65	71	>	75			25
26	Full	3 Elec	81	>	85	91	>	95												26
27	Full	4 Elec	23	27	43	47	53	66	>	70	76	>	80							27
28	Full	5 Elec	24	28	44	48	54	57	86	>	90	96	>	100						28
29	Full	6 E/Grndrw	130	>	135															29
30	Full	SL Sides	35	>	38	105	>	108	112	>	114	119	>	122						30
31	Full	SR Sides	31	>	34	101	>	104	109	>	111	115	>	118						31

Expression 3; 150 chan, 174 dim   Lighting by Steve Shelley 917.xxx.xxxx   Page 1 of 1

Figure 8.18 A Partial Group List for *Hokey*

5. The lighting designer considers the assigned purpose of the light beam to the reality of the situation, determining any adaptation that must take place in order to produce the overall desired result.

6. The lighting designer then directs the focusing electrician to point and shape the instrument's light.

7. When the light is focused to the designer's satisfaction, the next instrument's unit number is determined.

Since the time required to physically point and shape each instrument will vary for each unit, accelerating a focus session often starts by considering other surrounding variables. All methods or tactics that might reduce the time between the first instrument being completed and the next instrument being touched by the focusing electrician should be considered. Methods that rapidly define and communicate each instrument's channel and focus point to the lighting designer can be used to expedite that portion of the process. If the focus is expected to be repeated in the future, a written system is also needed to notate the finished focus of each instrument.

Since most focuses are performed in sequential hanging position order, the format of an instrument schedule is most often used to conduct the sessions. That format also allows the channel numbers for adjacent instruments to be rapidly identified. In the *Hokey* instrument schedule, a general focus is indicated in the "purpose" column, but quickly defining and communicating each instrument's specific focus point speeds the process between each light.

When the *Hokey* light plot was created, the section was used to define the up- and downstage coverage between the zones for the different systems. Front elevations determined side-to-side beam coverage and hanging placement between the instruments in each zone. Using those documents as a benchmark, the up- and downstage placement of the focus points can be measured from the section, while the left and right focus points can be measured from the front elevations.

Specifying those focus points on the stage often begins by dividing the stage into a grid. The reference line typically used is centerline, in order to define the playing area depth. The second reference line is usually perpendicular to centerline, and measured out to either side. So the usual tactic again is to start the measurements from groundplan zero. Measuring tapes or strips of jute webbing with distances marked in large numerals are attached to the stage, pinned at groundplan zero and stretched up and down on centerline, and to either side on plaster line. The next step is to translate the focus point coordinates for each system or special into documents that are easy to read.

One way to quickly communicate these focus points on stage is a list of written measurements, but for some they can be confusing, relatively easy to create mistakes, and not easy to double-check. Most folks instead prefer to instead use a series of pictographs. **Focus point groundplans** are often chosen as the fastest method to establish a focus point reference framework.

Focus Point Groundplans

Focus point groundplans contain the measurements that become reference marks on the performance surface. These marks combine to establish a framework that defines the playing area and focus points for light systems. When these marks are measured and placed onstage, they typically translate into different colors of cloth-backed tape called **spike marks**. Separate scenic groundplans are often used to measure out a second set of marks, indicating scenic or properties placement in a multi-scene production. Those situations quickly evolve into multi-color coded spike mark systems that can cover the floor. While the color-coding attempts to reduce confusion as to the identity or purpose of any given mark, the stage can quickly fill up with so many multi-colored dots and dashes that it quickly resembles an airport runway gone rogue.

Figure 8.19 shows the perimeters and spike marks indicated in the **performance area groundplan**. Defining the performance width starts at centerline. The onstage edge of the black masking legs are measured 18'-0" on either side of centerline. Dividing that distance in half defines the placement for the "quarter line" spikes, 9'-0" on either side of centerline.

In an effort to control the amount of spike tape, these spike marks are shown only at the up- and downstage edge of the lighting boundaries, the light lines. To avoid confusion, these spike marks are often assembled like the letter "T". The downstage T's labeled DSR quarter, DC, and DSL quarter will also define the downstage light line. The upstage T's labeled USR quarter, UC, and USL quarter serve the same purpose on the upstage side of the stage.

The distance from the downstage light line to the upstage light line is measured on centerline and divided by 2. That point is center-center, indicated with an "X" to distinguish it as the center-center point of the performance area.

Now that the performance area has been segmented into a grid, the rest of the lighting groundplans will indicate spike marks that will define focus points. During a focus, the lighting designer may be standing on a focus spike mark, but the hot spot of the instrument's beam is actually pointed toward the designer's head. If the show being focused involves a cast of tall performers, the short lighting designer may need to stand on tiptoe, a box, or take a short step away from the light beam in order to provide accurate focus points.

Figure 8.20 shows the first focus point groundplan, constructed for the frontlight system. In the *Hokey* light plot, each frontlight system consists of three zones. The section showed that the focus points for the three zones will be at 3'-0", 10'-0", and 16'-0" upstage of plaster line. The beam section illustrated

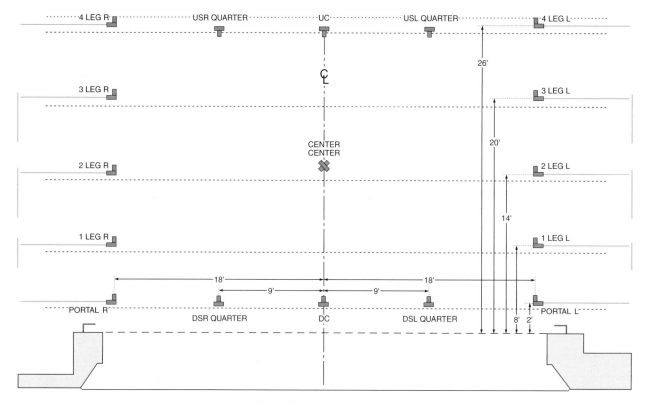

Figure 8.19 The Performance Area Groundplan for *Hokey*

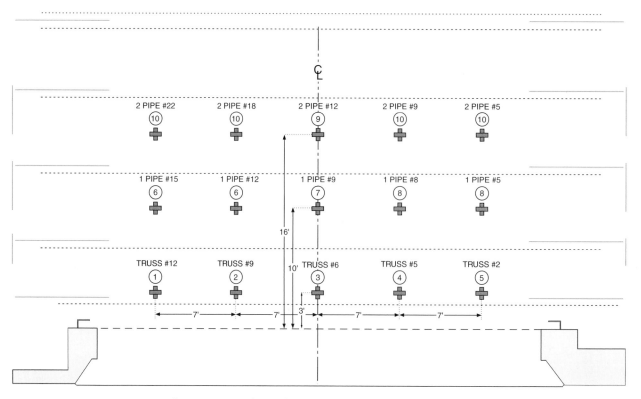

Figure 8.20 The *Hokey* Frontlight Focus Point Groundplan

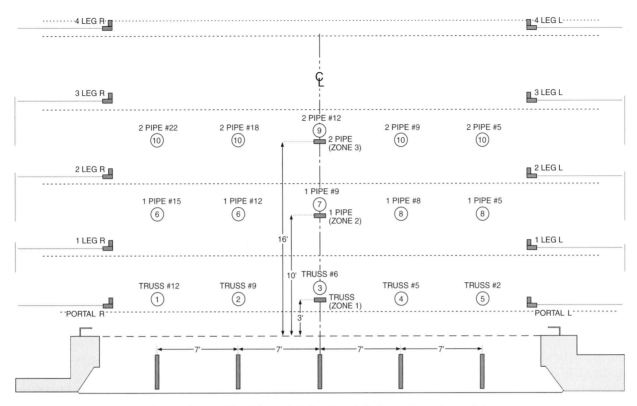

Figure 8.21 The Adjusted *Hokey* Frontlight Focus Point Groundplan

that the beam pools sufficiently overlapped, so the focus points are placed 7'-0" apart. These measurements are triangulated and marked with "plus" signs on the groundplan. The lighting designer will stand on each "+" to provide a target for the specified unit.

The channel number in each circle corresponds to the position and unit number indicated directly above it. These are the 15 instruments collectively assigned to the Roscolux 33 frontlight system. These spike marks will also be used as the focus points for the Lee 161 frontlight system.

Since focus points for other lighting systems will be in different locations on the stage, the prospect of placing a single spike mark for each focus point in each system can suddenly become a daunting task to consider—not to mention the amount of time and energy required. Even a multi-colored system of spike marks could quickly become confusing during the haste of a focus call. To reduce the possibility of confusion, the number of spike marks on the stage (and the amount of time required to place them) needs to be kept to a minimum.

Upon review, the 15 spike marks are based on five 7'-0" wide measurements, which are duplicated three times (for each of the three zones). Instead of the 15 marks, five pieces of tape on the apron can be used to establish the width measurements, while three

pieces of tape on centerline can be used to establish the zone measurements.

Figure 8.21 illustrates this plan: five long strips on the apron indicate the 7'-0" distance between each focus point, and three small pieces of tape measured on centerline define the depth location for each zone. During focus, the lighting designer will triangulate between the strips of tape on the apron, or apron strips, and the centerline pieces, to determine the X and Y coordinates of each focus point and stand in the right spot. The apron strips are longer, so they can still be seen when the designer is standing upstage in the third zone. (It will also be seen that the apron stripes will be useful for other lighting systems; their larger size will speed recognition of the distances for both the lighting designer and the focusing electrician.) While this system requires more thought, it reduces the amount of spike tape on the performance surface to eight pieces. More than that, it significantly reduces the amount of time required to measure and place them. Now that this system is in place, the remaining focus point groundplans can be separately created. Then they can all be combined, in order to see the overall number and placement of spike marks. Doing so will allow patterns to emerge, and reduce the overall amount of time required to place these marks before the focus session.

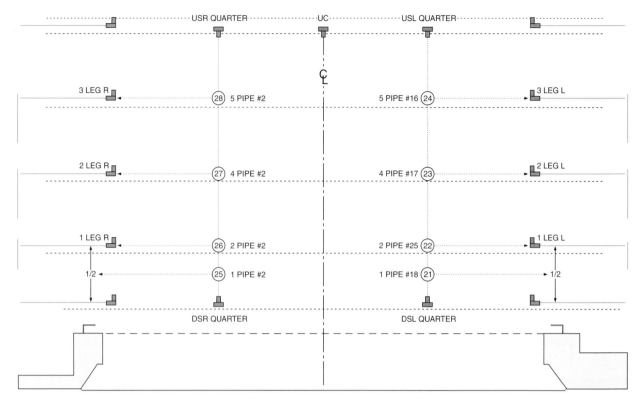

Figure 8.22 The *Hokey* Pipe End Sidelight Focus Point Groundplan

Figure 8.22 shows the triangulated focus point groundplan for the Roscolux 51 lavender pipe end system, assigned to channels 21 > 28. The instruments will focus across centerline to the far quarter line mark on the opposite side of the stage. To define the depth placement, the focus points are triangulated between the far quarter line spike marks and the black masking legs. Because it is a visual triangulation, there's no need for additional spike marks. These are the same focus points that will be used to focus the Roscolux 64 blue pipe end system, assigned to channels 41 > 48.

Figure 8.23 is the focus point groundplan for the no color template system, assigned to channels 51 > 54. The eight instruments (four on each side) have been plotted so that the focused system will produce a full stage template wash. The quarter lines and the masking legs define the offstage focus points. Rather than focus directly at center, the near focus points will cross-focus and overlap to blend with the offstage beams.

Figure 8.24 is the focus point groundplan for the Roscolux 20 amber downlight system, assigned to channels 61 > 70. The section placed the focus points for these two zones at 8'-6" and 16'-0" upstage of plaster line, so two pieces of spike tape will be placed on centerline at those two measurements. Since the five instruments are equidistantly plotted in each zone, the left-and-right distances can also be defined

by the 7'-0" apron strip spike marks that were originally laid down for the frontlight system. These same focus points will also be used for the Lee 124 downlight system, assigned to channels 71 > 80.

Figure 8.25 is the focus point groundplan for the no color backlight system, assigned to channels 81 > 90. The section placed the focus points for these two zones at 5'-6" and 18'-0" upstage of plaster line, so two more pieces of spike tape will be placed on centerline at those two measurements. Again, since the five instruments are equidistantly plotted in each zone, the left and right distances will be determined by the frontlight apron strip spike marks. These focus points will also be used for the Gam 850 backlight system, assigned to channels 91 > 100.

Figure 8.26 is the focus point groundplan for one side of the Roscolux 51 boom sidelight system, assigned to channels 35 > 38. The focus points are triangulated between the near quarter line and the opposite black masking legs. Since this is a visual triangulation, there's no need for additional spike marks. The preliminary plan is to use these focus points for each system of boom sidelight.

Figure 8.27 combines of all the focus point groundplans into a single document. While the other groundplans can be stored in the back of the notebook with the rest of the archives, this document will live in the front of the book in a plastic page protector,

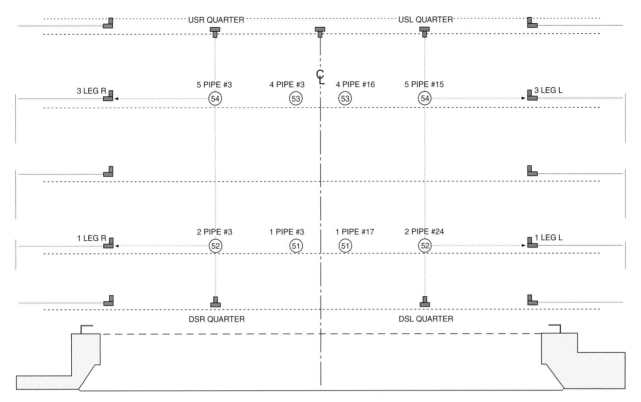

Figure 8.23 The *Hokey* Overhead Template Focus Point Groundplan

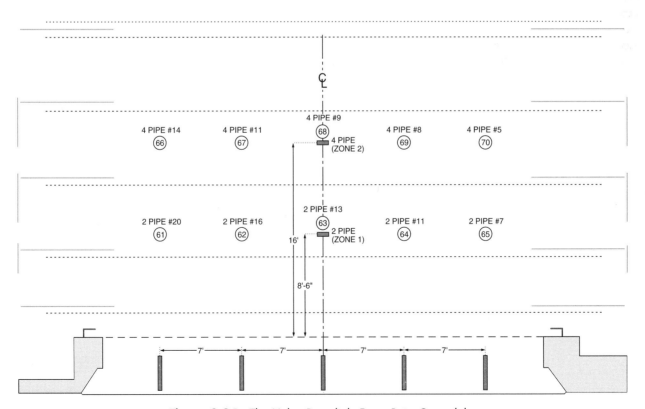

Figure 8.24 The *Hokey* Downlight Focus Point Groundplan

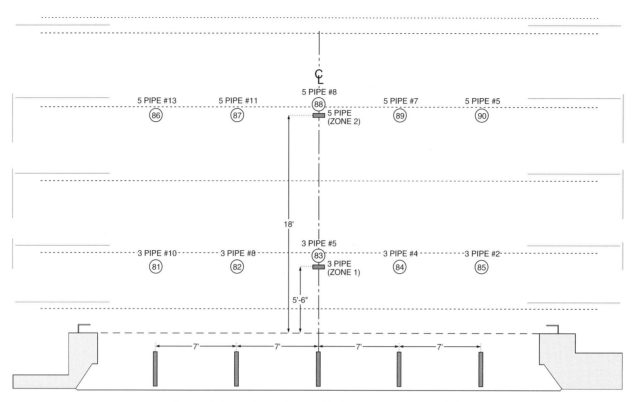

Figure 8.25 The *Hokey* Backlight Focus Point Groundplan

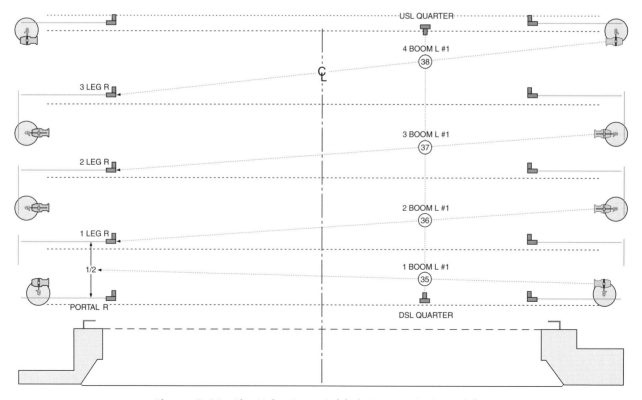

Figure 8.26 The *Hokey* Boom Sidelight Focus Point Groundplan

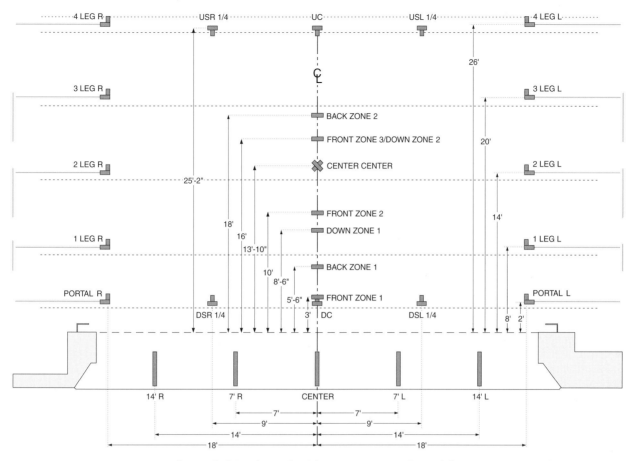

Figure 8.27 The *Hokey* Master Focus Point Groundplan

Focus Charts

ready to be used during load-in to rapidly spike the stage for the focus session.

Once the reference grid of focus point groundplans is established, it becomes a communication framework that defines the location of any light beam focused within its boundaries (in 2, 14′ Right, for example). The focus points can then be written on a reference document that will provide this information to the lighting designer during the focus session. This document may be altered versions of other paperwork, or it may be a unique document the lighting designer has in hand. Since the lighting designer typically moves around the stage establishing the focus points, regardless of what is used as a reference document, it needs to be compact, easy to read, and provide the ability to quickly cross-reference to other hanging positions in the light plot.

Since the focus session typically proceeds sequentially through each hanging position, some designers merely use a copy of the **instrument schedule**. This is often the focus document used if the designer can quickly understand the focus point location by translating the written indication in the "purpose" column, or its equivalent. Reading "Warm Area 5" as a purpose, for example, might be processed internally like this: (*Area 5, that would be the first zone, 14′-0″ left of center. Move!*).

If the lighting designer is more comfortable seeing a graphic layout, the focus document may be the **light plot**. Some designers prefer the light plot because it's visually simpler to compare the focus between two instruments from the same system in different zones. If the lighting designer's familiar with the plot and has the focus firmly in mind, he or she may merely make shorthand notes for specials. If the focus involves extensive scenery or numerous scenes, every note necessary to point and shape each light may be handwritten directly on the map. Doing so attempts to eliminate any need to refer to other paperwork. Depending on the complexity and scale size of the drawing, however, it may be difficult to handwrite or read all of the information so that it can easily be seen.

Figure 8.28 shows the stage left half of the FOH truss from the *Hokey* light plot with focus notes indicated above each instrument. Using the light plot

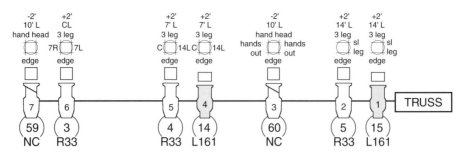

Figure 8.28 The Stage Left *Hokey* Truss with Focus Notes

graphically shows the designer the focus, color, and channel number. Presenting it in this arrangement attempts to speed the time between the activation of each channel and the physical pointing of the instrument. If handwritten focus notes will be required for every instrument, this version of the plot will need some amount of preparation time.

On the other hand, if the plan from the get-go is to use the light plot as the focus document, the drawing can be created with that in mind. Each unit's axis on the drafting can indicate not only the instrument's pre-hung direction, it can also telegraph the lighting instrument's system to the lighting designer. If the symbol's lens is pointed upstage, it is often then interpreted that the instrument will be focused as straight frontlight. Instruments drawn at a 45° angle toward the top of the document can represent area or diagonal frontlight. Lenses drawn sideways at 90° are usually sidelight, while lenses drawn straight down, toward the bottom of the document, often represent backlight or downlight. Finally, symbols drawn with lenses at a 45° angle toward the bottom of the page can represent diagonal backlight. Instruments

earmarked to be focused as specials can have dots or squares or other matching marks near the symbol to indicate their "special-ness" and visually make them "pop out" from the systems. The *Hokey* light plot is drawn in this manner, except that the specials are instead assigned a piece of additional text to remind the lighting designer of the special's location or purpose.

While this graphic method works for some lighting designers, others find a graphic presentation of the focus confusing. When that's the case, an adaptation of the instrument schedule can be used, presenting the same focus information in a spreadsheet layout known as a **focus schedule**.

Figure 8.29 shows the same instruments in the *Hokey* truss detailed for the same focus as before, but this time presented in a focus schedule format. To provide some visual separation, this version of the document is divided into three information groups: the database information (position, unit number, circuit, dimmer, channel), the instrument information (purpose or focus, unit type, wattage, color, notes), and the focus information. The X axis of each focus

Hybrid Theatre 2010   **HOKEY FOCUS SCHEDULE**   Date: 4/7/10

Pos	#	Cir	Dim	Chan	Purpose	Type	Watt	Color	Notes	U/D	L/R	Lens	Top	Bot	Left	Right	Pos	#
Truss	1	A-1	175	15	Cool Area 5	Alt 6 x 12	1kw	L161	Tophat	+2'	14'L	Med	3 Leg	Edge	7'L	SL Leg	Truss	1
Truss	2	A-2	174	5	Warm Area 5	Source 4-26°	575w	R33	Tophat	+2'	14'L	Med	3 Leg	Edge	7'L	SL Leg	Truss	2
Truss	3	A-3	173	60	DL Special	Source 4-19°	575w	NC	Tophat	-2'	10'L	Soft					Truss	3
Truss	4	A-4	172	14	Cool Area 4	Alt 6 x 12	1kw	L161	Tophat	+2'	7'L	Med	3 Leg	Edge	C	14'L	Truss	4
Truss	5	A-5	171	4	Warm Area 4	Source 4-26°	575w	R33	Tophat	+2'	7'L	Med	3 Leg	Edge	C	14'L	Truss	5
Truss	6	B-1	170	3	Warm Area 3	Source 4-26°	575w	R33	Tophat	+2'	C	Med	3 Leg	Edge	7'R	7'L	Truss	6
Truss	7	B-2	169	59	DC Special	Source 4-19°	575w	NC	Tophat	-2'	C	Soft					Truss	7
Truss	8	B-3	168	13	Cool Area 3	Alt 6 x 12	1kw	L161	Tophat	+2'	C	Med	3 Leg	Edge	7'R	7'L	Truss	8
Truss	9	B-4	167	2	Warm Area 2	Source 4-26°	575w	R33	Tophat	+2'	7'R	Med	3 Leg	Edge	C	14'R	Truss	9
Truss	10	B-5	166	12	Cool Area 2	Alt 6 x 12	1kw	L161	Tophat	+2'	7'R	Med	3 Leg	Edge	C	14'R	Truss	10
Truss	11	C-1	165	58	DR Special	Source 4-19°	575w	NC	Tophat	-2'	10'R	Soft					Truss	11
Truss	12	C-2	164	1	Warm Area 1	Source 4-26°	575w	R33	Tophat	+2'	14'R	Med	3 Leg	Edge	7'R	SR Leg	Truss	12
Truss	13	C-3	163	11	Cool Area 1	Alt 6 x 12	1kw	L161	Tophat	+2'	14'R	Med	3 Leg	Edge	7'R	SR Leg	Truss	13

Expression 3; 150 chan, 174 dim   Lighting design by Steve Shelley 917.xxx.xxxx   Page 1 of 7

Figure 8.29 The *Hokey* Truss Focus Schedule

point is listed in the "U/D" (upstage/downstage) column, while the *Y* axis is shown in the "L/R" (left/right) column. The "Lens" column tells the designer the sharpness of the beam edge, while the remaining four columns list the position of any shutters or barndoors.

One of this format's advantages is that, in addition to the focus information, all of the lighting database information is also included as well. This means that when something doesn't work during the focus, the lighting designer has just about everything immediately at hand in order to quickly troubleshoot the problem. There's no need to go digging in the production bag to find the instrument schedule or channel hookup. One downside to this format is that, to be a truly functional troubleshooting document, it can't be printed until the on-site database information is known. Printing the document with the wrong dimmer or circuitry numbers may not be a terrible thing, but it might add confusion to the mix when a problem's encountered and the wrong information is at hand. In many load-in situations, though, there may be a meal break, or an overnight rest period, between completing the light plot's hang and the focus. If the document is fully filled out prior to the load-in, then the only information that needs to be filled in might be changes in circuitry and dimming information. Presuming a quick printer's at hand, producing an accurate version of this document at the last minute, before the focus session begins, is not as impossible as it might seem.

Although methods have been discussed that define the focus points, and different forms have been examined to speed communication, there is no question that the focus will undoubtedly change in the performance space. As a matter of fact, on-site conditions may force extensive alteration to the focus of every instrument ("Gee, I don't remember seeing those house chandeliers during the advance"). There may not be time or room to keep track of those changes on the focus document.

For that matter, there may be those times when the focus is completely unknown until the instrument is turned on. ("Tom, what's the focus for that light?" "Hmm. I don't know, Steve, turn it on and let me see…"). In those kinds of situations, a separate written journal documenting the focus information for each instrument or electrical device may not be just a good idea, it may be the life jacket needed to hold on to sanity in the sea of chaos.

Focus Charts from Scratch

Focus charts are a written "snapshot" of the direction, beam edge, and shape of each lighting instrument in the light plot. Preparing and utilizing these documents can require some amount of time and effort. Before focus charts are produced, the need for their existence should be carefully judged.

The first question to be asked is this: Will this production (or any facet of it) ever have another life? If the production is a fund-raising benefit, for example, it may consist of pieces taken out of context and adapted to this singular performance. If the pieces already have a lighting design, the need to produce detailed focus charts may be unnecessary. If the benefit consists of pieces that have never existed before, however, there may be a possibility that one of the pieces may be performed again based on these light cues and this focus. In that case, the need for focus charts should be reconsidered.

In another scenario, if an entire production has never existed before, the possibility of a future incarnation of any portion of the show must be determined. That, of course, then requires the ability to see into the future, and know if a show will become that brilliant moment in the designer's career, or just another notch on the bedpost of lighting design experience. I've never figured it out—I've got focus charts for *lots* of shows in my file cabinet, still waiting for their next big break.

In any event, accurately analyzing light cues from an old show typically has to include information about the light cue coupled with accurate updated focus charts. With that in mind, if there's no doubt that this production has a short shelf life, then the focus can be approached as a once in a lifetime opportunity and save room in the file cabinet. On the other hand, experienced lighting designers can rattle off numerous "it will never be seen again" productions that have, of course, "returned from the dead." That being said, making the choice not to construct focus charts is a questionable one. If the personnel or time is available to record an original focus, it should be pursued.

The production's geographic location may also make the decision regarding the need for focus charts a simple one. If the theatre is located near a source of vibration such as a highway, a subway, a bridge, or an earthquake zone, the chance for instruments dropping out of focus is much greater. Audience reaction, such as stamping feet or clapping hands, may also cause vibration. If the show is performed outside, the additional element of weather strongly suggests that focus charts aren't a bad idea.

Other elements within the production may require the need for focus charts. If the possibility exists that scenery, costumes, properties, or performers may run into instruments during the course of a performance, the charts will be needed to check the focus of those instruments prior to each performance. A commercial production enjoying an extended run usually demands focus charts. In that situation, they're the reference document needed when instruments drop focus, get hit by scenery, need to be replaced, explode, or need to have the "focus broken" to replace burnouts. If the electrical staff changes over time during the course of the run and the lighting designer's not on site, the focus charts, coupled with the light cues, become precious elements required to maintain the original intent of the design. In most cases, focus charts become part of the archival packet once the show has opened. For all of these reasons, some focus charts in almost any sort have value. They should be constructed, filled out, and maintained.

All of the written information about the focus of each instrument usually won't fit onto a light plot, nor can it easily be recorded onto the instrument schedule. A separate focus chart format is strongly suggested in order to be certain that every action taken to each lighting instrument is accurately documented. Focus charts are usually sorted like an instrument schedule, grouping the units by hanging position, sequentially listing the numbered units, and listing all lighting database information. This allows the document to be used for troubleshooting without having to refer to a separate document.

Unlike an instrument schedule, however, the layout of focus charts often requires much more paper. In addition to including the lighting database information for each instrument, there needs to be enough room to manually fill out the form as the focus occurs.

As each instrument or electrical device is focused, a scribe simultaneously details each action applied to every unit. Often, focus charts utilize the reference gridwork to locate the focus point, and include places to note any movement of the barrel, lamp carriage, or shaping of the light beam.

As a focus proceeds, the channel-caller tells the board operator which channels to activate, while the scribe writes the actions taken to each instrument. At the completion of the call, these written "snapshots" of each instrument provide a description of the location of each light beam and how it was shaped. If time, or lack of personnel, doesn't permit the charts to be recorded during the focus, additional time may be necessary to perform the same function.

In addition to defining a structure in the choreography of the focus session, the scenic design may have a major impact on the appearance of focus charts. Multiple settings in a production may introduce the need for additional fields to inform the lighting designer of which scenery should be present when each instrument is focused.

One thing that must be included with a finished set of focus charts is a "key" explaining any focusing shorthand that was used while the focus was being recorded. Too often, old focus charts are brought out

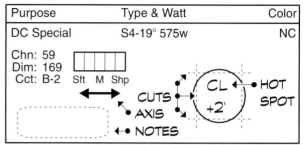

Figure 8.30 The *Hokey* Focus Key Cover Page

from the caverns for a revival only to find that they contain no information about the shorthand system that was used to record the focus.

Figure 8.30 is a compressed example of a focus key, which usually contains four sets of information. The most important note defines the "focus zero" placement—while the X axis is almost always on centerline, the Y axis may change, depending on the scribe's judgment. Some folks insist on using the groundplan zero-zero. In this case, the scribe has found it easier to merely attach the tape measure to the downstage edge. Usually there's no difference between the two, but if the focus key is lost, regenerating the focus from the distances in the notes (based on the wrong zero-zero) may cause confusion later in the process. The focus key usually also includes a graphic key to insure that each portion of the focus rectangle can be understood. A written example is sometimes included to provide an interpretation of the focus points. Finally, the vocabulary is listed to provide examples of all the written shorthand notations used during the focus.

Focus Chart Examples

Figure 8.31 is the first page of a focus chart for the same instruments in the truss position for *Hokey*. The document is broken into two sections. The top of the document includes the header, listing the name of the show, the position, and the title block information.

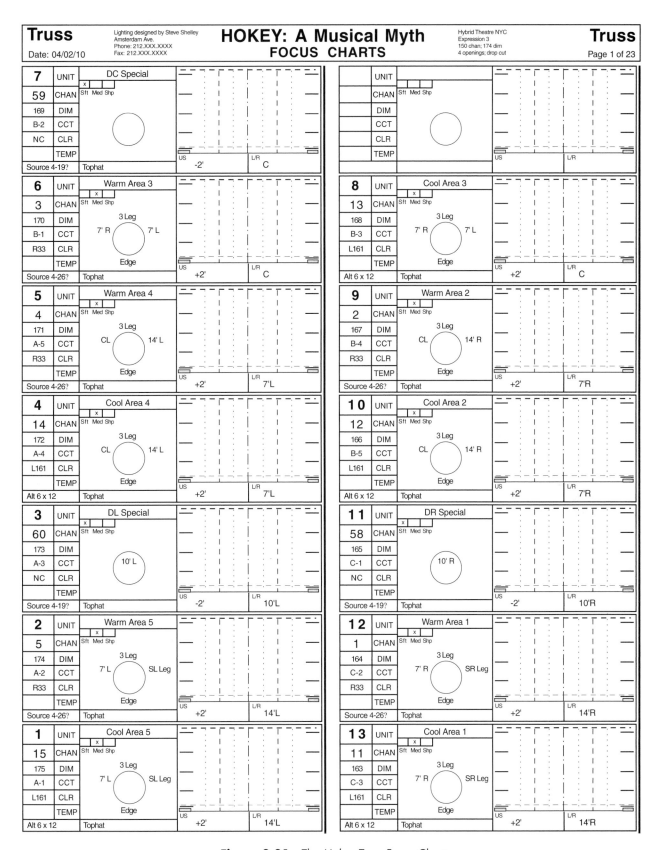

Truss

Date: 04/02/10

Lighting designed by Steve Shelley
Amsterdam Ave.
Phone: 212.XXX.XXXX
Fax: 212.XXX.XXXX

HOKEY: A Musical Myth
FOCUS CHARTS

Hybrid Theatre NYC
Expression 3
150 chan; 174 dim
4 openings; drop cut

Truss

Page 1 of 23

Figure 8.31 The *Hokey* Truss Focus Chart

Each large rectangle in Figure 8.31 represents a single instrument. Each rectangle is divided into three sections. The left side contains all of the lighting database information under the unit number. The right side shows a groundplan of the stage for any handwritten notes or for a drawing of the light beam's location. It also has space under the groundplan to indicate the X and Y coordinates of the focus point. The top of the middle section is the purpose or focus name of the instrument. Under that are boxes to check indicating the lens position (Soft, Medium, or Sharp). Under that a circle represents the beam of the instrument. Notes on the four sides indicate any shaping cuts anticipated with shutters or barndoors, usually drawn from the point of view of "behind" the instrument. During the focus session, lines will be drawn on the edges of the circle to indicate the true shaping of the beam.

The unit numbers on the left-hand side of the page start at the bottom and increase to the top of the page, wrap around and continue to increase down the right-hand side of the page. This is because unit 7 is on centerline, and the focus of the instruments often mirror each other. One side of the paper is the reverse of the other, in some cases allowing the focus of the instruments to match. When questions arise about the focus of the matching instrument on the opposite side of the hanging position, the eye can easily move across the page to retrieve the information.

Figure 8.32 is a different version of a focus chart for the same truss. It's the focus schedule from Figure 8.29, but it was printed out without any focus information included; all the focus information was added in by hand while the focus took place. While this format doesn't allow much room for any additional notes to be included, the form shouldn't be summarily dismissed. For a general open stage type of focus, in many cases, this form can be used without too much trouble. If the focus involves lighting lots of scenic units, drops, or different levels, however, there's very little room to allow for additional notation to be included.

These are two different layouts showing the same information presented in different ways. There are many other ways to present this information. Successful focus charts achieve two objectives; first, they are produced to include all of the lighting database information; the only manual marks required during the focus session are solely specific to how each light beam is pointed and shaped. Second, once filled out, the successful focus charts are simple to read, allowing the focus information to be quickly interpreted. The final design or presentation used for any focus chart is, as always, best left to the scribe who has to record it, or the person who has to maintain it.

Shelley's Notes: Digital Camera Focus Shots

There are other times when a picture really is worth a thousand words. Sometimes just looking at a picture of the focus, or the cue, is all that is really needed. Digital cameras now allow the focus to be quickly recorded as a series of digital photographs. Whether individual channels, moving light focus points, or special focuses cued into a show, the digital photo can be fed back into the laptop, and then converted to any number of different layouts.

Hybrid Theatre 2010   **HOKEY FOCUS SCHEDULE**   Date: 2/13/10

Pos	#	Cir	Dim	Chan	Purpose	Type	Watt	Color	Notes	U/D	L/R	Lens	Top	Bot	Left	Right	Pos	#
Truss	1	A-1	175	15	Cool Area 5	Alt 6 x 12	1kw	L161	Tophat	+2	14L	M	3LEG	EDGE	7'L	SLLEG	Truss	1
Truss	2	A-2	174	5	Warm Area 5	Source 4-26°	575w	R33	Tophat	+2	14L	M	3LEG	EDGE	7'L	SLLEG	Truss	2
Truss	3	A-3	173	60	DL Special	Source 4-19°	575w	NC	Tophat	-2	10L	S					Truss	3
Truss	4	A-4	172	14	Cool Area 4	Alt 6 x 12	1kw	L161	Tophat	+2	7L	M	3LEG	EDGE	C	14'L	Truss	4
Truss	5	A-5	171	4	Warm Area 4	Source 4-26°	575w	R33	Tophat	+2	7L	M	3LEG	EDGE	C	14'L	Truss	5
Truss	6	B-1	170	3	Warm Area 3	Source 4-26°	575w	R33	Tophat	+2	C	M	3LEG	EDGE	7R	7L	Truss	6
Truss	7	B-2	169	59	DC Special	Source 4-19°	575w	NC	Tophat	+2	C	S					Truss	7
Truss	8	B-3	168	13	Cool Area 3	Alt 6 x 12	1kw	L161	Tophat	+2	C	M	3LEG	EDGE	7R	7L	Truss	8
Truss	9	B-4	167	2	Warm Area 2	Source 4-26°	575w	R33	Tophat	+2	7R	M	3LEG	EDGE	C	14R	Truss	9
Truss	10	B-5	166	12	Cool Area 2	Alt 6 x 12	1kw	L161	Tophat	+2	7R	M	3LEG	EDGE	C	14R	Truss	10
Truss	11	C-1	165	58	DR Special	Source 4-19°	575w	NC	Tophat	-2	10R	S					Truss	11
Truss	12	C-2	164	1	Warm Area 1	Source 4-26°	575w	R33	Tophat	+2	14R	M	3LEG	EDGE	7R	SRLEG	Truss	12
Truss	13	C-3	163	11	Cool Area 1	Alt 6 x 12	1kw	L161	Tophat	+2	14R	M	3LEG	EDGE	7R	SRLEG	Truss	13

Expression 3; 150 chan, 174 dim   Lighting design by Steve Shelley 917.xxx.xxxx   Page 1 of 7

Figure 8.32   The *Hokey* Truss Spreadsheet Focus Chart

Figure 8.33 Digital Focus Photographs

Figure 8.33 shows three sample digital photos taken during a run-through of the channels (a **channel check**) for a presentation of Steve Reich's *The Cave*. These shots were imported into my laptop, cropped in GraphicConverter, and arranged in Vectorworks. These kinds of photos can be taken at the conclusion of the focus session, or during any of the other channel checks made as the system is being "booted up." Merely position the digital camera in the center of the house and snap a photo as each channel is activated during the channel check. In this case, the platforms and shutter cuts were complex, so in order to "see down" into the set, the photos were taken from the balcony perspective instead. Once the shots are assembled, they can be sorted in channel hookup or instrument schedule order. It's worth noting that while the photos are being taken, they should remain in order. Without some kind of placard or sign declaring the channel number, out-of-sequence photos can quickly make this task confusing.

Digital photographs or digital videos have become the method of choice to provide this kind of archival documentation for moving lights. I've found that taking the photos in black and white makes the contrast easier to see and it eliminates the need for a color printer to print the hard copy once the pictures are assembled. With proper contrast, a tripod, and the right amount of time, this visual diary can be imported into a Lightwright document, or become a separate archival storage device. The use and applications for this type of focus documentation are only beginning to be explored. While this can become an invaluable addition to the focus diary, be careful; it can easily expand into a much larger project than originally intended.

SUMMARY

Once the load-in and focus paperwork packet has been created, attention can turn to the packet of information that will be used to create and document the light cues and effects for the production.

Chapter 9

The Cue Construction Packet

INTRODUCTION

Once the instruments in the lighting package are focused it becomes a functional lighting system. This next paperwork packet facilitates and documents the creation of the lighting cues. The **magic sheet** is a concentrated map that graphically represents the entire light plot, and acts as an information receptacle to write any other useful information while the light cues are being constructed. The **cheat sheet** is a concentrated channel hookup that identifies the instruments in their dimmer or channel order. The **cue master** is a constantly evolving document based on the preliminary list used to originally create the light plot. Regardless of its current state, the cue master's purpose is to accurately reflect the current purpose and attributes of each light cue, and keep track of the progression of light changes for the show.

Board operator sheets, followspot cue sheets, and **repatch sheets** record the tasks assigned to other members of the electrics department. A set of forms may be used to monitor the status of the light cues and the lighting package as the design evolves, which include **light cue sheets, cue track sheets,** and **work note sheets.** Altogether, this paperwork packet assists in the creation, implementation, and documentation of the lighting cues for the production.

While each of these documents has separate purposes and goals, their design and intent are for speed. They're either quick-glance or quick-fill-in reference tools, whose objective is for them to be easily read and clearly understood. Successful versions of these documents allow the designer's eyes to spend as much time as possible looking at the stage and the cue, and as little as possible at any of the paper. Since the typical production table is inevitably cramped, the paperwork's also designed to be as compact, and when possible, combined. Keeping the overall number of documents needed on the table to the absolute minimum means that much less space is needed to simultaneously see all relevant information. The right combination of enough room at the production table, and few enough documents that fit onto it, means the designer's eyes can quickly refer to all necessary information without distractions scanning the table or un-piling stacks of paper to retrieve other information.

THE MAGIC SHEET

The magic sheet is the tool that compresses the entire lighting package into a single graphic map, combining focus locations, color, and control channel for every lighting instrument or electrical device involved in the lighting package. From an artistic point of view, the magic sheet is one view of the lighting designer's palette, showing the designer all of the components available to paint each stage picture. While an artist uses a palette to mix colors for the canvas, the lighting designer consults the magic sheet to identify channels of colored light that can be mixed on the stage. The difference is that, while an artist can stare at a canvas all day, the lighting designer may have only a brief moment in the present to view, analyze, and fix *that* look before it changes to the next cue.

For that reason, a magic sheet's success often lies in its layout, and how closely that mirrors the cognitive and subconscious recognition process of that particular lighting designer. And there are as many ways to construct a magic sheet as there are to design lights. In order to quickly scan the document and find the right channel number, most designers insist that they have to create each magic sheet themselves. As such, the magic sheet is usually viewed as the most personal document that expresses the lighting designer, next to the lighting design itself.

From a practical point of view, on the other hand, the magic sheet is the repository of all pertinent information required to create the light cues, along with any other information needed during the cueing process. Operators' names, scene lists, repeated sequences, and programming language are all examples of handwritten notes that may be added to the sheet during the cueing process. Any scrap of information that needs to be close at hand during the cueing process is fair game to be written onto the magic sheet.

The Magic Sheet Layout

Figure 9.1 is the *Hokey* magic sheet, which is an updated and expanded version of the preliminary magic sheet used in the first stage of the lighting design as one of the three core design documents. It's now been made official by reflecting the hookup of the show in this expanded graphic format. This completed version of the document is made up of three main areas. The top two-thirds of the page is devoted to all channel and device information. The bottom left-hand side of the page contains the submaster assignments, and the bottom right-hand portion of the page lists all of the group information.

Since the channel information will be referred to most often, it's listed on the top of the page. The submaster and group areas list the current state of their contents. Additional diamonds are left open in the group area, providing a place to write future channel combinations.

The channel information area is made up of small copies of the show's groundplan. The channel numbers on each groundplan refer to the hot spots of instruments focused on those locations. The diamond under each groundplan is the group number assigned to that entire system. The phrase under the diamond identifies the name and color of that group and system in the *Hokey* light plot.

The layout of *Hokey*'s magic sheet arranges the different systems of light in the same relationship as their location on the light plot. Using this layout means the eye is visually scanning the same relative area on the page as the light plot or the stage. The top of the page shown in Figure 9.1 shows the two backlight systems in No Color and Gam 850 (channels 81

> 90 and 91 > 100). Under the backlights are groundplans for the downlight systems, colored in Roscolux 20 and Lee 124 (channels 61 > 70 and channels 71 > 80). The two multi-rectangle boxes under the downlight are the channel numbers for the sidelight boom units. The bottom row of rectangles belongs to the first boom stage right (channels 31, 101, 109, and 115) and the first boom stage left (channels 35, 105, 112, and 119). Moving upward, each higher row identifies the channel numbers for each successive boom on either side of the stage.

All of the boom sidelight is assigned to group 40, shown by the large diamond just above and between the two sidelight rectangles. Underneath group 40 are a series of small diamonds indicating smaller groups for each opening. All instruments on the first boom, on both sides of the stage, are combined into group 41. These groups continue up to group 44, which controls all instruments on the fourth boom left and right. Another series of small diamonds indicate smaller groups for each system on the booms. To the left of group 40, a small diamond containing group 11 controls all of the top instruments on both sides of the stage, colored in Roscolux 51. Each system is assigned to its own group, ending with the shin in group 14. Activating groups 11 through 14, one at a time, will control each system of sidelight, while groups 41 through 44 control each opening of sidelight.

Below the multi-rectangle sidelight boxes are two groundplans showing the two frontlight systems in Roscolux 33 and Lee 161 (channels 1 > 10 and 11 > 20). While group 1 will activate the Roscolux 33 fronts, group 2 will activate the Lee 161 frontlight. Under the frontlight groundplans are a series of small circles with arrows. These refer to the box boom instruments (channels 29, 30, 39, 40, 49, and 50) listing their three respective colors.

On the top right-hand side, the two sets of rectangles are the channel numbers controlling the lighting behind the translucency. The top threesome with a vertical line on either side are essentially the same symbol as the groundrow striplights (channels 134 > 136), while the threesome underneath indicate the MR-16's hung on the sixth overhead electric (channels 131 > 133). The color is listed under each channel to prevent confusion. The two groundplans underneath the striplight rectangles contain a series of curves, which reverse and repeat on the opposite side of the page. These all refer to the pipe and systems (channels 21 > 28 and 41 > 48). The curves show the approximate location of each channel's beam edge once the instruments are focused.

Underneath the pipe end groundplans on the right side of the page is a groundplan containing circles and arrows. This groundplan shows the approximate

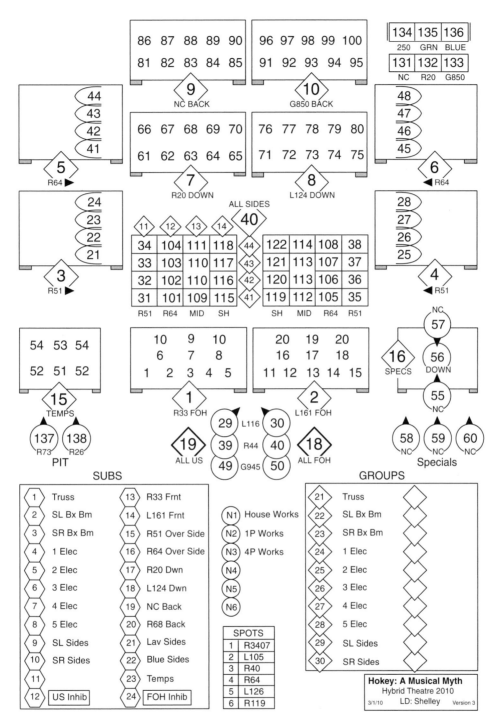

Figure 9.1 The Magic Sheet for *Hokey*

focus and location for all of the specials included in the light plot. For example, channel 57 will be focused as a No Color backlight to center-center, channel 56 will be focused as a downlight to the same area, while channel 55 will illuminate that area of the stage from a frontlight position. Finally, the groundplan on the opposite side of the page shows the approximate focus for the overhead template system (channels 51 > 54).

It's worth noting that the single-digit group numbers have been assigned to the basic building blocks that are predicted to be used the most when creating the cues for *Hokey*. That said, once the cueing session begins, if another group seems to be getting used more often, there is nothing preventing the lighting designer from reassigning group numbers, so that the single-digit groups are the ones used most often. •

While the physical layout of the document could be expanded a bit more, like using larger fonts or increasing the size of the miniature groundplans, leaving white areas around the perimeter of the document is a good thing. The open space can be used for handwritten reference notes that come up while creating or altering light cues, and reduce the need to refer to other documents. Because of those added notations, many designers make a copy of their updated magic sheet whenever they have the opportunity, and store it in a separate place other than their bag. Losing a magic sheet covered with scribbles in the middle of the tech process can be a serious blow; it's like losing a temporary friend.

THE CHEAT SHEET

The **cheat sheet** is the companion road map to the magic sheet. While the magic sheet sorts the dimmers or channels into graphic focus locations (right brain), the cheat sheet presents the same information as a compressed hookup (left brain). The purpose of the cheat sheet is to identify the contents and attributes of every handle or control channel in the same sequential order as the dimmer sliders or channels on the monitor display. When the designer doesn't recognize a channel number on the monitor display, the cheat sheet is the reference document that will identify what's in that channel.

When manual light boards couldn't be repositioned during technical rehearsals, and there was no remote monitor display at the production table, cheat sheets were often sorted by the dimmer number. In that scenario, it made sense to list the numbers in a vertical columnar format.

Figure 9.2 shows a partial cheat sheet using this basic format. The main intent was to show the dimmer number and the purpose. The color was also included to reiterate which system the dimmer belonged to. Since dimmers often moved together in groups, the color information often repeated in each row.

As spreadsheet applications grew more advanced, the ability to format cells provided more visual control over how information was presented in each cell.

Alignment, bold, and shading formats allowed cheat sheets to still list channels in a columnar format, but provide spatial information attributes somewhat like a magic sheet.

Figure 9.3 shows a partial example of the *Hokey* cheat sheet created in this format, using all of these additional formatting choices. The first column still indicates the channel, while the second column provides information about the color, along with the system or the hanging position. The third column spatially defines the channel's purpose; as the cell contents progress down the page, their left-to-right placement in the cell reflects where the instruments are focused left-to-right on the stage. In this way, the lighting designer can scan the second row in search of the color and then scan the third row to find the location. Channel 1 is focused downstage right, so its purpose is aligned to the left side of the cell. Channel 13 is focused down center, on the other hand, so its purpose is aligned to the center of the cell. Many lighting designers still use some variation of this format today.

HOKEY VERTICAL CHEAT SHEET

1	R33	DR		51	NC	>1C<
2		DRC		52	Temp	<1SD>
3		DC		53		>2C<
4		DLC		54		<1SD>
5		DL		55	NC	Frnt
6		MR		56	Pool	Dwn
7		CC		57		Bk
8		ML		58	NC	DR
9		UC		59	Truss	DC
10		UR UL		60		DL
11	161	DR		61	R20	DR
12		DRC		62	Down	DRC
13		DC		63		DC
14		DLC		64		DLC
15		DL		65		DL
16		MR		66		UR
17		CC		67		URC
18		ML		68		UC
19		UC		69		ULC
20		UR UL		70		UL
21	R51	SR> 1		71	124	DR
22		SR> 2		72	Down	DRC
23		SR> 3		73		DC
24		SR> 4		74		DLC
25		1 <SL		75		DL
26		2 <SL		76		UR
27		3 <SL		77		URC
28		4 <SL		78		UC
29	R51	<SL		79		ULC
30		SR>		80		UL

CH	Purpose	Color		CH	Purpose	Color
1	Warm DR	R33		51	Temps DC	NC
2	Warm DRC	R33		52	Temps DS	NC
3	Warm DC	R33		53	Temps UC	NC
4	Warm DLC	R33		54	Temps US	NC
5	Warm DL	R33		55	NC CC Pool Frnt	NC

Figure 9.2 A Partial Cheat Sheet for *Hokey* in Columnar Format

Figure 9.3 A Partial Spreadsheet Cheat Sheet for *Hokey* in Columnar Format

As computer lighting consoles have become the accepted norm in theatres, other lighting designers have changed the cheat sheet's layout to mimic the computer display. Almost all North American computer lighting consoles display channel numbers and intensity information in rows. In order to emulate that display, modern North American cheat sheets now commonly list channels in a horizontal format. Not only that, but they're now designed to specifically match the same number of channels on each row of the computer display; additional pages of channels on the monitor are often divided into separate rectangles of channels on the cheat sheet. The designer's eye moves from the spatial location on the monitor to the same spatial location on the paper.

When a new console is encountered, that often leads to a series of questions posed by the lighting department:

- The number of channels displayed on one row on the monitor screen?
- The total number of channels displayed on one monitor screen?
- Can the number of channels on a row be altered?
- Can the number of channels on one monitor screen be altered?

When a lighting console possesses the ability to change it's visual channel layout, the decision defining it's channel appearance is often "frozen" throughout the tech period. Otherwise, if the number of channels or their arrangement is changed on the monitor display after the paperwork has been produced, the ability of channels on the cheat sheet to mimic the same spatial location on the monitor display is lost.

Figure 9.4 is the cheat sheet for *Hokey*. It mirrors the computer monitor, displaying 25 channels per row. It also possesses additional rows of data in between the channel numbers, providing more information along with channel recognition. The text above each channel number indicates the channel's focus location on the stage. The text above the focus location indicates the channel's hanging location in the light plot. The letters at the top of each section of channels identifies the color and system name for that collection of channels. As an example, channel 1 is focused down right (DR), is hung on the truss (Truss), and is a portion of the Roscolux 33 frontlight system (R33 Front). In the case of sidelight, the "<" and ">" symbols are used to indicate the instrument's direction of origin. Double "<<" symbols are used to differentiate overhead sidelight.

Hybrid Theatre 2010   **HOKEY CHEAT SHEET**   Date: 2/13/10

R33 Front										L161 Front										R51>> Far 1/4				
TRUSS					1E			2E		FOH					1E			2E		1E	2E	4E	5E	1E
DR	DRC	DC	DLC	DL	MR	CC	ML	UC	Sd	DR	DRC	DC	DLC	DL	MR	CC	ML	UC	Sd	in1>	in2>	in3>	in4>	<in1
1	2	3	4	5	6	7	8	9	10	11	12	13	14	15	16	17	18	19	20	21	22	23	24	25

Far 1/4 <<R51			L116 Bx		R51 Bm Near 1/4				Near 1/4 Bm R51				R44 Bx		R64>> Far 1/4				Far 1/4 <<R64				G945 Bx	
2E	4E	5E													1E	2E	4E	5E	1E	2E	4E	5E		
<in2	<in3	<in4	>SR	SL<	in1>	in2>	in3>	in4>	<in1	<in2	<in3	<in4	>SR	SL<	in1>	in2>	in3>	in4>	<in1	<in2	<in3	<in4	>SR	SL<
26	27	28	29	30	31	32	33	34	35	36	37	38	39	40	41	42	43	44	45	46	47	48	49	50

Templates				NC Cen Pools			NC Spec			R20 Downs										L124 Downs DS				
1E	2E	4E	5E				Truss					2E					4E					2E		
DC	Sd	UC	Sd	1P	3P	5P	SR	C	SL	DR	DRC	DC	DLC	DL	UR	URC	UC	ULC	UL	DR	DRC	DC	DLC	DL
51	52	53	54	55	56	57	58	59	60	61	62	63	64	65	66	67	68	69	70	71	72	73	74	75

L124 Downs US					NC Backs										G850 Backs									
	4E					3E					5E					3E					5E			
UR	URC	UC	ULC	UL	DR	DRC	DC	DLC	DL	UR	URC	UC	ULC	UL	DR	DRC	DC	DLC	DL	UR	URC	UC	ULC	UL
76	77	78	79	80	81	82	83	84	85	86	87	88	89	90	91	92	93	94	95	96	97	98	99	100

R64 Bm Near 1/4				Near 1/4 Bm R64				Mids SR			Mids SL			Shins SR				Shins SL				Time Stamp		
in1>	in2>	in3>	in4>	<in1	<in2	<in3	<in4	in1>	2|3>	in4>	<in1	<2|3	<in4	in1>	in2>	in3>	in4>	<in1	<in2	<in3	<in4	Mon	Date	Year
101	102	103	104	105	106	107	108	109	110	111	112	113	114	115	116	117	118	119	120	121	122	123	124	125

Rovers				MR-16			Groundrow			Pit		Blackout Check											
DSL	USL	DSR	USR		NC	R20	G850	G250	Grn	Blue	R73	R26												
126	127	128	129	130	131	132	133	134	135	136	137	138	139	140	141	142	143	144	145	146	147	148	149	150

Expression 3; 150 chan, 174 dim   Lighting design by Steve Shelley 917.xxx.xxxx   Page 1 of 1

Figure 9.4 The *Hokey* Cheat Sheet

When the lighting designer sees a single channel by itself reading at a level of Full and can't remember what it is, or why it's currently turned on, this format of the cheat sheet provides a more complete explanation. If channel 118 is appearing on the screen at Full with no other channel intensities around it, the cheat sheet will inform the lighting designer that it's the shinbuster on the 4th boom stage right. Since the shinbuster's focus has no light hitting the floor, that explains why the designer can't see it. And if the performer isn't in the 4th wing, the shinbuster has nothing to do with the rest of the light cue. Channel 118 can be turned off for this cue and re-recorded.

THE CUE MASTER

The third document required to create light cues is the first core document created in the first stage of the lighting design, the **cue master**. Whether Post-it's stuffed into a score, dance track sheets covered with scribbles, doodles on a script, or printed-out spreadsheets, this document provides the lighting designer with the language of the show, and an updated record of the placement, speed, and purpose of each lighting change. No matter how messed up this document may become during the technical rehearsal process, the cue master needs to be constantly updated to somehow reflect on paper what's being produced as light cues or changes on the stage.

The cue master is also often used to communicate preliminary cue placement to the stage manager. In most cases, the stage manager wants this information recorded in his or her call book prior to the first technical rehearsal. Otherwise, more time may be spent in that first tech determining cue placement rather than figuring out how to make them run smoothly. Presuming the lighting designer and the stage manager are two different people, the appearance or structure of the cue master may need to be coordinated. Time constraints may be such that a meeting between the two prior to the first tech to discuss cue placement may not be possible. If the cue placement is recorded by the lighting designer in some format that can be passed on to the stage manager, the cues can be placed into the call book without the lighting designer's direct participation. Coordinating the cue master's format can reduce the amount of discussion necessary between the pair to transfer the information.

In the best of times, both folks will already know the general placement of many cues, since with luck they've watched run-through rehearsals together. In that situation, if a discussion about the timing or placement for a particular sequence in the show can't take place until the technical rehearsals begin, it won't be a major source of concern. When that doesn't take place, the stage manager may instead only get the designer's cue master the night before the tech to transfer numbers into the call book. While far from ideal, at least some cue numbers and a sense of their placement can still be sketched in before the long days of tech. If nothing else, it's still better than when the entire production team assembles at the production table for the first tech, and the stage manager asks: "So what number do I call to bring up the preset?"

The Spreadsheet Cue Master

Figure 9.5 is the expanded **spreadsheet cue master** for the opening scene of *Hokey*, version 5. While each cue may still not yet be named, a general description of each change or beat in the scene continues to be notated and updated. Each cue is listed on a single row with additional rows in between, giving extra space to still write in additional information. Some designers think it wise to triple space the cue master during initial light cue level setting sessions and technical rehearsals, when productions are particularly volatile or liquid. Rows will be eliminated in later versions, once the show settles down.

For multi-scene productions, the first column has changed from "Act" to "PG," short for page. For opera, an extra column could be added for the score's measure number. "SC" was eliminated; "Section" remains, as the knowledge about the piece has increased. The cue number and counts are now much more filled in, and what was "Song," "Folk," "Notes," and "Block," has now been converted and expanded into "On," "For," and "Action." The "on" column indicates the moment at which the stage manager says "the magic word." The "for" column indicates why the cue is happening. The "action" column gives a brief description of what lights actually move in each cue. At this point the cue master is based on meetings and descriptions. Many informational or descriptive points are still included that currently don't have a lighting change assigned to them. During run-throughs or the tech process, the points may be eliminated from the list, but at this point, they're still useful to provide a sequential description of the stage action, until it becomes more familiar to everyone connected with the show.

This version of the cue master now includes two new columns sketching preliminary thoughts about followspots. While these cues aren't definite, they provide the lighting designer with an initial idea about when the spots will be used. Including this information is the lighting designer's preference. While some designers don't want to include spots on

Hybrid Theatre 2010   **HOKEY CUE MASTER v5**   Date: 2/13/10

PG	SEC	CUE	CNT	ON	FOR	ACTION	SP2	SP1	SPOT NOTES
1	**Open**	100	3			Blocker			
		100.7	3		Preset	Pool in 4 L; blue bk			
			5	curtain out	Judy	SP3 pickup in wing	Judy		Tight; scrim
		101	5|10	Judy arm back	Move to center	Center up			
		102	7	2nd spin	1/2 group enter	Lav side/R20 back	Ø		Lag out
		103	10	End music phrase	Rest group enter	Bright; add NC back			
	Pook	104	7	Judy start X DL	Judy speech	DL Spec up	Judy		
				Judy X SL 1/4	Judy	Add ears	Roll		Color change
		105	5	Judy finish speak		DL Spec down	Ø		
	Tee-boo	106	7	Mitch X DC	Mitch speech	DC Spec up		Mitch	
				Put on crown				Roll	Color change
		107	5	Mitch finish speak		DC Spec down		Ø	Odds open for trio
	Pine	108	7	Lorraine X DR	Lorraine speech	DR Spec up	Lor		
				Lor put on cap			Roll		Color change
		109	5	Lorraine finish		DR Spec down	Ø		
2	**Storm**			End trio dance		spots out			
		110	7|10	End 2nd circle		Cooler			
		111	10	All start to center		Darker; green		Judy	Judy salsa
		112	7|10	All start leave cent	Judy @ center	Center up	Judy	Ø	Swap + color roll
		113	2|3	Judy X SR		DSR up; lose rest	Ø		

Expression 3; 150 chan, 174 dim   Lighting design by Steve Shelley 917.xxx.xxxx   Page 1 of 15

Figure 9.5 The Spreadsheet Cue Master for the Beginning of *Hokey*, Act 1

the cue master until they've seen a run-through, many designers feel having a preliminary spot plan means it's a plan that can be changed, rather than having no plan at all. Having a general idea of when the spots are used allows the lighting designer to quickly realize

when too many performers need spots in the action of a scene, and that he or she has run out of follow-spots. Better to know sooner, rather than later.

Though not as detailed as a followspot cue sheet, the form includes pickups, colors, and any live actions the followspots may need to accomplish. Depending on the complexity of the show, separate followspot cue sheets may be required. As *Hokey* is developing, there's no question that followspot cue sheets will be an absolute necessity. One of the tasks assigned to the assistant lighting designer will be the **spot wrangler**, directing spots and recording their cues during rehearsals.

The Movement Cue Master

One method used to record stage movement and cue placement information without a script or score is a format called a **movement cue master** or a **movement track sheet**. Figure 9.6 illustrates the same opening moments of *Hokey* in a movement cue master, constructed during run-throughs. It shows a more complete picture of the show's movement. Some lighting designers like this kind of tracking, since it provides a way to accurately place or move the cues. If the stage manager creates the document, he or she can glance at the page and see what action takes place immediately prior to each cue, allowing each cue to be anticipated.

The document is read from top to bottom. The header includes the pertinent information, including a space to include the date and the page number. A single column on both the left- and right-hand sides can be used for time notations. The simple groundplans repeat vertically down the page, so that the movements can be "tracked." The open area on the right side is provided for written notes that clarify or reiterate the movement pictograms made in the groundplans. The written boxes show the cue number and placement, while the small attached circles indicate the time counts. If the stage manager uses this page to call the opening sequence, he or she can gauge additional information by using a stop watch. From the timing notes in the left-hand column it appears that cue 102 will take place at a point between 0:32 and 0:48 seconds. After the clock reaches 0:32 the stage manager should listen for the end of the phrase and anticipate the group entering from both sides. As run-throughs progress, the stage manager can fill in more time information to provide more "timed" signposts for cue anticipation or near-placement.

The Script Cue Master

When a production involves a script, a **script cue master** can be constructed as a variation of a movement cue master. If the pages of the script are in a small format, they're often enlarged with a photocopy machine onto a single side of each page, making the text easier to read and allowing more room for notes. Miniature versions of the groundplan may

then be photocopied to the back of each page of the copied script, and the cue master script is assembled into a three-ring binder. Blocking notes can then be marked on the miniature groundplans on one page, which correlate to the enlarged script on the opposite page. When a production is based on movement and text, placement can be indicated in either the groundplans or the script.

Figure 9.7 shows the first page of *Hokey* in script format. While there's no room to indicate any movement during the dance numbers, it is possible to at least indicate cue placement relative to the lyrics or lines in the book. Since this show is moving from workshop to full production, it is presumed that there will be numerous rewrites of the script. To anticipate that, the shaded cue numbers are actually written on Post-it™ flags. As new pages of the script are issued, the cues can be moved from old page to new without constantly having to copy cue numbers from one page to the other. Using the Post-it flag system also means that, when cues need to get moved quickly, it's just a question of peeling the cue up and pasting it into another location.

FORMS

The next portion of the packet monitors the cues and actions taken by members of the lighting department during the course of the production.

Light Board Operator Sheets

During a live theatrical presentation, several actions must be coordinated for the lighting design to succeed. If the action taken for each light cue doesn't occur in the proper sequence, the lighting can be destroyed. Although the stage manager gives commands to initiate actions, the particular action that must occur for each command must be clearly understood by the light board operator. One of the lighting designer's responsibilities is to insure that the command and action for every lighting cue is clearly understood by the light board operator.

In a relaxed production, the light board operator's actions may only involve pressing the GO button on the computer lighting console and operating the house lights. A complex production, on the other hand, may require the board operator to initiate additional actions during cues. This may include operating other controls on the lighting console, activating special effects, or presetting fader banks. The **light board operator sheet** is a form that, when filled out, provides the light board operator with step-by-step written instructions describing what actions to

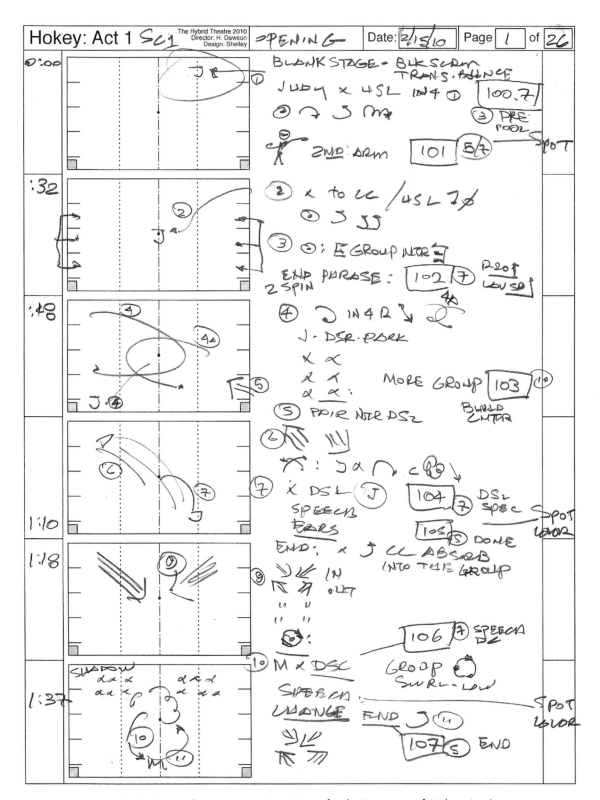

Figure 9.6 The Movement Cue Master for the Beginning of *Hokey*, Act 1

perform for each light cue. The form is laid out so that the cues are arranged in sequential rows that read from the top to the bottom of the page. The height of each row (or cue) is vertically compacted to allow the greatest number of cues to be viewed on each page. During rapid multi-cue sequences, less time spent flipping through cue sheets means more time spent making the actions properly happen. If a single cue requires extensive vertical space, it may be prudent to photocopy the final version of the cue

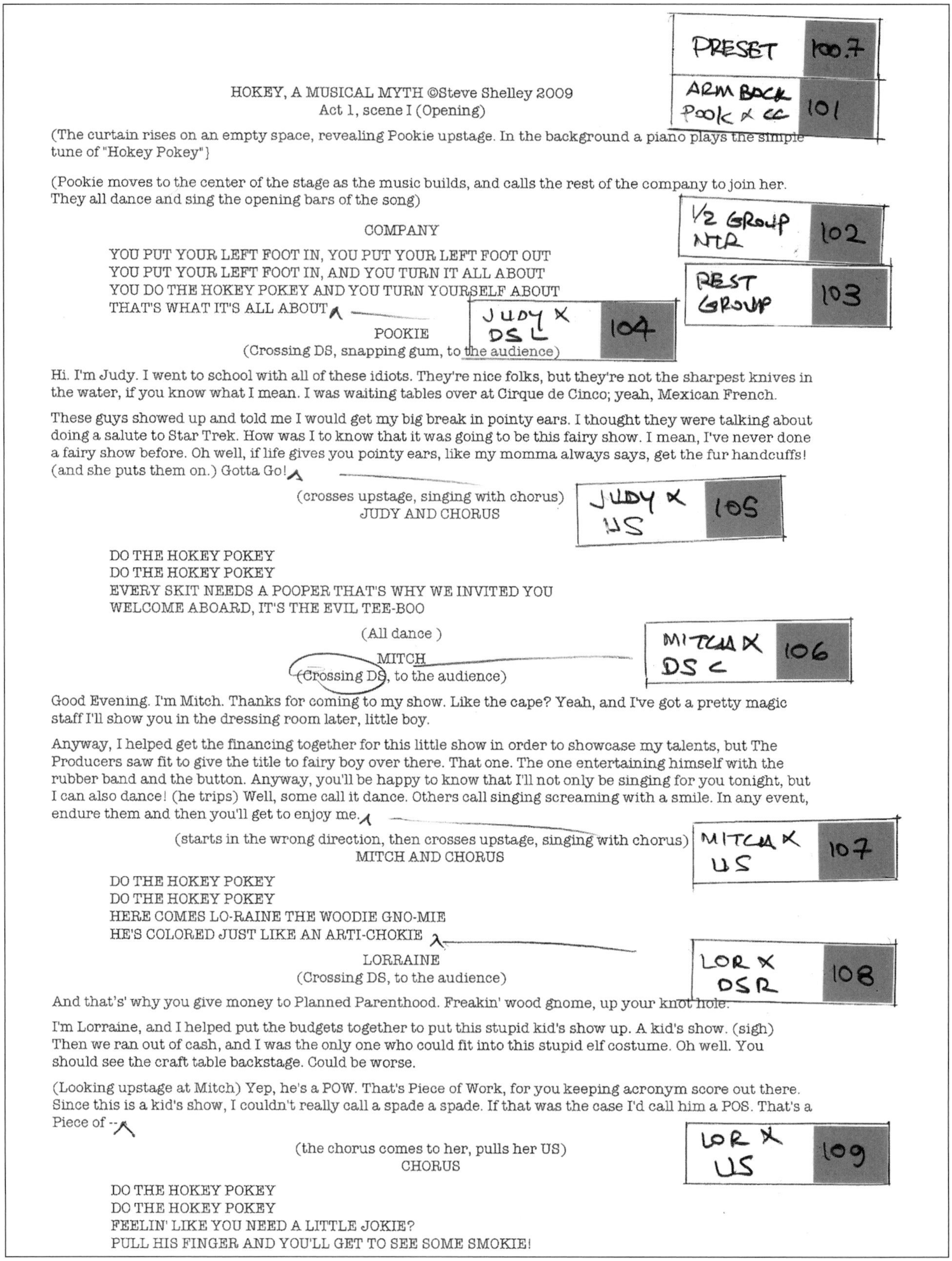

HOKEY, A MUSICAL MYTH ©Steve Shelley 2009
Act 1, scene I (Opening)

(The curtain rises on an empty space, revealing Pookie upstage. In the background a piano plays the simple tune of "Hokey Pokey")

(Pookie moves to the center of the stage as the music builds, and calls the rest of the company to join her. They all dance and sing the opening bars of the song)

COMPANY

YOU PUT YOUR LEFT FOOT IN, YOU PUT YOUR LEFT FOOT OUT
YOU PUT YOUR LEFT FOOT IN, AND YOU TURN IT ALL ABOUT
YOU DO THE HOKEY POKEY AND YOU TURN YOURSELF ABOUT
THAT'S WHAT IT'S ALL ABOUT

POOKIE
(Crossing DS, snapping gum, to the audience)

Hi. I'm Judy. I went to school with all of these idiots. They're nice folks, but they're not the sharpest knives in the water, if you know what I mean. I was waiting tables over at Cirque de Cinco; yeah, Mexican French.

These guys showed up and told me I would get my big break in pointy ears. I thought they were talking about doing a salute to Star Trek. How was I to know that it was going to be this fairy show. I mean, I've never done a fairy show before. Oh well, if life gives you pointy ears, like my momma always says, get the fur handcuffs! (and she puts them on.) Gotta Go!

(crosses upstage, singing with chorus)
JUDY AND CHORUS

DO THE HOKEY POKEY
DO THE HOKEY POKEY
EVERY SKIT NEEDS A POOPER THAT'S WHY WE INVITED YOU
WELCOME ABOARD, IT'S THE EVIL TEE-BOO

(All dance)
MITCH
(Crossing DS, to the audience)

Good Evening. I'm Mitch. Thanks for coming to my show. Like the cape? Yeah, and I've got a pretty magic staff I'll show you in the dressing room later, little boy.

Anyway, I helped get the financing together for this little show in order to showcase my talents, but The Producers saw fit to give the title to fairy boy over there. That one. The one entertaining himself with the rubber band and the button. Anyway, you'll be happy to know that I'll not only be singing for you tonight, but I can also dance! (he trips) Well, some call it dance. Others call singing screaming with a smile. In any event, endure them and then you'll get to enjoy me.

(starts in the wrong direction, then crosses upstage, singing with chorus)
MITCH AND CHORUS

DO THE HOKEY POKEY
DO THE HOKEY POKEY
HERE COMES LO-RAINE THE WOODIE GNO-MIE
HE'S COLORED JUST LIKE AN ARTI-CHOKIE

LORRAINE
(Crossing DS, to the audience)

And that's' why you give money to Planned Parenthood. Freakin' wood gnome, up your knot hole.

I'm Lorraine, and I helped put the budgets together to put this stupid kid's show up. A kid's show. (sigh) Then we ran out of cash, and I was the only one who could fit into this stupid elf costume. Oh well. You should see the craft table backstage. Could be worse.

(Looking upstage at Mitch) Yep, he's a POW. That's Piece of Work, for you keeping acronym score out there. Since this is a kid's show, I couldn't really call a spade a spade. If that was the case I'd call him a POS. That's a Piece of --

(the chorus comes to her, pulls her US)
CHORUS

DO THE HOKEY POKEY
DO THE HOKEY POKEY
FEELIN' LIKE YOU NEED A LITTLE JOKIE?
PULL HIS FINGER AND YOU'LL GET TO SEE SOME SMOKIE!

Handwritten cue boxes:
PRESET 100.7
ARM BACK POOK & CC 101
1/2 GROUP NTR 102
REST GROUP 103
JUDY X DSL 104
JUDY X US 105
MITCH X DSC 106
MITCH X US 107
LOR X DSR 108
LOR X US 109

Figure 9.7 The Script Cue Master for the Beginning of *Hokey*, Act 1

sheets onto either side of each copied page. This can then be assembled in a three-ring binder, and given to the board operator. During the performance, it will then be possible for the board operator to turn one page and see the next two pages of cue sheets.

Manual Light Board Operator Sheet

The layout of a manual light board operator sheet is designed so that one area informs the operator of the action required for each cue, while another area is set aside to note any actions to be performed prior to or after each cue. Some manual light boards require more than one board operator performing two different actions. In that case, two separate sets of board operator sheets may be required. Multi-bank preset light boards controlling numerous dimmers are one example of this situation. One set of forms is needed to provide instruction for the electrician operating the cross-fader and other masters. A second form sporting a completely different design is provided to the electrician charged with presetting each upcoming cue.

In any event, the form layout is designed to mirror the spatial arrangement of handles, knobs, or other control devices seen on the light board. Every handle, function, or option present on the light board is represented in the diagram, reducing the number of pencil strokes required to record the action of any cue to a minimum. Matching the document's layout to the physical configuration of the light board makes it simpler for the board operator to visually match the information between the two and properly anticipate and operate the light board.

Figure 9.8 shows the manual light board operator sheet for a LMI two-scene preset light board that was used during the workshop production of *Hokey*. The tall rectangles on the left side of the diagram reflect the same arrangement of the faders on the light board. The blackout switch (BLKOUT) is above the grand master (GM). The *X* and *Y* cross-faders (*X* and *Y*) are adjacent to the independent master (IND). The dimmer sliders (numbered 1 through 18) have tall rectangles below them to write preset intensities

and large arrows to indicate cues that involve slider movement. The rectangle above each dimmer represents the independent/master switch, located on the board in the same position above each slider.

The area above the switches includes a space for the cue name, the time, the preset scene, and the actual action required to execute that particular cue. The horizontal rectangle under the sliders is a space to write actions taken after each cue. In this example, the action of the cue is to fade the independent fader up to Full in 3 seconds. (The contents of the independent fader are sliders 11 and 16, denoted by the "X" above each number.) After the cue is complete, the board operator is instructed to repatch dimmer 18.

Computer Lighting Console Operator Sheet

The computer lighting console operator sheet also reflects the spatial layout of that particular console, showing the timed cross-faders, submasters, and other console functions. The document header includes the console's identity, the show, the disk, the date, and the page number of the cue sheet.

Figure 9.9 shows the same cue for *Hokey* that was previously run on the LMI preset light board. This particular light board has two split cross-faders and 24 submasters. The cue block on the left-hand side of the page includes the memory number (100.7) and its time duration (3). The rest of the row shows any cross-fade information and any notes that must occur prior to or after each light cue. The circled "GO" under the "A/B" rectangle indicates to the operator that when asked for, memory 100.7 should be loaded into the A/B cross-fader, using the GO button.

Followspot Cue Sheet

The three main attributes of a **followspot** (or a **spot**) that need to be included in cue sheets are the light beam's size, color, and fade speed (fade up or down). The beam's movement is presumed, and it's speed of movement is typically dictated by what it's following.

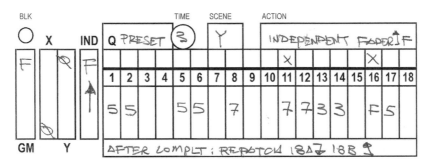

Figure 9.8 A Manual Light Board Operator Sheet

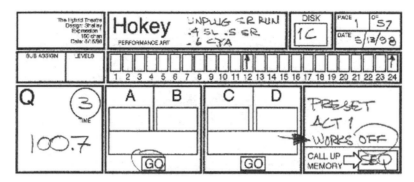

Figure 9.9 A Computer Lighting Console Operator Sheet

Determining if followspot cue sheets are required is based on a number of conditions. If the instruments are used only three or four times during the course of a show, their cues may be simple verbal instructions provided by the stage manager. The cues may be written in the margin of a script or a score, or if the performance involves movement, the cues may be written on a movement track sheet.

On the other hand, if there are numerous cues, live changes, or numerous followspots, followspot cue sheets may be a foregone conclusion. If the show will run for any length of time, substitute followspot operators will inevitably be required, and cue sheets will be needed. During tech rehearsals, the show may be complex enough to warrant a spot director to choreograph and initially call the followspot cues. When that's the case, part of the spot director's responsibility is to produce accurate cue sheets that can be read by someone else once the show has opened and the spot director is no longer on salary.

Three-Spot Cue Sheet

Figure 9.10 is a three-followspot cue sheet for the opening sequence of *Hokey*. During the tech process, updated copies of these cue sheets are distributed to the operators before each technical rehearsal. During the tech, the spot director makes updates to the sheets as he or she changes the cues. After each rehearsal, the spot op's copies are returned to the spot director so that any marks or notes missed during the heat of tech can be included in the next version. The updates are then printed and distributed for the next rehearsal and the process is repeated. The spot director creates the final version for opening night, and distributes copies to the stage manager, the lighting designer, and the archives.

Since the followspot operators are often attempting to read these cue sheets while operating their lamps, the layout and fonts used in this document are larger than usual. Not only does this enlarged format make the document easier to scan and read, enough white space remains so that written notes can be made directly onto the applicable cue.

The cue sheet is made up of two sections. The header lists the pertinent production information for the document. The body of the document consists of five columns. The left-hand column indicates the cue placement for each followspot action, while the next three columns are assigned to a specific spot. Each row is a separate cue, so that the actions of one followspot can always be "tracked" against the other three. For any cue, the spot director can see each spot's action in its separate cue block. The final column is left for notes, which might indicate sections of the show, or any useful information regarding that cue which doesn't fit in anyplace else.

The first row under the header is repeated on every page. It identifies the followspot number and the operator's name, so that information's always close at hand. The next row of blocks indicates the **defaults**, iris size and fade time, and lists the colors loaded into the boomerang of each followspot. The default color is highlighted. When one of those three areas is blank in any cue, the followspot operator presumes that the default value should be used. In simpler shows, the default row might also indicate a single character or performer in the show. The second row under the header defines the preset iris size and color for each spot at the top of Act 1 for *Hokey*. Once the followspots are preset, they're all ready for their first cue, whenever that may be. Spot 1 will start the show colored in frames 1 + 6 (noted in the color rectangle), with a waist-sized iris, while Spot 3 will be preset in frames 1 + 3 with a body-sized iris. The next row shows that both Spot 1 and 3 will fade up (or pick up) Judy on her entrance upstage left in 7 counts (noted in the time circle). Additional notes are indicated under the time circle.

On this cue sheet the area in each cue block indicates a performer. And typically the followspot's assignment for a show is to provide stage focus for the folks performing on the stage. It's worth noting, however, that followspots can highlight *anything* that needs focus while moving, or non-moving, for that matter, and anything that's the target of a followspot pickup can also be referred to as a **focus point**.

Hokey Hybrid 2010   **HOKEY FOLLOWSPOT CUE SHEET v4**   Date: 4/07/10

CUE	SPOT **3** Joel		SPOT **2** Kevin		SPOT **1** Ruth		NOTES
Key	1=R3407 4=G945 2=R51 5=G850 3=R64 6=R119	color	1=R3407 4=G945 2=R51 5=G850 3=R64 6=R119	color	1=R3407 4=G945 2=R51 5=G850 3=R64 6=R119	color	KEY
Line/cue	size	count	size	count	size	count	
Default		1+2		1+2		1+2	DEFAULT
	Body	3 cnt	Waist	3 cnt	Body	3 cnt	
Preset		1+3		1+2		1+2	
curtain out	Tight waist		Waist		Waist		
Curt	Judy ⤒ 5	1+3					
curtain out	in 4 SL						
101	Judy ↓ Ø						
J arm back	▼	3 cnt					
	Judy ⤒ 7	**1+2**					
Judy X CC	**body**	7 cnt					
104	Judy ↓ Ø		Judy ⤒ F				
Judy X DSL			DSL	2 cnt			
105			Judy ↓ Ø				Judy: "…get the fur hand<u>cuffs</u>"
Judy X US			▼				
106					Mitch ⤒ F		
Mitch X DSR					DSR	2 cnt	
107					Mitch ↓ Ø		Mitch: "…you'll get to enjoy <u>me</u>""
Mitch X US					▼		
108	Lorraine ⤒ F						
Lor X DSC	**waist** DSC	1 cnt					
109	Lorraine ↓ Ø						Lor: "…POS. That's a Piece <u>of</u>"
Lor X US		Ø cnt					

Lycian Stark; 1.2kw   Lighting design by Steve Shelley 917.xxx.xxxx   Page 1 of 21

Figure 9.10 A Three-Spot Cue Sheet for the Beginning of *Hokey*, Act 1

The first versions of this document during the tech process will be double-spaced. The open row between each cue provides space to add cues or write notes. After the followspot cues are more finalized, later versions of the document can be "tightened up" or single-spaced. The final page layout is designed to be vertically compact, in order to squeeze as many cues as possible onto a single page. This reduces the overall number of pages, and the number of times pages have to be turned during the show.

Repatch Sheets

Situations arise when the plot "runs out of dimmers": there are more instruments that need separate control than dimmers available to support them. This can be seen as an inconvenience, but it doesn't necessarily need to be a constraint. Although many instruments and their dimmers are used throughout the course of a production, some dimmers control specials or systems that don't get used that often. While one of those instruments is lying dormant, its dimmer may be used to control a different instrument. The circuit to the original special is unplugged or switched off, while an alternate instrument's circuit is plugged or switched on in the same dimmer. This action is known as **repatching**. Keeping track of what circuit is active in which dimmer at what point in the show often requires a **repatch sheet**. The design and management of a repatch system is often viewed as a skill, and not an activity to be entered into lightly. Many lighting designers avoid the exercise altogether, since it often means that a "repatch electrician" may be added to the labor for the show. Other designers consider the potential hazards of circuits accidentally getting "lost" or unplugged not worth the risk. On the other hand, repatching may be the only available solution to acquire the amount of control necessary for a lighting package.

Repatch Work Sheet

Before a repatch system can be considered, determine if the configuration of the lighting package will allow it. The key to any kind of repatch system is finding a central point where circuits can be switched off or unplugged. If a lighting package is plugged exclusively into pre-installed circuitry, this implies that each circuit is hard-wired to a dimmer. When that's the case, the only locations available to interrupt or swap circuits may be at permanent circuitry outlets, like raceway plugs or floor pockets. Other temporary dimmer racks may provide switches, but if the only available outputs from the dimmers are multicable plugs, like Socapex connectors, there may

be no quick way to interrupt the circuit. If repatching still needs to be considered under these conditions, the production electrician should become involved in the discussion.

Theatre lighting installations that contain an electrical **patch bay**, on the other hand, are ideal situations designed to allow repatching. The patch bay is a point where existing house circuitry can be re-routed to different dimmers. Touring dimmer racks, equipped with some kind of female stage plug outlets or circuit breakers, can also be considered for repatching. In any event, as long as two discrete circuits can somehow share a single dimmer, repatching is still a possibility.

Presuming that the hardware can be configured to allow physical repatching to be considered, the first step toward designing a repatch system is defining which dimmers will be dormant when an alternate instrument needs to be controlled.

Figure 9.11 is the **repatch worksheet** that was compiled during a workshop production of *Hokey*. All of the systems and specials that weren't used in every scene were listed in each row, while the different scenes or moments in the show were identified in each column. An X indicated when each system or special was active in the show. By visually comparing the presence or absence of the X's, it was then possible to pinpoint two items that didn't appear in the same or adjacent scenes. The arrows show four instances where two circuits were used that did not conflict with each other. Hypothetically, in each of those instances, each pair of items could share the same dimmer.

Figure 9.12 shows the repatch worksheet from the workshop production of *Hokey* resorted to show each pair of items next to each other. These eight items were eventually paired into four dimmers. Then the house dimmer rack was studied to see which dimmers would be the best for repatching. In the Quantum Theatre, there were more circuits than dimmer inputs. Using the dimmer's circuit breakers was not an option; they were on the wrong side of the rack. The circuits had to be physically plugged and unplugged into each dimmer. Dimmers 9 through 12 were selected as the repatch dimmers. They were the most accessible locations in the racks whose female dimmer sockets had the smallest chance of knocking adjacent plugs out of their dimmers while being replugged. To prevent confusion, the male plugs were then relabeled with gaff tape and identified by their respective dimmer number and a letter. Four circuits that would be repatched into dimmer 9 would be relabeled: 9A, 9B, 9C, and 9D. The rest of the circuits were also labeled with their new identity for dimmers 10, 11, and 12.

Quantumm Theatre 2006   **HOKEY REPATCH WORKSHEET**   Date: 2/13//07

System	Act One				Act Two			Act Three		
	Intro	Storm	Kidnap	After	Forest	Dream	Rock	Party	Duel	Finale
1E Front		X	X							X
3E Down	X				X		X			
5E Back			X	X					X	X
DSL Spec	X			X		X				
DC Spec						X			X	X
DSR Spec	X			X		X				
L180 Bx Bm		X		X		X			X	X
L124 Down		X	X	X	X	X			X	
Temps		X				X		X		
DSL Rover	X					X		X	X	
USL Rover		X							X	
DSR Rover	X					X				
USR Rover		X						X	X	
Fire							X			
Lanterns								X	X	
Railing									X	X

LMI 2 Scene; 18 dimmers   Lighting design by Steve Shelley 917.xxx.xxxx   Page 1 of 1

Figure 9.11   The Initial Repatch Worksheet for *Hokey*

System	Act One				Act Two			Act Three		
	Intro	Storm	Kidnap	After	Forest	Dream	Rock	Party	Duel	Finale
1E Front		X	X							X
Fire							X			
3E Down	X				X		X			
Lanterns								X	X	
5E Back			X	X					X	X
DSR Rover	X					X				
DSL Spec	X			X		X				
Railing									X	X

Figure 9.12   The Sorted Repatch Worksheet for *Hokey* Showing Mutually Exclusive Systems

Figure 9.13 is the final repatch sheet used for the workshop production of *Hokey*. The left-hand column lists the cue that was used to initiate the repatch. The following columns show the repatch action, the circuits, the affected instrument's focus, and the scenes in which the circuit was used. The scene columns aren't necessary from the electrician's point of view, but they're a visual aid for the lighting designer to track the path of the patch's components.

The reason repatching has to be approached with care is due to the fact that, if a repatch is performed when a dimmer is active (a "live" repatch), the repatched circuits pop off and on, rather than fading up and down with the rest of the cue. For the *Hokey* workshop, the sheet shows that the repatch in dimmer 11 occurred after light cue 27 was complete.

Dimmer 11 actually faded out in light cue 26, but the repatch action was assigned to take place one cue after the fadeout occurred. If the repatch had accidentally taken place during light cue 25 (while dimmer 11 was still active), the downstage right rover would have snapped off, and then the 5 Electric backlight would have popped on. Building in the additional "buffer cue" ensured that unwanted changes did not occur while dimmer 11 was possibly active.

Light Cue Sheet, Work Note Sheet, and Cue Track Sheet

Forms can be used that monitor the status of the light cues or the lighting package as the production evolves. While the looks for the show are being created, **light**

| Quantumm Theatre 2006 | | | HOKEY REPATCH WORKSHEET | | | | | | | | | Date: 2/13//07 |

CUE	PATCH		CIR	System	Act One				Act Two			Act Three		
					In	St	Lov	Tr	F	Dr	Tr	P	D	Fin
Preset	9A ↑ ON		1P12	1E Front	X	X								X
	9B ↓ OFF		SR2	Fire							X			
	10A ↑ ON		3P7	3E Down	X				X		X			
	10B ↓ OFF		SL 1	Lanterns								X	X	
	11A ↓ OFF		5P8	5E Back			X	X					X	X
	11B ↑ ON		SR1	DSR Rover	X					X				
	12A ↑ ON			DSL Spec	X			X		X				
	12B ↓ OFF			Railing									X	X
AFTER Q 27 Complete	11A ↑ ON		5P8	5E Back	X				X		X			
	11B ↓ OFF		SR1	DSR Rover								X	X	
1st Int.	9A ↓ OFF		1P12	1E Front	X	X								X
	9B ↑ ON		SR2	Fire							X			
	11A ↓ OFF		5P8	5E Back			X	X					X	X
	11B ↑ ON		SR1	DSR Rover	X					X				

LMI 2 Scene; 18 dimmers   Lighting by Steve Shelley 917.xxx.xxxx   Page 1 of 1

Figure 9.13 The Final Repatch Sheet for the *Hokey* Workshop

cue sheets may be necessary to document the channel intensities of each lighting state. **Work note sheets** can save time and energy during work calls, and provide a diary of any problems concerning the lighting package.

Once the show opens, one document that should always be acquired is a **light board printout**. After the show is frozen, there's no substitute for a complete printout to provide all of the light board information. The printed cue sheets and cue lists clarify any mysteries regarding the contents or timing of any light cues. The patch printout gives absolute confirmation regarding the channel assignment of any dimmer. The group printout identifies all of the building blocks, while the submaster printout identifies altered handles that were used for the show. All printouts should have a cover page with the basic show information, including the name of the show, the designer, the production electrician, the date of the printout, the dimmer configuration, the theatre location, the type of light board, and the software version. If the board doesn't have a functioning printer, off-line editing programs may provide an alternate solution.

Using them also means time isn't needed at the theatre in order to get the printout.

Other documents may be created that will aid in the analysis of the show for future productions. **Track sheets**, spreadsheet combinations of several light cues, are indispensable for analyzing the show or reproducing the lighting in future incarnations. During the rehearsal process, however, the core records that need to be documented revolve around the contents and timing of each light cue.

Light Cue Sheets

The main purpose of **light cue sheets** is to provide a moment-by-moment snapshot of each light cue. In today's world of computer hard drives, UPS's, and backups, it may seem old-school to even discuss the topic. But the lessons learned using those methods can still be applied to extreme situations today, and potentially save a non-backed-up show.

Back when manual light boards couldn't move to the production table, and computer monitor displays didn't yet exist, light cue sheets were the only tactic for lighting designers to have an up-to-date grasp of each light cue. When computer lighting consoles were first introduced, there was still the chance that the console could crash and all non-recorded cues in the RAM would be lost. Again, light cue sheets were the best answer to bad code, unstable power, fumble-fingered console operators, or impatient lighting designers.

Today's lighting consoles and hard drives make those early days of paperwork during light cue level setting sessions seem comparably labor-intensive. That said, when the lighting designer runs into a manual, non-moving console, or when there's no chance that a printout will ever be available, this is still the best recourse to provide the lighting designer with the ability to see not only the present light cue, but every cue that has been created before it. And just like all the other paperwork presented in this text, the successful document starts with the intent to make it fast and easy to use.

At first glance, each light cue sheet should reflect the channel intensities of its respective cue. During the level setting session, an assistant transcribes the directions given by the lighting designer to the board operator as each light cue is created. As each channel is activated, the assistant writes its intensity level in the proper location in the form. Listening, writing, and sorting through the cue sheets is a skill known as "tracking the cues." Sometimes cues are tracked to keep an up-to-the-moment record of each cue. If the show goes through major lighting changes, cue sheets can be "cut"; that is, they're dated, taken out of the sequenced stack, and stored at the end of the pile of cue sheets (just like the library memories discussed in Chapter 5). Just as simply, cue sheets can be "restored"—that is, pulled out of the pile in the back and reinserted back into the sequenced stack. Though requiring another person at the production table to create and maintain the sheets, there are conditions that can warrant the time and effort to have this hard copy of the light cues:

- When the computer lighting console crashes, losing all unrecorded memory. If a printout does not exist, the light cue sheets are the only record of the lost information. Re-feeding cues back into the console is much faster than reconstruction.
- When a monitor is not present at the production table, the cue sheet assumes that role. Constantly updated through the cueing process, the form becomes the "display screen," allowing the lighting designer to see the current state of the dimmers in any given look.

- When there is not a printer, and there never will be. The light cue sheets can assume the role of light board printout in order to provide an archive of the show's cue content.
- When a multi-scene preset console is being used, the light cue sheet can perform double duty. While the assistant records the presets during the level setting session, the preset operators concentrate solely on adjusting the dimmers. Once the session has concluded, the light cue sheets are photocopied, and the copy is then given to the preset operators. During the rehearsal process, the assistant updates the changes in the cue sheets. After each rehearsal, the updated light cue sheets are cleaned, photocopied, and then re-distributed to the preset operators for the next rehearsal.
- Sometimes the light cues can't be pre-programmed into the console prior to the load-in, and there may not be any time to look at any cues prior to the technical rehearsal. In that situation, loading the contents of pre-written light cue sheets into the console during the load-in might reduce the trauma or even save the day. In order for this process to work, the lighting designer must pre-think and pre-write each light cue without seeing any lights. While this takes time and some imagination, the exercise can clarify the movement and necessity for each cue. When the console is available during the load-in, the light cue sheets can be used to program the cues without the lighting designer's involvement.

Light Cue Sheet Layout

Regardless of the document's layout, each page should be limited to only one active light cue. That way, when a new cue is created between two existing cues, the new track sheet is merely inserted between the other two, and the cues remain in sequence. Likewise, no matter how large the piece of paper, all of the channels involved in a single cue sheet should fit onto a single piece of paper. On big light boards, that may mean special-sized light cue sheets, but this "one cue, one page" rule should be observed. Otherwise, there is always a chance that two or three pages might get separated.

The successful light cue sheet layout provides the maximum amount of information on the single page, so that the only information marked on it is specific solely to that light cue, and the tracked cue before it.

Figure 9.14 shows a light cue sheet for *Hokey*. It's divided into two sections, the header and the channel

CUE	MEM	TIME					COPY 2Q	GOTO Q	FADERS				HOKEY
		UP	DN	WT	DLY	Δ1 sc1			A	B	C	D	Expression 3
1	101	5	10			POOKIE X CC			X				Hybrid '10
													LD: Shelley

	R33 Front										L161 Front										R51>> Far 1/4				
	DR	DRC	DC	DLC	DL	MR	CC	ML	UC	Sd	DR	DRC	DC	DLC	DL	MR	CC	ML	UC	Sd	in1>	in2>	in3>	in4>	<in1
	1	2	3	4	5	6	7	8	9	10	11	12	13	14	15	16	17	18	19	20	21	22	23	24	25
																								O	
																								5	

Far 1/4 <<R51					R51 Bx				R51 Bm Near 1/4				Near 1/4 Bm R51				R44 Bx			R64>> Far 1/4				Far 1/4 <<R64				G945 Bx	
in2	in3	in4	>SR	SL<	in1>	in2>	in3>	in4>	<in1	in2	in3	in4	<in1	in2	in3	in4	>SR	SL<	in1>	in2>	in3>	in4>	<in1	in2	in3	in4	>SR	SL<
26	27	28	29	30	31	32	33	34	35	36	37	38	39	40	41	42	43	44	45	46	47	48	49	50

Templates				NC Cen Pools			NC Tr Spec			R20 Downs										L124 Downs DS				
DC	Sd	UC	Sd	1P	3P	5P	SR	C	SL	DR	DRC	DC	DLC	DL	UR	URC	UC	ULC	UL	DR	DRC	DC	DLC	DL
51	52	53	54	55	56	57	58	59	60	61	62	63	64	65	66	67	68	69	70	71	72	73	74	75
					5																			

L124 Downs US					NC Backs										G850 Backs									
UR	URC	UC	ULC	UL	DR	DRC	DC	DLC	DL	UR	URC	UC	ULC	UL	DR	DRC	DC	DLC	DL	UR	URC	UC	ULC	UL
76	77	78	79	80	81	82	83	84	85	86	87	88	89	90	91	92	93	94	95	96	97	98	99	100
															7	7	7	7	7	7	7	7	7	7
															5	5	5	5	5	5	5	5	5	5

R64 Bm Near 1/4				Near 1/4 Bm R64				Mids SR			Mids SL			Shins SR				Shins SL				Time Stamp		
in1>	in2>	in3>	in4>	<in1	in2	in3	in4	in1>	2l3>	in4>	<in1	<2l3	in4	in1>	in2>	in3>	in4>	<in1	in2	in3	in4	Mon	Date	Year
101	102	103	104	105	106	107	108	109	110	111	112	113	114	115	116	117	118	119	120	121	122	123	124	125
															5	5			5	5	O			
																						3		

Rovers				MR-16			Groundrow			Pit		Blackout												
DSL	USL	DSR	USR	NC	R20	850	250	Grn	Blue	R73	R26													
126	127	128	129	130	131	132	133	134	135	136	137	138	139	140	141	142	143	144	145	146	147	148	149	150
							3		5															
									3															

Figure 9.14 The Light Cue Sheet for *Hokey*, Light Cue 1

information area. The left-hand side of the header labels the cue and the memory if they're not the same. Adjacent to that is the cue's timing information (up, down, wait, or delay). Two blank areas are provided to name the cue or identify the moment. Next to that a space indicates whether the cue is a base cue for a restore (copy 2 Q). A space for traffic information is provided next, indicating if the next action is out of sequence (Goto Q). The rest of the sheet is specific information for a particular lighting console, noting any movement of the individual faders. Next to that is the title block, which is tucked on the right-hand side out of the way.

What's not apparent in this illustration is the layout of the light cue sheet on the photocopied page. In order to keep the light cue sheets archived in order, their preparation often includes being hole-punched for a three-ring binder. Because of that, these documents are always laid out slightly to the right, so that no printed or written information can be punched out on the left-hand side of the page.

The channel information area is a compressed version of the hookup. In fact, this cue sheet for *Hokey* is a modified version of the cheat sheet. By showing much of the same information as the cheat sheet, the lighting designer can analyze the cue without having to refer to the cheat sheet (or possibly the magic sheet). When the cheat sheet was discussed, it was pointed out that the number of channels per row should equal the number of channels on the monitor. In the case of a cue sheet, matching the numeric numbering and layout between the document and the monitor display is even more strongly suggested. Successfully matching that layout simplifies the task of visually transcribing the channel intensities from the screen to the paper cue sheet. This match can't be stressed enough, and understanding it importance may not be apparent until faced with a rapid light cue level setting session. Read on.

During level setting sessions, the lighting designer's concentration is aimed solely at the cue creation paperwork and the stage. The assistant is performing two tasks at once: recording every level change on the light cue sheet as it is requested, and simultaneously watching the monitor display to visually confirm that the request has been executed correctly. Since the assistant's eyes have to be in three different places at once, using light cue sheets where the layout doesn't match the channel positions on the monitor display can be a critical mistake. Preset board cue sheets used by the operators demand that the rows of dimmers match the spatial arrangement of the banks of dimmers. Otherwise, rapid presetting can become difficult, if not impossible.

Each row of channel numbers has the cheat sheet area above it, and two rectangles below it. The two rectangles under the channel numbers are filled in with two sets of numbers: the upper row of rectangles shows the channel intensities that have moved to achieve this lighting look, while the lower row of rectangles reflects the channel intensities from the preceding cue.

Cue Sheet Example

As the preset light cue (memory 100.7) is being created, the levels are written in the *top* row of rectangles, under the channel numbers. When the lighting designer gives the direction to record the completed state as memory 100.7, a blank cue sheet is then placed to the side of the just-recorded cue. All of the channel intensities of memory 100.7 are then copied onto the *lower* row of rectangles of the new cue sheet that will become cue 1 (memory 101). Once the copying is complete, the channel intensities of the documents match, except that the new cue sheet has the channel intensities written in the lower row of rectangles.

As the designer begins to build cue 1 from the preset cue, the assistant records the changes in the upper row of rectangles. If the channel doesn't change, then the channel intensity shown in the lower rectangle is duplicated in the upper rectangle. Figure 9.14 reflects this point in the cueing process. All of the lower rectangles reflect the channel intensities copied from memory 100.7; channels 24 + 91 > 100 @ 50%, and channels 122 + 136 @ 30%. When light cue 1 was created, the following changes occurred: channel 24 @ 00%, channel 57 @ 50%, channels 91 > 100 @ 70%, channels 116 + 117 + 120 + 121 + 136 @ 50%, channel 122 @ 00%, and channel 133 @ 30%.

Once the designer has instructed the board operator to record the new state as light cue 1, the assistant visually combines the readings for both rows of rectangles, and copies those levels to the bottom row of rectangles on the next blank page that will become light cue 2.

After becoming familiar with the cue sheet, the lighting designer can "read" the two cues on one page, seeing the previous cue in the lower row of rectangles, and the changes made to create the current light cue in the upper row of rectangles.

Work Notes Sheet

As soon as the load-in begins, work notes are constantly taken about problems to fix or adjustments to be made. At the end of each rehearsal period, the production electrician often needs the work notes list that will need to be addressed, so that he or she can determine the amount of labor that will be required for the next work call, and prioritize the schedule. Unfortunately, the work notes regarding physical labor may be buried in a legal pad, surrounded by notes ranging from light cue changes, to concept alterations for a section of the show. A list specifically detailing the amount of electrics work, generated by the end of the rehearsal, is often a necessity.

The **work notes sheet** is a form used to produce that list. The document is a single written location to centrally notate all work activities. At the end of each rehearsal period, the production electrician can scan this list to gauge the amount of work and the size of the crew that will be required for the next work call.

The layout of the form provides a method to speed corrections and coordinate efforts between technical departments. Figure 9.15 is the work notes sheet constructed specifically for the *Hokey* light plot. The document is laid out following the position sort of the instrument schedule. As the notes are written, they are sorted by hanging position. Once the document is scanned, personnel can be deployed to remote hanging positions, and areas of the stage can be kept clear to retain ladder access. The notes can specify

Hybrid Theatre 2010 · · · · · · · · · · HOKEY WORK NOTES SHEET · · · · · · · · · · DATE: 4/10/10 AFT

TRUSS	#	Chan	NOTE

BX L	#	Chan	NOTE
[F]	2	30	UNIT DROPPED

BX R	#	Chan	NOTE
	7	39	BOTTOM CUT

1 Elec	#	Chan	NOTE
	18	21	SHUTTER
	10	55	FOCUS TO STAIR?

2 Elec	#	Chan	NOTE

3 Elec	#	Chan	NOTE

4 Elec	#	Chan	NOTE
	L3	N3	SR WORK - BO?
	15a	141	ADD 36° STAIR

5 Elec	#	Chan	NOTE
	11	87	SOFTEN EDGE

STUFF	MOVE HAZER TO USR

1 Bm L	#	Chan	NOTE

2 Bm L	#	Chan	NOTE
	2	107	SWAP UNIT

3 Bm L	#	Chan	NOTE

4 Bm L	#	Chan	NOTE
	3	111	SCRIM

1 Bm R	#	Chan	NOTE
	1	31	BURNOUT?

2 Bm R	#	Chan	NOTE

3 Bm R	#	Chan	NOTE

4 Bm R	#	Chan	NOTE

Expression 3; 150 chan, 174 dim · · · Lighting design by Steve Shelley 917.xxx.xxxx · · · · · Page 1 of 1

Figure 9.15 The Work Notes Sheet for *Hokey*

other objects that may be required for focus notes, so that the proper departments can be informed of their need in advance.

Using a fresh copy of the form each day allows the dated documents to be kept as a diary of the lighting package. As work calls progress, the notes are crossed off, but the dated form is retained in a notebook. These "equipment track sheets" can be reviewed to "follow the trail" when specific problems become apparent. They can document patterns of equipment failure and provide a history of when and how problems were addressed. This information may become vital in negotiating any additional on-site emergency repair costs.

The day's work notes illustrated in Figure 9.15 can quickly be analyzed and sorted between the different hanging positions. The ladder crew will need the stage under the 1st and 4th Electric to remain clear. A Source Four-36° will be added to the 4th Electric, and a unit will need to be swapped on the 2 Boom L. During focus the black scrim may need to be flown in for the focus on 4 Boom L. At some point electricians will be required to touch the focus of instruments in both box booms. And the hazer needs to move, this time to somewhere on stage right.

Light Cue Track Sheet

If there's any possibility the show will have a future incarnation, there will undoubtedly be changes: a change in venue, dimmer size, or control, to name a few. The show's next life may be the opportunity to expand on the original concepts of the show. On the other hand, financial constraints may force the lighting designer to cut, change, or reconfigure the light plot.

In order to make informed decisions, one of the first things the lighting designer needs to know is how much and when each instrument was used in this first incarnation of the light plot. Upon analysis, it may be discovered that specials or channels within systems were sparingly used, if at all. It's entirely possible that other specials focused to the same area were utilized instead, and some instruments may have never been turned on. If the visual result was satisfactory, the unused units might be reassigned to a new purpose, or simply eliminated from the plot.

Attempting to determine the number of times that any given instrument was used through the course of a production is often only possible by comparing individual cue sheets to another. Comparing the cues in this manner is also often the only systematic method available to accurately determine the need for control separation between channels in any given system. That said, comparing cue sheets can take hours, and the results may still not be accurate. Without this level of analysis, though, decisions to eliminate instruments, or combine units into a single control channel, must be made based on gut instinct, rather than knowledge. It may not be realized until too late, the middle of the single dress rehearsal, that these instinctual decisions were errors in judgment.

In other scenarios, the show may be moving to a performance facility with a completely different lighting console, requiring a time-consuming re-feed of the light cues. It may be necessary to reconfigure the channel hookup or incorporate a repatch system. For that matter, the need for a repatch system may not become apparent until the middle of the load-in, when the true count of functioning dimmers is determined to be less than initially claimed.

The **cue track sheet** can address all of these situations. Not only does it show a spreadsheet format of channels and cues like the track screens found on some console displays, but also the cue track sheet adds elements of the cheat sheet and the cue master to create a single compact tool. Regardless of the size of the assembled document, the cue track sheet shows everything about the light cues for a production. It shows the moving and tracking channels in each cue, and the progression of intensities for each channel. When a cue doesn't work, it's possible to analyze the problem on paper, rather than spend time at the light board viewing the monitor display.

Light Cue Track Sheet Layout

Figure 9.16 shows a partial cue track sheet for *Hokey*. It's comprised of four basic components. The **title information** is in the upper left-hand corner. Underneath the title block are the **memory, count,** and **cue information columns.** The **channel numbers** and **cheat sheet** run across the top of the page, while the channel intensities (or **cue content**) makes up the rest of the document.

The title information lists the show, the portion of the show presented, and the key memory number. The header and footer can display additional information, including board type, dimmer configuration, the original creation date, and the version number of this particular document. Other data may include the name of the lighting designer, the name of the document creator, and the page number of the document.

The memory and cue information area starts with the cue or memory number in the left-hand column. The next column shows the time assignment for each cue, which can include split time fades, waits, or delays. As an example, light cue 109 has a time of 5 seconds, and a delay of 4 seconds. On this console, this implies that memory 109.5 is an autofollow. Tracing a cue across the sheet explains what is actually moving in that particular cue, so the "For" column from the cue master has been removed, leaving the "On" and "Action" columns.

The information above the channel numbers is copied from the cheat sheet. To eliminate confusion, the nomenclature from the cheat sheet is matched to the cue track sheet. The channel numbers are duplicated below the cue content area, making it easier to vertically scan and trace the path of a single channel.

Hybrid Theatre 2010   **HOKEY CUE TRACK SHEET**   Date: 2/13/10

Hokey: A Musical Myth Hybrid Theatre; Expression 3		Key: F-01-01		R33 Front											
				dr	drc	dc	dlc	dl	mr	cc	ml	uc	Sd	dr	drc
MEM	**CNT**	**ON**	**ACTION**	1	2	3	4	5	6	7	8	9	10	11	12
100	3		Blocker												
100.7	3		Preset												
101	5|10	Judy arm back	Center up												
102	7	2nd spin	Full stage	5	5	5	5	5	5	5	5	5	5		
103	10	End music phrase	Brighter	7	7	7	7	7	7	7	7	7	7	3	3
104	7	Judy start X DL	DL Spec up	7	7	7	7	7	3	3	3	3	3	3	3
105	5	Judy finish speak	DL Spec down	7	7	7	7	7	7	7	7	7	7	3	3
106	7	Mitch X DC	DC Spec up	3	3	3	3	3	0	0	0	0	0	3	3
107	5 D4	Mitch finish speak	DC Spec down	7	7	7	7	7	7	7	7	7	7	3	3
108	7	Lorraine X DR	DR Spec up	7	7	7	7	7	3	3	3	0	0	3	3
109	5	Lorrain finish speak	DR Spec down	7	7	7	7	7	7	7	7	7	7	3	3
109.5	10	Auto	Lose sides	5	5	5	5	5	5	5	5	5	5	3	3
110	7|10	End 2nd circle	Cooler	3	3	3	3	3	3	3	3	3	3	7	7
111	10	All start to center	Darker; green	0	0	0	0	0	0	0	0	0	0	5	5
112	7|10	All start leave cent	Center up											5	5
113	2|3	Judy X SR	DSR up; rest Ø											7	0
MEM	**CNT**	**ON**	**ACTION**	1	2	3	4	5	6	7	8	9	10	11	12

Expression 3; 150 chan, 174 dim   Lighting design by Steve Shelley 917.xxx.xxxx   Page 1 of 1

Figure 9.16 The Initial Cue Track Sheet for *Hokey*

The cue content area consists of a grid; following the path of a single row across shows the total contents of a single light cue, while the vertical columns show the progression of each channel's movement. The channel level information in the cue content area is formatted; the numbers that are bold and centered in the cell are receiving a "hard command," and **moving** in that cue. Non-bold numbers aligned to the right side of the cell aren't moving; they're **tracking** through the cue. The highlighted hard numerals make it easier to visually scan across the track sheet and see what channels are moving for any cue. Although a channel's intensity may read "70" on the monitor display, all zeros are typically truncated from the cue track sheet, making the level contents of each cell easier to read. The corresponding cell in the track sheet lists the intensity only as a "7."

By vertically scanning and comparing columns, it's easy to gauge the overall use of any channel. It's also possible to see the use and movement of channels within different systems. When the channels in a particular system are adjacent to one another, it's possible to scan down adjoining columns and compare the level information between the channels in the system. Figure 9.16 shows that channels 1 > 5 all consistently move together. This is also true for channels 6 > 8, and channels 9 + 10. Since those collections of channels have matching intensities through the entire example, then the channel numbers can be combined into a series of single columns.

Figure 9.17 shows the result of this cell compression. Columns of duplicate intensities have been eliminated. This reduces the width of the document, making it more compact and easier to read. Channel

	R33 Front		
	DS	MS	US
MEM	1>5	6>8	9>10
100			
101			
101			
102	5	5	5
103	7	7	7
104	7	3	3
105	7	7	7
106	7	3	0
107	7	7	7
108	3	0	0
109	7	7	7
110	5	5	5
110	3	3	3
111	0	0	0
112			
113			
MEM	1>5	6>8	9>10

Figure 9.17 The Condensed Cue Track Sheet for *Hokey*

separation in the hookup may be retained, however, to make the plot simpler to focus and use.

Since the hard commands for each cue are highlighted, it's also possible to make judgments while making changes in a cue. After consulting the cue track sheet, it can be quickly determined if the changes made in the cue should be re-recorded tracking or cue only.

After analysis of the cue track sheet, group and submaster lists may be adapted so that newly identified collections of channels can be more rapidly keystroked.

Program with Light Cue Track Sheets

The conventional method of programming memories into a lighting console (or "**feeding the cues**") is to program the level changes for a memory, and then record that memory. When cues are fed into the lighting console using this type of track sheet, the bold formatting makes it simpler to identify which channels are moving from the previous cue. Recognizing the bold formatting can reduce the amount of time and effort spent feeding several cues into the console. To compare the movement between nonadjacent channels, the cue track sheet can be accordion-folded, hiding intermediate columns. As an example, after folding the cue track sheet, it's easy to compare the intensity levels between channels 1 and 100.

In order to examine the progression of intensity changes for a single channel often requires the viewer to look at each memory, one at a time. Some lighting consoles can view the cue content like a spreadsheet (commonly referred to as "track sheet mode"). The memories are displayed as rows while the channels are shown as columns, like the cue track sheet. Some consoles allow intensity information for a single channel to be altered in more than one memory while viewing that screen. Instead of programming cues "horizontally," the cue track sheet makes it possible to utilize this display, and program level changes in a "vertical" direction.

Initially, all of the memory numbers are recorded without cue content, creating an empty grid. Since the channel path can be seen on both the cue track sheet and the computer display, the "vertical" movement of each channel can then be programmed. Depending on the number of channels or the number of intensity changes, this may reduce the number of keystrokes, and reduce the amount of programming time.

Repatch with Light Cue Track Sheets

If a repatch system must be designed within an existing light plot, the cue track sheet can be used to show channels that might be combined within the same scene, allowing a repatch to take place and reducing the need for an additional dimmer. The first step taken is to determine the total number of dimmers that are available for use, or the total number of dimmers that must be eliminated from the present channel hookup. In this example, two channels (and their respective dimmers) must be eliminated to fit within the new dimmer configuration.

Quickly scanning the partial cue track sheet on the left-hand side of Figure 9.18 shows columns that have few entries (or cue content). In this case, the column scan shows that channels 51 through 54, plus 56 and 57 are fairly active. Since the cells are centered and highlighted, the channels are moving quite a bit. That same scan, however, also reveals some relatively open columns. Channels 55, 58, 59, and 60 each appear briefly.

The right-hand side of Figure 9.18 isolates those four channels, showing that while channels 58 through 60 all move within one cue of each other, channel 55 is dormant until cue 111. One dimmer will be gained by repatching any of the 58 through 60 sequence with the contents of channel 55, since all of them will be at zero when channel 55 comes up. The effort to gain a second dimmer, though, is a bit more complex. Channel 60 shouldn't attempt a repatch with 58. They're both moving within one cue of each other and there's no buffer cue between the channel movements. The same situation exists for channels 58 and 59. Channel 60 fades out in cue 105, two cues before channel 59 is activated to Full in cue 108. Checking the "On" and "Action" columns on the left-hand side of the cue track sheet shows that there is some amount of time between cues 105 and 108.

The left-hand side of Figure 9.19 illustrates the solution. Channels 55 and 58 can repatch with each other, and channels 59 and 60 can repatch with each other. That means there will be two repatch cues. After cue 105 is complete, the contents of what is now channel 60 will be switched off, and the contents of what is now channel 59 will be switched on. After cue 107 is complete, the contents of what is now channel 58 will be switched off, and the contents of what is now channel 55 will be switched on. Analysis of the track sheet has shown one possible way to eliminate two dimmers. The contents of channel 58 are now hardpatched into the same dimmer controlled by channel 55, while the contents of channel 60 are hardpatched into channel 59.

The right-hand side of Figure 9.19 shows the reprogramming required for the repatch to succeed. Channels 55 and 59 have had the additional channel movements programmed to reflect the movements that used to be made by channels 58 and 60. The added movements have been italicized. A bullet has been added after the channel has gone to zero to

Figure 9.18 (left)

	Templates				NC CC Pools			NC Tr Spec		
	1E	2E	4E	5E	1P	3P	5P	SR	C	SL
	DC	Sd	UC	Sd						
MEM	51	52	53	54	55	56	57	58	59	60
100										
100.7										
101						5	7			
102						5	7			
103	5	5	5	5		5	5			
104	5	5	3	3		3	3			F
105	7	5	7	5		5	5			0
106	3	3	3	3		3	3	F		
107	5	5	5	5		5	5	0		
108	0	0	3	0		0	0		F	
109	5	5	5	5		3	3		0	
109.5	F	7	F	7		5	5			
110	7	7	7	7		5	5			
111	0	0	0	0	7	0	5			
112					F		F			
113					0		0			
MEM	51	52	53	54	55	56	57	58	59	60

Figure 9.18 (right) — Isolated Channels

	Templates				NC CC Pools			NC Tr Spec		
	1E	2E	4E	5E	1P	3P	5P	SR	C	SL
	DC	Sd	UC	Sd						
MEM	51	52	53	54	55	56	57	58	59	60
100										
100.7										
101						5	7			
102						5	7			
103	5	5	5	5		5	5			
104	5	5	3	3		3	3			F
105	7	5	7	5		5	5			0
106	3	3	3	3		3	3	F		
107	5	5	5	5		5	5	0		
108	0	0	3	0		0	0		F	
109	5	5	5	5		3	3		0	
109.5	F	7	F	7		5	5			
110	7	7	7	7		5	5			
111	0	0	0	0	7	0	5			
112					F		F			
113					0		0			
MEM	51	52	53	54	55	56	57	58	59	60

Figure 9.18 A Partial Cue Track Sheet on the Left; the Same Track Sheet Showing Isolated Channels on the Right

Figure 9.19 (left) — Channel Combinations

	Templates				NC Cen Pools			NC Tr Spec		
	1E	2E	4E	5E	1P	3P	5P	SR	C	SL
	DC	Sd	UC	Sd						
MEM	51	52	53	54	55	56	57	58	59	60
100										
100.7										
101						5	7			
102						5	7			
103	5	5	5	5		5	5			
104	5	5	3	3		3	3			F
105	7	5	7	5		5	5			0
106	3	3	3	3		3	3	F		
107	5	5	5	5		5	5	0		
108	0	0	3	0		0	0		F	
109	5	5	5	5		3	3		0	
109.5	F	7	F	7		5	5			
110	7	7	7	7		5	5			
111	0	0	0	0	7	0	5			
112					F		F			
113					0		0			
MEM	51	52	53	54	55	56	57	58	59	60

Figure 9.19 (right) — after Reprogramming

	Templates				NC Cen Pools			TR
	1E	2E	4E	5E	SR			SL
	DC	Sd	UC	Sd	1P	3P	5P	C
MEM	51	52	53	54	55	56	57	59
100								
100.7								
101						5	7	
102						5	7	
103	5	5	5	5		5	5	
104	5	5	3	3		3	3	*F*
105	7	5	7	5		5	5	*0*
106	3	3	3	3	*F*	3	3	·
107	5	5	5	5	*0*	5	5	
108	0	0	3	0	·	0	0	F
109	5	5	5	5		3	3	0
109.5	F	7	F	7		5	5	
110	7	7	7	7		5	5	
111	0	0	0	0	7	0	5	
112					F		F	
113					0		0	
MEM	51	52	53	54	55	56	57	59

Figure 9.19 A Partial Cue Track Sheet Showing Channel Combinations on the Left, after Reprogramming on the Right

help illuminate the moment when the repatch can occur. The four channels have been combined and programmed into two channels.

There is no question that the cue track sheet can be time consuming to compile. Once completed, however, the cue track sheet is one of the best tools in any designer's arsenal to analyze or reproduce lighting. The final document eliminates pounds of printouts, expedites cue analysis, and, considering the reduced number of pages, can be easily sent as a fax or a PDF. It can reduce delays and overnight delivery service charges.

Distributing the Paperwork

When the cue construction packet documents have been produced, the initial preparation of the paperwork packets for the production is complete. The initial copying and distribution of the complete packets can now take place, using the document distribution chart. If distribution consists of creating PDF documents and sending zipped email attachments, or involves trips to Kinko's® or their like in order to produce hard copies and send out overnight envelopes, or anything in between—the faster the packets are sent off, the sooner the lighting designer can take

a break. Whether it's short or long, the basic information is published and distributed so that everyone can now see the same thing.

SUMMARY

Now that all of the paperwork has been sent out, it's now time for a short "completion celebration." It should be taken, because it won't last for long. No matter how often preliminary documents have been sent to double-check ideas, thoughts, and assumptions—once the first version of "final" documents arrive on others' doorsteps, the next step in this process begins. Once all those involved see the complete overall plan proposed by the lighting designer; and have their own tangible copy to provide them with reference points, they'll provide feedback.

That will in turn start the next step in the process for the lighting designer: listening to their reactions, providing their adaptations, updating the plan's documents, and then the redistribution. And whether it's a short period of time or lasts over months, that cycle will continue into load-in, through the tech process, and up until opening night.

Chapter 10

Prior to the Load-In

INTRODUCTION

This chapter examines some of the events that take place between the time the paperwork packets have been sent out and up through the night before the load-in. First off, it's smart to confirm that whatever paperwork has been sent out, actually got there. Not very imaginatively, that activity is called **confirm paperwork distribution**.

While other departments prepare for the load-in, it may be necessary for the lighting design to **react to changes**, which may turn into more meetings and alterations to the production schedule.

As the load-in looms, the electrical package may get assembled and packed in a lighting rental shop, an activity known as **prepping the rental lighting package**. When the package is assembled, the **truck packing groundplan** shows how the gear will fit into the truck for the trip from the lighting rental shop to the performance facility, or between stops on a tour.

In many cases, while that is taking place, the designer will attend **run-throughs** of the show. Finally, there are the preparations made the **day and night before the load-in**.

CONFIRM PAPERWORK DISTRIBUTION

Once the packets have been assembled are sent out, call and make sure it got there.

If paperwork is sent to an out-of-town theatre, call and confirm that the theatre has received and distributed the paperwork to the proper parties. Do not assume that silence implies acceptance of the lighting package. It's not impossible that the package containing the information has been lost, misplaced, or misinterpreted.

Likewise, if paperwork is sent ahead to a lighting rental shop, a call to confirm the paperwork's arrival may seem redundant; until you call and it hasn't shown up. Overnight delivery services now provide many online tracking resources. At the time of this writing, the US Postal Service has the ability to send packages rapidly, but it's not always able to track the package's progress. When in doubt, most lighting designers agree that paying the extra money in order to track and trace the package once it's lost, is worth the extra money. On the other hand, just because it's arrived, doesn't always mean that it's gotten into the right hands.

 Shelley's Notes:
Confirm Paperwork Distribution

Back before the Internet and email attachments, I once produced an extensive lighting paperwork package and sent it off to the theatre barely meeting the contractual schedule defined by the producer. I heard nothing from the production electrician for weeks and presumed that everything had been received and approved. One week prior to load-in, I called him and discovered he had never received any paperwork from his production office. I immediately called the production office, since duplicating the paperwork package at this late date would involve no small amount of time and effort.

When I asked about the package in question, the receptionist in the production office immediately knew what I was talking about. "Oh yes," she said, "we received that package for Mr. Shelley weeks ago. And we're holding it here safe and secure until his arrival."

"That's very kind," I responded, "but this is Mr. Shelley. And I sent that package so that your staff would open it, study it, and respond to it a month ago. Please, don't wait for me. It's not a package that was sent *to* me, it was sent *from* me. Open the box and give the information to the house staff. There are no doubt issues that should be discussed now, not then."

Shelley's Notes: Don't Assume Communication

In these modern electronic days of immediate communication everyone slowly comes to assume that, as soon as we "reach out" and extend a communication to someone, the someone is there and available to listen. It has now reached the point where actors attempt to "sign out" of Broadway shows by texting messages to the Production Stage Manager.

Sometimes this is a gross assumption, which can blow up in your face. Just because you send an email, text message, or voicemail, doesn't mean the recipient at the other end is waiting for it, and is able to immediately respond. In the case of email, they may not be anywhere near their computer. They may not be able to get online. Their computer may be broken. Their computer's modem may be broken, in which case they can't even tell you the message hasn't been read.

Likewise, just because we call and leave a message on someone's cell phone, that doesn't automatically mean that they will immediately hear the message. Their phone may have the ringer turned down, or turned off, or the batteries might have run down. Or they may not be able to get the phone recharged. Or they forgot the charger. Or they're not in range.

It is foolish and unwise to assume that just because a message has been left, that the other person has any awareness of the message at all. If there are time-sensitive decisions that must to be made, and there is no response to your email, get off your derriere and contact them directly. If there is no response to your cell message, call their landline. Or fax them. Or call another friend who is with them. Or call their office or home.

Don't let your assumption of communication be proved to be the choke point in the process.

Vendor Double-Check

Many young lighting designers don't feel they need to be concerned with the financial aspect of the process, since it has nothing to do with the artistic vision. As a matter of fact, some designers choose to close their ears or leave the room when production meeting topics turn to budgetary matters for the show. It's not their problem. Well, at least, not until the special thingamajig that's going to save said show doesn't show up. Then they care. While it's banal and boring, it's a part of the business. And for that reason, this topic and the tactics involved are briefly examined.

The lighting package may consist of several different vendors, who all contribute purchased or rented goods to the project, and in so doing, get paid for their goods. When the package was originally assembled, contracts and deals were made with any number of folks so the lighting package and lighting design could be realized. In the time prior to the load-in, some lighting designers team up with their production electricians and create a calendar; scheduling when to make the double-check contact with each of the vendors. For some shows using several different resources, there may be a separate vendor contact sheet. Why go to all this trouble? Everything's taken care of, right?

Wrong. The number of things that can stop something from arriving on time is too long to list here. Suffice to say there are any number of ways even a simple package delivery can get screwed up; the wrong contact name, the wrong address, the wrong date; you imagine it, it can happen. As an example, I once had a package delivered on time, but refused, because it was addressed to a person not associated with the show, a "Steege Dour." So close, and yet so far; in this case, this snafu happened in spite of the fact I spelled out the name while making the arrangements: S-T-A-G-E D-O-O-R. And that's just delivery. There can be just as many ways a package can be derailed due to problems in accounting; establishing accounts can be a huge headache if it's not properly addressed. What if the producing company or theatre is non-profit? That's another whole book. And the number of times a problem just gets shuffled to the side, rather than re-addressed, is astounding. If the problem isn't noticed until the last minute, it could easily spell delay, exclusion, or knee-jerk replacement in order to get the piece on-site and get the show up.

That's why the double-check phone calls or emails are made. With a scheduling calendar and a vendor contact sheet, it's possible for the lighting department to contact each supplier and just make sure that everything is in place for on-time deliveries, and that there are no hitches in terms of payment, insurance or other delays that may impact the assembly of the lighting package.

The usual list of things to confirm typically includes:

- Whatever agreements requiring signatures have been properly signed.
- Whatever financial arrangements requiring additional forms or processing have been processed. Any checks, bank accounts, credit card numbers that need to be approved have been provided and processed.
- Any repeat billing (weekly, monthly, etc.) has been confirmed and arranged for.
- The delivery date and time, address, contact name and cell phone are on the invoice. Highlight this item if any of the information is different than the billing address and contact info, which it often is.
- For larger deliveries, the pick-up date and time for any empties.
- For one-off events, the pick-up date and time are on the invoice.
- And last but not least, the big gorilla in the room that has recently become important for lighting rentals, the Certificate of Insurance (COI).

Certificate of Insurance

The COI is a document issued by the producer's (or theatre's) insurance company that lists one specific vendor as the "lost payee." This document is legally binding proof that if the lighting rental package is destroyed or somehow hurts someone, the producer's insurance policy will pay to replace the gear, and/or assume the liability for anyone who got hurt by the rental package. The lighting rental shop doesn't have to pay to replace the destroyed rig, and is absolved of any liability if pieces of that rig hurt someone.

In these litigious days, many lighting rental shops now insist that this document is in their possession before the rental package will be released, and delivered to the venue. Some shops want it more than 48 hours in advance. While the Certificate of Insurance may often be limited to the lighting rental shop, it should not be excluded as a point of concern for any agreement involving borrowed or rented gear from any other source.

And that's the funny thing; each COI can only list one "loss payee" on each issued certificate, and often each certificate costs a fee. So if there are a lot of vendors asking for their own certificate, this can quickly add up to a whole new line item in the budget. While the producer or the general manager's office should handle all of this, the lighting designer needs to at least be aware of the implications. That way, when the lighting rental shop says to the lighting designer, at the last minute: "we don't have the COI, so we can't release the package," the next phone call is to management to get this sorted out ASAP.

Beyond rental items, there are many other sources for goods and gear to become involved in the lighting package. Their arrival at the theatre at the proper time during the tech process may require a second or third confirmation in order to be certain that they're included in the lighting package at the right time requiring the least amount of crisis. Other vendors worthy of this double-check might include:

- Any new beta products, or gear directly on loan from manufacturers.
- Drop-shipped custom items, such as custom gobos or gel string sixth.
- Other special effects rentals or loaners.
- Perishables from an external supplier; color, templates, black wrap, and so forth.

Double-checking may take some time to complete and may become an annoyance. Not double-checking may endanger a lighting design.

Truck Tactics

While the topic of getting gear to the theatre is being discussed, the discussion should also include general tactics about trucking. Every time a delivery is made to the venue, no matter where it comes be from, moving that freight costs money. The driver, the gas, the truck rental all need to be considered. There is the fact that the venue's loading dock, or the street outside of the theatre, may be blocked at different times of the day or night. Not to mention the potential cost of additional union employees ("loaders") who may be contracted to do nothing but get gear in and out of the door. The bottom line is, the fewer the trucks, the better.

For that reason, many designers and production electricians will direct large and small pieces of gear from outside sources to be delivered not to the venue, but to the lighting rental shop instead. Presuming that there's enough available room, and agreements can be made with the proper parties, the rental shop's loading dock can sometimes become a temporary staging area to pack all sorts of other gear into the shop's trucks on the day that the lighting package is scheduled to depart. This is a logistic challenge, and not one to be entered into lightly. The arrival of the external gear has to be carefully timed to make sure that it doesn't get in the way of the shop's scheduled business. Successfully arranging this scheme, though, means that many small pieces are all combined and delivered in single delivery. This is a common tactic that reduces the overall number of trucks arriving on-site, and saves time, money and delivery headaches.

It's also worth checking to see what truck sizes the rental shop uses, and how the shop charges for the trucks. Some rental houses now submit invoices not for round trips, but for each one-way drive. Back in the day of round-trip billing, the usual tactic was to schedule a second delivery, which was timed to also pick up the first truck's empties. Rather than taking two trips to accomplish both goals, it was completed more economically in a single trip. But that was then, and this is now. The lesson from this modern billing technique is: Don't send a truck back to the shop with a single empty crate on it. Doing so may potentially result in the show paying for the second truck run, which is money spent transporting one crate. Check the truck billing procedures of the rental shop before committing to an overall truck-hauling scheme.

Acknowledgments and Thank-yous

While vendors are being discussed, it's appropriate to talk about acknowledgments and thank-yous. Over the course of any production some number of favors, assistance, or help will accumulate. While not all of these helpful acts require attribution, it is customary to acknowledge the rental shops that have provided equipment for the show. In some cases, this may be as simple as sending an email to the rental companies and CC'ing the management offices. Other times it may be hardcopy letters that may then be filed away for future advertising use. Most often, however, it's as simple as the small print in the program that lists which vendors provided what elements of the technical aspects of the show. Depending on the program tradition, there may be several headings of thank-yous, ranging from "credits" to "acknowledgments." In some cases, acknowledgment attribution can become part of the negotiations in order to get loaned gear in the first place.

While it may seem mundane and superfluous, it is still very important. The lighting designer and the production electrician are the last double-checks to make sure that everyone is properly attributed in the credits of the program. A company's accidental exclusion from the acknowledgments in a program can adversely affect the relationship between a business supplying gear for the show and everyone involved in it. The lighting designer should be certain to not only check the program copy to make sure that everyone is included and listed the way they want to be, he or she should be certain to pass it by the production electrician to make sure no one is inadvertently omitted.

While programs are being discussed, it's also worthwhile to mention the topic of staff listings. By contract the lighting designer is often provided some amount of space in the "who's who" section to include their own bio. Standard procedure is for the final copy to be provided to the lighting designer for his or her final proof before it is submitted to the printer. At that point, the lighting designer is obligated to check the copy in order to be sure that everything is spelled and properly punctuated. But he or she should also take this chance to make sure everyone in the electrics department is properly credited, their names are spelled correctly, and their title is properly listed. While this may just be another show for some of the participants, it may just as easily be very important for other folks and should be done, no matter the level of production,. The lighting designer may be the final set of editing eyes checking this information, and everyone wants to show the program to their family.

REACTING TO CHANGES

One of the admirable qualities that all theatre people think they possess is the ability to "roll with the punch." While that may be true, to outsiders it may often seem more like a mandatory quality just to gain admission to the "Goofy Ride," also known as Theatre. While the process of mounting a production often seems like it's nothing *but* adapting to change, the process isn't limited to just the tech rehearsal process. More often than not, between the time the lighting package gets distributed and the load-in, some amount of adaptation is required on the part of all participants.

It always seems that, no matter how much preparation takes place and how many meetings are held, no one seems able to focus on the upcoming situation until just before it's scheduled to take place. Now that a plan is in place and published, it gets compared to the rest of the pre-existing information. Re-examination may show that portions of the venue's electrical infrastructure aren't quite as functional as originally advertised. Reviewing the plot might remind folks that new steel has been added to the grid, preventing the electric from being hung in that location.

In many cases, many of the last-minute "oh by the ways" can often be traced back to the fact that the original information passed on as being "state of the moment" was, in reality, years out of date. From this point forward, the amount of homework invested to confirm all the parameters (or the choice to ignore them) will come back to pay dividends, or just come back to haunt.

The lighting design for *Hokey* had to absorb a punch when the plot got chopped in the budget crunch. Once the plot was sufficiently reduced so the

slide along the track. Like the truss, electricians access the chairs from ladders or positions offstage of the rake, eliminating the need to move a ladder onto the slanted surface. This technique also relies on fall arrest protection, and qualified rigging safety oversight.

While any of these changes may require more on-site visits, conference calls, bar napkins sketches, or faxed restaurant placemats, everyone agrees that making changes and reacting to them is a good thing. Even if it's at the last minute and it's a pain, it's still better than having to consider choices and make decisions during the heat of the load-in. Instead, the choices are made and the load-in can focus on the task at hand, getting the show in and up on schedule.

PREPPING THE RENTAL LIGHT PACKAGE

On a small show, the production electrician may go into the shop for a day before the lighting package is delivered to the venue. On large shows, a team of electricians hired by the show can work at the lighting rental shop for weeks, getting all the gear prepped, marked, and packed. These days the shop prep time for a union crew to prep a Broadway play is 2 to 3 weeks, while a Broadway musical may budget the crew for 3 to 5 weeks.

Prepping a Show

So what are they doing that whole time? While some amount of it is spent waiting for gear to arrive from other returning rentals, the general idea behind prepping a package is to take every possible step, preparation, and action possible that can be done in the shop, instead of using stage time to perform the same activity in the theatre. As the package is getting prepped, it's also getting packed as tightly as possible to keep truck space to an absolute minimum. Each additional truck can cost a chunk of change for the delivery.

Before packing it, the ideal would be to gather all the equipment into one room, set it all up, and turn it on in order to test it—yep, that would be great. But it doesn't happen. There's not enough room, time, or money for that kind of activity. The entire thing is packed piece-meal, and depending on what becomes available when, completely out of order. That's where the smart folks come in; they assemble all of the pieces for the entire package together and pack it all into separate boxes, in a random order, so that it can still be quickly unloaded and installed at the venue. Not only that, when the whole lighting system is assembled in the theatre, everything snaps together, it all works, it's all complete, and there's enough extra gear built **in** so that most additional design requests

can still be accommodated without slowing down the design process.

The format and layout of the shop order is usually specific for that lighting rental shop–it's the process that works for them. Their choice of format will often reflect the way they process the order. Most shops now already have the elements of the shop order in their computer system.

Some shops pack the rental orders using copies of the paperwork they submitted to first get the bid. That document often mirrors the original shop order, and is laid out as a **departmental breakdown**, listing each equipment category on a separate page. That way each separate page can be distributed to the applicable department within the lighting rental shop. Using this format is acceptable when there's ample room on site to open a lot of crates at one time, since equipment will be loaded into the crates solely by type or size with no attention paid to position. It's highly likely that the Source 4-26° ellipsoidals for the box booms will be in the same road box as the Source 4-26° ellipsoidals on the fifth electric. If the shop order is processed using this system, areas on the paperwork can be assigned to note checkpoints in the process, including the road box's number and the date the equipment is packed. On large orders, a groundplan showing the load order of the road boxes in the truck (the **truck pack**) may be a handy idea as well.

Regardless of the format used when preparing the light package, the production electrician may choose to pack the entire lighting package like a series of modular kits. The **position breakdown** is a re-sort of the shop order, grouping all the pieces needed for each hanging position. In tight quarters, having everything needed for that specific hanging location in one box saves a lot of time otherwise spent looking for the box of top hats *somewhere* in the venue. While the format of this document can't answer questions about overall numbers in the shop order, the position breakdown compartmentalizes the load-in, reducing the number of road boxes necessary in the hot zone. Only the road boxes needed to hang each overhead position are brought in at any time. This can be a tactical advantage when onstage space is tight, but the pack has to be carefully overseen in order to make certain the lighting package doesn't expand into extensive road boxes to maintain compartmentalization.

Regardless of how the gear is assembled, the production electrician keeps detailed lists of where everything is packed, and constantly double-checks that the numbers for each sum of gear match with what was originally requested. While the ideal is for this to take place before the road boxes are all sealed, it doesn't always happen that way.

Even though each road box is labeled with its contents, there's no certainty that everything will be included on the list. Without the production electrician's detailed list tracing each movement of equipment out of the shop, claims can later be made that equipment was delivered to the job, while the equipment in question can't be found on-site. This can result in money being paid for equipment that was never received.

Typical prepping activities include:

- Test and check every lighting instrument.
- Test, patch, and label every dimmer rack.
- Test and label all the multicable.
- Build and pre-hang instruments on ladders, sidelight booms, overhead truss. Label all pipe.
- Inspect and label all feeder cable, multicable, individual cable, and data cable.
- Build all individual circuitry breakouts.
- Inspect and count all hardware.
- Inspect and count all power distribution boxes.
- Test and count all worklight switchboxes, cue light boxes.
- Construct all graphic diagrams for the truck pack, data maps for the installation, hang tapes for the overhead electrics.
- Cut and frame all color and templates.
- Cut tie-line. Lots of it.
- Physically assign the DMX identities to all devices and moving lights.
- Load custom gear into any devices; color scrolls into scrollers, custom gobos into movers.
- Program any infrastructure information into the lighting console.
- Label everything; instruments, movers, devices cable, plugs.
- Pack everything.
- Keep a running inventory list of everything.

While this doesn't include the entire gambit of activities that go on during a shop prep, it allows the reader to see that the electricians are actually pretty busy over there.

On top of that, they have to adapt and make any number of changes, any number of times, when the original gear specified gets replaced by different equipment that requires different power, data, or care. That would be part of the shop process called substitutions.

Substitutions

Regardless of the size or length of shop time, the incomplete parts to a future rental package are often set aside in the corner, waiting to be packed. The rest of the gear required to finish that rental order may still be out on another rental. Theatre being theatre, there's always the chance that the returning gear may get delayed. Can you say "substitution?" While lighting shops try to avoid this scenario, it's the nature of the beast, and it happens all the time.

To anticipate that, the savvy designer first calls the rental shop account representative to check in the day before the shop prep starts. At this point, this should merely be a check-in; presumably the lighting designer and the account rep have spoken several times about the show, the package, and the schedule. If there are any anticipated problems, this is the point where the account rep can present both the conflict and potential solutions to the designer, and the designer can react.

If there are any substitutions that take place during that conversation, the designer informs the production electrician. Regardless, the two speak before the next day begins, if for no other reason than that the designer informs the production electrician of his or her whereabouts for the entire time that the order is being prepped. To ensure communication, many designers will be certain not to schedule any doctor's appointments, be near hospitals, or even be in other production's performances during shop days in case the production electrician needs a rapid response.

When the call does come, experienced production electricians will first determine what exists in the shop that the lighting designer might be able to use instead. Obviously, when a designer gets the call "they don't have enough MR-16 striplights" the first thing the lighting designer will respond with is: "what DO they have?"

Reacting to Lighting Changes

Inevitably the phone call comes: "We don't have the ___." Again, the process is much the same. What are the alternatives, how long can the decision be delayed before dragging the process, and what are the financial implications? After a point, having to make changes in the shop is a case-by-case basis. In addition to everyone associated with the shop and the show, the lighting designer also has an entire group of other designers to use as consultants or a support system. Situations like this are one of many times to consider talking to anyone who's also gone through the same process.

When the crunch really hits, the designer may need to completely rethink the components of the lighting package. This goes back to knowing not only the latest lighting gear, but the older lighting gear as well. Does the show have to have LED fixtures? Really? Could a scroller do instead? Does the show have to have that many 2Kw Fresnels? Could a 750w parnel come close instead? Almost any cuts at this point in the game are exhausting, but it's rare that it can be avoided. Knowing the gear in the shop, knowing the folks in the shop, and knowing what's languishing on the shelves of the shop, are all good tools that can come into play to help the lighting designer in his or her time of need.

Perishables

While there are lots of activities while prepping the show, one of the basic tasks for any show is framing the color and prepping the templates. On the big shows, the crew does it in the shop. On the medium shows, the production electrician does it in the shop. On the small shows, the lighting designer is cutting it in his or her office. Regardless of the show size, having the color cut and the templates prepped and ready before the beginning of the load-in can't do anything but help the initial "in." First, it means that a pair (or two) of electrician's hands won't be lost boxing the color for some amount of time in the morning call. Second, it means that the lighting designer, trying to not lose those electricians, won't be trying to cut the color him or herself, instead of watching the load-in.

Console Pre-programming

If either the console rented for the show, or a matching console, is available for use without additional charge at the lighting rental shop, most shops will allow the lighting designer to come program whatever's desired while the show is being prepped. As long as the designer keeps the same hours as the production electrician, and the designer provides the storage media, he or she can often work on the console. If that becomes part of the plan, read up on the topic of "Program Information into the Computer Lighting Console" in Chapter 8. As a tip, however, come prepared. Don't show up to the shop, sit down in front of the console, and ask, "Does anyone have a spare floppy disk?"

Truck Pack

As the lighting package is prepped in the shop, one important job is to design the truck pack. While that may sound fairly simple, it's not. In any given lighting rental shop the number of different crate sizes, and what they're used for, can be stupefyingly diverse. There may also be constraints about how much weight each type of crate can support, or which hampers can fit onto what crates, or how the combined list fits into one type of truck but not another. On top of that, the size of any number of crates might or might not fit through specific doors or passages in the venue.

Another consideration is time; loading or unloading trucks without any sort of plan can quickly translate into hours of wasted labor. And while it's redundant, it's worth repeating; every trip in the truck can easily cost hundreds of dollars. For all of these considerations, many lighting designers and electricians believe that designing a successful electrics truck pack, and compactly fitting it into the fewest trucks possible, is its own separate art form.

Figure 10.1 is a packing groundplan, taken from the production electrician's notebook, for the first truck transporting the *Hokey* electrics package to the Hybrid Theatre. Not only does it show the rotation of the crates in order to fit inside the truck, it also lists the order that the crates are brought into the truck. In this way the crates can be lined up, prior to being loaded, in the shop, on the dock, or on the street. That way, as soon as one crate is packed and strapped in, there's no delay waiting for the next crate. Many shows have these groundplans pasted on the inside walls of their respective trucks, so the loaders can quickly call for the next crate.

The packing list also includes all packing bars, ratchet straps, and packing blankets. Not only does this insure that the right packing infrastructure is added at the right time, it also insures that there are enough packing materials provided by the shop or the truck rental agency.

One noteworthy item on the tail of this first truck is a **loading ramp**. In this situation the lighting rental shop has a loading dock, but the venue doesn't. If the truck doesn't have a built-in ramp or a lift gate, a ramp needs to be included to get the gear down to street level. Once unloaded, the ramp will remain in the theatre and be available for use with all of the trucks, until the final empties have been picked up.

THE PRODUCTION SCHEDULE

While the production schedule has been a consistent topic of discussion throughout this book, no matter how often it's discussed; impending clarity always somehow seems absent. For whatever reason, it often seems that folks just don't (or can't) focus on a project until it's imminently in their face. As the load-in looms closer, suddenly everyone seems to care more, think things though more, and come up with better suggestions (that would have been a great idea about a month ago).

Inevitably, everyone finally trains their focus on the two or three critical events in the production

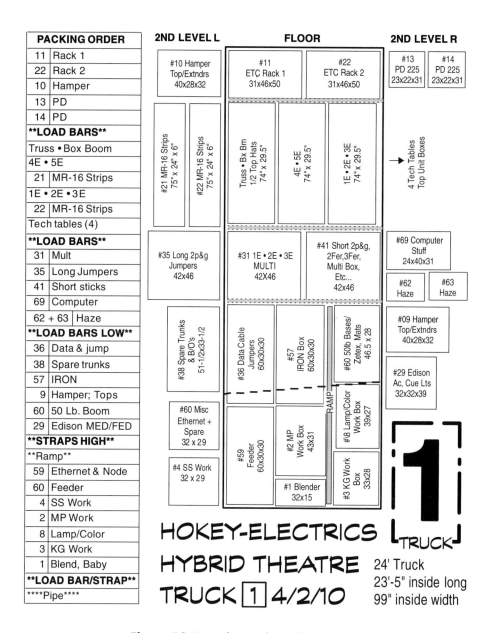

PACKING ORDER	
11	Rack 1
22	Rack 2
10	Hamper
13	PD
14	PD
LOAD BARS	
Truss • Box Boom	
4E • 5E	
21	MR-16 Strips
1E • 2E • 3E	
22	MR-16 Strips
Tech tables (4)	
LOAD BARS	
31	Mult
35	Long Jumpers
41	Short sticks
69	Computer
62 + 63	Haze
LOAD BARS LOW	
36	Data & jump
38	Spare trunks
57	IRON
9	Hamper; Tops
60	50 Lb. Boom
29	Edison MED/FED
STRAPS HIGH	
Ramp	
59	Ethernet & Node
60	Feeder
4	SS Work
2	MP Work
8	Lamp/Color
3	KG Work
1	Blend, Baby
LOAD BAR/STRAP	
****Pipe****	

Figure 10.1 *Hokey* Truck Number One Pack

schedule, which often includes the first technical rehearsal, and the first preview (or public performance). In order for them to be ready for those critical events, it often seems like the scheduled time prioritized for the lighting department gets pared down. This is the time needed for lighting to complete its own set of critical events; starting the focus, setting the cues, and being ready for the technical rehearsals.

Adapting Electrics to the Production Schedule

The changes that impact all of the technical departments of a show can also impact the amount of work they each have to achieve, and the amount of time required to achieve them. The performance surface that was an original painted groundcloth, has now turned into a rented assembled sprung floor, so more time must be allotted to allow that activity to fully take place. The main curtain that existed in the theatre can no longer be found, so time must be found somewhere in order to hang the traveler track and the goods.

The amount of time allocated for the electric department's activities is finite and already blocked off. So in many cases it's a question of what areas of the stage can be shared or abandoned, and when the stage can or can't get dark.

Some ideas to consider when the stage time clock runs out:

- Can any work be accomplished prior to the beginning of the load-in? Is it possible to pre-hang masking, other soft goods? Install the deck? Is it possible to bring any other trucks in before the load-in begins?
- How many hours of time exist prior to the first performance? If the call is departmentalized, how many people are allocated per department?
- Is there time allocated for the basic lighting tasks: a hang session, a hot test session, a focus session, a cue level setting session, a technical rehearsal, and a dress rehearsal? Can any tasks be combined?
- How much lighting equipment is being supplied by the show? How is the rental gear packaged? Any chance to change that, and speed the hang? Can any house gear be pre-hung that might save time? Or might it instead lose time?
- Is the show carrying its own lighting console? Is it possible to pre-write any cues prior to load-in, either in the shop, on another console, or using off-line editing software?

When all is said and done, no matter how badly other departments' bone-headed choices may negatively impact the lighting department's schedule, everyone has to work together. (For the purposes of this fictitious text, lighting would *never* make any scheduling gaffs. *ahem*). The lights can't be focused until the main components of the scenery are in place. Do all of them need to be in place before any focus can take place? Is it possible to focus some other area of the light plot while the final portion of the scenery gets installed? That's when experience and the ability to adapt come in to play.

While added events or left curves can significantly impact a production schedule, more often than not the overall number of days and work calls, once established back in the production meetings, often remain the same. The actual activities that take place during those work calls may eventually have absolutely nothing to do with what was originally scheduled. And no matter how far ahead the production may seem to be, relative to the original objectives laid out in the schedule, it is rare that a work call is ever cancelled. The work always seems to expand to fill the schedule.

The production schedule may be turned on its head, but that typically doesn't really start happening until all the "unforeseens" start to show themselves. More often than not, they remain concealed until the stage time clock starts, when the old adage "time is money" becomes painfully true.

While there are many important dates and meetings on the production schedule, one of the more important time periods prior to the load-in is the run-though. Or, if you're lucky, the run throughs.

WATCHING THE RUN THROUGH

The run-through is often the final scheduled work session for the cast in the rehearsal space. While more than one run-through may appear on the schedule, after the final one, the rehearsal hall is cleared of the production's equipment. The show gear and all the personnel then move into the theatre in order to start the technical rehearsals onstage. There are multiple reasons for a run-though.

From the director's perspective, the run-though may be the first and last time to see the overall rhythm and flow of the show, without getting slowed down by the technical elements like transitions, costume changes, or light cues. It's also the director's only shot to see if, as the show runs, the overall production concept succeeds. For the performers, the run-though is the first chance to consider where they'll need to be both on and offstage during each moment of the show. For the rest of the creative team, the run-through allows them to see how the individual scenes will fit (or not) into the environment waiting for them at the theatre.

For the lighting designer, on the other hand, the run-through is a big deal. A huge deal. On a complex show with a tight tech schedule, most designers consider attending the run-though critical. As opposed to all the meetings and descriptions and diagrams, the run-through shows the lighting designer the actual planned placement of every scene. It shows the designer all the transitions. It shows where everyone who isn't talking in the script or score has actually been blocked on the stage. It allows the lighting designer to place each lighting change, have a sense of the amount of time required for each change, and may allow the lighting designer to understand what needs to change for all those incomplete cues listed in the cue master. Finally the run-through will show the lighting designer all the 10-minute dance sequences that, up till now, have been indicated in the script as "Group Dance."

On top of that, the run-though might be the first *and only* time that the lighting designer ever gets to see anything about the show before the whole thing drops into his or her lap onstage. For that matter, this might be the first time the designer's seen *anything*, even though the plot's been approved and getting prepped while we speak.

While it may seem obvious the show should have several run-throughs before moving to the stage, that's rarely an option. Oftentimes the rehearsal schedule is just too tight to allow more than one run-through to take place. When that's the case, everyone connected with the show can only shrug, and work with what they've got. When more than one run-through takes place before the move, many lighting designers perceive that as a gift.

On those good days, viewing multiple run-throughs translates into several chances for the lighting designer to see the show, update the cue master, and refine the plot's focus before the focus or cue setting sessions take place. On bad days, the single run-through may not take place until the middle of the focus call. When that's the case, sadly, unless there's an assistant that can focus the show, or someone to videotape the run-through, the ability to pre-cue the show is going to suffer. In non-union situations, lighting designers often ask that the run-through be videotaped, so that it can be slowly analyzed, broken down, and played through numerous times. In union situations, Actor's Equity doesn't normally allow run-throughs to be taped without special or extenuating circumstances. Those are the times that having a really smart stage manager, who knows the rules for many different unions, can come in very handy. In times of desperation, however, one personal tactic that's proved successful is to take the stage manager out to dinner and have her act out the entire show at Chi-Chi's using salt-shakers and chips as substitutions for the performers, based on the promise of free margaritas and a taco.*

In any event, whenever the opportunity to watch a run-though is offered, the savvy lighting designer will take advantage of the invitation. Although the show is still coming together, and no doubt things will change once the cast gets on the stage, every chance to see the show provides the lighting designer with several opportunities. With each viewing, the lighting designer can improve and define the cue master, clarify the follow-spot choreography, discuss any number of thoughts or ideas with the director (or other members of the creative team), or just become more familiar with the show.

Prior to Attending the Run-Through

- Check the day before to make sure the run-through are still going to take place.
- Make sure you know where the rehearsal studio is located and how to get in.
- Make sure the cue master is up to date.
- Make sure your copy of the piece is up to date. If there are re-writes, arrange to have them

prior to, or immediately upon your arrival. It's always embarrassing to be following your script and then the performers start saying things that don't match your script, leaving your cues in a puddle on the floor.
- Make sure any groundplans included in the script/score/movement chart is up-to-date.
- Make sure all relevant batteries are charged; phone, laptop, etc.
- Make sure you have the contact sheet, especially the phone number for the lighting rental shop and the production electrician.
- Eat something or take food with you. Don't be the doofus who walks in and asks someone to go out and get him or her a sandwich.

General Run-through Tactics

- Check the schedule for the day. It may be that the scheduled run-through has changed, been adapted or aborted and you've just missed the memo. It's always embarrassing to find out just before the rehearsal that, instead of the run-through, they're instead going to beat the dead horse over that piece of business involving the dinner plate. And then you have to somehow collect your gear and subtly get out of the rehearsal room unnoticed.
- Arrive early and get a seat with a table, desk, or music stand so that you can write and take notes. It's counterproductive to try to update the cue master or make any notes juggling the production notebook on your knee.
- When possible sit next to the stage manager. Invariably there will be questions. The director may want to sit next to you as well; you should certainly be polite and ask the director of his or her preferences. This may also be hinged on the number of times you'll get to see a run-through.
- Identify the cast members and connect them to their characters; write notes about their names and any descriptive features.
- Introduce yourself to the cast so they know who you are.
- If need be, introduce yourself to the stage manager.
- Bring everything you need in order to write in your production book, make notes on a pad, or update documents on the laptop. Don't be the "needy" doofus designer who wastes the stage management team's time getting him or her settled before they can start the run-through.
- Identify all of the tape marks on the floor. See if they match with where you think the scenery has appeared on the groundplans provided to you.

---

*It's worth noting that this particular stage manager, after years of tolerance, agreed to become my wife.

- Take a look at the props; even if they're beat-up rehearsal items, make sure there are no last minute adds that have dropped through the cracks. "This is the new Staff of Tee-boo, the lights in it help suck the soul out of Pookie. We just added it yesterday."
- Check for the running time of each act. Don't be the one caught checking his watch.
- Make sure you mute or turn off your cell phone.
- Go to the bathroom before the run-through starts.
- If you bring anything to drink make sure it's covered so you can't spill it as easily.

Watching the Run-Through One Time

- If there are followspots, make sure the assistant is there to whack out the first prelim followspot cue sheets
- Make some kind of mark for each moment the lights change. Don't worry about numbers. Just mark when change takes place in the script, any idea of why and the amount of time for the change.
- Doodle in a general idea of blocking where the focus person is during light change.
- Note where other people are blocked during the scene.
- Try to quietly reach agreements with the assistant about when folks are in specials, or when they're in followspots.
- Immediately after the rehearsal, update the cue master and the piece.

Watching the Run-Through Two Times

- Preparation: Go through the piece and clean up, add, or clarify any possible marks. Update the cue master if used.
- Identify the portions of the show you completely missed because you were madly writing the first time.
- If possible, talk though the missing sequences with the stage manager before the rehearsal to define when focus or the lights should change.
- Immediately after the rehearsal, update the cue master and the piece.

Watching the Run-Through Three Times

- Preparation; Go through the piece and clean up, add, or clarify any possible marks. If possible, assign numbers to cues. If possible, give the cues to the stage manager, and possibly call it with them to provide them initial exact placement.

This way they can place each "go" in the call book before the tech rehearsals start. Big help.
- Fill in the rest of the blocking as needed. Call the show, if nothing else, to yourself and add cues, split cues as necessary.
- Immediately after the rehearsal, update the cue master and the piece.

Alternate Run-Through Tactics

Another way to watch run-throughs is based on hard scheduling. The designer knows the total number of run-throughs that will be possible to attend. While it accomplishes the same ends, it's structured slightly differently:

- Three run-throughs: 1-Track blocking, 2-Place cues, and 3-Time cues.
- Two run-throughs: 1-Track blocking, 2-Place and time cues.
- One run-through: Place and time cues, doodle blocking where you can.

End of Run-through Tactics

- Check that there is no post run-through informal production meeting.
- Say goodbye to the director/choreographer/driver of the boat. Make sure they don't have a pressing concern—if they do, stick around and find out what it is.
- Check notes, with the stage manager. Make dates to talk to everyone. Call the production electrician with any changes to the shop order or the hang or whatever.
- Go home, update the cue master and the piece.

Hokey Run-Through Notes

- The characters now assume many of their costume pieces after they have entered the stage. After the group assembles at center, Judy comes to the audience and speaks as Judy. As she finishes speaking, she puts on a costume piece and "becomes" Pookie. The color roll in the spot will hopefully be enough to reinforce her transformation.
- This is repeated three more times; Mitch becomes Tee-boo, Lorraine becomes the Knotty Piner, and George becomes Hokey.
- There is a *lot* of followspot activity. While it's been decided that the assistant lighting designer will choreograph and call the followspots in rehearsals, as important is the question: Who will call the followspot cues once the show is open?

The assistant lighting designer's only on contract through opening night. The same goes for the lighting designer's as well. If there's not an assistant stage manager assigned to the task, then it falls to one of the two followspot operators to take the lead. They may be paid a bit extra in their weekly salary, but with that they then assume the responsibility of watching the show in the stead of the lighting designer; adjusting pickups, giving notes on timing and movement, and instructing any followspot replacements.

FINAL PREPARATIONS FOR THE LOAD-IN

While you may not be leaving your home, in a sense, yes, you really are. Entering an extended tech period is a bit like going to a foreign country, or being somewhat separated from your typical surroundings.

You won't watch as much TV. You won't read as much of the paper. You won't be as prompt to return phone calls or messages that aren't show related. Matters outside of show-related information, ideas, or even gossip, may lose significance. Your world potentially tunnels in and becomes smaller.

That's not saying that this is a bad thing. It's just reality. So in order to prepare for this potential situation, below are some tips that might help at the other end, once the tech process is complete, the show is up and running, and you return to your regularly-scheduled life.

The Day (Week) Before the Load-in

- All current bills are paid.
- Library books are returned.
- If you've got a lawn, cut it.
- Confirm that there are no vital appointments during the tech period. If there are, tell the stage manager or the assistant.
- Send out all appropriate presents, cards, letters for all appropriate birthdays or anniversaries.
- Program the TV recording device to record all your favorite TV shows and sporting events.
- Stock up on food in the refrigerator. Food items that can be prepared with a minimum of effort, without a long preparation wait.
- Energy food and drink for the production table; non-perishable energy bars, pop tarts, nuts, liquids. This is also less expensive than buying in the deli next to the theatre every day.
- Coffee and coffee filters. For long tech periods, consider powered cream; regular milk goes bad relatively quickly.
- Favorite cold medication; Dayquil, Nyquil. Pain-reliever for tired legs; Ibuprofen or equivalent.·
- Purchase any alcohol or whatever allows you to relax.

The Night Before the Load-in

The night before a load-in, a lighting designer's emotions can range from a relaxed feeling of confidence to a feeling of paranoia and dread. The "night before" can often feel like the final period of time before the clock regulating stage time starts ticking. It's the last time that tasks can be approached in a leisurely manner. When nerves and anxiety try to take hold, regain your mental equilibrium by reviewing the load-in.

Remind yourself of the goals to be accomplished the next day, and imagine the steps required to complete each task. Are there enough copies of the paperwork available for additional last minute distribution? Is all of the paperwork prepared, allowing all questions to be rapidly answered? This may be the point when the designer discovers the need for another list.

Initial Paperwork and Tools

One decision the lighting designer needs to make prior to the load-in is the amount of information to have on hand when first walking in the door. The phrase "that paperwork is still on the electrics truck" takes on a whole new meaning when the electrics truck isn't the first to get unloaded, or when its axle breaks prior to reaching the dock, or when it's missing in the blizzard on the other side of the Continental Divide.

As the distinguished lighting designer Ms. Jennifer Tipton once said, "If you have a choice between taking your paperwork or your underwear, take the paperwork. You can light a show without undies, but you can't do much lighting with underwear."

Many lighting designers walk into theatres with that point of view, expecting delays with the arrival of equipment. They begin the day with enough paperwork to perform all work ignoring the contents of the truck, thereby avoiding any possible waste of stage time. Paperwork may include a copy of the light plot, the section, focus point groundplans, preliminary paperwork, infrastructure programming information, the magic sheet, and the cheat sheet. The focus document may also be included, so any changes made during the hang may be directly noted onto the paper that will be used during the focus session.

Since the amount of paperwork and equipment can quickly become cumbersome, many lighting designers coordinate their baggage with the production electrician. The road crew may also arrive with everything needed to accomplish every facet of work possible without the equipment packed in the electrics truck. This may include tape measures, scale rules, marking devices such as chalk or spike tape, and any hanging information. A copy of the show files will often travel separately from the electrics truck. If the show files contain any preprogramming, they may be loaded into the house lighting console, and the process of soft-patching dimmer information can begin. Even if the show files contain no information whatsoever, their presence may allow preprogramming to occur.

If house equipment is being used for the front of house positions, consider bringing precut or sheet color for those positions. If the overhead electrics are going to consist of house equipment, consider bringing the reference information needed to hang those positions as well.

Before the Lighting Designer Walks into the Theatre

Here's a last minute checklist for the paperwork, and for the lighting designer to feel reassured and prepared:

- Make certain that the plot is updated and that all distances from centerline are known.
- Check the section for all trim heights and focus point locations. Make any notes required.

- Make certain that the master focus point groundplan is updated and ready for use.
- Make certain that the focusing documents are updated. Consider rehearsing the focus at home, the night before the focus session. Some lighting designers quiz themselves by flipping to random instruments in the focus document. They see if every fact that may possibly be needed during the focus is present on the reference document.
- Determine which documents will be needed, and where to place them so that they are rapidly available.
- Don't store the light plot in the bottom of the carry-on bag.

A moment should be taken to remember other tools that the lighting designer possesses. The ability to prioritize, troubleshoot, problem solve, and communicate are all skills that will be called on throughout the production process. Superseding those abilities, however, are the lighting designer's good judgment, common sense, and a sense of safety.

SUMMARY

Once the paperwork and equipment have been packed for transport to the theatre, and the next day's production schedule has been reviewed, the lighting designer is prepared for the load-in.

Stage 3: Application

Using the Packets

Chapter 11

The Load-In and Setup

INTRODUCTION

This chapter examines events that occur at the beginning of stage time, between the start of load-in until the beginning of the focus session.

When the load-in for a production begins, it's often greeted with many emotions: equal parts confidence, calm, worry, concern, and anxiety, typically mixed with a healthy dose of relief. A great deal of time has been spent analyzing, discussing, and preparing every aspect and contingency of the schedule planned to mount this production. Until now the execution of these efforts has always been referred to in the future tense. Finally, it's the Monday morning of the load-in; the activities will begin to happen in the "now."

From a distance, the first day of a load-in is a quick-paced, exciting, terrific learning experience. If the process hasn't been thoroughly analyzed and prepared for, however, the load-in can be an exhausting, overwhelming exercise in backpedaling. On these days it seems that before one unexpected question is resolved, a second unexpected question is posed. When this situation occurs, and the questions can't be immediately answered, the best initial response is to define how soon an answer is required. Then find the personnel or documents that will provide an answer.

In the best of times, it's a joy to be able to see the often-discussed plans fit smoothly into place. At other times, it's irritating to see minor misunderstandings cost stage time. The worst of times is when problems continually crop up. At that point, disappointment can easily motivate a person into assigning blame. Conflict can rapidly surface. There may be conflicts between members of the crew, conflicts between members of the staff, or possibly conflicts between the crew and the lighting designer. Since each of these situations has the potential to impact the schedule, the lighting designer should be aware of these issues. If her or she remains oblivious to developing conflicts, that inaction may contribute to the possibility of an emotional outburst, which, feelings aside, will inevitably cost stage time.

The lighting designer, along with the rest of the production staff and department heads, is responsible for more than just making the show happen. Everyone needs to remain constantly vigilant to keep the situation safe. While everyone is subconsciously watching for safety, they also need to monitor the relationships and situations that can develop, so that bad feelings don't affect the speed of the load-in.

BEFORE THE LOAD-IN BEGINS

Before arriving at the theatre, the contact sheet should be reviewed in order to memorize the names of the crew heads. Calling individuals by their names shows a measure of respect, and it also reduces the miscommunication that occurs when someone doesn't know that he or she is being addressed. For the *Hokey* load-in, there's the production staff (or road crew) in addition to the staff of the facility (the house crew). All of the lighting designer's requests will first be directed to the production staff or crew. Regardless of the size of the show's staff, however, memorizing the house crew heads' names also enables the lighting designer to establish better working relationships.

The lighting designer does nothing but help his or her cause by arriving early at the theatre on the load-in day. Arriving before the work call begins provides several opportunities.

One optimal opportunity is that he or she will have the chance to see the performance space before it gets completely clogged up with gear and screaming people. Ideally, this isn't the lighting designer's initial viewing of the stage. Previous visits have clarified all of the observations, measurements, and questions about the performance space. The technical representatives or the crew heads have been introduced during preliminary meetings and discussions. On the other hand, if the combination of a distant location and a lack of financial funds has resulted in all information being transferred long distance, this may be the designer's first opportunity to view the space, and make initial face-to-face contact with the house crew.

If this is the first contact with the performance space, it's wise to quickly check the theatre's spatial relationships. The primary document for this task is the section, which should be consulted to confirm that the drawn document matches the reality of what's in the air above the stage. Next, the section and the light plot should be consulted to confirm that the drawn location and number of front of house positions really agree with the actual architecture.

A measuring tape can be used to check the sightline point for accuracy. If the distance from the plaster line to the sightline point is greater than originally thought, it may provide some amount of visual "cushion" in the vertical trim heights of the masking and the electrics. If the distance is less, the sightline point will be closer, and see higher into the flies. Nothing needs to be done about this right now, but being aware of this situation can be important, and will be examined in more detail when the trims are set later in this chapter. The distance from centerline to the sightline should also be compared to what's drawn on the groundplan. It may be discovered that the groundplan sent to the lighting designer may have left out an entire section of seats extending farther offstage than the drawn sightline point. In that situation, it may be necessary to reconsider the portal leg opening width, or the possibility of extending the masking farther offstage. If any changes are considered necessary, the production manager or technical director should be immediately consulted. Any alteration can quickly be agreed upon mutually and communication between the proper parties can take place before the beginning of the call.

Other locations in the theatre can be quickly visited and analyzed as well; the row location for the production table, the back sightline of the orchestra, and the onstage relationship with the FOH lighting positions. All of these are worth looking at, since they all may require modification of the plans in store for the electrics, masking, or cable runs.

Union Considerations

Most productions employ stagehands who may or may not belong to the **International Alliance of Theatrical Stage Employees** (**IATSE**, or the **IA**). The production heads working for the show (the road crew, or the production crew), along with the lighting designer and the rest of the creative team, supervise the installation of the production into the performance facility. The performance facility's technical staff (the house heads) provide and supervise any additional labor hired to perform the tasks necessary to mount the production, the house crew.

Many professional stagehands are IA members and belong to local chapters of the union. The professional union for lighting designers is the **United Scenic Artists** (**USA**). IA stagehands have a structured agreement that defines the number of hours a person can work in a single 24-hour period, with appropriate compensation for each one of those hours. This hourly structure can be unique in each union situation. USA designers, on the other hand, have no hourly theatrical rate in the present contract. Although the USA lighting designer is paid by the week, or by a fee, he or she must be aware of the clock. Along with the rest of the technical staffs working on the show, the lighting designer strives to make certain that the work is being completed in the budgeted amount of time, and that the stagehands are receiving the breaks required by their contract.

Until 1999, USA and IA were two different, separate unions. As such, the relationship between designers and stagehands was much more restrained. In April of that year USA members overwhelmingly voted to join the IA. While the pay rates are still the same as before, the fact that USA members are now union IA affiliates has allowed for an increased level of cooperation between the two groups.

Regardless of union affiliation, however, the understanding between lighting designers and stagehands is that the lighting designer provides the direction for the tasks (the light plot, the other paperwork, the objectives), while the stagehands provide the methods and labor to achieve these objectives. In practice, this means that the lighting designer's job is to watch the load-in without being distracted by performing physical labor. Or, simply put, when the lighting designer is working in a union house, he or she should not be required (nor, in some cases, allowed) to touch any equipment. Instead of expending effort on tasks that are assigned to others, the lighting designer should be concentrating on the accuracy of the work being performed. Together with the production electrician, the lighting designer considers the most time-efficient sequence that can be applied to the tasks necessary to produce the show.

Every union house has its own set of rules defining when coffee and meal breaks are required. Most designers agree that a positive working relationship with any crew can be developed by being polite, considerate, respectful, and simply following the rules. Additional simple advice often includes the gentle reminder to anyone who's a tenant, and not the owner, that they are the guest. Just as it's impolite to move furniture in your host's home, it's impolite to move equipment in someone else's theatre without asking. For example, ask permission to move a road box, or ask for assistance to do so, in order that your work measuring the stage can continue, rather than just shoving the road box. Be nice; there are many ways to accomplish the end means necessary to produce the show.

Regardless of the size or affiliation of the crew, knowing who's in charge and being aware of the local rules will reduce the number and severity of misunderstandings. The more union or house rules the lighting designer knows, the better equipped he or she can be to contribute to time-management decisions. In many cases, the leader of the road crew (the technical manager or the production manager) may have already memorized the local rules. Often these rules have been examined in other conversations when the options for the production schedule were considered.

Here are some of the questions that assist informed decisions to be made: Who's the **house union steward**? This position may be separate from the house heads. It is often the person responsible for payroll and checking everyone's contracts. In fact, the house steward is probably the person who will know the accurate answers to the rest of these questions:

- Is the crew departmentalized?
- How long can work proceed before a coffee break has to be taken?
- How long should a coffee break last?
- How long can work proceed before a meal break has to be taken?
- Does the entire crew have to break at the same time for meals?
- Can there be a "split" between crews? (This is discussed later in more depth.)
- How long, prior to the end of a work call, does "wash-up" occur (the point when the crew stops work to "wash their hands" prior to a meal break)?

- How late can the work call extend without going into overtime?
- Does the entire union load-in crew need to remain through the entire focus?

Two other basic questions should be addressed that may have a direct effect on a union call. If the production schedule has been altered or is unclear, the questions are worthy of consideration, since they will have a direct effect on the lighting designer's internal time clock:

- What time is the focus session scheduled to begin?
- What time is the focus session scheduled to end?

Information Distribution Check

After the initial introductions are made, casually inquire and confirm that everyone has the correct matching information. Presumably, the road crew has had the relevant paperwork for some time, so this double-check is hopefully limited to the house crew. The house master electrician should have the plot, the section, and the support paperwork. The house head fly-person should have some form of the hang plot and the section. The head carpenter should have the groundplans, the section, and the hang plot. If the paperwork has been misplaced, or never got to the house heads in the first place, this is the moment where having extra copies may save time. Otherwise, the lighting designer may start the day by determining the location of the theatre's photocopy machine and the amount of time required for it to warm up.

Being certain that everyone has the same information reduces misunderstandings. If the transferal of this information is not confirmed, these misunderstandings, which may not be discovered until much later in the load-in process, may result in hours of duplicated effort.

The First Misunderstanding

The first hours of a load-in can easily be thrown into disarray once the lighting designer is provided with accurate information. Those situations often started long ago with basic assumptions made by the lighting designer that will now prove to be based on inaccurate information. This information may be casually pointed out: "Yeah, the battens have always been 10'-0" shorter than what they show in the drawing," or "They keep saying in the tech packet that the circuits in the deck are different on either side. Heck, they repeat in every other floor pocket, and across the back for the groundrow."

HOKEY SOFT GOODS RENTAL			
ORIGINAL RENTAL REQUEST		**JUST UNLOADED OFF THE TRUCK**	
5	(Pairs) black legs 30'-0"H x 10'-0"W	1	(Pairs) black legs 26'-0"H x 4'-0"W
4	(Pairs) black legs 30'-0"H x 6'-0"W (tabs)	2	(Pairs) black legs 26'-0"H x 8'-0"W
		1	(Pairs) black legs 27'-0"H x 4'-0"W
		1	(Pairs) black legs 27'-0"H x 8'-0"W
		2	(Pairs) black legs 29'-0"H x 4'-0"W
		2	(Pairs) black legs 30'-0"H x 8'-0"W
5	Flat black borders 12'-0"H x 50'-0"W	2	Flat black borders 4'-0"H x 50'-0"W
		3	Flat black borders 6'-0"H x 50'-0"W
		1	Flat black border 10'-0"H x 50'-0"W
1	Black Sharkstooth Scrim 30'-0"H x 50'-0"W	1	Black Sharkstooth Scrim 24'-0"H x 50'-0"W
1	Black Traveler 2-30'-0"H x 30'-0"W (w/track)	1	Rosco Twin White Trans 28'-0"H x 50'-0"W
1	White Translucency 30'-0"H x 50'-0"W	1	White Bounce 28'-0"W x 50'-0"W
1	White Bounce 30'-0"W x 50'-0"W		

Figure 11.1 The *Hokey* Soft Goods Order: What Was Ordered, What Was Delivered

Thankfully, someone has informed you of the discrepancy. If the correct information drastically alters the shape or plan of the lighting design, it's unfortunate, but it happens. Don't waste time assigning blame. The house crew works with the physical objects on a daily basis, not the representational drawings. They rarely refer to the tech specs because they work with the equipment, not the lists. Without attending every production meeting for the show, it's impossible for them to understand the physical inter-relationships between the technical elements and the light plot. With luck, this accurate information will be received before the load-in begins. This time can be used to analyze the situation with a bare stage, drawings, and the appropriate personnel without the surrounding distractions of a load-in.

First, thank the individual for providing the information. Next, confirm the accuracy of the information. A course of action may be taken that allows the crew to continue work, while avoiding any tasks related to the potential problem. By temporarily avoiding the situation, alterations to the plan won't delay or duplicate any efforts. Take the time to specifically identify the problem and its potential effect on the production. Consult the members of the production team who might be affected by any change. When a solution is determined, the change should be communicated to all affected parties, and the paperwork should be updated to reflect the change.

The Masking Snafu

For the purposes of this text, however, the problem is going to be significant, and the lighting designer will be required to provide a remedy to the situation. It starts with the house carpenter walking into the production office with a receipt from the soft goods rental company. Saying "The guy that just dropped off the hampers and bags said that it wasn't quite what you ordered, but that it was pretty close," he gives the shipping receipt to the lighting designer.

Figure 11.1 is a comparison of the original order on the left-hand side, and the goods that were just unloaded on the right-hand side. They're not quite the same. Actually they don't have that much to do with each other. Actually, about the only thing that is similar between the two of them is that the masking is black.

In a realistic situation, this would be the point when the scenic designer, the production manager, the technical director, and the production carpenter would all get involved. While the lighting designer might still be involved in determining a solution, he or she would not be directly involved in all of the leg-work, but instead merely part of the process coming to a series of decisions. On the other hand, there's so little time before the lighting designer (and everyone else) needs the masking in place, he or she may be forced to be more pro-active in finding a solution or, at least, an initial course of action. For the purposes of this text, none of these folks is around, so the process can be viewed from a single perspective. The lighting designer is forced to consider all courses, take all actions, and quickly make all decisions in order to solve this potential schedule-wrecker. This scenario is being presented as an example of following theatrical protocol, presenting one method of thinking a problem through, and making decisions based on a process. First things first:

- All proper parties on-site should be made aware of the situation. Notify the leader of the road crew. In a typical situation it would then be their responsibility and judgment call to notify management. In this case, since there's no one else, the lighting designer will delay calling the management office until he or she has a complete grasp of the problem. Right now since this is only a hypothetical problem; there's no reason to "ring the alarm bell" until an accurate understanding of the extent of the potential disruption is determined.

- To that end, the supposed "erroneous soft goods rental" must be immediately counted and inventoried to confirm that the goods now in the building match what's shown on the rental agreement. This must be the second action taken; best-case scenario, it might turn out that the correct rental package arrived with the wrong slip. Realistic-case scenario, it may turn out that what's been delivered is exactly what's on the receipt. Worst-case scenario, the actual package that's been delivered has nothing to do with either the original rental or this delivery receipt—it's worse. Regardless, until the accuracy of the delivered inventory is confirmed, all subsequent actions may be unnecessary, fruitless, or need to be taken again.

- The third action must be to choose one of the three initial courses of action as quickly as possible: 1) These soft goods will be hung now in the best manner possible and not be replaced; 2) these soft goods will be hung now, in the best manner possible, and replaced at a later time; or, 3) these soft goods will not be hung now. They will be returned and an alternate source of soft goods will be hung instead in the (very) near future.

- Presuming the realistic-case scenario is indeed the true status of the situation, the delivery receipt is accurate, the next logical step is to consider the schedule: How much stage time remains before some kind of masking must be in place, and how long will the it take to properly complete the task? This might be the time for a mini-production meeting.

- First the completion time; all of the affected battens need to lower to the stage, get the goods tied on, get properly counterweighted, and then flown out. The borders need to have bottom pipe installed in their pipe pockets and trimmed. The scenic stack needs bottom pipe installed in all three pieces: the back scrim, the trans, and the bounce. All three of these need to be trimmed as well. This work cannot be done in the dark, nor can it be done in silence; there must be communication between the deck, the fly rail,

and the loading bridge above. Conservatively, this task could take anywhere from 2 to 4 hours.

- Next, the production schedule: how long can the overall load-in wait before starting the task to hang the masking and not slow the process?

Obviously, if the masking is hung and trimmed before the focus begins Tuesday afternoon, as scheduled, that would be best. But, if the goods are not in place during the focus, that can be worked around with spike tape and a solid focus plan. If the soft goods are not in place by the time the tech rehearsals begin, on the other hand, that's not acceptable. And frankly, if they're not in place by the time cues begin to be constructed, their absence will slow the process; there will potentially be too many other distracting tasks still happening offstage. So they (or their replacements) have to be in place by Wednesday afternoon for the cueing.

That said, the soft goods can't really wait until Wednesday morning to be installed; that's scheduled to be the main session allotted for focus. Trying to direct the focus call at the same time that the soft goods are being hung means that more worklight will be required for the carpenters, and there will be additional noise between the deck and the loading rail. Not good. The goods could be installed in a special Tuesday night work call but producers rarely (if ever) agree to pay the overtime penalty.

No, the latest that the soft goods can get installed is really Tuesday afternoon, while the FOH focus is taking place. While there will still be worklight and some amount of ruckus, the potential acoustic conflict will be lessened, since the electrics crew's noise will be confined to shouting commands to each other in the house, not on the stage.

In order for this sequence of events to take place, however, any replacement masking would then ideally arrive on site before the end of the Tuesday morning work call, before lunch. Since it will take some amount of time to assemble and transport the rental from whatever alternate source, that period of time will assumedly take place Tuesday morning. All told, as far as the lighting designer is concerned, the decision to commit to alternative masking must then be made before the end of business day today (Monday), or the entire schedule is endangered.

While this monologue has been solely concerned with the potential alternate masking's impact on electrics, the other departments need to also be considered and consulted as well. The delay or absence of masking may impact scenery, properties, or wardrobe's schedules in any number of ways that may not be apparent to the lighting designer.

- In this case, the count is complete and the result is the realistic scenario; the erroneous masking's exactly what was described on the delivery slip. Now that the mistaken inventory's confirmed, get on the phone to alert the production personnel and management of the snafu and to get their help. (In this case, none is forthcoming, so that all steps are examined.) Call the soft goods rental shop to confirm that the requested goods aren't available. It might be worth it to threaten to cancel the rental, but if there's not an alternative at hand, that's a fairly empty threat. Separate calls could be made to every other soft goods rental house, every other theatre, every rental house in adjacent cities, to see if the original order could still be produced and delivered to this theatre by the end of tomorrow's morning work call.

In the meantime, however, while all of these phone calls are being made (hopefully by others), the lighting designer must privately take the position that all efforts for immediate replacement will fail. While publicly providing support for other plans or options, the savvy lighting designer must privately presume the worst-case scenario, and plan as though the erroneous masking will be the soft goods that are hung in place potentially through the focus, the tech, and the opening of the show. If no one else is considering this alternate plan, the lighting designer better be. The lighting designer who chooses not to ponder this possibility does so at his or her own peril.

If the decision is made at the last minute to use the erroneous soft goods, without a prepared plan in place, the resulting chaos could be disastrous, and straightening it out at a later date will do nothing but lose precious stage time for the lighting designer. For that matter, the decision to abandon getting replacement goods could come at any time. The lighting designer has to approach this replacement exercise as if it is the only course of action. While it may later be perceived as an unnecessary exercise, it's useful to examine the process and method in order to see how it might be applied to other situations. For that matter, it might turn out that the alternate plan might be an acceptable alternative solution, eliminating the need to make any change in the delivered soft goods whatsoever.

From a logistical point of view, no one else may have considered any alternate plan; at this point, it's not as important, or it may not have yet been acknowledged as a possibility. In this situation, the person most likely to get stuck is the lighting designer. And, if nothing else, from merely a superstitious point of view, refusing to acknowledge this situation as a perfect demonstration of Murphy's Law, and failing to cobble together *some* kind of plan, could easily be perceived as hubris to the theatre gods, and invite the Fates to tip the scales into Murphy's favor.

With all that said, presuming this is the masking that must be used, how should it be hung in order to most closely resemble the original masking picture that was designed? What process can be used to quickly and efficiently see the whole picture and be able to make coherent decisions?

The Masking Snafu Analysis

In order to quickly analyze the situation and formulate a plan, the method used will be three-fold: Determine exactly what is needed in order to achieve the goal, compare all available resources to the listed needs in order to fulfill the goal, and then adapt as necessary to complete the task.

The first tool used to begin solving this puzzle is the latest version of the scaled section. At this point the small dotted sightlines are the key to determining the actual required height of each piece of goods, while the dashed horizontal lines provide signposts in order to make rough visual height measurements. If there are no sightlines indicated in the section, this is the time to quickly draft them. The sightlines can be used to define the soft goods heights actually needed to mask the show.

- Measure or gauge a visual guesstimate of the height where each sightline crosses the bottom of each border and touches each subsequent leg. Figure 11.2 shows a small white dashed circle at the juncture between sightline and leg height for linesets 3, 15, 27, 39, and 51. Write each height above each leg lineset. This is the actual height required to conceal the top of each set of legs.

- Measure or gauge a visual guesstimate of the height where each sightline stops on the face of each border. Another set of white dashed circles shows this juncture on linesets 1, 14, 26, 38, and 50. Write that height above each border lineset. This is the actual height required for each set of tab legs.

- Measure or gauge a visual guesstimate as to the distance from the bottom of each border to the same point where each sightline stops on the face of that same border. Write this vertical height as a dimension next to each border. This is the actual height required for each border.

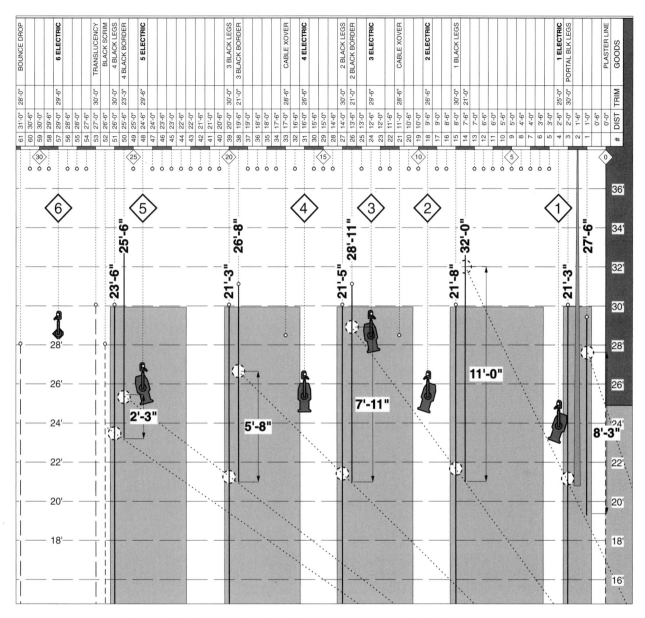

Figure 11.2 Actual Masking Dimensions Written on the Preliminary Section

Figure 11.2 shows the result of this exercise. Now that these distances are at hand, the second part of this step is to perform the same measured double-check of the width requirements for each set of masking goods in the groundplan. Once all of the actual dimensions are totaled, the combined heights and widths for each piece or pair of goods is then transferred to a single list.

Figure 11.3 shows this assembled list. The left-hand side shows the actual height and width measurements for each set of goods, along with their lineset number and distance from plaster line. The right-hand column shows the erroneous rental. Both columns are separated into four groups of soft goods;

the borders, the legs, the tab legs, and scenic stack, in order to make it as simple as possible to compare the relative sizes to one another.

Sneaky Tips: Shelley's Unwritten Rules of Masking

At this point it's appropriate to consider Shelley's Unwritten Rules of Masking:

- Shorter borders can often be assigned to the upstage openings farthest away from the sightlines on a proscenium stage. Taller borders

Hybrid Theatre 2010   **HOKEY SOFT GOODS SNAFU v1**   Date: 4/5/10

LINE	DIST.	MEASURED HOKEY MASKING REQUIREMENTS GOODS	HEIGHT	WIDTH		ERRONEOUS RENTAL GOODS GOODS	HEIGHT	WIDTH
1	1'-0"	Portal Border	8'-3"	45'-0"		Black Border	10'-0"	50'-0"
14	7'-6"	1 Black Border	11'-0"	45'-0"		Black Border	6'-0"	50'-0"
26	13'6"	2 Black Border	7'-11"	45'-0"		Black Border	6'-0"	50'-0"
38	19'-6"	3 Black Border	5'-8"	45'-0"		Black Border	6'-0"	50'-0"
50	25'-6"	4 Black Border	2'-3"	45'-0"		Black Border	4'-0"	50'-0"
						Black Border	4'-0"	50'-0"
3	2'-0"	Portal Black Legs	21'-2"	5'-6"		Pair of Legs	30'-0"	8'-0"
15	8'-0"	1 Black Legs	21'-8"	5'-6"		Pair of Legs	30'-0"	8'-0"
27	14'-0"	2 Black Legs	21'-5"	5'-6"		Pair of Legs	27'-0"	8'-0"
39	20'-0"	3 Black Legs	21'-3"	5'-6"		Pair of Legs	26'-0"	8'-0"
51	26'-0"	4 Black Legs	23'-6"	5'-6"		Pair of Legs	26'-0"	8'-0"
		Portal Tab Legs	27'-6"	2'-0"		Pair of Legs	29'-0"	4'-0"
		1 Tab Legs	32'-0"	5'-0"		Pair of Legs	29'-0"	4'-0"
		2 Tab Legs	29'-0"	4'-0"		Pair of Legs	27'-0"	4'-0"
		3 Tab Legs	26'-8"	3'-0"		Pair of Legs	26'-0"	4'-0"
		4 Tab Legs	25'-6"	2'-0"				
52	26'-6"	Black Sharkstooth Scrim	24'-0"	44'-0"		Black Sharkstooth Scrim	24'-0"	50'-0"
53	27'-0"	White Trans	24'-3"	45'-0"		Purchased White Trans	30'-0"	50'-0"
61	31'-0"	Bounce	26'-0"	45'-0"		Bounce	28'-0"	50'-0"

Expression 3; 150 chan, 174 dim   Lighting design by Steve Shelley 917.xxx.xxxx   Page 1 of 1

Figure 11.3 The Measured Masking Requirements Versus the Erroneous Rental Goods

are usually assigned to the downstage openings closest to the sightlines on a proscenium stage. (The sightline seats can see higher into the downstage openings.)

- If the border trims are all approximately the same, the leg heights may get slightly shorter the farther upstage the legs are from the sightlines.

- Almost any border does not need to hang on the next adjacent lineset downstage of the leg. It's the leg placements that really define the openings for performers or scenery. As a matter of fact, as long as the border is a matching, or close to the same, trim height as other nearby borders, it can be some distance away from any relative legs. The intermediate linesets in between are often then assigned to scenic legs or portals.

- The border with the cleanest edge should be hung on whichever lineset visually "tops" the translucency for a majority of the audience. That is typically *not* the portal border; instead it is often the first border downstage of the trans.

- The legs with the cleanest edge should be hung on whichever lineset visually "frames" the

sides of a translucency for the majority of the audience. Usually, that's also the first set of legs downstage of the trans as well.

- The height of a set of legs is ideally the same height as its relative tab pipes. If a pipe "L" bracket is inserted into the end of a leg pipe batten, then the extra leg fabric can be tied "around the corner" and act as its own tab.

- The height of the tab leg pipes should be the higher than the sightline point touching the face of the border immediately adjacent to it. Otherwise that same sightline point will see over the tab pipe.

- If midstage drops or other soft goods are hung immediately upstage of a border, they need to only travel higher than the bottom of that border to be hidden. If soft goods are hung immediately downstage of a border, they have to travel much higher in order to get out of sightlines. The soft goods also have to be that much taller in height to prevent their batten from being seen while the goods are at their "in" trim.

- Whenever possible, borders should be hung with bottom pipe. It prevents air currents from pulling the goods into backlight beams. Carpenters who hang borders without bottom pipe and insist that there's no difference are not lighting designers.

- Borders should not be hung as legs, and legs should not be hung as borders. For one reason, the ties are in the wrong place. For another, the nap of the fabric is running in the wrong direction. If light hits the fabric it will stand out and look peculiar. When necessity forces you to disregard this rule, try to use two borders as a pair of legs, so they match. Attempt to use the leg hung as a border so that it is not topping the translucency.

Masking Snafu Comparisons and Solutions

In a comparison between the two vertical columns, it's quickly apparent that the three pieces in the scenic stack that have been delivered are still large enough to be hung without any loss in the original intent of the design. Since the translucency is a purchase, it won't be returned. If both the black scrim and bounce have to be returned, at least the battens will already be weighted for their replacements. If the carpenters are in need of activities, they can hang the black scrim, the white trans, and the bounce. In the meantime, the rest of the list can be analyzed.

After a quick study of the overall numbers, it seems that the overall amount of masking is sufficient, or close to it. While there seems to be an extra border in the delivery, compared to what's needed on the left-hand side of the page, it's also obvious that lineset 14, the 1 black border, needs a border that is 11'-0" tall. The tallest border in the erroneous delivery is 10'-0" tall.

Because the unwritten law states that the taller legs need to be placed downstage, the erroneous rental goods have been resorted so that the tallest pieces are at the top of each list. The 8'-0' wide goods have been positioned adjacent to the black legs called for in the lineset schedule, while the 4'-0" wide goods have been sorted by tallest height across from the tab legs. It's apparent that there's been a bit of a miscommunication, since a set of tab legs is also missing from the erroneous order.

After no small amount of head scratching and erasures, a plan has been concocted. It's not perfect, and the initial plan to hang all of the tab legs on a single pipe at one trim has had to be abandoned.

Ideally, this plan has involved the carpentry staff, since it means that they'll be forced to hang some other arrangement in order for these tab legs to work.

Figure 11.4 shows the arrows detailing this plan. Since the single 10'-0" border wouldn't cover the 11'-0" tall vertical gap on line 14, it was delegated to line 26. Instead, two 6'-0" borders have been assigned to the line 14 area; one on 14, the other on line 13. The first few rows may notice the second border on 13, but they'll have to look pretty hard for it. The 4'-0" borders were a bit more tricky. One of them was easily assigned to line 50, since that vertical gap was only 2'-3". But the final 4'-0" can't possibly fill the vertical gap of 8'-3" measured on the portal border on line 1. After numerous alternatives are considered, a concession is made; the main curtain is swapped with the portal border. While this means the curtain won't be able fly out of sight (otherwise it'll expose line 1's system batten), it means the 4'-0" border now on line 2 will cover the new 3'-8" vertical gap. Since the border has moved 6" upstage, it means that the border's trim can be slightly increased, to 20'-0", which may possibly help the proportion of the stage picture.

The legs have worked out much like the unwritten laws said; the tallest legs are downstage, except for the portal black legs. Since those needed to be 5'-6" wide, and that area also needed a 2'-0" wide portal tab leg, the carpenters will provide an "L" bracket inserted into the end of lineset 3, and the single 8'-0" wide leg will tie around the corner to provide both leg and tab leg.

The rest of the tab legs were all 4'-0" wide, so there will still be a side masking hole on the downstage side of the 1 Tab Legs. But that will only be for the extreme sightlines.

Figure 11.5 shows the adjusted section, using the erroneous soft goods, and swapping lineset 1 and 2. A pair of positive notes; since the border is now on line 2, its trim can be raised 6" without altering the position of the 1st Electric. That in turn means that the followspots' focus range has slightly increased; their beams can raise up a bit more on the upstage shots if needed. On the down side, there's still a masking hole from the near sightline over the top of the 1 Tab Legs, as well as a small masking hole over the top of the portal tab legs. The riggers will be forced to either hang four tab pipes on either side of the stage, place "L" bracket extensions on the existing battens, or rig trapezes from a single upstage/downstage pipe. But above each leg and border there is a written indication of the soft goods height, and on each tab leg there's an indication of height and size.

Hybrid Theatre 2010   **HOKEY SOFT GOODS SNAFU v2**   Date: 4/5/10

MEASURED HOKEY MASKING REQUIREMENTS						ERRONEOUS RENTAL GOODS		
LINE	DIST.	GOODS	HEIGHT	WIDTH		GOODS	HEIGHT	WIDTH
2	1'-6"	Portal Border	3'-8"	45'-0"		Black Border	10'-0"	50'-0"
14	7'-6"	1 Black Border	11'-0"	45'-0"		Black Border	6'-0"	50'-0"
26	13'6"	2 Black Border	7'-11"	45'-0"		Black Border	6'-0"	50'-0"
38	19'-6"	3 Black Border	5'-8"	45'-0"		Black Border	6'-0"	50'-0"
50	25'-6"	4 Black Border	2'-3"	45'-0"		Black Border	4'-0"	50'-0"
						Black Border	4'-0"	50'-0"
3	2'-0"	Portal Black Legs	21'-2"	5'-6"		Pair of Legs	30'-0"	8'-0"
15	8'-0"	1 Black Legs	21'-8"	5'-6"		Pair of Legs	30'-0"	8'-0"
27	14'-0"	2 Black Legs	21'-5"	5'-6"		Pair of Legs	27'-0"	8'-0"
39	20'-0"	3 Black Legs	21'-3"	5'-6"		Pair of Legs	26'-0"	8'-0"
51	26'-0"	4 Black Legs	23'-6"	5'-6"		Pair of Legs	26'-0"	8'-0"
		Portal Tab Legs	27'-6"	2'-0"		Pair of Legs	29'-0"	4'-0"
		1 Tab Legs	32'-0"	5'-0"		Pair of Legs	29'-0"	4'-0"
		2 Tab Legs	29'-0"	4'-0"		Pair of Legs	27'-0"	4'-0"
		3 Tab Legs	26'-8"	3'-0"		Pair of Legs	26'-0"	4'-0"
		4 Tab Legs	25'-6"	2'-0"				
52	26'-6"	Black Sharkstooth Scrim	24'-0"	44'-0"		Black Sharkstooth Scrim	24'-0"	50'-0"
53	27'-0"	White Trans	24'-3"	45'-0"		Purchased White Trans	30'-0"	50'-0"
61	31'-0"	Bounce	26'-0"	45'-0"		Bounce	28'-0"	50'-0"

Expression 3; 150 chan, 174 dim   Lighting design by Steve Shelley 917.xxx.xxxx   Page 1 of 1

Figure 11.4 Drawing Arrows Between the Measured Masking Requirements and the Erroneous Rental Goods

While this may not be an ideal solution, it's a plan that can be a basis for discussion with other crews working on the show. Regardless of the final outcome, either the redrawn section or the diagrammed spreadsheet with arrows can be used as a basis for communication. If the decision is made to retain and install the delivered goods, either of these documents may become the reference archives used to record the installation of the erroneous soft goods rental order. In the meantime, calls can be made to management (if needed) to inform them the problem has been solved, and work can continue until the next unforeseen challenge.

THE LOAD-IN BEGINS

The beginning of a load-in can often be seen as controlled bedlam. Trucks are unloaded, equipment is moved into the space and distributed onto the stage, components of the house inventory are brought out of storage for use, and questions are being answered everywhere. Crates, boxes, racks of costumes, rolls of vinyl, pipe, scenery, soft goods, and numerous other components all seem to converge into the space.

During the initial load-in, keeping the hot zone clear and collectively shared between departments can be a challenge. Since it's the primary workspace used to perform most initial tasks, deciding who gets to use the hot zone for their departmental tasks can often turn into a test of wills. Scheduling activities in this area often requires combining the skills of a New York City traffic cop and the diplomacy of the State Department.

In constrained spaces, preserving the hot zone may result in equipment covering the seats of the house, filling the aisles, the concession areas, and even the lobby of the theatre. Everyone has a purpose, and is trying to get a jump on the day. The overall goal is to assemble and install all the lighting, scenery, properties, and sound equipment into their pre-designated locations in the time allowed.

While unloading equipment into a space can be seen as an exercise to "just get the gear in the door," the mechanics of a load-in are often approached from a different perspective. To avoid clogging the hot zone, much of the equipment must be placed in temporary storage locations. Those locations are often carefully considered before the load-in begins. Random dispersal of the gear may result in

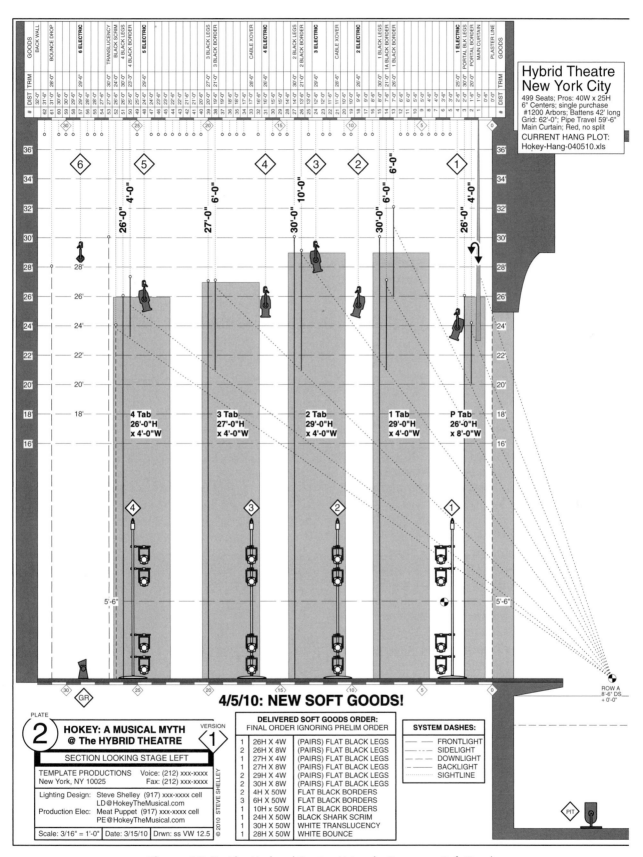

Figure 11.5 The Updated Section Using the Erroneous Soft Goods

additional time and effort spent retrieving the equipment back to the playing area when it's needed. Worse yet, it may end up "buried" in such a remote location that it might not be found again until the load-out. The people directing the equipment's distribution attempt to assign convenient temporary storage locations, and reduce the number of movements required by the equipment.

Before the load-in begins, the production manager, the road heads, and the house heads construct a general plan of equipment distribution. Initially, equipment is usually divided into two categories: things on wheels that can be placed almost anywhere, since moving them a second time doesn't require extensive time or effort, while items without wheels that won't have to be moved again until used should be placed in out-of-the-way locations. This plan attempts to allocate storage areas to each department so that the equipment is only moved twice. First, it is moved into the space so that when the trucks are empty, the hot zone is clear and ready for use. Its arrangement is also planned so that when the time comes, the equipment can be moved into the hot zone for assembly in a manner requiring the least amount of time and effort.

Usually, the production electrician or an assistant directs the lighting equipment to its locations. Equipment that will be installed in the front of house positions are often initially directed to an area adjacent to the front of house access, which may be the steps in the lobby. Additional dimmer racks brought in for the show are often placed in the location that will become their home. The reason for this is two-fold. First, by storing the racks "in place" they're available to be hooked up at any time. Second, nothing else can be stored there, and later get in the way. The instruments for the overhead electrics and any accompanying cable are stored on the sides of the stage, or nearby in the audience so that they'll be close at hand when it's time for the electrics to be hung.

The lighting designer's designated role during this time is to be an observer and a visible source of information. Although some requests for information may be questions regarding "when": ("How soon before you're going to want to start the focus?"), most of the questions directed to the lighting designer will be asking for definitions of "where." This may range from locating points ("Where do you want the production table?"), to confirming points of boundaries ("Where's the onstage edge of the legs?"), to establishing relationships between objects ("Before we hang the legs, where do you want the sidelight booms?"). In some cases, a defined "guesstimate" may be acceptable to

allow work to continue. In other cases, a concrete response may be required. Being able to provide comprehensible, accurate answers requires prior analysis, comprehension, and preparation for each aspect of the overall design.

The ability to provide a concrete response to the "where" questions is directly related to the lighting designer's ability to quickly define the performance space into spatial points of reference. Defining the space is often achieved by placing spike marks on the stage.

 **Shelley's Soapbox:
Keep the Hot Zone Clear**

I think of a load-in like a drafting. When I've got a light plot laid out on the drafting table, I try not to clutter up the workspace by piling books, paper, and other debris on top of the plot. When I let the clutter accumulate, the first thing I have to do is get the piles off the document before I can resume work on the plot.

Similarly, during the initial load-in, all cases, boxes, or equipment should ideally be placed somewhere else other than in the hot zone. Anything placed or temporarily stored under a batten used by the show will have to be cleared from that area before any work involving that batten can begin. If the choice must be made, things in the way that are castered are good. Things in the way that are not castered, requiring some amount of time to move again, are bad.

Key tip-off phrases include "Hey, Randy, let's just drag this pile of jumpers out to the center of the stage" or "Just dump all of the gel frames under the first electric. We'll sort out what we need." Find the production electrician and ask him or her to delicately intervene. Perhaps the pile could be located somewhere else. If it really has to be there, perhaps it could it be placed on or in something with wheels when it makes its debut onto the stage. Hopefully, those same wheels will allow it to rapidly disappear at the appropriate time.

 **Shelley's Soapbox:
Count the Gear**

When the rental package is prepped in the lighting shop, one set of tasks includes testing, sorting, and labeling the outgoing gear. Schedules or finances may prevent that from happening, though, and the rental package might appear on the doorstep of the theatre prepared by folks who have no vested interest in the final product.

Without anyone representing the show's interests present in the shop while the lighting package was assembled, it makes perfect sense to **check the counts** as the gear gets unpacked. Not only should counts be made of each category to make sure that the right number of doodads actually made it into the order, it's also worthwhile to confirm that the doodads even got included, and that they even work.

Determining mid-way through the load-in that there aren't as many two-fers as what was asked for in the shop order is one thing. Their absence may potentially slow down the final installation of the circuitry, or the wring-out.

Not discovering that the specific molded-end power cords required to power up the lighting console or the opto-isolators until after lunch, on the other hand, can quickly become a major headache. Unless quick action is taken, these power cords may not appear on site until the end of the day or the next work call after that. Their absence may delay the wring-out, and potentially, impact the schedule for the focus.

In this situation, the savvy lighting team requests a double-check of the counts when the lighting package comes in the door, to ensure that all the pieces and parts that are physically on site match the numbers that were originally on the shop order. Since no one in the theatre packed the boxes, performing the counts also means everyone knows where all the pieces are. And the sooner that it can be confirmed that the rental "will assemble into a fully functional system," then the faster it can be installed, instead of looking for the pieces in order to do so. Many folks use the "count-in" as the time to also distribute the gear to its intended destinations: console and associated pieces to the production table, color frames and template holders to the gel table, and so on.

Checking the counts also provides peace of mind on the load-out. Since the numbers were confirmed when the gear walked in, there's no question about the numbers when the gear gets loaded out. If the counts weren't checked during the load-in, (and the numbers were wrong when they came out of the shop), the show may potentially get charged to replace gear it never received.

Shelley's Soapbox: Test the Gear

The second part of that last soapbox is: When the electronics get unloaded, smart (read as: bitter) lighting designers open the rental console and run through its basic functions to make sure those aspects of the unit are in full and functional working order. For that

matter, experienced production electricians quickly cobble the entire rental electronics package together after it comes off the truck to confirm that everything made the trip intact. While that certainly starts with consoles, monitors, dimmer racks, opto-isolators, printers, and keyboards, it can also be extended to any other electronic devices in the package. In some cases, that might include a dimmer rack's control module, or numerous moving light fixtures.

While checking every mover before it's hung may not seem practical, experience has shown that the faster that any gear can be tested, the better. Countless stories can be told where the console wasn't unpacked, or set up until the dimmers were installed, and the entire light package was up in the air. Only then was it determined that the console didn't work. Without a backup console close at hand, all work allowing the process to proceed came to a complete, grinding halt. And remained so until something like a replacement arrived on site.

While I've personally experienced the failure of many devices, my specialty has always seemed to focus on the rental lighting console. For that reason, as soon as it's convenient for the production electrician, (if needed) I'll ask for the console to be sequestered somewhere off to the side, set up and tested, as early in the day as possible. That may not be possible until the morning coffee break. But if a problem is discovered, it can be addressed before lunch, and solutions can be found so that the afternoon call isn't jeopardized.

 One basic list of console functions to check after setting it up and turning it on:

- Turn on the console to confirm it boots up.
- Confirm that the monitors work and that their color settings are correct.
- Check the submasters, faders, any touch screens, and encoders.
- Confirm the console outputs DMX.
- Confirm the external keyboard works.
- Does the external printer work? Does a personal printer work with it?
- Confirm the internal disk drive writes to a storage device: a floppy drive, a flash stick, or a flash card.
- Verify the internal disk drive can read information from a storage device: floppy disk, flash stick, etc.
- Any DMX and video nodes are bootable and come on line.
- Check the data stream and confirm the count for opto-isolators, any Ethernet switches, and control cables.
- Check for spares.

Keep in mind that most shops typically have only one or two time periods a day when they can devote an employee and a vehicle to come to the theatre to make a delivery or pick something up. The sooner the problem can be perceived, the sooner the replacement or additional gear can be scheduled for delivery or exchange. If you don't discover the problem until late in the afternoon, or at night, scheduling nuances may force the show to lose a second day without the functional item. Either that, or you may be forced to arrange your own pick-up/drop-off using your own resources.

While all of this talk of "double-check" and "be careful" may seem unnecessary, keep in mind that any electronic device that breaks down inevitably takes some, if not all, of the lighting package down with it. In some cases, testing might pinpoint the need for a new fuse. On the other hand, it might also highlight a dead power supply. The sooner the problem is known, the faster it gets attention.

Shelley's Soapbox: Establish Your Base of Operations

During the first hours of a load-in, I've found it critical to define an area somewhere near the stage as my "base of operations." I want my information and tools close to me. I don't want the base to be moved, yet I want it secure and accessible. The first key word is "accessible." If the answer to the question is in your bag, but your bag is safely stowed in the production office on the third floor, everything can potentially come to a grinding halt while you scramble to the third floor to retrieve the answer. If your bag, which was offstage safely out of the way, suddenly got in the way, you may instead spend some time quizzing the entire crew to determine the new storage location of your bag.

During the initial load-in, I like to locate my base of operations down center. Usually, I find down center is typically out of everyone's way. Not only can I perform any work that's necessary, I can also monitor the entire stage. If there's enough room downstage of plaster line, I'll establish a base of operations on the edge of the apron. If I'm in the way, or if there's no apron, I'll establish the base in the first row of orchestra seats. If there's an orchestra pit, I'll move to a side area of the apron so that my bag stays on stage.

When there's enough room, this area of the stage can also become an ideal load-in location for the electric workbox, the color distribution box, or a table from which to work. When possible, I'll use an empty scenery hamper for the table of my

"office." It's on wheels. When I need to clear the area, or move the "office" to a different part of the stage, I can easily wheel the hamper to the location of my choosing.

Shelley's Notes: Paperwork Changes

Changes occur as soon as the load-in of a light plot begins. A change has three points in its lifetime. Initially, it's born when the decision is made to do something different from what was originally planned. Second, it receives an identity when it's recorded onto a document that uses it as a point of reference. Finally, it ceases to be a change when it is absorbed into an updated generation of documents, turning it into a known fact.

When the production electrician is informed of a change, he or she must write down the information into the appropriate paperwork, decide its significance, and choose whether or not to inform the lighting designer of the change. Likewise, when the lighting designer is informed of a change, he or she must record the change into the applicable documents, decide its significance, and choose whether or not to inform the production electrician of the change. These choices are based on the judgment of both individuals, which is why the communication between the lighting designer and the production electrician must constantly remain clear.

The point when revised documents are published varies by designer. For many designers, that time is after the focus session has been completed, and the lighting package has "settled down." The changes from all of the various documents used through the load-in are then updated into the lighting database and all other relevant paperwork. Once published, obsolete paperwork should be clearly marked as such. Although some lighting designers want reprinted plots, magic sheets, and cheat sheets before the light cue level setting session, others are more comfortable retaining their original version of these documents containing handwritten changes instead.

Shelley's Notes: Keeping Paper and Keeping Track

Throughout the course of the load-in, consider keeping copies of the important paperwork at your fingertips. There's no telling where or when a question may be asked, and if the paperwork isn't with me, time can be wasted searching for the answer. I've found that most initial questions can be answered by carrying a copy of the light plot, the section, the magic sheet, and the cheat sheet. By keeping these pieces of paperwork with me at all times, changes can be updated, regardless of my location. I've also found it useful to keep the paperwork in my pockets, not carried in my hands. Once it's set down on a crate, the crate may be moved while my back is turned and then the paperwork is gone.

When changes are made, the support paperwork will eventually need to be updated to include them. For the most part, though, I've found it simpler to record the changes on the documents that will be used when creating the light cues (magic sheet and cheat sheet) or on the base documents showing the overall design (plot and section). In addition to the typical changes of circuitry, color, and channel information, there may be additional or altered groups or submasters. When possible, I attempt to design the layout of the magic sheet to include extra white space for the purpose of recording additional groups or subs. Typically, I'll be looking at that document when I'm searching for a handle. I've found that those handles can be seen as tools, but if they're not identified, they may as well be forgotten tools in the cellar.

To maintain communication, and not introduce out-of-date data to the situation, a single location must be defined during the load-in as the repository of all current information. Common wisdom states that after the support paperwork leaves the hands of the lighting designer, the most current data regarding the lighting package is the version possessed by the production electrician. If told of any changes in circuitry after the load-in begins, I immediately take those changes to the production electrician and they're recorded into his or her support paperwork. Changes in purpose or focus, on the other hand, may not need to be immediately transferred to the lighting database since they don't impact the installation of the light plot.

Being able to quickly scan a page and see those changes, though, reduces the time spent updating information. I usually mark the changes in the appropriate document with a red pen. When changes are updated or communicated, I can find them. If the changes are made in a neutral color, they're easier to miss, and obsolete information may then be distributed. During updating sessions, I use a highlighter to mark on top of the red pen changes, reflecting the fact that the change has been included to the updated material. At the conclusion of an updating session, scanning each page for highlighter will confirm that all the changes have been made.

The need to assign additional control channels to devices may not become apparent until the middle of a load-in. At that point, the lighting designer should be given the choice to determine the additional channel assignment. If the device is assigned to a channel without informing the lighting designer, he or she may unknowingly assign an additional instrument to the same channel. The channel will be constantly changed to control the intensity of the instrument, while simultaneously altering the amount of voltage being fed to the device. If the device requires a constant voltage, this action may damage it. The lack of communication will cause improper programming to occur as the memories are constructed, and the location of the unlisted device may remain unknown until a crisis results due to its absence. Peripheral devices are peripheral only until they can't be found. Then they become a priority.

Shelley's Notes: Keeping Archives

As soon as the load-in begins, changes start to stack up. As soon as they're absorbed into the updated paperwork, the old versions start piling up. For years I decided that once the change was complete, there was no reason to keep that old paperwork around. So I threw all of the old versions away on a daily basis.

I followed this practice until the day when the director decided to return to a version of the show that had been long abandoned for over a week. When I couldn't find the critical piece of information in any wastebasket in the theatre, I resorted to emptying every trash can in the lobby. When the missing piece of information was found, it was very ripe. And I spent no small amount of time later cleaning up the lobby.

I learned my lesson. These days I search for an empty box; there's usually one in the photocopy room or the shipping room. I'll clearly mark it "archive" and leave it next to (or on top of) the production table. It doesn't matter whether anyone else throws his or her old paperwork in there as well. I know that, at least my old records are there and available at any time for retrieval. And since it's separate and exclusively paper, there's no way it can smell like that missing page.

Shelley's Notes: Delays During Load-in

Whenever a lighting package travels some amount of distance to a theatre, the possibility always exists that the transport may not arrive at the facility at the scheduled time. If the trucks don't show up at the beginning of the load-in, there may be a crew standing around with nothing to do. If the house equipment to be used includes instruments in the overhead electrics, the house electrician may be resistant to clogging up the hot zone with those units. This makes sense, since there's always the possibility that when the first electric is being hung, the truck will arrive, causing interruption and chaos.

If the front of house color, accessories, and console information are on site, however, work can still be accomplished. The house console can be programmed, while the front of house instruments can be prepared for focus. If the trucks are still absent by the time the programming has been completed and the instruments are prepared, consider focusing the front of house instruments without the rest of the light plot or any scenery. If the spike groundplans are accurate, the performance space can be spiked, and a limited focus can occur without clogging the stage.

Certainly, it's preferable to focus the entire light plot in a single session. Having the lighting and scenic package in performance positions ("the stage is set") means that the scenery doesn't have to be imagined, and the focus between systems and hanging positions can be accurate. On the other hand, since the focus will have to take place anyway, it may be prudent to take your best guess and focus what's available while the stage is otherwise dormant. When the trucks finally arrive, all concentration will be directed to the load-in and the entire schedule will be compressed. Waiting until the stage is set before focusing any front of house instruments will translate into that many more instruments that have to be focused in even less time.

SPIKING THE DECK

The moments before the beginning of a load-in are often perceived as "the calm before the storm"—the last time the deck is available to stretch out a tape and measure any points or boundaries. Leaving a measuring tape undisturbed on the stage for any length of time may not be possible again until all of the combined equipment is installed, assembled, and the peripheral items removed. Returning to that particular state, when the stage will again be calm, often seems to coincide with the beginning of the focus session—which is *not* the time to be making spike marks; that's the time to be focusing instruments as fast as you can. Nope, the best time to spike the deck is at the beginning of the day, before the maelstrom of load-in hits the fan. And the amount of time available to tape any spikes is brief, so it had best be completed with

precision and speed. If the spiking isn't done quickly, it will take twice as long to get the measuring tape into position undisturbed without getting run over by crates, ladders, stagehands, or your own staff. If the amount of load-in gear is even close to the footprint of the stage, it may be impossible to place the spike marks at all. And if the spike marks aren't right—like the mark for zero-zero—the entire layout of the stage may be off-center by that errant amount.

If there's not enough time at the beginning of the load-in to accomplish this activity, two scheduled periods of stage inactivity may be available to complete the task. Usually there's a coffee break mid-way through the morning call, or the lunch break may leave the stage unoccupied. If it becomes impossible to make spike marks on centerline, measuring the upstage/downstage spike marks can still be completed with relatively few interruptions on the side of the stage receiving the least amount of traffic. Often that's the side of the stage opposite from the loading door.

In order to place any spike marks based on measurements, a measuring tape is strongly suggested. While that may sound redundant and condescending, it's worth pointing out. Taping out the entire deck using only the 4′ × 8′ masonite sheets as signposts may seem to make perfect sense. Later discovering that the masonite was really only 3′-6″ × 7′-0″ is very deflating indeed. After the measuring tape is positioned, the marks can be accurately made.

Since the goal is to get the spikes down as fast as possible, prior thought should be devoted to define the minimal number of measuring tape positions that will be needed in order to produce the maximum number of spike marks. The initial mark that will define all measurements left and right is the centerline. Since the centerline is defined as the equidistant point bisecting the width of the proscenium opening, the simplest way to accurately determine that point is to measure the width of the proscenium and divide by 2. Any other method involving multiple measuring tapes is comparably haphazard, and the flawed information can indirectly lead to calamitous setbacks to the schedule.

Once the centerline is defined (creating the algebraic X axis), the Y axis must be determined. This second axis is often the plaster line, but the lineset for the main curtain, or the upstage side of the steel guides containing the fire curtain (the smoke pocket), are also used as an alternate line of reference. Although a case can be made defending each location's use as a demarcation, the reference choice rarely impacts the show's success. What's vital is that everyone who uses this demarcation point mutually agrees on the line of reference.

That reference line affects the location of everything from the location of added linesets, to the depth of an added built apron, to the location of spike marks for the Act 2 chair. To repeat: everyone connected to the show must agree on what is being used for the line of reference. Choosing a singular alternative can have dramatic impact on a production. Consider the scenario when the show deck containing thousands of dollars of automation didn't fit onto a stage. The resulting waste of time, effort, and money can be directly traced back to the one individual who chose to use the main curtain as the line of reference, instead of the otherwise mutually agreed-upon plaster line.

In this case, the plaster line will be used as the *Y* axis to locate the focus spike marks for *Hokey*. If there is no mark on centerline to define this line, one is often created using a carpenter's snap line stretched between the side walls of the proscenium arch. For some productions, this line of reference is all that's required in the opening moments of a load-in. The first installation activity of many productions is to install the performance surface, based upon these *X* and *Y* coordinates. When that's the case, the remaining spike marks can be made directly on the performance sur-face. If a performance surface is installed later in the load-in, however, it may be necessary to spike the deck a second time prior to the focus. Until that time, however, the first set of spike marks can act as the reference points during the scenic and electrical hang, and may end up being used during the focus session as well.

Now that the *X* and *Y* coordinates have been established, measurements can be made to create the spike marks, which will define the focus points, boundaries, and reference points within the performance space. The document that will be used as the template to create these points is the master system spike groundplan that was created in the load-in and setup packet of information.

Figure 11.6 is the master focus point groundplan, indicating all of the distances involved. At the intersection of centerline and plaster line (or the zero-zero point), a taped cross is placed to visually provide a temporary reference point. After the taped cross is made, a measurement is made directly upstage to match the distance from plaster line to the system pipe that will contain the black portal legs (2'-7"). At this point, a T is placed, marking the down center light line. Often, one of the first inquiries is in regard

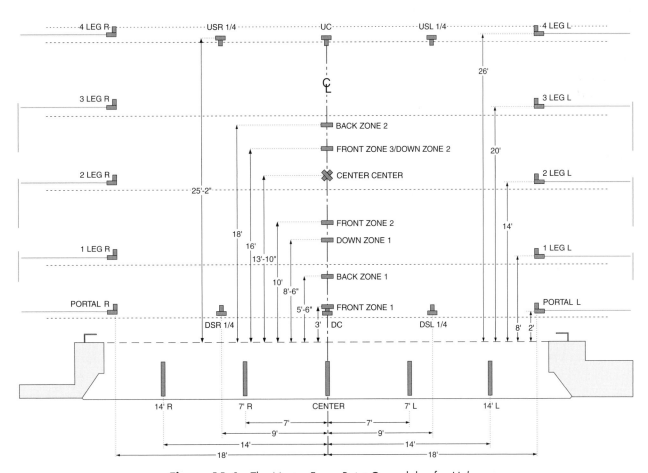

Figure 11.6 The Master Focus Point Groundplan for *Hokey*

to the location of the leg line, so the initial marks are made to either stage left or stage right. The measuring tape, attached to this T, is laid out to either side, parallel to the snap line chalk of the plaster line, offstage into the wings. After being tightened, the measuring tape is then used as the basis for the downstage quarter line light lines (9'-0"), the portal leg lines (18'-0"), the frontlight focus strips (7'-0" and 14'-0"), and the front of the sidelight boom lenses (26'-0").

Define Up Center

In many theatres, several marks have been made adjacent to or on the back wall denoting centerline. When no one can agree on which mark is the one and true centerline, all the existing marks are graffiti. When it's important to the show to have confidence in the up center mark, re-define the upstage centerline to your own satisfaction employing two (matching) tape measures. Each tape is attached to a matching point on each side of the proscenium arch, typically at the corners of the proscenium. They are then laid out diagonally, so that the two spools of the measuring tapes cross over each other close to the upstage wall. After the tapes are tightened, the two tapes are adjusted until the distances of both tapes match.

Figure 11.7 shows the two matching distances overlapping at 37'-1½". Presuming that both tapes are equal, the matching distance must be on centerline. The new improved upstage centerline point is marked, and then a second snap line is often applied to define the entire upstage/downstage length of centerline.

Once the snap line has been removed, one measuring tape is then reattached to the downstage taped reference cross, and laid out running straight upstage on the snap line. Since the master system groundplan has been drawn indicating distances from plaster line, the taped cross will be used as the downstage reference point. Once the measuring tape has been laid out and tightened, the centerline marks made on the master system groundplan will be duplicated onto the stage. For visual clarity, the three different zone marks are often made in different colors. The frontlight zones may be marked first (3'-0", 10'-0", and 16'-0"), followed by the downlight zones (8'-6" and 16'-0"), and finishing with the backlight zones (5'-6" and 18'0"). The center-center "X" (13'-10") is placed as an intermediate point of reference. Finally, the upstage light line "T" (25'-2") is spiked.

The measuring tape can then be attached to the upstage center T, and laid out to stage left or right, parallel to the plaster line. After being tightened, the upstage quarter line light line T's can be spiked (9'-0"), along with the onstage edge of the #4 leg

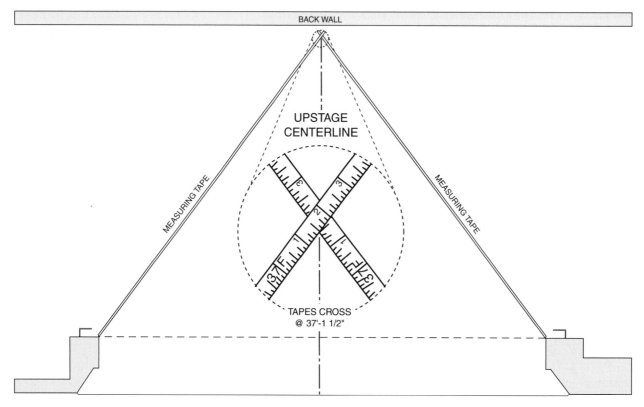

Figure 11.7 Crossed-Over Measuring Tapes Defining Up Center

(18'-0"), and the front of the sidelight boom lenses (26'-0"). The onstage edge of the intermediate black masking legs lines may be spiked by measuring up from the intersection cross to match the distance from plaster line to each of their system pipes (7'-3", 13'-2", and 19'-5"). After these marks are made, measurements are made offstage from centerline to each side of the stage (18'-0"). Later in the load-in process, carpenters may spike the onstage edge of the intermediate black masking legs. If the lighting designer doesn't anticipate the need for these marks during the load-in, the general location of the spike marks may be determined by standing at the black portal leg, and "sighting" upstage to the #4 leg. The decision not to spike the intermediate black legs will reduce the amount of time required for the overall spiking process.

Shelley's Soapbox: Provide Your Own Measuring Tape

Years ago I purchased a lightweight, compact 50'-0" fiberglass measuring tape that lives in my carry-on bag. It accompanies me to every load-in. Why carry a tape measure? If I combined the amount of time wasted watching a carpenter try to find his roadbox, or watching the stage manager open his roadbox drawers, or watching the production electrician empty his tool bag, I could have finished the spike marks. Besides, why should I place the responsibility on any of them to supply me with a tool I need at every stop? Having my own measuring tape allows me to perform my work at any time without dependence on others. I can make measurements anytime I want, without spending time requesting assistance.

Why add weight to the carry-on? When the luggage gets lost, measurements can still be made at any time. Presuming I arrive early at the performance facility with the tape in my bag, measurements can be made prior to the arrival of any show cargo. Why 50 feet? I've rarely trimmed a batten higher than 50 feet. I've never needed to locate a light boom farther than 50 feet from centerline. I've rarely had to contend with more than 50 feet of stage depth. Certainly, determining the centerline in some theatres has required a measuring tape longer than 50 feet, but that single measurement has typically been the sole distance requiring a longer length of tape.

Why fiberglass? I could circle the globe with the shards of my metal tapes that have been broken by ladders or crates wheeling over them, or people tripping over them. As a final thought, by not carrying a metal tape, the number of times my bag has been

dissected by airport security looking for that "dangerous-looking round thing" has been drastically reduced.

Shelley's Soapbox: My Spike Marks

Spike marks may have multiple uses in addition to being reference points for the lighting designer. If the carpenters don't place spike marks, the lighting designer's spikes may be utilized during the scenic hang to locate the center of each batten. They may also be used to determine the onstage edge of all of the masking and scenic legs. They may be referred to throughout the entire load-in process until the performance surface is installed.

Defining the space and providing reference points can be significant, and in my experience, I've found that I should place them myself. Allowing anyone other than me to make the spike marks can introduce an element of uncertainty. Regardless of who makes the marks, at some point during the load-in, their validity may be questioned. If I've performed the procedure myself, I don't need to be concerned with that uncertainty. I'll know that the mark has been correctly placed.

Tales from the Road: Spike Marks Without a Performance Surface

We were loading into the theatre on schedule. The light plot contained two zones of backlight, four zones of sidelight, and three zones of frontlight. Since the focus points were three distinct sets of distances from plaster line, I had placed the spike marks for the zones on centerline in three different colors of tape, along with apron stripes along the downstage edge. If the decision was made to focus the plot before the vinyl surface was installed, I was completely ready. If the choice was made to install the vinyl surface first, all I needed was a short amount of time once the vinyl was taped down to place another set of spike marks.

Suddenly both of those scenarios were thrown into doubt. The props head refused to lay the vinyl panels to create the performance surface until the focusing lift was off the stage. He had a point. Upon inspection, the focusing lift appeared to weigh about a ton, and the edges of the wheels looked like they could cut slits in the vinyl like a knife through warm butter. A review of the production schedule, however, showed that we were running out of time; the vinyl panels would need to be installed as the ladder moved upstage. Once the ladder completed each electric and moved upstage, the vinyl would immediately be installed in the freshly abandoned area.

Although I agreed in principle to this installation method, I was uncertain how I was going to accurately complete the focus session. Since the initial installation of the vinyl was to begin at the downstage edge of the stage, no apron stripes would remain uncovered. As each panel of vinyl was installed, another series of reference marks would be permanently obscured. Since I had no assistance, there was no one available who could replace the spike marks onto the vinyl as they were being covered. There was no time to interrupt the focus session while I wildly ran about with a measuring tape. How could focus be accurately performed without spike marks on the deck of the stage?

After some thought, I devised a plan. Since the focus points on the stage required triangulation anyway, I decided to extend the distance between the spike marks and the focus points. I went into the first row of the house, and sighted the locations of the apron stripes and the quarter lines to their matching locations in the first row of seats. At each location, I placed large strips of colored marking tape on the seat backs facing the stage. Presumably I'd be able to see these marks while standing upstage during the focus session. I then went to a location offstage of the planned edge of the vinyl floor. After laying out the measuring tape from plaster line running straight upstage, I duplicated the spike marks that had initially been placed on centerline, placing a second set of marks offstage in the wings. Since there were a variety of focus points for the different systems, I attached matching pieces of the colored tape on the light plot, so that while focusing, I would know which color referred to what zone. Finally, I rolled a rover offstage, plugged it into the wall, and focused it onto the new spike marks, so that they could be seen in the darkness during the focus.

The offstage spike marks functioned splendidly, and the focus session proceeded without hesitation or confusion on my part. The only hitch in the proceedings was when the props man noticed that someone had stuck a bunch of colored tape onto the front row of the audience seating, and began tearing the tape off before the focus was complete.

Tales from the Road: Spike Marks Without Walls

We were loading the electrics in for the show. The scenery truck containing the walls and ground cloth hadn't yet appeared. After the overhead electrics were up, plugged, and ready to focus, phone calls were made to find the scenery truck. It soon became clear that no one, including the dispatcher, had any clue as to the whereabouts of the scenery truck. Without a set, how could the focus be performed? We threw our hands in the air, proclaimed nothing could be focused (since it would all have to be redone once the scenery was in place), and proceeded to wait. And wait. As time wore on without the scenery truck's arrival, we started becoming concerned, since it was becoming apparent that whenever the set did arrive, there would be little time between the assembly of the set and the technical rehearsal. As the clock continued to tick, our concern grew to dread. The technical rehearsal was now in doubt. When (or if) the scenery showed up, there would barely be time to set it up and allow the performers to see the layout prior to the performance, much less focus the lighting. In an act of self-preservation, a plan was devised.

Together with the carpentry department, the set's location on the stage was defined. A groundplan was used to tape out the wall's locations on the stage. Since the stage would (eventually) be covered by the show's ground cloth, there was no concern about spiking the stage with small discrete pieces of tape; the walls became entire strips of tape. While this process was being completed, gallows humor suggested that, if nothing else, the performers could enact their blocking within the confines of the spike tape. The true test of their mime training, we decided, would be "walking up the stairs" stage right. After the tape on the stage traced the location of the walls in the groundplan, the points where tape crossed (the intersection of walls) were labeled with a large number, and the groundplan of the stage was ready for focus.

While the stage was being taped, four long pieces of 1 × 4 were located, all of which measured taller than the highest wall. These were broadly marked in 1-foot increments on both sides of the wood. Once these "walls" had been taped, the focus session began: four stagehands, each carrying one of the spiked pieces of wood, were assigned the roles of "wall intersections." They were directed to one of the large numbers marked on the stage (where two walls would meet) or other various locations to become "walls," "windows," or "doors." After they were directed to the proper location, the proper instrument would be turned on, pointed to the appropriate focus point, and the focusing electrician could accurately execute all of the required shutter cuts on the "walls." The number of directions required to position the "walls" during this time made the focus session sound like an extended square dance: "Dan, you move to wall point 3, Sabrina, swing around behind him to wall point 5." Although it took a little longer, in time the focus was complete. A spare A-frame ladder was cast in the role of the stairs so that the instruments could be focused to that area of the stage as well.

The set truck finally arrived, an hour before curtain. After the ground cloth was placed, rapid measurements were taken so that the walls of the set would be placed on the same points where the strips of tape had marked their location on the bare stage. The set pieces were assembled and the performance started a bit late, but the focus looked better than it had in some time.

HANGING THE LIGHT PLOT

Once all of the equipment has been brought into the facility, attention turns to the installation of equipment over the stage. Battens are lowered to chest height ("working height") so equipment can be attached to them. Typically, while the carpenters tie scenic goods to upstage battens, the electrics department starts hanging instruments onto battens downstage. The two departments attempt to complete their tasks while staying out of each other's way. The objective at this point is threefold: one, install the equipment and clear the stage as rapidly as possible so the performance surface can be installed. Two, safely install the equipment in such a manner that whatever flies up in the air stays there. Safety concerns aside, any overhead electric that has to later return to the deck will often cause a delay and cost stage time. Finally, three, hang the equipment and install it correctly so that it works the first time.

Before the Light Plot Is Hung

When the light plot's initially created on paper, the lighting designer makes specific choices that define the location for each instrument. While that may seem important on paper, for some lighting designers, the instrument's actual on-site position may not really be that vital. If the beam isn't seen, the need for absolute precision is often exchanged for speed during the installation. For other designers, the instrument's hang position is paramount and must be zealously observed. Although it might not be seen, the symmetry of the beam's placement is important to the focus. For some designers, this is especially true if atmospherics will be part of the show; without care and attention during the hang, the beams will not be symmetrical, and it will be noticeable from the production table.

In these situations, the production electrician and the crew must pay close attention and hang the lights at the distances dictated on the light plot. Likewise, in settings that involve foliage or multiple walls,

precision in the hang may be an absolute necessity in order to properly place light beams around the scenic elements. In these situations, a careless hang may affect the overall speed in which a lighting package is readied, and may ultimately have an impact on the integrity of the lighting design.

When all is said and done, if the coordinates of centerline and a Y axis (plaster line) are determined prior to the hang, replicating each hanging location shown on the drawing is really not that difficult to achieve; it merely requires some amount of effort and an attention to detail. The first step toward achieving this goal is to define the distance of each instrument from a single mutual reference point. Using an overhead electric as an example, the common reference point often used is the centerline. Mobile hanging positions like sidelight booms are typically defined by measurements taken from both centerline and plaster line. Measuring and marking the vertical pipe locations before hanging the instruments basically ensures that the instruments will end up in the right place.

Three methods are commonly used to define and communicate the hanging locations to the electricians. The first method transforms the distances shown in scale on the light plot into marks made on full-scale reference strips, ranging from rolls of adding machine paper, to drywall paper tape, to jute webbing. During the load-in these **hanging tapes** or **webbings** are either attached onto the battens or taped on the deck directly under the electrics batten while the units are being hung. Information about each instrument is marked on the tape at the proper intervals (unit type, color, circuit, channel), which is then used to prep the instrument when it's hung at that location. Once the instruments have been attached and prepped, they're checked for function and accuracy, after which the reference strips are usually removed.

The initial challenge to any of these tapes is how to mark them so they can be read, and in some cases, used more than once. A Sharpie can permanently write information directly onto a roll of jute webbing. If the information may shift around, it can be marked onto pieces of gaff tape, which are then stuck to the webbing at the proper location. Webbing rolls are large, and the tape can eventually get gooey. Adding machine tape is usually white, so Sharpies or pens can mark the info directly onto that surface at the proper locations. But adding machine tape isn't very wide, and it requires care. It can tear pretty easily while being used, and then delicate repair is needed to save the tape's value. For many electricians, drywall tape is the preferred way to go. It rolls up smaller than webbing, it's much more durable than adding machine tape, and it's usually about 2″ wide, providing a larger surface for providing written information. Rather than write instrument information at the dictated locations on the tape, smart production electricians now export the data directly from Lightwright into Microsoft Word templates designed for Avery preprinted label paper. Once the information is printed onto the labels, they're peeled off and stuck at their proper locations onto the drywall tape.

Since there are two sides to a hanging tape, it's possible to mark two different hanging positions on either side of this single reference strip, but this technique is not a good idea. When a show's being hung, it may not always be hung in the same sequential order. If one hanging tape has the information of two electrics marked on it, the tape can only be in one place at a time. During the course of a load-in, the point of confusion can come when one reference strip may simultaneously be needed at two different hanging positions at the same time. Most electricians agree that one exclusive hanging strip per overhead electric is a good rule to follow.

A second method cuts a copy of the light plot document into individual hanging positions. The pieces are then pasted onto multiple pieces of flat stock, such as cardboard or masonite, with a copy of the legend or key. Regardless of what they're mounted on, they're still often referred to as **hanging cardboards**, one cardboard for each hanging position. Since they're mounted on a backing, they don't need an additional clipboard in order to write information directly on the document. Since they're stiff, they're a little harder to lose, as compared to a piece of paper that can get tucked into a pocket and then forgotten. While the instruments get hung and plugged, the circuitry information gets written directly onto each cardboard and afterwards transferred back to the instrument schedule, channel hookup, or directly to the lighting database.

The third method utilizes the **instrument schedule**, with an additional column indicating the hanging location measurement from centerline, plaster line, or some other origin point. The measurements are verbally called out while the distances are marked directly onto the hanging position. Using this method means that the person handling the document must also verbally communicate all of the instrument attribute information directly to the electricians hanging the instruments, but it also requires the least amount of preparation.

Since these methods all use different formats to present the information, the lighting designer and the electrician (road or house) should agree on the method that will be used before the load-in. By doing so, the lighting designer will produce paperwork that the electrician will actually use. If the two don't communicate about the method to be used for the hang,

the paperwork produced by the lighting designer may be wasted effort, and have no value to the electrician or to the hang. For example, the lighting designer may produce an instrument schedule, which includes a written column of measurements from centerline. This may later be seen as a waste of time when it's discovered that the electrician plans to hang the show using cardboards. If the electrician doesn't communicate the desire for a copy of the light plot in a scale different from the one provided by the lighting designer, additional hours may be spent using photocopiers to reduce or enlarge drawings merely so they can properly fit onto the hanging cardboards and provide room for additional written notes.

Some situations allow the production electrician to pre-assign all of the circuits and dimmers in the electrical path prior to the hang. Although this technique is often used in productions that install a lighting package with little dependence on pre existing circuitry, it is also employed when some portion of an existing lighting package could potentially become a constraint. By defining each instrument's "electrical destination," a calculated guesstimate can be made about the amount of additional cable that will be required to plug the entire hanging position. In these situations the lighting designer needs to provide the electrician paperwork that will save time, not require a duplication of effort. If the two talk before the hang, the right paperwork will be created the first time.

As an overall observation, the electrician is in charge during the hang. No matter how foreign the format may seem to the lighting designer, any paperwork generated for that purpose should be tailored to the preference of the electrician who's running the hang.

Preparations to Speed the Hang

While the stated intent of the following checklist is "ways to expedite the hang," it could just as easily be subtitled as "ways to not slow down the hang." In general, come to the hang prepared. Make certain that the prepared paperwork will be used. Check the paperwork to make sure it's right. Don't presume that a facility is a general store; "common" tools may not be easily and quickly found at the facility. Time spent looking for things you should have brought with you is time not spent completing a task.

 A basic checklist to speed the instrument hang:

- Consult with the production, or house electrician, and provide the requested documentation for the hang.

- Arrive with reference tools used during the hang: a copy of the light plot, lighting database paperwork, a measuring tape, and a scale rule.
- Arrive prepared with hanging tapes, cardboards, or distances written on the instrument schedule.
- Bring the tools to mark the hanging positions, including chalk and spike tape.
- Arrive with the color pre-framed and sorted in the unit order of each hanging position. Electricians will be able to work on the hang, not preparing the color. If color may have to be cut on-site, bring the tools to perform that task: a paper cutter or a matte knife, brads (for metal gel frames), or a stapler (for paper frames).
- Arrive with the templates pre-trimmed and inserted in the correct orientation into template holders. On tours, consider carrying one set of templates prepackaged in holders, one set trimmed and loose, and one set fresh (for unique template slot sizes). Bring a tool that can trim the fresh templates, eliminating time spent acquiring the tool on-site.
- Arrive with any irises ready and prepped to be inserted into instruments. If iris instruments are required in the light plot, be certain that those are set aside or easily identified, to eliminate delay.
- Clearly mark any equipment being added to the existing house inventory to prevent confusion of ownership during load-out.

Hanging Procedures

In an ideal world, the lighting designer doesn't need to be present for the hang. This activity often takes place before the lighting designer arrives at the performance facility. Presuming that the paperwork package that has been sent ahead is accurate, the lighting designer may arrive on-site after the instruments have been hung, accessorized, circuited, tested, and ready for focus, and everything is just like it was drawn. In the real world, however, people make mistakes, assumptions are made, or the lighting designer may have unknowingly not provided a critical piece of information that wasn't noticed until the middle of the call. Hours of stage time can be lost, re-hanging entire systems or positions either prior to, or during a focus session. Whenever the situation presents itself, the lighting designer should consider either being present at the hang, or having an assistant on-site to answer questions or make decisions. If nothing else, the lighting designer should be reachable by phone, curtailing erroneous on-site decisions made based on incomplete information.

When the lighting package is hung, several procedures must occur. Initially, the correct instrument type with the right lamp is mounted in each location denoted on the light plot. The type and size of mounting hardware are typically defined by what it's being mounted *to*. Since the typical hanging position is made of steel pipe, c-clamps or sidearms are the usual mounting devices. The instrument is hung and locked down, which may require tightening additional bolts or nuts to make sure the unit is really secure. Many production electricians walk along an overhead electric and jerk each instrument's yoke to confirm that nothing moves before the batten flies out. This verifies that there are no loose c-clamps that might then slow down the focus or, worst-case scenario, fall off the batten.

Once securely hung, the instrument gets plugged into a circuit, which may be a pre-installed circuit or a length of cable. At that point the circuit's name, either marked on the female plug or next to the outlet, gets written onto some form of the support paperwork. Legibly writing the correct circuit number onto the paperwork helps speed the process if troubleshooting is later required.

Two basic rules are used during the hanging process. The first rule is to make sure that anything hung in the air stays there. Once the instrument is locked down to the hanging position, a **safety cable** is often added around each instrument to prevent the possibility of instruments falling from any position due to mounting hardware failure. While it is rare that a c-clamp snaps, for example, it has been known to happen. The safety cable is added to stop the fall if that failure occurs. The second rule is that once the instrument is hung, finish it off. Perform any preparation necessary so that when the light turns on to be focused, the only thing that needs to be done is focus the light. This means completing any preparation to the unit while the unit is close at hand: install any gobos, irises, or film loops; add any color frames, barndoors, tophats, or scrollers; and for movers or other devices, program any DMX addressing. Sometimes completing these tasks can take no small amount of time. While it may not seem like time well spent, consider the alternative: trying to complete these same tasks while standing on top of a focusing ladder in the dark. Yes, it may take longer now. But that's a much better alternative to waiting until later.

Aside from being comparably difficult to accomplish in the air, adding accessories during the hang also allows the total size, weight, and center of balance for each instrument to be known while the instrument is still close at hand. The added weight and bulk may require cranking down the instrument's c-clamp a little tighter onto the pipe, or tightening down the pipe to its hanging support for that matter, in order to make sure the added weight doesn't accidentally make the whole arrangement spin into view during the middle of a show.

Some lighting designers insist that the color can't be placed in the instrument until it's been focused. Personally, I think they're nutty. The delay caused by that choice may cost 10 to 20 seconds per instrument, while the electrician digs around to find the right color. On a 300-instrument show, that time quickly adds up. If the instruments are pre-colored prior to the focus, the focusing electrician's time on top of the ladder isn't spent sorting through several pieces of color to find the right one. Instead, his or her attention is directed solely to executing the lighting designer's requests.

Placing the color in each instrument during the hang is a good idea for many additional reasons. First, it can help identify the light: turn on the blue backlights without color—a bunch of lights turn on, so I guess they all work, right? Now, turn on the blue backlights that have been colored—aha! That no color one is cross-plugged. No way to quickly see that, without color in the lights. Second, placing color in the instrument during the hang will point out any broken color frame holders, a malady not always noticed during the hang. This may require swapping out the lens barrel or the entire instrument—an action easily performed on the deck, but one that can be an "adventure" in the air on a ladder. And finally, placing the color during the hang will also make it obvious if the color was cut to the wrong size color frame.

Speaking of wrong sizes, some years ago it seems that some kind of schism took place between ellipsoidal manufacturers. For whatever reason, the template slots in the same kind of instruments aren't a universal size. This means that anything fitting into the slot—templates, glass slides, gobo rotators, film loops, you name it—they all run the risk of being the wrong size and not fitting in the slot, or worse yet, falling out of the slot. Matching the correct template holder or device to the proper instrument can be a comedy of errors during the hang, but can quickly become serious business when causing delays during the focus session. It's best to discover that the template holders, or any devices traveling with the show, don't fit into the template slots of the house ellipsoidals when the instruments are close to the stage, not in the air.

After the instruments are hung, colored, and accessorized, they're then prepared for testing, which includes getting everything out of the way so the light can come out. Remove all shutters or barndoors out of the beam's path, so the light generated by the lamp can be seen when the instrument's turned on. If all that hardware is closed off, it may not be possible to see that the lamp is actually functional. And if the light's left on for any length of time, the heat buildup may warp the shutters, crack the lens, toast the internal wire, burn out the lamp, or start a fire inside the instrument. None of these is a good thing.

The instrument may also be prefocused, by locking the instrument off pointed in a specific direction. One basic choice the lighting designer makes is whether to prefocus the instrument in the direction of the eventual focus, or to avoid the focus point altogether. Prefocusing the unit in the direction of its assigned purpose may reduce the time required to achieve the instrument's final placement during the focus session. Prefocusing to avoid the focus point is a technique used when several instruments are assigned to a single control channel. When all of the instruments are turned on during the focus, each instrument, in turn, is aimed to the focus point, allowing the lighting designer to see the addition of each beam one at a time.

If PAR cans are included in the light plot, many designers prefocus their elliptical beams on the deck. The design of most PAR cans involves a metal retaining ring that clamps the bulb in place. Loosening the ring allows the bulb to spin around to the proper axis position. Accessing the ring and performing this operation, however, can be a time-consuming pain. While the beam can be rotated during the focus session, they sometimes get stuck and require additional prodding before they spin. Presetting the PAR lamp to the axis direction drawn on the plot, while the instrument is accessible on the deck, may reduce delays during the focus session.

Hanging overhead striplights is about making them all match, another step in the quest to create an even wash. They're all checked before they're hung to make sure they have matching bulb types, wattages, and if they're PAR bulbs, the same axis spin. They're all hung in the same direction, so that the cables at each end will gender-match and, if need be, plug directly to the next set of strips. They're hung with the same length hardware hangers, so they're all suspended at the same matching height below the batten. They're hung so that there's an equidistant gap between each of them, usually somewhere between 4″-6″ apart. They're hung so that the colors will be inserted from the same side—presumably that means that the reflector in each striplight cell is facing the same way. Once the striplights are all hung, plugged, and circuited, they're then turned on, one circuit at a time. Once the circuitry has been checked, then the circuits are turned on one at a time. Once a single circuit is up, it gets colored with one of the colors. After the strips are all colored, their bodies are all rotated to a matching prefocused orientation; in most cases, if the strips are within 2′-0″ of the goods, they're usually prefocused pointing straight down at the ground.

Once there, they are often equipped with a tape measure, all of the channels are turned on, and the overhead striplights are flown out to trim. Keeping them all turned on allows the designer to see how they are spreading on the goods as they fly out. It also allows everyone to see if, for some reason, a circuit unplugs on the way out to trim.

Striplights that make up the groundrow are preset much the same way. Again, matching the instruments to each other is of prime importance. Almost everything is the same between the two positions, regardless of the unit type. The usual difference, though, is in the way they prefocus. While overhead strips usually prefocus straight down, groundrow striplight bodies are typically preset slightly tipped, facing upstage into the bounce, or downstage into the trans. Because they tip, it's more important that the color frame holders slots are "up," so that the color frames can't fall out. The other main difference is one of timing and preset placement. If the groundrow's playing position is directly under the overhead striplights, it's often assembled some distance upstage or downstage of its final placement. That way a ladder, if need be, can move back and forth in its absence to focus the overhead position.

Using zoom ellipsoidals can be another element that may impact the speed of the focus. Trying to determine the positions of both lenses while on a ladder, especially for folks not familiar with the units, can slow a focus session to a crawl. Presetting the lens positions of zoom ellipsoidals (or the beam size of fresnels, for that matter) can be accomplished while the instruments are being hung. Typically, this technique is most useful when zoom instruments are plotted for entire systems of light. It requires a little homework on the part of the lighting designer, which is done prior to the load-in. First, a sectional beam drawing defines the actual throw distance for each instrument from each hanging position. If the zooms are used in a lot of different systems hung at different distances, some time will be spent constructing the drawings. As the hang is taking place, a single zoom is placed some distance from an un-obscured wall. The actual throw distance for each instrument or system is measured from the instrument to the wall. Likewise, the desired beam pool size is measured out on the wall. The sample zoom is then moved to each measured location, and its focus knobs are adjusted to match the desired diameter. The knob positions (or the number of rotations for fresnel instruments) are recorded for each actual throw distance, and then applied to each system's instrument in the hang.

Once the instruments are hung, plugged, colored, accessorized, and prefocused, the hang is complete and the instruments are ready to be tested.

POSITION THE BOOMS

Final on-site positions for sidelight booms are often defined by a combination of four elements: the initial plan, combined with the specific environment surrounding each location, personal experience, and gut instinct.

The ideal system is created when all of the positions are located equidistant from centerline, safely secured and hidden from the audience, and each system on the combined booms provide an even blend of light, covering the entire depth of the performance space. In order to achieve that even blend for each system, the lenses for all of those instruments on the booms are placed at the same distance from centerline. Presuming all of the instruments are the same type and the same wattage, the light beams in that system *should* then be matching intensities.

On and Offstage

The distance from centerline usually begins with a distance far enough offstage to be concealed by masking legs. That distance is then checked against the beam size produced by instruments focused on the near side of the stage. Usually, the field spread of those instruments is large enough so that light from the "near focus" instruments splashes the near masking legs. Often this means the instrument's lenses are placed somewhere between 8'-0" and 12'-0" offstage of the onstage edge of the black masking legs.

After that initial placement, however, the elements of the surrounding environment have to be considered. One element that may alter this location are the side sightlines from the audience. Common practice dictates that the lenses of the instruments should not be visible to the audience, and booms may need to move farther offstage to be concealed from view.

The length of the overhead battens can also affect the distance. When sidelight booms are located under overhead electrics, they're often positioned offstage of the end of the batten pipe, so the electric can still be lowered to the deck without hitting the sidelights. Often, however, the battens are just too long, and extend too far offstage. If the booms are moved far enough offstage to clear the battens, they may become ineffective. Often, the choice made is to place the boom directly underneath the overhead electric in that opening. The calculated gamble is that the electric batten will less likely need to be lowered to the deck than any adjacent battens, which may be weighted with scenery.

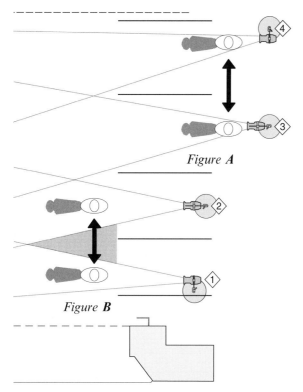

Figure A

Figure B

Figure 11.8 Onstage and Offstage Boom Placement

Shifting the position offstage may then involve consideration of the width of the masking leg. Figure 11.8A shows booms 3 and 4 placed "too far" offstage of the masking legs. The gap between the legs and the lens of the instruments may tempt performers to walk up- or downstage, in front of the instrument's light beams. Though hidden from the audience, the performer's movement through the light produces a visual "flicker" on the stage and the opposite legs, which can be distracting from the audience's point of view. This can be solved with spike marks restricting offstage traffic paths, shifting the booms onstage, or occasionally, a piercing glare.

The on- and offstage location of a sidelight boom can also be affected by the shutter cuts of the individual instruments. Typically, the ideal goal is to create an even wash with the combined light beams from each system, filling the entire upstage/downstage depth on the near side of each opening. While that may sound simple enough, the necessity of keeping light off the backdrop, and out of the audience, often means that side shutter cuts reduce the coverage of that depth. Figure 11.8B shows the common result of this dilemma. If booms 1 and 2 are too close to the onstage edge of the legs, their location, combined with their side shutter cuts, reduces the coverage width on the near side. The closer a performer gets to the near legs, the greater the possibility that the performer will pass between these shutter cuts, moving

up- or downstage through the shadowed "hole" in the sidelight coverage. The effect of bodies running in and out of light near the legs also produces a different type of visual "flicker"; in this case, the audience can also see the light momentarily striking the side of the performer's body. If the beam spread of the sidelight instruments is fixed, attempting to reduce the size of the holes and the flicker may require the boom to be shifted farther offstage.

Up and Downstage

The up- and downstage placement of a sidelight boom can be an equally complex dilemma. Figure 11.9 shows all sidelight booms placed in the downstage side of each opening. The upstage cuts required to keep light off the backdrop result in holes and sidelight flicker in the upstage side of each near opening (A). Because the upstage cuts are open in an effort to increase near coverage, more light (and performer shadows) will potentially be cast from the light on 1 Boom Left onto the face of the 2 Leg (or show leg) stage right (B). Finally, any performer standing in the upstage portion of the 4th opening stage left is in a "dead zone" and has no near coverage at all (C).

Figure 11.10 shows all the sidelight booms shifted upstage into the middle of each opening. Overall, this results in more even coverage. In order to keep light off the backdrop and the proscenium, there are still some holes and potential flicker on the near side of the stage (A), but they're much less than before. In this position, the upstage cuts can be shifted offstage, and off the face of the far legs; the upstage side cut on the 1 Boom Left is in far enough, so that there's no longer any performer shadow on the 2 Leg stage right (B). Finally, while the dead zone in the 4th opening stage left has been reduced (C), there's now starting to be another one created in the downstage side of the 1st opening (D).

If all of the sidelight booms continue to shift upstage, the result is almost a reversal of the first example, shown in Figure 11.11. Side shutters cutting light off the proscenium result in a loss of coverage in the downstage side of each near opening (A). As drawn, the coverage holes in this configuration are even worse than when the booms were initially in the downstage side of the opening. One positive note is that the upstage cuts can now be made off the face of the masking on the opposite side. The upstage shutter cut from the light on the 2 Boom stage left is in far enough so that there's no performer shadow, even while standing adjacent to the 2 Leg stage right (B). Finally, while the dead zone in the 4th opening upstage left is almost eliminated (C), the dead zone in the downstage side of the first opening is even more pronounced (D).

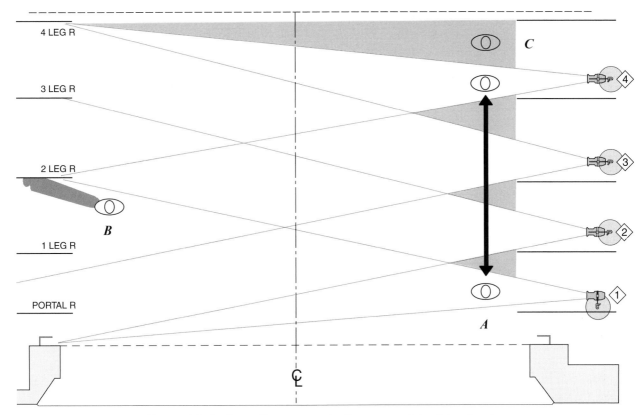

Figure 11.9 Boom Placement in the Downstage Side of the Opening

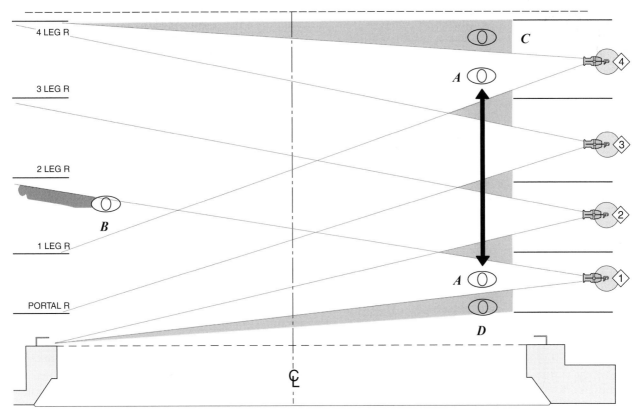

Figure 11.10 Boom Placement in the Middle of the Opening

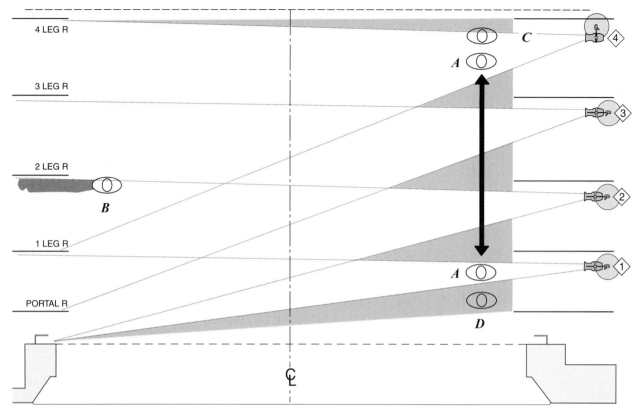

Figure 11.11 Boom Placement in the Upstage Side of the Opening

While these illustrations have been provided to show the impact of boom placement within each opening, the simple truth is that there is no easy solution for sidelight boom placement. Many lighting designers start with their own personal formula. For many, this is shown with Figure 11.12; the first boom is as far downstage as possible, the intermediate booms are in the middle of their respective openings, and the upstage boom is as far upstage as possible. While this still results in holes and flickers on the near side (A), that may be at least partially addressed by shifting all the booms more offstage. Some of the hole size is because of the upstage shutter cuts; in this case, all the shutters are kept off the face of the opposite masking legs (B). For sidelights mounted high enough on the boom, this upstage cut may not be necessary. Finally, keeping the 1st boom far downstage, and the 4th boom far upstage, attempts to fill the dead zones (C and D).

It's worth pointing out that all of these examples were drawn on an open stage. Numerous other factors can add additional layers of complexity to the decision of where to place a sidelight boom. Scenic elements, including scenic legs, midstage drops, downstage scrims, or the size of any scenery moving through each opening can quickly alter any plan for placement or shutter cuts. Practical on-site factors that may not be apparent until the middle of the load-in

can throw a complete curveball at any placement plan: the traffic pattern for the circuitry, how the circuitry is distributed to each boom, and even how long each piece of cable is ("Nope, the plugs end *here*"). At times it seems like the list of considerations is endless: the amount of peripheral movement offstage of the boom may alter its position (changing booths, scenic assembly), or the amount of equipment surrounding the position (monitor speakers, props tables, or wastebaskets) might cause a shift in its placement. On top of that, the focus of any special instruments on the boom, backstage traffic, and the stage manager's backstage calling position may affect the location as well. The final position of sidelight booms varies with each production, and the tighter the space, the more intricate the decisions. At the end of the day, it's like any other choice: get as much information as possible, consider all options, and make your best guess.

When the final location of the sidelight booms is determined on one side of the stage, standard operating procedure is to duplicate their positions on the opposite side. By mirroring the sidelight positions from one side to the other, the sidelight angles will look the same on both sides of objects on stage as the cues are created. In addition to that, the performers aren't forced to remember different spatial relationships between the booms and the surrounding

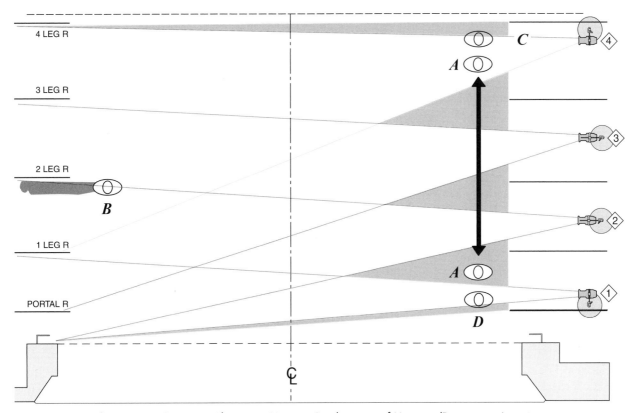

Figure 11.12 Boom Placement Using a Combination of Upstage/Downstage Locations

elements in each opening to the stage, on each side of the stage. When conditions force that standard to be tossed out the window, and every boom ends up in a different place, the common tactic is to highlight each boom's location with double the amount of colored tape, glow tape, or hazard tape; whatever it takes in order to insure that its placement can always be seen, in light or in the dark.

PROGRAMMING INFORMATION INTO THE COMPUTER LIGHTING CONSOLE

The amount of infrastructure information that's commonly preprogrammed into the computer lighting console can be extensive: the focus cues, the system wash cues, the hanging position cues, the groups, the submasters, and the blockers outlined in the disk master chart that were discussed in Chapter 8. If light cues from a prior incarnation of the production exist, they may also be programmed into the lighting console at this time.

While some lighting designers think programming infrastructure information into lighting consoles is a lot of extra unnecessary work, most lighting designers consider it vital, since it provides basic handles that can be used in almost every other board activity. The allocated time to program infrastructure information during the load-in, though, is limited and almost always secondary to getting the light package functional and focused. Almost every lighting designer who considers preprogramming important, just as quickly agrees that it must be completed before the instruments begin to get patched. Otherwise, once the patching and testing process begins, any other time to preprogram information ceases to exist except when work calls aren't taking place.

And that's not often. Other than coffee, or meal breaks, as soon as the instruments are patched, working, and in their focus positions, the lighting console is in constant use, bringing up channels or making cues. If the infrastructure programming has not been completed during the early hours of the load-in, it may never have the chance to get loaded into the console. If it looks like extensive console programming is going to be required, any alternatives to programming information during the load-in should be considered. Trying to preprogram under the gun and get finished before the patching needs to begin can be harrowing, and no matter what anyone thinks, programming always takes longer than expected. If a matching console is available for preprogramming use in a lighting shop or another space prior to load-in, either of those situations should be pursued. Major manufacturers provide sample consoles in their offices, which are often available for preprogramming. Use an off-line editing application for the console, if such an application exists. Manufacturers gladly provide the software required to perform this function. If the house console is going to be used, contact the performance facility and request permission to program the console prior to the load-in. If a rental console's unavailable until just prior to the load-in, arrange to transport the console to your home, preprogram the console on the kitchen table, and then transport the console directly to the load-in.

Presuming that none of those options is available, the lighting console should then be packed to be one of the first items taken off the truck. The programming can then take place while the instruments are initially being hung. The two activities can occur simultaneously until the instruments and circuits need to be patched. If the patching or channels being checked is extensive, that may conclude the preprogramming portion of the program. Efforts to continue preprogramming, while being interrupted by constant onstage requests, will become frustrating for the board operator, the lighting designer, and the electrician checking the instruments.

Attempting to read the information and then keypunch it into a console without assistance can require intensive concentration and consume a lot of time. If possible, an assistant should be assigned to the console operator. The assistant reads the information out loud, while the operator physically programs the information into the console. Ideally, the assistant is familiar with the documents. If he or she has never seen them before being assigned the task, unfamiliarity with the layout may slow the process.

Typically, a notebook is assembled that contains current copies of all of the paperwork, a light plot, and storage devices clearly identified with the name of the show, the date, the type of lighting console, and the system size. By labeling the disk in advance, the lighting designer and the console operator will always know its contents. Spare disks or storage media are also included in order to provide the console operator with some amount of comfort zone. The notebook should also contain board operator sheets, and may include a preliminary copy of the cue master. In most cases the production should not expect the house to provide the disks or storage media. By providing the storage media, there will never be an issue regarding how many copies of show information can be afforded to the production when the show loads out. By providing a storage location for the external show backup media, there's also less chance that any disks or flash drives will be left on speakers, under soft drinks, or underfoot, resulting in the possibility of lost data.

If there is concern that the number of cues in the show may be larger than allowed on a single disk or storage device, the production can be segmented between acts. When possible, though, it's advised to refrain from "splitting" the show between disks. Although the original infrastructure cues, groups, subs, and patch information can be duplicated on each act disk, any updates to the softpatch or infrastructure information will require careful monitoring so that the changes will be reflected on each of the act disks. Productions involving multiple repertory pieces may not have the luxury of this choice.

Ideally, all of the show information should fit into the one notebook that will be placed in the board operator's care. Not only will this make it simpler to store for archival purposes, but many light booths often contain extensive paperwork left over from different productions being presented in the facility. By providing a single information repository, including plastic sleeve jackets for the storage media, the possibility of losing paperwork or backups will be reduced. If there are disks from a previous incarnation of the show, those disks can be used to initially load information into the lighting console, but they should then be removed from the booth, to prevent accidental re-recording and loss of archival information.

Although many consoles are now being supplied with hard drives, it is still prudent to save information to a floppy disk or whatever storage medium is available at the end of the calls. Like all computers, experience has shown that the possibility of hard drive failure can occur at any time. It's often suggested that each segment of the show information should be saved to three copies of storage media, floppy disk or otherwise. Various methods are used in the sequence of recording the disks, to avoid loss of data during technical rehearsals. Often, the magic number of three means one can be used for off-line editing, leaving the remaining two as backup for the on-site console.

Set up the System

Presuming that the show is an original production, the first action that is usually taken is to define the system size that will be used for the show. The memory is flushed of all previous unnecessary information. This ensures that, during the current production, there will be no confusion with "left over" information from prior shows on the console. Then the individual system settings for the console are reset for the purposes of this show. The number of channels used by the show is reset in order to reduce the number of screens. The number of dimmers is also redefined. Once that's done, the system size settings are now complete. The sequence used to program information into the console may next be initially dictated by the lighting equipment that is permanently controlled by the existing dimmers.

If the console controls the permanent worklights or houselights, those channels or dimmers should be immediately softpatched or "parked" to reestablish worklight on the stage, and allow the load-in to continue. **Park** is a specific command function that supersedes any other command. It's often used to "freeze" a channel or dimmer at a level; neither of those can be "moved" until the command is given to "unpark." This command is often used to control electrical devices that should remain constant at a level and never change. It's also good to know that anything that's parked usually can't then be recorded in any cues for the show.

Once light on stage and in the house is restored, the console can continue to be programmed. If the dimmer assignments to any channels have been determined, that information can be programmed into the softpatch screen. The default softpatch setting in many lighting consoles pairs each dimmer to the same-numbered channel, known as a **one-to-one patch**. Dimmer 1 is assigned to channel 1, dimmer 2 is assigned to channel 2, and so on. Experienced designers and board operators typically eliminate this default setting and remove all dimmer assignments to any channels, an action known as **clearing the patch**. This makes certain that any dimmer that's used is intentionally softpatched to a channel, and eliminates any chance that a channel might activate a default-assigned dimmer. It also allows the patch screen to be used to confirm any unassigned (or unused) dimmers. The softpatch can be entered at any time, but ideally should be complete before channels are tested to confirm that their contents properly function. Once initial softpatching has taken place, programming infrastructure information can continue. Programming infrastructure information implies activating channels, and then recording them into cues, groups, or subs.

Programming channels in the "**live**" (or "stage") screens while instruments are being plugged into dimmers is a tactic that's typically avoided. Since channel activation typically occurs in zero seconds, sudden unexpected flashes of light from instruments can quickly cause an outcry on stage. The typical technique used in this situation is to program the console in the "**blind**" (or "preview") displays, thus avoiding any channel or dimmer activation. Any channels that need to remain constant through the hang can be activated in the live screen (or just parked) while programming continues in the background. Some consoles don't have the flexibility to program while in "blind" or "preview." When faced with this situation, it may be possible to turn the dimmers off during the hanging process. If the dimmers must remain on during the hang, one solution may be to unplug the DMX outputs from the console, allowing both activities to continue without inconvenience to either activity.

To expedite the eventual tedium of programming, consider determining the fewest number of keystrokes required to complete each series of channel changes. On some consoles, loading cues in "blind" or "preview" can speed the process. The execution of each channel activation records the command into the cue, eliminating the need to keystroke an entire record sequence. Since the logic and command sequences vary between consoles, familiarity with the console (or having a manual at hand) may answer any questions during the process.

When time runs short, the person reading the information to the board operator must gauge the amount of programming that remains. If the focus session is imminent, the priority may be to program the focus cues. If focus cues won't be used, then providing the handles to check hanging positions may be the next priority. If that doesn't appear to be an immediate concern, the handles that will be used to activate system washes during the light cue level setting session may be the programming that takes precedence. If written cues exist from a prior incarnation of the production, the memories that will be used as light cues during the technical rehearsal may be seen as the priority. When faced with a constrained amount of time, the assistant reading the information may need to consult with the lighting designer to prioritize the information that remains to be programmed.

Although programming infrastructure information can become boring, many lighting designers consider the benefits well worth the effort. Infrastructure programming provides the lighting console with numerous handles and methods to rapidly access channel information, and can save a lot of time.

Before any information is programmed, the programming sequence should be briefly considered. If infrastructure cues will also be recorded as a series of groups, the board's command structure should first be carefully examined. Although many light boards allow groups to be recorded into cues, those same boards may not allow cues to be loaded into groups. When this is the situation, the groups should be created first, and then each group should be activated and recorded to create the infrastructure cues. If the cues are programmed first without examining this one-sided relationship, this error in judgment may result in the costly use of time. To have the same channels available in the two separate functions, the same channel intensities will need to be keystroked a second time in order to be recorded as a group. That is the case for this particular console, so the groups for *Hokey* will be programmed first, followed by the submasters, and concluding with the infrastructure cues.

Program Infrastructure Groups

In many lighting consoles, creating groups in any display other than the group display is simply not possible. Groups are usually not listed on the monitor display until they are created. If several groups are to be created, the programming time can be reduced if all of the groups are initially created at one time. After the groups exist, it's then possible to view and program the channel intensities of each group by pressing the equivalent of the [next] or [last] keys, rather than individually "calling up" each group, requiring more keystrokes on the console. To load the groups for *Hokey*, the group list created in Chapter 8 would be used. After the groups are created, the individual channels are programmed into each group.

If time is short, a decision may need to be made as to which series of groups should be programmed first. If consultation with the lighting designer is not possible at the time, a review of the group's use may provide the answer. The groups for *Hokey* are divided into two separate functions. Groups 1 > 17 activate each system of light, while groups 21 > 44 activate each position. If the focus session is imminent, the ability to check the blending of system washes may supersede the need to activate all of the instruments in a single position. Activating several groups to confirm that all of the instruments in a single position are functional may require some amount of time, but having to activate numerous channels to check a system wash may take longer. The choice may be to program the system groups before the position groups.

Program Infrastructure Submasters

Unlike cue or group information, submasters usually actively exist and don't need to be created. Methods for recording channel information into different submasters may vary between consoles. Some consoles require that channel content only be activated while viewing the submaster screen, while other boards allow any activated channels or groups to be recorded into the contents of any sub. Since the recording procedures may vary between models and manufacturers, submaster recording procedures should be reviewed to reduce unnecessary keystroking.

The submasters for *Hokey* will be loaded using the submaster list that was created in Chapter 8. Since many of the submasters are repetitions of the channel intensities programmed into the groups, the amount of time this process will require is reduced.

Each submaster can be addressed, and then the proper group can be activated within that sub. The keystroking required to activate individual channels will be bypassed.

When the inhibitive submasters (12 and 24) are programmed, they should be double-checked to make certain they don't contain any ghost or infrastructure channels, including time stamp, key memory number, worklights, running lights, centering lights, house lights, music stand lights, or any devices that should constantly remain on throughout the performance.

Program Infrastructure Light Cues

When programming light cues into a computer console, a distinction should be made in the construction process. When written cues exist from a prior incarnation of the show, they should be programmed after the infrastructure cues have been recorded. If the production is an original presentation, however, the programming may be limited solely to the infrastructure cues, and provide the structure to be used as a framework by the lighting designer during the cue level setting session. This tactic will be more closely addressed at the conclusion of this section.

Initially, the first step often employed on tracking computer consoles is to program hard zeros into cues that will fade the stage to black, or be utilized as **blocker cues**. This ensures that any subsequent tracking channel changes will be forced to stop at the intended location, preventing them from tracking through the entire memory stack. When the hard zeros are programmed, any ghost channels that will be used as time stamp, key memory, or blackout information should be left unaffected. While referring to the disk master chart for *Hokey*, channels 1 > 122, and 126 > 138 will be "activated" to a level of zero (00%) and recorded into memories 100, 200, 400, 500, 600, 800, 900, and 950 to track.

Next, the **time stamp** information will be entered with the current date. In this example, the load-in is beginning on April 5, 2010. That being the case, channel 123 would be activated to 04%, channel 124 activated to 05%, and channel 125 activated to 10%. These levels would be recorded in memory 1 and allowed to track, so that they will appear in every memory.

With the basic blocks of memory now in place, the focus cues (memories 1 > 99), the system wash cues (memories 950 > 973), and the hanging position cues (memories 900 > 920) can be programmed. Since many of these cues consist of channel levels that already exist in the groups and submasters, these functions can be used to activate the channels when the memories are created.

Before beginning that process, however, a moment should be taken to consider what methods might reduce the amount of time required to complete the programming. The natural inclination may be to activate the channel levels, or **cue content** to be contained in each of the memories, along with any fade time information, and then record that singular cue. Programming information in this sequence, however, will require several different keystroke combinations in varying sequences. Performing repetitive keystroke combinations, on the other hand, often expedites the process. Consider programming **shell cues**: initially record all of the memories without channel content or time fade information in a single "pass." [Record Q 951 Enter], [Record Q 952 Enter], and so on. Once the "shells" (or "outside bodies") of the cues are created, the second step may be to assign all of the time fades to all of the cues in a second pass. Finally, a third pass can insert the intermittent waits, delays, or links between cues. On the final pass, the cue content (the "internal guts") for each memory can be programmed.

It is at this point that an important distinction in programming memories for light cues should be made. If the cues that remain to be programmed already exist on paper from a previous incarnation, the same sequence that was just described (shell cues) may be employed to program the cue content for the memories used in the show. If the production is an original presentation, however, and a preliminary cue master has been prepared, hesitation at this point is well advised. The assistant may be tempted to save the lighting designer time by programming the preliminary shell of the cue, along with its time fades. This should not be done without consulting the lighting designer to determine his or her preference. Many lighting designers use the lack of a cue number on the monitor display as a signpost to inform them of their progress during the initial cue level setting session. If all of the preliminary shells appear on the cue list screen, this may cause havoc, since it will no longer be possible for the lighting designer to scan for missing memory numbers to determine which light cues remain to be created.

Program Light Cues from Prior Incarnations

When written cues exist from prior incarnations of the show, the same methods employed to create the infrastructure memories can be used to speed the entry of the light cues for the show into the console. The shell cues can be created, then assigned fade times and other attributes. After those two passes are complete, the cue content can be sequentially programmed, starting with the first light cue in the show.

The sequence may be altered, however, when time grows short. When instruments and circuits are ready to be checked, the board may need to shift over to activating dimmers, channels, or programming the softpatch. As noted earlier, attempting to program cue information during that time can be difficult at best.

In that situation, consider programming only the cue information required to allow transitions between scenes to take place within the technical rehearsal. Though the internal cues within each scene will be missing, the rehearsal will still be able to practice the scene changes under show conditions, and the intermediate cues may be easier to program "on the fly." This may be as simple as programming cue information for the first, last, and any intermediate memories to complete each transition sequence. If time still remains after the transition cues have been programmed, the additional internal cues may be programmed in the same order in which scenes will be addressed during the technical rehearsal. If time runs out prior to completion of the programming, the first scene in the technical rehearsal can still occur without delay. Any time not utilized to alter cue information in the current scene can be used to continue programming internal cue information for scenes not yet encountered.

When time grows even shorter, consider ignoring the transitions, and program only the cue information for the first scene that will be addressed during the technical rehearsal. Though it may be frustrating not to complete the programming of most of the cues, the need to begin the technical rehearsal on time will have been addressed. If any time exists when the board is not required for onstage use, it may be possible to continue programming the cues in preview.

Record the Contents of Memory on Older Consoles

This is a critical moment. If the lighting designer is not familiar with this particular lighting console, he or she should be certain to observe this sequence closely, when the information that has been programmed into the RAM of the console is written onto whatever storage format is used. On older consoles, after a series of selections, one is usually confronted with a choice that looks something like this on the monitor display:

SAVE COPY TO DISK
LOAD TO BOARD

Different manufacturers use different nomenclature, and no matter how experienced the lighting designer may be, the display is often confusing. The two procedures that these statements represent reflect a choice of one of two things:

SAVE COPY TO DISK: The memory information in the brain (RAM) of the lighting console is about to be written onto the disk (or storage medium), and potentially *replace* whatever may have been previously recorded on that disk (or storage medium).

LOAD TO BOARD: The memory information that is stored on the disk (or storage medium) is about to be loaded into the computer's brain (RAM), and in some cases *replace* whatever may have been previously contained in the brain.

The lighting designer should be certain that he or she knows which action needs to be accomplished, and what selection should be chosen to accomplish that action. If the brain of the light board has just been programmed or changed, **DO NOT** choose LOAD TO BOARD. Taking that action will tell the computer to read all of the information from the disk and potentially replace the entire contents of the computer's brain. That means that all of the new information that was just programmed or changed in the light board would be lost. In this case, the correct procedure to choose is: SAVE TO DISK.

Numerous instances have been observed when memory transferal has been committed in the wrong direction without backup. Massive amounts of time have been lost, and tempers have flared, because not enough eyes were watching the screen during the critical moment when the memory transferal procedure was chosen. The lighting designer should watch the screen to make certain that he or she doesn't contribute to losing data by being unwilling to pay attention. At that moment, that's why the designer has eyes. The lighting designer is not a passive observer; he or she needs to be an involved participant. Nobody's perfect.

Memory transferal is not limited to the single act of understanding the directional flow of the information. If the show involves more than one series of disks, care should be taken to confirm that any time computer information is being transferred, the correct memory information is being recorded to (or loaded from) the correct disk. One habit many professional board operators practice is as soon as a disk has been involved in a memory transfer, the disk is removed from the disk drive. Why? Consider this scenario: changes for Act 2 have been programmed into the light board's brain, but the disk for Act 1 in still in the disk drive. If the command SAVE TO DISK is given, the Act 2 information will overwrite all of the information that had previously been stored on the disk

for Act 1. This is another good example of why it is important to have multiple copies of each series of disks.

Recording the Contents of Memory on Newer Consoles

Most modern lighting consoles have now adopted command and directory structures from Windows or Windows-based browsers. They've also eliminated disk drives from their list of hardware features because, as one manufacturer put it, "We can't get floppy disks any more." At the time of this writing, today's console storage media now includes hard drives, USB flash drives, or SD cards.

Between the change in hardware, software, and the relative sophistication of the typical console operator, show files are now treated like individual documents. But no matter what the operating system or command structure, the lighting designer and the console operator must still be vigilant whenever the contents of memory are shifted back and forth. Technology is always moving forward, but simple mistakes can always trump all progress.

 **Shelley's Golden Rule: Save Early and Often**

Anytime the board has received additional programmed information, and is temporarily dormant until its next use, the general rule is, whenever possible, write the contents of the light board's brain to a storage device. In order to do this, the request typically given to the console operator is "save the show." The board *will* crash someday, and no one knows when that will be.

Years ago we were cueing the Kirov Ballet at the Metropolitan Opera House, and we had just finished the entire first act, a process that had taken about 4 hours. At that time the Met had a Palette V6E, fully protected with surge suppression and voltage regulation; it had been dependable and error-free for years. So, naturally, *just* before we recorded to disk—that's right—the system crashed, rebooted, and the entire 4-hour session was lost.

Ever since then, I've been a little more respectful, and wary, of computers. Although computer lighting consoles may allow lighting designers to create art, the art isn't that much good to anybody when it turns into vaporware.

Check the Light Console Contents

Once the infrastructure information is in the console, if any time remains before the focus or light cue level setting session, the focus cues, groups, and submasters should be checked on their respective monitor displays. If the infrastructure information has been recorded from one function to the other (groups > memories, for example), then only one function will require visual confirmation. If it's anticipated that the groups will be used during the focus session to check system blending, the contents of the group system washes should be checked first. If there are inhibitive submasters, carefully check the attributes and contents of those subs, and be certain that the handles on the console are at Full. When inhibitive submasters are accidentally left at zero, they act like grand masters, and any channels assigned to them will not be activated.

Ideally, the contents of these functions can be checked live on stage once the lighting package is installed. If that somehow can take place as part of initial channel checks, any programming inconsistencies can be seen and then corrected. Sadly, there is no way to predict if that can take place, or if any time will be available later in the schedule. Checking the monitor displays, if nothing else, provides some measure of reassurance that no ghastly programming has accidentally taken place.

CHECK THE PRODUCTION TABLE

The production table is often the lighting designer's office and home in the theatre, where he or she creates and views the lighting cues for the production. The production table is usually a temporary structure that can be quickly installed or removed from the seats. It can range from an actual folding table with upholstery and legs, to a sheet of plywood laid on the seat backs, and just about anything in between. Regardless of appearance, what matters to most lighting designers is space: the footprint of the table area used by the lighting designer must be large enough to accommodate the monitor and the active paperwork needed to create the cues. With any luck, there will also be enough spare room for the rest of the files, printer, and archives.

The table is often initially shared between the lighting designer and the stage manager, and may also be occupied by other members of the design team, along with the director. In later rehearsals, the stage manager often moves to the base of operations where he or she will call the show during the performances. The director and the other designers may eventually scatter into different locations in the house to view the show from other perspectives. During initial technical rehearsals, however, everyone typically congregates at this single central viewpoint to discuss the timing and placement of all actions and movement on stage,

collectively shaping the stage picture. Face-to-face discussions facilitate communication, and reduce the amount of conversation on headset.

During the load-in, the production table is brought out and set up in the seats. If the table isn't constructed for a specific row, the lighting designer should decide in advance where the table should be located to provide an unobstructed view of the entire stage. Whenever possible, the production table should be positioned on centerline. When located in a decentralized location, the lighting designer's unable to see what is visually happening on the near side of the stage. Inevitably, there will be surprises in performance when the other side of the stage is seen for possibly the first time.

The table should be placed so that the bottom of the balcony doesn't obstruct the ability to see the entire height of the stage picture. If possible, the table may be placed in a row that possesses additional depth, allowing easier passage to and from the table. It's worth noting that any lighting designer wearing shorts can be easily spotted in a crowd by the distinct bruises on his or her legs, created when colliding with unforgiving armrests while trying to move to the production table via a row opening that's too narrow.

Since the lighting designer will often spend extensive hours at the production table, it should be made functional and comfortable. As a working space, it should be laid out with some amount of ergonomic concern. That concern hits home once it's remembered that the lighting designer is often tied to the space for at least 12 hours a day. Once the table has been set up, check the ergonomics of the space. Sit behind the table and pretend to write something down. Now pretend that action has been repeated for 12 hours. Often the distance or angle of the table relative to the location of the seat is disproportionate. Sitting on the armrests between the seats often solves this discomfort, but after 12 hours that can leave an aching impression. It's worth asking if a wide strip of wood can be placed to span the armrests, possibly with some kind of padding or support, allowing the lighting designer's attention to remain in front of him or her, instead of underneath.

Presuming the light board, the stage manager, or the followspots are in remote locations, the lighting designer must have a functioning headset. Headsets to other locations may be added as the situation demands. Although rock and roll presentations often demand headsets that cover both ears (double muff), most lighting designers prefer to have a headset covering only one ear (single muff). This reduces the need to constantly remove a portion of the headset to hear the performers or anyone adjacent to the production table. During the load-in, confirm that the correct numbers of headsets are at the table, the channel separation is correct, and the required channels are functioning. If possible, request separate channels for the followspots and the lighting console; the light board operator doesn't care about notes being given to the followspots, and the followspots certainly don't care about any of the numerous changes being made in every light cue.

If the lighting console is in a remote location, the production table must have a monitor display, allowing the designer to see the console's activities. In reality, the lighting designer really needs to see two displays: the equivalent of a cue list display (showing a numerical list of the memories with time and attribute information), and a cue content display, (showing as many channels and their intensities on a single screen). If one screen display can't include all of that information in a single view, then alternatives must be discussed. Either the console (and its full array of monitors) needs to be moved to the production table next to the lighting designer, or a "video switcher" needs to be installed at the table (allowing the lighting designer to swap between the screens), or two monitors need to be installed at the table. In lieu of that, the lighting designer can just drive the console operator crazy, constantly requesting "swap" so that the single screen can be changed back and forth, through the entire tech period.

When checking the table, confirm that the monitor or monitors connected to the computer lighting console are operational, that the proper screens are displayed, and that the contrast is set correctly for ease of viewing. If the monitor is monochrome, it should be as neutral a color as possible, to eliminate any color reaction to the designer's eyes. For the same reason, if the monitor is color, the background should be dark, while the channel colors are muted. Ideally, there should be enough room on the table between the monitors and the designer to accommodate the active paperwork. That way the only thing moving is the designer's head, pivoting up and down, to retain concentration on the stage.

The table should have a worklight to provide light on the paperwork. The worklight should have a hood, so that the lighting designer doesn't have to stare around a bare bulb. The worklight should be focused on the paperwork and out of the designer's eyes. Finally, the worklight should be dimmable, so the designer's eyes don't grow tired adjusting between a dark cue on stage and the reflective intensity of the paperwork.

If the production table is some distance from the stage, communicating with anyone onstage can be exhausting. In those situations, a microphone routed through the sound system to the monitor speakers (a "god" mike) allows directions from the production table to be heard. This microphone may become an important timesaving tool during rehearsals when staging is completely changed. Sometimes the god mike is preset elsewhere, indicating where the director will sit during the technical rehearsal.

A wastebasket should be placed adjacent to the table, to keep the workspace clear and simplify cleanup. If there's any length to the tech period, attempt to find a wastebasket that's waterproof for all the half-filled soft drinks and coffee cups that will inevitably be left on the production table, next to the electronic equipment and all of the paperwork.

And just a quick sidebar: Some designers believe that the production table is sacrosanct. Nothing will ever be touched, so it can remain a mess—they never need to worry about any paper piles being disturbed. While that might be an unwritten law regarding tech tables for theatre technicians and designers, experience has shown that cleaning crews haven't always heard about it. Bitter designers keep a three-hole punch, extra binders, file folders, or if nothing else, binder clips close at hand, to make a clear distinction between archive paperwork and piles ready for the recycling bin.

 Shelley's Soapbox: BYO Production Table Equipment

Working in different theatres can be exciting, but adapting to different production tables on a daily basis can become frustrating. Although it's rare that much can be done to change the seating or arrangement of the surface provided, the rest of the environment can become an irritating distraction. Time and effort can be wasted black wrapping or replacing the 100-watt non-dimmed bare bulb clip light that's been provided as a worklight. Wrestling with an antique headset to merely get the microphone placed near the designer's mouth can cause unnecessary agitation. To eliminate these distractions, many lighting designers carry their own headset and dimmable worklight. Though their carry-on weight is slightly increased, providing their own tools means that they don't have to adapt to the worklight or headset du jour.

Carrying your own tools isn't limited to lights or headsets. Some designers bring their own office. Figure 11.13 is a basic list of gear I bring for the production period. The amount of gear you carry into any theatre may be directly related to how close the theatre is to your home or your home city. For my money, being self-contained translates into that much more time spent on stage doing your job, and less time spent searching the theatre for the same equipment that's sitting in your home.

SHELLEY'S DOMESTIC PRODUCTION TABLE LIST		
COMPUTER PRODUCTS:	**STAGE:**	**REFERENCE:**
Headset, LittLite®	30', 50', 100' tape measures	Color swatch books
Computer, mouse, power brick, lock, USB light	Spike, Scotch, gaff, and glow tape	Template books
Backup CD's, DVD's	Flashlights	Cut Sheets
External hard drive, flash stick	Clipboard	Manuals
Printer, power brick, cable, lock	Laser Pointer	Theatre info
Plugging strip, extension cords	Monocular	
Battery charger, cell phone charger	Earplugs	**UPDATE & RECORD:**
Internet: Wi-fi card, CAT 5 cable	Leatherman	Digital Camera
	Continuity tester	Field Templates™
OFFICE PRODUCTS:	Voltage Detector	Scale rules, triangle
Plastic page protectors & binder pockets		Spare floppy disks
Folders, envelopes	**SOMETIMES:**	
Blank legal & letter paper	Focus Tapes	**PERSONAL:**
Stapler, staple remover, 3-hole punch	Hanging Tapes	Glasses
3-ring notebooks, spiral notebooks		Vitamins
Pencil, pen, highlighters, sharpie bag	**OTHER:**	Cold Medicine
White chalk, grease pencil, paint markers	Scissors	Lozenges
Spare printer cartridges, batteries, bulbs	Mat knife, zip knife, safety pins	Breath Mints
Post-it Flags, Labels, pencil leads, erasers	Couple of spare templates & trimmer	Hand Cleanser
Binder clips	Wastebasket	Ziplock storage bags

Figure 11.13 Shelley's Domestic Production Table Gear List

FOLLOWSPOTS

If followspots will be part of the show, their status should be addressed long before the technical rehearsal begins. Ideally, all of the followspots already exist in the performing facility, so time and effort aren't spent getting them in the door, up to the booth, assembled, and tuned. In most cases, if the facility owns followspots, the numbers and types of spots will be listed on the tech specs. Determining their current condition, however, is often not possible to judge until the load-in. Some facilities maintain the instruments, so that all of the beams have an even field and matching intensity. In many cases, however, the instruments are in need of a tune-up. And in some cases, the instruments need to be replaced.

Although the actual location, condition, and limitations of the followspots can often be seen by turning them on, taking time to perform that task in the middle of a load-in is often not a realistic option. Certainly, if someone offers to run up and turn them on, all effort should be made to have someone from the lighting department go with the person to the booth and perform a full analysis of the instruments. More often than not, however, the typical method used to gain information about the spots is to talk to an electrician who has recently operated one of them. Acquiring this information may reveal the need to rewrite the followspot cue sheets. If rewriting needs to occur, better to find that out during the load-in, rather than in the midst of a hectic technical rehearsal.

 Some questions that help define house followspots:

- How may followspots exist in the facility?
- What is the light source? Manufacturer? (Presumably, they'll all be the same instrument.)
- Where are they located? (Are they all located on centerline? If they are spread out, can the outside spots make pickups on their near sides, or do they hit architectural impediments? If the latter is the case, the spot cues may have to be designed so that the outside spots make "cross-shots," picking up entrances on the opposite side.)
- Do they all produce the same amount of light, and if not, which one is the brightest?
- Do the instruments have matching beam size?
- When was the last time they were serviced?
- How are the followspots identified or "numbered"? If the lighting designer renumbers the spots without asking, he or she may be introducing

a guaranteed confusion-creator. Consider that these spot operators may have been running these lamps, using the same identity number, before you were born. ("Whaddaya mean, I'm Spot Three? I've always been Spot One.")

- How many color frames are in each followspot's boomerang? What is the frame number closest to the nose (or front) of the instrument? If a frost is planned to diffuse the edge of the beam, is there a typical frame number used for that function? Is there a typical frost that has been used to produce a fuzzy beam edge? (This topic will be discussed in Chapter 13.)
- Do they all have dousers? (If not, now is the time to be aware of that fact and consider workarounds if needed. One possible solution is to use heat-resistant black foil as one of the "colors," and manually "fade" the light.)

At an appropriate time during the load-in, the pieces of followspot color should be provided to the house electrician, along with a list indicating the colors by frame number. This list should include the relative location of the instrument's nose to the frame numbers, reducing the chance of the color frames being loaded backwards into the boomerang. Discovering this numbering reversal immediately prior to the technical rehearsal may result in either delaying the proceedings while the color is straightened out, or hastily rewriting all of the followspot cue sheets.

HOT TEST THE POSITION

As the instruments are being hung and circuited, the circuit numbers are recorded onto some form of the paperwork. Then the circuits are hard patched into dimmers and (on a computer console) softpatched into channels. Prior to the electrician leaving the remote hanging position, or the overhead electric flying out, one of the final steps that should occur is to **hot test** the position. This troubleshooting process can also be referred to as "wringing out" (any problems at) the position. Though the phrase implies plugging each circuit directly into a hot wall outlet, the surge in voltage can cause bulbs to burn out prematurely. For that reason, the hot test often activates instruments through a dimmer.

The hot test is performed by activating each instrument in sequence to confirm that it functions, that it's in the correct dimmer or channel, and that it's ready to be focused. Using the instrument schedule or the light plot, each channel or dimmer number is sequentially brought up to an intensity to activate the instrument. Presuming that the instrument functions, it's then checked to see that it has the proper color, accessories, and prefocus. In

addition to confirming the readiness of each instrument, the activity also allows any problems to be corrected prior to the focus session. Once the overhead electrics have been trimmed, fixing problems will be more difficult and take more time during the focus session.

Sometimes the hot test is performed only to confirm that the electrical path between the dimmer to the instrument's bulb is functional. The console's softpatch is set to the default one-to-one patch, and the entire plot's circuitry is checked. Once the hot test for the entire plot has been performed, the entire plot is softpatched all at once. Some production electricians favor this tactic. In their opinion, it expedites any troubleshooting needed when instruments don't activate in channels. Since the circuit and the dimmer previously functioned, the problem must be confined to the softpatch.

In some situations, bundles or multicables are installed during the load-in, following the simplest path between the hanging position and the dimmer racks. When mults are used to connect overhead electrics to dimmer racks, performing a hot test while the electric batten is at working height often means that the mults can't be plugged into the racks. In those situations, hot testing the position can still occur. An additional cable or mult (the hot tester) bridges the gap between the dimmer racks and the end of the instrument's cable or the Socapex connector. After the dimmer is activated, each male plug of the electric's bundle is plugged, one by one, into the hot test cable. This confirms that the circuit number on the male plug of the cable is marked correctly, and that the path from the plug to each bulb is functional.

Once the mults from the overhead electrics are plugged into the dimmers, there may still be errors. When that's the case, however, the problem has to be confined to the hard patch or the softpatch, since the hot test showed that each instrument and circuit were in working order.

Although most of the instruments hung on the first electric of *Hokey* have been plugged into a raceway attached to the batten, there are more circuits required by the light plot (14) than exist in the raceway (12). To make up the difference, provide some insurance against circuit failure, and allow for possible instrument additions to the hanging position, a bundle of six cables has been added to the first electric during the hang. The position now contains a total of 18 circuits. The instruments have been plugged so that two circuits on the raceway and two circuits in the bundle remain as **spare circuits**. By splitting the spares between the two types of circuitry, a choice can still be made for the route and dimmers utilized for additions or substitutions.

Since the bundle can't conveniently plug into the road racks until the electric is flown out to trim, a hot test cable has been run from dimmer 31 to test the male plugs of the bundle, and dimmer 31 has been brought up to 50%. The instruments not plugged into the bundle have been plugged into the raceway, circuited to the house racks, and softpatched into their respective channels.

The hot test will begin with instrument 1. Since that instrument is plugged into the circuit marked 1E-1 in the bundle, the male plug at the end of the bundle with the matching label will be plugged directly into the hot test cable. Light comes out of the instrument, the color is correct, and the shutters have been pulled. The hot test is removed from the plug marked 1E-1. Instrument 2 has been plugged into bundle circuit 1E-2. When the labeled plug is found in the bundle, that plug is inserted into the hot test. No light comes out of the instrument. The plug from the instrument to the bundle is disconnected from the other end of 1E-2, and a test light is plugged into the circuit. If the test light turns on, the circuit is good; therefore the lamp or something else in the instrument is nonfunctional. If the test light doesn't turn on, the circuit or the connections in the plug are bad, or the labeling is incorrect, either the plug is mislabeled, or the plug requires rewiring, or one of the spare circuits will have to be used.

While the plugs are being opened to check the wiring, the hot test can continue. Instrument 3 is plugged into circuit 9 on the raceway, which is wired directly to dimmer 9, which has already been softpatched into channel 51. The board operator is asked to "bring up" channel 51 to 50%. When that's been done, instrument 3 doesn't turn on. When the softpatch is checked, it's discovered that dimmer 9 was assigned to channel 52. When the softpatch is corrected, the light from instrument 3 turns on.

This procedure continues through the entire electric, until the entire first electric has been hot tested and declared functional. The entire position can then be either flown out **above head height** (above 7 or 8 feet), or to its preliminary show trim. Before being flown out, however, the production electrician grabs and shakes the yoke of each instrument, confirming that all of the hanging connections are tight. The instruments won't be loose for the focus session, nor will the c-clamps be so loose that the instruments fall off the batten. The hot test procedure continues until every instrument in each position is functional or noted. Once all of the electric are hung, circuited, colored, hot tested, and prefocused, the next step is to fly the electrics out (or up) to trim.

Hot Test the Electronics and Their Data

While this text focuses mainly on conventional instruments, it's worthy to note that this is also the point, while battens or other hanging positions are still close at hand, to test any electronic devices. That would include making certain they each get proper power, that they each boot up, and that they each respond to data. If any devices require a DMX address, now is the time to set it and check that it's right. The tale is often told about the major lighting manufacturer who decided to wait until their entire rig was in the air at the trade show before they sent someone up on the ladder to set the DMX addresses for all their moving lights. After spending hours 30'-0" in the air hanging sideways from a lift with cable wrapped over the movers and dodging scenery, they realized the error of their ways.

Tales from the Road: Get Some Cable-Grow in Switzerland

While trying to quickly load into a theatre in Switzerland, we were faced with battens that contained no pre-installed circuitry. Instead, individual cables that ran to the end of each overhead electric batten were then pulled over to the pre-installed circuits in the gallery. The problem, in short, was the cable length. Or, to put it another way, the cables weren't long enough. When the batten was lowered to the deck, the cables weren't long enough to plug into the gallery circuits. To make matters worse, the instruments were rented from another city, so the male plugs of the instruments didn't match the female plugs of the cables. An adapter, containing a small circuit breaker, was placed between each cable and every instrument on every electric.

The production electrician refused to hot test the instruments by plugging each of the cables into a single hot test cable while the batten was on the deck. Instead, the entire hanging position was raised to trim, the cable bundle was swagged over to the gallery, and the cables were plugged into the gallery circuits. After the plugging was complete, the instruments were finally tested. And to no one's surprise, several of the instruments didn't work. That's when we discovered that none of the male ends of the cable, currently plugged into the gallery circuits, had been labeled. So the only way to determine which instruments didn't work was to turn on all of the circuits in the entire electric. That somewhat reduced the workload, since we were able to determine the "good lights." Unfortunately, we still had no idea of the circuitry identity for any of the "bad lights"—and there were a lot of them.

By not taking the time to hot test the entire batten and label the cables, two additional layers of confusion had been added. We had no idea if the lamp inside the instrument, the adapter, the cable, the circuit, or the softpatch was bad. And there was little or no way to troubleshoot around them At that point, the ladder was occupied with carpentry troubles, and we couldn't even get to the electric. With so many variables, finding any base from which to even start troubleshooting was a challenge. The answer chosen was to conduct an extended cross-plugging screaming match, from the stage to the gallery, and then from the stage to the lighting console. Simultaneously, the carpenters were screaming from the stage to the fly floor and the grid to solve the scenic problems. We wasted a lot of time, and no one was happy.

SETTING THE TRIMS

Once the overhead scenery, masking, electrics, and any other scenic goods are hung and ready, the next activity is to establish the performance positions of all of these elements in the air. This activity is known as **setting the trims** or a **trim session**. Every piece of goods is raised in the air, often to a predetermined height above the stage. The position of all of the goods is then adjusted as necessary, so that the ideal performance locations are determined. Each defined location is then spiked (a **trim**), so that the height of any goods can be moved and still be restored to its performance location. In a mechanical sense, setting the trims for a show often attempts to hide the technical elements (battens, electrics, and so on) from the vertical viewpoint of the audience, and physically actualize what was drawn in the section. From the lighting designer's perspective, successfully raising the goods to their drawn trims achieves two additional goals: First, it makes certain that the hanging positions are vertically high enough to allow the instrument's light beams to adequately spread and provide coverage, and second, it becomes possible to double-check that the designed focus range for all of the instruments at each hanging position will actually work before the focus session begins.

A trim session usually involves the lighting designer, the technical director or production carpenter, and a fly-person on the rail. Once the activity is complete, most of the audience will be unable to see anything above the stage except the black masking borders.

The actual seat designated as the sightline point can affect the success of a trim session. If the measurement between the plaster line and the sightline (taken at the beginning of load-in) matches the distance drawn in the section, applying the trim heights from the drawing to the goods on the stage should then achieve the desired result. If that physical distance is greater than what was drawn, the sightline seat won't be able to see as high, which may provide a lighting advantage. If needed, the overhead electrics may be lowered below their drawn locations, and still remain concealed. If that physical distance from plaster line

to the sightline is substantially less than what was drawn, on the other hand, the sightline seats are then actually closer to the stage. As such, the sightline seat can see "higher" into the fly system. In order to hide the technical goods, the entire procedure may require reevaluation. Or the sightline seat may need to be re-designated to another row farther from plaster line.

Very few designers like taking that course of action, but after a point, the process must move ahead in the available time allowed, and the needs of the many at some point have to overrule the wants of the few. Besides, as many sage production managers have noted, the first row or two of orchestra seating is often referred to as "the cheap seats." And as Dan Butt pointed out to me years ago, "If they're looking up, they're not looking at the stage. And if that's the case, we're all in trouble." Accepting the fact that some of the technical elements will be seen by row(s) of the audience close to the stage is a harsh reality. But the alternative may be that the light beams don't spread enough to provide coverage, or they can't make their focus without striking the masking goods. Sometimes, no matter what's drawn, reality wins.

A successful and rapid trimming session is often based on being provided accurate information on the tech specs that were then used to produce the section, or accurately marked masking goods that were hung when the initial load-in occurred. Presuming that the masking leg heights accurately match what's been drawn on the section, the chance of the border trims being too high (allowing the audience to see the leg battens) won't occur.

If the heights of the physical borders at least match the heights drawn in the section, the chance of "seeing over" a border that's too short may be avoided. If the batten's pipe travel distance has been accurately recorded, then the bottom of scenery intended to disappear after being flown out will truly rise into the air and be hidden behind the masking. If the cable running from the overhead electrics to the backstage road rack dimmers is the distance planned for in the section, the overhead electric battens can be elevated and remain plugged to the dimmers, while they're still concealed behind the masking.

The sequence used to set trims is variable; it's usually dependent on the amount and type of scenery, the number of scenes, and the number of overhead electric positions involved. The basic sequence, though, usually starts with the masking. In the case of *Hokey*, the masking replacement exchange that took place before the morning call began will now be seen as either a successful example of seat-of-the-pants planning, or a nice idea that will still need further corrections (read as: more masking) installed or exchanged in future work calls.

The sequence that will be used to trim *Hokey* will follow standard trimming procedures. The first step is to lower the masking legs and the backdrops to their performance positions, or "**playing positions**" or "**in-trims**." Once those goods have been lowered, so the bottom of the goods touch the stage, they're locked off. This initial step ensures that none of the final border trims will be higher than the top of the legs or backdrops, visually exposing the battens on which these soft goods are tied.

The second step is to trim the masking borders, which is often seen as the real key to setting trims. Once all of the borders are trimmed, they define the performance space height, and establish the vertical aspect of the stage picture. In most cases the borders are raised to a single trim and locked off. The electrics are then raised one at a time, and presuming the section drawing, sightline placement, and masking heights are accurate, the electric stops at its designated height. It's concealed from the audience; it's at the proper height to provide the beam spreads as drawn; and the lighting instruments have the proper focus range to provide light to all points required by the light plot. The lineset is locked off, and attention moves to the next overhead electric.

If the masking borders require multiple trims, on the other hand, the methods and tactics are much more involved. It often begins by first raising the borders to their highest out-trims, and locking them off. The electrics are then raised, and once successfully concealed by the borders in their higher locations, locked off and (hopefully) left there for the entire show. Since the higher border trims allow the sightline seats to see the "highest" into the fly system, once the electrics are successfully concealed under these conditions, they don't require a second lower trim. Once the borders are lowered to their lower trims, the electrics can (hopefully) remain untouched, and not require a second lower trim.

On the other hand, the border trims chosen to conceal initial electric trims may be the lower height, seen for a majority of the show. Both borders and electrics may then require two trims, one high and one low, in order for the borders to conceal the electrics, but also so the electrics provide the beam coverage drawn in the section in both positions. Whenever possible, however, the designed intent is to trim the electrics to a single performance position. Each time an electric changes height, it runs the risk of striking adjacent battens or goods, which may damage the goods or refocus the instruments.

In the case of *Hokey*, the black masking borders require only a single trim. Initially, the black portal border will be trimmed. It was converted to a 4′-0″ tall border and swapped with the main curtain during the load-in, moving to lineset 2. It was tied onto the batten, counterbalanced with weight, and flown out above head height. The bottom of the border is now lowered (dropped in) to working height, so a carpenter can attach a measuring tape to the bottom of the border with a piece of gaff tape. The section and the hang plot show that the bottom of the border should be trimmed to 20′-0″ above the stage. The carpenter signals the flyperson when that measurement is reached, and the lineset is locked off. The carpenter then jerks the measuring tape, which rips both it and the gaff tape off the bottom of the border. This process is repeated until all of the black borders are trimmed to the heights stated in the section or the hang plot.

At this point, the production carpenter, or the technical director, then sits in the sightline seat and looks up. He or she is checking two things: first, that the tops of the legs can't be seen, and second, that it's not possible to see over the tops of the borders. It appears that all of the erroneous masking is going to work. Even though most of the borders are shorter than what was originally ordered, by exactly matching the trims indicated on the section, all leg and border battens are concealed. The additional horizontal line looking at the bottom of the additional border on lineset 13 is the only visual anomaly. Since the horizontal line from that border will only be seen by the first rows, the border masking is deemed successful and complete, and the trimming session moves on to the electrics.

Lineset 4 (the first electric) is dropped to working height, and an electrician attaches the end of the measuring tape with a piece of gaff tape to the bottom of the batten pipe. At this point the area above the stage is rather dark, and all of the masking is black. Since the worklights in the first opening are hung on the first electric, seeing the silhouettes of the instruments (to make certain that they're concealed from the audience) may be difficult. To solve this dilemma, the lighting designer activates group 24, the hanging position group that is programmed to turn on every instrument on the first electric. Once the instruments are activated, the signal is given to the flyperson, who then raises the electric to its designated height. The electrician gives the flyperson a signal, the lineset is locked, and with a jerk, the measuring tape drops to the stage.

Although the electric is now at its designated trim, the carpenter, or technical director, in the audience can still see the illuminated lenses of the instruments "poking out" under the black portal border. There are now two choices: either the portal border must be lowered or the electric must be raised for the lenses of the first electric to be hidden from the sightline seats. In an effort to preserve the proportion of the stage opening, the carpenter or technical director asks the lighting designer if the electric can be raised. If the electric is raised too far, focused light from some of the instruments may splash onto the #1 black border (lineset 14), which has already been trimmed. In addition to that, the increase in height may hamper the focus range of any instruments targeted to focus points downstage of the portal border. To provide an accurate response, the lighting designer first consults the light plot, determining the farthest upstage and downstage focus points assigned to the instruments on that electric.

Since the instruments have not yet been focused, the section is also consulted. According to the light plot, the farthest upstage beam edges will be the first electric frontlight system controlled by channels 6 > 8 and 16 > 18. According to the section, those beams will land at 20'-0" upstage of plaster line. That measurement is in line with the #3 black masking legs. The lighting designer then crouches so that his or her head is at that location on the deck, and looks up at the first electric. If the lenses on the electric can be clearly seen, then the electric may be raised. If the lenses can't be seen, then either the #1 black border will have to be raised, or the electric will have to be lowered. If the electric is lowered, then the portal black border will have to drop in as well to conceal the first electric. When the lighting designer looks up, the lenses can't be seen. Rather than lower the downstage goods, the #1 border and the first electric are raised, until the lenses disappear behind the black portal border from the carpenter's viewpoint in the sightline seat and the lighting designer can still see the lenses of the first electric crouched at the 20'-0" mark on the stage. Since the #2 and #3 black borders are still at their original trim, the height of the stage picture is preserved. Once the lighting designer checks to confirm that beams from the first electric pipe end instruments will still be able to focus "under" the portal border to any downstage focus points as well, the current status of the battens is declared satisfactory, and both battens are locked off.

This process of negotiation continues upstage until all of the electrics are hidden, the focus of each lighting instrument is retained without being blocked by black borders, and the vertical height of the stage opening mirrors the drawn intent as closely as possible. Once the sixth electric is trimmed so that the MR-16 striplights are even with the system pipe of the translucency, the entire stage picture is viewed from the sightline in the audience to confirm that everything is hidden. Once declared that this is the final trim, the flyperson then places spike marks on the operating ropes, marking the performance positions of all of the goods. After all of the spike marks have been placed, the trim session is complete.

Shelley's Notes: Trimming

Although concealing the electrics is often the ideal, in reality that may not be possible. In the initial discussion, one realistic possibility was that the audience seating was too close to plaster line; successfully hiding the electrics from the designated sightline seat was counterproductive to the overall visual design of the production. In that situation, the choice is often made to retain the integrity of the stage picture for the majority of the audience. While the first or second row may look up and see the instruments' lenses, a seat in the second or third row is designated as the new on-site sightline seat.

If a midstage drop is involved in a quick transition during the production, its low trim is often established after the trim of the black surround has been completed. Dropping the goods so the bottom pipe loaded in the drop hits the stage then visually confirms that the top of the drop won't be seen. Once the in-trim has been spiked, however, the drop may merely be flown out for storage. This may result in the system batten possibly being taken all the way to the grid. If this isn't noticed, when the cue is given for the drop to fly in during the transition, seconds will be lost before the bottom of the drop is seen under the bottom of the borders. The overall time spent for the transition may be needlessly increased. To avoid that, once the drop's in-trim is spiked, the drop should then be flown out only until the bottom of the drop is above any instrument's focus and the masking border hides the bottom of the drop. Once hidden, the "out-trim" spike for the drop can then be marked.

When the midstage drop is lowered to establish its in-trim, and the top of the drop (and its batten) is revealed, the next black border immediately downstage of the drop may also have to be lowered in order to cover the top of the midstage drop. A second spike mark will also then be placed on the black border, and it will move in tandem with the same fly cues that lower and raise the midstage drop.

If the show has several pieces of scenery flying in and out during the course of the show, it's wise to establish and check all of the trims before telling the fly crew to spike the trims. Asking folks to do the same task again begins to chafe at their interest factor.

While electrics are being trimmed, the decision must be made whether to attach the measuring tape to the lens of the instrument or to the system pipe. I prefer now to attach the measuring tape to the pipe. It's easier to remember. When I was younger, I attached the tape to the lens of the longest instrument. People change.

In this written example, when *Hokey* was trimmed, all of the goods were dropped in, the measuring tape attached, and then flown out to trim. Often, this procedure is performed as the borders and electrics are each initially completed and flown out. After each border is hung and counterweighted, the tape is attached, the border is flown out (not above head height, but to trim), and the tape is removed. After each of the electrics is hot tested, the tape is attached to the batten pipe and the same process is performed. By setting the trims as the goods fly out, the amount of time consumed for the trim session is reduced.

Tales from the Road: The Shrinking Legs

One good reason to preset the legs at playing trim for focus revolves around my story of the shrinking legs. When I walked into the theatre before the load-in, I was told that the legs were 24'-0" tall. Without taking the time to lower the legs to their performance positions, I proceeded to trim the borders at 22'-0" above the stage. The pre-hung electrics were then trimmed so that they were concealed. After the focus was concluded and the performance surface had been installed, the legs were dropped in to playing trim. Imagine my surprise when it was discovered that the legs were really only 18'-0" tall. The bottom of the borders came nowhere close to covering the system battens or the top of the legs.

In that situation, the only available solution was to lower the borders. After all of the borders had been dropped in to hide the leg battens, all of the backlight on the electrics hit the borders. After all of the electrics were lowered to get light off the borders, none of the specials were close to their spike marks. Ah, the learning curve.

Tales from the Road: Trim the Overhead Electrics Without Borders

Late in the morning, as we were preparing to set the trims on a show, we were informed that the masking borders had not arrived from the scene shop. Consequently, none of the borders would be hung to meet the schedule. Initially, this raised eyebrows of concern because we were scheduled to focus in 2 hours. Although all of the legs were hung, how would we know how high to raise the electrics to make certain that they would be hidden? Since it was obvious that we wouldn't have the masking borders before focus began, how would we know that the electrics wouldn't have to be re-trimmed later to remain hidden, which could then result in a refocus of the affected electrics?

Since each border was assigned to its own lineset, we dropped each batten in to working height, attached a measuring tape to it, and then trimmed the batten to the same height as the bottom of the eventual masking border. Although there were no soft goods on the pipe, the pipe itself provided the straight horizontal line. While sitting in the sightline seat, the electrics were then raised until they were above the border's batten.

By using the battens as the substitute borders, the electrics were accurately trimmed the first time. Although the electrics could be clearly seen above the border's batten, they were trimmed above the bottom of where the masking borders would eventually hang. During the focus session, instead of cutting light off the borders, cuts were instead taken off the battens.

Two days later, the masking borders arrived on-site, and the carpenters hung them on their assigned battens. After the bottoms of the masking borders were trimmed to the same height that the battens had been trimmed to 2 days before, the trimming was finally complete. There was no need for any refocus, and no stage time was lost.

THE FIRST CHANNEL CHECK

Once the overhead electrics have been trimmed, and the sidelight booms have been positioned, some amount of the remaining time should be dedicated to performing an initial channel check of the entire lighting package. A **channel check** (or on manual light boards, a **dimmer check**), involves activating each channel individually, in the sequential hookup order. This confirms that the proper instruments function, that the electrical path for each instrument is accurate, and that the color and accessories for each instrument is correct. The amount of time required for this activity can be reduced if color media has been inserted in the instruments during the hang. During the initial channel check, irregularities are often only noted on the worksheet. After the status of the entire lighting package has been seen once, the troubleshooting process can begin.

If time remains after the channel check has been completed, it can be used to visually check the infrastructure programming. Regardless of whether the programming has been viewed on the monitor display, seeing the correct instruments turn on truly confirms the accuracy of the programming. Checking the contents within one infrastructure function (cues, groups, or subs) will often confirm the accuracy of the other two. If groups will be used initially during the focus session or the light cue level setting session, they are often the function checked. A moment should be specifically devoted to checking any inhibitive sub-masters, or submasters used for worklight. This is the time to discover and correct any errors in programming. Detecting mistakes at almost any time in the future may be inopportune and a cause for delay.

If none of this information can be checked live before the focus session, then that's not cataclysmic. If none of this info can be checked live before cues are created live, that's also not a terrible thing. If none of this information can be checked live before cues start getting created in blind, watch out. Programming cues blind and tracking without first checking infrastructure information live can potentially program bad things. Now, if the show will have numerous technical rehearsals, there may still be problems, but that can still be fixed. But if the cues are created blind,

and not seen live until the one-off performance, experience has shown that it may be prudent to fasten your collective seatbelts.

SUMMARY

Once the light plot is hung, colored, accessorized, prefocused, hot tested, and positioned, the installation of the lighting package is complete. At the same time, the scenery and the performance surface have been installed. The infrastructure and focusing cues are loaded into the light board, the production table is set, the followspots have been examined, the stage has been spiked, and the overhead goods have been trimmed. Although there may be many other tasks for the other departments to accomplish, the focus session can now take place.

Chapter 12

The Focus Session

INTRODUCTION

This chapter examines some of the events that occur during a focus session, and techniques that can be employed to expedite the process. Keep in mind that there are many different ways to focus front of house lights, overhead electrics, and boom sidelights. No one method is correct. This presentation is one combination presented to demonstrate different focus techniques.

OVERVIEW

In almost every union situation, the end of the focus session concludes the load-in portion of the schedule, which requires the largest number of stagehands. Once the final instrument has been touched, the size of the stagehand crew can be reduced to the "show crew" (or the "running crew"). In many non-union situations that same demarcation is true as well: finish the focus and lots of folks say good-bye. Whether the focus started on time, or got massively delayed by other factors, the pressure to finish at that point in the schedule is often placed on the shoulders of the lighting department. If the final instrument hasn't been touched by the end of the allocated time, the entire load-in crew's salary may escalate to a higher overtime rate. While these kinds of situations are not typical, they exemplify the basic skills required to run and finish a focus session on a stopwatch. Most designers agree that the best way to approach focus sessions is with tactical organization, ruthless calm, and directed concentration. With the support of the rest of the lighting department, maintain a rapid pace

and make certain that every lighting instrument is addressed by the end of the allotted time. In these crunch situations, time is precious—so performing any task a second time can be viewed as a waste of time. In many cases, fine-tuning the focus of the instruments ("touch-up focus") is delayed until work note calls are scheduled.

Sometimes the nature of the production requires multiple visits to the same hanging position. If the show is a multi-set production, some instruments may be specific for individual scenes. In that case, time management may be even more critical. The scenery for a single scene is assembled and positioned, after which the ladder passes along each electric, focusing only on the instruments that will be used within that scenic arrangement. After every instrument has been focused in that set, the scenery is changed to the next scene. Once the next scene is set, the ladder returns to each applicable hanging position to focus every instrument designated for that scene.

Since some scenes require longer set-up time to be assembled, while other scenes may be similar in nature, the lighting designer must provide a strong input into the sequential order in which the scenes are assembled for the focus. Indeed, multi-set productions may be focused completely out of order, defined solely by the time required to change from one scene to another. Regardless of the order, however, a common tactic is to determine the first scene that will be required in the next work session, and make that the final scene that is focused.

While directing the focus in these multi-set situations, the lighting designer must also be acutely aware of the spatial relationship between each scenic setup and the lighting instruments designed to be turned on for that scene. He or she needs to know where the ladder should be positioned in order to focus each instrument, and (ideally) not be in the way of the instrument's beam. Simultaneously, the lighting designer also needs to envision the ladder's overall traffic pattern, in order to focus all of the instruments in that scene as quickly as possible.

The sequence of a focus session usually begins with the instruments in the front of house hanging positions. The overhead electrics are usually focused next, followed by the instruments on the ladders. The booms, set mounts, and groundrows are usually the last positions to be focused, because they're often the units most accessible from the stage.

The focus session may involve other people besides the focusing electrician, the board operator, and the lighting designer. A **channel caller** may be present to quickly translate to the board operator the channel numbers or system handles requested by the designer. A **scribe** may also be on hand, notating the actions applied to each instrument onto the focus charts. If the focus is a regeneration of a prior design, the scribe may merely need to update the charts as changes take place, keep track of which instruments have been focused, and notate units that will require future attention. If the focus session is for an original production, on the other hand, the scribe may be very busy, writing down the location of the hot spots, the beam edge size or softness, and any shaping required for each instrument. In addition, he or she may also need to read information regarding focused instruments back to the designer, allowing the focus of the instrument at hand to be matched or reversed. When more than one instrument is being simultaneously focused, the two assistants must split their concentration. When these two positions are combined into the responsibility of a single individual, the caller/scribe need not be concerned about being bored. The constant need to record information, provide information, write notes in the proper location, and keep up with the designer while calling the channels over the span of an 8-hour focus session can test the mettle of most assistants.

While the caller and scribe are busy keeping up with their logistical tasks during the focus session, the lighting designer's perspective is completely different. The designer must constantly be thinking three or four steps ahead of the present situation. He or she must anticipate potential problems, and have ideas ready to correct them when they occur. When difficulties present themselves, the designer must know how to quickly solve the problem, or be able to prioritize the difficulty to a future work call. The designer must know what semantics to use while focusing, so that his or her directions are clearly understood and rapidly accomplished.

In addition to pointing the instruments to their desired locations, the lighting designer needs to simultaneously be aware of several additional factors. He or she needs to be aware of each beam's relationship with the entire surrounding environment, including the masking, architecture, the audience's eyes, and the performer's eyes. In addition to that, the designer also needs to remain aware of each instrument's beam in relation to other lights, so that the beams blend between several different instruments in a system. At the same time, the designer may have to coordinate scene changes, prioritize the tasks, direct the personnel, adapt the schedule, contend with the politics, be polite, and complete the focus call without going into overtime.

Though it's been said before, it cannot be stressed enough that a lighting designer's ability to concentrate on all of the aforementioned tasks is critically dependent on the rest of his or her team. And while any onstage situation may include folks providing excellent help as assistants or associates, the designer's success is undoubtedly dependent on a skilled production electrician and the support of trained electricians—not to mention the rest of the heads and crews on each work call. Without their combined skill, knowledge, and support, the lighting designer's job, not to mention his or her ability to be an artist, is significantly hampered. And at extremely pressured work calls, which the focus call typically is, many designers readily admit they could not achieve their success without the help of those other folks, union or non-union.

FOCUS ANALYSIS

Before discussing a focus session, it's worthwhile to first analyze why an audience sees a focused beam of light in particular ways. Understanding this can have a direct effect on the methods used to focus that particular instruments and systems. Then it's possible to consider different techniques and tactics used to focus lighting instruments.

The Audience Angle of Observation

In a typical light plot, instruments are focused onto the stage from many different angles and directions. Some instruments' beam edges are more apparent to the audience than others, which is often determined by the relative angles of each hanging position to the audience's angle of observation.

This can initially be explained by examining the **law of specular reflection**, which states, "the angle of incidence equals the angle of reflection." This law merely states that light striking a flat surface from one angle will bounce off the surface traveling at the same angle in the opposite direction. Or to put it another way, "The angle coming in is the same angle going out."

Figure 12.1 shows a beam of light as a dotted line. The "incoming light" is approaching at the angle of incidence, striking the mirror at a 45° angle. The "outgoing light" is departing at the angle of reflection, also a 45° angle. This figure is typically used to illustrate the movement of light affected by a reflector, but it can also be viewed as a sectional view of light bouncing off of a stage.

Light from an instrument at an angle to the stage (angle of incidence), striking a flat surface (the stage), will bounce off in a matching angle in the opposite direction (angle of reflection). Figure 12.2 shows frontlight, sidelight, and backlight in a proscenium theatre, all striking the stage from different angles. Frontlight, for example, bounces up toward the backdrop, sidelight bounces sideways, and backlight bounces out toward the audience. The three angles of light produce individual visual results.

Consider this example: a single ellipsoidal backlight whose barrel sharpness doesn't match the rest of the system is more apparent than a similarly mis-focused frontlight or sidelight. This is due to the viewer's angle of observation, the relationship created by the location of the source (the beam's angle of incidence coming from the instrument), bouncing off the stage, and reflecting into the viewer's eyes.

When viewing a light cue from the stage right wings looking onstage, it's difficult to see any beam edges from the stage right sidelights directly in front of you, because those instruments are focused in the same direction as your line of sight. That line of sight is following the beam's angle of incidence. On the other hand, it's comparatively easy to see the "sharpness" of the beam edges, reflecting off the stage from the stage left sidelights. From that perspective it is easier to see the beam edges of any lights focused toward your position on stage right: the stage left booms, ladders, or overhead pipe ends. This is because the line of sight is in line with those instruments' angles of reflection. Compared to the stage right sidelight, the beam edges of the frontlight and backlight systems are also easier to see than the stage right sidelight, since they're only 90 degrees from your angle of observation.

When more than one system of light strikes the same area of the stage, the beam edges that are most readily seen are the ones that are 180 degrees to the viewer's angle of observation. Beam edges from 90 degrees may also be seen, but with difficulty. Beam edges at 0 degrees, or originating from the same direction as the line of sight, are the most difficult to observe. In an uncolored light plot, this suggests three practical implications:

1. A backlight system, consisting of sharp-edged ellipsoidals, should be carefully matched and focused. If one of the backlights is brighter, dimmer, or softer-edged than the rest of the system, chances are greater that the audience will see the anomaly. Backlight or downlight beam edges are the most "exposed" to the audience's angle of observation.

2. When sidelight is combined with systems from other angles, it can often be focused as sharp as necessary to cut the beams off legs or scenery. The beam edges on the floor will not be as readily observed from the audience, since it is 90 degrees to the audience's angle of observation. If light cues are planned that use sidelight as the sole source of illumination, it may be necessary to soften the beam edges of the instruments. If the light cues in question combine backlight with the sidelight, any sharp beam edges from the sidelights will be obscured from the audience's point of view.

3. If the production intends to use relatively bright backlight, the shutter cuts in the frontlights may not need to be matching and precise. The backlight will wash out the irregular beam edges of the frontlight.

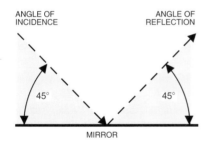

Figure 12.1 Specular Reflection

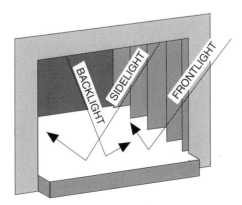

Figure 12.2 Stage Specular Reflection

Up to this point all attention on light bouncing back up toward the viewer's eye has been concerned with the angle of reflection. Now consider an example of the angle of incidence. When viewing a light cue from the audience, gaps in focus or irregular blending are most notable in the frontlight. When a performer's face darkens while crossing the stage, it's easily noted that he or she is moving through a hole in the coverage between two frontlights. If the focus of a frontlight is too sharp, the sharp beam edge can also be seen on the performer's face while he or she is crossing the stage.

It's much more difficult, however, for the viewer to see sharp beam edges or gaps in coverage from sidelight or backlight without looking at the deck. The lack of smooth blending or sharpness of the beam edges is only obvious to the eye when the angle of observation is the same as the instrument's angle of incidence. From the audience's angle of observation, this implies the following:

1. Frontlight systems need the smoothest coverage. To achieve this, frontlight beam edges are usually soft, rather than sharp.
2. In most cases, sidelights can be more sharply focused, because only the side sightlines of the audience will be able to see the reflected beam edges from the same angle of observation.

Although these implications are illustrated using a proscenium theatre as an example, they can be applied to other theatre configurations. When the audience views the stage from more than one perspective, like a thrust, arena, or alley configuration, these observations should be considered. It's prudent to consider the law of specular reflection and its impact before each focus session.

FOCUS TECHNIQUES AND NOTES

While focusing lighting instruments is an acquired skill, there are techniques and tactics that are shared here. It's important to keep track of which instruments have been completed, and which are in an unfinished state. It's also important to consider different ways to focus, and how to deal with environmental extremes during the focus session. Here are a few thoughts:

Paperwork Techniques

During the focus call, three documents are often updated. The lighting designer marks the focusing document, which may be a copy of the light plot, a focus schedule, or an instrument schedule. Constantly marking that document updates the progression and state of the focus session. The work notes sheet, or something like it, is marked to keep track of tasks to be completed at some point in the future, in order to make the light plot fully functional. The final document, usually a legal pad, is used to write down concepts, realizations, or any other notes not pertaining to physical labor.

During the focus session, instruments fall into three categories. Either the instruments haven't been focused, they have been focused, or they've been "touched." A "touched" instrument has been at least turned on, but may be only partially focused. It will require additional attention for its focus to be considered complete. Notes taken throughout the process keep track of each instrument's status. Some designers employ different colored highlighters or pens to indicate the current state of the focus. Other designers make two different kinds of marks on their focusing document next to each instrument: one indicates that the focus is complete, whereas the other shows the units that will require additional work. Often, both the "focus done" and the "more work" marks are made in pencil. In that way, when the "more work" action is completed, the note can be changed. When the page is scanned and no "more work" marks can be found, the entire hanging position can be considered focused. On the other hand, when an error in the focus is discovered, the "focus done" mark can be erased, replaced by the "more work" mark. A final scan of the hanging position displays the units that require additional attention.

Occasionally, it's necessary to change information about an instrument. A change in purpose, the planned electrical path, or other elements may require alterations in circuitry, patching, color, or focus. While these notes may be made directly on the focusing document, they're also recorded in the support paperwork. The cleaner the support paperwork is kept, the easier it will be to later update the database. Regardless of the system used to denote the changes, they shouldn't obliterate notes or information about the instruments that have been completed. Marking completed focus with a magic marker is not advised. When the information can't be seen, it can't be referenced later.

Keeping a separate work notes sheet, on the other hand, singles them out for the attention they deserve. Unless the note requires additional focus, many of them can be accomplished without the lighting designer's direct involvement. Throughout the focus, the electricians can attend to the work notes, without interrupting the designer's concentration.

A Focus Example

For most conventional fixtures, focusing a single instrument can often be reduced to four basic steps. In most cases, these steps are often made in the same sequence. Since the lighting designer is giving directions, he or she should *patiently* wait until each direction has been completed before requesting the next action. Likewise, the focusing electrician should communicate to the lighting designer when each requested action has been completed.

1. The lighting designer defines the location of the pool of light ("Hit me hot here" or "Edge of the beam there").
2. The lighting designer is satisfied with the location, and gives a command to immobilize the position of the instrument ("Lock it off"). Whatever immobilizes the "pan" (side-to-side movement) of the instrument is tightened, along with whatever immobilizes the "tilt" (vertical movement) of the instrument. Since the lighting designer may not be able to see when this is accomplished, the focusing electrician should respond when this action is complete.
3. The lighting designer adjusts the size of the pool or the sharpness of the beam ("Flood or spot the beam" or "Run the barrel in or out"), and indicates when the action is satisfactory. If the control for this action requires tightening some portion of the instrument, the focusing electrician also responds when this action is complete.
4. The lighting designer shapes the beam edges ("Put shutter cuts in here" or "Bring in a barndoor to here"). If this action is complex to achieve, the focusing electrician again responds when each action is complete.

In most cases, this process (or a variation of it) is repeated for each instrument. The more instruments in a light plot, the more often this sequence occurs. If the lighting designer establishes a consistent sequence, and repeats the same actions each time, the focusing electrician can keep up with, or even anticipate the lighting designer's requests. With constant communication between the two, and a repetition of the same actions, the amount of time between completed actions is often reduced and the focus gets done faster.

Positioning the Hot Spot

The first action in that example was to position the instrument's light beam. If not the first, at some point the beam has to be pointed somewhere and locked off. While there may be different times in the focus sequence to point the beam, there are just as many methods used to direct the beam's position. Usually, the lighting designer stands in a specific location so that his or her head is at the focus point. Then the beam is positioned so that the middle of the beam passes through the lighting designer's head.

When initially defining the focus point, some designers choose to stare into the light beam. By doing so, these "look-at" designers then see the filament of the lamp centered in the middle of the reflector. This implies that the hot spot of the instrument is centered on their face. When initially staring into the lamp, some amount of time elapses while the iris of the designer's eye "shutters down." It's an abrupt change for the eye to contend with, and during a single focus session, has to occur numerous times. To reduce the impact of this wear and tear, some designers hold a piece of saturated gel in front of their eyes while adjusting the hot spot to the focus point. Others hold up a piece of glass from a welder's mask.

Other designers "look away" from the light; they face away from the instrument to position the hot spot. By turning away from the instrument, it's then possible to see the hot spot while looking at the shadow, and also see where the beam is landing and what the beam is hitting. Look-away designers are also typically older. With age, their eyes take longer to recover after staring into the beam, which, in turn, means that it then takes longer to read paperwork. Look-away designers have also realized that, after seeing where the beam lands, it's often necessary to readjust the position of the hot spot a second time. Some look-away designers have refined the method so that they don't even stand at the focus point. They first ask for the instrument's beam to be horizontally centered where they stand. Then they ask for the beam to be raised or lowered so the beam's edge touches their foot, head, or hand.

Still other designers direct the positioning of the hot spot from a remote location, standing nowhere near the focus point. The key to their success is their ability to communicate with the focusing electrician.

Start the Focus from Center

When focusing multi-instrument system washes, such as straight fronts, downs, or backs, the first instrument focused by savvy designers is the unit pointing to centerline. This technique is especially useful when the beam spread, quality, or condition of the instruments is unknown. By starting the system's focus with the center instrument, the light beam requires fewer shutter cuts, as opposed to the instruments focused next to the side masking. Seeing the unshuttered center pool first can also make it easier to determine the next set of focus points in the same zone to create an even wash.

Another reason to start focus from center is the size of a beam chosen for a wash. Sometimes the beam spread of the instruments chosen for a system is smaller than what you thought. To achieve an even blend, the distance between focus points in the same zone may be shorter to avoid visual "dips" in wash coverage. In this scenario, if the system focus is started from one side of the stage, the coverage may "peter out" before reaching the opposite side. By starting the focus at center, the focus points in the same zone can be shifted equidistantly from centerline. After the system focus is complete, the coverage may still "peter out" before reaching the boundaries of the performance area, but starting the focus from center ensures that the system wash coverage will be symmetrical.

This technique also eliminates repetitive refocusing time. If a straight frontlight system focus begins with the offstage instruments, the dysfunctional instrument, destined to be focused at center, won't be discovered until midway through the hanging position. One solution to this dilemma is to shift the focus points in that zone closer to center, so that adjacent light beams will provide more "overlap" and ensure coverage. Although this is a viable solution, this tactic will require instruments to be refocused that were already considered complete. On the other hand, if the "middle" instrument focused first to centerline is discovered to be dysfunctional, the remaining focus points on either side of center can be shifted toward the inadequate pool. Using this technique, the rest of the instruments will then be focused once. No time is lost refocusing any instruments.

Focusing with Ambient Light

When worklights are on at full it's often a challenge to see the instrument beams for focus. While the obvious solution might be to turn off the works, the schedule may not allow that luxury. Other activities may still need to take place at the same time as the focus session. While it's generally understood that the faster the focus is finished, the sooner full worklight can be restored, most lighting designers can count on one hand the number of times they actually focused a show with all of the worklights off. Inevitably, they're presented with two options; they can have a dark stage for focus, then by delays during the cueing process because the scenery's now behind schedule. Or they can contend with some amount inconvenience (focusing with some amount of worklight), and hope the scenery will then be installed before the cueing session begins. Often the latter scenario is chosen, although it may elevate the frustration level brought on by bellowing focus directions over the sound of chain saws, or the inability to clearly see a beam of light.

Presuming there are worklights on different overhead electrics, one partial solution to this dilemma is to separate the worklights into downstage, midstage, and upstage handles. The designer can then keep the portion of the stage being focused relatively dim, while the rest of the stage can still be provided with adequate worklight. If that's not an option, it may be possible to use clip lights for the other activities surrounding the focus. Sometimes unfocused overhead instruments or rovers can be used to provide visibility for other tasks. At other times, it may be necessary to struggle through a focus session in full worklight with a smile on your face. If at all possible, break time is staggered, so that when the noisy folks take coffee, the stage can be darkened and the "focus" can actually be reviewed.

Sometimes contrast between the worklight and the focusing instrument can be used as a tool. When there's so much worklight, seeing the edge of the instrument's light beam may be difficult at best. In order to see the beam's edge, one technique often employed by the focusing electrician is to wave his or her hand through the beam of light, an action commonly referred to as **flagging the unit**, or **flag the lamp**. The flicker caused by the electrician's hand interrupting the beam helps the lighting designer to see the beam edge and determine the accuracy of that unit's focus.

If full worklight must be used during the focus session, consider searching for different locations of the beam edge that may be used as a signpost. As an example, searching for the bottom beam edge during boom sidelight focus can be frustrating. The top edge of the beam, however, may land high on the opposite wall, where the worklight isn't as bright. Consider matching subsequent beams to the top edge, rather than on the difficult-to-see beam edge on the deck.

Focusing with Other Activity

When the stage has to be shared with other departments during a focus session, it's typically due to a constrained schedule. Situations such as these can try the patience of any lighting designer. Frustration can grow high as inconvenience mounts, but this emotion should be tempered with the reminder that the other departments are probably not savoring the experience either. If they had exclusive use of the stage, it wouldn't be as difficult to see, they could make as much noise as they wished, nor would anyone be interrupted by the lighting designer bellowing instructions to the back of the house. Try to keep this in perspective, and attempt to peacefully share the working time.

If soft goods are being hung upstage during a frontlight focus, the scenery "in the way" may prevent the lighting designer from seeing where the upstage beam edge will land in relation to the upstage light line or the scenery stack. Rather than delay the focus, activate a single channel, focus the hot spot, and then stand on one side of the stage to see the beam "in section."

Mentally extend the edge of the beam upstage, gauge where the beam would land, and instruct the top cut accordingly. Afterwards, use the shutter cut of that instrument as a signpost. Park that channel at a low intensity, and cut the rest of the top shutters in the system to match.

Sometimes the offstage areas are crammed with so much gear there is no room to stand on either side of the stage. Viewing a focused frontlight beam from the side becomes an unattainable luxury. With the section, or a lineset schedule in hand, determine the location of the upstage shutter cut. Then walk upstage and stand on the light line, or under the batten that will eventually bear the downstage piece in the scenic stack, and direct the shutter cut to your feet.

At times, scenery "in the way" can be perceived as an advantage. Although battens at working height can make it difficult to discern upstage light lines during frontlight focus, they can also be used as signposts for shutter cuts. Presuming that the battens will remain locked at that height for some amount of time, they can be utilized as signposts for the focusing electricians: "Cut the top shutter in to the batten that's getting the black scrim." Sometimes inconveniences can be used as temporary advantages.

Focusing with Hand Signals

Sometimes the amount of background noise during a focus session is overwhelming. You're screaming to be heard and the electrician is still asking you to repeat your request. If the headset system has been set up, this is the perfect time to use wireless headsets. In lieu of that, call each other on your cell phones. On the really noisy days, however, the schedule may be so constrained that focus may have to occur at the same time as the jackhammers are literally cutting a trough through the audience. At that point, even headsets become irrelevant. In that situation, the lighting designer is forced to become a mime.

Agree upon the signals before the electrician goes to the position. Be clear and concise in your actions. If you are wearing mittens or gloves, make sure they are not black. If possible, keep the amount of paperwork in your hands or pockets to a minimum. Otherwise you'll inevitably put it down to make some motion with your hands and the paperwork will be swept away. Here's a selection of hand signals that have successfully worked in the past:

- A little bit, a "skosh": thumb and index finger close together.
- Beam larger: push out on either side of the mime's "box."
- Beam smaller: squeeze in on either side of the mime's "box."

- Check the connection: one hand with index and middle fingers extended (two prongs), moving into other hand gripping "ladder rung" (the body of the plug).
- Cross plug: make the "check the connection" gesture, then "criss-cross" with index fingers.
- Edge of the beam: one arm makes circular arc (pointing at edge of beam).
- Edge of beam here: one arm makes circular arc (pointing at edge of beam), other hand points to where the edge should go.
- Focus complete; move on: thumbs up, or small applause above your head.
- Focus complete; next channel on this pipe: wave circle in air.
- Hot spot here: point at own head.
- Lock: quickly twist hands together in opposition, like wringing out a wet washcloth.
- Nudge the fixture, don't adjust shutters: Butt hip pop.
- Open barndoors: hands sweep away from chest, like parting a curtain.
- Pan and tilt: thumb pointing in that direction like hitchhiking.
- PAR, twist the filament: extend both arms, like the guides on the airport landing strip.
- Sharpen: chop edge of flat hand into other flat hand.
- Skip a light: one hand "jumps over" the other hand.
- Shutter: chop edge of flat hand in air, then point to beam edge to be cut.
- Shutter edge: use two hands, not just one. Position fingers to edge of cut.
- Soften: fingers kneading dough.
- Stop: open hand, palm up, like crossing guard.
- Who made this mess: extend index finger and thumb to mime gun, point at own head.

When the orchestra rehearsal in the pit kicks into high gear during a focus session, communication can become just as difficult. With hand signals, it may be possible to focus in relative silence. The only speech required might be the channel numbers, which might still be provided to the board operator using a headset. One possible way to make this situation go smoother is to determine if there is a working fire curtain just upstage of plaster line. Usually, if it can stop fire, it will at least muffle sound. If readily available, it can be lowered to the deck and act as an acoustic damper, reducing the volume from the orchestra pit. If this rehearsal starts just as the overhead focus begins, double-check the focus points for any FOH frontlight systems that continue on overhead electrics. If the fire curtain will cover the downstage light line, anticipate the loss of this demarcation as well. Focus a single overhead sidelight, then lower the curtain to the deck. Once the curtain's in place, the side shutter cut can then be used as a signpost for the remainder of the instruments in the same system.

Sometimes the main curtain has to be used as the acoustic damper instead. Depending on air currents and current trims, though, the descending main curtain may strike the side shutter of the signpost instrument. If this happens, it may very well change the signpost line line cut. To avoid this, the common tactic is to hold one's hands up to the shutter cut while standing upstage of the curtain, and hold that pose while the curtain descends. If the curtain knocks the shutter, no matter. Once the curtain's in place, place spike tape at "hand height" on the curtain to signify the light line shutter cut, and proceed with the focus of the sidelight system. Not anticipating the need for this downstage light line signpost can be most embarrassing, since it may then be necessary to raise the fire curtain in order to establish the first downstage shutter cut.

Shelley's Notes: General Focus

On the day of focus, I'm more aware of my wardrobe. By wearing a light-colored shirt I provide the focusing electricians with a higher contrast target to be able to determine the relative location of the hot spot. While focusing, I often wear a baseball cap. Other than the fact that it protects my bald head, the visor can be used like a barndoor. Looking into a boom sidelight to see the beam edge, for example, often requires holding your hand in front your face to shade your eyes from the source of the instrument. Using the visor as a "hand," I'll merely tip my head down slightly, so that the visor of the cap blocks the source of the light. Without being blinded, I can see where the scallop of light or the shutter cut is hitting the floor.

When I check a system wash for blending, I don't use my hand. I'll walk between the focus points, and look at the blend of light on white paper attached to a clipboard, or the back of the light plot. I've found that "dips" in intensity are much easier to see on white, rather than on flesh.

If focus cues aren't used, it still makes good sense to reactivate the channel of the last focused instrument in that same system to compare beam edge placement or barrel softness. For example, after the first electric has been focused, activating channels 21 and 22 simultaneously brings up the lavender pipe ends on both the first and the second electric. This allows you to match the softness and beam edge location for channel 22 to channel 21 on the stage. If the matching beam edges aren't shuttered, this can reduce the task of positioning the hot spot to merely making certain that the second

electric's instrument is positioned in the middle of the opening. If the beam edges aren't supposed to match, on the other hand, seeing channel 21 will still allow the comparable barrel softness to be checked, along with the upstage/downstage blending between the two instruments.

There are times when using props can expedite a focus and reduce the lighting designer's physical labor. Any inanimate object can be placed as a signpost to define a focus point or a cut line. As an example, when the first frontlight is focused, I'll note where the shadow of my head lands on the stage. While the focus of the first instrument is being completed, I'll place a stool, a bucket, or a roll of tape where each head shadow will land. This eliminates the need to move to each focus point, and I can concentrate on the blending or shaping of the instruments.

Sometimes, there are just not enough props available to temporarily mark the stage. When there is no scenic stack in place, a shoe placed on each upstage quarter line gives the FOH electricians a visual signpost to refer to for the top cut, and reduces the amount of time I spend standing with my hands above my head screaming "cut the top shutter to my hands." If the theatre doesn't have enough clutter to be used as focus props, I occasionally end up disrobing bit-by-bit and leaving parts of my clothing around the stage. Although this may reduce the amount of effort on my part, these actions don't go unnoticed by clever carpenters who have screw guns and too much time on their hands. This becomes apparent when you finish the focus, walk to your shoes to put them back on, and discover that they've been screwed to the stage.

Shelley's Notes: Focusing More Than One Position

Occasionally, the combination of having enough skilled electricians, lifts, and support are such that it becomes possible to focus two lighting instruments, from two different locations, at the same time. On the other hand, the schedule may be running short and it may no longer be viewed as a luxury but a necessity instead. While the activity's the same, it can be met with two different mindsets. If you sense that the electricians are on your wavelength and you've got support, having the opportunity to focus twice the lights in the same amount of time means the entire crew might be able to break sooner for the night. If you feel like you're pulling everyone along, on the other hand, it can be an energy-sucking experience. Either way, if this plan is being seriously considered for an extended portion of the focus process, an analysis is warranted to define the amount of support that may be required.

First things first: Is the plot an original focus that is being recorded by no one else? If so, that's potentially a big thing. If only one instrument is being pointed at a time, it's certainly possible to provide direction and write notes at the same time. Occasionally, I've recorded the focus myself making shorthand on the instrument schedule or a copy of the plot. Adding the focus of a second instrument to the mix with the need for a little speed, and that task, along with keeping track of work notes will need to be assigned to someone else who has an idea of what's going on. Between bouncing back and forth between two positions, and keeping the numbers straight, I can no longer also write any of the notes without slowing the entire process. If there's no one available to be the scribe, it may be wiser to abandon recording the focus altogether during this session, and write the focus notes while observing a future channel check.

If it's regenerating a focus that I've done before, there may already be focus notes detailing the activity; in that case, the need for notes is reduced to actions specific for this situation.

So, if the focus is not being recorded, and just being regenerated, that makes it easier to do two units at once, right? Well, yes and no. If the focus is relatively straightforward, and if focus points and cuts have been already written on the plot or the paperwork, then shifting back and forth between two positions will merely require a little more concentration to visually shift back and forth between the two positions on the plot.

Regenerating a complex focus from charts, on the other hand, often requires visually flipping between two lighting positions to keep up with the electricians. Index separators or Post-Its™ can be used to define the different hanging locations within the paperwork. Quickly acquiring a channel caller means someone else can do the page flipping, read the info, and supply you with the purposes or focus points. If no one's available for those tasks, you'd be well advised to prepare the paperwork yourself; flipping between two pages, calling for the right channel, and keeping up with the electricians will make it necessary to process the information as rapidly as possible. And if you're not the original creator of the paperwork, a complex multi-position focus will require study, rehearsal, and possibly complete regeneration of the focus document into a language that you can then quickly process on the fly.

Adding the focus of a second instrument is also somewhat dependent on what positions are involved. If both instruments are frontlights, two electricians can be employed to focus channels that "mirror" each other. One electrician focuses instruments pointed on one side of the stage, while a second elec-

trician duplicates the same focus on the matching instrument focused on the opposite side. Box booms can also be focused in this manner, though the angles and size of the beams may overlap on the performance surface. Focusing box booms in this manner requires more careful coordination to avoid confusion. Pulling the color out of the unit being pointed can help isolate it from the rest of the lights in that channel, but the overlapping beams from both sides can quickly become overlapping pools of confusion, forcing all work to come to a halt in order for things to get sorted out.

When presented with the prospect of focusing three positions at once, my first reaction is to check the schedule. Is time so short that it warrants juggling three balls at the same time? In my mind, keeping up with two competent electricians can be an extended exercise in "too many plates, not enough sticks." Directing three electricians in different locations can be daunting, and not something to be entered into lightly. This situation is even more acute if there is no additional person to call out the channel numbers. One constraint that may squash this proposal is the number of available focusing ladders, or the number of available support personnel that will be required to move them.

The key to a successful three-position focus is anticipation, communication, and coordination. The tactical approach to this type of focus is to select non-adjacent hanging positions that won't "compete" with each other's beams—the instruments will point to mutually exclusive areas on the stage. One electrician on upstage backlight, the second downstage sidelight, and the third to the FOH, for example. The sequence in which hanging positions are focused may not make conventional sense. Careful location coordination reduces the slowdowns created when the light from one instrument washes out the beam from the second or third instrument. Before the electricians depart the stage, I'll memorize their names. This makes certain that the correct electrician and instrument are being addressed while giving directions, eliminating moments when the correct focus direction is applied to the wrong instrument. Then there are those days when all three electricians are named "Bob."

A three-position focus implies that the lighting designer will more heavily rely on the talents of good electricians. They'll be much more involved with the shape of the focus. In addition to having excellent focusing skills and an understanding of directions, it's a plus if they also know when to provide me with assistance, reminders, or alerts that they're ready for the next instrument. Since time to check a focus will be limited, I'll involve them much more in the process, asking for their visual judgment and opinions from their perspective.

This kind of focus is the ideal time to utilize additional spike tape, articles of clothing, or anything still not nailed down to indicate hot spots, edges of beams, or shutter cut lines. Having props to indicate locations means I no longer have to stand at a single position, waiting for the hot spot to be focused on my head. After instructing an electrician on the focus of an instrument, I'll leave him or her to follow my instructions, pointing and shaping the light while I attend to another instrument. I'll return to check the finished focus later.

For a three-electrician focus to succeed within a constrained schedule, everyone involved must agree that the electrics department has priority over everyone else on the stage. While the rest of the production team can continue work on other tasks, they should be on walkie-talkie. They are then available to respond to any needs or unanticipated problems that the lighting designer no longer has time to address. Often, one of those staff members will be assigned to stand nearby to take care of any situations that may impede the progress of the lighting designer. But whoever is near should not get into any extended non-show related conversations. Trying to focus and maintain concentration while the three "helpers" loudly discuss the best methods to wax cats quickly makes me lose my focus on the show, and instead mentally review if I'm carrying enough cash to bail me out of jail for three assaults, not just one.

If the call starts with three folks focusing at once, I'll utilize two of the electricians in FOH positions that can mirror each other, while the third electrician is assigned to an upstage overhead electric. Like before, the instructions for one frontlight's focus can be reversed and repeated for the same unit on the opposite side of the stage. If having two electricians on the same FOH position isn't a possibility, then start one electrician at one end of the FOH frontlight position, and send the second to the opposite box boom. Regardless, since the frontlights are typically focused downstage, the beams won't overpower or compete with the beams of the upstage instruments. Other possible combinations include focusing a boom downstage left, with a boom upstage right, plus an overhead. Or if there are enough electricians to move the ladders, two nonadjacent overhead positions can be juggled with a single boom.

Before agreeing to a three-position focus, all other options should be considered prior to committing to this course of action. Maintaining the pace, concentration, and speed of a three-position focus is exhausting. The only good thing is that it's not a four-position focus.

Designer Do's and Don'ts

During the focus, the most important task at hand is just that—the focus. Although appearing calm, relaxed, and polite, the lighting designer must constantly be aware of time management throughout the entire session. Here's a list of guidelines to consider during a focus session:

- Take command of the space. This is the only opportunity scheduled to focus the show— and the time is finite. If other departments are behind schedule, negotiate a compromise, so that all facets of work can continue, but if there's a scheduled end to the focus session, the focus is the priority. Establish a pace, and attempt to maintain it.
- Keep your concentration on the job at hand. Return phone calls, delay interruptions until break, or schedule meetings for another time. Just as designers can become irritated when crews are absent or dawdling, crews can get just as frustrated waiting for the designer.
- Don't get distracted by non-electrical matters. There are other members of the staff who can address crew call changes, wardrobe difficulties, or other pressing issues. You're the only one who can run the focus. Let the crew know that you respect them and their time, and your priority is to work with them and finish the task.
- Leave the stage as little as possible.
- Attempt to reduce delays in the process. Anticipate everything possible: channels, ladder movements, the next position to be focused, or scenic requirements. Communicate scenic needs prior to arriving at the instrument that requires its presence.
- When you run out of time and need to work through a break, respect the crew. Work with the production electrician to stagger the electricians' breaks so they all have a moment to relax, even if you work straight through it.
- Make certain that all notes are being recorded.
- Attempt to complete the focus for each lighting position to reduce the need for return access.
- Know the names of the people involved in the focus, write them down, and use them. The designer must give directions to many different individuals during a focus. If those instructions are given while turned away from the instrument, the electrician's name may be the only indication that the directions being given relate to the instrument.
- Be polite. When needed, ask for help. Respect your crew, your production team, and your hosts. You may be in charge of the focus, but you are the guest.

- Know when to continue, or when to stop the proceedings. If there's a problem, can it be fixed by someone else? Can it be worked on later? Can it be addressed while you continue somewhere else? Is there a workaround? Circuitry or color mix-ups may need to be reassigned as secondary "distractions" to getting the instruments pointed. On the other hand, if there's a problem that's safety related, stop your work immediately and get worklight up on the stage ASAP.

FOCUS TIPS

Consider these focus tips:

- Establish a communication with the focusing electrician. Make certain you both know when the other is waiting for instruction, confirmation, or a response.
- Be aware of any other elements adjacent to the beam of the instrument. Stand back and look for beam edges that may be striking architecture, masking goods, or scenery.
- Mentally rehearse the focus for the next instrument while the electrician completes the current unit. Consider other elements that may affect the focus. Scenery or additional spike marks may be required.
- Choreograph each position of the focus. Select the most difficult instrument to reach first. This prevents the first unit that has already been pointed from getting hit by the electrician while trying to focus the second unit.
- When focusing a system wash from a single hanging position, consider initially skipping other instruments and focusing that entire system. Repeating the same task can be faster. For example, if the electrician has memorized the focus for a system of backlight (the Fresnel is 3/4 flood, is hot on quarter and centerline, and top of the beam drops off the border), then activate those channels, and "run across the pipe," duplicating that focus. A second pass across the electric will allow the rest of the systems or specials to be focused.
- If two electricians are available to focus the front of house lights, consider using them to mirror the instruments on opposite sides.
- If time is limited to record an original focus, consider prewriting the focus on the charts in pencil. Written notes during the focus may be reduced to corrections or changes from the original plan.

- Delay any electrical or focus tasks accessible from the deck until last. The relative ease with which equipment in that position can be fixed, changed, and focused will make the end of the focus session go much faster.

Sneaky Tip: Focusing Ellipsoidals

One of the many reasons ellipsoidals are specified is the ability to shape their light beam edges with internal shutters. What some lighting designers constantly deny is the fact that the "fuzziness" or softness of the beam edge of an unshuttered ellipsoidal is often slightly different from the beam edge shaped by a shutter cut. When shutters are used, designers usually care more about the fuzziness of the shutter cut than the rest of the unshuttered beam.

The following sequence has been seen countless times in focus sessions:

- The lighting designer, staring at the beam edge of an unshuttered ellipsoidal, directs the electrician to run the barrel so that the beam edge is the desired fuzziness.
- The desired beam edge fuzziness is achieved. The designer is pleased. The focusing electrician locks the barrel's position.
- The designer directs the focusing electrician to push in a shutter cut. The electrician follows the direction, and a shutter cuts into the edge of the beam.
- The designer is no longer pleased. He or she then instructs the electrician to unlock and run the barrel again, so that the shuttered edge is now correctly softened.

If the amount of time consumed to run the barrel the second time is multiplied by the number of ellipsoidals, the result is time that could have been applied to a lot of other tasks.

If the softness of the shutter cut is important, bypass the first barrel run. Once the instrument has been pointed and locked, push a shutter into the beam of light (ideally one that will be used in the final focus). Run the barrel until the shutter is correctly softened. Then lock the barrel—once. Shape the light and move on.

Sneaky Tip: Focusing Orphans

Every light plot has an extra lighting instrument here and there that will be labeled "special." It's been placed there, as the legendary lighting designer Gilbert Hemsley would say, "as a GMOOT!—A Get

Me Out Of Trouble special!" Its purpose is vaguely defined, or it may presently have no purpose at all. But it's there just in case there's a need to isolate something, make something brighter, or become that extra special.

Before they have a purpose, however, these specials are orphans without an assigned intent. When possible, assign a dimmer and a channel to the orphans, and focus all of them. If dimmer allocation is tight, keep the circuits separated, but combine them into a single dimmer. If there hasn't been an opportunity to see a rehearsal, check with the stage manager, and focus the orphans to locations that seem like they might become important.

Before skipping the focus of an orphan, remember the amount of preparation and time it took for the electrician to reach that hanging position. Then point that orphan somewhere. Anywhere. Who knows, it might become the missing piece of inspiration.

Though they have no assigned purpose, if your assumptions are correct, an orphan may save the flow of a technical rehearsal. When the request is received to "make that area even brighter," it may be possible to turn *something* on. It may not be the right color, and it may not be the correct focus. But by responding immediately to the request, it may allow the rehearsal to continue. After the rehearsal, or in the next work call, refine the focus, color, and channel placement of the instrument to its new purpose. It's no longer an orphan. It has a home.

Shelley's Soapbox: Use the Hot Spot

Sometimes young lighting designers can be observed focusing the hot spot of an instrument at a focus point. While shaping the light, they then direct a shutter, or a barndoor, to be inserted in a manner that eliminates the hot spot. A typical example of this procedure can be seen in the focus of a pipe end instrument. After focusing an instrument's hot spot in line with a black masking leg, a side shutter cut then inserted to the very same leg. This would appear to be a waste of light.

The question to be asked is "What's the point?" If the beam of light has a purpose, don't defeat that purpose by trying to stick to the rules. Use as much of the light as possible. Focus the hot spot so that, after shaping the light, the hot spot still remains.

There are also many good practical reasons to include the instrument's hot spot in the focused light beam. When the shutter's shoved so far into the

instrument's body, the heat buildup can irrevocably warp the shutters or trash the instrument's reflector. More immediate, however, is that the heat built up inside the instrument can also cause the lamp to burn out, or to cause the instrument's socket to melt down. Ill-focused art can't be seen if the instrument doesn't work.

Shelley's Golden Rule: Is There a Light Cue Featuring This Instrument by Itself?

Sometimes in the middle of a focus session, an instrument's shutter suddenly sticks out like a sore thumb. It just won't cooperate. No matter what the focusing electrician does, the shutter still just can't get the right angle, location, or softness. After the third attempt, or when more than 3 minutes have been spent focusing that instrument, it's time to ask the question: "Will there be a light cue in the show featuring this instrument by itself?"

If the answer is no, then stop killing your electrician, your crew, and yourself. There's no reason to focus this instrument absolutely perfectly. A lot of other instruments probably remain that must be focused. Successfully beating the cranky instrument into submission to achieve the "right" cut, which only took 45 minutes to achieve, isn't much of a triumph if only half the plot is focused. On the other hand, if the full plot is focused with one reluctant shutter that's not quite right, then so be it. This single instrument will not make or break the show. Approximate a focus, and move on.

The bottom line is, keep moving. Don't allow a single problem to overwhelm, stall, or freeze you. Let someone else address that problem while you continue with the next position. If there is a problem in the overhead electrics, note the problem and continue through the rest of the focus. If there is time at the end of the focus to return to this nasty instrument, swap it for a different unit. If that can't occur, then the instrument is at least vaguely functional and will not be pointed into the director's eyes. Avoid the moment when the conclusion is made that, after the fact, the instrument wasn't that important anyway. If that time translates into overtime for the crew, you'll be very sorry.

One final note: this rule can be extended to entire systems of light. If the downstage shutter cuts on the frontlights don't exactly match, remember that in most cases there will be backlight on as well. The backlight may very well wash out the uneven shutter cuts in the frontlight from the audience's angle of observation.

Tales from the Road:
The Un-Called-for Channel

During a focus in a foreign country, I could not get the translated numbers in my head. No matter how I tried, every time I attempted to pronounce the identity of the next channel, the local crew would fall over laughing. While this didn't sour the mood, it did start to slow the process. First I pointed at the number on the page, and the translator would call the translated number to the console operator.

By the time we got to the two-color straight backlight systems, however, the hookup was so simple that I merely asked to switch between the two colors. I would focus the blue backlight, point my finger sideways, say "the other one," the translator would relay my request, the amber light would come on, and I would duplicate the focus.

Then we got to the show. There was no time for a technical rehearsal, so I had just pre-written light cues. The curtain opened on the blue-lit night scene for *Swan Lake, Act 2*, and it was . . . Day? Whoops. The colors had gotten swapped in the backlight, and since I didn't consistently call for it by channel, what should have been the blue backlight at Full was instead amber. As the dancers entered the stage, the scene became somewhat dimmer, as the amber backlight faded out. After a frenzied exchange on headset, the channel numbers were reversed, and the blue backlight faded up to complete the cue.

Since then I've learned my lesion. During focus, I always ask for each channel by number, rather than "the other one."

FOCUS CHECKLISTS

This next section contains a series of checklists worth reviewing before a focus session. Examining these lists can avoid delays.

The Environment

Items that are ideally complete
before the focus session begins:

- The electrics are wrung out, trimmed, set, and masked. The sidelight booms are immobilized and don't spin. The sidelight ladders are tied off. The deck rovers are plugged and positioned. There's been a channel check and possible problems have been noted on the instrument schedule, or focus schedule.

- The stage performance surface is clear. The area that you and the overhead focusing device will occupy has been swept so the lighting designer doesn't trip, and so the casters don't catch and threaten to tip the ladder/lift over.

- All spike marks and/or webbings are set. The designer has already rehearsed much of the focus in his or her head and believes that every spike mark that may be needed has been placed. Carrying a roll of spike tape in your pocket isn't a bad idea.

- The scenery is preset. Ideally, the performance surface is down. As much of the scenic package as possible is preset into position before the focus begins. Borders and legs are at trim. The downstage backdrop in the scenic stack has been landed to confirm the upstage light line. If all of the scenic goods are not available, spike marks have been placed to serve as signposts. Obviously, the ideal is for all scenery to be placed prior to the beginning of the focus. Less time spent mentally pretending where everything is going to be, allows more time to concentrate on the focus.

- The sound check is complete or scheduled for another time. The piano tuning is complete. Any audio that would compete with the lighting designer communicating with the focusing electrician, the board operator, or any assistants is complete.

- Other audio distractions are dispersed. People who need to scream at each other are convinced to take their discussion elsewhere. Projects involving noisy power tools are relocated. Musical instruments requiring tuning or practice are directed to a separate space or rescheduled for a different time.

- All extraneous light is reduced. The amount of ambient worklight is reduced or eliminated so that it's possible to see the beam of light and see everything the beam's hitting. The house lights are taken down to half or to a glow. If worklight must be on for work to continue, offstage worklights provide enough illumination to be used instead. When needed, the worklight control has been separated into three different channels: downstage, midstage, and upstage.

- The spare equipment and perishables are in accessible, lighted locations.

- If there's a scribe, an office position has been created onstage, so that the designer's directions can be heard, and the focus can be recorded. The office position includes a writing surface, a worklight, and enough copies of the forms. The scribe understands how to fill out, report, or update the focus charts.

- The channel caller has a worklight, accurate paperwork, and communication to the console operator. If the channel caller is the lighting designer, do you have a flashlight?
- The console operator knows how to run the console, can see the keypads, and can activate and deactivate channels, groups, subs, and can repatch, unpatch, and park dimmers.
- The ladder/lift used for overhead focus has some kind of drop line tied to a bucket, a spring clip, or a binder clip to get gear or accessories up to and down from the focusing electrician. Otherwise, much time will be lost going up and down, rather than focusing the instruments.
- A storage area has been created somewhere adjacent to the focusing electrician on top of the ladder. This may be as complex as an "apron" with pockets, or as simple as a bucket on a drop line. By providing a storage space, the electrician has both hands free to focus, and the time spent searching or acquiring the proper color or tool is reduced.
- If a staff electrician knows the focus, ask permission for him or her to focus the show. After they've seen the focus once, good electricians will begin to memorize the focus, and reduce the amount of time and communication required.
- If a staff electrician knows the show, the console, and the focus methods that are used, ask permission for him or her to run the lighting console for the focus. Many theatres will permit the "road electrician" to run the console. It often speeds the focus session.

The Lighting Designer

 Items the lighting designer should consider while preparing for the focus:

- Know the constrained vertical boundaries for the production; have a section handy to check the trims of all scenic goods and all masking borders.
- Know the constrained horizontal boundaries for the production; the spike marks show the different onstage edges of the leg and drop scenery, or the location of the not-quite-here-yet walls and doors.
- Know where the downstage and upstage edges of the performance surface are—(or will be).
- Know which lights are used relative to which scenery; make note of individual cuts in the documents referred to while pointing and shaping the lighting instruments.

- Focus tapes and/or spike marks are in place; have the system and special spike groundplans available, to either confirm locations or record additional marks.
- The lighting console is loaded with whatever infrastructure information will be required.
- Worklight control has been assigned; if there are no worklights in the light plot, or if the worklights are in a remote location, a full stage desaturated system wash has been assigned to a submaster for that additional task. It will then be possible to always get light on the stage.

Before the Electrician Departs the Stage

 Items to consider before the electrician leaves the stage for a hanging position:

- The channels have been checked for burnouts, color errors, and template accuracy. The electrician is equipped to address any problems with a test light, spare lamps, replacement color, diffusions, or accessories.
- Though it seems evident, the electrician has a wrench.
- The lighting designer (or the assistant) has accurate paperwork to call out accurate channels.
- The lighting designer (or the assistant) has focus charts that are readable and easily filled out.
- The electrician knows how to focus each instrument type at the hanging position.
- The lighting designer knows the mechanics and semantics to properly and rapidly direct the focus for each instrument type at the hanging position.

FOCUSING THE *HOKEY* LIGHT PLOT

These next sections examine some of the techniques, tactics, and workarounds used in focusing different systems in the *Hokey* light plot. An actual focus is conducted in an order resembling the instrument schedule; an electrician gains access to a hanging position, and the instruments are focused in order, one unit after another. In contrast to that, these sections will illustrate the focus of the *Hokey* light plot, system by system.

Front of House Positions

The hanging positions often selected as the first ones to start the focus session are in the front of house. In almost all cases they include the frontlight washes.

Typically, there are four main reasons for this. The first three are practical: first, those hanging positions are often hung and ready before many of the lighting locations onstage; second, they're usually ready for focus before many of the other departments have cleared their gear off the stage; and third, the basic parameters needed in order to focus many of the FOH instruments are minimal. Often, the downstage masking portal and the edge of the stage are the only items needed.

But all convenience or practicality aside, as far as lighting designers are concerned, the fourth reason to focus the FOH first is the most important; once the front of house frontlight washes are focused, designers then realistically know where the next upstage zone of frontlight focus points need to be placed in order to extend those smooth frontlight washes.

Think about it: the only lighting system washes that extend into the house are the frontlight washes. The rest of them—sidelight, downlight, backlight—are all contained on or over the stage. Now, if the frontlight washes aren't located both in the audience, and in overhead electrics over the stage, this isn't so important. If there's no frontlight in the overhead, most lighting designers will start the focus session wherever you tell them to. But nine times out of ten, as far as proscenium theatre is concerned, the frontlight has to originate both from positions over the audience and positions over the stage. And, in most cases, the only way to make sure there's an even blend of those systems between zones originating in the house, and zones originating from overhead, is to start the focus with the farthest systems downstage, over the audience.

So why is frontlight so important? In order to direct the audience's focus for most forms of theatre, they need to see the faces of the people who are speaking or singing. And, just like the concept of followspots, if the light beam drops off the performer's face, the audience becomes conscious of the sudden darkness. They're no longer in the moment of the show: now they're thinking: "Gee, that guy's face got dark." Shadows from the side, overhead, or back aren't as noticeable; they're not on the face. More often than not, it's the frontlight that's important. So in order to maintain the illusion of the theatrical moment, the basic unwritten law is that the frontlight *has* to be consistent. And the only way to maintain that consistency is to make sure there's not a visual intensity drop, or gap, between the downstage zones (over the audience) and the next zones (over the stage).

On top of that, consider this: in many theatres, the FOH positions can't move. They're typically the least flexible locations in the theatre, and in most cases, it's difficult, if not impossible, to change their position relative to the stage. The rest of the hanging locations upstage of plaster line, along with the scenery and masking, can all jiggle around with different trims and such, if need be, in order to accommodate architectural or scenic limitations. But in proscenium theatres with permanent FOH positions, those positions *are* the parameter.

Once the FOH focus is complete, the upstage boundaries of all the front of house systems are then known. This allows the lighting designer to judge the relative focus point locations for the remaining zones in each system. Now, as it was said, it may be necessary to shift the remaining upstage hanging positions, or focus points involved in those systems, to ensure an even blend of light between each of the downstage and upstage zones. But in most cases, focusing frontlight systems "out of order" is usually viewed as a risky proposition at best, and if considered, the lighting designer had best be committed to the focus point locations for each zone. Focusing the overhead instruments first, *before* focusing the FOH instruments, may result in a lack of downstage coverage from the first zone, or the dreaded intensity drop between the two zones. To fix this, it may be necessary to perform a second focus for the overhead instruments. "'Nuff said'."

A typical FOH focus often begins with the highest location. In the Hybrid Theatre, this means that the truss will be the initial starting point. After the truss is completed, the electricians will move to the box booms.

 A list to consider before focusing the FOH instruments:

- Vertical constraints (portal border, main curtain, midstage drops, scrims, and the scenic stack) are at playing trim or are indicated with spike marks. Specific shutter or barndoor cuts relating to the constraints are recorded on the lighting designer's focusing document.

- Horizontal constraints (onstage edge of black masking legs, or scenic legs, or onstage edges of walls) are placed at playing trim. If the actual goods aren't available, spike marks have been placed to identify the location of the goods. Specific shutter or barndoor cuts relating to these constraints are recorded on the lighting designer's focusing document.

- Any offstage constraints, like an adjustable proscenium or side house speaker stacks, are placed, spiked, or noted.

- Spike marks indicating the eventual center axis of each beam of straight frontlight have been placed along the apron, or on the seating in the house, or webbings have been taped down.
- The downstage edge of the performance surface has been defined. Or, if the performance surface isn't installed before the focus session begins, spike marks have been placed to indicate the future downstage edge.

Shelley's Notes: Where's the Downstage Edge?

Sometimes the frontlight gets focused before the performance surface can get installed. If the downstage edge of the frontlight will require a cut, the planned location of the downstage edge of the performance surface may become important to the lighting designer.

Why? If the performance surface is black but doesn't cover the light-colored apron, the frontlight may make the exposed apron glow like neon. Or the shadows from the backlight, otherwise undetected, may be seen on the apron, and might steal stage focus from the performers. The typical solution for this situation is to cover the surface of the exposed apron with velour or material matching the color of the performance surface. If the downstage edge of the performance surface ends up nowhere near the location agreed upon, on the other hand, alternate choices may have to be made. In most cases, efforts to mask the exposed apron will be faster and better for the show than changing the focus of the backlight. Better yet, if the downstage edge location can be determined prior to the focus, the appropriate cuts can be made, and the additional effort can be avoided altogether.

Whenever possible, avoid situations in which the entire electrics department is on hold, waiting for the downstage edge to be determined by being physically installed. I have memories of focusing electricians, sitting on ladders, surrounded by folks ready to move them, waiting at the edges of the stage, while I'm haggling with the production carpenter about the placement of the downstage edge. A conversation that should have taken place long before that particular moment. I remember that, and when it happens again, I now instead make a conservative estimate based on my best judgment, and move on. Stop waiting for the downstage edge.

In a larger sense, it's just as wise to define the location of the downstage edge of the stage prior to the focus session. Many theatres are equipped with hydraulic pit lifts, which can be lowered to increase the size of the orchestra pit, or raised to increase the size of the apron. If the decision is made to keep the pit lift in the "up" position for the show, then the frontlight can extend downstage onto the apron. This additional light may be useful to illuminate performers who cross downstage of the light line during the bows. If the pit lift's position is lowered after the focus, however, the frontlight focus should be immediately checked. The bottom beam edges may now be splashing onto the front edge of the stage, gaining much more visual attention than desired.

Straight Frontlight Focus

The *Hokey* light plot has two straight frontlight washes on the FOH truss, colored in Roscolux 33 and Lee 161. Instruments hung on the first and second overhead electrics provide the upstage zones for both washes.

Figure 12.3 shows channels 1 > 5, the instruments highlighted inside rectangles on the FOH truss. Colored in Roscolux 33, they'll be focused as the first zone in the pink straight frontlight system for *Hokey*. The apron spike marks, along with the front zone 1 centerline spike mark, provide the triangulation for the focus points. The same focus will be duplicated for channels 11 > 15, the Lee 161 blue frontlight wash. The first instrument that will be focused is unit #6, which will be focused on centerline.

Figure 12.4 is an abbreviated focus chart. The number in the small circle, located in the upper left-hand corner, is the channel number. The text under the circle is the position and the unit number. The large circle in the middle of the drawing represents the unshaped beam of light (seen as if the viewer were standing behind the instrument). The text inside the circle indicates the X and Y coordinates of the focus point. Lines running through the circle indicate shutter or barndoor cuts. The small rectangles on the right side show the barrel softness of the instrument (Soft, Medium, or Sharp).

In this case, truss unit #6 is controlled by channel 3. The focus point is on centerline, 3'-0" upstage of plaster line. The barrel will be moved to provide a medium soft beam edge. The upstage shutter cut will be 20'-0" upstage of plaster line or at the #3 leg line. The downstage cut will be out of the orchestra pit or to the edge of the performance surface.

Figure 12.5 shows channels 1 > 5, after the five instruments have been pointed. Channels 1 and 5 will require side cuts to keep light off the black masking legs. All five channels will require top cuts off of the scenic stack (or the #3 leg line), and bottom cuts to the edge of the performance surface.

Figure 12.6 shows channels 1 > 5 after the shutter cuts have been executed. To achieve side-to-side blending, all of the barrels are medium soft. Though these diagrams show all of the instruments pointed,

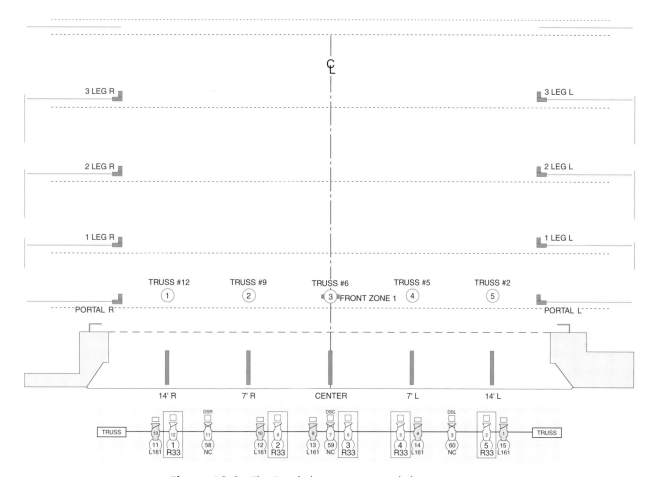

Figure 12.3 The Frontlight Instruments and Their Focus Points

and then shuttered in two separate steps, each instrument will be shuttered after it's been pointed during the actual focus. The focus of the first zone of pink straight frontlight is now complete.

Shelley's Notes: Straight Frontlight Tips and Workarounds

In many cases, when a theatre owns the frontlight equipment, the instruments have been hung in place for years. Without proper maintenance,

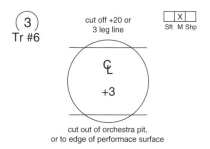

Figure 12.4 Focus Chart for Truss #6

there will be dysfunctional units. Since down center is often considered the most important location in most productions, that portion of the stage should be equipped to be brighter than the rest of the frontlight. If the instrument assigned to the down center frontlight is discovered to be dysfunctional, consider "swapping the focus" with another unit in the same system. A good instrument, previously assigned to focus on the quarter line, for example, can exchange focus assignments with the dysfunctional unit. The good instrument can focus to center, while the bad unit takes its place, and focuses to quarter line. Once focused, the softpatch can be altered so that the channel assignments are also exchanged.

Often, two zones of frontlight may be mounted above and below the same FOH hanging position. To retain the focus angle, conventional wisdom would suggest that the bottom hung instruments focus to the downstage zone, while the top hung instruments focus to the upstage zone. If the portal border prevents the top hung instruments from providing the desired upstage coverage, though, it may be necessary to ask, "Which instrument has the best opportunity

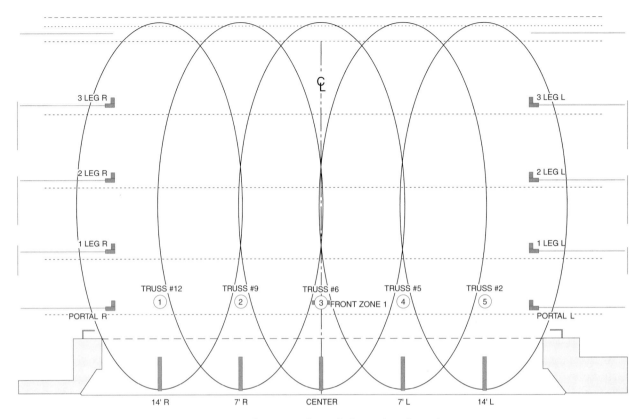

Figure 12.5 The Focused Frontlight Pools Before Shuttering

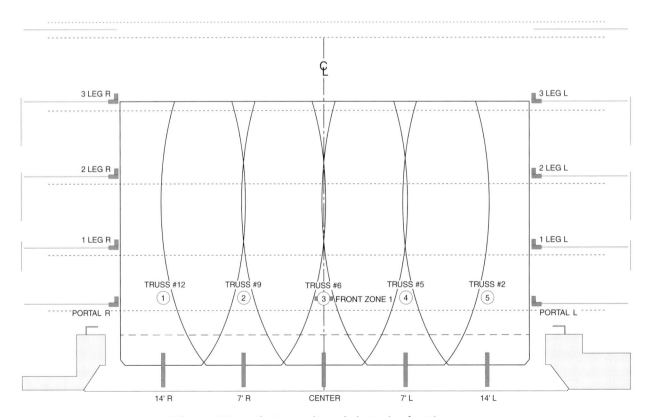

Figure 12.6 The Focused Frontlight Pools After Shuttering

to get to the desired focus point?" This may result in ignoring conventional wisdom and cross-focusing the instruments; the top hung instruments focus to the downstage zone, while the underhung instruments focus upstage, allowing them to shoot under the portal border and reach further upstage.

Front portals (or other soft goods) will occasionally be used for only a portion of a show. When these scenic pieces are in place, their side-to-side leg opening is usually less wide than the black masking legs directly upstage of them. If a frontlight system is turned on while the portal's in place, the offstage side shutter cuts must be pushed in further to keep the frontlight from splashing onto the onstage edges of the goods. Offstage instruments in other frontlight systems will still provide farther offstage coverage, since their side shutter cuts will remain open to the black masking. If all of the frontlight systems are turned on when the portal's in place, however, common wisdom dictates that the side shutters of all of the offstage instruments must cut in, off the portal. In that situation, the choice is often made to dedicate the side instruments of only one frontlight system for use when the portal is in place. The alternate solution is to add a duplicate pair of offstage instruments in the same color for each system. The first offstage instruments will be cut off the portal, and used when the portal is present. The added offstage instruments, in the same color, are used instead when the portal is removed, and frontlight coverage is required all the way offstage to the black masking legs.

Box Boom Focus

Focusing box booms can be the source of frustration and consternation for many lighting designers. Mention the box booms of specific road houses, and you'll hear sympathetic groans from designers who've endured focusing them. Architecture, the height and angle of the hanging location, scenery, and any equipment attached to the proscenium are only a few of the obstacles standing in the way of allowing systems hung in these locations from providing even coverage. In an effort to retain as much light as possible, while shuttering off unwanted distractions, the barrel focus of box boom instruments is typically sharper-edged than what the lighting designer originally wanted. Light frosts are often added in the color frame holders in an attempt to soften the edge and still retain control of the light beam. Their success is never guaranteed. Inevitably, the frost often scatters the light beam enough to provide more illumination where it's not wanted—on the face of the proscenium.

Figure 12.7 shows channel 30 controlling units #3 and #6 on the stage left box boom. Colored in Lee 116, they'll be focused as the stage left turquoise

box boom system for *Hokey*. The downstage light line spike marks, along with the stage right masking legs, provide the triangulation for the focus points. Unit #3 is a Source Four-26° ellipsoidal, which will focus to the far throw focus point, while unit #6, a 6 × 9 (40° beam spread) ellipsoidal, will focus to the near throw focus point. This focus will be duplicated for channels 40 and 50 on the stage left box boom, and mirrored on channels 29, 39, and 49 on the stage right box boom. Unit #3's hanging position is more difficult to access by the electrician, so it will be focused first, on the far throw focus point.

Figure 12.8 is an abbreviated focus chart showing that the preliminary focus point for unit #3 is 9'-0" stage right of centerline, and 5'-0" upstage of plaster line. The shutter cuts will eliminate the portions of the beam that splash light onto the black masking or onto the front of the stage. When the instrument is pointed, however, it quickly becomes apparent that shuttering successfully off the black masking legs will mean cutting through the hot spot of the light beam.

Figure 12.9 shows channel 30, after the focus points have been shifted, and the instruments have been pointed. This is the point at which the overlap and blend between the two instruments should be checked. If there's a "dark hole," or a drop in intensity between the two instruments, the focus points and their hot spots should be adjusted closer to each other. When the blend between the two beams is acceptable, the shutters should be applied. Unit #3 will still require shutter cuts to avoid splashing the black masking legs, while unit #6 will require a side cut to keep light off the stage left proscenium.

Figure 12.10 shows channel 30 after the shutter cuts have been executed. The side cuts between the two instruments were left open, to provide as much beam overlap as possible. Attempting to provide as much coverage as possible, while keeping light shuttered off the masking and architecture, means that the beam edges may be sharper than the straight frontlight system. The focus of the first stage left box boom system is now complete.

Shelley's Notes: Box Boom Tips and Workarounds

No matter how many beam sections are drawn, the final box boom focus may be completely different from what was planned. In theory, the box boom system is often used to provide a wash of frontlight from a different angle from straight frontlight. If reality demands that the focus points be shifted to create an even wash, adapt to the situation and move on. The previous example demonstrated this

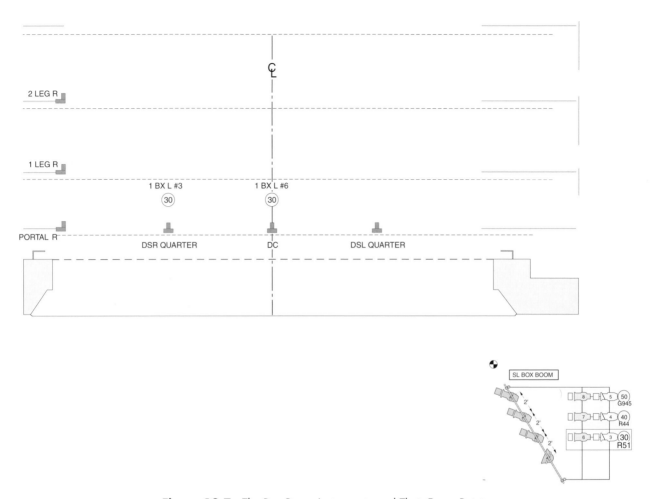

Figure 12.7 The Box Boom Instruments and Their Focus Points

adaptation. The objective is often reduced to merely using as much of the beam as possible. If the scenery isn't in place during the focus, knowing the placement of all scenic elements becomes important.

Usually, once the focus for the first box boom system is determined, that focus is copied for the other color systems. This will work well for *Hokey*, since the box boom instruments are all hung at the same height above the stage. Many theatres, though, have box boom positions that stack pairs of instruments

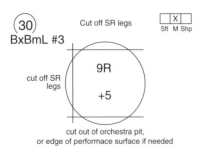

Figure 12.8 Focus Chart for Box Boom Left #3

below each other. In these situations, the top layer of instruments is usually focused first, so that the electrician "works down" the position. The challenge may develop with the lower layers of instruments. The system of focus points and shutter cuts that worked on the highest layer of instruments may not work at all two or three layers down. Since the lower instruments are at a reduced angle to the stage, duplicating the system of shutter cuts used on the top layer might result in thin slices of light.

If that's a possibility, consider plotting the most unsaturated colors at the top of the box boom, and the more saturated colors at the bottom of the position. While still providing facial coverage with the top units, the shutter cuts in the lower units can then be opened more, producing more light (and the resulting shadows from performers) onto the masking legs. If the color's saturated enough, however, the shadows won't be as noticed on the masking legs. Of course, if the legs are white, forget it; completely different shutter cuts should be considered.

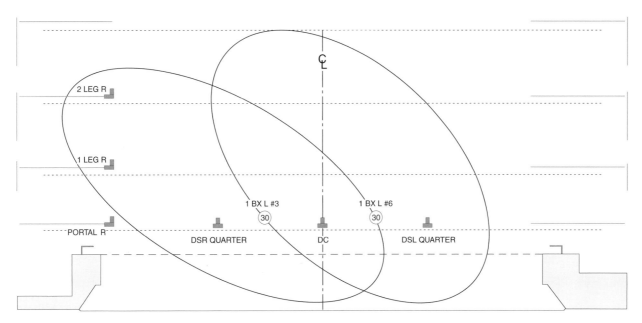

Figure 12.9 The Focused Box Boom Pools Before Shuttering

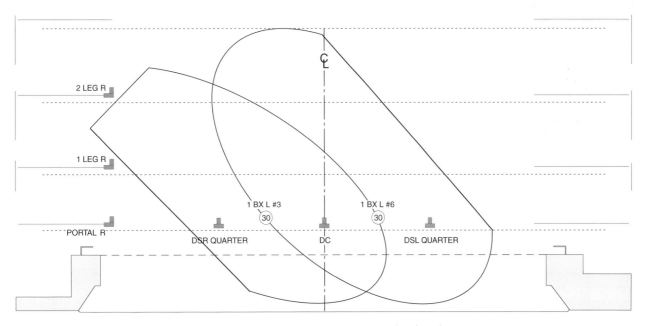

Figure 12.10 The Focused Box Boom Pools After Shuttering

When the location of the hanging position in relation to the stage is awkward, the alternatives may be few and time consuming as well. Choices include rehanging the instruments to a higher position, rehanging the instruments to a different position, or flinging your hands in the air and just eliminating the instruments altogether. Focusing the instruments in their present position may result in abandoning any structure where the focus points make any sense. The instruments are focused merely to provide as much coverage from that angle as possible, while cutting off the scenery and the architecture. If the choice is made to eliminate the units, and the plot doesn't include area frontlight, quick thinking may be required to provide light in the near corner of the stage, if the performers step out of the straight frontlight.

In some theatres, the box boom positions are difficult to access, and the instruments may have been hung there long ago. If that's the case, there's little doubt that they've received little maintenance. Shutters may be "sticky," absent, or just plain immovable. Recognizing this fact can alter the box boom focus priorities from pointing the ideal wash to getting light on the stage with the least movement, the fewest shutter cuts, using the least amount of time. This is a perfect situation to apply the golden rule: "Will there be a cue with this system on by itself?" If the answer given is a confident "no," then the task has been simplified: Get light on the stage, out of the pit, and off the scenery. Remember, there'll probably be backlight in the light cues, which will obliterate the beam edges or the peculiar shutter cuts from the audience's angle of observation.

If top shutter cuts will be inevitable, reducing the number of other cuts in the instrument may mean raising the hot spot of the instrument. This elevation may land the beam edge on the stage, and eliminate the need for a bottom shutter cut. Although the hot spots will no longer be at their designated focus points, the wash will be focused in half the time and the frustration level will remain low. Sometimes the opposite situation occurs; when the focus point is in the middle of the first opening, the hot spot may land on the far masking legs. If the top shutters are sticky, the solution may be to lower the focus point. Though this will "drop the focus," it will eliminate the need for a top shutter cut, and the focus can proceed.

Box Boom Cross Focus—Usually, instruments hung on box booms are assigned focus points so that the light beams from the instruments don't cross. When cross-focusing is attempted, the barrels of the instruments may bump into each other while trying to achieve their own focus. This barrel-bumping occurs when the units aren't hung far enough apart, and the focus can be slowed while the electrician rehangs one of the instruments to provide more space between them. In most cases, it's not worth the effort. In some theatres, though, the box boom's location may force a reevaluation of this plotting method.

Figure 12.11 is a groundplan showing the common method of plotting and focus assigned to box boom instruments. Unit #1 is focusing to the far throw focus point, while unit #2 is focusing to the near throw focus point. In some theatres, unit #2 can't focus "around" the near side of the proscenium. Although the instrument's beams can be focused closer together, unit #2 will still require extensive side shuttering.

Figure 12.12 is a groundplan showing the same two instruments "cross-focusing," contrary to common wisdom. Unit #1 is focusing to the near throw

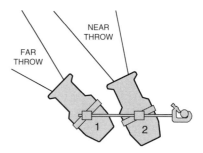

Figure 12.11 Typical Box Boom Focus

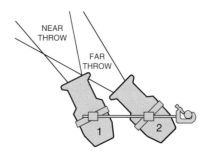

Figure 12.12 Cross Box Boom Focus

focus point, while unit #2 is focusing to the far throw focus point. The instruments have been hung farther apart on the sidearm to prevent the barrels from bumping into each other.

Filling in Box Boom Coverage—Sometimes the box boom position is so close to the proscenium it's not possible to utilize a near instrument. When the continuation of the color is more important to the design than matching the angle, consider adding another instrument from a different location.

Figure 12.13 is a groundplan showing box boom units #1 and #2 focused to the far and center throw focus points. Truss unit #3 provides the near throw

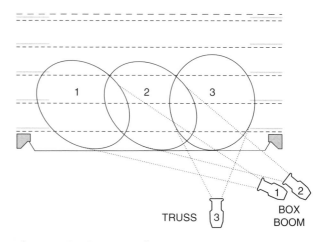

Figure 12.13 Near Fill Box Boom Coverage

focus point coverage. Although it's focused as a straight frontlight to the near side of the stage, it's colored to match the same color as the box boom units. Although the angle doesn't match, the color coverage will be consistent across the stage.

Sneaky Tip: Box Booms During Bows

Since it's downstage of the proscenium, box boom light can be used to cover performers during bows, when they're most likely to walk downstage of the light line to the front edge of the stage. To allow for this possibility, the shutter cuts of focused box boom lights can be left open downstage of the light line, to provide as much light downstage as possible. It may be possible to leave the bottom of the beam open, which can mean one or two fewer shutter cuts that have to be made. On the other hand, sometimes the apron is deep, but unused until the bows. Although the downstage side of the box boom light may remain unshuttered to cover the bows, this may result in too much light being seen downstage of the light line for the rest of the performance.

If there's enough instrumentation and hanging space available at the box boom position, focus an additional pair of units specifically for the bows on the apron and program them onto a pile-on submaster. The rest of the box boom lights can remain shuttered to the light line, and the stage manager can call for the submaster at his or her discretion. The added pair then doesn't need to be recorded as a separate cue.

Frontlight Drop Wash Analysis

When a show drop is used instead of a main curtain, the drop is often hung downstage of the first electric. If there isn't any room to squeeze in a set of striplights downstage of the drop, the choices are reduced. Alternate solutions that have been mentioned include using instruments mounted as footlights on the apron of the stage or in the orchestra pit.

Box booms or the frontlight hanging position have also been considered. In most cases, however, the first choice commonly selected is to use a frontlight drop wash from the balcony rail.

Frontlight Drop Wash Focus

When focusing a drop wash, it's advisable to start in the center to be certain that the wash will be symmetrical. To produce an overall wash of equal intensity, the beam edges are softened to blend together. When ellipsoidals are used, consider supplying the focusing electricians with several different kinds of diffusions to blend the beam edges in the middle of the drop.

A list to consider before focusing a drop wash system:

- The drop needs to be at in-trim. Period. This is one system that requires the goods to be seen to ensure an even blend, and eliminate the need for any touch-up.
- Any masking used specifically to mask the drop when it's at playing trim should also be at in-trim. If the drop isn't large enough to "fill" the portal opening, this might include an additional masking border and legs.
- Determine the staging for the scene. The location of the performers in relation to the drop may affect the height of the focus points on the drop, the location of any bottom cuts, or the focus arrangement of a template wash.

Figure 12.14A is a simple front elevation showing a masking border and two masking legs surrounding a downstage drop. The six circles represent pools of light from six instruments hung on the balcony rail. They have been pointed to provide full drop wash coverage. The pools overlap, so that the hot spots of the beams of light almost touch the edges of adjacent pools. The unshuttered light beams splash onto the masking, outside the drop area.

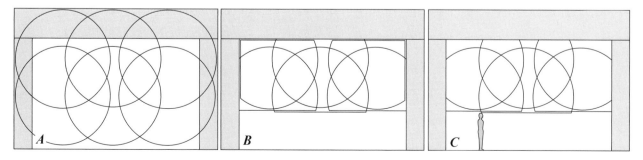

Figure 12.14 A Full Drop Focus Before and After Shuttering

Usually the top row is focused first, to reduce the chance that there will be dark spots between the top row and the bottom row. If the bottom row needs to be raised to achieve smooth coverage, facial front-light may fill in any darkness at the bottom of the drop. After all of the instruments are pointed and locked, Figure 12.14B shows how the shutters would be cut to the shape of the drop. When the shutter cuts are made, no tiny circular edges from the beams will be left in the corners of the drop.

While the drop is now evenly lit it's worth pointing out, however, that the hanging position is so low that anyone standing in front of the drop will cast his or her shadow onto the drop (Figure 12.14C). If there will be extensive performer activity, it may make sense to consider raising the focus of the instruments (or consider a higher hanging location).

Figure 12.15A shows the focus of what will be a partial drop wash. The focus points have been raised so that after shuttering, more light gets out of the instruments (Figure 12.15B). This provides more light on the drop, and reduces the amount of shutter burn inside the instrument. When shuttered, the bottom cuts are above the performer's head (Figure 12.15C).

The drop should be investigated before the plot is constructed, and examined before the focus session. If the drop has a painted sky or some other design element, Figure 12.16A shows how a reduced drop wash using only three instruments might be pointed.

Figure 12.16B shows the bottom cuts shuttered in to blend into the horizon line of the drop. After the shutter cuts are complete, the top "sky" of the drop is illuminated, and the bottom cuts are above the performer's head (Figure 12.16C).

Leg Wash Analysis

Unlike black legs that try to disappear, scenic legs contain a design element that's intended to be seen. In most cases, scenic legs are hung equidistant from center, so that each pair of legs provides the same leg opening width. Lighting scenic legs can be frustrating. Attempting to illuminate the legs with instruments hung directly downstage on the balcony rail will result in lighting only the first leg and leaving the rest of the legs in shadow. If the same instrument is panned across and focused onto the legs on the opposite side of the stage, however, all of the legs receive light. To light as much of the legs as far offstage as possible (and reduce the chance of shadows being cast on upstage legs), the instruments used for a leg wash often get hung as far from centerline as possible, and focused as cross-shots, across the stage.

The same light, focused onto the opposite legs, will also cast light on the proscenium or borders, causing sharp shadow lines on the legs. Because of that, the lowest border is often viewed as the vertical constraint. The top shutter, cutting light off the border, eliminates the sharp border shadow. Once the

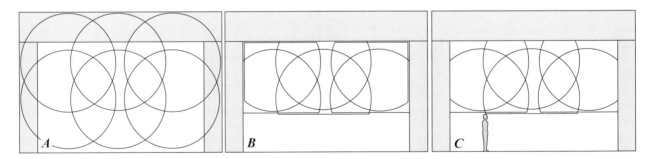

Figure 12.15 A Raised Partial Drop Focus Before and After Shuttering

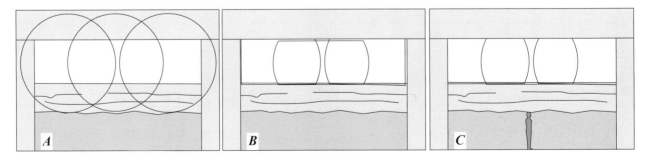

Figure 12.16 A Reduced Drop Focus Before and After Shuttering

light's shuttered off of the borders, though, the barrel focus may cause the shutter to produce as sharp an edge as the original border shadow. For that reason, the barrel of the instrument is typically softened, so that the beam edge is soft and fades into darkness.

Border trims define the top shutter cut, and since they may be lower than drawn on the section, the instruments used for a leg wash are usually hung as low as possible. The very bottom of the box boom or the ends of the balcony rail is the typical position of choice. The lower the better, allowing the beams to cast light higher up onto the scenic legs, and under the lowest border. The bottom cut is usually defined by the height of whatever shadow-causing objects may pass between the light beams and the scenic legs. These shadow-causing objects can include tall hats, spears, scenery, or performers being lifted during entrances or exits.

The number of instruments required for a leg wash depends on the throw distance, the beam spread of the selected units, the number of legs involved, and the overall depth of the stage occupied by the legs. If there are more than two sets of legs in a typical stage depth, that often implies at least two instruments needed from each side. This ensures that the shutter cuts can be achieved, and eliminates the possibility of curved beam edges being seen.

Leg Wash Focus

A list to consider before focusing a leg wash system:

- Either the scenic leg or spike marks indicating their onstage edges need to be placed prior to focus. If the legs are hung but can't come to their in-trim position during the focus session, the position of the spike marks should be double-checked by standing on each spike mark and looking straight up to confirm the leg's location.
- The borders, whether they're scenic or black, should be at their performance trim. Approximate top cuts can be made, but there may be no time to return to the hanging position for a touch-up focus.
- Whatever is downstage of the first scenic legs needs to be either in position or spiked. This scenic element is also masking the offstage edge of the first scenic leg. Usually, that scenic element is a black portal leg or the proscenium.

In Figure 12.17, two additional Source Four-26° ellipsoidals from the stage left box boom will be focused onto the stage right scenic legs. One formula that can be used to determine the location of the hot spots begins by measuring the distance from the masking downstage of the first scenic leg (in this case, the black portal leg) to the scenic backing (in this case, the black scrim). In the *Hokey* groundplan, that distance is 23'-3". When the distance is divided by three, the two intersections will be 7'-9" apart. These focus references will be spiked in line with the onstage edge of the legs.

Figure 12.18 shows the focus chart for the downstage instrument in the leg wash. Although the focus point is indicated, it will initially be used to indicate the center of the horizontal axis of the beam.

Once the instrument has been pointed towards the focus reference spike mark, the beam will be raised, so that the hot spot is halfway up the scenic leg.

Figure 12.19 shows the leg wash instruments after they have been pointed. When viewed from the front, the beams are pointed about halfway up the leg, so that the bottoms of the beams are close to the bottom of the leg. This is the point at which the overlap and blend between the two instruments should be checked. The instruments will receive side shutter cuts off the black portal masking leg and the black scrim upstage.

Figure 12.20 shows the leg wash instruments after the side shutter cuts have been applied. Top shutter cuts will eliminate light off the borders. Once the top cuts have been achieved, the designer will stand at the onstage side of the legs, and raise his or her hands above his or her head. The bottom shutters will cut in until they're touching the bottom of all of the legs. While they maintain that angle, the shutters will then continue cutting in until they reach the top of the designer's hands.

Figure 12.21 is a front view showing the completed leg wash focus, indicating where the top and bottom shutters were applied. In reality, the shutter cuts are usually soft and match between the units. The height of the top cut may be adapted if the border trims change height during the show. The bottom cut may be adapted depending on the height of performer traffic moving through the opening.

If shadow-causing objects are tall, the location of the bottom cut may need to be more extreme. Either the bottom cut needs to be pushed farther into the instrument, or the intensity of the leg wash will need to be reduced when the shadow-causing objects pass through the beam of light. The focus of one side of the leg wash system is now complete.

Shelley's Notes: Leg Wash Workarounds

If there isn't a balcony rail in the theatre, and the box boom doesn't get low enough to provide an adequate shot, the leg wash system can be hung in a third location.

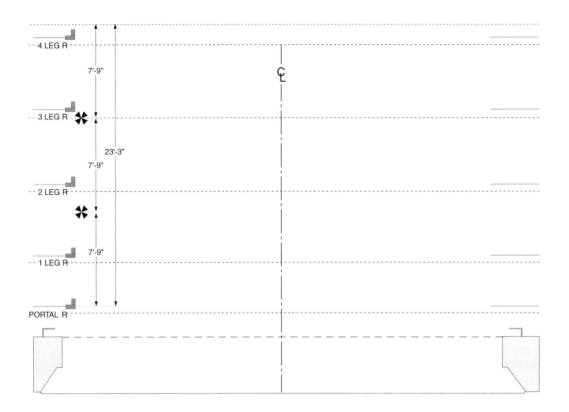

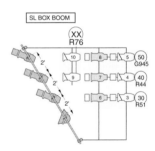

Figure 12.17 The Leg Wash Instruments and Their Focus Points

Figure 12.22 is a groundplan showing an instrument mounted on a boom in the first opening stage left, offstage and out of the audience's sightlines. It can provide some light on the scenic legs. The instrument will be mounted higher on the boom than any shadow-causing object. Otherwise, if the object moves through the first opening stage left while the leg wash instrument is on, the object will suddenly be very bright and distract attention from the scene.

Sometimes the leg wash can be placed on a separate boom or other hanging locations downstage of the proscenium, though this may require additional masking or crew time to install new hanging hardware. For that matter, it may be possible to place a boom in the seating area, though this should be carefully considered and cleared with the theatre's management.

Overhead Positions

The focus of the overhead electrics usually involves a focusing electrician perched on top of a ladder, lift, or hoist. On the side, while many theatres have

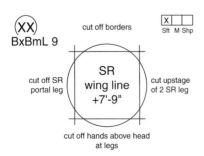

Figure 12.18 Focus Chart for Box Boom Left #9

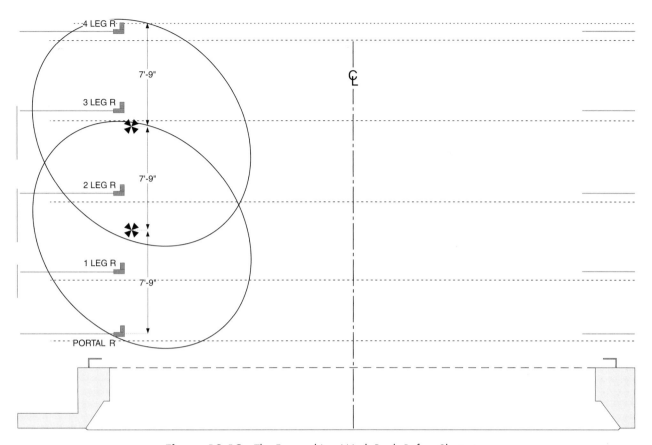

Figure 12.19 The Focused Leg Wash Pools Before Shuttering

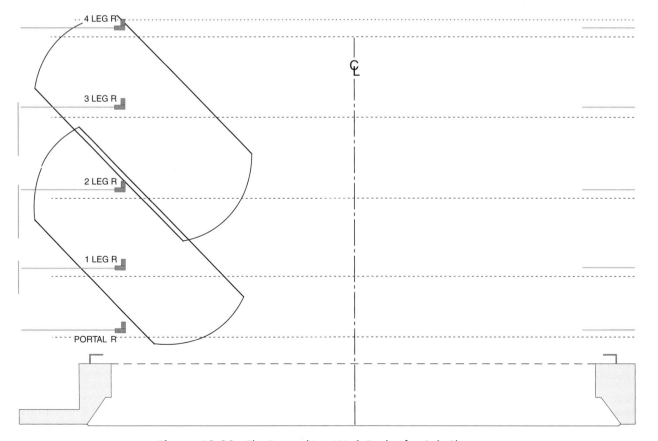

Figure 12.20 The Focused Leg Wash Pools After Side Shuttering

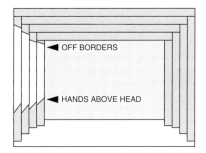

Figure 12.21 The Focused Leg Wash Pools After Top and Bottom Shuttering

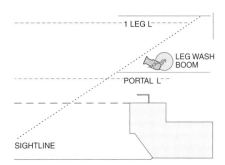

Figure 12.22 A Third Leg Wash Hanging Position

banned using A-frame ladders on their stages due to safety concerns, the noun is still constantly interchanged with the word "lift"—like this following statement: "the lift is usually castered so a ladder crew can move it about the stage." When overhead focusing was first discussed, it was pointed out that moving a personnel lift from one opening to another can take some amount of time. This is the demonstration of that condition; rather than focus each instrument in a single system, an overhead electric focus usually addresses each electric, one instrument at a time. The lift starts at one end of the electric, and moves across the stage as each instrument is focused, finishing at the opposite end of the same electric. Once the final instrument has been completed, the lift is moved to the next electric position upstage. Instruments in the overhead electrics are often assigned to several different systems that focus to different locations on the stage. Because of that, placing the lift in a position that allows the electrician to focus each instrument, while staying out of the way of its light beam, can be an extensive and time-consuming amount of movement. Depending on the type of lift or ladder used, minutes can go by merely maneuvering it from the downstage side to the upstage side of the same electric. For that matter, some amount of time is necessary to move the ladder from one side of the stage to the other. The fewer number of ladder movements, the faster the focus.

For this reason, the ladder's choreography is almost always taken into account, and in many ways, ends up "leading the dance." When up or downstage movement of the ladder takes too much time, it makes sense to limit those movements. If the ladder's on one side of the electric, it will be faster to focus only the instruments or systems on that electric that require the ladder on that side. Then the ladder gets repositioned to the opposite side of the electric—once. After repositioning, a second pass will be taken to focus the remaining instruments on the same electric.

When the ladder finishes one electric, it may be faster to start the next electric from the same side of the stage, rather than take time to move the ladder across. For example, Figure 12.23 shows the first two overhead electrics. After unit #19 (the final instrument on the first electric) has been focused, the common tactic is to move the ladder directly upstage to unit #26 on the second electric, rather than back across the stage to second electric unit #1.

The prefocus and final focused positions of the instruments should also be considered before the focus begins. Often, instruments are prefocused hanging straight down, so that several light beams, from instruments in the same channel, don't obliterate the ability to see the single beam in question. If there's a series of pipe end sidelights, consider beginning with the most onstage unit of the series. Otherwise, unit #2 may block the focus of unit #1.

This is the portion of the focus when the focus cues can come into play. If that's the plan, then be certain everyone knows the ladder choreography, which has been determined by the order of memories 1 > 100 that were programmed into the lighting console.

A list to consider before focusing overhead electrics:

- Confirm that the borders are at playing trim.
- Confirm that all legs are at playing trim, or spike marks are present to define their location.
- Confirm that any scenic portals are lowered to trim.
- If any scenery needs to be flown in and out during the focus, a stagehand is assigned to the fly rail, and knows that you may be requiring this scenery to move.
- The stage is clear of nails or screws that might trip the casters under the ladder.
- There are enough stagehands assigned to the bottom of the ladder to move it efficiently.

- The stagehands are listening to the electrician, who's at the top of the ladder, for his or her movement directions.
- Perform a channel check (if one has not yet been performed) of the entire overhead to determine nonfunctioning instruments. If time allows, examine the softpatch for errors to reduce the number of possible explanations for inoperable instruments.

Although the instruments in overhead electrics are realistically focused in sequential order, the focus for each system in the *Hokey* light plot will continue to be individually illustrated. The overhead frontlight focus will be examined first.

Overhead Frontlight Focus

The overhead frontlight washes may be a continuation of the frontlight system originating from the front of house. In this case, the two frontlight washes for *Hokey* consist of three zones each. The first zone was hung on the front of house truss. The next two zones are hung on the first and second electrics.

Figure 12.23 shows channels 6 > 10, the instruments on the first and second electric, colored in Roscolux 33. When focused, they'll act as the second and third zone in the pink straight frontlight system for *Hokey*. The apron spike marks, along with the front zone 2 and 3 centerline spike marks, provide the triangulation for the focus points. The masking leg spike marks will provide signposts for side shutter cuts if the legs aren't in place during the focus session, while the upstage T's (the light line) provide the signposts for top cuts if the scenic stack is absent. This focus will be duplicated for channels 16 > 20, the Lee 161 blue straight frontlight wash. The first instrument that will be focused is 1 electric unit #9, which will be focused on centerline. This unit will be focused first to ensure that the upstage frontlight will be focused symmetrically side-to-side.

Figure 12.24 shows the focus chart for unit #9 on the first electric. The preliminary focus point is on centerline, 10'-0" upstage of plaster line. The beam is intended to remain open, except for a possible top shutter cut off of the #1 black border upstage of the electric, or the black scrim in the scenic stack.

The placement of the second zone of focus points should be double-checked before the focus of the entire first electric frontlight system has begun. This is accomplished by standing on the centerline focus point in the second zone, and activating the center channel of the first zone of frontlight. In this case, that would be unit #6 on the truss, controlled by channel 3. If the light from channel 3 is hitting the lighting designer above eye level, the first

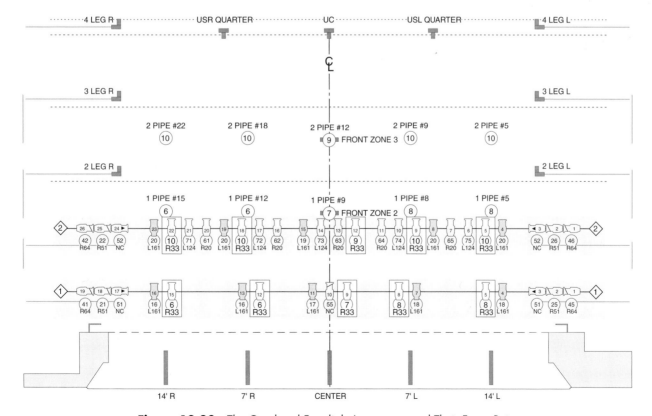

Figure 12.23 The Overhead Frontlight Instruments and Their Focus Points

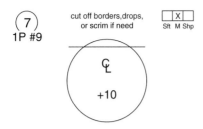

Figure 12.24 Focus Chart for 1 Electric #12

electric beams should adequately overlap, and the second zone focus points' placement should be correct. If the upstage edge of channel 3 isn't reaching the designer's eyes, the second zone focus points may need to shift downstage, or the top cuts in the first zone instruments may need to be opened up to retain an up- and downstage blend between the two zones. After the focus of 1 Electric #9 has been completed, the combined beams of the two centerline instruments, channels 3 and 7, should result in a blended frontlight system between the two zones. The same double-check should be performed between channels 7 and 9 before the entire second electric frontlight system is focused as well.

Figure 12.25 shows channels 6 > 10 after the 10 instruments have been pointed. The offstage instruments in channels 6, 8, and 10 will require side cuts to keep light off the black masking legs. Channels 9 and 10 will require top cuts to eliminate unwanted portions of the beams from the black scrim.

Figure 12.26 shows channels 6 > 10 after the shutter cuts have been executed. To achieve side-to-side blending, the barrels are all medium soft. Though these diagrams show all of the instruments pointed, and then shuttered in two separate steps, each instrument will be shuttered after it's been pointed during the actual focus. The focus of the second and third zones of pink straight frontlight is now complete. Group 1 can be activated to check the overall focus and blend of the entire pink straight frontlight system.

Overhead Sidelight Focus

The *Hokey* light plot has two pipe end systems, colored in Roscolux 51 and 64. Although a templated instrument can be seen adjacent to the pair, its focus will be different. The focus of the two pipe end systems will be discussed first.

Figure 12.27 shows the instruments and the focus points for channels 25 > 28, controlling the second instruments on the first, second, fourth, and fifth electrics. Colored in Roscolux 51, they'll be focused as the stage left lavender pipe end system for *Hokey*.

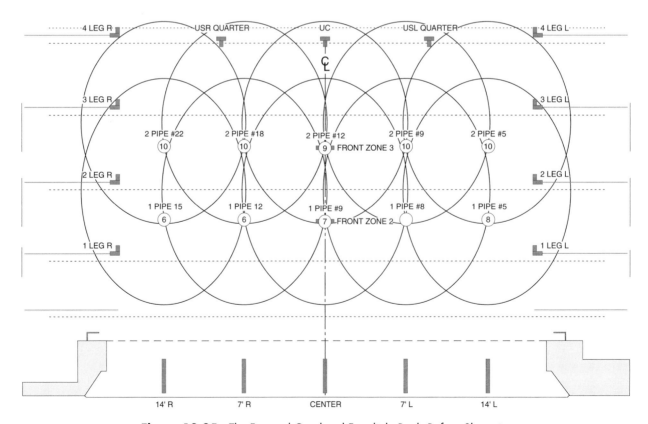

Figure 12.25 The Focused Overhead Frontlight Pools Before Shuttering

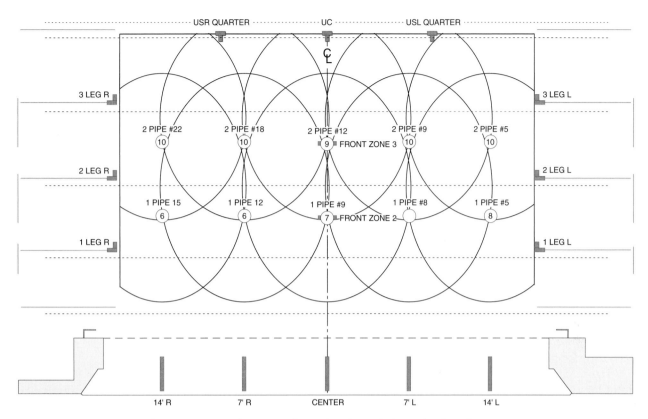

Figure 12.26 The Focused Overhead Frontlight Pools After Shuttering

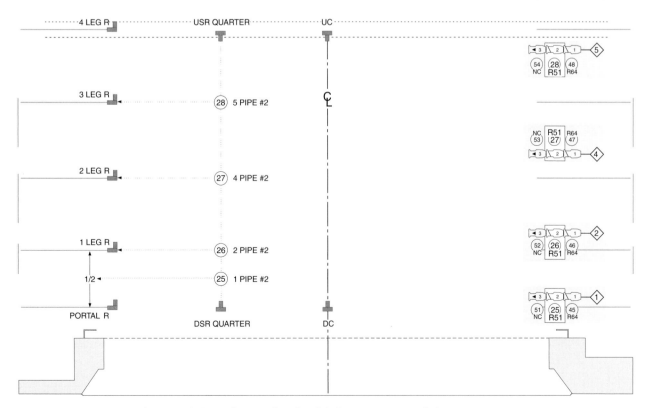

Figure 12.27 The Overhead Sidelight Instruments and Their Focus Points

The downstage and upstage quarter line spike marks, along with the stage right masking legs, provide the triangulation for the focus points.

The focus points for both the overhead sidelight and the boom sidelight may be shifted up- or downstage, depending on the amount of black masking that's attempting to be "concealed." In this case, the finished focus for the system will attempt to eliminate as much of the light on the face of the black masking legs as possible. To do so, the focus points of the three upstage pipe ends are shifted downstage from the middle of each opening. While the focus point for channel 25 is in the middle of the first opening, the focus points for the rest of the system are located at the intersection between the stage right quarter line and the black masking leg downstage of each electric. The locations of the leg spike marks will be used not only to locate the focus points, they'll also be the objects of the side shutter cuts as well. This focus will be duplicated for channels 45 > 48, the stage left blue pipe end system.

Figure 12.28 shows that the preliminary focus point for unit #2 is 9′-0″ stage right of centerline, and in the middle of the first opening. The shutter cuts will eliminate the portions of the beam that splash light onto the black masking on either side of the opening.

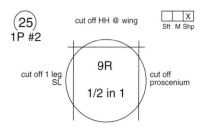

Figure 12.28 Focus Chart for 1 Electric #2

It is believed that the performers will not be lifted in the air near the onstage side of the legs, so the top shutter will cut the beam above the top of the tallest performer's head standing next to the black legs.

Figure 12.29 shows channels 25 > 28 after the instruments have been pointed. Side cuts will be required on all of the instruments to keep light off the black masking legs. The other three instruments will also receive the same top shutter cut as channel 25.

Figure 12.30 shows channels 25 > 28 after the shutter cuts have been executed. To keep light off the black legs, while using as much of the beam as possible, the units have a sharp focus. The focus of the stage left lavender pipe end system is now complete. Group 4 can be activated to check the system's overall focus and blend.

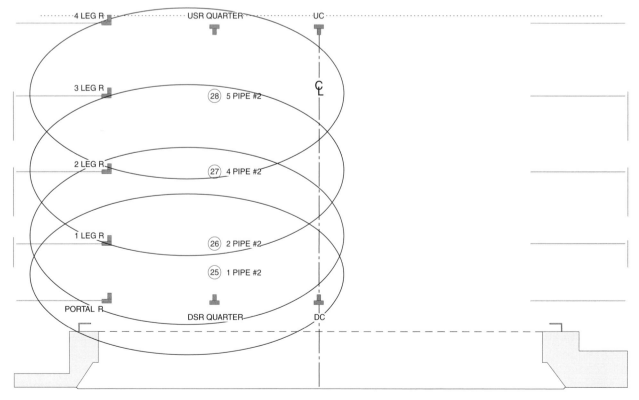

Figure 12.29 The Focused Overhead Sidelight Pools Before Shuttering

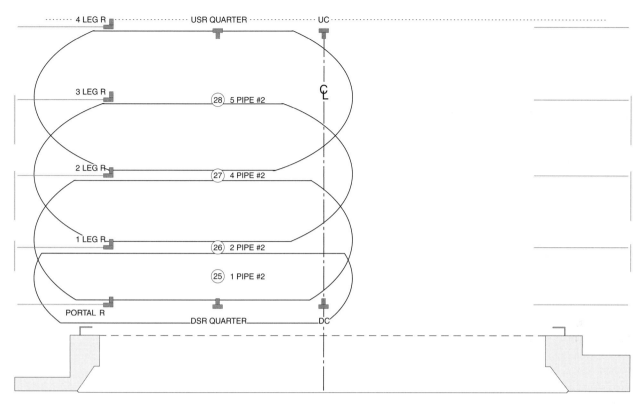

4 LEG R • USR QUARTER • UC

3 LEG R (28) 5 PIPE #2 C̸L

2 LEG R (27) 4 PIPE #2

1 LEG R (26) 2 PIPE #2

(25) 1 PIPE #2

PORTAL R DSR QUARTER DC

Figure 12.30 The Focused Overhead Sidelight Pools After Shuttering

Depending on the relative trims of the electrics and the borders, it may be necessary to cut the shutters even more. If light is hitting the back of a border, it should be shuttered to eliminate that spill. Although some light may be lost, it will prevent light from bouncing off the back of the downstage border, onto the next border upstage of the electric. Not shuttering the light would reduce the effect of a clean black environment. More than that, however, it's also a matter of safety.

 **Shelley's Golden Rule: Cut Light off Close Combustibles**

Sometimes instruments are hung in locations so tight that the units are close to soft goods or other objects that can burn. Flame-retardant products can be applied to fabric to reduce the chance that the heat from an instrument could start a fire. In addition, several different fabrics that are constructed of heat-insulating material can be draped between the instrument and anything combustible.

As the lighting designer, you shouldn't have to worry if the hanging location of the instruments is close to soft goods or scenery. From a perspective of time management, however, it's wise to watch for these potential problems. Unnoticed, fixing fire

safety issues can later consume time that was scheduled to complete electrical tasks. Setting the trims can be delayed when the electrics have to be lowered down to the stage so heat-resistant material can be tied to the batten. Worse yet is losing focus time while the focusing electrician ties heat-insulating material to the batten in the air. If there's no material to insulate the instrument, it may be necessary to rehang the unit, the electric, or just turn the instrument off.

In addition to the heat of the instrument itself, the heat of the beam coming out of the unit can be intense enough to start a fire. As such, beams splashing on soft goods close to the instrument can not only be a visual distraction, they can, more important, be a potential fire-starter. Overhead sidelight, downlight, backlight, and boom sidelight are all systems that may require an additional shutter cut to be certain there's no chance that their beams could make the masking smolder. During the focus, be aware of this hazard and address it. Never allow carelessness on your part contribute to a disaster.

If you're not convinced, look up any of the numbers of tragedies involving fire in the history of theatre. It's sobering, and often the fire's cause was eventually traced to a thoughtless person. As a member of the theatrical community, matters of fire safety should be burned deep in your mind. As one of the people in charge, you should contribute to setting safety standards. Strive to be aware of, and address, any potential hazards.

Overhead Template Focus

The *Hokey* light plot has a single overhead template system using Rosco Designer Pattern 77733 templates. The system is hung in a pipe end sidelight configuration. Each unit will be focused to a different area, so the combined instruments' pattern will cover the entire stage.

Figure 12.31 shows one side of the instruments and the focus points for channels 51 > 54, controlling the third instruments on the first, second, fourth, and fifth electrics. Specified as No Color units, they'll be left un-gelled and focused as the stage left side overhead pipe end template system for *Hokey*. The downstage and upstage right quarter line spike marks, along with the #1 and #3 stage right masking legs, provide the focus point triangulation for channels 52 and 54. The same masking legs provide the upstage/downstage placement of channels 51 and 53. During focus, those templates will be focused to overlap at centerline and fill the stage with the pattern.

The focus points for the template system may be shifted on- or offstage, so that the beams from channels 52 and 54 can remain as "open" as possible without using shutters. The focus points may also shift up or downstage, so that the pattern reaches as far offstage as possible (without striking the downstage side of the black masking legs exposed to the audience), or closer to the center of the stage (to ensure overlap coverage between the upstage and downstage zones). Out of all of the overhead system focuses, this is the one that is the most organic.

Figure 12.32 shows that the preliminary focus point for unit #3 is 3′-0″ stage right of centerline, and in line with the first black masking leg. The beam's task is to cover both the first and the second opening, while overlapping at center and blending with channel 52 farther offstage.

Since the template system's primary purpose is to cover the stage with a consistent pattern, less attention is paid to performer location. When the system is used as a primary source of light in the nighttime forest scene, it's planned that the additional templates inserted in the boom sidelights (channels 109 > 114) will "fill in" any locations not covered by the overhead system.

Figure 12.33 shows one side of channels 51 > 54 after the instruments have been pointed. The individual holes of light from the templates are not shown. This illustration is shown as if the templates have been removed.

Figure 12.34 shows channels 51 > 54 after the shutter cuts have been executed in the offstage instruments. The shutter cuts are used in the offstage

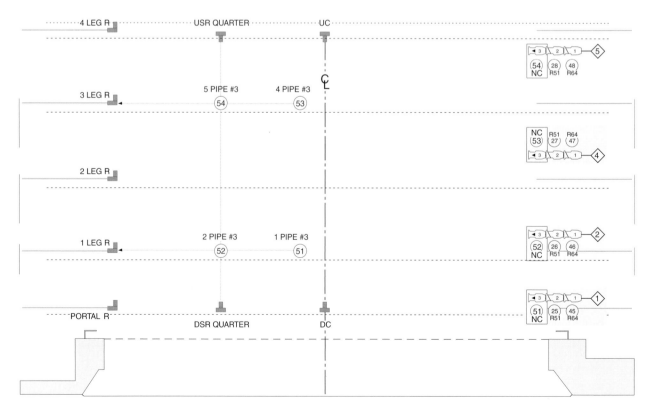

Figure 12.31 The Overhead Template Instruments and Their Focus Points

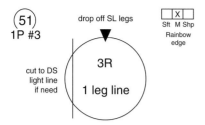

Figure 12.32 Focus Chart for 1 Electric #3

instruments only to keep light off the black legs and the black scrim. The focus of the stage left template pipe end system is now complete. Once the other side of templates is focused, group 15 can be activated to check the system's overall focus and blend.

Overhead Downlight Focus

The light plot for *Hokey* contains two downlight systems. Channels 61 > 70 are colored in Roscolux 20, and channels 71 > 80 are colored in Lee 124. Since a separate channel controls every instrument, the intent of the systems is to isolate areas of the stage or combine to wash the entire performance surface with a color. Though the two zones shown in the section cover the depth of the stage on the floor, the fact that there are only two zones, combined with the position of the electrics, doesn't provide any coverage at head height in the upstage side of the fourth opening.

Figure 12.35 shows channels 61 > 70, the instruments on the second and fourth electric, colored in Roscolux 20. When focused, they'll act as the first and second zone in the amber downlight system for *Hokey*. In this figure the positions of the electrics have been moved, so the focus points can be seen. The apron spike marks, and the down zone 1 and 2 centerline spike marks, provide the triangulation for the focus points. The masking leg spike marks will again provide signposts for side shutter cuts if the legs aren't in place during the focus session, while the upstage and downstage T's provide the signposts for the edges of the beams. This focus will be duplicated for channels 71 > 80, the Lee 124 green downlight wash. The first instrument that will be focused is 2 electric unit #13, which will be focused on centerline. Again, this unit in the zone will be focused first in order to ensure that the system will have side-to-side symmetry. If circumstances dictated, 4 electric unit #9 could be the first instrument focused, followed by the rest of the instruments on that electric.

Figure 12.36 shows that the preliminary focus point for unit #13 is 8′-6″ upstage of plaster line, standing on centerline. An additional note points out that the downstage edge of the beam should land at plaster line. The section has shown that the unit will be able to remain unshuttered. The barrel softness for the entire system will be medium soft.

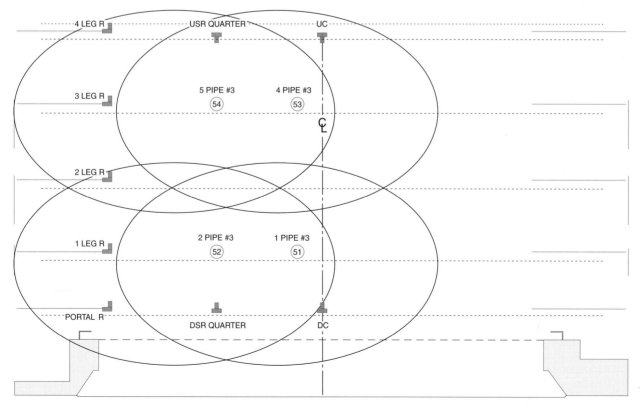

Figure 12.33 The Focused Overhead Template Pools Before Shuttering

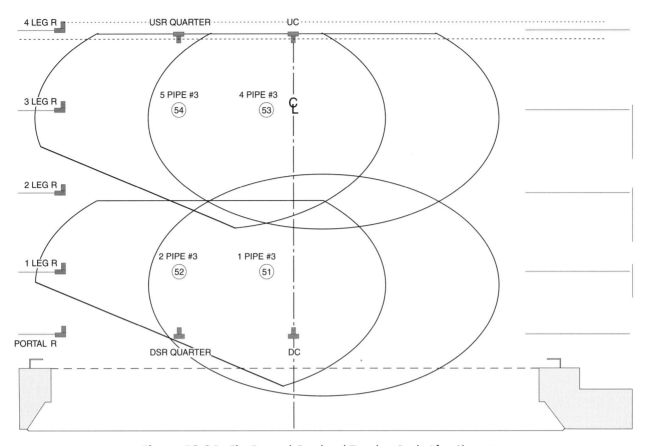

Figure 12.34 The Focused Overhead Template Pools After Shuttering

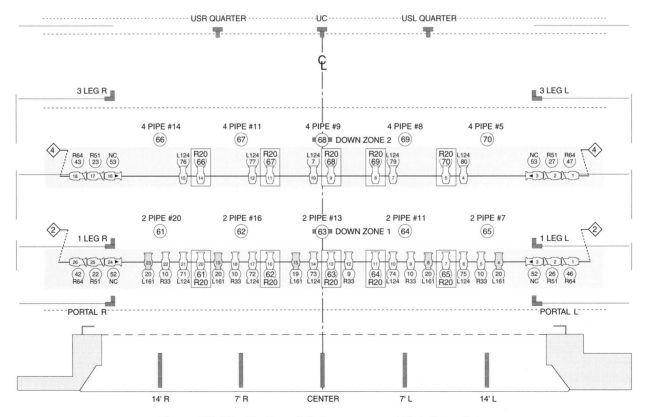

Figure 12.35 The Downlight Instruments and Their Focus Points

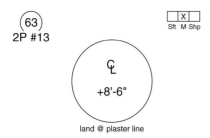

Figure 12.36 Focus Chart for 2 Electric #13

Figure 12.37 shows channels 61 > 70 after the ten instruments have been pointed. The offstage instruments in channels 61, 65, 66, and 70 will require side cuts to keep light off the black masking legs. The beam edges have landed in their positions without the beams hitting the borders, and no top or bottom cuts will be required.

Figure 12.38 shows channels 61 > 70 after the side shutter cuts have been executed. The focus of the amber downlight system is now complete. Group 7 can be activated to check the system's overall focus and blend.

Overhead Backlight Focus

The light plot for *Hokey* contains two backlight washes. Channels 81 > 90 have no color, and channels 91 > 100 are colored in Gam 850. Since a separate channel controls every instrument, the intent of both systems is to isolate areas of the stage in either color.

Figure 12.39 shows channels 81 > 90, the no color instruments on the third and fifth electric. When focused, they'll act as the first and second zone in the no color backlight system for *Hokey*. The apron spike marks, and the back zone 1 and 2 centerline spike marks, provide the triangulation for the focus points. The masking leg spike marks will again provide signposts for side shutter cuts if the legs aren't in place during the focus session, while the upstage T's provide the signposts for the upstage edges of the beams. This focus will be duplicated for channels 91 > 100, the Roscolux 68 blue backlight wash. The first instrument that will be focused is 3 electric unit #5, which will be focused on centerline. Again, this unit in the zone will be focused first to ensure that the system will have side-to-side symmetry.

Figure 12.40 shows that the preliminary focus point for unit #5 is 3'-0" upstage of plaster line, standing on centerline. Although this is the focus for a backlight, the focus chart still views the beam of light from behind the instrument. The note seen at the top of the circle indicates the top of the unshuttered beam should drop off the #1 black border on lineset 14.

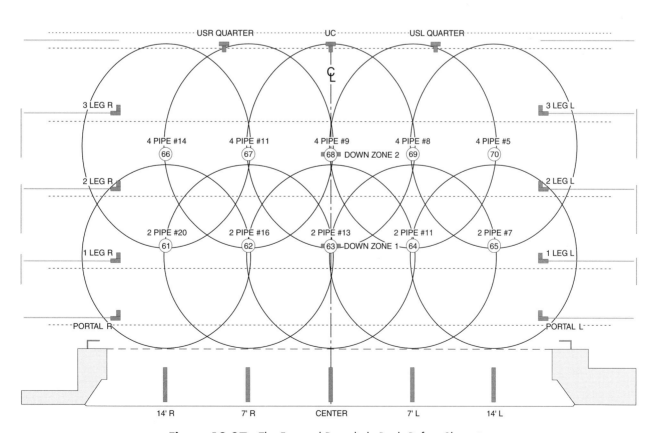

Figure 12.37 The Focused Downlight Pools Before Shuttering

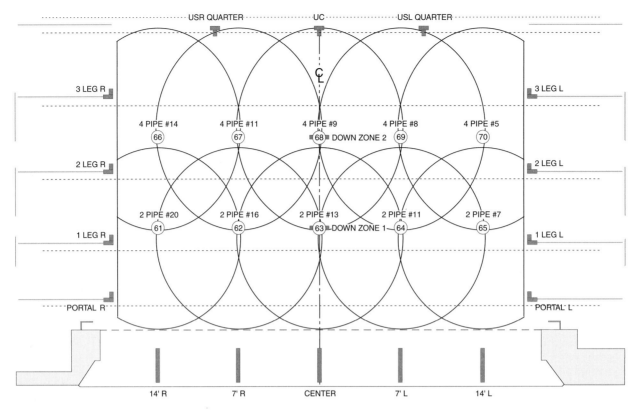

Figure 12.38 The Focused Downlight Pools After Shuttering

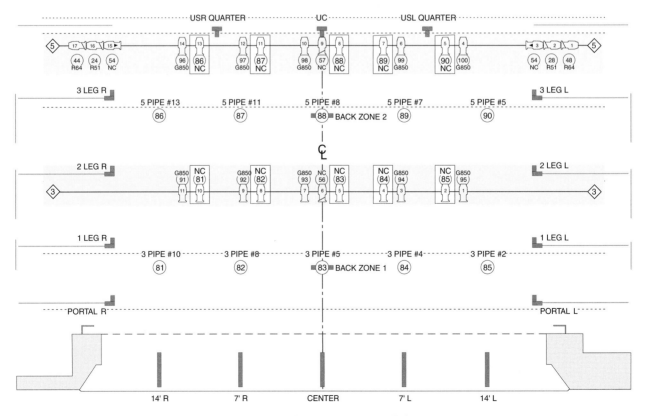

Figure 12.39 The Backlight Instruments and Their Focus Points

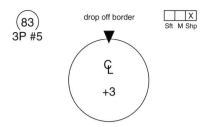

Figure 12.40 Focus Chart for 3 Electric #5

This instrument could be focused by standing on the focus point, or an alternate method can also be used. The lighting designer can stand at the downstage light line, with hands held above his or her head. The instrument is then slowly tipped toward the audience until the downstage beam edge reaches the hands. When combined with the rest of the downstage zone beams, this should ensure backlight coverage at head height across the light line, but may also provide more light upstage. If the audience seating is close to the stage, a top shutter may be used to cut light below the audience's eyes.

Figure 12.41 shows channels 81 > 90 after the 10 instruments have been pointed. The offstage instruments in channels 81, 85, 66, and 90 will receive side cuts to keep light off the black masking legs. The beam edges have landed as planned, and no top or bottom cuts will be required.

Figure 12.42 shows channels 81 > 90 after the side shutter cuts have been executed. The focus of the no color backlight system is now complete. Group 9 can be activated to check the system's overall focus and blend.

Boom Sidelight Positions

Sidelight booms are often the next hanging positions to be addressed in the focus session. Since the positions are lower and more accessible from the deck, more instruments can be simultaneously focused in a shorter amount of time.

If a ladder is required, its position relative to the boom is essential to the speed of the focus. Successfully placing a focusing electrician in the air somewhere near the instrument has little value if the electrician's hands can't get to the focusing apparatus of the instrument. It can also be counterproductive if the ladder placement doesn't allow the electrician to see the beam of light that he or she is focusing. For those reasons, attention must be paid to the amount of deck equipment that is intended to be stored around the base and offstage of the booms. When possible, this equipment should not be placed until

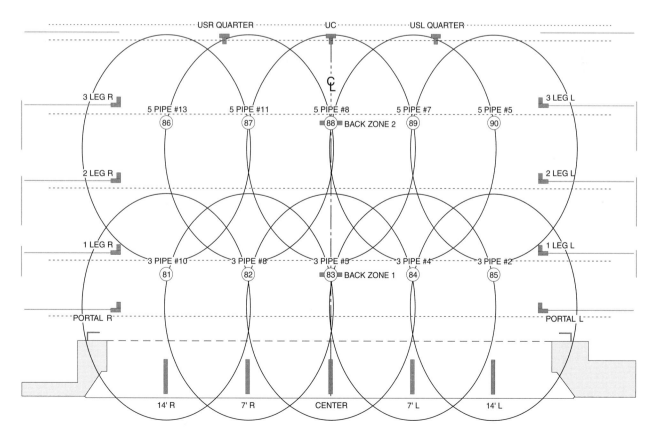

Figure 12.41 The Focused Backlight Pools Before Shuttering

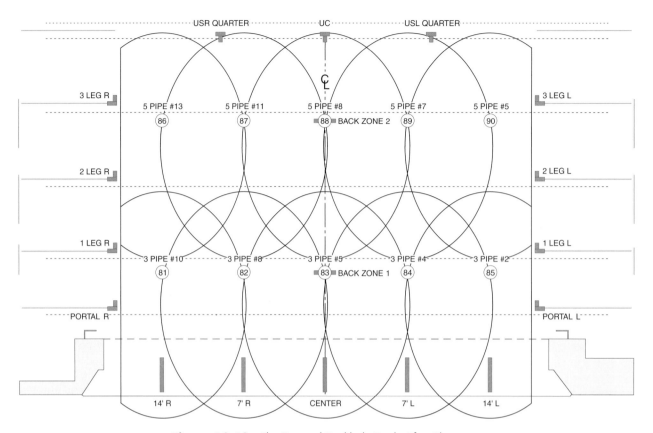

Figure 12.42 The Focused Backlight Pools After Shuttering

the instruments requiring ladder access have been focused. Even without the interference of deck equipment, the lack of backstage space may force the legs to be flown out, so that the ladder can be navigated into a working position for the focus. To accurately define the location for any side shutter cuts in that situation, the spike marks indicating the onstage edge of the black legs can then be used.

If the booms are tall, their height and balance can be a safety concern. When the boom is initially hung, attempts should be made to hang the side-arms and yokes of the instruments as they will be focused. When the boom is then tied off, its center of balance won't radically change as instruments are later rehung into performance positions. Hanging the instruments in performance positions also eliminates the time-consuming effort of rehanging the instruments during the focus session. It goes without saying that any stabilization required for the boom needs to take place before the focus begins; if the vertical pipe is loose, tighten it before any lights are turned on. In order to tighten the vertical pipe after the focus is complete means that the pipe will need to be rotated. After the pipe is twisted tight, every instrument hung on the boom will probably need to be focused again.

Since booms are the closest major hanging position to the stage, they often become repositories

for many other departments. The position is often employed as a location for monitor speakers, either on the ground or hung in the air with the lighting instruments. Booms may also be asked to support masking, or perform other totally unplanned-for structural functions. Although everyone works for the same goal, communication between departments will avoid situations where focused booms become involved in a secondary role that results in a need to refocus the entire boom.

Boom Sidelight Focus

Before focusing instruments at this position, it's worth remembering that almost any boom sidelight will initially splash light onto the performance surface and the face of the black legs on the opposite side. The shadows of performers on those surfaces might conceivably be a distraction from the audience's angle of observation. Addressing those shadows, and any shutter cuts, is another choice that is individual to each designer, and often to each boom light system.

The shutter shaping may depend on many elements, including the position of the boom, the unit's mounting height on the boom, any scenic legs, or what the system is trying to illuminate. Although there are many shuttering techniques that can be employed, one method that can be used matches the side cuts employed by the pipe end systems. Instruments focusing to the near quarter line are sometimes mounted high enough on the boom so that their top shutters are used to cut unwanted light off the legs and the side cuts are left open, thus allowing for better coverage at the near leg opening. Occasionally, the bottom beam edge hitting the stage can appear to be brighter than the light on the performer, and therefore a distraction. Bottom shutter cuts can be used to eliminate this beam edge.

If the shuttering for a particular system doesn't seem to be effective, most designers agree that taking a consistent course of action is often the best first step. Even if it looks like the end result won't be a complete success, instigating any system is another step toward completing the initial focus. Since the booms are so relatively easy to access, refocusing all of them in a work notes session is relatively simple.

 A list to consider before focusing boom sidelights:

- The position of the booms has been checked and approved.
- Confirm that all masking and scenic borders are at performance trim.
- Confirm that all legs are at in-trim, or spike marks are present to define their location.
- If the booms change color during the course of the production, the instruments have been colored with the series of gels that will initially be used during the light cue level setting session. Pre-coloring the boom instruments will also confirm that all of the instruments have been hung right side up, so that the color won't fall out of the instrument.
- Perform a channel check of the entire boom package to determine which units don't work. Note the nonfunctioning instruments. If possible swap caps with adjacent instruments in order to get the units focused in this call.
- The hardware used to construct the boom is tight and immobilized. Discovering the entire boom can freely pan up or downstage while working on the final instrument may result in the need to refocus the entire position. And really boring.

The light plot for *Hokey* includes four boom sidelight washes. At the top of the boom, channels 31 > 38 are colored in Roscolux 51, while channels 101 > 108 are colored in Roscolux 64. When focused, these

will become the lavender and blue boom sidelight systems. The booms are also equipped with instruments in channels 109 > 114, and channels 115 > 122. Since the light cue setting session for *Hokey* will begin with Act 1, all of these instruments have already been colored, respectively, in Roscolux 76 and No Color, the color used for that act. The separation of control implies that the instruments will be used to isolate zones of the stage or wash the entire performance area.

Figure 12.43 shows the instruments and the focus points for channels 35 > 38, controlling the top instrument on each sidelight boom. Colored in Roscolux 51, they'll be focused as the stage left lavender boom sidelight system for *Hokey*. The stage left quarter line spike marks, along with the stage right masking legs, provide the triangulation for the focus points.

Like the overhead sidelight, the focus points for the boom sidelight may be shifted up- or downstage, depending on how important it is to "hide" the black masking. In this case, the finished focus for the system will attempt to eliminate as much light on the face of the black masking legs as possible. To do so, the focus points of the three upstage boom instruments are shifted downstage from the middle of each opening. While the focus point for channel 35 is in the middle of the first opening, the focus points for the rest of the system are located at the intersection between the stage left quarter line and the black masking leg on the opposite side of the stage of each boom. The locations of the far leg spike marks will be used to not only locate the focus points; they'll also become the objects of the side shutter cuts as well. This focus will be duplicated for channels 101 > 108, the stage left blue boom sidelight system.

Figure 12.44 shows that the preliminary focus point for unit #1 is 9'-0" stage left of centerline and in the middle of the first opening. The side shutter cuts will eliminate the portions of the beam that splash light onto the black masking on either side of the opening. The bottom shutter cut will be made to eliminate the near beam edge. It is believed that the performers will not be lifted in the air near the onstage side of the legs, so the top shutter cut will be made to "HH" or "hands above head" (while standing at the opposite leg). To achieve clean shutter cuts, the barrel will be sharp to the shutter.

Figure 12.45 shows channels 35 > 38 after the instruments have been pointed. Upstage side cuts will be required on all of the instruments to keep light off the far black masking legs. Channel 35's downstage cut will be placed in the stage right smoke pocket. The rest of the downstage cuts will remain open, unless they splash on the upstage side of the near leg.

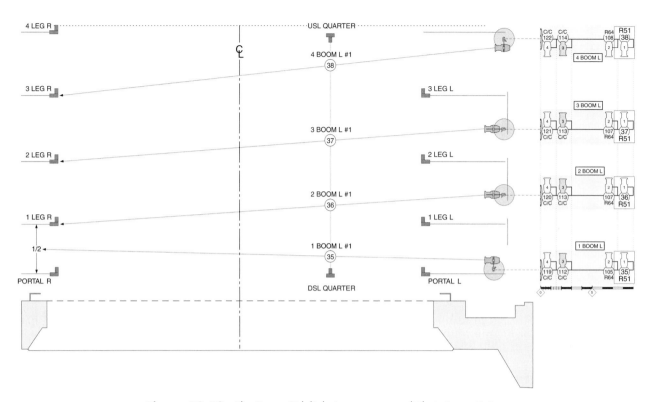

Figure 12.43 The Boom Sidelight Instruments and Their Focus Points

Figure 12.46 shows channels 35 > 38 after the shutter cuts have been executed. To keep the maximum amount of light off the black legs, while using as much of the beam as possible, the shutter cuts have a sharp focus. The focus of the stage left lavender boom sidelight system is now complete.

The rest of the instruments, mounted on each boom, use the same focus point as the top unit. The pair of instruments at the bottom of the boom, however, will have radically different top and bottom shutter cuts. As a reminder, the bottom instrument on a boom closest to the floor is the shinbuster, since that's what it does to anyone who runs into it. The unit above it is commonly referred to as a mid.

Figure 12.47 shows that the focus point and the side shutter cuts for the mid-unit #3 are the same as unit #1, shown in Figure 12.44. Like unit #1, the shutters are in sharp focus. The top and bottom shutters,

however, are much different. The top cuts off at the intersection where the leg meets the border on the opposite side, while the bottom shutter is cut off the deck. This focus is duplicated for unit #4 in channel 119.

Figure 12.48 is a front view showing instruments 3 or 4 focused as a system of mids or shinbusters with the top and bottom cuts open.

The top cut off the borders eliminates the shadows from performers running in front of the instrument. The bottom cut of the instruments deserves special attention. After the other cuts have been completed, the bottom of the beam could remain unshuttered. A second choice might be to cut the bottom shutter to the near quarter line. The choice in this case, however, will be to cut the bottom shutter just off the deck.

Figure 12.49 is a front view showing the same sidelight systems with top shutter cuts off the borders and bottom shutter cuts off the deck. With a sharp focus eliminating halation from glazing the deck, this will result in a wash of light that covers the entire stage, but will only illuminate the onstage edge of the opposite black masking legs. Depending on the intensity and the angle of the opposite legs, this system can light performers as if the light were coming from "nowhere." The performance surface can be colored by the backlight in a completely different color from the sidelight.

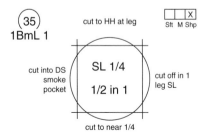

Figure 12.44 Focus Chart for 1 Boom Left #1

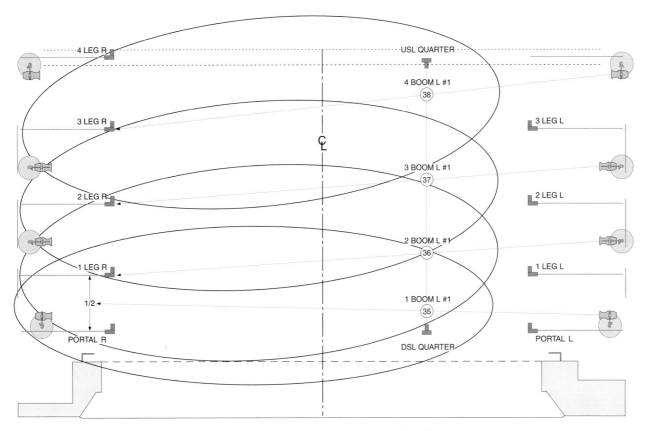

Figure 12.45 The Focused Boom Sidelight Pools Before Shuttering

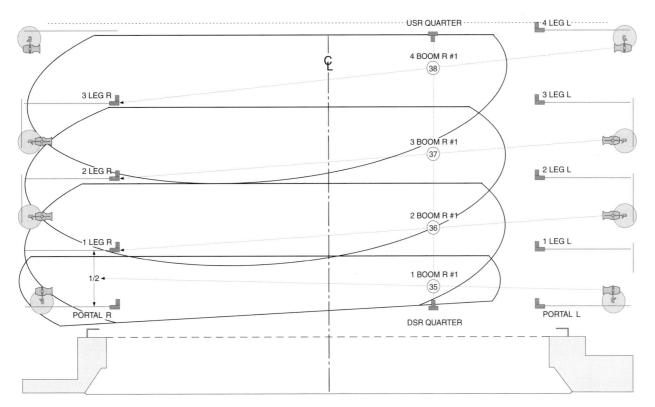

Figure 12.46 The Focused Boom Sidelight Pools After Shuttering

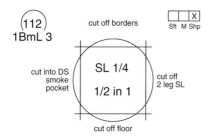

Figure 12.47 Focus Chart for 1 Boom Left #3

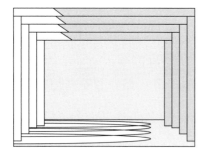

Figure 12.48 The Focused Mid or Shin Pools Before Shuttering

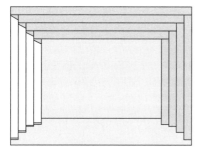

Figure 12.49 The Focused Mid or Shin Pools After Shuttering

If this focus is considered, the affected instruments should be mounted as close to the floor as possible to provide the maximum vertical coverage. In addition to that, the barrel focus of the instrument must be as sharp as possible. If sharp-focused instruments produce halation, a donut in front of the lens may be one solution to consider.

 ### Shelley's Notes: Boom Sidelight Tips and Workarounds

When presented with the choice, consider focusing sidelights requiring ladder access first, leaving instruments accessible from the deck until last. The ladder often requires additional electricians, who can then be available to focus the instruments low on the booms.

When possible, cut the side shutters off any near masking legs. In addition to safety considerations, any light hitting legs upstage of the boom will be seen by the audience, while light splashing legs downstage of the boom will bounce upstage. This is even more apparent when scenic legs are involved. Any scenic legs that are hung without a black backing may show sidelight "bleeding through" if light strikes them on the upstage side.

Instruments mounted high on booms may be targeted to focus points on the opposite quarter line. If there are no dance lifts, tall hats, or spears above head height next to the legs on the opposite side, cut the top shutter to just above head height while standing next to those legs. Get rid of the unnecessary light hitting the far legs.

Sometimes there are not enough channels for sidelight, and a single channel is assigned to matching instruments on booms directly facing each other. While the two instruments may always move together as a single channel, attempting to focus them together at the same time can be frustrating. If the instrument on 1 Boom Left is on at the same time as the same instrument on 1 Boom Right, both electricians will be blind and it will take longer to focus either of them. When possible, alter the hookup of the sidelight channels so that one side of booms has exclusive control from the opposite side. If this isn't possible, consider switching off the circuits for one side of instruments while the opposite side is focused. If possible, avoid unplugging instruments. Once instruments are unplugged, it may become difficult to find the proper plugs and properly restore the circuitry. Some folks just hold a clipboard up in front of one boom's light while the other side gets focused.

If two electricians are available to focus sidelight, rather than assign each to a single boom on either side of the stage, consider focusing the same instrument on two adjacent booms on one side of the stage. Having both electricians on one side means that instructions only need to be given to one side. It also reduces the number of instructions: "Both of these instruments will be hot on my head here and here. Paula, your hot spot will be at the top of the 1 Boom Right. Jerry, your hot spot will be at the top of the 2 Boom Right." If four electricians are available for sidelight focus, each of them can be assigned to a different boom on the same side of the stage, one electrician per boom.

If the focus points duplicate between instruments, inform the electricians of their location prior to the focus. If the same system is being simultaneously focused on different booms, focus the hot spot of the first beam, and instruct the rest of the electricians to match the top or bottom of their beams to the focused instrument. If that's not a possibility, consider running strips of tape up- and downstage, giving the focusing electricians a reference location for the bottom of the instrument's beams, or for bottom shutter cuts.

If any infrastructure information has been programmed into the light board, this is the perfect time to activate entire matching systems of sidelight. Having this information programmed into submasters will make the activation process even faster.

Scenic Stack Focus Analysis

Plotting the proper instrumentation to illuminate backdrops, cycs, and translucencies was initially discussed in Chapter 1. Choosing the proper lighting instruments and placing them in the most advantageous hanging locations are two steps towards creating an even wash. Knowing then how to focus an even wash with minimal effort is good. Focusing that even wash quickly is *really* good.

Focusing any kind of drop wash in less than ideal conditions can be challenging and test the mettle of entire electric crews. Focusing the same drop wash, without experience or knowledge of diffusions and their use, can quickly eat up twice the stage time. If there's ever a time to consider when to experiment with diffusions in the studio before encountering the real deal on stage, this is it. Either that, or be braced for the slew of last-minute phone calls trying to arrange for rolls of frost to be delivered to the venue post-haste.

When creating system washes on goods in the scenic stack was first examined, the typical theatrical instrument choice was some kind of striplight. In this case, there are both the overhead strips on the sixth electric, and the groundrow on the deck. When strips are plotted in this configuration, the overhead striplights are usually the first instruments focused. Practically speaking, the ladder doing the focus may have to move in the same alley as where the groundrow will eventually be placed. If the groundrow is focused first, it may all then need to be moved or shifted, in order to allow the ladder passage to move across the electric and touch the overhead strips.

The typical overhead striplight focus usually starts at the end of the electric, rather than the middle of it. Focusing a single unit at one end means that light's relatively isolated, and not obscured by the adjacent striplight on either side of it. That said, the focusing ladder is moved to the end of the electric. When in position, the most desaturated circuit is turned on, which makes it simpler to see the edge of the beams, not to mention any wrinkles, puckers, or other anomalies. The lighting designer stands down center and the farthest offstage striplight is then rotated slightly, one way or the other, until the most even wash is produced on the drop. Producing this even wash might also include changing the trim height of the batten, adding diffusion, or altering the drop's angle by kicking the bottom pipe up- or downstage.

Once the offstage unit receives approval, that striplight is locked off, and the lineset's trim (if need be) is re-spiked. After that, the next step taken is one of two tactics: either the the focusing electrician moves across the overhead electric, rotating each striplight to match the first unit's angle, and locking them off, one by one, or the entire overhead electric is lowered to working height, and all of the units are rotated to match. If diffusion needs to be added, it's a lot easier to do from the deck, even if added circuitry to the overhead electric has been picked up in the air and tied off out of the way. Regardless of the technique, the single circuit of desaturated color remains on at some level to confirm the matching beam edges of the striplights on the drop as each strip is eventually rotated and locked.

Overhead Scenic Stack Focus

 A list to consider before focusing overhead striplights:

- The striplights are all matching: unit type, lamp, hang height, and color.
- The striplight circuits all function, and the batten is at the recorded trim.
- The masking goods are at trim. The scenic stack is at trim. Initially, all goods are landed so their bottom pipe is directly under their respective batten.
- The electrician is in position in the ladder or lift, ready to tip the unit.
- The electrician has strips of diffusion that can be taped over several bulbs in one circuit of the striplight, along with gaff tape, BlackWrap, and Blacktak.
- The lighting designer is in position down center, ready to look at the unit. In some cases, it may be necessary for the lighting designer to move to the house. In that case, someone may be needed to relay instructions.
- The upstage worklights are dimmed or turned off so that the only light hitting the stack is from the overhead or groundrow striplights.
- The amount of ambient noise is reduced. Since the two can't see each other, audio communication can quickly become critical.

The light plot for *Hokey* includes a three-color overhead MR-16 striplight wash in channels 131 > 133. Prefocused straight down, channel 131 is turned on. Since the striplights are upstage of the translucency, the lighting designer asks the electrician to flag a number of the bulbs, in order to get a sense of the exact area of the translucency to look at. The unit's handles are unlocked, and the unit is rotated into different positions.

The batten is unlocked with the direct communication between the focusing electrician and the flyperson, and the batten is raised slightly to compare the spread of the striplight. The designer moves to the area offstage of the gap between the translucency and the bounce to see the spread of the circuit, and gauge if a diffusion is warranted. Blacktak or BlackWrap may be temporarily added to any vent holes to prevent pinholes of light to strike the back of the translucency.

After a point, the unit's handles are locked, the batten trim is spiked, the diffusion is chosen, and the Blacktak position of blocking light leaks is confirmed. The lift crew moves the electrician's lift away from the batten, and the batten is lowered to the deck. All of the striplights are rotated to match the first unit, diffusion is added as needed, and Blacktak is added where needed. All of the circuits are turned on to check focus and functionality, the batten is returned to the new trim, and the focus of the sixth electric is now complete.

Groundrow Scenic Stack Focus

The light plot for *Hokey* includes a three-color R-40 groundrow wash in channels 134 > 136. First the groundrow is checked to make certain that all of the trunions used to support the striplights are of matching height. If not, they are changed, or replacement trunions are constructed out of plywood cut into duplicate shapes.

The groundrow is next moved into position. Some folks snap a line parallel to the trans or the plaster line to make sure that all of the instruments start the same distance away from the goods—both the translucency and the bounce. Once positioned, the strips are then tested to make sure they're all plugged and colored properly, and if any diffusion is planned, it's properly installed and matching for every affected bulb. The bulbs are also checked to confirm they're all matching wattages and beam spreads. After they've passed this test for function and unanimity, the circuitry cable is then cleaned up while all the strips are tipped into a matching rotation. Standard operation procedure is to tip the strip so the bulb is pointed straight up. This makes it easier to tell when any one unit is tipped differently, no matter whether it's located on centerline or at the offstage end of a row. If room is tight, this is now the point when everyone except the focusing electrician(s) move out of the alley between the trans and the bounce, and the goods are flown in to playing trim. In this way there are only one or two people potentially causing shadows while adjustments are being made. If there are too many folks working in the alley at the same time, it results in nothing but confusion and slows the focusing process.

Channel 134 is activated. Again the offstage unit is unlocked, rotated, shifted in position farther or closer to the trans. Diffusions are added, changed, rotated. Eventually the lighting designer approves the final "recipe." Sometimes the offstage instrument doesn't show up as well as one closer to center. Or it may be necessary to make matching adjustments to three or four adjacent units in order for the lighting designer to see the result.

The strips are turned off and the same process is repeated to make all the units match. Once the work is complete, channel 134 is again turned on to check the focus of the single circuit. With approval, the other two channels are checked one at a time for any light leaks. Once the groundrow's focus has been approved, the position of each floor trunion supporting the groundrow is spiked with tape, and the circuitry cable is dressed out of the way as much as possible. The focus of the groundrow is now complete.

Shelley's Notes: Scenic Stack Tips and Workarounds

Here are some ideas to consider when dealing with goods in the scenic stack:

- If there's not enough room between a trans and a bounce, create it. Lower the goods' battens in slightly, and kick the bottom pipe of the soft goods away from each other to create more room for the lights to spread and diffuse.
- Usually the first set of goods to kick is the bounce. It usually has more room than the trans, and dropping the system batten of the trans is more likely to create wrinkles that will then be seen from the audience.
- If any bottom pipes are kicked, they must remain parallel to the groundrow, or the effect on the lighting won't be consistent all the way across the goods.
- Once the goods are kicked, use stage weights to keep the offstage ends of the bottom pipe

breasted into the kicked position. Not on centerline (if it's the trans), which will cause a shadow of the brick.

- Whenever any scenic goods are kicked, or shifted from their flown locations, spike tape should be close at hand to mark the altered position on the stage, and any change on the operating line. Getting it right the first time often means taking a little more time to get everything adjusted *just so*. Spiking everything allows it all to be restored after the goods have been flown out for the mopping call.

- If the scrim's pipe pocket is ripped, drop the lineset in enough so the pipe pocket is laying on the deck, not just touching it. Place a piece of pipe onto the back of the goods to flatten the face of the goods out. Often bottom pipe isn't heavy enough to keep the scrim taut; typical 1.5″ I.D. schedule 40 pipe usually packs enough heft to keep the goods flat. This can come in handy for drops or translucencies as well.

- Do *not* view two scrims flown in at the same time unless the scene calls for complete disorientation. It creates a visual state called *moiré* and it can make the entire audience queasy. Look at the two scrims under worklight (without an audience) and you'll become a believer.

- Not enough battens? Hang the scrim and the trans on the same pipe if they're close to the same height.

- Not enough room for a bounce drop? Paint the back wall white (of course, if the back wall is used as a bounce, then the onstage crossover for performers is lost).

Shelley's Notes: The Black Band

If the striplights aren't tipped or rotated properly, the overall light coverage may dip in the middle of the goods, creating the Black Band across the middle of the goods. This is most apparent on translucencies, and it seems to be accentuated when standing closer to the goods on stage, rather than in the middle of the house. Here are some suggested workarounds for addressing the Black Band. Good luck.

- Check where the hot spot of the strips is focused. Rotate or "tip" the striplight focus so their hot spot is closer to the vertical center of the goods. Or tip in the opposite direction, pointing the striplights more into the bounce. Shift the entire groundrow unit to a different location in the alley between the trans and the

bounce. Watch out that the bottom or top of the goods don't start getting dark, though.

- Add additional "stretch" diffusion media in front of the striplight bulbs to make the light disperse more vertically. Be aware that there must still be air between the diffusion and any color. Otherwise heat may fuse the two pieces of plastic together and eventually require the entire color system to be replaced. Cha-ching!

- Add some other kind of light that shoots in from the side to provide more punch to either the drop or the bounce. Focusing to the bounce has less of a chance of revealing wrinkles on the translucency.

- Add another set of striplights with a tighter beam spread that focuses more to the middle of the drop or bounce.

What about painted drops? What happens when they have the Black Band? Or the bottom half is dark? Here are a couple of ideas to consider that might get a more even blend on the front of the drop:

- Check where the hot spot of the frontlight strips is focused. Is there a lot of light on the stage just downstage of the drop? Kick the drop downstage into the light.

- Add a second set of frontlight strips with a tighter beam focused to the bottom of the drop.

- Add a drop wash from several individual units hung on an overhead electric, focused and diffused specifically for the bottom of the drop.

- Add a drop wash from the balcony rail. Care should be taken; washes from the balcony rail may result in performer's shadows on the drop.

- Hang a black scrim downstage of the frontlight strips, to visually help smooth the beam spread.

It should be pointed out that, when the phrase "add another set of strips" is used, it should first be carefully considered. Another row or batten of striplights requires not only the instruments, the dimmers, the circuitry, the cable, and the color, but also the time for the installation. Adding a set of striplights at the last minute ain't for sissies. That doesn't mean it should be summarily dismissed; it should be one of many remedies considered. In most cases, however, it should not be proposed as the first last-minute remedy for the Black Band.

The Slinky Method Applied to the Focus Session

Now that the basic focus of the *Hokey* lighting systems has been examined, more advanced focusing techniques can be discussed, based on the Slinky

Method. These techniques can quickly confirm that the light beams in a system are being focused into an even, consistent, wash. While it is a reaffirmation of the procedures used when the systems were initially being constructed, the guidelines can also be used as a quick visual double-check as washes are being focused.

As a brief reminder, when the *Hokey* light plot was originally being constructed, the method used to construct a single zone or multiple zones was based on the concept of overlapping pools. This Slinky Method's fundamental concept has been reiterated in many ways throughout this book: to achieve proper beam pool overlap between two similar light pools, the first instrument's beam edge should land in the center of the second instrument's beam. In addition to applying that concept to the system construction, the Slinky Method can also be applied to the focus session.

The Slinky Method of Calculating Focus

In the middle of a focus session, there are many moments when sudden adjustments must be made to adapt the focus of a system to the physical reality of the situation. The plan for the system focus just won't work. At other times, frontlight washes have to be quickly focused without knowing the identity or the beam spread of the house instruments. And then there are those times when every drawing or predetermined set of focus points can just be thrown out the window.

In each of those situations, the Slinky Method can be used to ensure that the adjusted focus of a system wash will still adequately provide blended coverage. To fully understand the methodology, here's a quick review of how the zones were constructed:

1. Define the field angle of the instrument.
2. Draw a beam section to determine the actual throw distance.
3. Draw the perpendicular line centered at stage level to measure the overall beam pool width.
4. Divide that distance by 2. That "½ of the beam pool" width is also the rough estimated width of the internal cone of light, the beam angle.

The ½ beam pool width was used in Chapter 5 to construct the backlight system. It can also be used to quickly confirm adequate zone coverage created by instruments with matching beam spreads from the same hanging position. In the first plotting example, the section showed that the field pool of a Source Four-36° hung in the first opening was 18'-0" on the stage floor. Now, in the middle of the focus, it's questioned if the five instruments will provide adequate side-to-side coverage. The answer? Multiply

the ½ beam pool by the number of instruments *plus one*. The calculations:

- 18'-0" divided by 2 = ½ beam pool width (9'-0").
- Number of instruments hung for wash = 5.
- ½ beam pool (9'-0") × 6 instruments (5 instruments *plus one*)= 54'-0".

If the leg opening width is 40'-0", there will be 7'-0" of extra light beam on each side of the zone. Five instruments will provide ample side-to-side beam angle coverage from leg to leg. Now, where should the focus points be spiked for an even blended focus? The off-stage focus point can't be placed at 18'-0" from centerline because, the side shutter will cut through the beam's hot spot. Regardless of where the instruments have been hung, the Slinky Method calculations can evenly space the focus points. Divide the leg opening by the number of instruments:

- Leg opening (40'-0") divided by 5 instruments = 8'-0".
- Odd number of instruments, so the middle focus point is placed on centerline.
- The next two are measured on either side at 8'-0" and 16'-0".

In the midst of a focus, it might suddenly be questioned if the number or focus of downlight zones (3) will adequately cover the depth of a performance space (38'-0"). The answer? Multiply ½ beam pool width by number of zones (*plus one*) and adjust. The quick calculation:

- ½ beam pool width = 9'-0".
- Depth of stage = 38'-0".
- 9'-0" × 4 (3 zones *plus one*) = 36'-0".

Since the product is less than the desired depth, the upstage-downstage distance between zones will have to increase slightly. Each subsequent zone may need to shift 1'-0" farther upstage than the middle of the first and second zone's beam pool, in order for the upstage edge of the third zone's beam pool to land at 38'-0". A small caveat to this calculation: when calculating zone-to-zone coverage, the Slinky Method can quickly turn into little more than a guideline. Several different hanging positions, trim heights, shutter cuts, and possibly more than one instrument type may be involved.

The Slinky Method of Focusing

Putting this technique to practical use, the lighting designer can use the Slinky Method to calculate approximate focus points and the probability of success for almost any system after focusing only one instrument in the system. In most cases, this can be achieved without even knowing the identity or field angle of the instruments involved. After completing the focus of the first instrument in a system, stand at the edge of that beam and focus the middle of the *second* pool at the focus point created by your head: at the *edge* of the first light pool. This technique can also be used to focus different zones of the same system to assure blended up and downstage coverage.

Figure 12.50 shows the groundplan of 5-36° instruments, plotted to cover one zone of overhead frontlight. Using the Slinky Method, this system is focused using this sequence:

- Point the hot spot of the center instrument (unit 3) at the focus point defined as head height on centerline in the first opening (C). After unit 3 is locked off, walk to the stage right beam edge of unit 3 (focus point B).
- Activate unit 4, and point its hot spot onto focus point B. After unit 4 is locked off, walk to the stage right beam edge of unit 4 (focus point A).
- Activate unit 5, and point its hot spot onto focus point A. After unit 5 is locked off, cut the side shutter off the stage right masking legs.
- Walk to the stage left beam edge of unit 3 (focus point D). Turn off units 4 and 5.
- Activate unit 2, and point its hot spot onto focus point D. After unit 2 is locked off, walk to the stage left beam edge of unit 2 (focus point E).

- Activate unit 1, and point its hot spot onto focus point E. After unit 1 is locked off, cut the side shutter off the stage left masking legs. The focus of the frontlight zone is complete.

In theory, this will result in the five beam angles touching or overlapping at head height. The side-to-side intensity of frontlight should remain consistent while traveling stage left or right in the first opening.

This next example illustrates how the Slinky Method can be used during focus to ensure blended coverage for one side of a single zone of overhead sidelight.

Figure 12.51 shows a front elevation of 3-26° instruments, plotted to cover the first zone of one side of overhead pipe end sidelight. This system is focused using this sequence:

- Point the hot spot of the most onstage instrument (unit 3) at the focus point defined as head height at the stage left quarter line in the first opening (C). After instrument 3 is locked off, activate instrument 2.
- Tip the stage left beam edge of instrument 2's pool so that it passes through instrument 3's focus point (C). After instrument 2 is locked off, walk onstage until standing in the hot spot (B), instrument 2's focus point. Activate instrument 1.
- Tip the stage left beam edge of instrument 1's pool so that it passes through instrument 2's focus

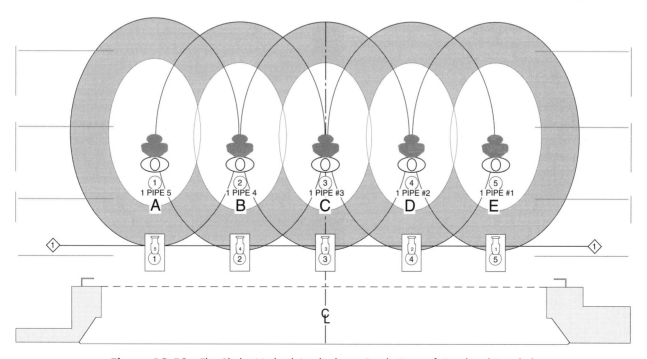

Figure 12.50 The Slinky Method Applied to a Single Zone of Overhead Frontlight

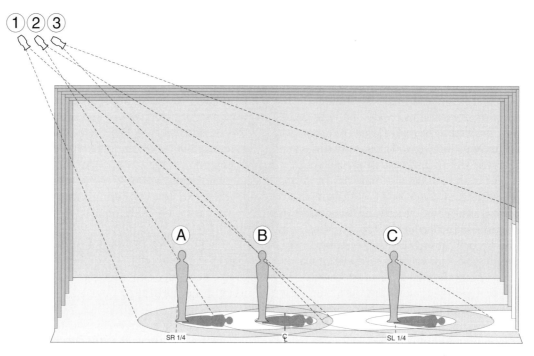

Figure 12.51 The Slinky Method Applied to a Single Zone of Overhead Sidelight

point (B). After instrument 1 is locked off, the focus of the overhead sidelight system is complete.

In theory, this will result in the three beam angles touching or overlapping at head height. The intensity of sidelight from stage right should remain consistent while traveling stage left or right in the first opening. If more coverage on the near side is desired, options may include changing the near instruments to a larger beam spread, adding an instrument to the system from the sidelight boom in the same opening, or the shifting the focus points of the existing three instruments toward stage right.

The Slinky Method can also be used to confirm up and downstage coverage between overhead sidelight zones.

Figure 12.52 is a section showing the four beam edges from a pipe end sidelight system hung on the first, second, fourth, and fifth electrics. Using the Slinky Method, the four instruments are focused to create a blended zone-to-zone sidelight wash in this sequence:

• Focus the instrument on the first electric while standing at the downstage focus point (A). After the first electric instrument is locked off, activate the instrument on the second electric (2).
• Tip the downstage edge of the second electric's beam to pass through or overlap the same focus point (A). After the second electric instrument is locked off, walk directly upstage until standing in the hot spot (B) of the second electric's beam.

• The unit on the fourth electric is activated (4). Tip the downstage edge of its beam to pass through the second focus point (B). After the fourth electric instrument is locked off, walk directly upstage until standing in the hot spot (C) of the fourth electric's beam.

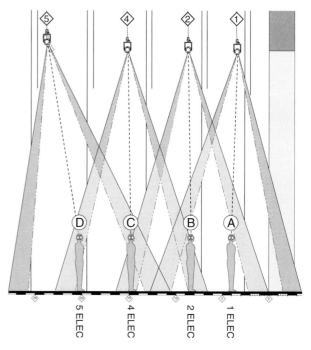

Figure 12.52 The Slinky Method Applied to Overhead Sidelight Zones

• The unit on the fifth electric is activated (5). Tip the downstage edge of its beam to pass through the third focus point (C). After the fifth electric is locked off, the focus of the overhead sidelight system is complete.

The beam angle width of each pool at head height is greater than the distance between any of the focus points. At these trim heights, the beam angles more than overlap between the four pools, and the sidelight intensity at head height will remain consistent up and downstage.

Although other methods can be used during the plotting process to define the focus points, the Slinky Method can be used in practice, during the focus session, to visually confirm that there are no gaps in the system coverage. Once a system has been focused and shaped, the entire system can be activated, allowing the following observations to be made:

• If the edges of *every other* beam aren't touching, the intensity consistency between the beams should be checked; there may be "holes" (or dips of intensity) in the coverage.
• If each beam doesn't overlap into an adjacent pool so that it *bisects* its neighbor's beam of light, the intensity consistency between the beams should be checked; same thing—there may be holes in the coverage.

The Slinky Method can be applied in this manner to many overhead systems, including downlight or backlight. The next example illustrates how the method can be used during focus to ensure blended coverage between zones of frontlight.

Figure 12.53 is a section view looking stage left. Using the Slinky Method, three instruments (one on the truss and two on the overhead electrics) are focused to create a blended up and downstage multizone frontlight wash, in this sequence:

• Focus the hot spot from the centerline instrument hung on the truss (T), while standing at the first zone focus point (A). After the truss instrument is locked off, activate the centerline instrument on the first electric (1).
• Tip the downstage beam edge of the first electric's pool (1) until it reaches the first zone focus point (A). After the first electric instrument is locked off, activate the matching instrument on the second electric (2).
• Walk directly upstage until standing in the hot spot of the first electric's pool (B), now established as the second zone focus point.

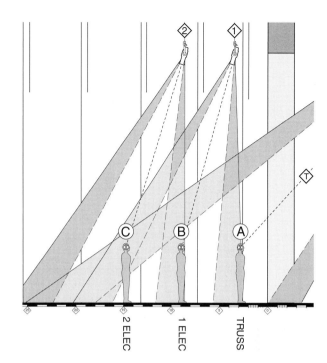

Figure 12.53 The Slinky Method Applied to Frontlight Zones

• Tip the downstage beam edge of the second electric's pool (2) until it reaches the second zone focus point (B). After the second electric instrument is focused (2), the three-zone frontlight system should be accurately focused.

The Slinky Method states that if the three beam angles overlap at head height, the coverage should remain consistent up- and downstage. Due to possible differences in instrumentation type and the actual throw distances between zones, the intensity between zones may require balancing.

The Slinky Method can also be used while focusing diagonal frontlight or backlight. The next example illustrates how the method can be used while focusing to ensure blended coverage between instruments hung in a box boom position.

Figure 12.54 is a front elevation showing three instruments hung at the stage left box boom position. Using the Slinky Method, the three instruments are focused to create a blended system in this sequence:

• Stand on the far quarter line (A) and focus the hot spot of the far box boom instrument (1) on the focus point. Lock off the first instrument. Activate the second instrument (2).
• Walk to the edge of the first instrument's pool of light (B). Focus the hot spot of the center box boom instrument (2) to that focus point (B),

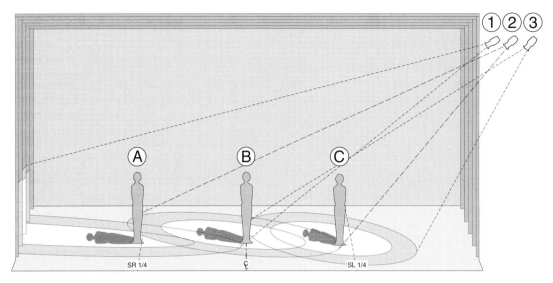

Figure 12.54 The Slinky Method Applied to Box Boom Light in a Single Zone

and lock off the second instrument. Activate the third instrument.

- Walk to the edge of the second instrument's pool of light (C). Focus the hot spot of the near box boom instrument (3) to that focus point (C), and lock off the third instrument.

In theory, since the edge of each pool is bisecting the adjacent pool's beam, this should result in the beam angles touching or overlapping at head height, and the intensity of the box boom system should remain consistent. Due to differences in beam spreads of each of the instruments, additional adjustment of these relative beam intensities may be required as well.

The Slinky Method can be used as a benchmark to define and adjust washes of light during the plotting process or during on-site focus sessions. It can be used to define the distances between focus points in a single zone and distances between adjacent zones.

After a Hanging Position Has Been Focused

It's frustrating to see simple errors after the electrician has left the position. It's even worse to tell the electrician who has just returned to the stage that he or she must return to the just-departed hanging position. And beyond all of that, it's also time consuming. The time taken by the electrician to return to the focus position, complete the note, and return to the stage is all time during which the electrician could have been doing something else.

After the focus of a hanging position is complete, turn on all the instruments and do a "last look" at all the light beams before the electrician leaves the position:

- If the position contains color washes, activate the systems using groups or submasters. This "final check" ensures that the right color is in the right instruments, and gives the lighting designer a final opportunity to check beam blending.
- Turn on the entire position and check the bottom cuts. Now is the best time to discover the instrument that slipped after being focused, or the instrument that was skipped and then later forgotten.
- The position may be movement sensitive; when the electrician moves from the hanging location, the beams of light "bounce." Turn on all the instruments using a hanging position group or submaster as the electrician leaves the position. If the vibration of his or her movement causes the focus of an instrument to drop, it's immediately known and can be addressed.

 Shelley's Notes: Turn off the Works Before Leaving the Position

If the production electrician is otherwise occupied when a hanging position's been completed, remind the focusing electrician to turn off the worklights prior to his or her departure. Unnoticed worklights can later cause unexpected delays. It's surprising how bright worklights can be, especially when they're not noticed until the house is dark at the beginning of a technical rehearsal. The tech rehearsal can often come to a screeching halt for no reason, other than waiting for those *^&@$* lights to be turned off.

After the Focus Has Concluded

After the final instrument has been focused, work notes taken during the session are given to the production electrician. Combined with his or her list of notes, the entire scope of work yet to be accomplished can be prioritized and executed at appropriate times.

After the worklights have been turned on, the lighting designer may consider "cleaning up" after him or herself and removing any spike marks. If the focus occurred on top of the performance surface for the show, this action could take place, leaving only the spike marks that the lighting designer may need as reference points. If the performance surface has not yet been installed, however, the lighting designer should reconsider the decision to remove all of the spikes. If there is any delay in the installation of the performance surface, the designer's spike marks may be the only reference points currently placed on the stage. If any other work will be performed that may rely on them as guides, removing any of these spike marks may result in time taken to replace them before the performance surface is installed.

SUMMARY

Now that the focus session has been completed, the light plot has become a fully functional lighting package. The lighting designer's palette is now prepared. The next step is to create the cues in the light cue level setting session.

Chapter 13

The Light Cue Level Setting Session and Technical Rehearsals

INTRODUCTION

This chapter examines some of the events that take place during the light cue level setting session and the technical rehearsals. Although they are two distinct events, for the purposes of this text, they have been combined into a single chapter. That's based on the perception that, once the lighting designer begins to create and modify the cues, the activity doesn't stop until opening night.

LIGHT CUE LEVEL SETTING SESSION ANALYSIS

The purpose of the light cue level setting session is to create and record the electrical actions that will occur each time the lighting changes during the production. Typically, it's also the first opportunity to view, discuss, and analyze the light cues with the director and the rest of the creative staff without the pressure imposed by the technical rehearsals. Any other technical elements that create the different looks of the production are preset to complete each stage picture. Scenery may be changed, properties might be preset, and pieces of wardrobe may be left on stage during different scenes, so the visual impact and progression of the entire production can be viewed without the performers. Each stage picture and every light change can be created, studied, and collaborated with the director and the design team.

Many people can be involved in a level setting session. The lighting designer directs the activation of the channels, or functions of the lighting console,

and the console operator executes those directions. Depending on the complexity of the show, there may be one or more assistants recording different facets of the action. One assistant may be assigned to record each of the different cues and actions of the lighting console onto light cue sheets, while a second assistant may be recording the choreography of the followspots on the followspot cue sheets. Out of that pair, someone is keeping track of the work notes. The stage manager is present to confirm the placement and timing of each cue in the call book, and to keep the process moving. It's rare for the direct or not to be present at this chance to finally see the combined design elements come together on the stage. It's his or her opportunity to comment and collaborate on all technical aspects of the show, approve the appearance of the cues, and provide his or her input into the visual components of the production.

During the cueing process, it may be necessary to see the contrast of light intensities on faces in various locations on the stage. In non-union situations, members of the crew trade off standing onstage to provide the tech row with faces that mimic the blocking for the show. Union situations often require folks otherwise unassociated with the production to act as "walkers." Sometimes they're assigned to wear colored garments that approximate the costumes that will be used in the show. Following the stage directions given by the director, the walkers allow the director to see the different staging compositions that have been blocked with a substitute cast.

In other situations, though, the piece being lit and created really needs the participation and collaboration of the original cast. While this method of

403

setting light cues can be applied to almost any theatrical form, it's most often seen in dance. While a substitute might provide a facial canvas for frontlight, and a dimensional canvas for the rest of the lighting systems by standing in place on the stage, only the actual dancer or performer can provide the feedback to the lighting designer and director about a host of information: the dancer's ability to get to the focus point, slightly altering the dancer's body to take on the light, slightly altering the light to better join with the dancer, where the dancer can move, where the dancer gets lost out of light, when the cue feels right, how the cue provides energy, and so forth. Creating cues in this manner is often slower, more careful, and more deliberate. As long as enough time is scheduled to allow this process to take place, the final lighting cues, as well as the entire technical participation in this environment, can often be perceived as a true collaboration, crafted by all of the participants.

While some lighting designers feel strongly about who will be on the stage during the level setting session, other designers are thrilled when anyone is there in the first place. Presuming the show has a production staff of any size, members of the other departments are also sitting in the house and watching the action. They're present to more fully understand the show, answer questions, take notes, or quickly make alterations to help move the process along. While everyone attending provides assistance and contributions as needed, this is also when the members of all departments become fully aware of the technical components involved within each scene.

At this point, the main reference sources and the place to record most changes shifts to the primary paperwork included in the cue construction packet. That doesn't mean that the rest of the paperwork gets tossed; the light plot, section, support paperwork, and so on are all still in the background and are occasionally used as reference or documents to store updates. But from this point on, the main documents that the lighting designer carries with him or her until opening night are the magic sheet, the cheat sheet, and the cue master.

As a cue is being created, the lighting designer first refers the cue master to mentally refresh the "for" and "action" attributes of that lighting "look" and the other cues surrounding that look in a sequence. He or she then refers to the magic sheet and selects the proper channels or handles to quickly turn on the right channels, in the right color, in the right areas of the stage. During this portion of the process, the working relationship between the lighting designer and the director now takes another step. Some lighting designers prefer to assemble each light cue and then present it to the director for his or her approval, while other designers provide explanations and invite collaboration as the cues are being assembled. There are many exchanges, negotiations, and interactions between these two, the stage manager, and the rest of the creative team as the broad looks and individual lighting changes are one by one created, molded, and recorded. The light cue level setting session often marks the beginning not only for the collected assembly of the technical components of the show, but the formation of working relationships between all members of the creative and production team.

At this point, the cheat sheet isn't used that much; it's a cross-reference guide that's used more to inform the lighting designer of a displayed channel's identity. Right now the intent is merely to create the pictures. The cue sheets, board operator sheets, repatch sheets, and followspot cue sheets are all used to record the actions of the different lighting elements as they are used in the show. They'll be distributed to the running crew for the technical rehearsals. While the rest of the paperwork isn't currently being used, it's all assembled in notebooks or piles as a reference of the light plot's current state, and documents to note changes that take place as the lighting design evolves into a finished product.

Setting light cues begins by activating channels. On manual light boards, channels are activated by manually moving sliders, dials, or handles. On computer lighting consoles, this is usually accomplished by typing commands into the keypads or using the touchpads of the lighting console. The keystroke sequences used to activate the channels vary between lighting consoles, but the combination of channel intensities creates each desired "look." After that look has been approved, the different intensities are recorded, both on paper and as memories within a computer lighting console, and a fade time is assigned to each light cue. In many cases, the light cues are often created in the same sequence that they'll be seen during the performance. Once a series of cues is constructed, they're often quickly compared to one another so that everyone can see the changes, contrasts, and focus point changes between each light cue.

With ample time, cueing can be viewed as a slow crafting of the images that were mentally imagined and collaborated between the lighting designer, the director, and the design team long ago. On the other hand, if there are a lot of cues to create, and little time to create them, the pace of a cueing session can feel like the visual equivalent of base coating paint on espresso, activating systems like broad bristle paintbrushes, and slapping on coats of light. Much like the multiset focus, transitions may be secondary to lighting "like" scenes and reduce the time expended changing from scene to scene. This then allows more time to make the light cues and make sure that, if nothing else, each scene has a base cue to get the show into the dry techs or the technical rehearsals.

When the lighting cues are created, the lighting designer attempts to simultaneously play the roles of artist, programmer, and time manager. On the artistic level, he or she needs to quickly transform the mental images into concrete lighting states that achieve the objectives of light, reinforce the production concept, provide focus, and emotionally underscore the action onstage. At the same time, the lighting designer is a mechanic, understanding how to quickly assemble those looks by speaking the proper console language to the operator in order to construct the cue. Finally, along with the stage manager, the lighting designer has to keep an eye on the clock to be certain that some form of primary light cues for the show are created and recorded before the scheduled light cue level setting time runs out.

General Cueing Concepts

Although the light cues and their step-by-step construction are unique for every show, a number of general cue concepts and the methods used to quickly create them are consistent for many productions.

At almost every moment in almost every theatrical presentation, the action on the stage is directed to an area of particular focus. It may be the entire stage, one whole side of the stage, or it could be a very tiny isolated area. In the course of almost every production, this stage focus shifts between different locations. One of the primary purposes of each light cue in a production, then, is to telegraph these focus shifts to the audience, and thereby reinforce the stage focus. Since the eye is subconsciously drawn to the brightest point on a stage, one basic property of light that is used to direct the stage focus is intensity. Although the other properties of light play as much of a role in each lighting design, the purpose for each light cue is often initially constructed with that in mind; the area of focus, in that light cue, is brighter than the rest of the stage.

From that perspective, every light cue can be constructed based on contrast. A light cue can be **built up,** by adding a brighter area of focus to a comparably dim surrounding, or a light cue can be **built down,** from a bright focus to a comparably lower intensity. Most light cues are usually constructed using one of these two methods.

Built-up light cues are constructed by first activating channels at lower intensities, and then adding channels at brighter intensities to establish the points of stage focus. Light cues for large group scenes often illustrate this method. The general washes are layered in first, to ensure visibility on the stage. Then brighter intensities are added, to highlight the lead performers or otherwise direct the stage focus. Built down light cues reverse that method. The bright focus of the light cue is activated first, followed by adding washes or specials in lower intensities to illuminate the surrounding environment. This method is often used to create light cues for highly focused or isolated scenes.

Not only is it important for the designer to understand the focus of each light cue, it's also technically important to compare the contrast of that look with the light cues that precede and follow it. Cues constructed without being compared to their "neighbors" may not be as visually successful when viewed in sequence during the production.

In some cases, light changes indicated on the cue master just don't have enough information filled in to their rows. While it may seem that a change is needed or justified, the lighting designer may ultimately be unable to figure out what the change needs to be. These are the cues that are often the easiest ones to skip or cut. If you're unable to figure out what visually needs to change in the cue, then maybe that moment in the show doesn't need a cue there in the first place. Tech rehearsals will provide clarity and either the cue will make sense or be eliminated altogether.

General Cueing Tactics

From a mechanical point of view, time allocated to a cueing session should be spent viewing and discussing completed looks, rather than watching the lighting designer trying to decide how they should appear or how to construct them. Each look has been predetermined in the lighting designer's mind prior to the cueing session, using some form of the cue master. What's left is then to tactically plan in advance how to construct each cue as rapidly as possible. Some designers pre-write recipes on the cue master directing which groups to quickly activate to achieve the basic look. Other designers pre-write base cues in off-line editing programs in order to have something loaded in the console before the session begins. Once the cue has been constructed, it can then be viewed, discussed, and modified (and often is) by the rest of the collaborative team. The point is to reduce the amount of time that everyone has to wait before the next cue can be viewed.

Even with pre-written information, one obvious tactic to speed up the light cue construction process is to use handles to paint the broad strokes. This is one primary reason to program the infrastructure cues, groups, or submasters. Another not-so-obvious tactic is to recognize when the same number of keystrokes have been made more than once. Type them in the third time and record them as a new group or sub. The fewer number of keystrokes required to construct a light cue, the faster it's made, which translates to more time available to actually look at it.

 Suggestions to consider prior to the beginning of the cueing session:

• Decide which cues may be built based on other (base) cues, and which cues need to be unique looks built from a clean (black) stage.

• Know how to quickly create and modify group or submaster handles on that particular lighting console, live or in preview.

• Consider the choreography of the cue creation. Once the base cue is approved, know what needs to be changed, *in the fastest sequence*, in order to record all intermediary cues built on that initial look.

• Identify sections of the show that involve transitions, or active sequences. Consider padding the cue master with several whole numbers. If the sections later require additional called cues, enough whole-numbered cues will exist, avoiding the possibility of numerous point cues that must be called by the stage manager in rapid succession.

• Always place a mark on the cue master, next to each cue, to confirm that cue has been recorded. If cue are being created out of order, or if the console contents consist only of shell cues, marking the cue master may be the only way the lighting designer knows where he or she is within the cueing process.

• As cues are added or changed, update the cue master so that it matches the console's display. Cue number and fade time are notations that must be added; an idea of what the change accomplishes is also good to know the next run-through.

Sometimes, the cueing session is too brief, or the scheduled time is suddenly shortened. While neither of these conditions may be the fault of the lighting designer, either of these constraints may translate into speeding up the pace of the cueing session. The overall goal of the cueing session may quickly shift from analyzing each cue's reinforcement of the production concept, to just making sure that enough light cues exist in order for a subsequent technical rehearsal to take place.

 Some suggestions to consider prior to a cueing session under pressurized conditions:

• Block in the structure. Create, and check, any blackout or fade to black cues.

• Skip internal cues and concentrate on the beginning of scenes, the end of scenes, and the transition sequences. Attempt to provide the programming so that the transitions can be called in real time.

• Use broad strokes to build light cues. Temporarily lower your standards for visual acceptability so that information is recorded into the console. Be less concerned with detail and more concerned with visibility. Skip nuance; omit adding the little touches or practicals until later. Don't get stuck in the construction of a single light cue. Keep moving.

• If a cue's purpose is solely to activate a single channel, skip the cue or record it from the previous cue. Come back later to finish the cue.

• Record cues as other cues. Consult the cue master and steal previously recorded cues that are close to the same appearance of cues not yet recorded. If a bright cue has been constructed in scene 1, it may be completely different from the bright cue required for scene 2, but under these conditions it's a bright cue that will provide light on the stage. Record it and move on.

• When cues are recorded, either assign a default time to all of the cues, or skip entering time fade information altogether. After all of the primary cues have been created, go back through the cues and assign all of the time fades at once.

• Keep notes of what you are doing. Check off the cues that have been created. Draw arrows indicating the source of stolen cues. Be able to retrace the steps if there are problems.

• Save to the storage media. Save to the storage media. Save to the storage media.

BEFORE THE CUEING SESSION

Let's back up. Before the light cue level setting session begins, several events should take place. A meeting with the light board operator is certainly one of them, and several other items to consider are presented in separate checklists.

Meeting with the Light Board Operator

Presumably, a meeting with the board operator occurred during the beginning of the load-in, when the notebook containing disks or other storage media, paperwork regarding the production, and infrastructure information were exchanged. Prior to the cue level setting session, a second meeting with the board operator may be valuable to discuss the use of the console and the methods that will be employed to construct the light cues.

Ideally, both the lighting designer and the board operator know the command structures, functions, and limitations of the lighting console. A general discussion about the way the console will be used, however, may reveal previously unknown limitations or capabilities of the device or either individual. Although both folks may know the console well, a different version of system software may make a difference in the manner in which cues are constructed.

Here are some basic functions and commands that may be requested during the light cue level setting session and the technical rehearsals.

Functions that are typically required while programming a computer lighting console:

- Turn the light console on and off properly.
- "Save show" to hard drive or external storage media.
- "Open show" from hard drive or external storage media.
- Understand how to manipulate the display contents and format.
- Use of the Grand Master and submasters.
- Repatch, unpatch, park, or profile dimmers.
- Patch moving lights or other devices.
- Set channel information.
- Create or edit groups.
- Create or edit submasters.
- Create or edit referenced data for moving lights.
- Create cues and modify cue attributes.
- Create, manipulate, and run effects.
- Link cues to other cues.
- Print out show data (to a printer or as a PDF).

Basic commands to create and manipulate light cue information in the "live" or "stage" screen:

- Build from a clear state or an existing cue.
- Activate channels, groups, or submasters.
- Use referenced data.
- Record a light cue in track or cue only mode.
- Preset (mark) moving lights.
- Update to modify all record targets.
- Re-record a light cue in track or cue only mode.
- Assign or alter a time fade.
- Split a time fade (up/down).
- Create a block cue.
- Alter a cue to be an autofollow cue.

- Delay a cue.
- Divide a light cue into "parts." (This will be explained during the cueing process later in this chapter.)
- Delete a light cue.
- Playback a cue in time.
- Manually override cue timing.

Basic commands to create and manipulate light cue information in the "blind" or "preview" screen:

- Build from a new cue.
- Alter channels, groups, or submasters.
- Alter channel data in track or cue only mode.
- Assign or alter a time fade.
- Split a time fade (up/down).
- Create a block cue.
- Alter a cue to be an autofollow cue.
- Delay a cue.
- Divide a light cue into "parts." (This will be explained during the cueing process later in this chapter.)
- Delete a light cue.

Basic commands to create and manipulate light cue information on a manual light board:

- Activate a dimmer in the active scene.
- Activate a scene.
- Cross-fade between scenes.
- Switch a dimmer to the independent master.
- Preset a nonactive scene.
- Record a preset and a light cue.

Depending on the complexity of the production, other functions may need to be employed. Providing the console operator with a list of the functions that will be used to construct the cues may also help the lighting designer define each "look." If that list is provided with enough time prior to the cueing session, the console operator will have time to study an unfamiliar command language.

This meeting is also the beginning of a working relationship. The lighting designer and board operator will soon be attached to each other through a headset cable. This also allows the lighting designer and operator an opportunity to discuss how they will communicate with each other. As a coworker, the lighting designer needs to be considerate. If the designer doesn't anticipate what infrequently used functions may be required during the programming period, it's impolite to expect a console operator to have those command structures memorized. If neither party is intimate with a light board's operation, a console manual, a dealer's cell, or the console rep's cell number may answer most programming questions. This will allow the session to be devoted to creating the light cues, instead of figuring out how to properly program them.

Checklists Before Cueing

 Working Environment

- The production table is set up. The worklight and headset work, and are properly arranged. The light plot and support paperwork are nearby and available.
- The lighting package has been focused, and all devices have been tested.
- Other onstage work has been completed, so that the worklights can be turned off.
- Other onstage work has to continue; are there offstage worklights instead? All worklight is controlled so that they'll not be recorded into the light cues.
- All lobby doors have been closed. All the curtains, preventing daylight spilling into the space, have been closed. All theatre tours have been canceled or delayed.
- The scenery, floor surface, and masking are in place. The correct items in the scenic stack are in place. It's very discouraging to discover the black scrim was accidentally left in through the entire cueing session. When it's correctly removed for the tech, time can be wasted altering the channel levels controlling the translucency, rather than observing the flow of the cues. (Tip: Profile the trans dimmers.)
- The lighting groundrow is in place and focused.
- If the performance includes an orchestra, all of the appropriate music stand lights have been turned on. If there is no music for the stands, white pieces of paper have been distributed in their place.
- If costume pieces are to be viewed, they're on site.
- If walkers have been arranged for, they're ready and familiarized with the situation.
- The board operator's in place.
- A channel check has been performed and the work notes sheet has been updated. If work notes need to be addressed, it's been determined that this can occur while cues are being constructed. It has been determined if dimmers can be activated without being recorded into the cues.
- If there are repatches, all the affected dimmers been checked for their proper contents.

- Strobes, scrollers, hazers, foggers, or any other special devices have been tested and preset.

 Computer Lighting Console

- All defaults or system settings (time fade, channel display, mode of tracking, number of channels displayed on a row, etc.) have been altered to the preferred setting.
- The RAM in the console has been labeled with an alphanumeric keyboard (if available). If not, a key memory system has been loaded into the time stamp channels.
- Group, submaster, or channel handles have been built to quickly control the worklights (downstage, upstage, offstage). They've been checked for accuracy. They've been written down.
- Group, submaster, or channel handles have been constructed in preparation to build light cues. They've been checked for accuracy. Any updates or adds have been written down.
- The submasters are labeled.
- The lighting package has been checked for missing, miscolored, or misfocused instruments. Any units that appear brighter or dimmer than the rest of the system have been noted.
- The board operator's been informed about what light board functions will be required.
- If a storage media management system is in place, are the preset cue numbers known?
- If the light board has tracking capability, are blockers built into the cues?

 Manual Light Board

- The dimmers on the light board have been labeled.
- All of the sliders, as well as the Grand Master, have been checked for smoothness of operation.
- Any subs, scene masters, or independent masters have been checked for smoothness of operation. All of the independent switches have been checked in their proper scenes. Nonfunctioning switches have been noted and taped.
- The accuracy of repatch dimmers has been checked. All inactive elements of the repatch have been switched off to prevent overloading. The repatch sheets are ready to be filled out or updated.
- The board operator has been informed what light board functions will be required.
- The board operator has enough copies of the board operator sheets or preset sheets.

Lighting Designer

- Do you know how to use the lighting console? Do you know the limitations and workarounds, so that the cues can be constructed rapidly with the fewest possible keystrokes?
- Have you preassigned the memory numbers that will be used?
- Do you have a plan of attack? Do you know how much time is available to you to program the light cues before the worklights have to be turned on for another task?
- Do you have a method for taking work notes that will be comprehensible?
- Do you have a method for taking cue notes that will be comprehensible?
- Have you determined the amount of time that can be dedicated to each light cue before the session falls behind? Or to each scene? Or to each act?
- If the show is multi-scene, has a scene sequence been devised? Has a list been defined showing the order in which the scenes will be lit, involving the fewest possible set changes, concluding with the first scene required in the next call?

Lighting Designer's Tools and Environment

- The magic sheet, the cheat sheet, the cue master.
- Enough cue sheets, board operator sheets, followspot cue sheets, or repatch sheets are available.
- Work note sheets.
- A copy of the updated light plot, section, and support paperwork.
- A keyboard layout sheet and/or a lighting manual.
- Something to drink, since the lighting designer will be talking for hours. Ideally with a lid or cap, for those dyspraxic moments.
- Something to nibble on when the blood sugar drops.
- Go to the restroom when the opportunity presents itself.

Shelley's Golden Rule: Save Early and Often—Again

Although this was mentioned during the load-in, it's worthwhile to repeat again while the cues are being created. When the light board is inactive, save the contents of the RAM to the storage media. I can't stress enough what effect the loss of board content will have on the tempo of the pre-performance period. The board will crash someday, and no one knows when that moment will occur.

If a storm is brewing outside, save to the storage media often and remove it from the console. There's no telling what lightning can do to electronics. Not only can cues be lost, but enormous amounts of time and effort can also disappear when the light board unexpectedly reboots.

I save at every convenient opportunity. During the cueing session, I've gotten into the habit of making different marks on the cue master, after each time the RAM has been saved to the storage media. In this way, when the board crashes, I'll know what cues have been lost and where to begin. This technique is especially helpful after the memories have been created. If no additional cues have been created in a notes session, the only signpost that shows which memories have been recorded to the storage media are my marks on the cue master.

Shelley's Golden Rule: Avoid Unannounced Blackouts Onstage

In almost every production some of the lighting memories are programmed to be blackouts, or cues are built from a black stage. When working with a computer lighting console, the natural inclination is to program the light cues in sequence. Almost all light boards have the ability to remove all light from the stage, and board operators are often well versed in rapidly completing this function. It is common practice to take the stage to black numerous times in the course of a light cue level setting session.

Too often the number of cues that need to be constructed far outweighs the amount of time dedicated to the session. The pace that is required to complete this task often demands the total concentration of the lighting designer. Throughout the light cue level setting session, however, the lighting designer must remain aware of any personnel who may still be working on the stage. If the worklights have been turned off during the session while people are still working on the deck, the golden rule to remember is this:

Don't take the stage to black (without warning) if there are people working on stage.

If the stage lights are abruptly turned off while a crucial action is taking place onstage, the sudden loss of light could potentially cause an injury or accident. If power tools are involved in the onstage activity, the importance of adhering to this golden rule is even greater.

Several methods can be used to avoid that situation, and allow both activities to continue. One method is to program or check all blackout memories while viewing the preview display, rather than seeing them live onstage. If work onstage is confined to a static area, consider setting up a worklight not controlled by the lighting console, or select a lighting instrument focused to that location and park it so it can't be recorded into any cues. If that's not an option, then keep the worklight turned on until the stage light in the cue is established. Then turn off the worklights to see the cue. If it's absolutely necessary to see the timing of a fade to black, loudly announce to the stage that this is about to happen, and wait for a response from the onstage personnel before taking any action. Anyone who can't contend with darkness at that moment will give you an opinion regarding your intent.

THE CUEING SESSION

No matter how much preparation has taken place, any number of lighting designers have experienced anxiety at the beginning of a light cue level setting session. That's absolutely normal. Typically, everyone involved in a cueing session can be a little nervous. It's the first time that all of the technical elements will be seen in their proper perspective. The best remedy is to just start. Even if the appearance of the first series of cues isn't satisfactory, take notes and move on. Once a rhythm is established, it will get better. Knowledge will be gained from discussions with the director, and the rest of the design team, during the course of the session. That knowledge may provide clarity about the appearance of those opening cues. There will be time to get back to those cues later.

Avoid or delay any unnecessary interruptions to the rhythm of a cueing session. If possible, take notes. Don't turn the time into a work or focus call, unless the problem will affect the cueing process. The cue level setting session should be reserved for the cue construction process.

The Opening: Act 1, Scene 1

The performance of *Hokey* will begin with a short musical introduction, with the curtain closed. After the house lights and the curtain warmers have faded out, the curtain will rise to reveal Pookie in the fourth opening upstage left. The musical theme begins slowly as she performs a series of movements, and then moves to center. She beckons to other members of the cast, who join her onstage as the increased tempo and volume of the second verse begin.

The cue master has been constructed so that memory 100.7 will be the preset that reveals Pookie as the curtain opens. After Pookie completes her initial movement, memory 101 will build the center area up, and eliminate the opening isolated area up left. When the group joins her, memory 102 will use washes to build a full-stage warm look.

Since the opening look will not be bright, memory 100.7 will be initially built with low intensities of light, and then highlight the point of focus for the cue.

- Constructing memory 100.7 will begin by starting from a clear fader, to be certain that there are no erroneous channel intensities. The time stamp and key memory information, along with any infrastructure channels, are activated so they will be recorded through all of the cues. If there are many infrastructure channels requiring different levels, this blank look may be recorded as memory 100.1, to be used as a template for all other cues that will be built from black.
- The background will be used to establish a location. Initially, the opening look is a quiet, "predawn" moment, and the focus should remain low and close to the stage. With that in mind, the blue groundrow (channel 136) is brought up to 30%. Since the light is being seen through both the black scrim and the translucency, the level of light seen from the audience's angle of observation will be lower.

Now is the time to quickly compare keystrokes against infrastructure information. The next action taken will be to activate the Gam 850 backlight system to 50%. Activating the channels on the computer lighting console could be accomplished by stroking the keys that would then appear in this manner on the command line: 91 > 100 @ 5 [Enter]. (On most consoles, when keystroking intensity information, the zero is automatically added and this keystroke sequence activates the channels to 50%.) On most consoles, typing this sequence requires nine keystrokes. If this series of channels will be frequently activated and moved together, the group that was programmed for this purpose can be used instead. The keystrokes might appear in this manner on the display: Group 10 @ 5 [Enter], and would require only six keystrokes.

While that might not seem to make much of a difference, consider the amount of keystroking that is required for a typical show. Presuming that an average production may consist of 100 built memories, it's probable that each memory will consist of at least 20 channel activations to construct each cue. When those two numbers are multiplied, the result is

2000 channel activations. Now imagine that during each technical rehearsal, an average of 5 channel intensities may be changed for each cue. The number of keystrokes can quickly add up. This is another reason to use groups when frequently activating the same series of channels.

For this reason, the group list for *Hokey* was constructed so that each system was given a group assignment. More to the point, the group identity numbers were assigned so that the single-digit groups would activate the largest series of channels that would most frequently be activated together. This is also the reason why the group numbers were so large on the *Hokey* magic sheet. The diamond icon and larger font size were used specifically to allow the system group numbers to be easily seen. Instead of activating the series of channels for the Gam 850 backlight system, group 10 will be used instead. (And when it's necessary to get the blue backlight up *fast*, and there's not as much concern about being exactly at 50%, submaster 20 could instead just be slapped up to something like 50% and the cueing can continue.)

- Group 10 is activated to a level of 50%. This washes the performance surface with a blue light.
- Pookie is preset in the fourth opening stage left. The closest downlights (channels 70 and 80) can't be utilized to shape her body, since they aren't focused far enough upstage to provide head high coverage in the fourth opening. Instead, the Roscolux 51 pipe end is used (channel 24). It's brought up to 50% in order to highlight the performer's body from the onstage side.
- To help shape the performer from the offstage side, the stage left shin in the fourth opening is also brought up (channel 122). The performer is close to the boom, so the intensity is only 30%. Since the shinbusters are cut off the deck, the only light that is seen from stage left is on the performer's body.

This "look" is recorded as memory 100.7. Since the cue will be preset on stage before the curtain is raised, it will contain no frontlight downstage of the curtain. The instruments will fade up to their assigned levels in a time of 3 seconds. A time of 0 seconds would bump the instruments to their assigned intensities, but there's no need for that speed; it's potentially jarring to the performers backstage, and the surge in voltage to the filaments might cause lamps to burn out.

Now memory 101 will be constructed. It's been decided that Pookie's cross to center should be a shift in focus on the stage, so the cue should be

built from memory 100.7. When the cue is complete, there should no longer be any isolation upstage left. The center area should receive focus instead.

- To eliminate the isolation upstage left, channels 24 and 122 are taken to zero.
- To brighten the stage for Pookie and prepare for the following cue, the color in the background and the color on the floor will get a little brighter. Channel 136 is brought up to 50%, and group 10 is brought up to 70%. In addition, channel 133, controlling the blue MR-16's at the top of the translucency, is brought up to 30%.
- To isolate center, the no color center backlight special (channel 57) is brought up to 50%.
- To shape the performer and provide color consistency, the Roscolux 51 shinbusters will be activated. To be certain that the performer isn't left in the dark while crossing from upstage left to center, the shinbusters in 2 and in 3 on both sides of the stage (channels 116, 117, 120, and 121) are activated to 50%.

This "look" is recorded as memory 101. Initially, the cue is recorded as a 5-second cross-fade from memory 100.7, but the dimmers don't respond quickly enough. When the cross-fade is run in time, it appears that the "isolation channels" up left fade too quickly before the performer moves to center. The time is changed to 5 seconds up and 10 seconds down to ensure that there will be light on Pookie from the time she leaves up left through the time she stops at center.

The next cue in the sequence, memory 102, will build levels on the entire stage as the group enters, so it could be built from memory 101. On the other hand, it's a unique look. The stage will get much brighter and warmer than the first two cues, so it will be built from a clean black stage. "Stage going to Black!"

- Initially, cue 100.1 is loaded into the fader, to retain the infrastructure channels.
- It has been decided that the motivation for the brightness of this cue will be a stylized "dawn." Channel 133, the top blue of the translucency, is brought up to 50% while channel 131, the no color MR-16's, is brought up to 15%. Channel 136, the bottom blue of the translucency, is brought up to 60%, while channel 134, the Gam 250 bottom of the translucency, is brought up to 20%.
- Group 7, controlling the Roscolux 20 downlight, is brought up to 50% to color the floor. To shape the bodies of the group, the Roscolux 51 will color them from stage right, while the Roscolux 64 will

color them from stage left. Channels 21 > 24 (Group 3), the stage right lavender pipe ends, are brought up to 50%, along with channels 31 > 34 on the stage right lavender booms. Channels 45 > 48 (Group 6), the stage left blue pipe ends, are brought up to 40%, along with 105 > 108 on the stage left blue booms.

- Frontlight will also be added at a lower intensity to see the group's faces as they enter. Group 1, controlling the Roscolux 33 frontlight, is brought up to 30%. Channels 29 and 30, the Roscolux 51 box booms, are brought up to 50% to fill in the shadows.

This look is recorded as memory 102. Initially assigned a 7-second fade time, it seems too fast when seeing the cross-fade from memory 101 to memory 102 in time. There also seems to be a visual "dip" as the center area fades down and the rest of the cue fades up. To correct these notes, the upfade time is slowed to 10 seconds, while the downfade time is slowed to 13 seconds.

The first three cues for *Hokey* have now been written. The cue list on the monitor display looks like Figure 13.1.

The Storm: Act 1, Scene 2

The rest of the cues for the first scene are recorded, concluding with memory 124. That cue will be used for the end of Hokey and Pookie's love song in bright daylight at center-center, surrounded by the rest of the group. The show then moves into the second scene of the first act, beginning with the storm conjured by Tee-boo. This would have been the time to write a series of effect sequences with the strobes, but they are only a small part of the "Chapter 6 Massacre," when the preliminary plot was cut down. The flashes to represent the storm will be from ellipsoidals. Either the director will like the effect without the strobe lights, or she'll have to speak to the producer. Sadly, the lighting designer has no say at this point but to provide the cues in this manner.

The choice was also made long ago in all of the meetings to use the common visual convention for

Q	Cnt	Label
100	2.5	Block
100.1	2.5	Black w/ infrastructure channels
100.7	3	Preset; Pookie USL
101	5\10	Center up; USL down
102	10\13	Dawn; Group enter 1
300	2.5	Block

Figure 13.1 The Cue List for *Hokey*, Act 1, scene 1

evil (Tee-boo), the color green. This is part of the comic-book analogy.

The visual sequence description is as follows: As the applause dies down at the end of the song, the lights will change into scene 2 with memory 130, a "darker and more foreboding look." The background music slightly wanders and is non-harmonious, with imposing bass notes. The performers, concerned, surround Hokey and Pookie, waving Chinese silk to represent the impending storm, which will be memory 131.

On a sound cue, the lights flash, followed by a bump of the focus with a huge evil musical chord for Tee-boo's entrance downstage left. Actually he'll be preset in the dark during the flashes with the Tee-boo-ettes. The flash sequence will be programmed into memory 132 and autofollows. Since it's uncertain how many flashes will be needed over what period of time, cue numbers will then be skipped, so that Tee-boo's entrance will be recorded as memory 136. This still gives three whole numbers to record intermediate called cues, if needed, prior to Tee-boo's entrance.

- Since memory 130 will be a different look from memory 124, the cue will be built from black. Again, memory 100.1 (containing the infrastructure channels) is loaded into the fader.
- Memory 130 is an intermediate cue; it is providing the visual punctuation point between the song and the storm. The general feeling of the cue is attempting to be "the storm approaching." With that in mind, channels 135 and 136 are brought up to 50%, to achieve a blue-green mix (evil on the horizon). Group 10 (the Gam 850 backlight) is brought up to 70%.
- Since the lovers at center are still the focus, the cue will be built so that the warmth comes from center. Groups 3 and 4, controlling the Roscolux 51 pipe ends, are brought up to 50%, while the cool boom sidelights, assigned to group 12, are also brought up to 50%.
- To provide facial light for the rest of the performers, group 2, controlling the Lee 161 frontlight, is brought up to 50%. If stage focus needs to be directed to a specific person in the group, the followspots will be used, or individual channels in the Roscolux 33 frontlight system may be brought up to a low level so their faces can be seen.
- The cue will be finished by adding specials to center to "punch up" the lovers. Channel 56, controlling the center center downlight, is brought up to 70%. To prevent the lovers' faces from being too sharply shadowed, channel 59, controlling the 1 pipe center frontlight, is brought up to 50%.

This look is recorded as memory 130, with a time of 7 seconds. When memory 130 is recorded, most computer consoles recognize that any active channels from the previous memory (in this case memory 124) not reading in memory 130 will automatically be assigned a level of zero. This means that any channel in memory 124 not active in memory 130 will automatically be recorded to fade out to zero in 7 seconds.

Memory 131 will need to be darker and more ominous than memory 130. The initial plan is to use no system frontlight, only sides, downs, and backs. Faces will be covered with followspots.

- First, the background will be addressed. The green bottom of the translucency, channel 135, is brought up to 70%. The blue bottom of the translucency, channel 136, is taken down to 30%.
- The warmth from memory 130 will be taken out. Groups 3 and 4 are taken to zero, and groups 5 and 6, controlling the Roscolux 64 pipe ends, replace them at 30%.
- The color of the floor will shift. Group 10 is taken down to 30%, dimming the blue backlight. In its place, group 8 (controlling the Lee 124 downlight) is brought up to 70%.
- Likewise, the cool booms in group 12 are taken down to 20%, while the blue-green mids in group 13 are brought up to 50%.
- To provide visual contrast to the rest of the scene, the Gam 945 box booms in channels 49 and 50 are brought up to 30% to fill in the front shadows with saturated lavender.

Memory 131 is now recorded, with a time of 10 seconds. Since most of the cue is lower in intensity, it may be necessary to split the time, and make the downfade time longer so that there is no visual "dip" as the channels cross-fade. Memory 131 has tinges of green, but is still mixed with other color systems. The saturated colors will remain reduced until the entrance of Tee-boo.

Next, memory 132 will be recorded with the base intensities, so that all of the other subsequent cues or effects will be "layered" on top of it. Whenever other cues are not running, the channel content of memory 132 will provide the basic illumination on stage.

- To make sure that the flashes will be seen, the entire base cue will be a lower version of memory 131. All of the channels are activated (except for the infrastructure channels), and the entire cue is "pulled down" 25%. That look is now recorded as memory 132, with a time of zero. This means that when the cue is loaded, the entire look of the stage will drop down 25% in a bump.

Now it's time to construct the storm cues. Although the entire sequence could be programmed in an effect loop, the amount of time between the initiation of the storm and Tee-boo's appearance in rehearsal, times out to approximately 5 seconds. For that reason, the choice is made to build this sequence as a series of autofollows, so that altering the sequence will be easier and more controllable. The memories will skip numbers so that other memories, if need be, can be inserted in between.

- Since the more dramatic angles in this case are perceived to be from the side or the back, the frontlight systems will not be used. To pop through the saturation, the desaturated Roscolux 51 and the Roscolux 64 pipe ends and booms will be employed. Initially a flash will be programmed upstage left and downstage right. Channels 24 and 35 are brought to Full. This look is recorded as memory 132.2, with a time of zero seconds up and 1 second down (Ø\1).
- Next, a flash midstage right and left will be recorded. Channels 24 and 35 are taken to zero, and channels 23 and 26 are brought up to Full. This look is recorded as memory 132.4, also with a time of zero seconds up and 1 second down (Ø\1).
- Now a flash upstage right and downstage left will be recorded. Channels 23 and 26 are taken to zero, and channels 48 and 31 are brought to Full. This look is recorded as memory 132.6, also with an upfade time of zero seconds, and a downfade time of 1 second (Ø\1).

On this particular lighting console, a memory that is assigned a delay time automatically assigns the following cue as an autofollow. The delay time is also defined as the amount of time elapsed between the initiation of the first cue, and the automatic initiation of the second cue. If memory 132 is assigned a delay time of 2 seconds, then memory 132.2 will automatically begin 2 seconds after memory 132 begins. To break up the rhythm of the flashes, the console is programmed with a variety of delay times assigned to memory 132, 132.2, 132.4, and 132.6.

The final cue that needs to be constructed is Tee-boo's entrance, memory 136. Following the director's intent, the stage will be filled with variations of green. Since this is a new look, the memory can be built from black. The fader is cleared, and the infrastructure memory 100.1 is loaded once again.

- The background will become completely green by bringing up channel 135 (the green bottom translucency) to Full. The floor will become green by activating group 8 (the Lee 124 downlight)

Q	Cnt	Delay	Label
124	5		End of love song; applause
130	7		Pull to center, turq cyc
131	10		Cool stage, greener cyc
132	0	0.3	Thunder crash; BASE Q
132.2	0\1	0.5	Flash UL/DR (.3 after 132)
132.4	0\1	0.2	Flash ML/MR (.5 after 132.2)
132.6	0\1	0.2	Flash UR/DL (.2 after 132.4)
136	1		Tee-boo entrance DSL

Figure 13.2 The Cue List for the Transition from Act 1, scene 1 to Act 1, scene 2

to Full. The mids in group 13 (colored in Roscolux 76) are brought to Full. Channel 65, the Roscolux 20 downlight downstage left, is brought to 50% to provide focus for Tee-boo. The Roscolux 44 box boom focused to his side of the stage, channel 39, is brought up to 50%.

This look is recorded as memory 136, with a time fade of 1 second. The initial sequence is now complete. The cue list on the monitor display looks like Figure 13.2.

Because the delays are listed on the screen, it is easy to see that the memories between 132 and 136 are auto-follows. Once the stage manager has called cue 132, the board will automatically run through the next three memories until the stage manager calls for cue 136.

Since all of the flash cues are zero count upfades, the total length of time for the entire sequence can be determined by adding all of the delay times. In this case, the length of time between the initiation of memory 132 through the completion of memory 132.4 will be only 1 second.

Unfortunately, the flashing sequence needs to occupy 5 seconds, so additional action needs to be programmed. Otherwise, after the stage manager calls cue 132, the three flashes will occur and the stage will be static for 4 seconds before Tee-boo enters downstage left. Presuming the director wants an "active" stage during the thunder crashing, either the delay times between flashes need to be increased so that there is a longer amount of time between flashes, or more memories need to be constructed to fill those 4 seconds. Depending on the timing and choreography, increasing the length of the delay times might be the solution, or it may make the entire sequence look like a mistake.

One solution might be to construct another 12 memories with different channels flashing, which would probably be more visually interesting. If this entire sequence hasn't been thought through prior to the level setting session, however, there may not be enough time to build that sequence.

Another possible solution that would fill the 5-second flash time would be to repeat the sequence or to create a "loop." If the light board has the capability to link memories, a command can be assigned to memory 132.6, instructing the light board to automatically reload memory 132. The memories then progress to the end of the sequence, and then start over again, and repeat indefinitely, until the GO button is pressed to clear the fader and load the new memory. Since there's only one base memory and three flash memories, the rhythm may visually appear too regular.

- The solution that is chosen is to duplicate the flash cues and alter the delay times to make the times of the flashes irregular. After loading memory 132, record that cue as memory 133, memory 134, and memory 135.
- After loading memory 132.2, record that cue as memory 133.2, 134.2, and memory 135.2.
- Continue the duplication of recording through 135.6, and then add and alter the delay times for the entire range of cues between 132 and 135.6, to break up the rhythm of the flashes.

Twelve additional memories have now been created to fill the 5-second sequence. After successfully running the sequence in time, the next problem that becomes apparent is that the instruments don't flash bright enough (bumping up to Full in 0 seconds), before they fade out in the down time of 1 second. If this is the case, the solution may be to preheat the filaments.

Preheat is the term applied to a low channel intensity, that allows just enough voltage to make a lamp's filament glow. It's not enough voltage, however, to make the filament bright enough to create a beam of light. By recording that preheat intensity in every flash cue not involving the active channels, the filaments are warmed up, and can react more quickly to the zero time fade-up command.

First, the preheat intensity is defined for the channels used in the flash sequence (23, 24, 26, 31, 35, and 48). While looking into the lens of each instrument, each channel will be individually brought up to a level (typically somewhere between 09% and 14%), so that the filament of each lamp glows without causing enough light to reach the stage. The channel intensity may be different for each instrument, depending on the dimmers. Each of those preheat intensities is written down.

Next, the board must be programmed. Since there's so little elapsed time between the base cue and the first flash, all of the preheats will be programmed starting with memory 131. While looking at the cues in the preview display, each of the flash channels is programmed with the preheat intensity and recorded in the cue to track. This means the preheat intensities will be at the same levels in memory 132, the base cue. In memory 132.2, channels 24 and 35 come to Full while the rest of the channels continue to track. In memory 132.4, channels 24 and 35 go to zero. Those two channels are reprogrammed to their preheat intensities, again recording to track. This time-consuming process must be repeated through the entire sequence, so that whenever a flash channel is not at Full the channel is only reduced to its preheat intensity, not zero.

One way to avoid this situation is to decide, while building memory 131, which channels will be the flash channels. Those channels are then recorded at preheat intensities in memory 131, which becomes the "template" cue to record all of the other flash cues. The preheat intensity for the nonactive channels is directly recorded into the cues.

After all of the cues are built, the delays assigned, and the preheat intensities programmed, the cue sequence is then run in real time to see its visual effect. Variation to break up the rhythm is achieved by altering the delay time, the up- and downfade time, and the channel intensity in each flash memory. If additional channels are added to the cues, their preheat intensity should first be programmed into memory 131 to track.

Finally, memory 136 is viewed in the blind or preview display. Any of the flash channels that are not used in the cue are programmed to zero and tracked, which eliminates the possibility of the preheat intensities tracking through the rest of the scene. The entire sequence is run again in real time, and finally deemed a success.

While this is only one way to program an effects sequence, it's hopefully now more apparent that programming sequences are not to be taken lightly. Without proper planning, any programmed linking, looping, effect, or sequential memories can consume extensive programming time. Mentally visualizing the sequence on paper, prior to the level setting session, forces the lighting designer to select the channel numbers, delay times, and memory numbers that will be involved. Otherwise, an entire cue level setting session can easily be reduced to programming one involved sequence for what may possibly be a relatively brief moment during the production. As a result, the rest of the memories may not have been created in the time allotted to the cueing session.

If the director agrees to move on, take a note, write this sequence later in the day, or before the tech rehearsal tomorrow, and show it to her then. If the director decides that this sequence needs to be worked out today, perhaps it can be written during the lunch break. But if the director decides that this sequence *has* to be programmed now, before the rest of the session can continue, consider calling for a coffee break for everyone but yourself and the console operator. With his or her permission, you will be able to program much more rapidly without everyone else's eyes staring at you, waiting for you to complete the programming.

The Beginning of Act 2, Scene 1

The first scene in the second act of *Hokey* is the nighttime forest scene, when the Knotty Piners join Hokey. The sequence will begin with the house lights fading out while intro music is being played. Then the main curtain will rise on a dark stage. With 17 seconds of music, the forest scene will slowly be revealed. Initially the translucency will fade up, followed by the blue light on the floor. Then the leafy templates will appear on the floor, followed by the sidelight fading up. Finally, the frontlight will fade up as Hokey enters the scene.

According to the cue master, memory 200.7 will be recorded as a "black preset" cue, and memory 201 will be called by the stage manager. Memory 201 will be constructed as a five-part cue. Each part will be assigned its own fade and wait time.

When a memory is made up of parts, the visual end result is the same as building a series of overlapping autofollow memories. The difference is that they are all contained in a single memory. To create a single look that consists of five different actions moving at five different speeds, for example, that sequence is typically created by activating a series of channels and recording a separate memory five times with five different time fades. To construct the same sequence using the part feature, the final "look" is created once, recorded once, and then the five components of the memory are separated into parts. Each part is then assigned an individual fade time, wait, or delay to achieve each separate movement.

After creating the typical five-memory sequence, it's decided that the overhead pipe end templates, for example, should fade up later in the sequence. Typical cue construction requires activating those channels in a later memory, recording that memory, and then deleting the channel levels from the earlier memory. To complete the same action in the part cue, the same channels are merely activated in a later part.

The advantage of a part cue is the fact that it's a single memory. Channels can be "shifted" from part to part with relative ease. The limitation of a part cue, on the other hand, is that it's a single memory. Although channels can easily be shifted, they can only be activated to a single intensity level. If the desired sequence requires the overhead templates to initially fade up to a high intensity, and then immediately fade down to a lower intensity, the sequence must be constructed with two separate memories.

Working with parts may require different methods on different consoles. On some consoles, programming a memory into parts may be restricted to a specific monitor display. Other consoles may require the parts to be created before channels can be assigned to each part. Most consoles that provide this feature are designed to provide at least six parts in any memory.

In this case, memory 201 will be broken into five parts. When the GO button is pushed, the five different parts will automatically occur with individual time fades. The wait times will be programmed to relate to the single push of the GO button. As discussed in Chapter 1, a wait on this lighting console is defined as the amount of time that elapses between the moment that the GO button is pressed, and when the unit of memory (in this case, a part) begins. When programming this amount of complexity, the cue list may not adequately show the time relationships. Sometimes drawing a time map can help illustrate the movement of the cue. Here is one way to illustrate the five-part memory 201 sequence, using the graphic layout that was shown in Chapter 1.

Figure 13.3 shows the same information as the cue list, but graphically indicates the time line for all of the parts of memory 201. To record this sequence:

- Load memory 100.1, and record that as memory 200.7.
- Now create memory 201. The translucency will be blue green, so channel 136 (blue bottom translucency) is brought up to 50%. Channel 135 (green bottom translucency) is brought up to 25%. The floor will be blue, dappled with templates; group 10 (Gam 850 backlight) is brought up to 50%, while group 15 (overhead templates in channels 51 > 54) is brought up to 70%. The blue sidelight booms (in channels 101 > 108) will help shape the initial look of the performers, so group 12 is brought up to 30%. Finally, the blue frontlight will be added; group 2 is brought up to 30% as well.

After this look is recorded as memory 201, the five parts will be created in the preview or blind display.

- Part 1 will bring up the background. After activating channels 135 and 136, part 1 is recorded and assigned a time of 5 seconds.
- Part 2 will bring up the blue backlight. After activating group 10, part 2 is recorded and assigned a time of 5 seconds as well, but with an added wait of 3 seconds. This means that after the GO button is pushed for memory 201, 3 seconds will elapse before part 2 begins its 5-second fade.
- Part 3 will bring up the template system. After activating group 15, part 3 is recorded and assigned a time of 7 seconds, with a wait time of 6 seconds.
- Part 4 will bring up the blue booms. After activating group 12, part 4 is recorded and assigned a time of 7 seconds, with a wait time of 9 seconds.
- Finally, part 5 will bring up the blue frontlight. After group 2 is activated, part 5 is recorded and assigned a time of 7 seconds, with a wait time of 12 seconds.

The programming for the parts of memory 201 is now complete. The cue list on the monitor looks like Figure 13.4.

When the GO button is pressed to load memory 201, part 1 will fade up the background in 5 seconds. Three seconds into that fade, part 2 will begin to fade up the blue backlight on the floor in 5 seconds. Three seconds into that fade, part 3 will begin to fade up the template system in 7 seconds. Three seconds into that fade, part 4 will begin to fade up the blue booms in 7 seconds. Finally, 12 seconds after the GO button was pushed, part 5 will begin to fade up the blue frontlights. The entire cue will be complete in 17 seconds.

If it's necessary to see a single part, on some consoles this can occur by pressing the GOTO button and loading that part into the fade. On other consoles, it may be necessary to search for other workarounds.

Q	Cnt	Wait	Label
200.7	3		Preset A2-1; Black on stage
201 P1	5		Blue-Green background
201 P2	5	3	Blue backs on floor
201 P3	7	6	Templates
201 P4	7	9	Blue booms
201 P5	5	12	Blue fronts

Figure 13.4 The Cue List for *Hokey*, Act 2, scene 1

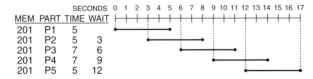

Figure 13.3 A Time Map of Memory 201

The End of Act 2, Scene 1

The end of the forest scene concludes with Hokey and the Knotty Piners singing the rousing song "Knots are Tight," as they agree to join forces in the quest to free Pookie from Tee-boo's spell. The scene has been staged so the entire group finishes the song down center. After they finish singing, the group remains in a pose as the curtain descends.

Memory 227 has been defined as the cue that will be called as the group assembles downstage. Memory 228 will be called by the stage manager, timed so that all frontlights will have faded out before the curtain descends, leaving the group in light. Constructing this sequence will be relatively simple, by using the inhibitive submaster controlling the front of house channels.

- Memory 227 is currently loaded into the active fader.
- Move the handle for submaster 24 (the front of house inhibitive sub) to zero. All of the front of house lights should now be at zero.
- Record memory 228, assigning a 3-second time fade.
- Restore submaster 24 to Full. The front of house lights should remain inactive, since memory 228 has been recorded with those channels at zero.

After memory 227 is reloaded into the active fader, the cue restores all of the front of house light in the memory. When the GO button is pressed, the channels upstage of the plaster line remain unaffected, while the front of house lights fade to zero in 3 seconds. The cueing for the end of Act 2, scene 1 is complete.

This is a brief glimpse of some of the methods used to create light cues. There are many other ways to manipulate cue information, using other displays, setups, and command structures such as "rem-dim" or "record minus sub" to expedite cue creation. The manufacturer and model of the computer lighting console that is being used helps define the amount of flexibility.

Although each lighting console may have its own particular advantages and quirks, the largest limitation may be a lack of understanding about how to program the lighting console on the part of the lighting designer. If time runs short, inadequate preparation or lack of knowledge on the part of the lighting designer can cause delay. If you don't know how to use a console, find someone who does before the light cue level setting session and learn. If that's not a choice, ask that person to be your guest at the light cue level setting session and buy him or her lunch. Don't walk into the session without knowledge or assistance.

After the Cueing Session

After the final memory has been recorded, turn on the worklights, change the time stamp, and save to the storage media. Save to the storage media. Save to the storage media. If it's warranted, do a printout. Take the time to be certain that every cue that has been recorded has been marked on the cue master as having been constructed. Note all changes in channeling, submaster assignment, or group identity on the appropriate paperwork. Make note of any cue work that will be delayed until a future time. Give work notes, if needed. If possible, take a moment, get out of the theatre, take some deep breaths, and collect your thoughts. Take something to write on. After seeing the entire show once, inspiration or clarity can strike at any time.

FOLLOWSPOTS

When the followspot cue sheets were prepared, the instrument's attributes were mentioned: the iris size, the color boomerang, and the douser. This section considers followspot concepts, analyzes their use, and suggests tactics to make them simple to use in a production.

Followspot Concepts

The justification used for followspotting comes from three sources, provided by the world of art and scientific research. Almost any classical painting is a demonstration of the tenet which states that the eye is subconsciously attracted to the brightest point of light. Scientific observation has confirmed that the eye is subconsciously attracted to movement, while research has determined that there's a corollary between visibility and sound, justifying the old adage "what isn't seen, isn't heard."

A followspot can be used to implement those tenets. By moving and making one area of the stage brighter, it directs the stage focus, identifies the source of the speech or sound, and thus allows the performer to be heard. In the early days of vaudeville, the followspot achieved these goals while blatantly being seen and being part of the show. In today's theatrical situations, on the other hand, while still providing that focus, today's spot attempts to downplay its existence. To do this, the intensity and the softness of the beam edge are carefully controlled. Other times, the need for stage focus may overrule any desire for subtlety. Successfully providing stage focus during bright scenes may result in the followspots returning to their vaudeville appearance, being used uncolored and hard-edged. Sometimes that's part of the design; the hard-edged followspot defines the "theatrical" location. When the "performance" occurs, the hard-edged beam subconsciously telegraphs to the audience that the action is taking place "onstage."

Most of the time, though, a followspot is trying to perform its function while remaining hidden. Concealing a followspot's existence is often tied directly to the hot spot, the fade speed, and the smoothness of its movement. In most circumstances, when performers are being followed, the hot spot will be on their face. Regardless of the beam's size, in this situation, the unwritten law is that the spot needs to always remain at least on the head of the performer. Since the performer is spotted, the audience is focused on his fact. If the spot suddenly misses the target, the performer's face will suddenly go "dark" by moving out of the followspot, and the absence of the followspot will steal stage focus. To keep the spot unnoticed, the time fades of the spot strive to be smooth and unobtrusive. When the spot follows a performer to an exit, for example, the light typically fades before the shadow of the performer is seen on the scenic legs or background. The fade-out is not done quickly; even a one-count fade would result in the audience's conscious recognition of the absence of light, and the stage focus is stolen again. When a followspot tracks a performer moving about the stage, it's typically designed to exactly match the performer's speed and appear in tandem with his or her general movement, only smoother. If a followspot's beam movement is herky-jerky and somewhat stutter step relative to the movement of the performer, it's not matching the speed or movement, and the followspot's existence will be exposed. This is especially visible when the performer and followspot are seen against scenery or a backdrop. The "smooth" followspot will be subconsciously noted, accepted by the audience, and attention will return to the stage focus. The movements of a "jerky" spot will constantly divert attention from the performer.

Followspot Analysis

It was earlier mentioned that a followspot helps direct stage focus by making one area of the stage brighter. Typically, this is accomplished by "irising down," or reducing the size of the beam to a single performer. Although the priority of most followspots is to concentrate on the face, different iris sizes are often associated with specific genres of theatre. In dance, spots often use a **full body shot** (the most "open"), which is larger than the body of a rapidly moving dancer, including especially the feet but also the hands. In musicals, the spot beams may be irised slightly smaller

to what's referred to as a **body shot**, highlighting the entire body of a performer from head to toe during songs and scenes staged with less vigorous movement. Opera spots often tighten the iris to **waist shots** during solos, covering only from above the head to the waist, to direct attention to the singer's face and mouth. In some cases, the spots iris is tighter to **head shots**, highlighting only the singer's face. **Pin spot** refers to the smallest iris size possible in that particular instrument, and isn't specific to any particular genre. Followspots in drama don't have an identifiable size; they're used less frequently, so they often end up providing focus as a subtly moving frontlight special in any size.

Regardless of the show's genre, in most cases the followspot gets the "provide the focus, don't be seen" assignment. In addition to smooth moves and subtle fades, its stealth also depends on possessing a soft beam edge and not being too bright. That said, successfully running a followspot and providing even coverage on a moving performer with a soft-edged beam is a skill, and don't let any one tell you different. It's not easy, but it all starts with the fuzzy edge.

The design and construction of many followspots result in incredibly bright beams, but in many cases their projected beam of light is slightly out of focus—it often includes a high-contrast hot spot that is often off-center, on one side of the beam. Efforts to eliminate the hot spot or center it in the middle of the beam by "tuning" the lamp's relationship to the reflector is rarely successful. Adjusting the lens focus at the front of the instrument, in an effort to soften and smooth the beam, usually does little more than slightly soften the hot spot and produce exaggerated halation (the little rain-bowies) on the beam edge.

When touring productions encounter these kinds of followspots, efforts to create a smooth beam with a soft, fuzzy edge are often reduced to an extended process of trial and error. A portion of a work call may be set aside for a **show and tell**, starring the followspots. That's when worklights are dimmed, and individual or multiple pieces of different diffusions are held in front of the beam in the spot booth and compared, one at a time, much like the optometrist's office: ("R114? Or R132? R114? Or R119? 2-R132's? Or R114"). The lighting department, meanwhile, stands in the house, stares at the followspot's beam and its edges, and casts their ballots. While some portion of the show and tell may be spent determining the best diffusion recipe, additional time may be devoted to figuring out where to put it; placed in a boomerang frame, taped to the nose of the instrument, or taped between the lenses in the barrel of the unit. Other tactics may abandon the use of diffusions altogether in favor of old-school tactics, such as smearing petroleum jelly in the middle of individual colors, or just using plastic baggies purchased from the supermarket instead.

In many cases, the show and tell is usually a two-part affair. In addition to ugly beam characteristics, some uncolored modern followspots often change performers' skin tone to look like they just got released from a hospital. Because of that, the second part of a show and tell often tries to color correct that particular spot lamp so the cast doesn't look like the Living Dead. ("Add another piece of ½ CTO? Another straw? Two straws?") All of this takes much longer than anyone would like to admit; while originally scheduled for only 15 minutes, the show and tell work call often results in someone ordering a pizza.

The placement of theatrical followspots usually falls into two categories:

1. Productions that only use spots as frontlight, in order to direct the stage focus. In this situation, the architectural limitations built into most theatres typically dictate no more than three spotlights, since that's often the maximum number of instruments that can fit into the spot booth.
2. Productions that can afford to place followspots in both the front and from additional locations. Sometimes it's the box boom, sometimes the torm, sometimes the gallery, or sometimes as backlight. In these cases, while the overall number of spots makes the labor a bit more expensive, the additions make the focus points more interesting to look at. The spots are often added in pairs, one from each side. Doing so makes it much easier to balance the spotlight intensity using the same number of followspots from either side.

While the lighting designer or an assistant (spot wrangler) may initially choreograph the spots until the cues are set, by the time the show opens the followspots' actions are called by someone else. The complexity of the production and the need to call other cues may not afford the stage manager the time to provide direction to the spots. In that case the lead followspot operator is often assigned the task, providing the cues to the rest of the operators, usually on a separate headset channel.

Followspot Tactics

Before the technical rehearsals begin, the followspots are often assigned a series of defaults: if the followspot activity will be constrained to a few lead performers, or leads, it may be possible to assign default performers to the followspots as well. The cue sheets then only need to record what is unique to each spot cue, rather than detail the preset for every upfade, or **pickup**.

Before the rehearsal begins, followspots are often assigned an identity number. If only two followspots are used, the brighter instrument typically receives the label "1," and that spot is usually then always on the number one performer. When three or more front spots are used, common conventions begin numbering them from stage left, utilizing the same numbering system as the instruments on overhead electrics. If the followspots are scattered around the theatre, the numerical labels are usually assigned in a circular pattern. Starting at one instrument (usually in the front), the instruments are numbered in a continual sweep around the theatre. If stacking occurs, number top to bottom. Using this system allows the followspot director to refer rapidly to half of the followspots as "odds," and the other half "evens," cueing alternate spots on either side.

Labeling can be expanded far beyond numbers. In ice shows, every third spot can also be assigned the letter "A," "B," or "C." That way the spots can be quickly directed during pieces starring three performers. Another label might be a position, so that one group can be summoned with the call for "runway fronts." When enough followspots are in the show that each spot is given multiple names (spot 4-A-Left Front), the spot wrangler often writes each name on white gaff tape and sticks it directly on each spot. That way each operator can quickly check his or her "name" during the show.

Labeling the followspots forces the lighting designer to consider their position and the way they'll be used. For example, suppose followspots are located solely at the box boom positions, far from centerline. The performers consistently need spots as soon as they appear from the wings. The clear option is to assign each pickup to the followspot on the opposite side of the stage. In this situation, any system assigning followspots to specific performers must be abandoned. Rather, the pickups are determined solely by which side of the stage a performer makes his or her entrance.

Since the brightest followspot needs to be on the most important focus point, it's smart to determine which one that is before the rehearsal starts. One of the first things a spot wrangler does is compare all of the beam intensities on a communal wall or curtain. If the followspots are nonmatching intensities, he or she will note which one is the brightest. In dance, that spot is usually on the woman. In opera, it's often assigned to the highest-billed singer. While the labeling and calling structure will often differ between shows, it's always important to know which spot physically puts out more light so spot usage can be properly allocated.

During bright scenes, if the intensity of a single followspot isn't sufficient to cut through the light and highlight the focus point, a second followspot is often piled on top of the first spot to brighten the focus point. When that's still insufficient, it may be necessary to just un-gel the spot (commonly known as "drop the color") to get more intensity.

When there are too many performers requiring stage focus at different times, assigning a default performer is typically not a possibility. Initially identifying the performers for the followspots may be difficult without costumes. The costumes may not be available (or complete) for the rehearsal, and identifying pickups by name may mean nothing to spot operators unfamiliar with the cast. For that matter, understudies or alternates may be leading the rehearsal, rather than the cast who will perform that night. On those occasions, identify the performers by identifying features: red sweats, yellow shirt, and so on. Building on that idea, it may be possible for the leads to wear pieces (t-shirts, pants) in their character's colors during initial rehearsals. If future rehearsals are anticipated to insert understudies into leading roles, it may be worthy to purchase loose t-shirts of related colors to be used specifically for these uncostumed rehearsals.

Designing followspot choreography in a production with constantly shifting focus points can be an exciting challenge, but the complexity can also quickly create conundrums. Inevitably, there are moments when there are more focus points required than there are followspots, and the lighting designer is forced to make choices. First, the most important point of focus must be determined. Once that has been defined, the current position of the followspots needs to be considered. If two performers are adjacent to each other, it may be possible to open the iris of one spot to cover both performers, while slowly fading out the second followspot. The now-available followspot can then pick up the additional focus point. Moments can occur when a spot, following one performer, suddenly needs to pick up a different performer. If a moment occurs where the two performers are staged close together, consider using that moment to change (or **swap**) the spot's focus to the second performer.

Since followspots can affect the stage focus, their use doesn't have to be constrained to only highlighting performers. They're viewed as frontlight get-me-out-of-trouble specials. From that perspective, their use can be expanded, providing stage focus for anything on the stage. This may range from highlighting properties, to illuminating entire pieces of "unplanned-for" scenery. When utilized for these types of pickups, the followspots' fade time may need to be carefully matched with the speed of the light cues. Colors may be chosen that have nothing to do with the performers and are used solely to complement the inanimate objects.

Shelley's Notes: Followspot Language

One of the challenges of calling followspots is to be as brief as possible. In typical use, the amount of followspot choreography that needs to be verbally communicated (until the spots learn the sequence) can potentially be so extensive that by the time you've related one set of commands, you've missed the next three cues. Here's one list of additional followspot lingo, where a short phrase can express coverage, action, or speed:

- Ballyhoo: Move the spot in a figure 8 on its side. This pattern is often asked for on show drops. If there are two spots they try to stay opposite of each other.
- Bump: Regardless of the action, it's performed as quickly and cleanly as possible. Same as zero count.
- Cover near: Usually used when two spotted performers are adjacent to one another, but not close enough for one spot to cover both. In this case, the spot would cover the performer closest to him or her.
- Cover far: In this case the spot would cover the performer farthest from him or her (and try to avoid the near performer).
- Cloverleaf swap: Always covers the far person; if two people come together at center and then part company, each followspot always stays with the performer farthest away from it.
- Frame: Colors in the boomerang. Frame 1 is always closest to the operator.
- Hold: Freeze the position of the followspot, allowing the performers to walk in and out of its light.
- Isolate: Tighten or change the iris size, or shift the beam location, so that the beam hits only the assigned focus point. Stay off anything that isn't the focus point.
- Inclusive: The opposite of "isolate"; do whatever is necessary to include whoever is close to the assigned focus point. When other performers get close, open the iris to include them in the spot's coverage. The interaction between the two performers is the focus point designed to receive stage focus.
- Primary coverage: One performer is designated as the primary; when other people get close to that performer, they're included in the followpot's coverage. The interaction between the anyone and the primary is the focus point that should receive stage focus.
- Open or Open out: Increase iris size.

- Pickup: Same as focus point or the action of fading up.
- Pop: Action taken in zero counts.
- Roll: A live action changing from one color to another. Typically requires dexterity to "cross-fade" between two colors in the boomerang with one hand while following with the other.
- Spot spikes: Using the small bits of light that escape the body of the followspot (light leaks) and hit the glass or walls in the spot booth to position the spot for difficult critical pickups. Followspots are typically anchored and marks show where the light leaks must be placed for the spot to make the pickup.
- Sweep: Broad action like a ballyhoo but without the change in height; a rapid pan.
- Tighten or Tighten in: Decrease iris size.

Followspots Before the First Technical Rehearsal

Meet with the followspot operators before the first encounter on headset. One purpose of the meeting is to allow the lighting designer to explain the numbering and defaults being used and to identify the main performers who will be picked up and any special pickups. The meeting's second purpose is to allow the lighting designer the opportunity to attach faces to names and establish a working relationship with the operators. With larger shows, this meeting may be the opportunity to distribute the color. The spot operator then has the responsibility to load the color into the boomerang correctly.

When calling followspots on a headset, the first rule to remember is to be brief. The followspot director should rehearse the semantics of his or her directions, so that the largest amount of information can be conveyed in the fewest possible words. The followspot director who chatters away incessantly through a performance may soon discover that he or she is alone on the channel. The operators have grown tired of the banter and have taken off their headsets.

Before giving any instructions, confirm that all operators are on headset and that they can hear the spot director. Unless time is short, giving instructions can wait until everyone is on, so that the instructions only need to be given once. After confirming that all involved know their individual label, ask for all of the followspots to turn on, and cast their beams on a common wall to match the focus and intensity of the instruments. Make all of the spots the same size, drop all color and diffusion, and focus all the spots as best they can for an even field and a sharp beam edge. Once the spots are focused, note the units that seem brighter or darker for future work calls. Next, check the mechanical elements of the instruments, confirm

that the colors are loaded in the correct sequence ("run through the colors"), check the largest and smallest iris sizes, and check that the dousers are fully functional in both directions (faded out, faded up).

If people are on stage, drop one spot pickup a person, and define any typical iris sizes that will be used for the production, including full body, body, waist, or head shot. Physically mark the iris control position on that spot. Once the instrument has been marked, have it rejoin the other light pools back up on the wall, and mirror the iris sizes to the other spots. That way the rest can mark their irises as well. After all the instruments have been calibrated, explain the location of typical entrances or other areas of the stage where the spots will fade up (commonly known as "pickup points") to be used in the show. Typical pickup points include "in 1" left and right, "in 4" left and right, down center, and center-center. Providing the spots with this location information and asking each to go there also confirms that all of the followspot beams can reach each of the pickup points.

If there are any special sequences, consider rehearsing those sequences before the rehearsal begins. Typical sequences may include a slow opening or closing of the iris on a performer ("Tighten to a head shot in 7 counts" or "Even spots open to a waist shot in 10 counts") or changing color in zero counts ("Odd spots swap color to frame three in a bump"). Other sequences may involve individual pickups made in black ("Spot one in a pin spot on the glove down center in three counts"), or swirling patterns on show curtains ("Ballyhoo on the show drop").

When inexperienced spot operators are being thrown into a tech rehearsal, some designers try to help by constructing a quick cheat sheet. Figure 13.5 includes a map of the stage from the followspot's perspective on the left-hand side of the page, with labels indicating "in 1 SR," "in 2 SL," and so on. Labels in between indicate basic nomenclature including "proscenium," "border," and "scenic stack." Next to the stage diagram is a quick reference guide for the colors and their relative location in the boomerang, along with a basic headset list of channels and "who's who." Under that is a diagram showing how to use the basic knobs to control the beam. Below that is a basic cast list, indicating colors for the leads. Sometimes it pays off to photocopy portions of the costume sketches to provide identifying features of performers. At full size the text of this document is oversized, making it easy to read from a distance. That way it can be taped on the glass or the wall of the spot booth as quick, easy-to-glance at reference. Basically, any notes that might provide guidance should be included on the document, in an effort to provide clarity, eliminate some of the questions, and reduce headset chatter.

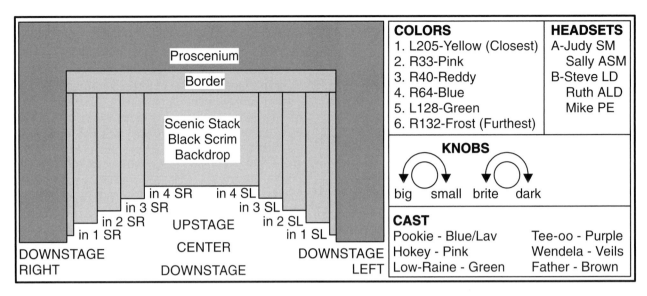

Figure 13.5 Followspot Cheat Sheet

The followspot director and operators are now ready to begin the technical rehearsal.

Shelley's Notes: Followspots as Guide Lights

The lamps in most followspots are relatively delicate; many folks think they take more wear and tear being ignited (striking up) than they do if they're just left on. For that reason, if the break time between periods of spot usage is relatively short, they're often just left on. Whether this practice is good or bad is a discussion best left to the lamp experts. For me, though, if the followspot is going to remain on, it can be put to good use as an illumination source pointed anywhere on the stage.

During breaks or in rehearsal when the stage is being re-set, console programming may still be taking place, but the brightness of a spot's beam won't get in the way. Rather than douse the followspots so their beams can't be seen, I'll direct the spots toward critical areas of the stage that are otherwise in complete darkness, and then ask the spot ops to lock their beams off. Critical areas might include stairs leading to the house, the edge of the stage, the aisles in the house, ladders, or piles of scenery that have things sticking out of it. Areas of the stage that have traffic typically receive no illumination or are potentially precarious when it's dark.

During breaks in the tech, or breaks over coffee, "parking" the spot beams at these predetermined locations means that folks can still move about the stage in semi-darkness and console cueing can still take place, without the need to fumble around and turn on the worklights. If need be, the followspots can be doused out by the operator.

During rehearsals I'll assign each followspot to a default location; my first choice is often the stair access between the audience and the stage. As soon as a scene has been halted, I give the instruction "spots, please move to your park points," and the spots leave their pickups on stage (presuming they're not needed for light cue work), move to their respective guide points, and lock off. The followspots can then relax for a moment, and the critical areas of movement are lit. When the rehearsal's ready to start back up, I'll give the instruction "spots unlock and back to your positions at the top of the scene." If someone is still moving through a parked spot at a guide point, that will be seen and accounted for. In this way, no matter when performers want to move to or from the stage, or move about the stage, they're not traversing in darkness. Using the followspots as guide lights speeds the rehearsal process, and increases the safety of working in the dark.

THE TECHNICAL REHEARSAL

Some say that the primary objective of **technical rehearsals** is to safely add performers to the technical elements of the production. While most agree that statement is true, from a broader perspective, the technical rehearsal is a whole slew of things: it's also the first peek toward the production's visual concept, and the first step toward realizing the overall flow of the show. The technical rehearsal is the opportunity for the director and the creative team to clarify the stage pictures, and to decide if all the choices that have been made, design or otherwise, will fully (or have a snowball's chance) to succeed. To achieve this goal, the initial objective of the technical rehearsal is to address every problem that might potentially slow or stop the production from more fully assembling in subsequent rehearsals. This may require several repetitions of the same sequence to "work through" a particular transition. The first rehearsal with performers can also be referred to as a "stop and start." Once the flow of the production is achieved, and the performers have refined their performance, it will be possible to see if the overall concept has successfully evolved. Since the amount of time dedicated to this portion of the rehearsal process is finite, the secondary objective of these rehearsals is to complete an entire work-through of the show in the scheduled amount of time.

In a complex production, different technical rehearsals may be dedicated to different acts of the production. Although the performers attempt to perform the show without interruption in "real time," any problems that may hamper the production in future rehearsals warrant a stoppage of the action. During these rehearsals, light cues are altered and shaped in their appearance. Together with the other technical elements, the placement and timing of each cue are rehearsed in real time. Simultaneously, many other refinements are often taking place as well. The director may alter staging for the performers, scenery may be repositioned, and properties may be respiked. To an outside observer, it often resembles barely organized chaos.

Initial techs are often scheduled without adding the additional complexity of wardrobe, or any live music. Sometimes cue sequences and transitions are rehearsed before the performers even get to the stage during **dry techs**. On the other hand, after the entire show has been teched with the performers, rehearsals that solely address transitions can take place, called **cue-to-cues**. Costumes, hair pieces, and makeup are added for the **dress rehearsal**(s). When an orchestra is added, and the performers wear their costumes, the rehearsal is known as an **orchestra dress**. After a point, rehearsal labels can become confusing, but usually once the performers begin their work on the stage, the light cues will always be rehearsed. Due to that fact, for the purpose of this text, all of these rehearsals will be collectively referred to as the technical rehearsal.

If the number of technical rehearsals is reduced, the need to correct problems immediately becomes intensified. If the first technical rehearsal is also the final orchestra dress, hold onto your hats; it's gonna be an **all-skate**. In this situation, everyone has his or her own agenda. The director and choreographer may think that the rehearsal is solely to allow them to space or stage the performers. Performers may believe the rehearsal is to correct the conductor about the tempos. Conductors may believe the rehearsal is to get the correct tempos, mix, and color from the orchestra. The stage manager is trying to call the transitions and cue sequences correctly. The scenic designer may take advantage of a break in the action to direct rehanging of a backdrop. Meanwhile, the lighting designer is checking the intensity, blend, and timing of each light cue, while reacting to the numerous demands, requests, and suggestions of everyone around the production table.

Hopefully, those situations are few and far between. *Hokey*'s production schedule is a relatively relaxed one. Now that the light cues have been created, and the elements of the transitions rehearsed, preference is given to the director, or choreographer to insert the performers into the stage picture and adapt to their presence. Initially, the stage manager is with the lighting designer at the production table. This allows the pair to discuss the timing or placement of light cues and have face-to-face discussions with the director.

Prior to the Technical Rehearsal

 A list to consider prior to the technical rehearsal:

- Priority one: All required components at the production table work. This is very important. Few things get a tech off to a rougher start than discovering at the last minute that the monitor is flickering, the headsets aren't working, or, when the house lights dim out, discovering that the worklight at the production table is burned out.
- All of the primary cue construction paperwork is present, updated, and arranged. Adequate numbers of forms are available. Work note sheets are dated and prepared.
- A channel check has been performed for both instruments and any electrical devices. Any problems have been noted.
- A blackout check has been performed. The running lights and spotting lights are functioning, and unnecessary worklights (including the grid worklights) have been turned off.
- Any repertory work has been accomplished (color changes or refocusing in the sidelight booms, reset rovers, groundrow movements, etc.).
- Repatch is set for the top of the rehearsal and has been checked for accuracy.
- The cue light system is functioning.
- The lighting console is in the preset cue.
- All members of the electrics department have checked in on headset and know their initial actions.

- The seating area between the stage and the production table has been cleared. (Since the eye is unconsciously attracted to movement, observers sitting in that area may otherwise distract the lighting designer.)
- A path of easy access has been determined between the production table and backstage. (The last thing needed three minutes prior to the start of the tech is the opportunity to play treasure hunt because the labyrinthine route between the two locations has changed. Again.)

The lighting designer and the electrics department are now ready to begin the technical rehearsal.

Shelley's Soapbox: Headset Etiquette

The headset is a tool for communication. Although its contribution to theatre can't be stressed enough, wearing even the most comfortable headset for 12 hours can still make anyone's head throb. While trying to work in a fairly intense situation, distractions can often become twice as irritating. If one of your ears is trapped inside of plastic and foam and you have no choice about what comes through the speaker in your ear, the last thing that's needed is unknowing personnel not following proper headset etiquette. The headset is not a telephone for casual conversation—it is a business tool.

Additional do's and don'ts when wearing a headset:

- If you're not speaking with someone over your headset, turn off your microphone.
- Have the location of the headset's microphone switch memorized. Use it often. If uncertain, check with the sound department so you know how the microphone switches on the beltpack work. If the headset has a call button, know how to turn the headset on and off, without accidentally hitting that button instead. If there is any confusion, label the switches or buttons with tape.
- Remain calm, even in emergencies. Don't lose your patience while talking over a headset. Don't ever scream into a headset. Don't even think of taking your headset off in a huff and slamming it onto the table with the microphone on.
- Speak clearly into the headset. Don't talk while the microphone is under your chin or above your head. Do not mumble, hum, whistle, sing, or cluck while the microphone is on. Don't eat,

chew gum, drink, sneeze, or yell to someone in the distance while the headset microphone is turned on.
- Don't believe that the headset is its own private confessional. Be aware that your headset conversation may be broadcast on monitor speakers backstage, or into green rooms or management offices. Personal opinions about the talent, state of the show, or any of the individuals with whom you are working should not be expressed over headset.

The Technical Rehearsal Begins

When the technical rehearsal begins, the lighting designer looks at each light cue to see what is right and what needs to be corrected. This may include the channel intensities, the length of the time fades, and the called placement of the cue. Additionally, the designer is also making certain that the visual purpose of the cue is correct and works with the action on the stage. Meanwhile, the stage manager is attempting to run the rehearsal by calling cues for the first time and providing direction. There's usually a *lot* of activity on the headset.

The most important thing that needs to be remembered by the lighting designer is safety. Certainly, there may be times that require darkness while performers are present onstage. If a cue must be rebuilt from scratch, the most expedient method may be to start from a clean slate—a black stage. The lighting designer must be aware that the performers may not yet be used to being in the dark. Remember the Golden Rule: never go to black onstage unannounced. That goes double when performers get onstage. Doing so could easily cause accident or injury. If a black stage is required, announce the fact loudly to the entire theatre. Or if the stage manager has a God mic, ask him or her to do it for you, so you can return to your notes.

The second thing the lighting designer must keep in mind is the overall purpose of the activity. If at all possible, the flow of the technical rehearsal should not be delayed by the lighting designer making changes, refocusing lights, or hanging additional moving light fixtures. If the lighting designer refuses to interrupt cue or other work for the sake of the rehearsal, consider this thought; although the corrected light cues may now look better, while that work was performed, the entire cast, crew, and design team was unable to do their jobs while a series of level intensities was altered. Unless those changes drastically affect the sequence to be rehearsed, the lighting designer must stop changing levels when the stage manager is ready to continue, so that the console operator can prepare to run the sequence again.

The third thing the lighting designer needs to do is maintain composure; write things down, avoid distractions, and remain conversational and calm at all times. If the entire cue sequence has been lost due to a mistake, turn off your headset and breathe before you say something you'll regret. For that matter, even nervous energy can be easily transferred over a headset, and can lead to a jumpy atmosphere, or even accidents. While at times it may seem impossible, **Stay Calm**.

Working with the Stage Manager

The lighting designer especially needs to be cognizant of the stage manager, who may be patiently waiting for the lighting designer to finish reprogramming before the rehearsal continues. Even more important than the stage manager, the lighting designer should stop whatever he or she is doing as quickly as possible whenever the director wants to have a chat.

In many tech situations, the lighting designer and the stage manager have to share the same headset channel, and the two must work together. While every lighting correction may seem important in the moment, the lighting designer must keep the larger objective in mind. Although lighting changes must be programmed, in order to be seen, when the stage manager is ready to move on, the lighting designer needs to take a back seat. Stop speaking, take notes, and let the stage manager do his or her job. Don't become an obstruction to the rehearsal flow. When the stage manager is attempting to call cue sequences, be silent and don't vocally get in the way on headset. Stop making corrections and allow the sequence to be run again. If there are numerous notes, chances are that other departments involved in the sequence will also need adjustment, or will need to run the sequence again as well. So take notes—if there is no opportune time during the tech, fix the light cues during the next break, or later while viewing the preview screen. One way to reduce headset traffic, and still communicate with the rest of the electrics crew, is to have walkie-talkies. For quick conversations, consider using cell phones.

While teching involved sequences, there may be confusion about cue placement. Part of that may be due to clumsy cueing on the part of the lighting designer. During difficult transitions, the lighting designer also needs to listen to the stage manager. If there are repeated problems, ask if anything can be done to help out; make cues autofollows, link cues differently, or change the cue numbers in order to make it easier to rapidly speak all the numbers in the midst of the other commands.

On the other hand, it may not be semantics or structure, but mere unfamiliarity causing the transition to run into a wall. In those cases, the simplest solution

may be for the lighting designer to ask permission to call portions of the rehearsal so the stage manager can watch the sequence. Whether the sequence is perfect or a complete fiasco, the stage manager has had the chance to watch the sequence from a different perspective.

The Assistant

On a smaller show, the assistant may be the scribe, taking notes for the lighting designer, and keeping them sorted for the end of the rehearsal. Work note, cue note, stage manager note, and so on. On other shows the assistant may be updating the cue master on a laptop, so that at the end of the rehearsal a fresh cue master can be printed out. At the same time, the assistant is usually charged to make sure the light plot and the lighting database match with the reality in the theatre. Along with that, he or she also has to update, produce, and distribute all updated plot information or running sheets.

On larger shows with more gear, the assistant may be assigned to also be the spot wrangler, the moving light wrangler, or the fill-in-the-blank wrangler. The assistant may work with the production electrician to oversee work on the deck, including focus checks, work calls, quick fixes during breaks in the action, and deck moves during the show. The assistant may be the advance warning device, running backstage to get house lights or worklights turned off or on. The assistant may be another pair of eyes, watching the programmer's command line, watching (and recording cue numbers for) live scroller or live mover moves, or watching the clock. The assistant may be assigned as the buffer, to intercept everyone except the producer or director from interrupting the lighting designer's work on stage.

Does this sound like too many activities? In some cases it is. Larger shows can often have so many lighting elements simultaneously working at the same time that one assistant can't possibly update, record, negotiate, watch, and buffer the whole thing. Convincing some of the folks in management that not enough hands can cripple a show in a tight schedule, though, can be a tough sell. Sadly, this book has no suggestions how to explain that fact to a general manager. Maybe sock puppets.

Talking: Not on Headset

When the assistant is otherwise engaged, or possibly non-existent, a person may appear at the production table and wish to speak to the lighting designer, while he or she is working at cues onstage. At that point the designer may be listening to the console operator over headset. The person may not be aware that you're speaking to someone else, because they can't hear them. If you're in the midst of an involved sequence, be polite. Acknowledge the person with a wave of the hand or a nod. By acknowledging the person, they won't feel like they're being ignored, and they'll be less likely to get impatient until you're at a point where you can pause, in order to speak to them.

If you remove your headset in order to have the conversation, announce your departure: "Going off headset for a couple of minutes." That way folks know not to ask for you until your return, and the console operator will know there's time to save the show file and with luck, a bathroom break.

That said, not everyone who wishes to speak with you is going to have the best intentions of the show at heart. Or for that matter, have anything to do with the show. When possible, know the source of any face-to-face notes, and be able to prioritize their significance to the process. Lighting designers typically memorize the names or faces of the administrative and creative staff, or have a copy of the contact sheet nearby, in order to be attentive to opinions provided by new faces in the process—especially the producer. On the other hand, I once stopped working in the midst of a tech at the Metropolitan Opera House in order to take a note from someone I didn't recognize. While writing the note, I determined that the note-giver was a new usher.

The Laptop During the Tech

Most lighting designers avoid using their laptops during the rehearsal itself. They keep their eyes glued to the stage and the primary paperwork in front of them. They may update information back into their machine during breaks, but most folks get the machine out of the way so that the concentration can re-focus on the show in front of them.

The assistants, on the other hand, are another matter completely. In that role, the computer is the lifeline. While there may be a notepad available to scribble whatever information flies in their direction, most of the rehearsal is taken up with filtering all the notes and updates back into the machine. The laptop can be used to sort the information into lists that can be printed and distributed as each rehearsal ends. Usually there's the list of work notes ("Move the hazer to the loading rail"), the list for stage management ("Light cue 136 can be called together with the spots on Tee-boo downstage left"), cue notes ("the Producer thinks 124 should be more romantic"), or followspot notes ("Spot 2, watch out. I can see you presetting your pickup on Low-Raine before her appearance at the top of Act 2. Get a spot spike for that one").

While Internet connections are an invaluable tool for research or logistic updates in the middle of the

rehearsal, most folks will limit checking their email during breaks in a rehearsal.

Tech Rehearsal Lighting Tactics

When the technical rehearsal is stopped for a requested change in the lighting, come to an understanding of what change is needed, and then react as rapidly as possible. Inform the stage manager of any changes in the cue placement. Rewrite the affected cues. Consider the possibility of using another cue that has already been approved. If the cue must be built from scratch, consider which handles can be used to construct the light cue as rapidly as possible.

If cues are to be deleted, record the rejected sequences into the library block, instead of eliminating them completely. Keep a supplemental cue list, and when possible use the same numerical sequence in order to know where the cues came from. When cues get moved, always record cues into the library block in the correct mode (track or cue only). The mode often used for singular recording is cue only, not track.

Later rehearsals may be smooth enough to check the cues from other vantage points in the house. Sitting in the back of the house may reveal that a light cue is too dim. The balcony view may allow the designer to see unsightly, or misfocused, gobo patterns on the floor.

Before the End of the Technical Rehearsal

On most commercial shows, when the technical rehearsal ends the day, the people who sit around and talk about it usually include members of the creative team and the management office. Other heads may also be involved, but the crew only wants to know when they need to return, and they then put on their jackets, and go home. They're on the clock. In order to tell them their next starting time, or to "set the call," a plan must be in place before the end of the rehearsal. That plan may already be known. If it's not, however, the creative team and the production staff need to be individually prioritizing what needs to be fixed or ready for the next rehearsal, before this one is finished.

To that end, toward the end of the rehearsal, the assistant may be updating information and printing out work notes for the production electrician. At the same time, while compiling a list of scenes or transitions that need to be fixed before the next tech rehearsal begins, the lighting designer is still watching and making corrections in the current rehearsal.

During long rehearsals everyone needs to take occasional breaks, both bathroom and mental. Not only does that include the assistant and the stage manager, but the lighting designer should also occasionally step outside and clear his or her head as well. While the lighting designer is aware of the stage manager and console operator's status, if followspots are on their own channel, they may potentially be forgotten. If an assistant is with them on the other headset channel, it's his or her job to keep the designer aware of their current state. Regardless, if followspots are a part of the show, the lighting designer must remain aware of their status, and make sure they get breaks as well.

In addition to that, toward the end of rehearsals, while trying to prioritize, sort work notes, and finish lighting the rehearsals, lighting designers try to provide the followspots with a small nod of respect. During intense rehearsals, the followspots and the console operator are typically tied to their chairs maintaining sustained concentration longer than anyone else in the electrics department. And while both positions can be mentally grueling, the spot op's job is generally regarded as the more physically punishing of the two.

Combined with the fact that the spot ops often require more advance time to get to and from their spot positions, typical protocol is to send the spots up early (so they're in position when the tech begins), and shut them off early and bring them down (if they're no longer being used) before the end of the tech rehearsal call. Bringing them down before the end of the rehearsal requires good judgment; the director could have a sudden change of heart, and once the spots have left they may be needed again before the end of the night. Oops. The designer needs to be careful and not bring them down too early, but whenever possible, get the spot ops down. Not only is this a show of respect for their contribution, it also prevents the awkward moment when the spot operators arrive on an empty stage, ready for notes, only to discover that everyone else has left for the night.

End of the Technical Rehearsal

If the next work call has not already been finalized before the conclusion of the technical rehearsal, the production manager (or whoever is setting the departmental calls for the next day) ought to be at the production table before the tech rehearsal ends. Once the rehearsal is concluded, a miniature production meeting with the director, the stage manager, the creative team, and the production staff can quickly establish the technical priorities for the next rehearsal. This is the lighting designer's chance to submit the list of scenes and transitions that need to be fixed before the next rehearsal. Sometimes other folks want to fix those problem areas as well, sometimes not.

With the production electrician and the other department heads at hand, once the list of priorities has been established, it is then time to quickly determine what labor will be needed, and each department sets its call. Doing this quickly prevents the entire crew, waiting with their coats on, to hear the starting time for the next day, while the production staff slowly assembles at the production table for notes.

BEFORE THE FINAL REHEARSAL

The morning before the final rehearsal brings with it some amount of relief. On the good shows, most of the work and programming notes have been addressed. On the time-crunched shows, the morning call is the last chance to get all of the work notes that have been getting pushed back for days finally completed. Regardless of the insanity level, at least there will now be a punctuation point in the process, one way or the other. Before that can come, however, some thought has to be given to the bigger picture.

 A list to consider before the final rehearsal:

- Confirm the viewing position for the first performance, or get the tickets from the box office.
- Clean up and store all archive information. That way you won't get asked "Is this important?" by the cleaning crew while you're trying to make changes after the final rehearsal.
- If you haven't already, create the final set of show paperwork, including all cue sheets. That way, folks can use it during the final dress. If there are any mistakes, it will be noticed then, not during the first performance. Also, printing this now means you can pack the printer.
- Clean up the trash around the production table. That way, you won't be trying to make changes after the final rehearsal, as people surround you, furiously cleaning up around the production table.
- Once the final printout is complete, pack up the entire production table kit, so that it can merely be picked up and moved after the rehearsal. Keep it there at the table during the final rehearsal; that way you won't need it.

End of the Final Rehearsal

Before the final rehearsal starts, the schedule should be examined. Presumably, there will be a portion of time designated for cleanup. The production schedule may read "Tech Notes, 5:30 P.M. to 6:00 P.M." This time is typically scheduled to complete final notes, and clean the house. This may also be the final opportunity to make changes in the lighting cues while still looking at the both the stage and the monitors. Seeing cue changes onstage is always preferable to altering information on paper, or in a preview display. If the console notes can be separated into two categories (need to see to change, can change blind), prioritizing the board notes that require viewing will be clear. The need for prioritization can become more urgent, though, because the amount of time available isn't really 30 minutes. While the final tech note period is listed on the schedule as a 30-minute block of time, typical union protocol states that "wash-up" begins 5 to 15 minutes before the end of that call. Therefore, if tech notes are scheduled between 5:30 and 6:00, the lighting designer may really only have until 5:45 to make cue corrections while looking at the stage, before the stagehands arrive in the house to remove the production table.

With that time constraint in mind, as soon as the rehearsal has concluded, inform the production electrician of any refocus or work notes that will be required. A ladder crew will be organized and in place by the time the console notes are complete. If there is a choice between work notes or console notes, work on stage requiring the lighting designer's attention often takes precedence over console work. Depending on the complexity of the preshow check and preset call, it may be difficult to get a ladder crew onstage after half an hour without disrupting the preset flow of the production. Usually, any incomplete console notes can be addressed after the preshow check is complete, while looking at the preview display. However, depending on the number and severity of cue notes that need to be seen, it may be necessary to continue to work at the production table until the crew is sent out to take the table away.

After the final console note has been recorded, and the memory has been saved to the storage media, the console may only be needed to activate channels for work notes. If there are still many console notes, consider using an off-line editing program during the dinner break.

Let's briefly flip the schedule and look at it backwards. Depending on many variables, the show call for the stagehands may not begin until the house opens, or after the house has opened to seat the audience. If that's the case, the all work in the house must be completed before the crew has left the theatre for their dinner break. Lighting equipment, color, and focusing ladders must all be removed. The headsets need to be cleared, the cue light switch boxes may need to be moved to the stage manager's calling position, and the production table has to be completely struck. On top of that, the house invariably needs to be cleaned. Prioritize the activities that must take place before the performance begins. If it's important that a front of house instrument gets refocused, then that has to be addressed immediately; the curtain will be closed when the crew returns from dinner.

If you foresee running out of time, consider what could be delayed until after the crew returns from dinner. Present the situation to the production electrician and the house electrician; they're there to help you. If there are overhead instruments that require a refocus, that task might be delayed until after half an hour when the crew has returned, and the main curtain is closed. On the other hand, at the end of the rehearsal, the deck electricians could recolor the sidelight until final changes to the lighting cues have been completed. Then the overhead lighting instruments could possibly be refocused while the tech table is being struck.

As the tech table is being struck, before taking the bag of production table gear back to the stage manager's office, this time period, before the house is open, may be the last chance to determine and check out the viewing location, the lighting designer's office during the performance.

The Viewing Location

During the course of the show, the lighting designer's role usually shifts from being a participant in the production to being an observer. Depending on several factors, the viewing location may be provided with a headset allowing him or her to notate cue placements for any problems within the electrics department. In a broader sense, however, the lighting designer may be the only person on headset watching the show from the audience's perspective, and not occupied or assigned to perform cues or specific tasks. If that's the case, the lighting designer may be requested to take notes about any other visual or timing aspect of the show. To function in that capacity, the lighting designer should ideally be located with a complete view of the stage and have the ability to hear and speak to the board operator, stage manager, and the followspots. If it is possible to acquire a two-channel headset, the typical request is to be given the ability to both hear and speak to the stage manager and board operator on one channel, and the followspots on the second channel. Since presetting this headset configuration may take some time, the request should be made long before the beginning of the first performance.

Ideally, the viewing location will be somewhere other than in the light booth. Although there may be occasion for the lighting designer to speak to the board operator during the show, in most cases the board operator must concentrate solely on listening to the stage manager. The last thing a board operator needs is a lighting designer attempting to fix light cues live in front of an audience. Unless a situation develops that may involve the safety of someone in the theatre, respect the board operator's role in the performance. When given the choice, the lighting designer should choose to be in a separate location. Live changes made in haste can potentially contribute to opening night crises.

On occasion, the architectural design of the theatre may dictate that the lighting designer has to sit in the audience; no other location exists. Although a headset will inform the lighting designer of the current memory or cue, discretely taking notes with a flashlight is a challenge and typically there's very little available room for paperwork. Since the documents may no longer be immediately accessible, notes may be less specific, harder to understand, or completely illegible. If the note is not executed, the same problems will be repeated in the same cues during the next performance.

Like the route to the production table before the first tech, it's smart to determine the path to the viewing position sooner, rather than later. Waiting until just before curtain to determine the route or examine the viewing location can be catastrophic–everyone is busy with their own job trying to get the audience into their seats, or get ready to do the show. No one, at that point, has time to explain the path, unlock the door, get a worklight, or troubleshoot the headsets. Determine the route to be taken to the viewing location and, if needed, the light booth before the house opens. If the viewing location's perspective is restricted, this is also the time to determine how to move easily and quietly into the house to see the unobscured stage picture, which may include the top of the scenery, the downstage edge, or one side of the wings. This time can also used to meet the ushers who will allow the lighting designer uninterrupted passage during the performance.

While determining the route out to the viewing location is important, it is also smart to figure out the fast and quiet route to get backstage. There may be one route used during the production and intermission, whereas a second path might be necessary for the end of the show. In order to stay through the end of the curtain call, watch the house lights come up, and then quickly get backstage without getting caught in the traffic of the departing audience–it may actually be quicker using little-known fire exits rather than typical public access. Inquiries with the house heads and the front of house staff may unveil faster and quicker routes.

SUMMARY

Once the house has been cleared, and all possible work notes have been executed or scheduled for the preshow time period, the stage is often abandoned to a state much like the quiet before a storm. This is an excellent opportunity for the lighting designer to update any remaining paperwork that will reference documents while watching the show. If that process is complete, the time can be used to leave the space and do other things—for instance, go eat.

Chapter 14

The Performance

INTRODUCTION

This chapter examines the typical sequence of events that surround the performance, beginning with preshow checks, followed by a preset of the technical elements involved in the production. After the final preshow checks, the performance begins. At the conclusion of the first act, several changes may occur during the intermission.

After the conclusion of the performance, meetings may occur to exchange and discuss observations made during the show. Generally, these observations are collectively referred to as "notes." The number and severity of the notes often then determine how many changes and how much work needs to be accomplished before the next performance.

Typically, one performance is declared "opening night." It's often scheduled to include marketing, reviewers, and with luck, a party. In most situations, after opening night, major changes are no longer made to the production; the show is "frozen," and notes are often no longer given. In most cases this is because the director and the rest of the creative team have completed their contracts, and no longer attend the show on a nightly basis. As part of the creative team, once opening night takes place, the lighting designer's contract typically ends as well.

In preparation for the lighting designer's absence, the show is usually staffed so that once the production is open, all tasks are performed without his or her involvement. As such, during the initial performances the lighting designer is transformed from being an active participant into an observer, watching the show for light cue and timing notes. Instead of directing preshow focuses and overseeing intermission activities, the designer takes a step back and watches, to make sure that the lighting design will be properly executed once he or she is no longer actively participating in the show.

BEFORE THE PERFORMANCE

The time prior to a union-staffed performance is often broken into two distinct periods of time. The **preshow call** is the time when a reduced crew (if nothing else, the department heads) perform preshow checks to confirm that all technical elements related to the production are operational, and to note anything that must be fixed. Typically, this period of time is strictly confined to only observe and note the status of the technical elements. Nothing can be repaired, adjusted, or preset until the **show call**, when all of the technical personnel are required by contract to be in the theatre (the **show crew**). During the show call, any notes are addressed, and the stage is preset for the performance. Usually, the preshow call is scheduled for 90 minutes prior to the beginning of the performance, while the show call begins 30 minutes before the performance.

One factor that may affect this schedule relates to what the audience sees onstage when entering the theatre, known as the "stage preset." If the production doesn't use a main curtain, then all onstage work must be complete before the scheduled time the audience is admitted into the theatre. This preshow time period, when the lobby doors are opened to admit patrons, typically begins the moment "**the house is open.**" In many theatres in North America, the house opens 30 minutes prior to the scheduled beginning of the performance. If the preset for a union show is an open stage without a curtain, then the show call is sometimes moved back at least 30 minutes before the house opens, or 1 hour before the performance begins.

Obviously, the other main choice to present to the audience on their entrance is the main curtain being in. When that's the case, the management for the production may dictate that the show crew not be called until "half hour," the same 30-minute time period as "house open." When that is the case, the audience is often briefly delayed while the electrics crew quickly checks the front of house channels. Presuming there are no problems, the main curtain is then quickly flown in, the doors are opened to the audience, and the light check continues upstage of the curtain while the audience is seated in the house. In this scenario, the ability to rapidly check the function and focus of the lighting package gains new significance. Any burnouts downstage of the main curtain need to be rapidly located and identified. Reaching any FOH position takes some amount of time. Discovering any FOH problems before the house is open means a quick judgment must be made to determine if the affected instrument is critical to the show. If so, it may result in a delay opening the house while it's fixed. Unless it's a critical special, though, the non-functional instrument may merely be noted for lamp replacement during the next available work call. For this reason, critical FOH specials are often plotted next to a duplicate instrument that acts as a non-active twin. If the original special burns out, the second instrument is preset in every aspect. The two plugs are swapped at the dimmer, and the house opens without incident.

The Preshow Call

The electrics department begins the preshow call by activating each lighting instrument and checking every electrical device used or related to the production. The purpose of this **preshow check** is to be certain that everything is in working order, that the instruments have retained their focus, and that the color media has not faded or burned out. Although the lighting designer may have focus notes, and light board corrections, none of these notes can technically be addressed until the lighting system is checked and the show call begins.

The reason for this is simple: performing any notes or corrections makes no sense if the lights aren't functioning and the show can't take place. The only way to determine that the show is preserved, and the lighting system is functioning, is to do a complete preshow check. Therefore, the preshow check takes precedence. Besides, the preshow check may uncover other notes that can be addressed at the same time as the designer's work notes.

On the other hand, if there are major problems, priority instantly shifts to making certain that the lighting system is functional and the show can go on. In those situations, the designer's notes may be quietly set aside.

Electrics Preshow Check

Although the main curtain is in for the stage preset of *Hokey*, the entire show crew has been called to begin work "at hour" (60 minutes before curtain). While this will inevitably change once the show has gotten into a performance rhythm, initially having this extra breathing room allows the preshow checks to be relaxed, and everyone has time to double-check everything before the first performance.

Even though the light plot for *Hokey* doesn't include a large number of instruments, the overall list of items to be checked includes more than merely the instruments in the light plot. Many show-related electrical items used on stage are often the responsibility of the electric department. Worklights, running lights, cue lights, and any special effects are all checked to confirm that they are operational. In some cases, house lights, hall lights, or aisle lights may also be a part of the electric department's responsibility.

The preshow light check can be called many names, including dimmer check, burnout check, or channel check. Initially, the lighting designer may run the preshow check, or observe it and take notes. At some point before the show opens, the production electrician assumes this responsibility, and the lighting designer becomes another pair of eyes watching the work take place. Once the show opens, there may not be time before every performance to run an extensive preshow check of the entire light plot. Unless the overhead electrics were hit before the end of the technical rehearsal (or there's been an earthquake), it's often assumed that the focus of the instruments won't radically change, except for an occasional instrument that drops its focus. Extensive electric preshow checks are often selectively scheduled on an individual show-by-show basis.

Many folks believe that whenever filaments are quickly activated, the surge in voltage may cause them to prematurely burn out. To avoid this, once the system has been turned on, a programmed memory is often loaded that contains all of the instruments at a low percentage to "warm the filaments." These light cues were programmed in the *Hokey* disk as memories 900.7 and 950.7. All of the channels used in the show fade up to 30% in 10 counts to perform this function.

In most cases, before any of these checks are performed, the overall brightness of the space is reduced. Some of the worklights are turned off and the houselights are dimmed, in order to increase contrast and make the lights and the light beams more visible. If there are lights in the grid, those are usually left on, making it possible to see the silhouette of a nonfunctioning instrument.

Four different methods are commonly used to confirm that the instruments in the light plot are functional and focused. The **individual channel check** is exactly what it implies, sequentially looking at each channel one by one. Like the check performed after the hang, it's performed to confirm that the contents of each channel works and that the focus of the instruments hasn't changed. Starting with channel 1, each channel is activated to Full so that its beam can be seen. For a large light plot, this may not be time effective. If the time between the preshow call and the house opening is short, this type of preshow check will need to be performed rapidly. While the lighting designer, the production electrician, and most of the electrics department often have the focus for the entire show memorized, the console operator still needs to be nimble-fingered.

A second method that only checks for nonfunctioning instruments is referred to as the **burnout check**. Every channel that contains an instrument is activated to the same percentage (25 to 50%). Each position is visually scanned to confirm that every instrument has light coming out of it. Although this is faster than an individual channel check to determine burnouts, it also means that the focus of each instrument isn't addressed. With all of the lighting instruments on at one time, this check often requires a mental pattern while examining the entire light plot. Otherwise, while attempting to view all of the different locations simultaneously, any distraction may result in an entire position being visually skipped and forgotten.

A third method used to check burnouts is the **position channel check**. This is comprised of a series of cues programmed into computer lighting consoles. The cues are constructed so that only one position is activated in each cue. If a channel contains two instruments located in two positions, then the channel will come up in two different cues. This method provides a structure to the burnout check. By activating all of the instruments in a single position, it's possible to rapidly scan the entire position and see a dark spot, which may indicate a burned-out lamp. The intensity of the channels is usually recorded at a lower percentage, so that eyes aren't strained if looking into the lenses of the instruments. Since a single position is the focus of concentration, and every channel involved in the show is programmed into one of the memories, the possibility of accidentally skipping a position or an instrument is reduced. Programming the 900 cue

series into the console during load-in was for this purpose. If this method is used, the cues need to be updated with any changes or additions to the light plot before they're used. This prevents the possibility of mistaking an absent channel for a burnout.

Although this is a more systematic approach to the burnout check, this method still doesn't address the issue of focus. Unless the instrument has completely dropped focus, seeing any focus irregularities will be difficult.

Although the issue of focus isn't addressed, a position channel check still has its advantages. Since all of the channels are programmed into cues, the need to individually activate channels is eliminated. This means that anyone can hit the GO button to advance to the next light cue (and the next hanging position). If the console is in a remote location, the position channel check reduces the need for communication between the production electrician and the board operator. Instead of interpreting numbers shouted over a tiny sound monitor, the board operator only has to listen for the next GO. If the production electrician is the only electrician called to perform a preshow check, the cues in the position channel check sequence can be linked together as a series of autofollows. By programming a delay between each cue, the GO button can be pressed once; the production electrician can then move to the stage and scan each position as the cues load in sequence. If more time is required at a single position, the delay time can be lengthened.

A fourth method that allows both burnouts and focus to be checked is called a **system channel check**. This preshow check is also comprised of a cue series programmed into computer lighting consoles. In this case, the cues are constructed so that only one light system is activated in each cue. Since the focus of each system involves overlapping and matching beam edges, it's possible to rapidly identify any deviations in focus between instruments. Once the appearance of each system has been memorized, the entire light plot can be checked rapidly for both burnouts and focus. The primary purpose of the 950 cue series was to provide handles while constructing memories for the show. Their secondary purpose, however, is for this application. Since matching light systems are in adjacent memories, seeing burnouts, or focus anomalies, is relatively simple. Due to the fact that the number of systems is greater than the number of positions, there are more memories in the system channel check. Hypothetically, this means that the system channel check takes more time to complete, but a more complete picture of the light plot's current status will be known.

The other advantage of this method is the same as the position channel check. The GO button is the only keystroke used, communication is simplified, and the cues can be linked as autofollows, allowing the check to be performed by a single person. The only time paperwork may need to be consulted is when memories containing special channels aren't properly updated.

Shelley's Golden Rule: Complete the Check Before Fixing the Problems

When a nonfunctioning instrument is discovered during the electric preshow check, the first course of action is *not* to check the lamp, swap the plugs, or any other troubleshooting activity. The first thing to do when encountering an instrument that doesn't work is to:

Finish the electric preshow check.

Continue through the entire light plot to be certain that all of the problems are known. Then the troubleshooting can begin. Although this seems basic, it can often be overlooked. On more than one occasion, I've seen this basic rule forgotten. While an electric preshow check is being performed, a burnout will be discovered. The preshow check is interrupted to get a ladder onstage. The burnout is replaced and the ladder struck. After this interruption, the preshow check then continues, and a second nonfunctional instrument in the same position is discovered. The ladder must return to the stage, requiring a duplication of effort.

On the side, it's worthy to note that the culprit of a non-functioning instrument may not always be a burned-out bulb. A blown fuse in a dimmer rack may be the problem, causing several lamps to appear to be burnouts. Repairing a blown component may take little time to complete, but several minutes of troubleshooting may be required to identify the true source of the problem. If the preshow check is interrupted to address a single instrument, some amount of the finite time available may be consumed merely in gaining access to that unit. Only after the replacement lamp also fails to function will it become obvious that a larger problem exists, and time has now been lost that could have been applied to the troubleshooting process.

Anyway, it's worth noting that a nonfunctioning lamp may be the least of the problems encountered before a performance. Electronic components can fail at any time, most often when a system is turned on. This action sends a surge of voltage through the entire system. The more electronic devices involved in any production directly translates into that many more possibilities of things not working. Since every action consumes some amount of time, spending that time fixing a single instrument will be shown for the error

it is when an entire dimmer rack is later discovered to be nonfunctional. The status of the entire lighting system must first be determined. Time spent interrupting the preshow check to fix a single burnout may delay seeing the larger problem, which could ultimately delay or cause a performance to be lost.

Shelley's Notes: Electrics Preshow Checks

During the electrics preshow check, the worklights often need to remain on so that other tasks can happen at the same time, and it may be difficult to see the focus of the instruments. In these situations, the angle of observation can be used to the lighting designer's advantage. If the lighting designer stands in the path of the reflection of the beam, even under most worklights, the beam edges will be much more visible. As an example, activating channels 1 > 5 would turn on the downstage frontlight zone hung on the truss. To see the edge of the beams, rather than stand downstage facing the backdrop, the lighting designer would stand upstage, facing the instruments, and the reflection of light bouncing upstage. The downstage edge of the multiple beams will be seen on the floor. If the beams match, the focus is correct. If one beam edge is in a different plane, the instrument might have dropped and may require refocusing.

If worklights must remain on throughout the entire preshow check, the lighting designer can use this method to check the focus of the systems. By anticipating the direction from which the next system's beams will originate, the designer can move to a position on the stage to see the light reflected from the stage and the beam edges of that particular system.

Although submasters are often assigned to control systems during the performance, their use as preshow checking devices should not be dismissed. If a series of electrical devices is used in the light plot, the submasters can allow many of them to be checked, requiring only the activation of a handle instead of numerous channels. If color scrollers are used in a production, for example, one submaster can be assigned to all of the color scrollers, while a second submaster can be assigned to all of the channels controlling the instruments behind the scrollers. Using this method not only means that all of the color scrolls can be checked at one time, but it also means anyone can run the board instead of a trained console operator.

THE SHOW CALL

Once the show call begins, all work notes can be addressed, and the stage can be preset for the top of the show. Although the technical departments go about their tasks to preset the stage in a relaxed fashion, the activities are performed with a sense of purpose. Much of this pace is due to the fact that the schedule is finite. Problems may be discovered that were not apparent in the preshow checks, and if they need to be solved, they must be rapidly addressed. What's avoided is the possibility of having to delay the beginning of the performance. Not only does this make the evening that much longer, it might possibly extend the overall length of the show call beyond the length of time allowed. When that occurs, members of several different unions may automatically be escalated into the higher additional pay rate of overtime.

Overhead Work Notes

If the notes include any work in the overhead electrics, standard operating procedure is to keep performers offstage or away from the affected area until all ladder work is complete. Although this varies from production to production, the reason is twofold: first, performers are kept away from the work area to be certain that they remain absolutely safe. Second, if the ladder needs to move around the stage, additional people just get in the way. To reduce this inconvenience, effort is made to complete the notes and presets with controlled dispatch. The sooner the stage can be "given over" to the performers, the more quickly the stage environment's preshow rhythm can be restored.

In this effort to clear the stage, any electrical work notes are addressed first. Because the ladder may be buried behind offstage equipment, some time may be involved in accessing it. While the ladder is being brought to the stage, the work notes are identified by location. The traffic pattern of the ladder is then determined so that it spends as little time as possible on the performance surface, and begins the notes at the farthest location first. In that way, if time runs short, the ladder won't be caught in the most distant location. Unless instruments are hung too high to reach with a regular ladder, any work or focus notes involving the sidelight booms are delayed until the overhead ladder has been returned to its storage area.

Sidelight Check

Once the overhead work notes are complete, the sidelight boom instruments are often then recolored, and any electrical tasks on the deck are performed. These activities are accomplished, and checked, using the color cards. Usually, the sidelight booms aren't checked until after their color and templates have been preset for the top of the show. Since they're the closest instruments to the stage, sidelights often receive the roughest treatment and require the most attention.

More than that, however, waiting to check the sidelights until after they've been recolored means that the color units will match the color cards, and any unintentional refocusing that may have occurred while the units were being prepared will be spotted. Once the sidelights are checked for focus and color, the rest of the systems, specials, and rovers can be checked for their function and focus using the floor cards.

The key to accelerating these checks is to determine what channels need to be seen, define how to quickly confirm that the instruments are correct, and how to rapidly activate them. If the same collection of channels will be requested in the same order before every performance, consider recording the sequences into cues or groups. Although the sidelights can be checked channel-by-channel, it may be quicker to record groups that activate one side of one system at a time. By matching the shutter cuts and the beam edges, the focused accuracy of an entire sidelight system can more rapidly be checked. A different approach might be to create a handle that contains all of the channels assigned to a single boom. When activated, all of the side shutter cuts can be compared. A third approach is to create a handle that contains all of the instruments on one side of the stage. The *Hokey* light plot has been programmed so that submasters 10 and 11 perform this function.

When one of these two submasters is used to check one side of the boom sidelights, the sub is initially brought up to a low level, so that the focus of the units can be checked. This is achieved by walking up and downstage while looking into the instruments to see the centered filament in the reflector. Afterwards, the submaster is brought to Full, to check side shutter cuts off of the scenic backing, and top shutter cuts off of the borders. If it's necessary to check sidelight focus under worklights, consider using the angle of observation to see the edges of the beams. Stand at center and look down at the stage. The bottom beam edges should be visible, along with the side shutter cuts. If the side cuts are compared to the locations of the black masking legs, it's possible to determine which instruments will require a shutter adjustment. To finish the sidelight check, any rovers used for that portion of the performance are activated and focused.

Lighting Console Notes

If the console notes were corrected with an off-line editing program during dinner, the lighting designer need only view or assist with the preshow checks. He or she can then proceed to the viewing location. On the other hand, if no off-line editing could take place, updating any console notes should be avoided until the initial checks have been completed, and the console operator can listen to the lighting designer give corrections.

Depending on the number of notes and the amount of time available, it may be necessary to prioritize the notes. When the console operator or stage manager says "stop," stop. Allow the console operator a chance to prepare for the show. In addition to that, the lighting designer now needs to move to the viewing location.

When programming console notes, a light cue may need to be seen on stage to determine the problem and apply the correction. Presuming that the problem is coming from an instrument upstage of the main curtain, this is one situation that may utilize the FOH inhibitive submaster. This scenario is one of the reasons why the curtain warmers, conductor special, and house lights are not programmed into that sub. Deactivate the front of house inhibitive sub for *Hokey* (sub 24), and then load the cue into the lighting console. Since no current channels in the FOH are affected, there will be no visual light change from the audience's perspective. Backstage, however, it will be possible to examine the problematic light cue and correct the memory. Once the problem has been determined, it can be recorded into the memory using the preview display, after which the fader can be cleared. If there is FOH light in the cue, it must be recorded in the preview display. If recorded live, the FOH light may be erased from that cue. When the process is complete, don't forget to restore the FOH inhibitive submaster to its show level. Otherwise, the FOH light will remain inactive for the entire act.

Final Light Board Check

At this point, the entire lighting package should be ready for the performance. As a final double check, however, the preset sequence programmed at the beginning of each act is viewed.

In the case of *Hokey,* the following preset sequence has been programmed into the computer console:

- *Memory 100.4* = All of the stage left sidelights (used in the act) brought up to a level of 70%. The intensity isn't so bright that it hurts the eyes to look into the lights, but it's bright enough to see errant shutters spilling on masking or scenery. Comparing the sidelights to a color card will confirm that the instruments have been correctly colored. Standing in the focus points and looking into the reflectors of the instruments will confirm that the lamp is centered in the reflectors.
- *Memory 100.5* = All of the stage right sidelights (used in the act) brought up to a level of 70%. Again, the colors of the instruments can be checked, along with the focus and the shuttering.

- *Memory 100.6* = All of the cues (used in the act) are "piled on" together. After that, the FOH inhibitive submaster (sub 24) is then taken to zero, and the cue is recorded. This cue is known as the "super cue," since it contains the highest recorded level for each channel in that specific act. Since the channels in the super cue reflect only their highest intensity in the cues, it's possible to see if a problem warrants immediate attention. As an example, although an errantly-focused instrument is discovered while looking at the super cue, the severity of the problem is lessened because its intensity is only 30%. On the other hand, if the channel is reading at 100%, a check of the cues may be warranted. If it is programmed at Full in cues with few other instruments, the problem channel may be visually apparent during the performance. If so, time should be taken to restore its focus.

The super cue is often viewed from down center just upstage of the main curtain, the closest approximation of the audience's perspective. From this viewpoint, any abnormalities will be most apparent. If the scenery stack is reset to a translucency and a black scrim, be certain to activate the channels upstage of the translucency before the show begins. Be certain there are no light leaks under the drops, and check that no groundrow instruments have been knocked out of focus. Although other sidelight notes can be addressed once the curtain flies out, when problems involving the translucency are seen in front of the audience, there's little that can be done to fix them.

After these checks have been accomplished, the final preshow check of the lighting system is complete. The light board can now be loaded with the first memory of the show, in this case, memory 100.7. If the preset is a black stage, a submaster containing a backlight or downlight system upstage of the main curtain can be activated to provide some light on the stage. After the worklights have been turned off, the stage manager can ask the board operator for the submaster to be taken to zero to be ready for the first light cue. The light board is ready for the performance.

The Viewing Location

Ideally, when the lighting designer determined the path to the viewing location, it was also possible to check the environment of the space. The headset, along with the monitors, and the sound feed were all operational. The dimmer controlling the worklights in the space was functional. When returning to the viewing location immediately before the show, double-check all of these elements. If possible, arrive in the viewing area early to arrange the workspace and be ready for the performance.

THE PERFORMANCE

If there's no one else on headset taking notes for the production, the lighting designer should be certain to be at the viewing position before the performance begins. During initial performances, the stage manager may still be fine-tuning the cue placement for several elements during difficult transitions. In that situation, the lighting designer can also be an analytic observer. Presuming that the lighting designer and the stage manager now have a working relationship, the lighting designer's separate perspective may be valuable to the stage manager, providing feedback about complex cue sequences. Before the show begins, the lighting designer should report to the stage manager on headset, and then say nothing else unless requested.

Notes Taken During the Performance

Most of the notes taken by the lighting designer can be divided into four categories: cue content and timing, cue placement, work notes, and followspots. The primary documents used to construct the cues now becomes the reference material used while taking the notes: the cue master, the magic sheet, the cheat sheet, the color cards, the floor cards, and the followspot cue sheets. The light cues, or a printout, may be on hand to display the latest cue content for each memory, if no monitor is available. The light plot can be used as an instrument schedule.

The notes regarding cue content, fade times, and placement are typically written on one sheet of paper. Since the cue content and timing changes need to be given to the console programmer, and the cue timing and placement changes need to be provided to the stage manager, the single document can be used for verbal note sessions with both of them. In the lighting designer's absence, the document can be photocopied and a separate copy provided to both personnel.

Notes regarding physical changes or tasks to be addressed in the next work notes calls can be recorded on a fresh work notes sheet and given to the production electrician after the show. If followspots are used in the production, those notes are usually written directly on the followspot cue sheets, so that they can be photocopied or updated before the next performance.

Fresh, dated pages should be used for each performance. The notes are written as legibly as possible, since an incomprehensible note merely guarantees that the note will be taken again. The cue number is clearly written for each note. If the note is directed to a specific person, the initial of the person's name may be written next to the note.

When the notes are delivered and changed, one method is to draw a single line through the note, but taking care not to obscure it. Being able to still see the note, after it's been given, allows the board and work notes sheets to remain readable as archival documents, stored in a folder or notebook. Maintaining this archival record allows the lighting designer to trace the changes that were made in each memory or cue. It also means that when the new console operator makes an honest mistake, time is not lost. If the storage media is loaded into the just-updated RAM by accident, the notes can be re-read, and the changes can be fed back into the lighting console a second time. If need be, these documents can be photocopied and given to the proper parties prior to the next performance.

Shelley's Notes: Identifying the Mystery Hot Spot

Sometimes it's not possible to have a monitor at the viewing location, displaying the contents of the cue. Granted, the stage manager will state the cue number on each call. When watching the show, however, a cue may appear that suddenly includes an unwanted hot spot in the middle of the stage. If several systems are involved in the cue, it can be frustrating trying to define the problem instrument.

Presumably, a single instrument is creating the hot spot. If the show is using an extensive instrument inventory, however, even that assumption may be erroneous. Taking a note is certainly recommended, but it may be possible to visually determine the channel. As performers walk through the hot spot, study the shadows on the floor. The number and direction of the shadows will provide clues to the origin of the light that's hitting that portion of the stage. Better yet, the hot instrument is probably causing the darkest shadow. Between the direction and the depth of shadow, an educated guess might be made as to the exact cause of the hot spot.

Intermission

Typically, the lighting designer will go backstage at intermission. Regardless of what happened during the first act, the lighting designer should not give any notes unless requested. Ideally, the only reason for the lighting designer to be backstage at intermission is to answer any questions posed by other personnel.

In some cases, however, the lighting designer may be requested to come backstage and make a design decision during a complex intermission change. Or there may be a different translucent backdrop that should be checked. It may be realized that the note regarding a focus change in a rover may not have been passed on. If any of these scenarios possibly occurs, then the lighting designer must not only return backstage at intermission, he or she needs to be there as soon as the intermission starts. Waltzing in after the work has been completed, only to ask for the same work to be performed again, is not fair to the crew. As soon as the curtain closes on the final cue, leave the viewing location and proceed backstage. Have respect for the crew's time by being on time.

If there is a color change in the sidelights, the preset memories for the second act should allow any instruments requiring a second focus to be seen. The super cue will show any instruments that may be suddenly hitting scenery.

Attempt to return to the viewing position before the second act begins.

The Bows

In many shows, the bow cue involves two memories. Much like the method used to create the memories at the end of Act 2, scene 1, in *Hokey*, the bow cues at the end of the show utilize the FOH inhibitive submaster. Initially, a cue was created that lit the entire stage and included frontlight (memory 486). This was recorded as the bow ride. After the inhibitive FOH submaster was pulled down to zero, the remains of the cue were recorded as the memories prior to and after the bow ride, becoming the bow preset (memory 485) and bow postset (memory 487). If the bows are strictly choreographed, this structure can continue to be recorded into the memories, so that the light cues match each opening and closing of the curtain.

Although it may seem unnecessary to watch the bows, cues still occur that need to be checked. On opening night, though, actions may take place that not only require the lighting designer's perspective for analysis after the fact, but they may possibly demand his or her active participation.

During opening night bows, people can do funny things. Directors can change their mind without telling anyone. Leads can suddenly be inspired to create their own bow sequence and walk downstage where there is no light. Or the audience may applaud longer than expected. At this point, the bows can suddenly become a free-for-all. The stage manager may have to abandon memory numbers, and for the first time, ask for specific actions instead. When these situations develop, the handles that have been programmed into the computer light board may be able to help prevent the wheels from falling off. If a main curtain is used, the first handle that should be considered is the front of house inhibitive submaster (sub 24), which will fade and restore the front of house light while

leaving the rest of the stage unchanged. If the stage manager needs to fade the entire stage to black and then restore, the Grand Master may be used. If no Grand Master exists, then the upstage inhibitive submaster (sub 12) can be faded and restored simultaneously with the FOH inhibitive sub (sub 24).

During these moments of intensity, the first thing that the lighting designer should do is get on the headset and not say a word. If the stage manager and the console operator need help, they'll ask. Unless your perspective allows you to see an accident about to occur, stay out of the way. Your voice will interfere with the stage manager being heard. If you're addressed, give the information requested as succinctly as possible, telling the console operator numbers, not labels, and then turn the microphone off. Don't offer advice, encouragement, or comments about the magic of the moment.

Spontaneous moments like these provide excellent examples of why it's advised not to release followspot operators after their final cue on opening night. Suddenly there may be the need for the followspots to cover the lead couple in the dark on the apron. In addition, consider that numerous people may be onstage during the bows who aren't used to being blinded by light. Disoriented, they may attempt to exit backstage, but instead go to locations on the stage that are dark. The momentary blindness and disorientation may possibly lead to severe injury if they're close to the edge of the stage. Though the followspots may be used to direct focus during the bows, during moments like these they should be considered beacons, to light the floor in front of people in the dark, so that the edge of the stage can be seen.

If the wheels do indeed fall off, and the board is without any more memories to load, choices must be made on the spot. If there's silence on the headset, find a memory number to load, and be ready to give it over the headset. On the other hand, it may make more sense to remain silent, and just leave the board where it is. This may result in the front of house lights crashing onto the main curtain. Or the choice may be made to fade the light board to black as the curtain closes. Let the stage manager make these choices.

AFTER THE SHOW

Presuming that the bows have been uneventful, get backstage as quickly as possible. There may be a production meeting immediately following the performance that may alter the work calls in the morning. In addition to that, the lighting designer must be certain that the director is given the opportunity to give notes. The director may have a limited amount of time available to meet after the show, and if the meeting doesn't take place, there's no guarantee that the notes will be addressed by the next performance. To be able to instigate the notes, some amount of time may be required to analyze, organize, and prioritize the next day.

A private production meeting may be required with the production electrician, to devise a plan of attack for the next work call. Then he or she can prioritize and ask for the proper number of crew people. If the work call has already been previously decided by the time the lighting designer reaches backstage, it may be deserted. Leave any notes in prespecified locations and leave the theatre.

The Departure

If it's the last night of the lighting designer's contract, notes may still be received. Although these notes are probably about the performance just seen, they may also be applicable to future incarnations of the same production. Sometimes, they may be desperate notes that require extensive blind programming in the lighting designer's absence. If that's the case, remember that no programming can take place until the next show call. There's time to devise a plan that will attempt to meet those demands.

Before the lighting designer's departure, the production electrician must be provided with accurate, up-to-date documentation so that the production runs smoothly in the lighting designer's absence. Even if the paperwork has scribbles on it, the information is then accurate. Although updating archival paperwork may be boring, if or when it's needed, it had best be accurate for the sake of the show.

Distribute any last work notes and board notes. Thank everyone on the crew for his or her help and support in mounting the production. Without everyone's involvement, effort, and support, the production would never have been possible.

Out of the Theatre

Go home. If needed, update the paperwork and resend it out to the appropriate folks as either softcopy documents or PDF's. Consider writing the notes as emails, when applicable, and send them to all the relevant folks. That way, things that can be accomplished prior to receiving the notes at the theatre can take place.

Analyze what went right and what went wrong. As always, there are many lessons to be learned from the experiences of the day, and from the show. If time is taken to examine what went wrong, it may be possible to avoid making the same mistakes again in the future.

If you'll be back the next day, analyze, prioritize, and prepare the notes that you'll bring with you. The morning work call will typically begin with projects that require lots of worklight. If the console operator isn't involved in those activities, he or she may then be available to program console notes. If an off-line editing program can be utilized, consider using it. If there's a lot of work to be completed before the stage can be set to look at light cues, stay out of the crew's way. After the notes requiring worklight are completed, the stage will be set to look at light cues. Construct a preliminary list of the scenes and light cues to be viewed. Consider scheduling the sequence so that the last scene before lunch will be the first scene worked on in the afternoon rehearsal. After consultation with the carpentry staff, the list will be used to schedule the scene order.

On the other hand, the lighting designer might have seen the show for the last time. On most productions, the lighting designer is present only through the opening. The notes have been distributed and it's time to pack the bags.

SUMMARY

This concludes *A Practical Guide for Stage Lighting*. Though this text has presented one practical viewpoint of the events surrounding the installation of a production, there are many more variations and unknowns that can affect any show.

Experience is the harshest instructor. A willingness to learn is what prevents the same mistake from happening more than once. On the other hand, there are situations when, no matter what the lighting designer may be prepared for, the events can border on the catastrophic. Here is one lesson that the reader will hopefully never have the opportunity to experience.

Tales from the Road: A Lifetime in Italy One Night

One time long ago, Ballet Trockadero de Monte Carlo was touring Italy. The Trocks, as they are known, are an all-male dance company that performs parodies of dance classics. As such, all of the guys wear ballet toe shoes, which is no small feat (or feet, in the case of Shannon, who wore 13-1/2 double EEs). When we initially started performing on the Italian raked stages, performances were often punctuated by offbalance pirouettes resulting in spinout sprawls rivaling the Indy 500. By the time we arrived in a small port city in the "heel" of the country, everyone had adjusted to the slanted stages.

I had been told that the theatre owned a dance floor, which was a relief, since we didn't travel with one. I was thrilled with the prospect that, for a change, we were actually going to be performing on a surface that didn't have gaps in the stage, allowing us to see through the floor into the basement. I had also been told that they had all of the lighting equipment that we required. I was mis-informed on both counts.

The theatre had a proscenium and a small ante-proscenium, which is essentially a second proscenium opening and a small offstage area downstage of the actual picture frame opening. The ante-proscenium is where the curtain was controlled, but the space wasn't large enough for the huge tripods we eventually used for sidelight booms. After we arrived, I discovered that the dance floor was actually kitchen linoleum. I also found out that the lighting equipment was being rented from a remote location. Little did I know that meant another part of the country. But that's all later. The day started when Chewie and I showed up at the theatre. Chewie was our interpreter and thought we were a fun dance company. The load-in crew greeted us onstage: two carpenters.

I had gotten used to the Italian method of rigging. I ran around the stage placing pieces of wood on the deck, stating as I went "This is a border, this is a leg, this is an electric." The carps nodded, scrambled up to the grid, and proceeded to nail the Italian version of sheaves (which look a lot like large sewing thread spools) into the wooden grid. They then proceeded to drop down several lines of 1/4-inch hemp, returned to the deck, scabbed together several pieces of 1×2, tied the 1/4-inch hemp to it, and presto! It's a batten!

This is a batten? Not to my young eyes. Certainly this method was adequate for the legs and borders. None of the masking moved during the show, so it didn't matter if goods weren't counterweighted. There wasn't that much weight on each batten, because the fabric was so lightweight it was translucent at best. Unfortunately, this was also the construction method they intended to use for the electrics. While I was dubious at best, I couldn't get too concerned about this "detail" since there didn't seem to be any instruments to hang on said "electric" battens.

Around 10:30 A.M. the electricians arrived and unloaded the electrics package they had transported from a distant province. They had almost completed unloading all of the lighting equipment when the head electrician slapped himself on the forehead. This translates into almost any language: "Damn! I forgot the...."

It turned out what had been left behind were the c-clamps needed to hang the instruments from the battens. I was getting a little nervous about amount of remaining stage time and didn't want them to leave

again. They suggested gaff taping the instruments to the 1×2. I expressed my concern that the focus might not work real well, as well as my lack of confidence that the lights would stay up in the air. This entire train of thought was expressed rather simply: barely shake head, squint eyes, and say "No." That also translates pretty well into any language. So far, Chewie had been fairly bored, since there was little for him to do.

Eventually, someone came up with a spool of metal containing a series of holes that, in English, is called plumber's tape. After some discussion this became our c-clamps. A piece of plumber's tape was wrapped around the 1×2, and then bolted together through the hole in the yoke. Although it wasn't very pretty, or very secure, it was certainly more functional, and a little safer, than the gaffer tape. We all laughed and bonded and applauded our new method of hanging instruments.

That's about the time that the head electrician slapped himself on the forehead again, which this time translated into "Damn! The gel frames." Well, I still really didn't want them to leave since I wasn't sure how far this gear had actually traveled, and we still had a lot of plumber's tape. After four pieces were cut, they were then bolted together. It's a gel frame!

A gel frame? Well... sure. Except the bolts were too large to slip through the color frame holders, and the tape was too stiff to be bent. Well, so much for any color changes. We proceeded to bolt the color into the instruments. The rest of the afternoon was spent raising the non-counterweighted electrics to something like trim without killing anyone, pointing the instruments in the proper direction, and cajoling the salt water dimming system to function. After initial misgivings, the somewhat nervous dancers were convinced to perform their onstage warm-ups wearing pre-World War II hard hats.

Our evening opened with confidence; the performance began with *Yes Virginia, Another Piano Ballet*. A sendup of Robbins's *Dances at a Gathering*, the original is a pleasant collection of simple dances performed by 10 dancers, a grand piano, and a pianist. The Trocks version approached the piece with a lone piano onstage, one man, and three "ballerinas" with attitude. At one point in the choreography, petty rivalries between two of the ballerinas would result in a moment of slapstick. A line of three dancers was formed upstage, with the man in the middle holding the two ballerinas' hands. This line then swept in an arc around the front of the stage past the piano. One of the women, intent on harming her rival, would purposefully place herself as a pivot during this arc like the children's game "crack the whip," which would result in the second woman slamming into the piano.

One of the divas in the company named Zami could play the second woman's role in this moment to perfection. Not only could he come to a screeching halt against the piano without harming himself, he would "mount" the piano and hold himself off the floor, with both legs in the air straddling the keyboard. Since the stage was raked, we had placed chocks under the wheels of the piano to prevent it from moving. What we didn't know was that the chocks weren't very effective. So there we were in mid-performance. I was calling cues from stage right while the threesome joined hands. They swung the arc. The other "woman" whipped Zami into the piano. As expected, there was huge laughter.

And then the piano started to move. With Zami pasted to the corner of the piano like a fly on the windshield, the baby grand imperceptibly shuddered, and then started oh so slowly to inch its way downstage on the rake toward the orchestra pit.

My jaw slacked. Little sounds made their way out of my throat. Then I started looking around. Fast. One of the stagehands standing next to me had a cane. I grabbed it (sorry about that) and reached around the corner of the masking leg with the cane, snaking the hook of the cane around the upstage leg of the piano. This at least slowed it down. Unfortunately, this was an excellent demonstration of the laws of motion. Moreover, the laws were winning. Zami, the piano, the cane, and I were all slowly being dragged into the pit, with Zami still astride the piano.

Chewie grabbed my legs. An electrician grabbed his. Suddenly a human chain was formed backstage, one end clutching the radiator mounted to the side wall. In the back of my mind I began to wonder where the ice was. Finally, Zami got off the piano and continued to dance. Granted, he looked a little terrified; hey, if I had been riding a piano to my certain doom, I would have looked a little funny too.

But we made it to the end of the piece. The piano didn't move any more, we finished the piece, we did bows, we were going to make it out of this mess and regroup at intermission . . . and then the curtain didn't close. Chewie screamed incessantly into the headset without effect. Finally, after some amount of screaming from the electricians on the opposite side, the curtain slowly jerked to a close.

Ralph, the curtain operator, seemed like a nice enough fellow, but either his family tree didn't fork, or he was equipped with the attention span of a dinner plate. Regardless, the situation had to be addressed; something had to be done to get the curtain under control. After some amount of discussion, it was determined that his tardiness was due to his inability to pull the ropes controlling the curtain while keeping the telephone handset next to his ear to hear the cues. As intermission ended, I turned around in time to see the crew gaff taping the handset to Ralph's head while Chewie sternly explained to him in no uncertain terms that he should pull his rope any time he heard the word "Go."

The second act started with the Trockadero tribute to the Olympics, a duet for two in Greek togas called *Spring Waters*. During the piece, the sailors in the audience felt it appropriate to throw money at the dancers and scream encouragement in Italian. Since none of us understood any Italian, we thought they were screaming "Bravo." Apparently, though, the sailors were enthusiastically informing the dancers how much fun a sailor could be. Anyway, the dance ended. We did the bows. Ralph and his taped head closed the curtain on cue. We were a hit, but now we had to reset the stage and continue with the next piece.

During the pause, I ran onstage to get the coins swept out of the way, chase the dancers onto the stage who were to perform in the next piece, *Pas de Quatre*, and chase the *Spring Waters* dancers off, who were busy picking up the coins. I met Chewie down center. I said quickly "As soon as we get this cleaned we'll be ready to *go*," when I looked behind him to see Ralph's taped head snap up at the magic word and pull the curtain open. Chewie dove offstage into the middle of the saltwater dimmers and the tape deck. I was not so fortunate. I ended up diving into the ante-pro with Ralph, who was so busy congratulating himself for finally hearing a cue that he didn't realize that I shouldn't be standing there in his arms in the first place.

I almost panicked. Should I just casually stroll around the proscenium in full view of the audience? Or do I just hope that Chewie would notice I was missing, and be able to read my call sheets? I was frozen like the proverbial deer in the headlights. Suddenly I saw a hole in the proscenium wall. I bent over and could see the tape deck through the hole! I shoved my arm into the hole, and could feel my hand sticking out of the other side of the wall.

I looked at the stage, with the four dancers now in preset position, and raised my index finger in the direction of the tape deck. When the proper moment arrived, I dropped my finger . . . and the music started! I then raised my finger in the direction of the saltwater dimmer operators and, at the proper moment, dropped my finger . . . and the lights changed! Using my index finger to call the show, the piece ran flawlessly, even the numerous cues involved in the curtain call. And Ralph even got the curtain right. After the end of the show, Chewie and I sat at the piano and bonded over a bottle of tequila.

Glossary

Actual Throw Distance (ATD)   The shortest measured distance between an instrument and its focus point, which defines the size and intensity of the light beam.

All-skate   Based on skating rink session periods when anyone can get on the rink and do anything they want. In a theatrical context, an all-skate is the rehearsal or work call where too much needs to take place in too little time. The compressed schedule results in everyone executing what's individually perceived as tasks necessary to achieve the common goal, but without any regard how those tasks may impact anyone else's ability to achieve their individual goals as well.

Attribute   Quality or characteristic belonging to functions, commands, or structures in a computer lighting environment or an automated lighting fixture.

Autofollow   A light cue or any action that begins at the moment the previous cue or action has completed its time duration. More loosely, any light cue that is linked to a previous cue. Its initiation may begin before the previous cue has completed its time fade.

AutoPlot   A collection of macros written in the Vectorworks environment by Sam Jones, with initial encouragement by Stan Pressner and Craig Miller.

Baby-sit the rig   Overseeing and performing basic maintenance on a light plot that's only being used for performance; replacing burned out lamps, burned out color, or tipping instruments up that have dropped their focus.

Back   Restore, return to a former state. Also refers to the button on lighting consoles that is pressed to load the sequential memory into a fader immediately prior to the current one.

Backstage   The area of the stage typically concealed from the audience's view.

Batten   A hanging location suspended over a performance space, typically comprised of steel pipe. When part of a *counterweight system*, its height above the stage can be changed. Usually the batten has scenery, masking, or lighting equipment hung from it.

Beam angle   The internal cone of a light beam created by an instrument. Usually defined in degree increments, it is the area of the light beam where the light is 50% of the intensity of that instrument's hot spot.

Beam spread   The overall size or width of a light beam created by an instrument. Often defined in degree increments. See *field angle*.

Beating a Dead Horse   The point when the same sequence has been tech'ed so many times that everyone at the production table can act the scene, dance the dance, or sing the songs. Meanwhile the director/choreographer/person in charge still isn't satisfied. After ten times, the phrase is officially upgraded to "puree-ing the dead horse". After twenty times, lots are drawn to see who wins and gets to be the horse.

Blackout   A lighting state in which all intensity to all lighting instruments is off; complete darkness. Also referred to in the speed at which the state is achieved, usually in zero seconds.

Blamestorm   The point when all is in ruins and shards, and the only thing left is for everyone to find someone else to blame. More often than not, the catastrophe is the fault of whoever is absent. See *Equity Deputy Elections*.

Blind record   The process of altering channel intensity or other information contained within the lighting console without the results being seen on stage.

Blind screen   A computer display showing the channel level information of a light cue without the channels being activated to their displayed levels. Also shortened to *blind*. Depending on the console, also called *preview*.

Blocker cue   A cue that contains hard commands for all channels from previous cues. Tracking channels recognize the hard command and assume the level programmed in the cue. The same channel following the blocker cue assumes the level provided within the blocker.

Blocking   The physical movement patterns of performers onstage (or offstage) during a straight play. For large groups, typically in opera, it's more often referred to as "staging". In dance, the movement patterns are typically more involved, and referred to as "choreography."

Border   A narrow horizontal masking piece typically suspended above the stage, designed to conceal overhead lighting instruments and goods from the audience, and to provide an upper visual limit to the scene. Also called a *teaser*.

Center-center   A reference point in the middle of the playing area. Typically located on centerline midway between the up and downstage light lines.

Centerline   Architectural term typically based on the imaginary point that is the bisected width of plaster line. That point, extended as a perpendicular line, is the centerlin.

Chromatic aberration   The prismatic fringe seen at the edge of a pool of light like a rainbow; often seen when an ellipsoidal is focused to a sharp edge.

Color Frame   A frame which holds the color filter in the guides (color frame holder) at the front of a lighting instrument. Usually constructed from metal or flame-resistant cardboard.

Column   Vertical line of information.

Command line   Location on a computer display reflecting keypad function instructions given to a lighting console.

Console   An electronic mechanism containing the CPU, RAM, and control apparatus that, when connected to dimmers, remotely controls their voltage output to instruments and other devices.

Continuity hour   Phrase typically used in a union labor situation. It refers to physical labor other than typical work involved in show call, taking place for 1 hour. Typically applied to a separate hour of pay, either immediately prior to the half-hour show call, or immediately following the performance.

Cross-fade   The act of changing to a new visual look on stage. Using a manual preset board, the term often means moving a master fader between two banks or rows of dimmers preset in different configurations. When using a computer console, the term often means loading a new memory into a fader.

Cue   A single lighting state, also called a look, or a memory, usually assigned a fade time. For a manual light board, the specific level assignments for dimmers or other physical handles. For a computer lighting console, a unit of RAM memory containing specific channel intensities. The word is also used

as the command given, usually by a stage manager, to initiate a predetermined action.

Cue content   The level intensity information for all channels in a cue.

Cue information   The level intensity information for all channels, and any other associated time or function attributes associated with the same cue.

Cue list screen   A monitor display listing a sequential list of recorded cues and any associated attributes.

Cue only   Type of recording function that memorizes the change in channel intensity for only the affected cue. Channels changed in the cue revert to intensity from the previous cue in the next cue.

Cue screen   A monitor display typically showing the intensity and attribute levels for each channel.

Cue to cue   Period of time when technical elements, sequences, and transitions of production are rehearsed, with or without performers. Stage action is abbreviated to the action solely required to provide a timed standby before a cue. See *dry tech*.

Cyclorama   Fabric drop or wall, typically placed upstage of the performance area, often used to represent sky or distance. Shortened name is *cyclo* or *cyc*. Fabric versions constructed from a single piece in order to be used as translucencies are often referred to as *seamless*.

Dead   The state of equipment, gear, or containers no longer having a purpose applicable to the current situation. See *empty*.

Default   A preset value that a lighting console or device assumes, or a course of action that either will take, when the user or programmer specifies no overriding value or action.

Delay   Dependent on software platform, one of the two time durations that can occur with the initiation of a memory on a computer lighting console. Usually defined as amount of time between initiation of first memory (pressing the GO button), and automatic initiation of next programmed memory. See *wait*.

Device   An electronic thing made for a particular purpose, typically requiring either power, or a control signal, or both.

Dichroic   Glass color filters which reflect all light except the color shown. Longer lasting and more expensive than plastic gelatin.

Disk Master   A document assigning portions of memory storage in the RAM of a lighting console to specific tasks, ranging from memories used to playback cues for the production, to infrastructure information used to help program and oversee the health of the lighting package, to storage areas for light cues not currently used in the production. While storage devices are now rarely floppy disks, the misnomer persists.

Dimmer Device that regulates voltage to other devices. Usually controls brightness of lighting instruments.

Display A specific arrangement of information on a computer monitor.

DMX512 A serial form of digital language that initially allowed computer lighting consoles to communicate intensity information with dimmers. Over the years it has expanded to send information to many other electronic devices as well.

Donut Metal insert placed in ellipsoidal color frame holders to eliminate halation or chromatic aberration outside edge of beam pool. The hole in the donut is typically the same diameter as the gate of the instrument on which it will be used.

Downfade Any channel intensities in a fade that are decreasing from previous state or cue, often related to in terms of time.

Downstage The area of a proscenium stage closest to the audience (the lowest portion of a raked stage), or movement in that direction.

Dress rehearsal Time period when all elements of the production are brought together, ideally as it will then be performed on opening night.

Dry tech Period of time when technical elements, sequences, and transitions of production are rehearsed without performer involvement. See *cue to cue*.

Dyslexia Any of various reading disorders associated with impairment of the ability to interpret spatial relationships or to integrate auditory and visual information.

Dyspraxia A development disorder which entails some inability to coordinate and perform certain purposeful movements and gestures, or "difficulty getting our bodies to do what we want when we want them to do it" (from Wikipedia).

Electrical path The singular electric and electronic route for each lighting instrument or device in a light plot, defined by the intersections in the route. Usually includes a circuit, dimmer, and sometimes a control channel.

Empty State of a crate or container after all show goods have been removed. "Is this box live?" "No, it's an empty." More than one empty crate or container: Empties. See *dead*.

Equity Deputy Elections The dreaded moment in the first Equity rehearsal when union actors elect one of their own to represent them in all union matters, throughout the length of the contract. Also known as the worst possible moment to go to the bathroom, since upon return you'll discover you've been voted to be the deputy.

Ethereal Refined or spiritual; of or pertaining to heavenly or celestial.

Fade A gradual change of channel intensities from one lighting state to another.

Fader In manual light boards, a physical handle that controls the levels of a series of dimmers. In computer lighting consoles, a portion of the electronics and software controlling predetermined contents of a single cue.

Feeding the cues Programming previously existing cues into a computer lighting console.

Field angle The overall size or width of a light beam created by an instrument. Usually defined in degree increments, it is the area of the light beam where the light is 10% of the intensity of that instrument's hot spot. See *beam spread*.

Focus point The location on the stage, scenery, or in space where the hot spot of an instrument's beam is pointed. When instruments are assigned to illuminate performers, the location on the stage or the location of the designer's head used to define the placement of the instrument's hot spot can be both referred to as the focus point.

Focus session Period of time when the lighting instruments are aimed at specific locations from directions given by the lighting designer.

Footer Bottom line of information that is duplicated on separate pages of a single document.

Four wall theatre A theatre empty and void of all equipment. The only things provided in the rental agreement are the four walls. All support equipment necessary for the production are provided from remote locations.

Frozen Usually referred to as the moment when no more changes will be made or sometimes allowed to the production. May or may not be associated with opening night. See *liquid*.

Full The channel intensity of 100%.

Gel A generic term for coated color media (usually plastic) that absorbs all other wavelengths than the color shown in the media. Usually produced in sheets or rolls, then cut and placed in color frame holders. Short for *gelatin*.

Ghost channel   A channel without an assigned dimmer. The level intensity displayed by the channel provides information about the current contents of the memory or the RAM contained in the lighting console.

Go   The command given to initiate a cue or action. Also known as "the magic word", so that it may be alluded to on headset without actually stating the word (and possibly instigating an erroneous cue). Also refers to the button on lighting consoles that is pressed to load a memory into a fader.

Gobo Rotator   An electronic device that fits into a gobo slot (or template slot) of an ellipsoidal. The device is fitted with a motor and a gobo cut into a circular pattern. Once inserted, the gobo is in the proper location of the gate of the instrument so that it can be focused like a static gobo. The motor is typically assigned to a separate control channel; when activated, it turns the gobo at various speeds.

Grand Master   A fader that overrides all other intensity levels. Typically the grand master only possesses the inhibitive attribute.

Groundplan zero-zero point   The theatrical point of reference from which all relative measurements are made. Typically, the intersection of the centerline and either plaster line or the smoke pocket line. In CAD drafting, also known as *datum*.

Group   Software function given to a unit of memory containing unrelated channels at any intensity level. Software equivalent of a submaster, but intensity level is controlled by keypad on light board. As such, a group can act as either pile-on or inhibitive.

Halation   Unwanted scattered light bouncing off inside of ellipsoidal. Often solved by using a donut.

Half hour   The 30-minute period of time prior to a performance. Often the same time as *house open*.

Hang Plot   The stand-alone document listing the goods hung in the air, sorted in sequential order. Typically more detailed and inclusive than matching lists included on either the light plot or the lighting section. The term is also interchangeably used with *lineset schedule*.

Hard command   Phrase used in computer light boards, referring to tracking systems. Describes a new level intensity assigned to a channel in a particular cue. The "hard command" instruction forces the channel to assume the new level intensity.

Hardpatch   The act of physically plugging cables or circuits into dimmers, manually assigning the control of an instrument or electrical device.

Head height   The horizontal plane in space above a stage, defined by the lighting designer's head, used as the generic height to determine focus points. Most often seen in sectional view drawings to illustrate beam overlap of different zones within a single system.

Header   Top line of information that is duplicated on separate pages of a single document.

Hot spot   The brightest portion of a light beam created by an instrument, usually in the center of the beam.

Hour before half hour   A 1-hour period of time prior to half hour, used to perform preshow checks of the technical elements of the production. Not to be confused with continuity hour.

House   Term used to refer to the entire audience seating area.

House open   The moment when the doors to the theatre are opened, allowing the audience to be seated.

Infrastructure cues   Light cues, other than memories created to play back "looks" in a production, that are used to provide additional handles or other functions in a computer lighting console.

Inhibitive   An attribute often associated with submasters that overrides the intensity of its contents. Like a grand master. See *pile-on* or *timed*.

Integer   A whole number that has no fraction or numbers following a decimal point.

Intensity   The actual brightness of light generated by the lamp inside the instrument.

Key memory number   A numeric system used to identify a portion of, or entire contents of RAM within a computer lighting console. When a recorded level from a designated ghost channel is visually combined with the initial memory number of a collection of light cues, the resulting key memory number identifies not only the intended purpose of those light cues, but also the disk where the light cues are stored.

Leg   A vertical masking piece, typically constructed of fabric, designed to conceal the backstage area on the perimeter of the performance area, and to provide a side visual limit to the scene. Also called a *tormentor*.

Light board   Device that controls intensity of instruments or other devices. May be manual, preset, or computer. See *console*.

Lighting Rental shop   An organization often containing all of the components required to package a light plot. May also provide service, support, maintenance, and sales of equipment and perishables.

Light Leak Little holes or vents in the housings of lighting instruments where light escapes into an otherwise dark environment. Light leaks coming out of followspot bodies have often been used to mark pickup placements.

Light line Imaginary boundary defining the collective edge of coverage for primary lighting systems.

Link A jump to any other memory recorded in the lighting console, usually other than the next sequential numeric memory.

Liquid The period of time before final decisions are made defining what will technically occur during each moment of a production. Every option is examined as a stage moment before the final version is defined. See *frozen*.

Live screen The monitor display showing the present levels of the channels, reflecting the current output of all active faders. Also known as *stage screen*.

Lightwright A software database application written specifically for the lighting entertainment industry by John McKernon.

Load-in Beginning the installation or mounting of equipment for a production. May or may not involve equipment being "loaded into" the theatre. The term is applied to a time increment that may affect the amount of money and people required for labor. A loose call dependent on the management in charge.

Load-out The period of time following the final performance. Typically begins when equipment starts being disassembled and ends when the performance facility has been restored to the same state of existence before production loaded in. Often concludes with final truck pulling away from the loading dock. Sometimes also referred to as *strike*.

Macro A recorded series of keystrokes or actions that performs a repeated effect. Can be initiated on different contents.

Masking A set of curtains or scenic elements used to constrain the visual sightlines of the audience, and to prevent them from seeing backstage.

Memory A single unit of information within the RAM of a lighting console, also referred to as a *cue*.

Mock-up A trial setup using inexpensive or quickly-assembled substitute components in order to evaluate elements of a design, and make a judgment. In theatre, a mock-up is often created to analyze aspects of scenic, lighting, or costume designs, proposed moments in a show, or overall visual effects.

Monitor A computer display device. Also referred to as a CRT.

Moving Lights A generic term for automated fixtures. Usually follows one of two design philosophies: either the entire body moves and swivels on a yoke, or the body is fixed and only the mirror moves. Also commonly referred to as "movers" or "wiggle lights".

Murphy's Law The adage in Western culture that broadly states: "Anything that can go wrong, will go wrong."

Non-dim A physical device controlling the voltage output to another device or instrument controlled by a computer lighting console. Often limited to only outputting zero or full voltage in zero seconds.

Notes session Period of time following end of rehearsal session spent analyzing rehearsal, coordinating solutions, and deciding future production schedule.

Offstage The area of the stage further from, or movement away from, centerline.

Onstage The area of the stage closer to, or movement towards, centerline.

Opaque The visual state seen when light is not transmitted nor objects seen through a material. See *translucent* and *transparent*.

Opening night The first performance viewed by a paid audience, or reviewed by critics.

Orchestra dress Period of time when all elements of a production are rehearsed with a live orchestra and wardrobe.

Orchestra tech Period of time when all elements of a production, except for wardrobe, are rehearsed with a live orchestra.

Overtime An escalation of pay rates, after a set number of labor hours have concluded.

Page In the world of lighting consoles, a button or software command that initiates one of two things; it either advances the monitor display to the next sequential series of items that are the object of the screen (channels, dimmers, etc), or it loads the next sequential series of channel levels labeled with numeric "handle" values higher than the hardware associated with them. Loading the second page of submasters (25-48) to a 24-handle submaster console, for example.

Park A software command or state that overrides all other commands or handles, often associated with dimmers. If a dimmer is "parked" at a level, its intensity cannot be altered. By "parking" dimmers containing worklight at full, memories can still be recorded without programming the worklight channels into the cue.

Part A recorded lighting state that is assigned unique time durations within a single light cue. Often several parts can exist in any lighting memory.

Patch Specifies the control assigned to each instrument. See *hardpatch* and *softpatch*.

Patch screen The monitor screen that shows the dimmer assignments to the channels.

PC The initials used to refer to either a single Plano-Convex lens, or the lighting instruments solely utilizing that lens. A close relative to the Fresnel lens.

Perishables Consumable items such as tape, pens, markers, or gel, templates, and special effects fluids. Once used, the items cannot be returned for refund.

Pile-on Term describing the action of "highest level takes precedence," so that the higher intensity level overrides other level information. The higher level is being "piled on" to the existing level. Pile-on is an attribute usually associated with submasters. See *inhibitive* or *timed*.

Plaster line Architectural term describing the upstage plane of the proscenium arch. Typically referenced as the imaginary line drawn between the two points where each side of the arch touches the stage. Usually one-half of the reference lines used to define ground-plan zero-zero.

Playback The act of loading a pre-existing memory into a fader, activating the contents of the memory.

Postset The appearance seen on stage, or the sound heard by the audience, after the bows have been completed and the performers have left the stage.

Prehang Period of time prior to official beginning of load-in, usually performing reduced scenic or electrical activities and requiring less labor. Typically involves only electrics or rigging equipment.

Preset The state when activity, spatial location, or actions are in a state of readiness and preparation for a production or a specific moment. Can also refer to a type of manual light board, or a single row of controllers for that light board.

Preshow The period of scheduled time prior to a performance. May or may not be the same as half hour. Can also refer to actions involving that take place before the actual production begins.

Previews Performances given to nonpaying audience, or prior to the arrival of critics.

Profile patch Commands instructing a dimmer to alter its perception of what is "full" or any other portion within the curve of the dimmer.

Pull the order Physical act of assembling, testing, and packing a lighting inventory from a lighting rental shop.

Record Giving a label to a particular state of light. On a manual light board, writing the level intensities for the dimmers. On a computer light board, assigning a numeric label to a particular arrangement of channel levels.

Replug The physical act of altering the circuit and connected instrument to a dimmer. May be performed by pulling one plug out of a dimmer input and inserting a second plug in its place. May also be achieved by switches that control separate inputs.

Road Rash Worn out by use, or overuse. Often applied to old soft goods that should be retired.

Row Horizontal line of information.

Run-through Often the final rehearsals with performers prior to moving to the stage. The objective is to "run through" the entire show, without stopping, to get a feeling for the flow of the entire piece without interruption.

Scene master Physical handle on light board that controls a bank or row of sliders controlling dimmers.

Scrim Cloth with a relatively coarse weave, can be dyed or painted. Opaque when lit obliquely from the front, transparent when the scene behind it is lit.

Show call Period of time defined in union labor for presetting of all equipment for performance. Often does not involve other labor associated with maintenance or work call. Typically refers to the number of stagehands required to run the technical elements during a performance.

Slider Physical handle on light board that controls a range of functions, ranging from a single dimmer to a series of channels.

Smoke Pocket Vertical steel troughs bolted on either side of the upstage side of the proscenium. Together they provide a channel that surrounds the side edges of the fire curtain and maintains a protective shield. An imaginary line drawn between the two upstage sides of the troughs is sometimes used as a reference line instead of plaster line. Also referred to as *the steel*.

Softpatch The act of assigning dimmer control to a channel on a computer lighting console using software; often achieved with a keypad.

Squint Affectionate nickname for an electrician. Other alternatives include "sparky" "juicer" "wrencher" "spanner".

Stage Cable Electrical cable used to connect theatrical lighting instruments. Typically equipped with stage pin connectors, or connectors that allow the cable to be used to connect the instruments to dimmers.

Standby The heightened moment or preparatory command given prior to the command to initiate a cue (go).

Step A sequential repetitive action. Step through cues, step through channels, etc. Also refers to unit of memory associated with effect packages in computer light boards.

Stinger A generic term for an electrical adaptor, typically from stage pin plug to Edison plug. A <u>M</u>ale <u>ED</u>ison to female stage pin plug adaptor is often shortened to "a MED". A <u>F</u>emale <u>ED</u>ison to male stage pin plug adaptor is often shortened to "a FED".

Strike See *load-out*.

Submaster A physical handle, often controlling unrelated channels. On lighting computer consoles, can be programmed to have different attributes, including pile-on, inhibitive, or timed.

Super group Collection of related channels in a single system, or a whole bunch of channels.

System At least two instruments equipped with matching color filters that are focused to different or adjacent areas of the stage. When overlapping light beams in the same color create a consistent intensity wider than the width of a single beam angle, can also be referred to as a wash. The term is also used to refer to an entire lighting package.

Tab A masking leg or blackout drop hung to be parallel to centerline. *German box*

Technical rehearsal Period of time when technical elements of the production are combined with performers to define timing and effect. Usually doesn't include wardrobe or orchestra. Often called a tech.

Template Thin pieces of metal containing holes. When a template is inserted into an ellipsoidal, light projected through the lens of the instrument mirrors the shape of the holes. Also called gobos or patterns.

Time stamp channel Ghost channel designated to display a calendar date or time not associated with the time clock chip contained in a computer lighting console. Used to define the last date that the contents of the RAM was altered.

Timed An attribute often associated with submasters which, when activated, automatically fades up its contents, maintains a preprogrammed intensity, and fades the contents back out. See *pile-on* or *inhibitive*.

Time fade Duration of seconds for a light cue or action to be completed.

Title block Area of logistical information that may or may not be confined in a particular area. In paperwork, often found in headers or footers.

Track To keep track of something; to track light cues. Also, type of recording function that memorizes the change in channel intensity and instructs the channel to continue through succeeding cues until it encounters a hard command.

Track screen Usually refers to the monitor display arranged in a grid or spreadsheet format; rows indicate each sequential cue, while columns indicate an individual channel. Contents of each row of the grid show the channel levels for each cue, while contents of each column show the level progression for each channel.

Translucent The visual state seen when light is transmitted but objects are not distinctly seen through a material. See *transparent* and *opaque*.

Transparent The visual state seen when light passes through or objects are distinctly seen on the other side of a material. See *translucent* and *opaque*.

Traveler A curtain on a track that can be opened or closed to reveal or mask a portion of the stage. Travelers are typically two panels that overlap on centerline, or one panel that performs the same function from one side called a *one way draw*.

Trim The act of physically moving objects in the air to a predetermined distance or to a visual location from a sightline point. Also a reference to a specific vertical location.

Triage Theatre Primary meaning: the process of prioritizing medical emergencies to increase the number of survivors. In this book, it relates to the second meaning; determining priorities for action in an emergency or high-pressure situation.

Upfade Any channel intensities in a fade that are increasing to a higher level than the previous cue, often related to in terms of time.

Upstage The area of a proscenium stage furthest from the audience (the highest portion of a raked stage), or movement towards that direction.

Venue   Location or site of performance typically involving an audience.

Wait   Dependent on software platform and can mean one of two things. Either the duration of time between the initiation of a memory (pressing the GO button) and the initiation of the following memory in a sequence, or the duration of time between the initiation of a memory (pressing the GO button) and the actual moment at which the same memory begins to load into the fader. See *delay*.

Walk-away   Phrase indicating that no stage work will commence following a performance. The only official stage activity is "walking away" from the stage.

Warning   A preparatory command given prior to or in place of a standby.

Wash   At least two instruments focused so that their overlapping beams create a consistent hue and intensity over a portion or all of a performance area. Can also be referred to as a system.

Wheels fall off   The point in a technical rehearsal or a performance when all coherence and direction is lost.

Wind Screen   A blackout drop hung upstage of the scenic stack (including the bounce drop). It's purpose is to reduce the amount of air currents caused by performers rapidly crossing from one side of the stage to the other upstage of the bounce. Without a wind screen, the rapid movement causes ripples in the cyc or drop that can be seen from the audience.

Working Height   A generic term applied to the distance above the stage that a batten is locked off, so that work can be performed on it or its contents. For scenic goods, the batten height is often slightly below armpit height, so that knots can be easily tied onto the batten while soft goods are being attached. For electrics, the working height is slightly higher, so that the shutters and color frame holders of the instruments are at armpit height instead. When borders are being trimmed, the working height applies to the bottom of the goods receiving the measuring tape, not the batten.

Wysiwyg   Both a software product and a method to provide pre-visualization.

YMMV   Your Mileage May Vary.

Zero-Zero Point   The point where centerline and plaster line intersect on a proscenium stage; the origin point used in a non-traditional venue. This point is also refers to elevation; commonly referring to the plane of the stage as the beginning of all vertical measurements on the "z" plane.

Zone   At least two light beams focused to create a single band of light aimed at focus points equidistant from plaster line, so that the overlapping beams create a consistent hue and intensity between the two focus points, and typically across the width of a stage. Overlapping zones are often combined to create a system or a wash.

Selected Bibliography

A Method of Lighting the Stage
Stanley McCandless
Theatre Arts Books
333 Sixth Avenue
New York, NY 10014
Automated Lighting
Richard Cadena
Focal Press

Concert Lighting 3rd Edition
James L. Moody and Paul Dexter
Focal Press
Control Systems for Live Entertainment
John Huntington
Focal Press

Designer Drafting for the Entertainment World
Patricia Woodbridge
Focal Press

Fieldbook for Boys and Men
Boy Scouts of America
New Brunswick, New Jersey

HEADS! and Tales
Bill Sapsis
Sapsis Rigging, Inc.
233 N. Lansdowne Ave.
Landsdowne, PA 19050

Designing with Light, Second Edition
J. Michael Gillette
Mayfield Publishing Company
1240 Villa Street
Mountain View, CA 94041

Lighting Handbook
Westinghouse Electric Corporation
Lamp Divisions
Bloomfield, New Jersey 07003

Photometrics Handbook
Robert C. Mumm
Broadway Press
3001 Sprintcrest Drive
Louisville, KY 40241

Pocket Ref
Thomas J. Glover
Sequoia Publishing
Aggeon Cal, Inc.
123-33T Gray Avenue
Santa Barbara, CA 93101

Stage Rigging Handbook, Revised, 2nd Edition
Jay O. Glerum
Southern Illinois University Press
1915 University Press Drive
Carbondale, Illinois 62901

Stage Lighting
Richard Pilbrow
Von Nostrand Reinhold Company
450 West 33rd Street
New York, NY 10001

The Dramatic Imagination
Robert Edmond Jones
Theatre Arts Books
333 Sixth Avenu
New York, NY 10014

The Magic of Light
Jean Rosenthal and Lael Wertenbaker
Little, Brown and Company-Boston-Toronto
In association with Theatre Arts Books
333 Sixth Avenue
New York, NY 10014

Index

Note: Page numbers followed by *f* indicates figure and *t* indicates table.